McGra

McGraw-Hill Dictionary of
COMPUTERS

Sybil P. Parker
EDITOR IN CHIEF

McGraw-Hill Book Company

New York   St. Louis   San Francisco

Auckland   Bogotá   Guatemala   Hamburg
Lisbon   London   Madrid   Mexico
Montreal   New Delhi   Panama   Paris   San Juan
São Paulo   Singapore   Sydney   Tokyo   Toronto

On the cover: Graphical representation of mathematical formulas executed by the Calcomp digital computer. (California Computer Products, Inc.)

McGRAW-HILL DICTIONARY OF COMPUTERS
The material in this Dictionary has been published previously in the McGRAW-HILL DICTIONARY OF SCIENTIFIC AND TECHNICAL TERMS, Third Edition, copyright

2 3 4 5 6 7 8 9 0   FGFG   8 9 1 0 9 8

ISBN 0-07-045415-9

Library of Congress Cataloging in Publication Data
McGraw-Hill dictionary of computers.

1. Computers—Dictionaries.   I. Parker, Sybil P.
II. McGraw-Hill Book Company.
QA76.15.M395   1985   001.64'03'21   84-27863
ISBN 0-07-045415-9 (pbk.)

Editorial Staff

Sybil P. Parker, Editor in Chief

Jonathan Weil, Editor
Betty Richman, Editor
Edward J. Fox, Art director
Joe Faulk, Editing manager
Frank Kotowski, Jr., Editing supervisor

Consulting and Contributing Editors
from the McGraw-Hill Dictionary of Scientific and Technical Terms

Prof. Roland H. Good, Jr.—Department of Physics, Pennsylvania State University. PHYSICS.

Phillip B. Jordain—Senior Research Officer, First National City Bank of New York. COMPUTERS.

John Markus—Author and Consultant. ELECTRONICS.

How to Use the Dictionary

ALPHABETIZATION

The terms in the *McGraw-Hill Dictionary of Computers* are alphabetized on a letter-by-letter basis; word spacing, hyphen, comma, solidus, and apostrophe in a term are ignored in the sequencing. For example, an ordering of terms would be:

> **read-around ratio**
> **Read diode**
> **reader**
> **read error**
> **readout**
> **read/write channel**

CROSS-REFERENCING

A cross-reference entry directs the user to the defining entry. For example, the user looking up "read-back check" finds:

> **read-back check** *See* echo check.

The user then turns to the "E" terms for the definition.

Cross-references are also made from variant spellings, acronyms, abbreviations, and symbols.

> **i-f** *See* intermediate frequency.
> **kVp** *See* kilovolts peak.
> **RAM** *See* random-access memory.

The user turning directly to a defining entry will find the above type of information included, introduced by "Also known as . . . ," "Also spelled . . . ," "Abbreviated . . . ," "Symbolized . . . ," "Derived from . . . ."

McGraw-Hill Dictionary of
COMPUTERS

A AND NOT B gate *See* AND NOT gate.

A battery The battery that supplies power for filaments or heaters of electron tubes in battery-operated equipment.

ABC *See* automatic brightness control.

abend An unplanned program termination that occurs when a computer is directed to execute an instruction or to process information that it cannot recognize. Also known as bomb; crash.

abnormal glow discharge A discharge of electricity in a gas tube at currents somewhat higher than those of an ordinary glow discharge, at which point the glow covers the entire cathode and the voltage drop decreases with increasing current.

abnormal statement An element of a FORTRAN V (UNIVAC) program which specifies that certain function subroutines must be called every time they are referred to.

abrupt junction A *pn* junction in which the concentration of impurities changes suddenly from acceptors to donors.

abs A special function occurring in ALGOL, which yields the absolute value, or modulus, of its argument.

absolute address The numerical identification of each storage location which is wired permanently into a computer by the manufacturer.

absolute addressing The identification of storage locations in a computer program by their physical addresses.

absolute code A code used when the addresses in a program are to be written in machine language exactly as they will appear when the instructions are executed by the control circuits.

absolute programming Programming with the use of absolute code.

absolute-value computer A computer that processes the values of the variables rather than their increments.

absorber A material or device that takes up and dissipates radiated energy; may be used to shield an object from the energy, prevent reflection of the energy, determine the nature of the radiation, or selectively transmit one or more components of the radiation.

absorption circuit A series-resonant circuit used to absorb power at an unwanted signal frequency by providing a low impedance to ground at this frequency.

absorption control *See* absorption modulation.

absorption modulation A system of amplitude modulation in which a variable-impedance device is inserted in or coupled to the output circuit of the transmitter. Also known as absorption control; loss modulation.

2   absorption wavemeter

absorption wavemeter A frequency- or wavelength-measuring instrument consisting of a calibrated tunable circuit and a resonance indicator.

abstract automata theory The mathematical theory which characterizes automata by three sets: input signals, internal states, and output signals; and two functions: input functions and output functions.

accelerating electrode An electrode used in cathode-ray tubes and other electron tubes to increase the velocity of the electrons that contribute the space current or form a beam.

accelerating potential The energy potential in electron-beam equipment that imparts additional speed and energy to the electrons.

acceleration time The time required for a magnetic tape transport or any other mechanical device to attain its operating speed.

acceleration voltage The voltage between a cathode and accelerating electrode of an electron tube.

accentuation The enhancement of signal amplitudes in selected freuency bands with respect to other signals.

accentuator A circuit that provides for the first part of a process for increasing the strength of certain audio frequencies with respect to others, to help these frequencies override noise or to reduce distortion. Also known as accentuator circuit.

accentuator circuit See accentuator.

accept A data transmission statement which is used in FORTRAN when the computer is in conversational mode, and which enables the programmer to input, through the teletypewriter, data the programmer wishes stored in memory.

acceptor An impurity element that increases the number of holes in a semiconductor crystal such as germanium or silicon; aluminum, gallium, and indium are examples. Also known as acceptor impurity; acceptor material.

acceptor atom An atom of a substance added to a semiconductor crystal to increase the number of holes in the conduction band.

acceptor circuit A series-resonant circuit that has a low impedance at the frequency to which it is tuned and a higher impedance at all other frequencies.

acceptor impurity See acceptor.

acceptor material See acceptor.

access The reading of data from storage or the writing of data into storage.

access arm The mechanical device which positions the read/write head on a magnetic storage unit.

access-control register A storage device which controls the word-by-word transmission over a given channel.

access-control words Permanently wired instructions channeling transmitted words into reserved locations.

access gap See memory gap.

access mechanism The mechanism of positioning reading or writing heads onto the required tracks of a magnetic disk.

access method A set of programming routines which links programs and the data that these programs transfer into and out of memory.

access mode A programming clause in COBOL which is required when using a random-access device so that a specific record may be read out of or written into a mass storage bin.

access time The time period required for reading out of or writing into the computer memory.

accounting machine A machine that produces tabulations or accounting records of a specified unvarying format.

accounting package A set of special routines that allow collection of information about the usage level of various components of a computer system by each production program.

accumulated total punching A checking procedure to ensure that no punch-card item has been dropped from a file.

accumulating reproducer An electromechanical device which reads a sorted deck of cards and creates a set of subtotals on additional cards according to some preset criterion.

accumulator A specific register, in the arithmetic unit of a computer, in which the result of an arithmetic or logical operation is formed; here numbers are added or subtracted, and certain operations such as sensing, shifting, and complementing are performed. Also known as accumulator register; counter.

accumulator jump instruction An instruction which programs a computer to ignore the previously established program sequence depending on the status of the accumulator. Also known as accumulator transfer instruction.

accumulator register See accumulator.

accumulator shift instruction A computer instruction which causes the word in a register to be displaced a specified number of bit positions to the left or right.

accumulator transfer instruction See accumulator jump instruction.

accuracy control system Any method which attempts error detection and control, such as random sampling and squaring.

ac/dc receiver A radio receiver designed to operate from either an alternating- or direct-current power line. Also known as universal receiver.

acorn tube An ultra-high-frequency electron tube resembling an acorn in shape and size.

acoustic amplifier A device that amplifies mechanical vibrations directly at audio and ultrasonic frequencies. Also known as acoustoelectric amplifier.

acoustic bridge A device, based on the principle of the electrical Wheatstone bridge, used for analysis of deafness.

acoustic convolver See convolver.

acoustic delay line A device in which acoustic signals are propagated in a medium to make use of the sonic propagation time to obtain a time delay for the signals. Also known as sonic delay line.

acoustic detector The stage in a receiver at which demodulation of a modulated radio wave into its audio component takes place.

acoustic memory A computer memory that uses an acoustic delay line, in which a train of pulses travels through a medium such as mercury or quartz.

acoustic mode The type of crystal lattice vibrations which for long wavelengths act like an acoustic wave in a continuous medium, but which for shorter wavelengths approach the Debye frequency, showing a dispersive decrease in phase velocity.

acoustic phonon A quantum of excitation of an acoustic mode of vibration.

acoustic receiver The complete equipment required for receiving modulated radio waves and converting them into sound.

acoustic-wave amplifier An amplifier in which the charge carriers in a semiconductor are coupled to an acoustic wave that is propagated in a piezoelectric material, to produce amplification.

acoustoelectric amplifier *See* acoustic amplifier.

acoustoelectric effect The development of a direct-current voltage in a semiconductor or metal by an acoustic wave traveling parallel to the surface of the material. Also known as electroacoustic effect.

acquire 1. Of acquisition radars, the process of detecting the presence and location of a target in sufficient detail to permit identification. **2.** Of tracking radars, the process of positioning a radar beam so that a target is in that beam to permit the effective employment of weapons. Also known as target acquisition.

action entries The lower right-hand portion of a decision table, indicating which of the various possible actions result from each of the various possible conditions.

action period The period of time during which data in a Williams tube storage device can be read or new data can be written into this storage.

action portion The lower portion of a decision table, comprising the action stub and action entries.

action stub The lower left-hand portion of a decision table, consisting of a single column listing the various possible actions (transformations to be done on data and materials).

activate To treat the filament, cathode, or target of a vacuum tube to increase electron emission.

activated cathode A thermionic cathode consisting of a tungsten filament to which thorium has been added, and then brought to the surface, by a process such as heating in the absence of an electric field in order to increase thermionic emission.

activation The process of treating the cathode or target of an electron tube to increase its emission. Also known as sensitization.

activation record A variable part of a program module, such as data and control information, that may vary with different instances of execution.

active area The area of a metallic rectifier that acts as the rectifying junction and conducts current in the forward direction.

active component *See* active element.

active computer When two or more computers are installed, the one that is on-line and processing data.

active device A component, such as an electron tube or transistor, that is capable of amplifying the current or voltage in a circuit.

active electronic countermeasures The major subdivision of electronic countermeasures concerning electronic jamming and electronic deceptions.

active element Any generator of voltage or current in an impedance network. Also known as active component.

active filter A filter that uses an amplifier with conventional passive filter elements to provide a desired fixed or tunable pass or rejection characteristic.

active jamming *See* jamming.

active leg An electrical element within a transducer which changes its electrical characteristics as a function of the application of a stimulus.

active logic Logic that incorporates active components which provide such functions as level restoration, pulse shaping, pulse inversion, and power gain.

active master file A relatively active computer master file, as determined by usage data.

active master item A relatively active item in a computer master file, as determined by usage data.

active material The material of the cathode of an electron tube that emits electrons when heated.

active region The region in which amplifying, rectifying, light emitting, or other dynamic action occurs in a semiconductor device.

active substrate A semiconductor or ferrite material in which active elements are formed; also a mechanical support for the other elements of a semiconductor device or integrated circuit.

active transducer A transducer whose output is dependent upon sources of power, apart from that supplied by any of the actuating signals, which power is controlled by one or more of these signals.

activity The use or modification of information contained in a file.

activity level 1. The value assumed by a structural variable during the solution of a programming problem. 2. A measure of the number of times that use or modification is made of the information contained in a file.

activity ratio The ratio between used or modified records and the total number of records in a file.

actual argument The variable which replaces a dummy argument when a procedure or macroinstruction is called up.

actual decimal point The period appearing on a printed report as opposed to the virtual point defined only by the data structure within the computer.

actual instruction *See* effective instruction.

actual key A data item in COBOL computer language which can be used as an address.

acyclic feeding A method employed by alphanumeric readers in which the trailing edge or some other document characteristic is used to activate the feeding of the succeeding document.

acyclic machine *See* homopolar generator.

adapter A device which converts bits of information received serially into parallel bit form for use in the inquiry buffer unit.

adaptive system A system that can change itself to meet new requirements.

adaptive system theory The branch of automata theory dealing with adaptive, or self-organizing, systems.

ADCON *See* address constant.

adconductor cathode A cathode in which adsorbed alkali metal atoms provide electron emission in a glow or arc discharge.

adder 1. A computer device that can form the sum of two or more numbers or quantities. 2. A circuit in which two or more signals are combined to give an output-signal amplitude that is proportional to the sum of the input-signal amplitudes. Also known as adder circuit.

adder circuit *See* adder.

adding circuit A circuit that performs the mathematical operation of addition.

adding machine A device which performs the arithmetical operation of addition and subtraction.

addition item An item which is to be filed in its proper place in a computer.

addition record A new record inserted into an updated master file.

addition table The part of memory that holds the table of numbers used in addition in a computer employing table look-up techniques to carry out this operation.

address The number or name that uniquely identifies a register, memory location, or storage device in a computer.

address computation The modification by a computer of an address within an instruction, or of an instruction based on results obtained so far. Also known as address modification.

address constant A value, or its expression, used in the calculation of storage addresses from relative addresses for computers. Abbreviated ADCON. Also known as base address; presumptive address; reference address.

address conversion The use of an assembly program to translate symbolic or relative computer addresses.

address counter A counter which increments an initial memory address as a block of data is being transferred into the memory locations indicated by the counter.

address field The portion of a computer program instruction which specifies where a particular piece of information is located in the computer memory.

address format A description of the number of addresses included in a computer instruction.

address-free program A computer program in which all addresses are represented as displacements from the expected contents of a base register.

address generation An addressing technique which facilitates addressing large storages and implementing dynamic program relocation; the effective main storage address is obtained by adding together the contents of the base register of the index register and of the displacement field.

addressing mode The specific technique by means of which a memory reference instruction will be spelled out if the computer word is too small to contain the memory address.

addressing system A labeling technique used to identify storage locations within a computer system.

address interleaving The assignment of consecutive addresses to physically separate modules of a computer memory, making possible the very-high-speed access of a sequence of contiguously addressed words, since all modules operate nearly simultaneously.

addressless instruction format *See* zero address instruction format.

address modification *See* address computation.

address part That part of a computer instruction which contains the address of the operand, of the result, or of the next instruction.

address register A register wherein the address part of an instruction is stored by a computer.

address sort routine A debugging routine which scans all instructions of the program being checked for a given address.

address track A path on a magnetic tape, drum, or disk on which are recorded addresses used in the retrieval of data stored on other tracks.

address translation The assignment of actual locations in a computer memory to virtual addresses in a computer program.

add-subtract time The time required to perform an addition or subtraction, exclusive of the time required to obtain the quantities from storage and put the sum or difference back into storage.

add time The time required by a computer to perform an addition, not including the time needed to obtain the addends from storage and put the sum back into storage.

add-to-memory technique In direct-memory-access systems, a technique which adds a data word to a memory location; permits linear operations such as data averaging on process data.

ADF *See* automatic direction finder.

A display A radar oscilloscope display in cartesian coordinates; the targets appear as vertical deflection lines; their Y coordinates are proportional to signal intensity; their X coordinates are proportional to distance to targets.

adjacency A condition in character recognition in which two consecutive graphic characters are separated by less than a specified distance.

adjacent-channel selectivity The ability of a radio receiver to respond to the desired signal and to reject signals in adjacent frequency channels.

adjusted decibel A unit used to show the relationship between the interfering effect of a noise frequency, or band of noise frequencies, and a reference noise power level of -85 dBm. Abbreviated dBa. Also known as decibel adjusted.

Administrative Terminal System A system developed by the International Business Machine Corporation to enable the handling by computer of texts that would otherwise require copying by a typist. Abbreviated ATS.

ADPE *See* automatic data-processing equipment.

advanced signal-processing system A portable data-processing system for military use; its complete configuration may consist of the analyzer unit, a postprocessing unit (for data-processing and control tasks), and an advanced signal-processing display unit. Also known as Proteus.

advance feed tape Computer tape punched so that the leading edges of its feed holes will line up with the leading edges of the data holes in the tape usage device.

aerial *See* antenna.

aerospace electronics The field of electronics as applied to aircraft and spacecraft.

AFC *See* automatic frequency control.

a format A nonexecutable statement in FORTRAN which permits alphanumeric characters to be transmitted in a manner similar to numeric data.

AGC *See* automatic gain control.

agenda 1. The sequence of control statements required to carry out the solution of a computer problem. 2. A collection of programs used for manipulating a matrix in the solution of a problem in linear programming.

agendum call card A punch card that contains one item in an agenda for manipulation of a matrix in the solution of a linear programming problem.

aggressive device A unit of a computer that can initiate a request for communication with another device.

A indicator *See* A scope.

air cell A cell in which depolarization at the positive electrode is accomplished chemically by reduction of the oxygen in the air.

air-core coil An inductor without a magnetic core.

aircraft antenna An airborne device used to detect or radiate electromagnetic waves.

air gap 1. A gap or an equivalent filler of nonmagnetic material across the core of a choke, transformer, or other magnetic device. 2. A spark gap consisting of two electrodes separated by air.

airwave A radio wave used in radio and television broadcasting.

alarm signal The international radiotelegraph alarm signal transmitted to actuate automatic devices that sound an alarm indicating that a distress message is about to be broadcast.

Alaska Integrated Communications Exchange A network of radio stations, generally using scatter-propagation equipment, that links early-warning radar stations. Also known as Alice; White Alice.

algebraic manipulation language A programming language used in the solution of analytic problems by symbolic computation.

ALGOL An algorithmic and procedure-oriented computer language used principally in the programming of scientific problems.

algorithmic language A language in which a procedure or scheme of calculations can be expressed accurately.

algorithm translation A step-by-step computerized method of translating one programming language into another programming language.

alias An alternative entry point in a computer subroutine at which its execution may begin, if so instructed by another routine.

Alice *See* Alaska Integrated Communications Exchange.

alignment The process of adjusting components of a system for proper interrelationship, including the adjustment of tuned circuits for proper frequency response and the time synchronization of the components of a system.

all-diffused monolithic integrated circuit Microcircuit consisting of a silicon substrate into which all of the circuit parts (both active and passive elements) are fabricated by diffusion and related processes.

allocate To place a portion of a computer memory or a peripheral unit under control of a computer program, through the action of an operator, program instruction, or executive program.

allowed energy bands The restricted regions of possible electron energy levels in a solid.

alloy junction A junction produced by alloying one or more impurity metals to a semiconductor to form a p or n region, depending on the impurity used. Also known as fused junction.

alloy junction diode A junction diode made by placing a pill of doped alloying material on a semiconductor material and heating until the molten alloy melts a portion of the semiconductor, resulting in a pn junction when the dissolved semiconductor recrystallizes. Also known as fused-junction diode.

alloy-junction transistor A junction transistor made by placing pellets of a p-type impurity such as indium above and below an n-type wafer of germanium, then heating until the impurity alloys with the germanium to give a pnp transistor. Also known as fused-junction transistor.

all-pass network A network designed to introduce a phase shift in a signal without introducing an appreciable reduction in energy of the signal at any frequency.

all-purpose computer A computer combining the specific capabilities of a general-purpose computer and a special-purpose, scientific or business computer.

all-wave receiver A radio receiver capable of being tuned from about 535 kilohertz to at least 20 megahertz; some go above 100 megahertz and thus cover the FM band also.

alphabetic coding 1. Abbreviation of words for computer input. 2. A system of coding with a number system of base 26, the letters of the alphabet being used instead of the cardinal numbers.

alphabetic shift The status of a card punch when the program control is off (star wheels are raised).

alphabetic string *See* character string.

alpha cutoff frequency The frequency at the high end of a transistor's range at which current amplification drops 3 decibels below its low-frequency value.

alphameric characters *See* alphanumeric characters.

alphameric typebar A metal bar containing the alphabet, the ten numerical characters, and the ampersand, in use in electromechanical accounting machines.

alphanumeric characters All characters used by a computer, including letters, numerals, punctuation marks, and such signs as $, @, and #. Also known as alphameric characters.

alphanumeric display device A device which visibly represents alphanumeric output information from some signal source.

alphanumeric instruction The name given to instructions which can be read equally well with alphabetic or numeric kinds of fields of data.

alphanumeric reader A device capable of reading alphabetic, numeric, and special characters and punctuation marks.

alphascope An interactive alphanumerical input/output device that consists of a cathode-ray tube, keyboard, method of generating characters, method of refreshing the display, and communications equipment, and that forms part of a computer-based system requiring a short response time for retrieving answers to queries from a computer random-access memory.

alteration switch A hand-operated switch mounted on the console of a computer, used to feed a single bit of information into a program. Also known as sense switch.

alternate track The disk track used if, after a disk volume is initialized, a defective track is sensed by the system.

alternating-current coupling A coupling which passes alternating-current signals but blocks direct-current signals.

alternating-current/direct-current Pertaining to electronic equipment capable of operation from either an alternating-current or direct-current primary power source.

alternating-current dump The removal of all alternating-current power from a computer intentionally, accidentally, or conditionally.

alternating-current erase The use of an alternating current to energize a tape recorder erase head in order to remove previously recorded signals from a tape.

alternating-current erasing head In magnetic recording, an erasing head which uses alternating current to produce the magnetic field necessary for erasing.

alternating-current magnetic biasing Biasing with alternating current, usually well above the signal frequency range, in magnetic tape recording.

alternating-current transmission In television, that form of transmission in which a fixed setting of the controls makes any instantaneous value of signal correspond to the same value of brightness for only a short time.

altitude delay Synchronization delay introduced between the time of transmission of the radar pulse and the start of the trace on the indicator to eliminate the altitude/height hole on the plan position indicator–type display.

altitude hole The blank area in the center of a plan position indicator–type radarscope display caused by the time interval between transmission of a pulse and the receipt of the first ground return.

altitude signal The radio signals returned to an airborne electronics device by the ground or sea surface directly beneath the aircraft.

AM *See* amplitude modulation.

amateur radio A radio used for two-way radio communications by private individuals as leisure-time activity. Also known as ham radio.

ambiguity The condition in which a synchro system or servosystem seeks more than one null position.

ambiguity error An error in reading a number represented in a digital display that can occur when this representation is changing; for example, the number 699 changing to 700 might be read as 799 because of imprecise synchronization in the changing of digits.

amendment record *See* change record.

AM field signature The characteristic pattern of an alternating magnetic field, as displayed by detection and classification equipment.

amorphous memory array An array of memory switches made of amorphous material.

amorphous semiconductor A semiconductor material which is not entirely crystalline, having only short-range order in its structure.

amplification factor In a vacuum tube, the ratio of the incremental change in plate voltage to a given small change in grid voltage, under the conditions that the plate current and all other electrode voltages are held constant.

amplified back bias Degenerative voltage developed across a fast time-constant circuit within a stage of an amplifier and fed back into a preceding stage.

amplifying delay line Delay line used in pulse-compression systems to amplify delayed signals in the super-high-frequency region.

amplitron Crossed-field continuous cathode reentrant beam backward-wave amplifier for microwave frequencies.

amplitude discriminator *See* pulse-height discriminator.

amplitude distortion *See* frequency distortion.

amplitude-frequency distortion *See* frequency distortion.

amplitude gate A circuit which transmits only those portions of an input signal which lie between two amplitude boundary level values. Also known as slicer; slicer amplifier.

amplitude limiter *See* limiter.

amplitude-limiting circuit *See* limiter.

amplitude modulation Abbreviated AM. **1.** Modulation in which the aplitude of a wave is the characteristic varied in accordance with the intelligence to be transmitted. **2.** In telemetry, those systems of modulation in which each component frequency f of the transmitted intelligence produces a pair of sideband frequencies at carrier frequency plus f and carrier minus f.

amplitude response The maximum output amplitude obtainable at various points over the frequency range of an instrument operating under rated conditions.

amplitude selector *See* pulse-height selector.

amplitude separator A circuit used to isolate the portion of a waveform with amplitudes above or below a given value or between two given values.

amplitude suppression ratio Ratio, in frequency modulation, of the undesired output to the desired output of a frequency-modulated receiver when the applied signal has simultaneous amplitude and frequency modulation.

amplitude versus frequency distortion The distortion caused by the nonuniform attenuation or gain of the system, with respect to frequency under specified terminal conditions.

analog A physical variable which remains similar to another variable insofar as the proportional relationships are the same over some specified range; for example, a temperature may be represented by a voltage which is its analog.

analog adder A device with one output voltage which is a weighted sum of two input voltages.

analog channel A channel on which the information transmitted can have any value between the channel limits, such as a voice channel.

analog comparator 1. A comparator that checks digital values to determine whether they are within predetermined upper and lower limits. 2. A comparator that produces high and low digital output signals when the sum of two analog voltages is positive and negative, respectively.

analog computer A computer is which quantities are represented by physical variables; problem parameters are translated into equivalent mechanical or electrical circuits as an analog for the physical phenomenon being investigated.

analog data Data represented in a continuous form, as contrasted with digital data having discrete values.

analog device A control device that operates with variables represented by continuously measured voltages or other quantities.

analog indicator A device in which the result of a measurement is indicated by a pointer deflection or other visual quantity.

analog multiplexer A multiplexer that provides switching of analog input signals to allow use of a common analog-to-digital converter.

analog multiplier A device that accepts two or more inputs in analog form and then produces an output proportional to the product of the input quantities.

analog network A circuit designed so that circuit variables such as voltages are proportional to the values of variables in a system under study.

analog recording Any method of recording in which some characteristic of the recording signal, such as amplitude or frequency, is continuously varied in a manner analogous to the time variations of the original signal.

analog signal A nominally continuous electrical signal that varies in amplitude or frequency in response to changes in sound, light, heat, position, or pressure.

analog simulation The representation of physical systems and phenomena by variables such as translation, rotation, resistance, and voltage.

analog switch 1. A device that either transmits an analog signal without distortion or completely blocks it. 2. Any solid-state device, with or without a driver, capable of bilaterally switching voltages or current.

analog-to-digital converter A device which translates continuous analog signals into proportional discrete digital signals.

12 analog-to-frequency converter

analog-to-frequency converter A converter in which an analog input in some form other than frequency is converted to a proportional change in frequency.

analog voltage A voltage that varies in a continuous fashion in accordance with the magnitude of a measured variable.

analytical engine An early-19th-century form of mechanically operated digital computer.

analytical function generator An analog computer device in which the dependence of an output variable on one or more input variables is given by a function that also appears in a physical law. Also known as natural function generator; natural law function generator.

analyzer 1. A routine for the checking of a program. 2. One of several types of computers used to solve differential equations.

AND circuit *See* AND gate.

Anderson bridge A six-branch modification of the Maxwell-Wien bridge, used to measure self-inductance in terms of capacitance and resistance; bridge balance is independent of frequency.

AND gate A circuit which has two or more input signal ports and which delivers an output only if and when every input signal port is simultaneously energized. Also known as AND circuit; passive AND gate.

AND/NOR gate A single logic element whose operation is equivalent to that of two AND gates with outputs feeding into a NOR gate.

AND NOT gate A coincidence circuit that performs the logic operation AND NOT, under which a result is true only if statement A is true and statement B is not. Also known as A AND NOT B gate.

AND-OR circuit Gating circuit that produces a prescribed output condition when several possible combined input signals are applied; exhibits the characteristics of the AND gate and the OR gate.

AND-OR-INVERT gate A logic circuit with four inputs, a_1, a_2, b_1, and b_2, whose output is 0 only if either a_1 and a_2 or b_1 and b_2 are 1. Abbreviated A-O-I gate.

angle jamming An electronic countermeasure in which azimuth and elevation information, from a scanning fire control radar present in the modulation components on the returning echo pulse, is jammed by transmitting a pulse similar to the radar pulse but with modulation information out of phase with the returning target angle modulation information.

angle modulation The variation in the angle of a sine-wave carrier; particular forms are phase modulation and frequency modulation. Also known as sinusoidal angular modulation.

angle tracking noise Any deviation of the tracking axis from the center of reflectivity of a radar target; it is the resultant of servo noise, receiver noise, angle noise, and amplitude noise.

angular resolver *See* resolver.

annotation Any comment or note included in a program or flow chart in order to clarify some point at issue.

annular transistor Mesa transistor in which the semiconductor regions are arranged in concentric circles about the emitter.

anode 1. The collector of electrons in an electron tube. Also known as plate; positive electrode. 2. In a semiconductor diode, the terminal toward which forward current flows from the external circuit.

anode circuit Complete external electrical circuit connected between the anode and the cathode of an electron tube. Also known as plate circuit.

anode-circuit detector Detector functioning by virtue of a nonlinearity in its anode-circuit characteristic. Also known as plate-circuit detector.

anode current The electron current flowing through an electron tube from the cathode to the anode. Also known as plate current.

anode detector A detector in which rectification of radio-frequency signals takes place in the anode circuit of an electron tube. Also known as plate detector.

anode dissipation Power dissipated as heat in the anode of an electron tube because of bombardment by electrons and ions.

anode efficiency The ratio of the ac load circuit power to the dc anode power input for an electron tube. Also known as plate efficiency.

anode fall A very thin space-charge region in front of an anode surface, characterized by a steep potential gradient through the region.

anode impedance Total impedance between anode and cathode exclusive of the electron stream. Also known as plate impedance; plate-load impedance.

anode input power Direct-current power delivered to the plate (anode) of a vacuum tube by the source of supply. Also known as plate input power.

anode modulation Modulation produced by introducing the modulating signal into the anode circuit of any tube in which the carrier is present. Also known as plate modulation.

anode neutralization Method of neutralizing an amplifier in which the necessary 180° phase shift is obtained by an inverting network in the plate circuit. Also known as plate neutralization.

anode pulse modulation Modulation produced in an amplifier or oscillator by application of externally generated pulses to the plate circuit. Also known as plate pulse modulation.

anode rays Positive ions coming from the anode of an electron tube; generally due to impurities in the metal of the anode.

anode resistance The resistance value obtained when a small change in the anode voltage of an electron tube is divided by the resulting small change in anode current. Also known as plate resistance.

anode saturation The condition in which the anode current of an electron tube cannot be further increased by increasing the anode voltage; the electrons are then being drawn to the anode at the same rate as they are emitted from the cathode. Also known as current saturation; plate saturation; saturation; voltage saturation.

anode sheath The electron boundary which exists in a gas-discharge tube between the plasma and the anode when the current demanded by the anode circuit exceeds the random electron current at the anode surface.

anotron A cold-cathode glow-discharge diode having a copper anode and a large cathode of sodium or other material.

antenna circuit A complete electric circuit which includes an antenna.

antenna loading 1. The amount of inductance or capacitance in series with an antenna, which determines the antenna's electrical length. 2. The practice of loading an antenna in order to increase its electrical length.

anticapacitance switch A switch designed to have low capacitance between its terminals when open.

anticathode The anode or target of an x-ray tube, on which the stream of electrons from the cathode is focused and from which x-rays are emitted.

anticipatory staging Moving blocks of data from one storage device to another prior to the actual request for them by the program.

anticlutter gain control Device which automatically and smoothly increases the gain of a radar receiver from a low level to the maximum, within a specified period after each transmitter pulse, so that short-range echoes producing clutter are amplified less than long-range echoes.

anticoincidence circuit Circuit that produces a specified output pulse when one (frequently predesignated) of two inputs receives a pulse and the other receives no pulse within an assigned time interval.

antifading antenna An antenna designed to confine radiation mainly to small angles of elevation to minimize the fading of radiation directed at larger angles of elevation.

antiferroelectric crystal A crystalline substance characterized by a state of lower symmetry consisting of two interpenetrating sublattices with equal but opposite electric polarization, and a state of higher symmetry in which the sublattices are unpolarized and indistinguishable.

antiferromagnetic domain A region in a solid within which equal groups of elementary atomic or molecular magnetic moments are aligned antiparallel.

antiferromagnetism A property possessed by some metals, alloys, and salts of transition elements by which the atomic magnetic moments form an ordered array which alternates or spirals so as to give no net total moment in zero applied magnetic field.

antihunt circuit A stabilizing circuit used in a closed-loop feedback system to prevent self-oscillations.

antijamming Any system or technique used to counteract the jamming of communications or of radar operation.

Anti-Submarine Detection Investigation Committee See asdic.

anti-transmit-receive tube A switching tube that prevents the received echo signal from being dissipated in the transmitter.

A-O-I gate See AND-OR-INVERT gate.

APC See automatic phase control.

aperture An opening through which electrons, light, radio waves, or other radiation can pass.

aperture grill picture tube An in-line gun-type picture tube in which the shadow mask is perforated by long, vertical stripes and the screen is painted with vertical phosphor stripes.

aperture plate A small part of a piece of perforated ferromagnetic material that forms a magnetic cell.

apodization A technique for modifying the response of a surface acoustic wave filter by varying the overlap between adjacent electrodes of the interdigital transducer.

A power supply See A supply.

Applegate diagram A graph of the electron paths in a two-cavity klystron tube, showing how electron bunching occurs.

application development language A very-high-level programming language that generates coding in a conventional programming language or provides the user of a data-base management system with a programming language that is easier to implement than conventional programming languages.

application package A combination of required hardware, including remote inputs and outputs, plus programming of the computer memory to produce the specified results.

applications program A program written to solve a specific problem, produce a specific report, or update a specific file.

application study The detailed process of determining a system or set of procedures for using a computer for definite functions of operations, and establishing specifications to be used as a base for the selection of equipment suitable to the specific needs.

applied epistemology The use of machines or other models to simulate processes such as perception, recognition, learning, and selective recall, or the application of principles assumed to hold for human categorization, perception, storage, search, and so on, to the design of machines, machine programs, scanning, storage, and retrieval systems.

APT *See* Automatic Programming Tool.

APT system *See* automatic picture transmission system.

aquadag Graphite coating on the inside of certain cathode-ray tubes for collecting secondary electrons emitted by the face of the tube.

arbiter A computer unit that determines the priority sequence in which two or more processor inputs are connected to a single functional unit such as a multiplier or memory.

arbitrary function generator *See* general-purpose function generator.

arcback The flow of a principal electron stream in the reverse direction in a mercury-vapor rectifier tube because of formation of a cathode spot on an anode; this results in failure of the rectifying action. Also known as backfire.

arc converter A form of oscillator using an electric arc as the generator of alternating or pulsating current.

archiving The storage of files, in the form of punch cards, microfilm, or magnetic tape, for very long periods of time, in case it is necessary to regenerate the file due to subsequent introduction of errors.

arc-through Of a gas tube, a loss of control resulting in the flow of a principal electron stream in the normal direction during a scheduled nonconducting period.

area A section of a computer memory assigned by a computer program or by the hardware to hold data of a particular type.

area effect In general, the condition of the dielectric strength of a liquid or vacuum separating two electrodes being higher for electrodes of smaller area.

area search A computer search that examines only those records which satisfy some broad criteria.

A register *See* arithmetic register.

argument A value applied to a procedure, subroutine, or macroinstruction which is required in order to evaluate any of these.

arithmetic address An address in a computer program that results from performing an arithmetic operation on another address.

arithmetical element *See* arithmetical unit.

arithmetical instruction An instruction in a computer program that directs the computer to perform an arithmetic operation (addition, subtraction, multiplication, or division) upon specified items of data.

arithmetical operation A digital computer operation in which numerical quantities are added, subtracted, multiplied, divided, or compared.

arithmetical unit The section of the computer which carries out all arithmetic and logic operations. Also known as arithmetical element; arithmetic-logic unit (ALU); arithmetic section; logic-arithmetic unit; logic section.

arithmetic check The verification of an arithmetical operation or series of operations by another such process; for example, the multiplication of 73 by 21 to check the result of multiplying 21 by 73.

arithmetic circuitry The section of the computer circuitry which carries out the arithmetic operations.

arithmetic-logic unit *See* arithmetical unit.

arithmetic register A specific memory location reserved for intermediate results of arithmetic operations. Also known as A register.

arithmetic scan The procedure for examining arithmetic expressions and determining the order of execution of operators, in the process of compilation into machine-executable code of a program written in a higher-level language.

arithmetic section *See* arithmetical unit.

arithmetic shift A shift of the digits of a number, expressed in a positional notation system, in the register without changing the sign of the number.

Armstrong oscillator Inductive feedback oscillator that consists of a tuned-grid circuit and an untuned-tickler coil in the plate circuit; control of feedback is accomplished by varying the coupling between the tickler and the grid circuit.

array 1. A collection of data items with each identified by a subscript or key and arranged in such a way that a computer can examine the collection and retrieve data from these items associated with a particular subscript or key. **2.** A group of components such as antennas, reflectors, or directors arranged to provide a desired variation of radiation transmission or reception with direction.

array processor A multiprocessor composed of a set of identical central processing units acting synchronously under the control of a common unit.

artificial antenna *See* dummy antenna.

artificial delay line *See* delay line.

artificial intelligence The property of a machine capable of reason by which it can learn functions normally associated with human intelligence.

artificial language A computer language that is specifically designed to facilitate communication in a particular field, but is not yet natural to that field; opposite of a natural language, which evolves through long usage.

A scan *See* A scope.

A scope A radarscope on which the trace appears as a horizontal or vertical range scale and the signals appear as vertical or horizontal deflections. Also known as A indicator; A scan.

asdic Acronym for Anti-Submarine Detection Investigation Committee; British term for sonar and underwater listening devices.

aspect card A card on which is entered the accession numbers of documents in an information retrieval system; the documents are judged to be related importantly to the concept for which the card is established.

asperomagnetic state The condition of a rare-earth glass in which the spins are oriented in fixed directions, with most nearest-neighbor spins parallel or nearly parallel, so that the spin directions are distributed in one hemisphere.

assembler A program designed to convert symbolic instruction into a form suitable for execution on a computer. Also known as assembly program; assembly routine.

assembly The automatic translation into machine language of a computer program written in symbolic language.

assembly language A low-level computer language one step above the binary machine language.

assembly list A printed list which is the by-product of an assembly procedure; it lists in logical instruction sequence all details of a routine, showing the coded and symbolic notation next to the actual notations established by the assembly procedure; this listing is highly useful in the debugging of a routine.

assembly program *See* assembler.

assembly routine *See* assembler.

assembly system An automatic programming software system with a programming language and machine-language programs that aid the programmer by performing different functions such as checkout and updating.

assembly unit 1. A device which performs the function of associating and joining several parts or piecing together a program. 2. A portion of a program which is capable of being assembled into a larger program.

assign A control statement in FORTRAN which assigns a computed value i to a variable k, the latter representing the number of the statement to which control is then transferred.

assignment problem A special case of the transportation problem in a linear program, in which the number of sources (assignees) equals the number of designations (assignments) and each supply and each demand equals 1.

association trail A linkage between two or more documents or items of information, discerned during the process of their examination and recorded with the aid of an information retrieval system.

associative key In a computer system with an associative memory, a field used to reference items through comparing the value of the field with corresponding fields in each memory cell and retrieving the contents of matching cells.

associative memory A data-storage device in which a location is identified by its informational content rather than by names, addresses, or relative positions, and from which the data may be retrieved. Also known as associative storage.

associative processor A digital computer that consists of a content-addressable memory and means for searching rapidly changing random digital data stored within, at speeds up to 1000 times faster than conventional digital computers.

associative storage *See* associative memory.

associator A device for bringing like entities into conjunction or juxtaposition.

assumed decimal point For a decimal number stored in a computer or appearing on a printout, a position in the number at which place values change from positive to negative powers of 10, but to which no location is assigned or at which no printed character appears, as opposed to an actual decimal point. Also known as virtual decimal point.

astable circuit A circuit that alternates automatically and continuously between two unstable states at a frequency dependent on circuit constants; for example, a blocking oscillator.

astable multivibrator A multivibrator in which each active device alternately conducts and is cut off for intervals of time determined by circuit constants, without use of external triggers. Also known as free-running multivibrator.

astigmatism In an electron-beam tube, a focus defect in which electrons in different axial planes come to focus at different points.

Aston dark space A dark region in a glow-discharge tube which extends for a few millimeters from the cathode up to the cathode glow.

astrionics The science of adapting electronics to aerospace flight.

A supply Battery, transformer filament winding, or other voltage source that supplies power for heating filaments of vacuum tubes. Also known as A power supply.

asymmetrical cell A cell, such as a photoelectric cell, in which the impedance to the flow of current in one direction is greater than in the other direction.

asymmetrical deflection A type of electrostatic deflection in which one deflector plate is maintained at a fixed potential and the deflecting voltage is supplied to the other plate.

asynchronous Operating at a speed determined by the circuit functions rather than by timing signals.

asynchronous computer A computer in which the performance of any operation starts as a result of a signal that the previous operation has been completed, rather than on a signal from a master clock.

asynchronous data Information which is sampled at irregular intervals with respect to another operation.

asynchronous input/output The ability to receive input data while simultaneously outputting data.

asynchronous inputs The terminals in a flip-flop circuit which affect the output state of the flip-flop independently of the clock.

asynchronous logic A logic network in which the speed of operation depends only on the signal propagation through the network.

asynchronous operation An operation that is started by a completion signal from a previous operation, proceeds at the maximum speed of the circuits until finished, and then generates its own completion signal.

asynchronous working The mode of operation of a computer in which an operation is performed only at the end of the preceding operation.

asyndetic 1. Omitting conjunctions or connectives. 2. Pertaining to a catalog without cross references.

atmospheric noise Noise heard during radio reception due to atmospheric interference.

atom A primitive data element in a data structure.

A trace The first trace of an oscilloscope, such as the upper trace of a loran indicator.

ATS *See* Administrative Terminal System

attack director An electromechanical analog computer which is designed for surface antisubmarine use and which computes continuous solution of several lines of submarine attack; it is part of several antisubmarine fire control systems.

attended time The time in which a computer is either switched on and capable of normal operation (including time during which it is temporarily idle but still watched over by computer personnel) or out of service for maintenance work.

attenuation equalizer Corrective network which is designed to make the absolute value of the transfer impedance, with respect to two chosen pairs of terminals, substantially constant for all frequencies within a desired range.

attenuation network Arrangement of circuit elements, usually impedance elements, inserted in circuitry to introduce a known loss or to reduce the impedance level without reflections.

attenuator An adjustable or fixed transducer for reducing the amplitude of a wave without introducing appreciable distortion.

attribute A data item containing information about a variable.

audio amplifier *See* audio-frequency amplifier.

audio-frequency amplifier An electronic circuit for amplification of signals within, and in some cases above, the audible range of frequencies in equipment used to record and reproduce sound. Also known as audio amplifier.

audio-frequency oscillator An oscillator circuit using an electron tube, transistor, or other nonrotating device to produce an audio-frequency alternating current. Also known as audio oscillator.

audio oscillator *See* audio-frequency oscillator.

audit The operations developed to corroborate the evidence as regards authenticity and validity of the data that are introduced into the data-processing problem or system.

audit trail A system that provides a means for tracing items of data from processing step to step, particularly from a machine-produced report or other machine output back to the original source data.

augmented operation code An operation code which is further defined by information from another portion of an instruction.

aural radio range A radio-range station providing lines of position by virtue of aural identification or comparison of signals at the output of a receiver.

aurora gating Operator-controlled gating to eliminate undesirable radar returns from aurora.

authoring language A programming language designed to be convenient for authors of computer-based learning materials.

auto-abstract 1. To select key words from a document, commonly by an automatic or machine method, for the purpose of forming an abstract of the document. 2. The material abstracted from a document by machine methods.

autoalarm *See* automatic alarm receiver.

autocode The process of using a computer to convert automatically a symbolic code into a machine code. Also known as automatic code.

autocoder A person or machine producing or using autocode as a part or the whole of some task.

autocorrelation A technique used to detect cyclic activity in a complex signal.

autocorrelator A correlator in which the input signal is delayed and multiplied by the undelayed signal, the product of which is then smoothed in a low-pass filter to give an approximate computation of the autocorrelation function; used to detect a non-periodic signal or a weak periodic signal hidden in noise.

autodecrement addressing An addressing mode of minicomputers in which the register is first decremented and then used as a pointer.

autodyne circuit A circuit in which the same tube elements serve as oscillator and detector simultaneously.

autoincrement addressing An addressing mode of minicomputers in which the operand address is gotten from the specified register which is then incremented.

autoindexing *See* automatic indexing.

automated tape library A computer storage system consisting of several thousand magnetic tapes and equipment under computer control which automatically brings the tapes from storage, mounts them on tape drives, dismounts the tapes when the job is completed, and returns them to storage.

automatic abstracting Techniques whereby, on the basis of statistical properties, a subset of the sentences in a document is selected as representative of the general content of that document.

automatic alarm receiver A complete receiving, selecting, and warning device capable of being actuated automatically by intercepted radio-frequency waves forming the international automatic alarm signal. Also known as autoalarm.

automatic back bias Radar technique which consists of one or more automatic gain control loops to prevent overloading of a receiver by large signals, whether jamming or actual radar echoes.

automatic background control *See* automatic brightness control.

automatic bass compensation A circuit related to the volume control in some radio receivers and audio amplifiers to make bass notes sound properly balanced, in the audio spectrum, at low volume-control settings.

automatic brightness control A circuit used in a television receiver to keep the average brightness of the reproduced image essentially constant. Abbreviated ABC. Also known as automatic background control.

automatic carriage Any mechanism designed to feed continuous paper or plastic forms through a printing or writing device, often using sprockets to engage holes in the paper.

automatic C bias *See* self-bias.

automatic character recognition The technology of using special machine systems to identify human-readable symbols, most often alphanumeric, and then to utilize this data.

automatic check An error-detecting procedure performed by a computer as an integral part of the normal operation of a device, with no human attention required unless an error is actually detected.

automatic chroma control *See* automatic color control.

automatic chrominance control *See* automatic color control.

automatic code *See* autocode.

automatic coding Any technique in which a computer is used to help bridge the gap between some intellectual and manual form of describing the steps to be followed in solving a given problem, and some final coding of the same problem for a given computer.

automatic color control A circuit used in a color television receiver to keep color intensity levels essentially constant despite variations in the strength of the received color signal; control is usually achieved by varying the gain of the chrominance bandpass amplifier. Also known as automatic chroma control; automatic chrominance control.

automatic computer A computer which can carry out a special set of operations without human intervention.

automatic connection Ability of electronic switching equipment to make a connection between users without human intervention.

automatic contrast control A circuit that varies the gain of the radio-frequency and video intermediate-frequency amplifiers in such a way that the contrast of the television picture is maintained at a constant average level.

automatic data-processing auxiliary equipment Equipment which is related in function to automatic data-processing equipment, other than peripheral equipment, and whose use is not exclusively and directly used with an automatic data-processing system; when it is so used, it supports the system in off-line operations such as card-punching equipment and paper-tape-preparing equipment; for example, a flexowriter.

automatic data-processing equipment Electronic data-processing equipment and punched-card accounting machines, irrespective of use, application, or source of funding. Abbreviated ADPE.

automatic data-processing system The equipment, personnel program, and application operations involved in the utilization of electronic data-processing equipment, along with associated electric accounting machines, to solve business and logistics data-processing problems, with a minimum of human intervention.

automatic data-processing system specifications A description (devoid of any orientation to the specific equipment of particular suppliers) of a requirement for, and operations to be performed by, automatic data-processing equipment, and generally including a workload description in terms of representative programs (benchmarks) and extension factors.

automatic degausser An arrangement of degaussing coils mounted around a color television picture tube, combined with a special circuit that energizes these coils only while the set is warming up; demagnetizes any parts of the receiver that have been affected by the magnetic field of the earth or of any nearby home appliance.

automatic dialer A device in which a telephone number up to a maximum of 14 digits can be stored in a memory and then activated, directly into the line, by the caller's pressing a button. Also known as mechanical dialer.

automatic dictionary Any table within a computer memory which establishes a one-to-one correspondence between two sets of characters.

automatic direction finder A direction finder that without manual manipulation indicates the direction of arrival of a radio signal. Abbreviated ADF. Also known as radio compass.

automatic exchange A telephone, teletypewriter, or data-transmission exchange in which communication between subscribers is effected, without the intervention of an operator, by devices set in operation by the originating subscriber's instrument. Also known as automatic switching system; machine switching system.

automatic-feed punch A card punch having a hopper, a card track, and a stacker; movement of cards through the punch is automatic.

automatic fine-tuning control A circuit used in a color television receiver to maintain the correct oscillator frequency in the tuner for best color picture by compensating for drift and incorrect tuning.

automatic frequency control Abbreviated AFC. 1. A circuit used to maintain the frequency of an oscillator within specified limits, as in a transmitter. 2. A circuit used to keep a superheterodyne receiver tuned accurately to a given frequency by controlling its local oscillator, as in an FM receiver. 3. A circuit used in radar superheterodyne receivers to vary the local oscillator frequency so as to compensate for changes in the frequency of the received echo signal. 4. A circuit used in television receivers to make the frequency of a sweep oscillator correspond to the frequency of the synchronizing pulses in the received signal.

automatic gain control A control circuit that automatically changes the gain (amplification) of a receiver or other piece of equipment so that the desired output signal remains essentially constant despite variations in input signal strength. Abbreviated AGC.

automatic grid bias *See* self-bias.

automatic indexing Selection of key words from a document by computer for use as index entries. Also known as autoindexing.

automatic interrupt Interruption of a computer program brought about by a hardware device or executive program acting as a result of some event which has occurred independently of the interrupted program.

automatic light control Automatic adjustment of illumination reaching a film, television camera, or other imaging device as a function of scene brightness.

automatic mathematical translator An automatic-programming computer capable of receiving a mathematical equation from a remote input and returning an immediate solution.

automatic peak limiter *See* limiter.

automatic phase control Abbreviated APC. 1. A circuit used in color television receivers to reinsert a 3.58-megahertz carrier signal with exactly the correct phase and frequency by synchronizing it with the transmitted color-burst signal. 2. An automatic frequency-control circuit in which the difference between two frequency sources is fed to a phase detector that produces the required control signal.

automatic picture control A multiple-contact switch used in some color television receivers to disconnect one or more of the regular controls and make connections to corresponding preset controls.

automatic picture transmission system A system in which a meteorological satellite continuously scans and transmits a view of a transverse swath directly beneath it; transmissions can be recorded by simple ground equipment to reconstruct an image of the cloud patterns within a thousand kilometers of the ground station. Abbreviated APT system.

automatic programming The preparation of machine-language instructions by use of a computer.

Automatic Programming Tool A computer language used to program numerically controlled machine tools. Abbreviated APT.

automatic routine A routine that is executed independently of manual operations, but only if certain conditions occur within a program or record, or during some other process.

automatic scanning receiver A receiver which can automatically and continuously sweep across a preselected frequency, either to stop when a signal is found or to plot signal occupancy within the frequency spectrum being swept.

automatic sensitivity control Circuit used for automatically maintaining receiver sensitivity at a predetermined level; it is similar to automatic gain control, but it affects the receiver constantly rather than during the brief interval selected by the range gate.

automatic sequences The characteristic of a computer that can perform successive operations without human intervention.

automatic stop An automatic halting of a computer processing operation as the result of an error detected by built-in checking devices.

automatic switching system *See* automatic exchange.

automatic tape punch A device that punches holes in a paper tape upon reception of electronic signals from a central processing unit.

automatic threshold variation Constant false-alarm rate scheme that is an open-loop of automatic gain control in which the decision threshold is varied continuously in proportion to the incoming intermediate frequency and video noise level.

automatic tint control A circuit used in color television receivers to maintain correct flesh tones when a station changes cameras or switches to commercials, by correcting phase errors before the chroma signal is demodulated.

automatic video noise leveling Constant false-alarm rate scheme in which the video noise level at the output of the receiver is sampled at the end of each range sweep and the receiver gain is readjusted accordingly to maintain a constant video noise level at the output.

automatic voltage regulator *See* voltage regulator.

automatic volume control An automatic gain control that keeps the output volume of a radio receiver essentially constant despite variations in input-signal strength during fading or when tuning from station to station. Abbreviated AVC.

automation source data The many methods of recording information in coded forms on paper tapes, punched cards, or tags that can be used over and over again to produce many other records without rewriting. Also known as source data automation (SDA).

automaton A robot which functions without step-by-step guidance by a human operator.

automonitor A computer program used in debugging which instructs a computer to make a record of its own operations.

autonomous channel operation The rapid transfer of data between computer peripherals and the main store in which an entire block of data is transferred, word by word; the cycles of storage time for the word transfer are stolen from those available to the central processing unit.

autoplotter A machine which automatically draws a graph from input data.

autopolarity Automatic interchanging of connections to a digital meter when polarity is wrong; a minus sign appears ahead of the value on the digital display if the reading is negative.

auxiliary instruction buffer A section of storage in the instruction unit, 16 bytes in length, used to hold prefetched instructions.

auxiliary operation An operation performed by equipment not under continuous control of the central processing unit of a computer.

auxiliary processor Any equipment which performs an auxiliary operation in a computer.

auxiliary routine A routine designed to assist in the operation of the computer and in debugging other routines.

auxiliary storage Storage device in addition to the main storage of a computer; for example, magnetic tape, disk, or magnetic drum.

availability Of data, data channels, and input-output devices in computers, the condition of being ready for use and not immediately committed to other tasks.

available line Portion of the length of the scanning line which can be used specifically for picture signals in a facsimile system.

available machine time Time during which a computer has the power turned on, is not under maintenance, and is known or believed to be operating correctly.

available power The power which a linear source of energy is capable of delivering into its conjugate impedance.

available power gain Ratio, in an electronic transducer, of the available power from the output terminals of the transducer, under specified input termination conditions, to the available power from the driving generator.

available space list A pool of inactive memory cells, available for use in a list-processing system, to which cells containing items deleted from data lists are added, and from which cells needed for newly inserted data items are removed.

avalanche 1. The cumulative process in which an electron or other charged particle accelerated by a strong electric field collides with and ionizes gas molecules, thereby releasing new electrons which in turn have more collisions, so that the discharge is thus self-maintained. Also known as avalanche effect; cascade; cumulative ionization; Townsend avalanche; Townsend ionization. **2.** Cumulative multiplication of carriers in a semiconductor as a result of avalanche breakdown. Also known as avalanche effect.

avalanche breakdown Nondestructive breakdown in a semiconductor diode when the electric field across the barrier region is strong enough so that current carriers collide with valence electrons to produce ionization and cumulative multiplication of carriers.

avalanche diode A semiconductor breakdown diode, usually made of silicon, in which avalanche breakdown occurs across the entire pn junction and voltage drop is then essentially constant and independent of current; the two most important types are IMPATT and TRAPATT diodes.

avalanche effect *See* avalanche.

avalanche-induced migration A technique of forming interconnections in a field-programmable logic array by applying appropriate voltages for shorting selected base-emitter junctions.

avalanche noise 1. A junction phenomenon in a semiconductor in which carriers in a high-voltage gradient develop sufficient energy to dislodge additional carriers through physical impact; this agitation creates ragged current flows which are indicated by noise. **2.** The noise produced when a junction diode is operated at the onset of avalanche breakdown.

avalanche oscillator An oscillator that uses an avalanche diode as a negative resistance to achieve one-step conversion from direct-current to microwave outputs in the gigahertz range.

avalanche photodiode A photodiode operated in the avalanche breakdown region to achieve internal photocurrent multiplication, thereby providing rapid light-controlled switching operation.

avalanche transistor A transistor that utilizes avalanche breakdown to produce chain generation of charge-carrying hole-electron pairs.

AVC *See* automatic volume control.

average-calculating operation A common or typical calculating operation longer than an addition and shorter than a multiplication; often taken as the mean of nine additions and one multiplication.

average-edge line The imaginary line which traces or smooths the shape of any written or printed character to be recognized by a computer through optical, magnetic, or other means.

average effectiveness level *See* effectiveness level.

average noise figure Ratio in a transducer of total output noise power to the portion thereof attributable to thermal noise in the input termination, the total noise being summed over frequencies from zero to infinity, and the noise temperature of the input termination being standard (290 K).

average power output Radio-frequency power, in an audio-modulation transmitter, delivered to the transmitter output terminals, averaged over a modulation cycle.

axial ratio The ratio of the major axis to the minor axis of the polarization ellipse of a waveguide. Also known as ellipticity.

azel display Modified type of plan position indicator presentation showing two separate radar displays on one cathode-ray screen; one display presents bearing information and the other shows elevation.

azimuth blanking Blanking of the radar receiver as the scan traverses a selected azimuth region.

azimuth gain reduction Technique which allows control of the radar receiver system throughout any two azimuth sectors.

azimuth gating The practice of selectively brightening and enhancing the gain-desired sectors of a radar plan position indicator display, usually by applying a step waveform to the automatic gain control circuit.

azimuth marker *See* electronic azimuth marker.

azimuth versus amplitude Electronic counter-countermeasures receiver with a plan position indicator type of display attached to the main antenna and used to display strobes due to jamming aircraft; it is useful in making passive fixes when two or more radar sites can operate together.

B

back bias 1. Degenerative or regenerative voltage which is fed back to circuits before its originating point; usually applied to a control anode of a tube or other device. 2. Voltage applied to a grid of a tube (or tubes) or electrode of another device to reduce a condition which has been upset by some external cause.

back echo reflection A radar echo produced by radiation reflected to the target by a large, fixed obstruction; that is, the ray path is from antenna to obstruction to target to antenna, instead of antenna to target to antenna.

back-emission electron radiography A technique used in microradiography to visualize, among other things, the presence of material of different atomic numbers in the surface of the specimen being observed; the polished side of the specimen is facing and in close contact with the emulsion side of a fine-grain photographic plate; a light-tight cover holds the specimen and plate in place to be subjected to hardened x-rays.

backfire *See* arcback.

background processing The execution of lower-priority programs when higher-priority programs are not being handled by a data-processing system.

background reflectance The reflectance, relative to a standard, of the surface on which a printed or handwritten character has been inscribed in optical character recognition.

backing Flexible material, usually cellulose acetate or polyester, used on magnetic tape as the carrier for the oxide coating.

backing storage A computer storage device whose capacity is larger, but whose access time is slower, than that of the computer's main storage or immediate access storage; usually slower than main storage. Also known as bulk storage.

backlash A small reverse current in a rectifier tube caused by the motion of positive ions produced in the gas by the impact of thermoelectrons.

backplane A wiring board, usually constructed as a printed circuit, used in microcomputers and minicomputers to provide the required connections between logic, memory, and input/output modules.

back porch The period of time in a television circuit immediately following a synchronizing pulse during which the signal is held at the instantaneous amplitude corresponding to a black area in the received picture.

back resistance The resistance between the contacts opposing the inverse current of a metallic rectifier.

backspace To move a recording medium one unit in the reverse or background direction.

backtalk Passage of information from a standby computer to the active computer.

backtracking A method of solving problems automatically by a systematic search of the possible solutions; invalid solutions are eliminated and are not retried.

Backus-Naur form A metalanguage that specifies which sequences of symbols constitute a syntactically valid program language. Abbreviated BNF.

backward-acting regulator Transmission regulator in which the adjustment made by the regulator affects the quantity which caused the adjustment.

backward diode A semiconductor diode similar to a tunnel diode except that it has no forward tunnel current; used as a low-voltage rectifier.

backward error analysis A form of error analysis which seeks to replace all errors made in the course of solving a problem by an equivalent perturbation of the original problem.

backward-wave magnetron A magnetron in which the electron beam travels in a direction opposite to the flow of the radio-frequency energy.

backward-wave oscillator An electronic device which amplifies microwave signals simultaneously over a wide band of frequencies and in which the traveling wave produced is reflected backward so as to sustain the wave oscillations. Abbreviated BWO. Also known as carcinotron.

backward-wave tube A type of microwave traveling-wave electron tube in which electromagnetic energy on a slow-wave circuit flows opposite in direction to the travel of electrons in a beam.

badge reader A device that can read data appearing in the form of holes in plastic badges or prepunched cards.

baffle An auxiliary member in a gas tube used, for example, to control the flow of mercury particles or deionize the mercury following conduction.

balance control A control used in a stereo sound system to vary the volume of one loudspeaker system relative to the other while maintaining their combined volume essentially constant.

balanced amplifier An electronic amplifier in which there are two identical signal branches connected so as to operate with the inputs in phase opposition and with the output connections in phase, each balanced to ground.

balanced detector A detector used in frequency-modulation receivers; in one form the audio output is the rectified difference between voltages produced across two resonant circuits, one being tuned slightly above the carrier frequency and one slightly below.

balanced input A symmetrical input circuit having equal impedance from both input terminals to reference.

balanced modulator A modulator in which the carrier and modulating signal are introduced in such a way that the output contains the two sidebands without the carrier.

balanced oscillator Any oscillator in which, at the oscillator frequency, the impedance centers of the tank circuits are at ground potential, and the voltages between either end and their centers are equal in magnitude and opposite in phase.

balanced output A three-conductor output (as from an amplifier) in which the signal voltage alternates above and below a third, neutral wire.

balanced ring modulator A modulator that uses tubes or diodes to suppress the carrier signal while providing double-sideband output.

balance error An error voltage that arises at the output of analog adders in an analog computer and is directly proportional to the drift error.

balancing capacitor A variable capacitor used to improve the accuracy of a radio direction finder. Also known as compensating capacitor.

band 1. A set of circular or cyclic recording tracks on a storage device such as a magnetic drum, disk, or tape loop. 2. A restricted range in which the energies of electrons in solids lie, or from which they are excluded, as understood in quantum-mechanical terms.

band gap An energy difference between two allowed bands of electron energy in a metal.

band-pass A range, in hertz or kilohertz, expressing the difference between the limiting frequencies at which a desired fraction (usually half power) of the maximum output is obtained.

band-pass amplifier An amplifier designed to pass a definite band of frequencies with essentially uniform response.

band-pass filter An electric filter which transmits more or less uniformly in a certain band, outside of which the frequency components are attenuated.

band-pass response Response characteristics in which a definite band of frequencies is transmitted uniformly. Also known as flat top response.

band printer A line printer that uses a band of type characters as its printing mechanism.

band scheme The identification of energy bands of a solid with the levels of independent atoms from which they arise as the atoms are brought together to form the solid, together with the width and spacing of the bands.

band selector A switch that selects any of the bands in which a receiver, signal generator, or transmitter is designed to operate and usually has two or more sections to make the required changes in all tuning circuits simultaneously. Also known as band switch.

band-spread tuning control A tuning control provided on some shortwave receivers to spread the stations in a single band of frequencies over an entire tuning dial.

band-stop filter An electric filter which transmits more or less uniformly at all frequencies of interest except for a band within which frequency components are largely attenuated. Also known as band-elimination filter; band-rejection filter.

band theory of solids A quantum-mechanical theory of the motion of electrons in solids that predicts certain restricted ranges or bands for the energies of these electrons.

bang-bang circuit An operational amplifier with double feedback limiters that drive a high-speed relay (1–2 milliseconds) in an analog computer; involved in signal-controlled programming.

bang-bang control Control of programming in an analog computer through a bang-bang circuit.

banked winding A radio-frequency coil winding which proceeds from one end of the coil to the other without return by having, side by side, many flat spirals formed by winding single turns one over the other, thereby reducing the distributed capacitance of the coil.

bantam tube Vacuum tube having a standard octal base, but a considerably smaller glass tube than a standard glass tube.

bar code The representation of alphanumeric characters by series of adjacent stripes of various widths, for example, the universal product code.

bar-code reader *See* bar-code scanner.

bar-code scanner An optical scanning device that reads texts which have been converted into a special bar code. Also known as bar-code reader.

Bardeen-Cooper-Schrieffer theory A theory of superconductivity that describes quantum-mechanically those states of the system in which conduction electrons cooperate in their motion so as to reduce the total energy appreciably below that of other states by exploiting their effective mutual attraction; these states predominate in a superconducting material. Abbreviated BCS theory.

bar generator Generator of pulses or repeating waves which are equally separated in time; these pulses are synchronized by the synchronizing pulses of a television system, so that they can produce a stationary bar pattern on a television screen.

BARITT diode *See* barrier injection transit-time diode.

Barkhausen-Kurz oscillator An oscillator of the retarding-field type in which the frequency of oscillation depends solely on the transit time of electrons oscillating about a highly positive grid before reaching the less positive anode. Also known as Barkhausen oscillator; positive-grid oscillator.

Barkhausen oscillation Undesired oscillation in the horizontal output tube of a television receiver, causing one or more ragged dark vertical lines on the left side of the picture.

Barkhausen oscillator *See* Barkhausen-Kurz oscillator.

bar pattern Pattern of repeating lines or bars on a television screen.

barrel printer A computer printer in which the entire set of characters is placed around a rapidly rotating cylinder at each print position; computer-controlled print hammers opposite each print position strike the paper and press it against an inked ribbon between the paper and the cylinder when the appropriate character reaches a position opposite the print hammer.

barrier-grid storage tube *See* radechon.

barrier injection transit-time diode A microwave diode in which the carriers that traverse the drift region are generated by minority carrier injection from a forward-biased junction instead of being extracted from the plasma of an avalanche region. Abbreviated BARITT diode.

barrier layer *See* depletion layer.

barrier-layer cell *See* photovoltaic cell.

barrier-layer photocell *See* photovoltaic cell.

barrier-layer rectification *See* depletion-layer rectification.

barrier voltage The voltage necessary to cause electrical conduction in a junction of two dissimilar materials, such as *pn* junction diode.

base 1. The region that lies between an emitter and a collector of a transistor and into which minority carriers are injected. **2.** The part of an electron tube that has the pins, leads, or other terminals to which external connections are made either directly or through a socket. **3.** The plastic, ceramic, or other insulating board that supports a printed wiring pattern. **4.** A plastic film that supports the magnetic powder of magnetic tape or the emulsion of photographic film. **5.** *See* root.

base address *See* address constant.

base bias The direct voltage that is applied to the majority-carrier contact (base) of a transistor.

base electrode An ohmic or majority carrier contact to the base region of a transistor.

base language The component of an extensible language which provides a complete but minimal set of primitive facilities, such as elementary data types, and simple operations and control constructs.

base line The line traced on amplitude-modulated indicators which corresponds to the power level of the weakest echo detected by the radar; it is retraced with every pulse transmitted by the radar but appears as a nearly continuous display on the scope.

base-line break Technique in radar which uses the characteristic break in the base line on an A-scope display due to a pulse signal of significant strength in noise jamming.

base modulation Amplitude modulation produced by applying the modulating voltage to the base of a transistor amplifier.

base pin *See* pin.

base register *See* index register.

base-spreading resistance Resistance which is found in the base of any transistor and acts in series with it, generally a few ohms in value.

BASIC A procedure-level computer language well suited for conversational mode on a terminal usually connected with a remotely operated computer. Derived from Beginners All-purpose Symbolic Instruction Code.

basic batch The least complex level of computer processing, in which application systems are normally made up of small programs that are run through the computer one at a time and that can process transactions only from sequential files.

basic instruction An instruction in a computer program which is systematically changed by the program to obtain the instructions which are actually carried out. Also known as presumptive instruction; unmodified instruction.

basic linkage Computer coding that provides a standard means of connecting a given routine or program with other routines and that can be used repeatedly according to the same rules.

basic software Software requirements that are taken into account in the design of the data-processing hardware and usually provided by the original equipment manufacturer.

basic variables The m variables in a basic feasible solution for a linear programming model.

basket coil *See* basket winding.

basket winding A crisscross coil winding in which successive turns are far apart except at points of crossing, giving low distributed capacitance. Also known as basket coil.

bass boost A circuit that emphasizes the lower audio frequencies, generally by attenuating higher audio frequencies.

bass compensation A circuit that emphasizes the low-frequency response of an audio amplifier at low volume levels to offset the lower sensitivity of the human ear to weak low frequencies.

bass control A manual tone control that attenuates higher audio frequencies in an audio amplifier and thereby emphasizes bass frequencies.

bass response A measure of the output of an electronic device or system as a function of an input of low audio frequencies.

batch A set of items, records, or documents to be processed as a single unit.

batching Grouping records for the purpose of processing them in a computer.

batch processing A technique that uses a single program loading to process many individual jobs, tasks, or requests for service.

batch terminal A computer terminal that provides access similar to that provided by the computer's input/output devices, but at a location convenient to the user, so that an entire task or job can be submitted at one time.

batch total The total for a specified constituent quantity in a batch; used to verify the accuracy of operations on the batch.

Batten system A system of information retrieval that uses cards in which holes have been punched. Also known as Cordonnier system; peekaboo system.

battery eliminator A device which supplies electron tubes with voltage from electric power supply mains.

Bayard-Alpert ionization gage A type of ionization vacuum gage using a tube with an electrode structure designed to minimize x-ray-induced electron emission from the ion collector.

B battery The battery that furnishes required direct-current voltages to the plate and screen-grid electrodes of the electron tubes in a battery-operated circuit.

BBD *See* bucket brigade device.

B box *See* index register.

BCD system *See* binary coded decimal system.

B display The presentation of radar output data in rectangular coordinates in which range and azimuth are plotted on the coordinate axes. Also known as range-bearing display.

beacon delay The amount of transponding delay within a beacon, that is, the time between the arrival of a signal and the response of the beacon.

beacon presentation The radarscope presentation resulting from radio-frequency waves sent out by a radar beacon.

beacon skipping A condition where transponder return pulses from a beacon are missing at the interrogating radar.

beacon stealing Loss of beacon tracking by one radar due to stronger signals from an interfering radar.

beam blank *See* blank.

beam coupling The production of an alternating current in a circuit connected between two electrodes that are close to, or in the path of, a density-modulated electron beam.

beam current The electric current determined by the number and velocity of electrons in an electron beam.

beam-deflection tube An electron-beam tube in which the current to an output electrode is controlled by transversely moving the electron beam.

beam-forming electrode Electron-beam focusing elements in power tetrodes and cathode-ray tubes.

beam holding Use of a diffused beam of electrons to regenerate the charges stored on the screen of a cathode-ray storage tube.

beam-indexing tube A single-beam color television picture tube in which the color phosphor strips are arranged in groups of red, green, and blue.

beam lead A flat thick-film lead, sometimes of gold, deposited on a semiconductor chip chemically or by evaporation, as a connecting lead for a semiconductor device or integrated circuit.

beam lobe switching Method of determining the direction of a remote object by comparison of the signals corresponding to two or more successive beam angles, differing slightly from the direction of the object.

beam magnet *See* convergence magnet.

beam parametric amplifier Parametric amplifier that uses a modulated electron beam to provide a variable reactance.

beam power tube An electron-beam tube which uses directed electron beams to provide most of its power-handling capability and in which the control grid and screen grid are essentially aligned. Also known as beam tetrode.

beam recording A method of using an electron beam to write data generated by a computer directly on microfilm.

beam splitting Process for increasing accuracy in locating targets by radar; by noting the azimuths at which one radar scan first discloses a target and at which radar data from it ceases, beam splitting calculates the mean azimuth for the target.

beam steering Changing the direction of the major lobe of a radiation pattern, usually by switching antenna elements.

beam storage A magnetic storage device that employs electron beams to enter information into, or retrieve information from, storage cells; for example, a cathode-ray-tube storage.

beam switching Method of obtaining more accurately the bearing or elevation of an object by comparing the signals received when the beam is in directions differing slightly in bearing or elevation; when these signals are equal, the object lies midway between the beam axes. Also known as lobe switching.

beam-switching tube An electron tube which has a series of electrodes arranged around a central cathode and in which an electron beam is switched from one electrode to another. Also known as cyclophon.

beam tetrode *See* beam-power tube.

bearing resolution Minimum angular separation in a horizontal plane between two targets at the same range that will allow an operator to obtain data on either target.

beat frequency The frequency of a signal equal to the difference in frequencies of two signals which produce the signal when they are combined in a nonlinear circuit.

beat-frequency oscillator An oscillator in which a desired signal frequency, such as an audio frequency, is obtained as the beat frequency produced by combining two different signal frequencies, such as two different radio frequencies. Abbreviated BFO. Also known as heterodyne oscillator.

beating-in Interconnecting two transmitter oscillators and adjusting one until no beat frequency is heard in a connected receiver; the oscillators are then at the same frequency.

beat note The beat frequency whose signal is produced by two signals having waves that are sinusoidal.

beat reception *See* heterodyne reception.

beat-time programming A type of programming which requires that data be made available to the computer during some ongoing process prior to a particular point in time.

BEGIN An enclosing statement of ALGOL used to indicate the beginning of a block; any variable in a block enclosed by BEGIN and END is normally local to this block.

beginning-of-information marker A section of magnetic tape covered with reflective material that indicates the beginning of the area on which information is to be recorded.

B eliminator Power pack that changes the alternating-current powerline voltage to the direct-current source required by plant circuits of vacuum tubes or semiconductor devices.

bench-mark problem A problem to be run on computers to evaluate their performances relative to one another.

bender element A combination of two thin strips of different piezoelectric materials bonded together so that when a voltage is applied, one strip increases in length and the other becomes shorter, causing the combination to bend.

beta The current gain of a transistor that is connected as a grounded-emitter amplifier, expressed as the ratio of change in collector current to resulting change in base current, the collector voltage being constant.

beta rule *See* reduction rule.

bias 1. A direct-current voltage applied to a transistor control electrode to establish the desired operating point. 2. *See* grid bias.

bias cell A small dry cell used singly or in series to provide the required negative bias for the grid circuit of an electron tube. Also known as grid-bias cell.

bias current 1. An alternating electric current above about 40,000 hertz added to the audio current being recorded on magnetic tape to reduce distortion. 2. An electric current flowing through the base-emitter junction of a transistor and adjusted to set the operating point of the transistor.

bias distortion Distortion resulting from the operation on a nonlinear portion of the characteristic curve of a vacuum tube or other device, due to improper biasing.

biased automatic gain control *See* delayed automatic gain control.

biased relay *See* percentage differential relay.

bias oscillator An oscillator used in a magnetic recorder to generate the alternating-current signal that is added to the audio current being recorded on magnetic tape to reduce distortion.

bias resistor A resistor used in the cathode or grid circuit of an electron tube to provide a voltage drop that serves as the bias.

bias voltage A voltage applied or developed between two electrodes as a bias.

biconditional gate *See* equivalence gate.

bidirectional clamping circuit A clamping circuit that functions at the prescribed time irrespective of the polarity of the signal source at the time the pulses used to actuate the clamping action are applied.

bidirectional clipping circuit An electronic circuit that prevents transmission of the portion of an electrical signal that exceeds a prescribed maximum or minimum voltage value.

bidirectional counter *See* forward-backward counter.

bidirectional transducer A transducer capable of measuring in both positive and negative directions from a reference position. Also known as bilateral transducer.

bidirectional transistor A transistor that provides switching action in either direction of signal flow through a circuit; widely used in telephone switching circuits.

bidirectional triode thyristor A gate-controlled semiconductor switch designed for alternating-current power control.

big M method A technique for solving linear programming problems in which artificial variables are assigned cost coefficients which are a very large number M, say, $M = 10^{35}$.

bilateral Having a voltage current characteristic curve that is symmetrical with respect to the origin.

bilateral amplifier An amplifier capable of receiving as well as transmitting signals; used primarily in transceivers.

bilateral transducer *See* bidirectional transducer.

bimag core *See* bistable magnetic core.

bimorph cell Two piezoelectric plates cemented together in such a way that an applied voltage causes one to expand and the other to contract so that the cell bends in proportion to the applied voltage; conversely, applied pressure generates double the voltage of a single cell; used in phonograph pickups and microphones.

bin A magnetic-tape memory in which a number of tapes are stored in a single housing.

binary Possessing a property for which there exists two choices or conditions, one choice excluding the other.

binary arithmetic operation An arithmetical operation in which the operands are in the form of binary numbers. Also known as binary operation.

binary cell An elementary unit of computer storage that can have one or the other of two stable states and can thus store one bit of information.

binary chain A series of binary circuit elements so arranged that each can change the state of the one following it.

binary code A code in which each allowable position has one of two possible states, commonly 0 and 1; the binary number system is one of many binary codes.

binary coded character One element of a notation system representing alphanumeric characters such as decimal digits, alphabetic letters, and punctuation marks by a predetermined configuration of consecutive binary digits.

binary coded decimal system A system of number representation in which each digit of a decimal number is represented by a binary number. Abbreviated BCD system.

binary coded decimal-to-decimal converter A computer circuit which selects one of ten outputs corresponding to a four-bit binary coded decimal input, placing it in the 0 state and the other nine outputs in the 1 state.

binary coded octal system Octal numbering system in which each octal digit is represented by a three-place binary number.

binary counter *See* binary scaler.

binary dump The operation of copying the contents of a computer memory in binary form onto an external storage device.

binary encoder An encoder that changes angular, linear, or other forms of input data into binary-coded output characters.

binary image A representation in a computer storage device of each of the holes in a punch card or paper tape (for example, by indicating the places where there are holes with a 1 and the places where there are no holes with a 0), to be differentiated from the characters represented by the combinations of holes.

binary incremental representation A type of incremental representation in which the value of change in a variable is represented by one binary digit which is set equal to 1 if there is an increase in the variable and to 0 if there is a decrease.

binary loader A computer program which transfers to main memory an exact image of the binary pattern of a program held in a storage or input device.

binary logic An assembly of digital logic elements which operate with two distinct states.

binary magnetic core A ferromagnetic core that can be made to take either of two stable magnetic states.

binary operation *See* binary arithmetic operation.

binary point The character, or the location of an implied symbol, that separates the integral part of a numerical expression from its fractional part in binary notation.

binary row Pertaining to the binary representation of data on punched cards in which adjacent positions in a row correspond to adjacent bits of the data.

binary scaler A scaler that produces one output pulse for every two input pulses. Also known as binary counter; scale-of-two circuit.

binary search A dichotomizing search in which the set of items to be searched is divided at each step into two equal, or nearly equal, parts.

binary signal A voltage or current which carries information by varying between two possible values, corresponding to 0 and 1 in the binary system.

binary word A group of bits which occupies one storage address and is treated by the computer as a unit.

B indicator *See* B scope.

binding time The instant when a symbolic expression in a computer program is reduced to a form which is directly interpretable by the hardware.

binistor A silicon *npn* tetrode that serves as a bistable negative-resistance device.

binode An electron tube with two anodes and one cathode used as a full-wave rectifier. Also known as double diode.

bipolar amplifier An amplifier capable of supplying a pair of output signals corresponding to the positive or negative polarity of the input signal.

bipolar circuit A logic circuit in which zeros and ones are treated in a symmetric or bipolar manner, rather than by the presence or absence of a signal; for example, a balanced arrangement in a square-loop-ferrite magnetic circuit.

bipolar integrated circuit An integrated circuit in which the principal element is the bipolar junction transistor.

bipolar memory A computer memory employing integrated-circuit bipolar junction transistors as bistable memory cells.

bipolar transistor A transistor that uses both positive and negative charge carriers.

bipotential electrostatic lens An electron lens in which image and object space are field-free, but at different potentials; examples are the lenses formed between apertures of cylinders at different potentials. Also known as immersion electrostatic lens.

biquartic filter An active filter that uses operational amplifiers in combination with resistors and capacitors to provide infinite values of Q and simple adjustments for band-pass and center frequency.

bistable circuit A circuit with two stable states such that the transition between the states cannot be accomplished by self-triggering.

bistable magnetic core A magnetic core that can be in either of two possible states of magnetization. Also known as bimag core.

bistable multivibrator A multivibrator in which either of the two active devices may remain conducting, with the other nonconducting, until the application of an external pulse. Also known as Eccles-Jordan circuit; Eccles-Jordan multivibrator; flip-flop circuit; trigger circuit.

bit 1. A unit of information content equal to one binary decision or the designation of one of two possible and equally likely values or states of anything used to store or convey information. **2.** A dimensionless unit of storage capacity specifying that the capacity of a storage device is expressed by the logarithm to the base 2 of the number of possible states of the device.

bit count appendage One of the two-byte elements replacing the parity bit stripped off each byte transferred from main storage to disk volume (the other element is the cyclic check); these two elements are appended to the block during the write operation; on a subsequent read operation these elements are calculated and compared to the appended elements for accuracy.

bit density Number of bits which can be placed, per unit length, area, or volume, on a storage medium; for example, bits per inch of magnetic tape. Also known as record density.

bit location Storage position on a record capable of storing one bit.

bit pattern A combination of binary digits arranged in a sequence.

bit position The position of a binary digit in a word, generally numbered from the least significant bit.

bit-sliced microprocessor A microprocessor in which the major logic of the central processor is partitioned into a set of large-scale-integration circuits, as opposed to being placed on a single chip.

bit stream 1. A consecutive line of bits transmitted over a circuit in a transmission method in which character separation is accomplished by the terminal equipment. 2. A binary signal without regard to grouping by character.

bit string A set of consecutive binary digits representing data in coded form, in which the significance of each bit is determined by its position in the sequence and its relation to the other bits.

bit zone 1. One of the two left-most bits in a commonly used system in which six bits are used for each character; related to overpunch. 2. Any bit in a group of bit positions that are used to indicate a specific class of items; for example, numbers, letters, special signs, and commands.

black-and-white groups See Shubnikov groups.

black level The level of the television picture signal corresponding to the maximum limit of black peaks.

black scope Cathode-ray tube operating at the threshold of luminescence when no video signals are being applied.

black-surface field A layer of p^+ material which is applied to the back surface of a solar cell to reduce hole-electron recombinations there and thereby increase the cell's efficiency.

blank To cut off the electron beam of a television picture tube, camera tube, or cathode-ray oscilloscope tube during the process of retrace by applying a rectangular pulse voltage to the grid or cathode during each retrace interval. Also known as beam blank.

blank character A character, either printed or appearing as a blank, used to denote a blank space among printed characters. Also known as space character.

blank form See blank medium.

blanking circuit A circuit preventing the transmission of brightness variations during the horizontal and vertical retrace intervals in television scanning.

blanking level The level that separates picture information from synchronizing information in a composite television picture signal; coincides with the level of the base of the synchronizing pulses. Also known as pedestal; pedestal level.

blanking pulse A positive or negative square-wave pulse used to switch off a part of a television or radar set electronically for a predetermined length of time.

blanking signal The signal rendering the return trace invisible on the picture tube of a television receiver.

blanking time The length of time that the electron beam of a cathode-ray tube is shut off.

blank medium An empty position on the medium concerned, such as a column without holes on a punch tape, used to indicate a blank character. Also known as blank form.

blank tape A portion of a paper tape having sprocket holes only, to indicate a blank character.

blank tape halting problem The problem of finding an algorithm that, for any Turing machine, decides whether the machine eventually stops if it started on an empty tape; it has been proved that no such algorithm exists.

blast To release internal or external memory areas from the control of a computer program in the course of dynamic storage allocation, making these areas available for reallocation to other programs.

bleed In optical character recognition, the flow of ink in printed characters beyond the limits specified for their recognition by a character reader.

bleeder A high resistance connected across the dc output of a high-voltage power supply which serves to discharge the filter capacitors after the power supply has been turned off, and to provide a stabilizing load.

B line *See* index register.

blinking Electronic-countermeasures technique employed by two aircraft separated by a short distance and within the same azimuth resolution so as to appear as one target to a tracking radar; the two aircraft alternately spot-jam, causing the radar system to oscillate from one place to another, making an accurate solution of a fire control problem impossible.

blip 1. The display of a received pulse on the screen of a cathode-ray tube. Also known as pip. **2.** An ideal infrared radiation detector that detects with unit quantum efficiency all of the radiation in the signal for which the detector was designed, and responds only to the background radiation noise that comes from the field of view of the detector.

blip-scan ratio The ratio of the number of times a target appears on a radarscope to the number of times it could have been seen.

Bloch wall A transition layer, with a finite thickness of a few hundred lattice constants, between adjacent ferromagnetic domains. Also known as domain wall.

block 1. A group of information units (such as records, words, characters, or digits) that are transported or considered as a single unit by virtue of their being stored in successive storage locations; for example, a group of logical records constituting a physical record. **2.** The section of a computer memory or storage device that stores such a group of information units. Also known as storage block. **3.** To combine two or more information units into a single unit.

block body A list of statements that follows the block head in a computer program with block structure.

block data A statement in FORTRAN which declares that the program following is a data specification subprogram.

blocked F-format data set *See* FB data set.

blockette A subdivision of a group of consecutive machine words transferred as a unit, particularly with reference to input and output.

block head A list of declarations at the beginning of a computer program with block structure.

block identifier A means of identifying an area of storage in FORTRAN so that this area may be shared by a program and its subprograms.

block ignore character A character associated with a block which indicates the presence of errors in the block.

blocking 1. Combining two or more computer records into one block. 2. Applying a high negative bias to the grid of an electron tube to reduce its anode current to zero. 3. Overloading a receiver by an unwanted signal so that the automatic gain control reduces the response to a desired signal. 4. Distortion occurring in a resistance-capacitance-coupled electron tube amplifier stage when grid current flows in the following tube.

blocking capacitor *See* coupling capacitor.

blocking factor The largest possible number of records of a given size that can be contained within a single block.

blocking layer *See* depletion layer.

blocking oscillator A relaxation oscillator that generates a short-time-duration pulse by using a single transistor or electron tube and associated circuitry. Also known as squegger; squegging oscillator.

blocking oscillator driver Circuit which develops a square pulse used to drive the modulator tubes, and which usually contains a line-controlled blocking oscillator that shapes the pulse into the square wave.

block input 1. A block of computer words considered as a unit and intended or destined to be transferred from an internal storage medium to an external destination. 2. *See* output area.

block length The total number of records, words, or characters contained in one block.

block loading A program loading technique in which the control sections of a program or program segment are loaded into contiguous positions in main memory.

block mark A special character that indicates the end of a block.

block sort A method of sorting a file, usually with punched card sorters, in which the file is first sorted according to the value of the digit in the highest digit position of the key; the resulting collections of records can next be sorted independently in smaller operations, and the separate sections then joined.

block standby Locations always set aside in storage for communication with buffers in order to make more efficient use of such buffers.

block structure In computer programming, a conceptual tool used to group sequences of statements into single compound statements and to allow the programmer explicit control over the scope of the program variables.

block transfer The movement of data in blocks instead of by individual records.

blooming 1. Defocusing of television picture areas where excessive brightness results in enlargement of spot size and halation of the fluorescent screen. 2. An increase in radarscope spot size due to an increase in signal intensity.

blue glow A glow normally seen in electron tubes containing mercury vapor, due to ionization of the mercury molecules.

BNF *See* Backus-Naur form.

bobbing Fluctuation of the strength of a radar echo, or its indication on a radarscope, due to alternate interference and reinforcement of returning reflected waves.

Bode diagram A diagram in which the phase shift or the gain of an amplifier, a servomechanism, or other device is plotted against frequency to show frequency response; logarithmic scales are customarily used for gain and frequency.

bomb *See* abend.

bombardment The use of induction heating to heat electrodes of electron tubes to drive out gases during evacuation.

bonded NR diode An n^+ junction semiconductor device in which the negative resistance arises from a combination of avalanche breakdown and conductivity modulation which is due to the current flow through the junction.

bonding pad A metallized area on the surface of a semiconductor device, to which connections can be made.

bookkeeping operation A computer operation which does not directly contribute to the result, that is, arithmetical, logical, and transfer operations used in modifying the address section of other instructions in counting cycles and in rearranging data. Also known as red-tape operation.

Boolean A scalar declaration in ALGOL defining variables similar to FORTRAN's logical variables.

Boolean data type *See* logical data type.

Boolean search A search for selected information, that is, information satisfying conditions that can be expressed by AND, OR, and NOT functions.

boost To augment in relative intensity, as to boost the bass response in an audio system.

booster 1. A separate radio-frequency amplifier connected between an antenna and a television receiver to amplify weak signals. 2. A radio-frequency amplifier that amplifies and rebroadcasts a received television or communication radio carrier frequency for reception by the general public.

booster battery A battery which increases the sensitivity of a crystal detector by maintaining a certain voltage across it and thereby adjusting conditions to increase the response to a given input.

booster voltage The additional voltage supplied by the damper tube to the horizontal output, horizontal oscillator, and vertical output tubes of a television receiver to give greater sawtooth sweep output.

boot button *See* bootstrap button.

bootstrap button The first button pressed when a computer is turned on, causing the operating system to be loaded into memory. Also known as boot button; initial program load button; IPL button.

bootstrap circuit A single-stage amplifier in which the output load is connected between the negative end of the anode supply and the cathode, while signal voltage is applied between grid and cathode; a change in grid voltage changes the input signal voltage with respect to ground by an amount equal to the output signal voltage.

bootstrap driver Electronic circuit used to produce a square pulse to drive the modulator tube; the duration of the square pulse is determined by a pulse-forming line.

bootstrap instructor technique A technique permitting a system to bring itself into an operational state by means of its own action. Also known as bootstrap technique.

bootstrap integrator A bootstrap sawtooth generator in which an integrating amplifier is used in the circuit. Also known as Miller generator.

bootstrap loader A very short program loading routine, used for loading other loaders in a computer; often implemented in a read-only memory.

bootstrap memory A device that provides for the automatic input of new programs without erasing the basic instructions in the computer.

bootstrapping A technique for lifting a generator circuit above ground by a voltage value derived from its own output signal.

bootstrap sawtooth generator A circuit capable of generating a highly linear positive sawtooth waveform through the use of bootstrapping.

bootstrap technique *See* bootstrap instructor technique.

bottom-up analysis A reductive method of syntactic analysis which attempts to reduce a string to a root symbol.

boundary An interface between *p*- and *n*-type semiconductor materials, at which donor and acceptor concentrations are equal.

boundary-layer photocell *See* photovoltaic cell.

bounds register A device which stores the upper and lower bounds on addresses in the memory of a given computer program in a time-sharing system.

boxcar circuit A circuit used in radar for sampling voltage waveforms and storing the latest value sampled; the term is derived from the flat, steplike segments of the output voltage waveform.

B power supply *See* B supply.

branch 1. Any one of a number of instruction sequences in a program to which computer control is passed, depending upon the status of one or more variables. **2.** *See* jump.

branching The selection, under control of a computer program, of one of two or more branches.

branch instruction An instruction that makes the computer choose between alternative subprograms, depending on the conditions determined by the computer during the execution of the program.

branch point A point in a computer program at which there is a branch instruction.

breadboarding Assembling an electronic circuit in the most convenient manner, without regard for final locations of components, to prove the feasibility of the circuit and to facilitate changes when necessary.

break A reflected radar pulse which appears on a radarscope as a line perpendicular to the base line.

breakdown impedance Of a semiconductor, the small-signal impedance at a specified direct current in the breakdown region.

breakdown region Of a semiconductor diode, the entire region of the volt-ampere characteristic beyond the initiation of breakdown for increasing magnitude of bias.

break-in device A device in a radiotelegraph communication system allowing an operator to receive signals in intervals between his own transmission signals.

breakoutput An ALGOL procedure which causes all bytes in a device buffer to be sent to the device rather than wait until the buffer is full.

breakover In a silicon controlled rectifier or related device, a transition into forward conduction caused by the application of an excessively high anode voltage.

breakover voltage The positive anode voltage at which a silicon controlled rectifier switches into the conductive state with gate circuit open.

breakpoint A point in a program where an instruction, instruction digit, or other condition enables a programmer to interrupt the run by external intervention or by a monitor routine.

breakpoint switch A manually operated switch which controls conditional operation at breakpoints, used primarily in debugging.

breakpoint symbol A symbol which may be optionally included in an instruction, as an indication, tag, or flag, to designate it as a breakpoint.

breakthrough An interruption in the intended character stroke in optical character recognition.

B register *See* index register.

bridge hybrid *See* hybrid junction.

bridge limiter A device employed in analog computers to keep the value of a variable within specified limits.

bridge magnetic amplifier A magnetic amplifier in which each of the gate windings is connected in series with an arm of a bridge rectifier; the rectifiers provide self-saturation and direct-current output.

bridge oscillator An oscillator using a balanced bridge circuit as the feedback network.

bridge rectifier A full-wave rectifier with four elements connected as a bridge circuit with direct voltage obtained from one pair of opposite junctions when alternating voltage is applied to the other pair.

bridging amplifier Amplifier with an input impedance sufficiently high so that its input may be bridged across a circuit without substantially affecting the signal level of the circuit across which it is bridged.

bridging connection Parallel connection by means of which some of the signal energy in a circuit may be withdrawn frequently, with imperceptible effect on the normal operation of the circuit.

bridging loss Loss resulting from bridging an impedance across a transmission system; quantitatively, the ratio of the signal power delivered to that part of the system following the bridging point, and measured before the bridging, to the signal power delivered to the same part after the bridging.

brightness control A control that varies the luminance of the fluorescent screen of a cathode-ray tube, for a given input signal, by changing the grid bias of the tube and hence the beam current. Also known as brilliance control; intensity control.

brilliance 1. The degree of brightness and clarity of the display of a cathode-ray tube. 2. The degree to which the higher audio frequencies of an input sound are reproduced by a radio receiver, by a public address amplifier, or by a sound-recording playback system.

brilliance control *See* brightness control.

Brillouin scattering Light scattering by acoustic phonons.

broad-band amplifier An amplifier having essentially flat response over a wide range of frequencies.

broad-band klystron Klystron having three or more resonant cavities that are externally loaded and stagger-tuned to broaden the bandwidth.

broadcast transmitter A transmitter designed for use in a commercial amplitude-modulation, frequency-modulation, or television broadcast channel.

broad tuning Poor selectivity in a radio receiver, causing reception of two or more stations at a single setting of the tuning dial.

brush encoder An encoder in which brushes that make contact with conductive segments on a rotating or linearly moving surface convert positional information to digitally encoded data.

brush station A location in a device where the holes in a punched card are sensed by brushes sweeping electrical contacts.

B scan *See* B scope.

B scope A cathode-ray scope on which signals appear as spots, with bearing angle as the horizontal coordinate and range as the vertical coordinate. Also known as B indicator; B scan.

B store *See* index register.

B supply Anode high voltage and screen-grid power source in vacuum tube circuits. Also known as B power supply.

B trace In loran the second trace of an oscilloscope which corresponds to the signal from the B station.

bubble *See* magnetic bubble.

bubble memory A computer memory in which the presence or absence of a magnetic bubble in a localized region of a thin magnetic film designates a 1 or 0; storage capacity can be well over 1 megabit per cubic inch. Also known as magnetic bubble memory.

bucket A name usually reserved for a storage cell in which data may be accumulated.

bucket brigade device A semiconductor device in which majority carriers store charges that represent information, and minority carriers transfer charges from point to point in sequence. Abbreviated BBD.

buffer 1. An isolating circuit in an electronic computer used to prevent the action of a driven circuit from affecting the corresponding driving circuit. 2. *See* buffer amplifier; buffer storage.

buffer amplifier An amplifier used after an oscillator or other critical stage to isolate it from the effects of load impedance variations in subsequent stages. Also known as buffer; buffer stage.

buffer capacitor A capacitor connected across the secondary of a vibrator transformer or between the anode and cathode of a cold-cathode rectifier tube to suppress voltage surges that might otherwise damage other parts in the circuit.

buffered computer A computer having a temporary storage device to compensate for differences in transmission speeds.

buffered I/O channel A storage device located between input/output (I/O) channels and main storage control to free the channels for use by other operations.

buffered terminal A computer terminal which contains storage equipment so that the rate at which it sends or receives data over its line does not need to agree exactly with the rate at which the data are entered or printed.

buffer pooling A technique for receiving data in an input/output control system in which a number of buffers are available to the system; when a record is produced, a buffer is taken from the pool, used to hold the data, and returned to the pool after data transmission.

buffer stage *See* buffer amplifier.

buffer storage A synchronizing element used between two different forms of storage in a computer; computation continues while transfers take place between buffer storage and the secondary or internal storage. Also known as buffer.

buffer zone An area of main memory set aside for temporary storage.

bug 1. A defect in a program code or in designing a routine or a computer. 2. A semiautomatic code-sending telegraph key in which movement of a lever to one side produces a series of correctly spaced dots and movement to the other side produces a single dash. 3. An electronic listening device, generally concealed, used for commercial or military espionage.

build To increase in received signal strength.

built-in check A hardware device which controls the accuracy of data either moved or stored within the computer system.

built-in function A function that is available through a simple reference and specification of arguments in a given higher-level programming language. Also known as built-in procedure; intrinsic procedure.

built-in procedure *See* built-in function.

bulk-acoustic-wave delay line A delay line in which the delay is determined by the distance traveled by a bulk acoustic wave between input and output transducers mounted on a piezoelectric block.

bulk diode A semiconductor microwave diode that uses the bulk effect, such as Gunn diodes and diodes operating in limited space-charge-accumulation modes.

bulk effect An effect that occurs within the entire bulk of a semiconductor material rather than in a localized region or junction.

bulk-effect device A semiconductor device that depends on a bulk effect, as in Gunn and avalanche devices.

bulk lifetime The average time that elapses between the formation and recombination of minority charge carriers in the bulk material of a semiconductor.

bulk memory A high-capacity memory used in connection with a computer for bulk storage of large quantities of data.

bulk photoconductor A photoconductor having high power-handling capability and other unique properties that depend on the semiconductor and doping materials used.

bulk resistor An integrated-circuit resistor in which the *n*-type epitaxial layer of a semiconducting substrate is used as a noncritical high-value resistor; the spacing between the attached terminals and the sheet resistivity of the material together determine the resistance value.

bulk storage *See* backing storage.

bump contact A large-area contact used for alloying directly to the substrate of a transistor for mounting or interconnecting purposes.

buncher *See* buncher resonator.

buncher resonator The first or input cavity resonator in a velocity-modulated tube, next to the cathode; here the faster electrons catch up with the slower ones to produce bunches of electrons. Also known as buncher; input resonator.

bunching The flow of electrons from cathode to anode of a velocity-modulated tube as a succession of electron groups rather than as a continuous stream.

bunching voltage Radio-frequency voltage between the grids of the buncher resonator in a velocity-modulated tube such as a klystron; generally, the term implies the peak value of this oscillating voltage.

bundled program A computer program written, maintained, and updated by the computer manufacturer, and included in the price of the hardware.

burn-in Operation of electronic components before they are applied in order to stabilize their characteristics and reveal defects.

burn-through *See* jammer finder.

burst 1. To separate a continuous roll of paper into stacks of individual sheets by means of a burster. **2.** The transfer of a collection of records in a storage device, leaving an interval in which data for other requirements can be obtained from or entered into the device. **3.** A sequence of signals regarded as a unit in data transmission. **4.** An exceptionally large electric pulse in the circuit of an ionization chamber due to the simultaneous arrival of several ionizing particles. **5.** A radar term for a single pulse of radio energy.

burst amplifier An amplifier stage in a color television receiver that is keyed into conduction and amplification by a horizontal pulse at the instant of each arrival of the color burst. Also known as chroma band-pass amplifier.

burster An off-line device in a computer system used to separate the continuous roll of paper produced as output from a printer into individual sheets, generally along perforations in the roll.

burst mode A method of transferring data between a peripheral unit and a control processing unit in a computer system in which the peripheral unit sends the central processor a signal to receive data until the peripheral unit signals that the transfer is completed.

burst separator The circuit in a color television receiver that separates the color burst from the composite video signal.

bus One or more conductors in a computer along which information is transmitted from any of several sources to any of several destinations.

Butterworth filter An electric filter whose pass band (graph of transmission versus frequency) has a maximally flat shape.

button 1. A small, round piece of metal alloyed to the base wafer of an alloy-junction transistor. Also known as dot. **2.** The container that holds the carbon granules of a carbon microphone. Also known as carbon button.

buzz The condition of a combinatorial circuit with feedback that has undergone a transition, caused by the inputs, from an unstable state to a new state that is also unstable.

BWO *See* backward-wave oscillator.

bypass filter Filter which provides a low-attenuation path around some other equipment, such as a carrier frequency filter used to bypass a physical telephone repeater station.

byte A sequence of adjacent binary digits operated upon as a unit in a computer and usually shorter than a word.

byte mode A method of transferring data between a peripheral unit and a central processor in which one byte is transferred at a time.

C

cable delay The time required for one bit of data to go through a cable, about 1.5 nanoseconds per foot of cable.

cache A small, fast storage buffer integrated in the central processing unit of some large computers.

CAD *See* computer-aided design.

cadmium selenide cell A photoconductive cell that uses cadmium selenide as the semiconductor material and has a fast response time and high sensitivity to longer wavelengths of light.

cadmium sulfide cell A photoconductive cell in which a small wafer of cadmium sulfide provides an extremely high dark-light resistance ratio.

cadmium telluride detector A photoconductive cell capable of operating continuously at ambient temperatures up to 750°F (400°C); used in solar cells and infrared, nuclear-radiation, and gamma-ray detectors.

CAI *See* computer-assisted instruction.

CAL A higher-level language, developed especially for time-sharing purposes, in which a user at a remote console typewriter is directly connected to the computer and can work out problems on-line with considerable help from the computer. Derived from Conversational Algebraic Language.

calculated address *See* generated address.

calculating machine *See* calculator.

calculating punch A calculator having a card reader and a card punch.

calculator A device that performs logic and arithmetic digital operations based on numerical data which are entered by pressing numerical and control keys. Also known as calculating machine.

call To transfer control to a specified closed subroutine.

call announcer Device for receiving pulses from an automatic telephone office and audibly reproducing the corresponding number in words, so that it may be heard by a manual operator.

call by location A method of transferring arguments from a calling program to a subprogram in which the referencing program provides to the subprogram the memory location at which the value of the argument can be found, rather than the value itself.

call by name A method of transferring arguments from a calling program to a subprogram in which the actual expression is passed to the subprogram.

call by value A method of transferring arguments from a calling program to a subprogram in which the subprogram is provided with the values of the argument and on path leads back to the referencing program.

call in To transfer control of a digital computer, temporarily, from a main routine to a subroutine that is inserted in the sequence of calculating operations, to fulfill an ancillary purpose.

call indicator Device for receiving pulses from an automatic switching system and displaying the corresponding called number before an operator at a manual switchboard.

calling device Apparatus which generates the pulses required for establishing connections in an automatic telephone switching system.

calling sequence A specific set of instructions to set up and call a given subroutine, make available the data required by it, and tell the computer where to return after the subroutine is executed.

call number In computer operations, a set of characters identifying a subroutine, and containing information concerning parameters to be inserted in the subroutine, or information to be used in generating the subroutine, or information related to the operands.

CAM *See* computer-aided manufacturing.

camera *See* television camera.

camera tube An electron-beam tube used in a television camera to convert an optical image into a corresponding charge-density electric image and to scan the resulting electric image in a predetermined sequence to provide an equivalent electric signal. Also known as pickup tube; television camera tube.

cancellation circuit A circuit used in providing moving-target indication on a plan position indicator scope; cancels constant-amplitude fixed-target pulses by subtraction of successive pulse trains.

canned program A program which has been written to solve a particular problem, is available to users of a computer system, and is usually fixed in form and capable of little or no modification.

capacitance relay An electronic relay that responds to a small change in capacitance, such as that created by bringing a hand near a pickup wire or plate.

capacitive-discharge ignition An automotive ignition system in which energy is stored in a capacitor and discharged across the gap of a spark plug through a step-up pulse transformer and distributor each time a silicon controlled rectifier is triggered.

capacitive-discharge pilot light An electronic ignition system, operating off an alternating-current power line or battery power supply, that produces a spark for lighting a gas flame.

capacitive feedback Process of returning part of the energy in the plate (or output) circuit of a vacuum tube (or other device) to the grid (or input) circuit by means of a capacitance common to both circuits.

capacitive tuning Tuning involving use of a variable capacitor.

capacitor box A box-shaped structure in which a capacitor is submerged in a heat-absorbing medium, usually water. Also known as condenser box.

capacitor-input filter A power-supply filter in which a shunt capacitor is the first element after the rectifier.

capacity *See* storage capacity.

capture effect The effect wherein a strong frequency-modulation signal in an FM receiver completely suppresses a weaker signal on the same or nearly the same frequency.

carbon button *See* button.

carbon resistor A resistor consisting of carbon particles mixed with a binder, molded into a cylindrical shape, and baked; terminal leads are attached to opposite ends. Also known as composition resistor.

carcinotron *See* backward-wave oscillator.

card An information-carrying medium, common to practically all computers, for the introduction of data and instructions into the computers either directly or indirectly.

card bed The metal plate along which the card travels to the punching and reading stations.

card checking The verification carried out by the computer to ensure that all the data keypunched on a card has been correctly read into the memory.

card code The representation of characters on a punched card by means of punching one or more holes per column.

card face The printed side of a punched card or, if printing is on both sides, the side of chief importance.

card feed A device that inserts cards into a machine one at a time.

card field A specified group of card columns used for a particular category of data.

card fluff Small bits of paper that may be left attached to the edge of a hole punched in a punch card, which may cause misfeeding or misreading of the card.

card hopper A device that holds cards and makes them available to a card-feed mechanism. Also known as hopper.

card image A one-to-one representation of the contents of a punched card, such as a matrix in which a 1 represents a hole and a 0 represents the absence of a hole.

cardinal point effect The increased intensity of a line or group of returns on the radarscope occurring when the radar beam is perpendicular to the rectangular surface of a line or group of similarly aligned features in the ground pattern.

card jam A condition in which one or more punch cards become jammed along the card bed of a machine that is processing them. Also known as card wreck.

card loader A programming routine which permits a deck of cards to be read into a memory.

card machine 1. Any of several small computers which perform particular operations called for by instruction cards, concurrently with the reading of data cards. 2. Loosely, any type of peripheral equipment which reads or punches cards.

card punch A computer output device that punches holes in a punch card upon reception of signals from the central processing unit.

card punch buffer A temporary storage device into which the output of a computer is transmitted before it is entered on a punch card by a card punch, and in which the data remain if for any reason the card punch cannot operate.

card reader A mechanism that senses information punched on cards, using wire brushes, metal feelers, or a photoelectric system. Also known as punched-card reader.

card reproducer A machine that makes a duplicate of a punched card.

card row A row of punching positions parallel to the long edge of a punched card.

card sorter A machine used to arrange punched cards into an appropriate sequence for further processing. Also known as punched-card sorter; sorter.

card system A computer system whose only input unit is a card reader and whose only output units are a card punch and a printer.

card-to-card transceiving A system that makes possible instantaneous and accurate duplication of punched cards over telephone and telegraph networks between locations separated by either just a few miles or thousands of miles.

card-to-disk conversion A straightforward operation which consists in loading the data in a deck of cards onto a disk by means of a utility program.

card-to-print program A small computer program that uses punch cards in concert with a printer listing the information on the cards and that does not use either tape or disk storage equipment.

card-to-tape conversion A straightforward operation which consists in loading the data in a deck of cards onto a magnetic tape by means of a utility program.

card verifier An electromechanical device which allows the operator to check that a card has been properly key-punched.

card wreck *See* card jam.

carriage return The operation that causes the next character to be printed at the extreme left margin, and usually advances to the next line at the same time.

carriage tape *See* control tape.

carrier *See* charge carrier.

carrier amplifier A direct-current amplifier in which the dc input signal is filtered by a low-pass filter, then used to modulate a carrier so it can be amplified conventionally as an alternating-current signal; the amplified dc output is obtained by rectifying and filtering the rectified carrier signal.

carrier density The density of electrons and holes in a semiconductor.

carrier mobility The average drift velocity of carriers per unit electric field in a homogeneous semiconductor; the mobility of electrons is usually different from that of holes.

carrier repeater Equipment designed to raise carrier signal levels to such a value that they may traverse a succeeding line section at such amplitude as to preserve an adequate signal-to-noise ratio; while the heart of a repeater is the amplifier, necessary adjuncts are filters, equalizers, level controls, and so on, depending upon the operating methods.

carrier terminal Apparatus at one end of a carrier transmission system, whereby the processes of modulation, demodulation, filtering, amplification, and associated functions are effected.

carrier transfer filters Filters arranged as a carrier-frequency crossover or bridge between two transmission circuits.

carry-complete signal A signal generated by a digital parallel adder, indicating that all carries from an adding operation have been generated and propagated, and that the addition operation is completed.

carry flag A flip-flop circuit which indicates overflow in arithmetic operations.

carry lookahead A circuit which allows low-order carries to ripple through all the way to the highest-order bit to output a completed sum.

carry-save adder A device for the rapid addition of three operands; consists of a sequence of full adders, in which one of the operands is entered in the carry inputs, and the carry outputs, instead of feeding the carry inputs of the following full adders, form a second output word which is then added to the ordinary output in a two-operand adder to form the final sum.

carry signal A signal produced in a computer when the sum of two digits in the same column equals or exceeds the base of the number system in use or when the difference between two digits is less than zero.

carry time The time needed to transfer all carry digits to the next higher column.

cartridge disk A type of disk storage device consisting of a single disk encased in a compact container which can be inserted in and removed from the disk drive unit; used extensively with minicomputer systems.

cartridge tape drive A tape drive which will automatically thread the tape on the takeup reels without human assistance. Formerly known as hypertape drive.

cascade *See* avalanche.

cascade amplifier A vacuum-tube amplifier containing two or more stages arranged in the conventional series manner. Also known as multistage amplifier.

cascade-amplifier klystron A klystron having three resonant cavities to provide increased power amplification and output; the extra resonator, located between the input and output resonators, is excited by the bunched beam emerging from the first resonator gap and produces further bunching of the beam.

cascade connection A series connection of amplifier stages, networks, or tuning circuits in which the output of one feeds the input of the next. Also known as tandem connection.

cascaded carry A carry process in which the addition of two numerals results in a sum numeral and a carry numeral that are in turn added together, this process being repeated until no new carries are generated.

cascaded feedback canceler Sophisticated moving-target-indicator canceler which provides clutter and chaff rejection. Also known as velocity shaped canceler.

cascade image tube An image tube having a number of sections stacked together, the output image of one section serving as the input for the next section; used for light detection at very low levels.

cascade junction Two *pn* semiconductor junctions in tandem such that the condition of the first governs that of the second.

cascade limiter A limiter circuit that uses two vacuum tubes in series to give improved limiter operation for both weak and strong signals in a frequency-modulation receiver. Also known as double limiter.

cascade noise The noise in a communications receiver after an input signal has been subjected to two tandem stages of amplification.

cascode amplifier An amplifier consisting of a grounded-cathode input stage that drives a grounded-grid output stage; advantages include high gain and low noise; widely used in television tuners.

case In computers, a set of data to be used by a particular program.

cassette-cartridge system An input system often used in minicomputers; its low cost and ease in mounting often offset its slow access time.

cassette memory A removable magnetic tape cassette that stores computer programs and data.

catalog 1. All the indexes to data sets or files in a system. 2. The index to all other indexes; the master index. 3. To add an entry to an index or to build an entire new index.

cataloged procedure A group of control cards (job control language statements) that has been placed in a cataloged data set.

catalog-order device A logic circuit element that is readily obtainable from a manufacturer, and can be combined wih other such elements to provide a wide variety of logic circuits.

catcher Electrode in a velocity-modulated vacuum tube on which the spaced electron groups induce a signal; the output of the tube is taken from this element.

catching diode Diode connected to act as a short circuit when its anode becomes positive; the diode then prevents the voltage of a circuit terminal from rising above the diode cathode voltage.

categorization Process of separating multiple addressed messages to form individual messages for singular addresses.

catena A series of data items that appears in a chained list.

catenate To arrange a collection of items in a chained list or catena.

cathode 1. The primary source of electrons in an electron tube; in directly heated tubes the filament is the cathode, and in indirectly heated tubes a coated metal cathode surrounds a heater. Designated K. Also known as negative electrode. 2. The terminal of a semiconductor diode that is negative with respect to the other terminal when the diode is biased in the forward direction.

cathode bias Bias obtained by placing a resistor in the common cathode return circuit, between cathode and ground; flow of electrode currents through this resistor produces a voltage drop that serves to make the control grid negative with respect to the cathode.

cathode-coupled amplifier A cascade amplifier in which the coupling between two stages is provided by a common cathode resistor.

cathode coupling Use of an input or output element in the cathode circuit for coupling energy to another stage.

cathode dark space The relatively nonluminous region between the cathode glow and the negative flow in a glow-discharge cold-cathode tube. Also known as Crookes dark space; Hittorf dark space.

cathode disintegration The destruction of the active area of a cathode by positive-ion bombardment.

cathode drop The voltage between the arc stream and the cathode of a glow-discharge tube. Also known as cathode fall.

cathode emission A process whereby electrons are emitted from the cathode structure.

cathode fall *See* cathode drop.

cathode follower A vacuum-tube circuit in which the input signal is applied between the control grid and ground, and the load is connected between the cathode and ground. Also known as grounded-anode amplifier; grounded-plate amplifier.

cathode glow The luminous glow that covers all or part of the cathode in a glow-discharge cold-cathode tube.

cathode interface capacitance A capacitance which, when connected in parallel with an appropriate resistance, forms an impedance approximately equal to the cathode interface impedance. Also known as layer capacitance.

cathode interface impedance The impedance between the cathode base and coating in an electron tube, due to a high-resistivity layer or a poor mechanical bond. Also known as layer impedance.

cathode keying Transmitter keying by means of a key in the cathode lead of the keyed vacuum-tube stage, opening the direct-current circuits for the grid and anode simultaneously.

cathode modulation Amplitude modulation accomplished by applying the modulating voltage to the cathode circuit of an electron tube in which the carrier is present.

cathode ray A stream of electrons, such as that emitted by a heated filament in a tube, or that emitted by the cathode of a gas-discharge tube when the cathode is bombarded by positive ions.

cathode-ray oscillograph A cathode-ray oscilloscope in which a photographic or other permanent record is produced by the electron beam of the cathode-ray tube.

cathode-ray oscilloscope A test instrument that uses a cathode-ray tube to make visible on a fluorescent screen the instantaneous values and waveforms of electrical quantities that are rapidly varying as a function of time or another quantity. Abbreviated CRO. Also known as oscilloscope; scope.

cathode-ray output A cathode-ray tube used in a computer to display output information in graphic form or by character representation.

cathode-ray storage tube A storage tube in which the information is written by means of a cathode-ray beam.

cathode-ray tube An electron tube in which a beam of electrons can be focused to a small area and varied in position and intensity on a surface. Abbreviated CRT. Originally known as Braun tube; also known as electron-ray tube.

cathode-ray tuning indicator A small cathode-ray tube having a fluorescent pattern whose size varies with the voltage applied to the grid; used in radio receivers to indicate accuracy of tuning and as a modulation indicator in some tape recorders. Also known as electric eye; electron-ray indicator; magic eye; tuning eye.

cathode resistor A resistor used in the cathode circuit of a vacuum tube, having a resistance value such that the voltage drop across it due to tube current provides the correct negative grid bias for the tube.

cathode spot The small cathode area from which an arc appears to originate in a discharge tube.

cathodoluminescence Luminescence produced when high-velocity electrons bombard a metal in vacuum, thus vaporizing small amounts of the metal in an excited state, which amounts emit radiation characteristic of the metal. Also known as electron-oluminescence.

cathodophosphorescence Phosphorescence produced when high-velocity electrons bombard a metal in a vacuum.

CATT *See* controlled avalanche transit-time triode.

catwhisker A sharply pointed, flexible wire used to make contact with the surface of a semiconductor crystal at a point that provides rectification.

cavity impedance The impedance of the cavity of a microwave tube which appears across the gap between the cathode and the anode.

cavity magnetron A magnetron having a number of resonant cavities forming the anode; used as a microwave oscillator.

cavity oscillator An ultra-high-frequency oscillator whose frequency is controlled by a cavity resonator.

CAW *See* channel address word.

C bias *See* grid bias.

CCW *See* channel command word.

C display In radar, a rectangular display in which targets appear as blips with bearing indicated by the horizontal coordinate, and angles of elevation by the vertical coordinate.

cellar *See* push-down storage.

cell-type tube Gas-filled radio-frequency switching tube which operates in an external resonant circuit; a tuning mechanism may be incorporated in either the external resonant circuit or the tube.

cellular automation A theoretical model of a parallel computer which is subject to various restrictions to make practicable the formal investigation of its computing powers.

cellular chain A chain which is not allowed to cross a cell boundary.

cellular multilist A type of multilist organization composed of cellular chains.

cellular splitting A method of adding records to a file in which the records are grouped into cells and each cell is divided into two when it becomes full.

center-coupled loop Coupling loop in the center of one of the resonant cavities of a multicavity magnetron.

center-feed tape Punched tape in which the centers of the sprocket holes are in line with the centers of the holes carrying the data or message.

centering control One of the two controls used for positioning the image on the screen of a cathode-ray tube; either the horizontal centering control or the vertical centering control.

center line *See* stroke center line.

centralized data processing The processing of all the data concerned with a given activity at one place, usually with fixed equipment within one building.

central processing unit The part of a computer containing the circuits required to interpret and execute the instructions. Abbreviated CPU. Also known as frame; main frame.

central terminal A communication device which queues tellers' requests for processing and which channels answers to the consoles originating the transactions.

ceramic amplifier An amplifier that utilizes the piezoelectric properties of semiconductors such as silicon.

ceramic-based microcircuit A microminiature circuit printed on a ceramic substrate.

ceramic tube An electron tube having a ceramic envelope capable of withstanding operating temperatures over 500°C, as required during reentry of guided missiles.

Cerenkov rebatron radiator Device in which a tightly bunched, velocity-modulated electron beam is passed through a hole in a dielectric; the reaction between the higher velocity of the electrons passing through the hole and the slower velocity of the electromagnetic energy passing through the dielectric results in radiation at some frequency higher than the frequency of modulation of the electron beam.

cesium-antimonide photocathode A photocathode obtained by exposing a thin layer of antimony to cesium vapor at elevated temperatures; has a maximum sensitivity in the blue and ultraviolet regions of the spectrum.

cesium-beam sputter source A source of negative ions in which a beam of positive cesium ions, accelerated through a potential difference on 20–30 kilovolts, sputters the cesium-coated inner surface of a hollow cone fabricated from or containing the element whose negative ion is required, and an appreciable fraction of the negative ions leaving the surface are extracted from the rear hole of the sputter cone.

cesium beam tube *See* cesium electron tube.

cesium electron tube An electronic device used as an atomic clock, producing electromagnetic energy that is accurate and stable in frequency. Also known as cesium beam tube.

cesium hollow cathode A cathode in which cesium is heated at the bottom of a cylinder serving as the cathode of an electron tube, to give current densities that can be as high as 800 amperes per square centimeter.

cesium phototube A phototube having a cesium-coated cathode; maximum sensitivity in the infrared portion of the spectrum.

cesium thermionic converter A thermionic diode in which cesium vapor is stored between the plates to neutralize space charge and to lower the work function of the emitter.

cesium-vapor lamp A lamp in which light is produced by the passage of current between two electrodes in ionized cesium vapor.

cesium-vapor Penning source A conventional Penning source modified for negative-ion generation through the introduction or a third, sputter cathode, made from or containing the element of interest, which is the source of negative ions, and through the introduction of cesium vapor into the arc chamber.

cesium-vapor rectifier A gas tube in which cesium vapor serves as the conducting gas and a condensed monatomic layer of cesium serves as the cathode coating.

chad The piece of material removed when forming a hole or notch in a punched tape or punched card. Also known as chip.

chadless tape Paper tape in which the perforations for code characters are made by an incomplete circular cut, with the resulting flap of material folded aside.

chad tape Paper tape in which perforations for code characters are completely punched out.

chain 1. A series of data or other items linked together in some way. **2.** A sequence of binary digits used to construct a code.

chain code A binary code consisting of a cyclic sequence of some or all of the possible binary words at a given length such that each word is derived from the previous one by moving the binary digits one position to the left, dropping the leading bit, and inserting a new bit at the end, in such a way that no word recurs before the cycle is complete.

chain command Any input/output command in a sequence of input/output commands such as WRITE, READ, SENSE.

chain data flag A value of 1 given to a specific bit of a channel command word, commonly used with scatter read or scatter write operations.

chained list A collection of data items arranged in a sequence so that each item contains an address giving the location of the next item in a computer storage device.

chained records A file of records arranged according to the chaining method.

chaining A method of storing records which are not necessarily contiguous, in which the records are arranged in a sequence and each record contains means to identify its successor.

chaining search A method of searching for a data item in a chained list in which an initial key is used to obtain the location of either the item sought or another item in the list, and the search then progresses through the chain until the required item is obtained or the chain is completed.

chain printer A high-speed printer in which the type slugs are carried by the links of a revolving chain.

challenger *See* interrogator.

chance-constrained programming Type of nonlinear programming wherein the deterministic constraints are replaced by their probabilistic counterparts.

changed memory routine A selective memory dump routine in which only those words that have been changed in the course of running a program are printed.

change dump A type of dump in which only those locations in a computer memory whose contents have changed since some previous event are copied.

change of control 1. A break in a series of records at which processing of the records may be interrupted and some predetermined action taken. 2. *See* jump.

change record A record that is used to alter information in a corresponding master record. Also known as amendment record; transaction record.

change tape A paper tape or magnetic tape carrying information that is to be used to update filed information; the latter is often on a master tape. Also known as transaction tape.

channel 1. A path along which digital or other information may flow in a computer. 2. The section of a storage medium that is accessible to a given reading station in a computer, such as a path parallel to the edge of a magnetic tape or drum or a path in a delay-line memory. 3. One of the longitudinal rows of intelligence holes punched along the length of paper tape. Also known as level. 4. A path for a signal, as an audio amplifier may have several input channels. 5. The main current path between the source and drain electrodes in a field-effect transistor or other semiconductor device.

channel address word A four-byte code containing the protection key and the main storage address of the first channel command word at the start of an input/output operation. Abbreviated CAW.

channel bank Part of a carrier-multiplex terminal that performs the first step of modulation of the transmitting voice frequencies into a higher-frequency band, and the final step in the demodulation of the received higher-frequency band into the received voice frequencies.

channel command The step, equivalent to a program instruction, required to tell an input/output channel what operation is to be performed, and where the data are or should be located.

channel command word A code specifying an operation, one or more flags, a count, and a storage location. Abbreviated CCW.

channel control command An order to a control unit to perform a nondata input/output operation.

channel design The type of channel, characterized by the tasks it can perform, available to a computer.

channel effect A leakage current flowing over a surface path between the collector and emitter in some types of transistors.

channel-end condition A signal indicating that the use of an input/output channel is no longer required.

channel mask A portion of a program status word indicating which channels may interrupt the task by their completion signals.

channel program The set of steps, called channel commands, by means of which an input/output channel is controlled.

channel read-backward command A command to transfer data from tape device to main storage while the tape is moving backward.

channel read command A command to transfer data from an input/output device to main storage.

channel sense command A command commonly used to denote an unusual condition existing in an input/output device and requesting more information.

channel shifter Radiotelephone carrier circuit that shifts one or two voice-frequency channels from normal channels to higher voice-frequency channels to reduce cross talk between channels; the channels are shifted back by a similar circuit at the receiving end.

channel status table A table that is set up by an executive program to show the status of the various channels that connect the central processing unit with peripheral units, enabling the program to control input/output operations.

channel status word A storage register containing the status information of the input/ output operation which caused an interrupt. Abbreviated CSW.

channel synchronizer An electronic device providing the proper interface between the central processing unit and the peripheral devices.

channel-to-channel adapter A device which provides two computer systems with interchannel communications.

channel write command A command which transfers data from main storage to an input/output device.

character 1. An elementary mark used to represent data, usually in the form of a graphic spatial arrangement of connected or adjacent strokes, such as a letter or a digit. **2.** A small collection of adjacent bits used to represent a piece of data, addressed and handled as a unit, often corresponding to a digit or letter.

character adjustment An address modification affecting a specific number of characters of the address part of the instruction.

character boundary In character recognition, a real or imaginary rectangle which serves as the delimiter between consecutive characters or successive lines on a source document.

character data type A scalar data type which provides an internal representation of printable characters.

character density The number of characters recorded per unit of length or area. Also known as record density.

character display terminal A console that can display only alphanumeric characters, and cannot show arbitrary lines or curves.

character emitter In character recognition, an electromechanical device which conveys a specimen character in the form of a time pulse or group of pulses.

character fill To fill one or more locations in a computer storage device by repeated insertion of some particular character, usually blanks or zeros.

character generator A hard-wired subroutine which will display alphanumeric characters on a screen.

characteristic overflow An error condition encountered when the characteristic of a floating point number exceeds the limit imposed by the hardware manufacturer.

characteristic underflow An error condition encountered when the characteristic of a floating point number is smaller than the smallest limit imposed by the hardware manufacturer.

character-oriented computer A computer in which the locations of individual characters, rather than words, can be addressed.

character outline The graphic pattern formed by the stroke edges of a printed or handwritten character in character recognition.

character reader In character recognition, any device capable of locating, identifying, and translating into machine code the handwritten or printed data appearing on a source document.

character recognition The technology of using a machine to sense and encode into a machine language the characters which are originally written or printed by human beings.

character skew In character recognition, an improper appearance of a character to be recognized, in which it appears in a tilted condition with respect to a real or imaginary horizontal base line.

character string A sequence of characters in a computer memory or other storage device. Also known as alphabetic string.

character string constant An arbitrary combination of letters, digits, and other symbols which, in the processing of nonnumeric data involving character strings, performs a function analogous to that of a numeric constant in the processing of numeric data.

character stroke *See* stroke.

character style In character recognition, a distinctive construction that is common to all members of a particular character set.

character-writing tube A cathode-ray tube that forms alphanumeric and symbolic characters on its screen for viewing or recording purposes.

charge carrier A mobile conduction electron or mobile hole in a semiconductor. Also known as carrier.

charge-coupled devices Semiconductor devices arrayed so that the electric charge at the output of one provides the input stimulus to the next.

charge-coupled image sensor A device in which charges are introduced when light from a scene is focused on the surface of the device; image points are accessed sequentially to produce a television-type output signal. Also known as solid-state image sensor.

charge-coupled memory A computer memory that uses a large number of charge-coupled devices for data storage and retrieval.

charge coupling Transfer of all electric charges within a semiconductor storage element to a similar, nearby element by means of voltage manipulations.

charge exchange source A source of negative ions, generally negative helium ions, in which positive ions generated in a duoplasmatron are directed through a donor canal, usually containing lithium vapor, where they pick up sequentially two electrons to form negative ions.

charge-injection device A charge-transfer device used as an image sensor in which the image points are accessed by reference to their horizontal and vertical coordinates. Abbreviated CID.

charge neutrality The condition in which electrons and holes are present in equal numbers in a semiconductor.

charge-storage transistor A transistor in which the collector-base junction will charge when forward bias is applied with the base at a high level and the collector at a low level.

charge-storage tube A storage tube in which information is retained on a surface in the form of electric charges.

charge-storage varactor A varactor that uses semiconductor techniques to achieve power outputs above 50 watts at ultra-high and microwave frequencies.

charge-transfer device A semiconductor device that depends upon movements of stored charges between predetermined locations, as in charge-coupled and charge-injection devices.

Chebyshev filter A filter in which the transmission frequency curve has an equal-ripple shape, with very small peaks and valleys.

check A test which is necessary to detect a mistake in computer programming or a computer malfunction.

check bit A binary check digit.

check character A redundant character used to perform a check.

check digit A redundant digit used to perform a check.

check indicator A console device, usually a light, informing the operator that an error has occurred.

check indicator instruction A computer instruction which directs that a signal device is turned on to call the operator's attention to the fact that there is some discrepancy in the instruction now in use.

checking program A computer program which detects and determines the nature of errors in other programs, particularly those that involve incorrect coding or punching of wrong characters. Also known as checking routine.

checking routine *See* checking program.

check number A number denoting a specific type of hardware malfunction.

checkpoint That place in a routine at which the entire state of the computer (memory, registers, and so on) is written out on auxiliary storage (tape, disk, cards) from which it may be read back into the computer if the program is to be restarted later.

check problem *See* check routine.

check register A register in which transferred data are temporarily stored so that they may be compared with a second transfer of the same data, to verify the accuracy of the transfer.

check routine A routine or problem designed primarily to indicate whether a fault exists in a computer, without giving detailed information on the location of the fault. Also known as check problem; test program; test routine.

check row A row (or one of two or more rows) on a paper tape which contains the cumulated sum of existing rows, column by column, resulting in either 1 or 0 by column, thus verifying that all rows have been properly read.

check sum A sum of digits or numbers used in a summation check.

check symbol One or more digits generated by performing an arithmetic check or summation check on a data item which are then attached to the item and copied along with it through various stages of processing, allowing the check to be repeated to verify the accuracy of the copying processes.

check word A computer word, containing data from a block of records, that is joined to the block and serves as a check symbol during transfers of the block between different locations.

Child-Langmuir equation *See* Child's law.

Child-Langmuir-Schottky equation *See* Child's law.

Child's law A law stating that the current in a thermionic diode varies directly with the three-halves power of anode voltage and inversely with the square of the distance between the electrodes, provided the operating conditions are such that the current is limited only by the space charge. Also known as Child-Langmuir equation; Child-Langmuir-Schottky equation; Langmuir-Child equation.

chimney A pipelike enclosure that is placed over a heat sink to improve natural upward convection of heat and thereby increase the dissipating ability of the sink.

Chinese binary *See* column binary.

chip 1. The shaped and processed semiconductor die that is mounted on a substrate to form a transistor, diode, or other semiconductor device. 2. An integrated microcircuit performing a significant number of functions and constituting a subsystem. **3.** *See* chad.

chip capacitor A single-layer or multilayer monolithic capacitor constructed in chip form, with metallized terminations to facilitate direct bonding on hybrid integrated circuits.

chip circuit *See* large-scale integrated circuit.

chip resistor A thick-film resistor constructed in chip form, with metallized terminations to facilitate direct bonding on hybrid integrated circuits.

chopper amplifier A carrier amplifier in which the direct-current input is filtered by a low-pass filter, then converted into a square-wave alternating-current signal by either one or two choppers.

chopper-stabilized amplifier A direct-current amplifier in which a direct-coupled amplifier is in parallel with a chopper amplifier.

chopper transistor A bipolar or field-effect transistor operated as a repetitive "on/off" switch to produce square-wave modulation of an input signal.

chopping The removal, by electronic means, of one or both extremities of a wave at a predetermined level.

chroma band-pass amplifier *See* burst amplifier.

chroma control The control that adjusts the amplitude of the carrier chrominance signal fed to the chrominance demodulators in a color television receiver, so as to change the saturation or vividness of the hues in the color picture. Also known as color control; color-saturation control.

chroma oscillator A crystal oscillator used in color television receivers to generate a 3.579545-megahertz signal for comparison with the incoming 3.579545-megahertz chrominance subcarrier signal being transmitted. Also known as chrominance-subcarrier oscillator; color oscillator; color-subcarrier oscillator.

chromatic aberration An electron-gun defect causing enlargement and blurring of the spot on the screen of a cathode-ray tube, because electrons leave the cathode with different initial velocities and are deflected differently by the electron lenses and deflection coils.

chromatron A single-gun color picture tube having color phosphors deposited on the screen in strips instead of dots. Also known as Lawrence tube.

chrominance demodulator A demodulator used in a color television receiver for deriving the I and Q components of the chrominance signal from the chrominance signal and the chrominance-subcarrier frequency. Also known as chrominance-subcarrier demodulator.

chrominance gain control Variable resistors in red, green, and blue matrix channels that individually adjust primary signal levels in color television.

chrominance modulator A modulator used in a color television transmitter to generate the chrominance signal from the video-frequency chrominance components and the chrominance subcarrier. Also known as chrominance-subcarrier modulator.

chrominance-subcarrier demodulator *See* chrominance demodulator.

chrominance-subcarrier modulator *See* chrominance modulator.

chrominance-subcarrier oscillator *See* chroma oscillator.

chrominance video signal Voltage output from the red, green, or blue section of a color television camera or receiver matrix.

chromium dioxide tape A magnetic recording tape developed primarily to improve quality and brilliance of reproduction when used in cassettes operated at 1⅞ inches per second (4.76 centimeters per second); requires special recorders that provide high bias.

chromium-gold metallizing A metal film used on a silicon or silicon oxide surface in semiconductor devices because it is not susceptible to purple plague deterioration; a layer of chromium is applied first for adherence to silicon, then a layer of chromium-gold mixture, and finally a layer of gold to which bonding contacts can be applied.

chronistor A subminiature elapsed-time indicator that uses electroplating principles to totalize operating time of equipment up to several thousand hours.

chronometric encoder An encoder that uses an electronic counter to time or count electrical events and deliver in digital form a number equivalent to the input magnitude.

chronopher Instrument for emitting standard time signal impulses from a standard clock or timing device.

chronotron A device that measures nanosecond time intervals between pulses on a transmission line to determine the time between the events which initiated the pulses.

chute blades Thin metal bands which form channels to the various pockets of a sorter.

CID *See* charge-injection device.

CIM *See* computer input from microfilm.

cinching Creases produced in magnetic tape when the supply reel is wound at low tension and suddenly stopped during playback.

C indicator *See* C scope.

ciphony equipment Any equipment attached to a radio transmitter, radio receiver, or telephone for scrambling or unscrambling voice messages.

circle-dot mode Mode of cathode-ray storage of binary digits in which one kind of digit is represented by a small circle of excitation of the screen, and the other kind by a similar circle with a concentric dot.

circuit conditioning Test, analysis, engineering, and installation actions to upgrade a communications circuit to meet an operational requirement; includes the reduction of noise, the equalization of phase and level stability and frequency response, and the correction of impedance discontinuities, but does not include normal maintenance and repair activities.

circuit efficiency Of an electron tube, the power delivered to a load at the output terminals of the output circuit at a desired frequency divided by the power delivered by the electron stream to the output circuit at that frequency.

circuit protection Provision for automatically preventing excess or dangerous temperatures in a conductor and limiting the amount of energy liberated when an electrical failure occurs.

circuitron Combination of active and passive components mounted in a single envelope like that used for tubes, to serve as one or more complete operating stages.

circuit shift *See* cyclic shift.

circular buffering A technique for receiving data in an input-output control system which uses a single buffer that appears to be organized in a circle, with data wrapping around it.

circular shift *See* cyclic shift.

circular sweep generation The use of electronic circuits to provide voltage or current which causes an electron beam in a device such as a cathode-ray tube to move in a circular deflection path at constant speed.

circular wait *See* mutual deadlock.

circulating memory A digital computer device that uses a delay line to store information in the form of a pattern of pulses in a train; the output pulses are detected electrically, amplified, reshaped, and reinserted in the delay line at the beginning. Also known as circulating storage; delay-line memory; delay-line storage.

circulating register A shift register in which data move out of one end and reenter the other end, as in a closed loop.

circulating storage *See* circulating memory.

clamp *See* clamping circuit.

clamper *See* direct-current restorer.

clamping The introduction of a reference level that has some desired relation to a pulsed waveform, as at the negative or positive peaks. Also known as direct-current reinsertion; direct-current restoration.

clamping circuit A circuit that reestablishes the direct-current level of a waveform; used in the dc restorer stage of a television receiver to restore the dc component to the video signal after its loss in capacitance-coupled alternating-current amplifiers, to reestablish the average light value of the reproduced image. Also known as clamp.

clamping diode A diode used to clamp a voltage at some point in a circuit.

Clapp oscillator A series-tuned Colpitts oscillator, having low drift.

class A amplifier 1. An amplifier in which the grid bias and alternating grid voltages are such that anode current in a specific tube flows at all times. 2. A transistor amplifier in which each transistor is in its active region for the entire signal cycle.

class AB amplifier 1. An amplifier in which the grid bias and alternating grid voltages are such that anode current in a specific tube flows for appreciably more than half but less than the entire electric cycle. 2. A transistor amplifier whose operation is class A for small signals and class B for large signals.

class A modulator A class A amplifier used to supply the necessary signal power to modulate a carrier.

class B amplifier 1. An amplifier in which the grid bias is approximately equal to the cutoff value, so that anode current is approximately zero when no exciting grid voltage is applied, and flows for approximately half of each cycle when an alternating grid voltage is applied. 2. A transistor amplifier in which each transistor is in its active region for approximately half the signal cycle.

class B modulator A class B amplifier used to supply the necessary signal power to modulate a carrier; usually connected in push-pull.

class C amplifier 1. An amplifier in which the bias on the control element is appreciably greater than the cutoff valve, so that the output current in each device is zero when no alternating control signal is applied, and flows for appreciably less than half of each cycle when an alternating control signal is applied. 2. A transistor amplifier in which each transistor is in its active region for significantly less than half the signal cycle.

clause A part of a statement in the COBOL language which may describe the structure of an elementary item, give initial values to items in independent and group work areas, or redefine data previously defined by another clause.

cleanup Gradual disappearance of gases from an electron tube during operation, due to absorption by getter material or the tube structure.

clear 1. To restore a storage device, memory device, or binary stage to a prescribed state, usually that denoting zero. Also known as reset. 2. A function key on calculators, to delete an entire problem or just the last keyboard entry.

clear area In optical character recognition, any area designated to be kept free of printing or any other extraneous markings.

clear band In character recognition, a continuous horizontal strip of blank paper which must be obtained between consecutive code lines on a source document.

clipper *See* limiter.

clipper diode A bidirectional breakdown diode that clips signal voltage peaks of either polarity when they exceed a predetermined amplitude.

clipper-limiter A device whose output is a function of the instantaneous input amplitude for a range of values lying between two predetermined limits but is approximately constant, at another level, for input values above the range.

clipping *See* limiting.

clipping circuit *See* limiter.

clipping level The level at which a clipping circuit is adjusted; for example, the magnitude of the clipped wave shape.

clock A source of accurately timed pulses, used for synchronization in a digital computer or as a time base in a transmission system.

clocked flip-flop A flip-flop circuit that is set and reset at specific times by adding clock pulses to the input so that the circuit is triggered only if both trigger and clock pulses are present simultaneously.

clocked logic A logic circuit in which the switching action is controlled by repetitive pulses from a clock.

clock frequency The master frequency of the periodic pulses that schedule the operation of a digital computer.

clock oscillator An oscillator that controls an electronic clock.

clock pulses Electronic pulses which are emitted periodically, usually by a crystal device, to synchronize the operation of circuits in a computer. Also known as clock signals.

clock rate The rate at which bits or words are transferred from one internal element of a computer to another.

clock signals *See* clock pulses.

clock time *See* internal cycle time.

clock track A track on a magnetic recording medium that generates clock pulses for the synchronization of read and write operations.

closed file A file that cannot be accessed for reading or writing.

closed loop A loop whose execution continues indefinitely in the absence of any external intervention.

closed-loop voltage gain The voltage gain of an amplifier with feedback.

closed shop A data-processing center so organized that only professional programmers and operators have access to the center to meet the needs of users.

closed subroutine A subroutine that can be stored outside the main routine and can be connected to it by linkages at one or more locations.

closefile A procedure call in time sharing which enables an ALGOL program to close a file no longer required.

close routine A computer program that changes the state of a file from open to closed.

cloud pulse The output resulting from space charge effects produced by turning the electron beam on or off in a charge-storage tube.

cluster In a clustered file, one of the classes into which records with similar sets of content identifiers are grouped.

clustered file A collection of records organized so that items which exhibit similar sets of content identifiers are automatically grouped into common classes.

clustering algorithm A computer program that attempts to detect and locate the presence of groups of vectors, in a high-dimensional multivariate space, that share some property of similarity.

clutch point The moment in time at which the clutch is engaged in a peripheral device such as a card punch.

clutter gating A technique which provides switching between moving-target-indicator and normal videos; this results in normal video being displayed in regions with no clutter and moving-target-indicator video being switched in only for the clutter areas.

CMI *See* computer-managed instruction.

CMOS device A device formed by the combination of a PMOS (*p*-type-channel metal oxide semiconductor device) with an NMOS (*n*-type-channel metal oxide semiconductor device). Derived from complementary metal oxide semiconductor device.

C network Network composed of three impedance branches in series, the free ends being connected to one pair of terminals, and the junction points being connected to another pair of terminals.

coated cathode A cathode that has been coated with compounds to increase electron emission.

coated filament A vacuum-tube filament coated with metal oxides to provide increased electron emission.

coaxial bolometer A bolometer in which the desired square-law detection characteristic is provided by a fine Wollaston wire element that has been thoroughly cleaned before being axially located and soldered in position in its cylinder.

coaxial cavity magnetron A magnetron which achieves mode separation, high efficiency, stability, and ease of mechanical tuning by coupling a coaxial high Q cavity to a normal set of quarter wavelength vane cavities.

coaxial cylinder magnetron A magnetron in which the cathode and anode consist of coaxial cylinders.

coaxial diode A diode having the same outer diameter and terminations as a coaxial cable, or otherwise designed to be inserted in a coaxial cable.

coaxial transistor A point-contact transistor in which the emitter and collector are point electrodes making pressure contact at the centers of opposite sides of a thin disk of semiconductor material serving as base.

COBOL A business data-processing language that can be given to a computer as a series of English statements describing a complete business operation. Derived from common business-oriented language.

codan A device that silences a receiver except when a modulated carrier signal is being received.

code-check To remove mistakes from a coded routine or program.

code checking time Time spent checking out a problem on the computer, making sure that the problem is set up correctly and that the code is correct.

code converter A converter that changes coded information to a different code system.

coded character set A set of characters together with the code assigned to each character for computer use.

coded decimal *See* decimal-coded digit.

coded program A program expressed in the required code for a computer.

coded stop A stop instruction built into a computer routine.

code error A surplus or lack of a bit or bits in a machine instruction.

code holes The informational holes in perforated tape, as opposed to the feed holes or other holes.

code line In character recognition, the area reserved for the inscription of the printed or handwritten characters to be recognized.

code position A location in a data-recording medium at which data may be entered, such as the intersection of a column and a row on a punch card, at which a hole may be punched.

code practice oscillator An oscillator used with a key and either headphones or a loudspeaker to practice sending and receiving Morse code.

coder A person who translates a sequence of computer instructions into codes acceptable to the machine.

coding 1. The process of converting a program design into an accurate, detailed representation of that program in some suitable language. **2.** A list, in computer code, of the successive operations required to carry out a given routine or solve a given problem.

coding sheet A sheet of paper printed with a form on which one can conveniently write a coded program.

codistor A multijunction semiconductor device which provides noise rejection and voltage regulation functions.

COGO A higher-level computer language oriented toward civil engineering, enabling one to write a program in a technical vocabulary familiar to engineers and feed it to the computer; several versions have been implemented. Derived from coordinated geometry.

cohered video The video detector output signal in a coherent moving-target indicator radar system.

coherence distance *See* coherence length.

coherence length A measure of the distance through which the effect of any local disturbance is spread out in a superconducting material. Also known as coherence distance.

coherent detector A detector used in moving-target indicator radar to give an output-signal amplitude that depends on the phase of the echo signal instead of on its strength, as required for a display that shows only moving targets.

coherent echo A radar echo whose phase and amplitude at a given range remain relatively constant.

coherent oscillator An oscillator used in moving-target indicator radar to serve as a reference by which changes in the radio-frequency phase of successively received pulses may be recognized. Abbreviated coho.

coherent-pulse radar A radar in which the radio-frequency oscillations of recurrent pulses bear a constant phase relation to those of a continuous oscillation.

coherent pulses Characterizing pulses in which the phase of the radio-frequency waves is maintained through successive pulses.

coherent reference A reference signal, usually of stable frequency, to which other signals are phase-locked to establish coherence throughout a system.

coherent signal In a pulsed radar system, a signal having a constant phase; it is mixed with the echo signal, whose phase depends upon the range of the target, in order to detect the phase shift and measure the target's range.

coherent transponder A transponder in which a fixed relation between frequency and phase of input and output signals is maintained.

coherent video The video signal produced in a moving-target indicator system by combining a radar echo signal with the output of a continuous-wave oscillator; after delay, this signal is detected, amplified, and subtracted from the next pulse train to give a signal representing only moving targets.

coho *See* coherent oscillator.

coil neutralization *See* inductive neutralization.

coincidence amplifier An electronic circuit that amplifies only that portion of a signal present when an enabling or controlling signal is simultaneously applied.

coincidence circuit A circuit that produces a specified output pulse only when a specified number or combination of two or more input terminals receives pulses within an assigned time interval. Also known as coincidence counter; coincidence gate.

coincidence counter *See* coincidence circuit.

coincidence gate *See* coincidence circuit.

coincident-current selection The selection of a particular magnetic cell, for reading or writing in computer storage, by simultaneously applying two or more currents.

cold cathode A cathode whose operation does not depend on its temperature being above the ambient temperature.

cold-cathode counter tube A counter tube having one anode and three sets of 10 cathodes; two sets of cathodes serve as guides that direct the flow discharge to each of the 10 output cathodes in correct sequence in response to driving pulses.

cold-cathode discharge *See* glow discharge.

cold-cathode ionization gage *See* Philips ionization gage.

cold-cathode rectifier A cold-cathode gas tube in which the electrodes differ greatly in size so electron flow is much greater in one direction than in the other. Also known as gas-filled rectifier.

cold-cathode tube An electron tube containing a cold cathode, such as a cold-cathode rectifier, mercury-pool rectifier, neon tube, phototube, or voltage regulator.

cold emission *See* field emission.

cold junction The reference junction of thermocouple wires leading to the measuring instrument; normally at room temperature.

collate To combine two or more similarly ordered sets of values into one set that may or may not have the same order as the original sets.

collating sequence The ordering of a set of items such that sets in that assigned order can be collated.

collating unit An electromechanical device capable of performing singly or simultaneously the merging, sequence-checking, selection, and matching of punched cards. Also known as collator.

collator *See* collating unit.

collector 1. A semiconductive region through which a primary flow of charge carriers leaves the base of a transistor; the electrode or terminal connected to this region is also called the collector. **2.** An electrode that collects electrons or ions which have completed their functions within an electron tube; a collector receives electrons after they have done useful work, whereas an anode receives electrons whose useful work is to be done outside the tube. Also known as electron collector.

collector capacitance The depletion-layer capacitance associated with the collector junction of a transistor.

collector cutoff The reverse saturation current of the collector-base junction.

collector junction A semiconductor junction located between the base and collector electrodes of a transistor.

collector modulation Amplitude modulation in which the modulator varies the collector voltage of a transistor.

collector resistance The back resistance of the collector-base diode of a transistor.

collector voltage The direct-current voltage, obtained from a power supply, that is applied between the base and collector of a transistor.

colliding-beam source A device for generating beams of polarized negative hydrogen or deuterium ions, in which polarized negative hydrogen or deuterium atoms are converted to negative ions through charge exchange during collisions with cesium atoms.

collinear heterodyning An optical processing system in which the correlation function is developed from an ultrasonic light modulator; the output signal is derived from a reference beam in such a way that the two beams are collinear until they enter the detection aperture; variations in optical path length then modulate the phase of both signal and reference beams simultaneously, and phase differences cancel out in the heterodyning process.

color balance Adjustment of the circuits feeding the three electron guns of a television color picture tube to compensate for differences in light-emitting efficiencies of the three color phosphors on the screen of the tube.

color-bar generator A signal generator that delivers to the input of a color television receiver the signal needed to produce a color-bar test pattern on one or more channels.

color burst The portion of the composite color television signal consisting of a few cycles of a sine wave of chrominance subcarrier frequency. Also known as burst; reference burst.

color center A point lattice defect which produces optical absorption bands in an otherwise transparent crystal.

color coder *See* matrix.

color control *See* chroma control.

color decoder *See* matrix.

color-difference signal A signal that is added to the monochrome signal in a color television receiver to obtain a signal representative of one of the three tristimulus values needed by the color picture tube.

color encoder *See* matrix.

color fringing Spurious chromaticity at boundaries of objects in a television picture.

color killer circuit The circuit in a color television receiver that biases chrominance amplifier tubes to cutoff during reception of monochrome programs. Also known as killer stage.

color kinescope *See* color picture tube.

color oscillator *See* chroma oscillator.

color-phase detector The color television receiver circuit that compares the frequency and phase of the incoming burst signal with those of the locally generated 3.579545-megahertz chroma oscillator and delivers a correction voltage to a reactance tube to ensure that the color portions of the picture will be in exact register with the black-and-white portions on the screen.

color picture tube A cathode-ray tube having three different colors of phosphors, so that when these are appropriately scanned and excited in a color television receiver, a color picture is obtained. Also known as color kinescope; color television picture tube; tricolor picture tube.

color purity Absence of undesired colors in the spot produced on the screen by each beam of a television color picture tube.

color-saturation control *See* chroma control.

color-subcarrier oscillator *See* chroma oscillator.

color television picture tube *See* color picture tube.

Colpitts oscillator An oscillator in which a parallel-tuned tank circuit has two voltage-dividing capacitors in series, with their common connection going to the cathode in the electron-tube version and the emitter circuit in the transistor version.

column A vertical arrangement of characters or other expressions, usually referring to a specific print position on a printer or a vertical area on a card.

column binary The binary representation of data on punched cards in which adjacent positions in a column correspond to adjacent bits of data. Also known as Chinese binary.

column binary card A punched card containing data in column binary representation.

column indicator The visible column on the program card which shows to the punch card operator the next column to be encountered.

column order The storage of a matrix $a(m,n)$ as $a(1,1)$, $a(2,1),\ldots,a(m,1),a(1,2),\ldots$.

column printer A small line printer used with some calculators to provide hard-copy printout of input and output data; typically consists of 20 columns of numerals and a limited number of alphabetic or other identifying characters.

column split A device on a punched card machine that senses a column in two parts, used to treat certain punch positions in the column differently from others or to treat the column as two separate characters.

COM *See* computer output on microfilm.

coma A cathode-ray tube image defect that makes the spot on the screen appear comet-shaped when away from the center of the screen.

comb filter A wave filter whose frequency spectrum consists of a number of equispaced elements resembling the teeth of a comb.

combinational circuit A switching circuit whose outputs are determined only by the concurrent inputs.

combined head *See* read/write head.

combiner circuit The circuit that combines the luminance and chrominance signals with the synchronizing signals in a color television camera chain.

COMIT A user-oriented, general-purpose, symbol-manipulation programming language for computers.

command A signal that initiates a predetermined type of computer operation that is defined by an instruction.

command code *See* operation code.

command control program The interface between a time-sharing computer and its users by means of which they can create, edit, save, delete, and execute their programs.

command interpreter A program that processes commands and other input and output from an active terminal in a time-sharing system.

command language The language of an operating system, through which the users of a data-processing system describe the requirements of their tasks to that system. Also known as job control language.

command mode The status of a terminal in a time-sharing environment enabling the programmer to use the command control program.

command pulses The electrical representations of bit values of 1 or 0 which control input/output devices.

comment An expression identifying or explaining one or more steps in a routine, which has no effect on execution of the routine.

comment code One or more characters identifying a comment.

common area An area of storage which two or more routines share.

common-base connection *See* grounded-base connection.

common-base feedback oscillator A bipolar transistor amplifier with a common-base connection and a positive feedback network between the collector (output) and the emitter (input).

common business-oriented language *See* COBOL.

common-collector connection *See* grounded-collector connection.

common control unit Control unit that is shared by more than one machine.

common declaration statement A nonexecutable statement in FORTRAN which allows specified arrays or variables to be stored in an area available to other programs.

common-drain amplifier An amplifier using a field-effect transistor so that the input signal is injected between gate and drain, while the output is taken between the source and drain. Also known as source-follower amplifier.

common-emitter connection *See* grounded-emitter connection.

common-gate amplifier An amplifier using a field-effect transistor in which the gate is common to both the input circuit and the output circuit.

common language A machine-readable language that is common to a group of computers and associated equipment.

common language family Various types of business machines, capable of being operated automatically and interchangeably by the same piece of punched paper tape, are said to be of a common language family.

common mode Having signals that are identical in amplitude and phase at both inputs, as in a differential operational amplifier.

common-mode error The error voltage that exists at the output terminals of an operational amplifier due to the common-mode voltage at the input.

common-mode gain The ratio of the output voltage of a differential amplifier to the common-mode input voltage.

common-mode input capacitance The equivalent capacitance of both inverting and noninverting inputs of an operational amplifier with respect to ground.

common-mode input impedance The open-loop input impedance of both inverting and noninverting inputs of an operational amplifier with respect to ground.

common-mode input resistance The equivalent resistance of both inverting and non-inverting inputs of an operational amplifier with respect to ground or reference.

common-mode rejection The ability of an amplifier to cancel a common-mode signal while responding to an out-of-phase signal. Also known as in-phase rejection.

common-mode signal A signal applied equally to both ungrounded inputs of a balanced amplifier stage or other differential device. Also known as in-phase signal.

common-mode voltage A voltage that appears in common at both input terminals of a device with respect to the output reference (usually ground).

common return A return conductor that serves two or more circuits.

common-source amplifier An amplifier stage using a field-effect transistor in which the input signal is applied between gate and source and the output signal is taken between drain and source.

common storage A section of memory in certain computers reserved for temporary storage of program outputs to be used as input for other programs.

communication protocol The exchange of a special sequence of control characters between a computer and a remote terminal in order to establish synchronous communication. Also known as protocol.

communication receiver A receiver designed especially for reception of voice or code messages transmitted by radio communication systems.

communications zone indicator Device to indicate whether or not long-distance high-frequency broadcasts are successfully reaching their destinations.

commutating capacitor A capacitor used in gas-tube rectifier circuits to prevent the anode from going highly negative immediately after extinction.

commutating reactance An inductive reactance placed in the cathode lead of a three-phase mercury-arc rectifier to ensure that tube current holds over during transfer of conduction from one anode to the next.

commutation The transfer of current from one channel to another in a gas tube.

commutator pulse One of a series of pulses indicating the beginning or end of a signal representing a single binary digit in a computer word. Also known as position pulse (P pulse).

compacting garbage collection The physical rearrangement of data cells so that those cells whose contents are no longer useful (garbage) are compressed into a contiguous array.

compaction A technique for reducing the space required for data storage without losing any information content.

companding A process in which compression is followed by expansion; often used for noise reduction in equipment, in which case compression is applied before noise exposure and expansion after exposure.

compandor A system for improving the signal-to-noise ratio by compressing the volume range of the signal at a transmitter or recorder by means of a compressor and restoring the normal range at the receiving or reproducing apparatus with an expander.

comparator A device that compares two transcriptions of the same information to verify the accuracy of transcription, storage, arithmetical operation, or some other process in a computer, and delivers an output signal of some form to indicate whether or not the two sources are equal or in agreement.

comparator circuit An electronic circuit that produces an output voltage or current whenever two input levels simultaneously satisfy predetermined amplitude requirements; may be linear (continuous) or digital (discrete).

comparator probe A component of a hardware monitor that is used to sense the number of bits that appear in parallel, as in an address register.

comparing brushes Sets of metallic brushes which verify that all the cards in a gang-punching operation have been properly punched.

comparing control change See control change.

comparing unit An electromechanical device which compares two groups of timed pulses and signals to establish either identity or nonidentity.

comparison A computer operation in which two numbers are compared as to identity, relative magnitude, or sign.

comparison bridge A bridge circuit in which any change in the output voltage with respect to a reference voltage creates a corresponding error signal, which, by means of negative feedback, is used to correct the output voltage and thereby restore bridge balance.

comparison indicators Registers, one of which is activated during the comparison of two quantities to indicate whether the first quantity is lower than, equal to, or greater than the second quantity.

compatibility The ability of one device to accept data handled by another device without conversion of the data or modification of the code.

compatible monolithic integrated circuit Device in which passive components are deposited by thin-film techniques on top of a basic silicon-substrate circuit containing the active components and some passive parts.

compensated amplifier A broad-band amplifier in which the frequency range is extended by choice of circuit constants.

compensated-loop direction finder A direction finder employing a loop antenna and a second antenna system to compensate for polarization error.

compensated semiconductor Semiconductor in which one type of impurity or imperfection (for example, donor) partially cancels the electrical effects on the other type of impurity or imperfection (for example, acceptor).

compensating capacitor See balancing capacitor.

compensation The modification of the amplitude-frequency response of an amplifier to broaden the bandwidth or to make the response more nearly uniform over the existing bandwidth. Also known as frequency compensation.

compensator A component that offsets an error or other undesired effect.

compile To prepare a machine-language program automatically from a program written in a higher programming language, usually generating more than one machine instruction for each symbolic statement.

compiler A program to translate a higher programming language into machine language. Also known as compiling routine.

compiler-level language A higher-level language normally supplied by the computer manufacturer.

compiler system The set consisting of a higher-level language, such as FORTRAN, and its compiler which translates the program written in that language into machine-readable instructions.

compiling routine See compiler.

complementary Having *pnp* and *npn* or *p*- and *n*-channel semiconductor elements on or within the same integrated-circuit substrate or working together in the same functional amplifier state.

complementary logic switch A complementary transistor pair which has a common input and interconnections such that one transistor is on when the other is off, and vice versa.

complementary metal oxide semiconductor device *See* CMOS device.

complementary symmetry A circuit using both *pnp* and *npn* transistors in a symmetrical arrangement that permits push-pull operation without an input transformer or other form of phase inverter.

complementary transistors Two transistors of opposite conductivity (*pnp* and *npn*) in the same functional unit.

complement number system System of number handling in which the complement of the actual number is operated upon; used in some computers to facilitate arithmetic operations.

complete carry In parallel addition, an arrangement in which the carries that result from the addition of carry digits are allowed to propagate from place to place.

complete operation An operation which includes obtaining all operands from storage, performing the operation, returning resulting operands to storage, and obtaining the next instruction.

complete routine A routine, generally supplied by a computer manufacturer, which does not have to be modified by the user before being applied.

complex data type A scalar data type which contains two real fields representing the real and imaginary components of a complex number.

complex declaration statement A nonexecutable statement in FORTRAN used to specify that the type of identifier appearing in the program is of the form $a + bi$, where i is the square root of -1.

complex relative attenuation The ratio of the peak output voltage, in complex notation, of an electric filter to the output voltage at the frequency being considered.

component name *See* metavariable.

composite circuit A circuit used simultaneously for voice communication and telegraphy, with frequency-discriminating networks serving to separate the two types of signals.

composite filter A filter constructed by linking filters of different kinds in series.

composite pulse A pulse composed of a series of overlapping pulses received from the same source over several paths in a pulse navigation system.

composite set Assembly of apparatus designed to provide one end of a composite circuit.

composite wave filter A combination of two or more low-pass, high-pass, band-pass, or band-elimination filters.

composition resistor *See* carbon resistor.

compound cryosar A cryosar consisting of two normal cryosars with different electrical characteristics in series.

compression 1. Reduction of the effective gain of a device at one level of signal with respect to the gain at a lower level of signal, so that weak signal components will not be lost in background and strong signals will not overload the system. **2.** *See* compression ratio; data compression.

compression ratio The ratio of the gain of a device at a low power level to the gain at some higher level, usually expressed in decibels. Also known as compression.

compressive intercept receiver An electromagnetic surveillance receiver that instantaneously analyzes and sorts all signals within a broad radio-frequency spectrum by using pulse compression techniques which perform a complete analysis up to 10,000 times faster than a superheterodyne receiver or spectrum analyzer.

compressor The part of a compandor that is used to compress the intensity range of signals at the transmitting or recording end of a circuit.

computed go to A control procedure in FORTRAN which allows the transfer of control to the ith label of a set of n labels used as statement numbers in the program.

compute mode The operation of an analog computer in which input signals are used by the computing units to calculate a solution, in contrast to hold mode and reset mode.

computer A device that receives, processes, and presents data; the two types are analog and digital. Also known as computing machine.

computer-aided design The generation of computer automated designs for display on cathode-ray tubes. Abbreviated CAD.

computer-aided management of instruction See computer-managed instruction.

computer-aided manufacturing The use of computers to communicate work instructions to automatic machinery for the handling and processing needed to produce a workpiece. Abbreviated CAM.

computer analyst A person who defines a problem, determines exactly what is required in the solution, and defines the outlines of the machine solution; generally, an expert in automatic data processing applications.

computer animation The use of a computer to present, either continuously or in rapid succession, pictures on a cathode-ray tube or other device, graphically representing a time developing system at successive times.

computer architecture The art and science of assembling logical elements to form a computing device.

computer-assisted instruction The use of computers to present drills, practice exercises, and tutorial sequences to the student, and sometimes to engage the student in a dialog about the substance of the instruction. Abbreviated CAI.

computer center See electronic data-processing center.

computer code The code representing the operations built into the hardware of a particular computer.

computer control counter Counter which stores the next required address; any counter which furnishes information to the control unit.

computer control register See program register.

computer efficiency 1. The ratio of actual operating time to scheduled operating time of a computer. 2. In time-sharing, the ratio of user time to the sum of user time plus system time.

computer entry punch Combination card-reader and key punch that enters data directly onto a computer's memory drum.

computer graphics The process of pictorial communication between human and computers, in which the computer input and output have the form of charts, drawings, or appropriate pictorial representation; such devices as cathode-ray tubes, mechanical plotting boards, curve tracers, coordinate digitizers, and light pens are employed.

computer input from microfilm The technique of reading images on microfilm and transforming them into a form which is understandable to a computer. Abbreviated CIM.

computer-limited Pertaining to a situation in which the time required for computation exceeds the time required to read inputs and write outputs.

computer-managed instruction The use of computer assistance in testing, diagnosing, prescribing, grading, and record keeping. Abbreviated CMI. Also known as computer-aided management of instruction.

computer memory *See* memory.

computer network A system of two or more computers interconnected by communication channels.

computer operation The electronic action required in a computer to give a desired computation.

computer output on microfilm The generation of microfilm which displays information developed by a computer. Abbreviated COM.

computer performance evaluation The measurement and evaluation of the performance of a computer system, aimed at ensuring that a minimum amount of effort, expense, and waste is incurred in the production of data-processing services, and encompassing such tools as canned programs, source program optimizers, software monitors, hardware monitors, simulation, and bench-mark problems. Abbreviated CPE.

computer programming *See* programming.

computer science The branch of knowledge concerned with information processes, the structures and procedures that represent these processes, and their implementation in information-processing systems.

computer security Measures taken to protect computers and their contents from unauthorized use.

computer storage device *See* storage device.

computer system 1. A set of related but unconnected components (hardware) of a computer or data-processing system. 2. A set of hardware parts that are related and connected, and thus form a computer.

computer theory A discipline covering the study of circuitry, logic, microprogramming, compilers, programming languages, file structures, and system architectures.

computer utility A computer that provides service on a time-sharing basis, generally over telephone lines, to subscribers who have appropriate terminals.

computer word *See* word.

computing machine *See* computer.

computing power The number of operations that a computer can carry out in 1 second.

computing unit The section of a computer that carries out arithmetic, logical, and decision-making operations.

concatenate To unite in a sequence, link together, or link to a chain.

concatenation 1. An operation in which a number of conceptually related components are linked together to form a larger, organizationally similar entity. 2. In string processing, the synthesis of longer character strings from shorter ones.

concentrator Buffer switch (analog or digital) which reduces the number of trunks required.

concept coordination The basic principles of various punched-card, aspect, and mechanized information retrieval systems in which independently assigned concepts are used to characterize the subject content of documents, and the latter are identified during searching by means of either such assigned concepts or their combination.

conceptual modeling Writing a program by means of which a given result will be obtained, although the result is incapable of proof. Also known as heuristic programming.

concurrency Referring to two or more tasks of a computer system which are in progress simultaneously.

concurrent conversion The transfer of data from one medium to another, such as card to tape, under computer control while programs are being run on the same computer.

concurrent input/output The simultaneous reading from and writing on different media by a computer.

concurrent operations control The supervisory capability required by a computer to handle more than one program at a time.

concurrent processing The capability of a computer to process more than one program at the time.

concurrent real-time processing The capability of a computer to process simultaneously several programs, each of which requires responses within a time span related to its particular time frame.

condensed instruction deck The card output from an assembly program in which several instructions per card are punched in machine language; input to the assembly program may consist of one instruction per card, so the output is condensed.

condenser box *See* capacitor box.

condensing routine A routine that converts a program format having one instruction per card to a program format having several instructions per card.

conditional Subject to the result of a comparison made during computation in a computer, or subject to human intervention.

conditional assembly A feature of some assemblers which suppresses certain sections of code if stated program conditions are not met at assembly time.

conditional branch *See* conditional jump.

conditional breakpoint A conditional jump that, if a specified switch is set, will cause a computer to stop; the routine may then be continued as coded or a jump may be forced.

conditional expression A COBOL language expression which is either true or false, depending upon the status of the variables within the expression.

conditional jump A computer instruction that will cause the proper one of two or more addresses to be used in obtaining the next instruction, depending on some property of a numerical expression that may be the result of some previous instruction. Also known as conditional branch; conditional transfer; decision instruction; discrimination.

conditionally stable circuit A circuit which is stable for certain values of input signal and gain, and unstable for other values.

conditional transfer *See* conditional jump.

condition code Portion of a program status word indicating the outcome of the most recently executed arithmetic or boolean operation.

conditioned stop instruction A computer instruction which causes the execution of a program to stop if some given condition exists, such as the specific setting of a switch on a computer console.

condition entries The upper-right-hand portion of a decision table, indicating, for each of the conditions, whether the condition satisfies various criteria listed in the condition stub, or the values of various parameters listed in the condition stub.

conditioning Equipment modifications or adjustments necessary to match transmission levels and impedances or to provide equalization between facilities.

condition portion The upper portion of a decision table, comprising the condition stub and condition entires.

condition stub The upper-left-hand portion of a decision table, consisting of a single column listing various criteria or parameters which are used to specify the conditions.

conduction band An energy band in which electrons can move freely in a solid, producing net transport of charge.

conduction current A current due to a flow of conduction electrons through a body.

conduction electron An electron in the conduction band of a solid, where it is free to move under the influence of an electric field. Also known as outer-shell electron; valence electron.

conductivity modulation Of a semiconductor, the variation of the conductivity of a semiconductor through variation of the charge carrier density.

conductivity modulation transistor Transistor in which the active properties are derived from minority carrier modulation of the bulk resistivity of the semiconductor.

conformable optical mask An optical mask made on a flexible glass substrate so that it can be pulled down under vacuum into intimate contact with the substrate for accurate circuit fabrication.

conformal array A circular, cylindrical, hemispherical, or other shaped array of electronically switched antennas; provides the special radiation patterns required for Tacan, IFF, and other air navigation, radar, and missile control applications.

confusion jamming An electronic countermeasure technique in which the signal from an enemy tracking radar is amplified and retransmitted with distortion to create a false echo that affects accuracy of target range, azimuth, and velocity data.

confusion matrix In pattern recognition, a matrix used to represent errors in assigning classes to observed patterns in which the ijth element represents the number of samples from class i which were classified as class j.

congruential generator A method of generating a sequence of random numbers x_0, x_1, x_2, . . . , in which each member is generated from the previous one by the formula $x_{i+1} \equiv ax_i + b$ modulus m, where a, b, and m are constants.

conical beam The radar beam produced by conical scanning methods.

conical scanning Scanning in radar in which the direction of maximum radiation generates a cone, the vertex angle of which is of the order of the beam width; may be either rotating or nutating, according to whether the direction of polarization rotates or remains unchanged.

conjugate bridge A bridge in which the detector circuit and the supply circuits are interchanged, as compared with a normal bridge of the given type.

conjunctive search A search to identify items having all of a certain set of characteristics.

connect function A signal sent over a data line to a selected peripheral device to connect it with the central processing unit.

connecting circuit A functional switching circuit which directly couples other functional circuit units to each other to exchange information as dictated by the momentary needs of the switching system.

connection box A mechanical device for altering electrical connections between various terminals, used to control the operations of a punched-card machine; its function is similar to that of a plug board.

connector A switch, or relay group system, which finds the telephone line being called as a result of digits being dialed; it also causes interrupted ringing voltage to be placed on the called line or of returning a busy tone to the calling party if the line is busy.

connect time The time that a user at a terminal is signed on to a computer.

consequence finding program A computer program that attempts to deduce mathematical consequences from a set of axioms and to select those consequences that will be significant.

consistency routine A debugging routine which is used to determine whether the program being checked gives consistent results at specified check points; for example, consistent between runs or with values calculated by other means.

console The section of a computer that is used to control the machine manually, correct errors, manually revise the contents of storage, and provide communication in other ways between the operator or service engineer and the central processing unit.

console display The visible representation of information, whether in words, numbers, or drawings, on a console screen connected to a computer.

console file adapter A special input/output device which allows the operator to load reloadable control storage from the system console.

console receiver A television or radio receiver in a console.

console switch A switch on a computer console whose setting can be sensed by a computer, so that an instruction in the program can direct the computer to use this setting to determine which of various alternative courses of action should be followed.

console typewriter A typewriter by means of which the computer operator can monitor system and program operations.

constant area A part of storage used for constants.

constant-conductance network *See* constant-resistance network.

constant-current characteristic The relation between the voltages of two electrodes in an electron tube when the current to one of them is maintained constant and all other electrode voltages are constant.

constant-current filter A filter network intended to be connected to a source whose internal impedance is so high it can be assumed as infinite.

constant-current generator A vacuum-tube circuit, generally containing a pentode, in which the alternating-current anode resistance is so high that anode current remains essentially constant despite variations in load resistance.

constant-current source A circuit which produces a specified current, independent of the load resistance or applied voltage.

constant-false-alarm rate Radar system devices used to prevent receiver saturation and overload so as to present clean video information to the display, and to present a constant noise level to an automatic detector.

constant instruction A nonexecutable instruction.

constant-k filter A filter in which the product of the series and shunt impedances is a constant that is independent of frequency.

constant-k network A ladder network in which the product of the series and shunt impedances is independent of frequency within the operating frequency range.

constant-resistance network A network having at least one driving-point impedance that is a positive constant. Also known as constant-conductance network.

constraint matrix The set of equations and inequalities defining the set of admissible solutions in linear programming.

construction operator The part of a data structure which is used to construct composite objects from atoms.

contact-mask read-only memory *See* last-mask read-only memory.

contact rectifier *See* metallic rectifier.

content analysis A method of automatically assigning words that identify the content of information items or search requests in an information retrieval system.

content indicator Display unit that indicates the content in a computer, and the program or mode being used.

contention The condition arising when two or more units attempt to transmit over a time-division-multiplex channel at the same time.

contention resolver A device that enables a central processing unit, memory, or channel whose attention is being requested over several pathways to give its attention to one pathway and ignore all others.

contents The information stored at any address or in any register of a computer.

context-driven line editor A line editor in which the user need not know or keep track of line numbers but can call up text by line content; the computer will then search for the indicated pattern.

context-free grammar A grammar in which any occurrence of a metavariable may be replaced by one of its alternatives.

context-sensitive grammar A grammar in which the rules are applicable only when a metavariable occurs in a specified context.

contingency interrupt A processing interruption due to an operator's action or due to an abnormal result from the system or from a program.

continue statement A nonexecutable statement in FORTRAN used principally as a target for transfers, particularly as the last statement in the range of a do statement.

continuous comparator *See* linear comparator.

continuous film scanner A television film scanner in which the motion picture film moves continuously while being scanned by a flying-spot kinescope.

continuous forms In character recognition, any batch of source information that exists in reel form, such as tally rolls or cash-register receipts.

continuous stationery A continuous ribbon of paper consisting of several hundred or more sheets separated by perforations and folded to form a pack, used to feed a computer printer and generally having sprocket holes along the margin for this purpose.

continuous stationery reader A type of character reader which processes only continuous forms of predefined dimensions.

continuous-tone squelch Squelch in which a continuous subaudible tone, generally below 200 hertz, is transmitted by frequency-modulation equipment along with a desired voice signal.

continuous-wave jammer An electronic jammer that emits a single frequency which gives the appearance of a picket or rail fence on an enemy's radarscope. Also known as rail-fence jammer.

continuous-wave tracking system Tracking system which operates by keeping a continuous radio beam on a target and determining its behavior from changes in the antenna necessary to keep the beam on the target.

contour analysis In optical character recognition, a reading technique that employs a roving spot of light which searches out the character's outline by bouncing around its outer edges.

contouring control The guidance by a computer of a machine tool along a programmed path by interpolating many intermediate points between selected points.

contour model A model for describing the run-time execution of programs written in block-structured languages, consisting of a program component, the data component, and the control component.

contourograph Device using a cathode-ray oscilloscope to produce imagery that has a three-dimensional appearance.

CONTRAN Computer programming language in which instructions are written at the compiler level, thereby eliminating the need for translation by a compiling routine.

contrast In optical character recognition, the difference in color, reflectance, or shading between two areas of a surface, for example, a character and its background.

contrast control A manual control that adjusts the range of brightness between highlights and shadows on the reproduced image in a television receiver.

contrast ratio The ratio of the maximum to the minimum luminance values in a television picture.

control 1. The section of a digital computer that carries out instructions in proper sequence, interprets each coded instruction, and applies the proper signals to the arithmetic unit and other parts in accordance with this interpretation. 2. A mathematical check used with some computer operations. 3. An input element of a cryotron.

control and read-only memory A read-only memory that also provides storage, sequencing, execution, and translation logic for various microinstructions. Abbreviated CROM.

control bit A bit which marks either the beginning or the end of a character transmitted in asynchronous communication.

control block A storage area containing (in condensed, formalized form) the information required for the control of a task, function, operation, or quantity of information.

control break A key change which takes place in a control data field, especially in the execution of a report program.

control card A punched card containing input data or parameters which are necessary to begin or modify a program, or containing instructions needed for the specific application of a general routine.

control change A change of function that occurs when successive records (such as those entered on punched cards) differ in the data entered in the control field; for example, a punched-card tabulator may change from adding to printing at the end of a series of items. Also known as comparing control change.

control character A character whose occurrence in a particular context initiates, modifies, or stops a control operation in a computer or associated equipment.

control characteristic 1. The relation, usually shown by a graph, between critical grid voltage and anode voltage of a gas tube. 2. The relation between control ampere-turns and output current of a magnetic amplifier.

control circuit 1. One of the circuits that responds to the instructions in the program for a digital computer. 2. The circuit that feeds the control winding of a magnetic amplifier.

control computer A computer which uses inputs from sensor devices and outputs connected to control mechanisms to control physical processes.

control counter A counter providing data used to control the execution of a computer program.

control data Data used for identifying, selecting, executing, or modifying another set of data, a routine, a record, or the like.

control electrode An electrode used to initiate or vary the current between two or more electrodes in an electron tube.

control field A constant location where information for control purposes is placed, such as specified columns on punched cards.

control grid A grid, ordinarily placed between the cathode and an anode, that serves to control the anode current of an electron tube.

control-grid bias Average direct-current voltage between the control grid and cathode of a vacuum tube.

control-grid plate transconductance Ratio of the amplification factor of a vacuum tube to its plate resistance, combining the effects of both into one term.

control head gap The distance maintained between the read/write head of a disk drive and the disk surface.

control hole *See* designation punch.

control inductor *See* control winding.

control instructions Those instructions in a computer program which ensure proper sequencing of instructions so that a programmed task can be performed correctly.

controlled avalanche device A semiconductor device that has rigidly specified maximum and minimum avalanche voltage characteristics and is able to operate and absorb momentary power surges in this avalanche region indefinitely without damage.

controlled avalanche rectifier A silicon rectifier in which carefully controlled, nondestructive internal avalanche breakdown across the entire junction area protects the junction surface, thereby eliminating local heating that would impair or destroy the reverse blocking ability of the rectifier.

controlled avalanche transit-time triode A solid-state microwave device that uses a combination of IMPATT diode and *npn* bipolar transistor technologies; avalanche and drift zones are located between the base and collector regions. Abbreviated CATT.

controlled mercury-arc rectifier A mercury-arc rectifier in which one or more electrodes control the start of the discharge in each cycle and thereby control output current.

controlled rectifier A rectifier that has provisions for regulating output current, such as with thyratrons, ignitrons, or silicon controlled rectifiers.

control limits In radar evaluation, upper and lower control limits are established at those performance figures within which it is expected that 95% of quality-control samples will fall when the radar is performing normally.

control logic The sequence of steps required to perform a specific function.

control mark *See* tape mark.

control-message display A device, such as a console typewriter, on which control information, such as information on the progress of a running computer program, is displayed in ordinary language.

control module The set of registers and circuitry required to carry out a specific function.

control panel 1. An array of jacks or sockets in which wires (or other elements) may be plugged to control the action of an electromechanical device in a data-processing system such as a printer. Also known as plugboard; wiring board. 2. *See* panel.

control point 1. The numerical value of the controlled variable (speed, temperature, and so on) which, under any fixed set of operating conditions, an automatic controller operates to maintain. 2. One of the hardware locations at which the output of the instruction decoder of the processor activates the input to and output from specific registers as well as operational resources of the system.

control program A program which carries on input/output operations, loading of programs, detection of errors, communication with the operator, and so forth.

control punch *See* designation punch.

control register Any one of the registers in a computer used to control the execution of a computer program.

control section The smallest integral subsection of a program, that is, the smallest unit of code that can be separately relocated during loading.

control sequence The order in which a set of executions are carried to perform a specific function.

control signal A set of pulses used to identify the channels to be followed by transferred data.

control state The operating mode of a system which permits it to override its normal sequence of operations.

control statement *See* job control statement.

control supervisor The computer software which controls the processing of the system.

control symbol A symbol which, coded into the machine memory, controls certain steps in the mechanical translation process; since control symbols are not contextual symbols, they appear neither in the input nor in the output.

control systems equipment Computers which are an integral part of a total facility or larger complex of equipment and have the primary purpose of controlling, monitoring, analyzing, or measuring a process or other equipment.

control tape Loop of paper tape to control the carriage operation of character printers. Also known as carriage tape.

control total The sum of the numbers in a specified record field of a batch of records, determined repetitiously during computer processing so that any discrepancy from the control indicates an error.

control unit An electronic device containing data buffers and logical circuitry, situated between the computer channel and the input/output device, and controlling data transfers and such operations as tape rewind.

control winding A winding used on a magnetic amplifier or saturable reactor to apply control magnetomotive forces to the core. Also known as control inductor.

control word A computer word specifying a certain action to be taken.

convection current The time rate at which the electric charges of an electron stream are transported through a given surface.

convective discharge The movement of a visible or invisible stream of charged particles away from a body that has been charged to a sufficiently high voltage. Also known as electric wind; static breeze.

conventional grouping When a unit record containing a coding field is used for a single item code and the set of codes of the terms which describe the item, the grouping is conventional; for example, a personnel file in which each individual is represented by a card on which are punched codes for his or her age, sex, education, and salary.

conventional programming The use of standard programming languages, as opposed to application development languages, financial planning languages, query languages, and report programs.

convergence A condition in which the electron beams of a multibeam cathode-ray tube intersect at a specified point, such as at an opening in the shadow mask of a three-gun color television picture tube; both static convergence and dynamic convergence are required.

convergence coil One of the coils used to obtain convergence of electron beams in a three-gun color television picture tube.

convergence control A control used in a color television receiver to adjust the potential on the convergence electrode of the three-gun color picture tube to achieve convergence.

convergence electrode An electrode whose electric field converges two or more electron beams.

convergence magnet A magnet assembly whose magnetic field converges two or more electron beams; used in three-gun color picture tubes. Also known as beam magnet.

Conversational Algebraic Language *See* CAL.

conversational compiler A compiler which immediately checks the validity of each source language statement entered to the computer and informs the user if the next statement can be entered or if a mistake must be corrected. Also known as interpreter.

conversational processing The operating mode of a computer system which enables a user to have each statement he keys into the system processed immediately.

conversational time-sharing The simultaneous utilization of a computer system by multiple users, each user being equipped with a remote terminal with which he communicates with the computer in conversational mode.

conversion *See* data conversion.

conversion equipment Equipment used for conversion of data from one recording medium to another, as from card to tape.

conversion gain 1. Ratio of the intermediate-frequency output voltage to the input signal voltage of the first detector of a superheterodyne receiver. 2. Ratio of the available intermediate-frequency power output of a converter or mixer to the available radio-frequency power input.

conversion program A set of instructions which allows a program written for one system to be run on a different system.

conversion rate The number of complete conversions an analog-to-digital converter can perform per unit time, usually specified in cycles (or conversions) per second.

conversion routine A flexible, self-contained, and generalized program used for data conversion, which only requires specifications about very few facts in order to be used by a programmer.

conversion time The time required to read in data from one code into another code.

convert To transform the representation of data.

converter **1.** A computer unit that changes numerical information from one form to another, as from decimal to binary or vice versa, from fixed-point to floating-point representation, or from punched cards to magnetic tape. Also known as data converter. **2.** The section of a superheterodyne radio receiver that converts the desired incoming radio-frequency signal to the intermediate-frequency value; the converter section includes the oscillator and the mixer-first detector. Also known as heterodyne conversion transducer; oscillator-mixer-first detector. **3.** An auxiliary unit used with a television or radio receiver to permit reception of channels or frequencies for which the receiver was not originally designed. **4.** In facsimile, a device that changes the type of modulation delivered by the scanner. **5.** Unit of a radar system in which the mixer of a superheterodyne receiver and usually two stages of intermediate-frequency amplification are located; performs a preamplifying operation. **6.** *See* remodulator.

converter tube An electron tube that combines the mixer and local-oscillator functions of a heterodyne conversion transducer.

convolver A surface acoustic-wave device in which signal processing is performed by a nonlinear interaction between two waves traveling in opposite directions. Also known as acoustic convolver.

Conwell-Weisskopf equation An equation for the mobility of electrons in a semiconductor in the presence of donor or acceptor impurities, in terms of the dielectric constant of the medium, the temperature, the concentration of ionized donors (or acceptors), and the average distance between them.

cooled infrared detector An infrared detector that must be operated at cryogenic temperatures, such as at the temperature of liquid nitrogen, to obtain the desired infrared sensitivity.

cooperative phenomenon A process that involves a simultaneous collective interaction among many atoms or electrons in a crystal, such as ferromagnetism, superconductivity, and order-disorder transformations.

Cooper pairs Pairs of bound electrons which occur in a superconducting medium according to the Bardeen-Cooper-Schrieffer theory.

coordinate data receiver A receiver specifically designed to accept the signal of a coordinate data transmitter and reconvert this signal into a form suitable for input to associated equipment such as a plotting board, computer, or radar set.

coordinate data transmitter A transmitter that accepts two or more coordinates, such as those representing a target position, and converts them into a form suitable for transmission.

coordinated geometry *See* COGO.

coordinate indexing An indexing scheme in which equal-rank descriptors are used to describe a document, for information retrieval by a computer or other means.

coordinate storage *See* matrix storage.

coplanar electrodes Electrodes mounted in the same plane.

copper oxide photovoltaic cell A photovoltaic cell in which light acting on the surface of contact between layers of copper and cuprous oxide causes a voltage to be produced.

copper oxide rectifier A metallic rectifier in which the rectifying barrier is the junction between metallic copper and cuprous oxide.

copper sulfide rectifier A semiconductor rectifier in which the rectifying barrier is the junction between magnesium and copper sulfide.

copy A string procedure in ALGOL by means of which a new byte string can be generated from an existing byte string.

copying program A system program which copies a data or program file from one peripheral device onto another.

cordwood module High-density circuit module in which discrete components are mounted between and perpendicular to two small, parallel printed circuit boards to which their terminals are attached.

core *See* magnetic core.

core array A rectangular grid arrangement of magnetic cores.

core bank A stack of core arrays and associated electronics, the stack containing a specific number of core arrays.

core-dump To copy the contents of all or part of core storage, usually into an external storage device.

core-image library A collection of computer programs residing on mass-storage device in ready-to-run form.

core logic Logic performed in ferrite cores that serve as inputs to diode and transistor circuits.

core memory *See* magnetic core storage.

core memory resident A control program which is in the main memory of a computer at all times to supervise the processing of the computer.

core rope storage Direct-access storage consisting of a large number of doughnut-shaped ferrite cores arranged on a common axis, with sense, inhibit, and set wires threaded through or around individual cores in a predetermined manner to provide fixed storage of digital data; each core rope stores one or more complete words, rather than just a single bit.

core stack A number of core arrays, next to one another and treated as a unit.

core storage 1. The main memory of a computer. 2. *See* magnetic core storage.

corner cut A corner cut off a punched card at an oblique angle to aid in orientation.

coroutine A program module for which the lifetime of a particular activation record is independent of the time when control enters or leaves the module, and in which the activation record maintains a local instruction counter so that, whenever control enters the module, execution begins at the point where it stopped when control last left that particular instance of execution.

corrective maintenance The maintenance performed as required, on an unscheduled basis, by the contractor following equipment failure. Also known as remedial maintenance.

correlation-type receiver *See* correlator.

correlator A device that detects weak signals in noise by performing an electronic operation approximating the computation of a correlation function. Also known as correlation-type receiver.

cosine winding A winding used in the deflection yoke of a cathode-ray tube to prevent changes in focus as the beam is deflected over the entire area of the screen.

count cyle An increase or decrease of the cycle index by unity or by an arbitrary integer.

counter 1. A register or storage location used to represent the number of occurrences of an event. 2. *See* accumulator; scaler.

counter circuit *See* counting circuit.

counter coupling The technique of combining two or more counters into one counter of larger capacity in electromechanical devices by means of control panel wiring.

counter decade *See* decade scaler.

counter-free machine A sequential machine that cannot count modulo any integer greater than 1.

countermeasures set A complete electronic set specifically designed to provide facilities for intercepting and analyzing electromagnetic energy propagated by transmitter and to provide a source of radio-frequency signals which deprive the enemy of effective use of his electronic equipment.

counter tube An electron tube having one signal-input electrode and 10 or more output electrodes, with each input pulse serving to transfer conduction sequentially to the next output electrode; beam-switching tubes and cold-cathode counter tubes are examples.

counting circuit A circuit that counts pulses by frequency-dividing techniques, by charging a capacitor in such a way as to produce a voltage proportional to the pulse count, or by other means. Also known as counter circuit.

counting-down circuit *See* frequency divider.

counting rate–voltage characteristic *See* plateau characteristic.

couple Two metals placed in contact, as in a thermocouple.

coupled transistors Transistors connected in series by transformers or resistance-capacitance networks, in much the same manner as electron tubes.

coupling capacitor A capacitor used to block the flow of direct current while allowing alternating or signal current to pass; widely used for joining two circuits or stages. Also known as blocking capacitor; stopping capacitor.

coupling coefficient The ratio of the maximum change in energy of an electron traversing an interaction space to the product of the peak alternating gap voltage and the electronic charge.

CPE *See* computer performance evaluation.

C power supply A device connected in the circuit between the cathode and grid of a vacuum tube to apply grid bias.

CPU *See* central processing unit.

crash *See* abend.

crater lamp A glow-discharge tube used as a point source of light whose brightness is proportional to the signal current sent through the tube; used for photographic recording of facsimile signals.

creation operator The part of a data structure which allows components to be created.

creep A slow change in a characteristic with time or usage.

crippled leap-frog test A variation of the leap-frog test, modified so the computer tests are repeated from a single set of storage locations rather than a changing set of locations.

crippled mode The operation of a computer at reduced capacity when certain parts are not working.

critical anode voltage The anode voltage at which breakdown occurs in a gas tube.

critical area *See* picture element.

critical current The current in a superconductive material above which the material is normal and below which the material is superconducting, at a specified temperature and in the absence of external magnetic fields.

critical field The smallest theoretical value of steady magnetic flux density that would prevent an electron emitted from the cathode of a magnetron at zero velocity from reaching the anode. Also known as cutoff field.

critical frequency *See* cutoff frequency.

critical grid current Instantaneous value of grid current when the anode current starts to flow in a gas-filled vacuum tube.

critical grid voltage The grid voltage at which anode current starts to flow in a gas tube. Also known as firing point.

critical magnetic field The field below which a superconductive material is superconducting and above which the material is normal, at a specified temperature and in the absence of current.

critical voltage The highest theoretical value of steady anode voltage, at a given steady magnetic flux density, at which electrons emitted from the cathode of a magnetron at zero velocity would fail to reach the anode. Also known as cutoff voltage.

CRO *See* cathode-ray oscilloscope.

CROM *See* control and read-only memory.

Crookes dark space *See* cathode dark space.

Crookes tube An early form of low-pressure discharge tube whose cathode was a flat aluminum disk at one end of the tube, and whose anode was a wire at one side of the tube, outside the electron stream; used to study cathode rays.

cross-color In color television, the interference in the receiver chrominance channel caused by cross talk from monochrome signals.

cross-correlator A correlator in which a locally generated reference signal is multiplied by the incoming signal and the result is smoothed in a low-pass filter to give an approximate computation of the cross-correlation function. Also known as synchronous detector.

crossed-field amplifier A forward-wave, beam-type microwave amplifier that uses crossed-field interaction to achieve good phase stability, high efficiency, high gain, and wide bandwidth for most of the microwave spectrum.

crossed-field backward-wave oscillator One of several types of backward-wave oscillators that utilize a crossed field, such as the amplitron and carcinotron.

crossed-field device Any instrument which uses the motion of electrons in perpendicular electric and magnetic fields to generate microwave radiation, either as an amplifier or oscillator.

crossed-field multiplier phototube A multiplier phototube in which repeated secondary emission is obtained from a single active electrode by the combined effects of a strong radio-frequency electric field and a perpendicular direct-current magnetic field.

crossfoot To add numbers in several different ways in a computer, for checking purposes.

crosshatch generator A signal generator that generates a crosshatch pattern for adjusting color television receiver circuits.

cross-neutralization Method of neutralization used in push-pull amplifiers, whereby a portion of the plate-cathode alternating-current voltage of each vacuum tube is applied to the grid-cathode circuit of the other vacuum tube through a neutralizing capacitor.

crossover distortion Amplitude distortion in a class B transistor power amplifier which occurs at low values of current, when input impedance becomes appreciable compared with driver impedance.

crossover voltage In a cathode-ray storage tube, the voltage of a secondary writing surface, with respect to cathode voltage, on which the secondary emission is unity.

cross-referencing program A computer program used in debugging that produces indexed lists of both the variable names and the statement numbers of the source program.

crosstalk *See* magnetic printing.

CRT *See* cathode-ray tube.

cryoelectronics A branch of electronics concerned with the study and application of superconductivity and other low-temperature phenomena to electronic devices and systems.

cryogenic conductor *See* superconductor.

cryogenic film A storage element using superconducting thin films of lead at liquid-helium temperature.

cryogenic transformer A transformer designed to operate in digital cryogenic circuits, such as a controlled-coupling transformer.

cryolectronics Technology concerning the characteristics of electronic components at cryogenic temperatures.

cryosar A cryogenic, two-terminal, negative-resistance semiconductor device, consisting essentially of two contacts on a germanium wafer operating in liquid helium.

cryosistor A cryogenic semiconductor device in which a reverse-biased *pn* junction is used to control the ionization between two ohmic contacts.

cryotron A switch that operates at very low temperatures at which its components are superconducting; when current is sent through a control element to produce a magnetic field, a gate element changes from a superconductive zero-resistance state to its normal resistive state.

cryotronics The branch of electronics that deals with the design, construction, and use of cryogenic devices.

crystal A natural or synthetic piezoelectric or semiconductor material whose atoms are arranged with some degree of geometric regularity.

crystal activity A measure of the amplitude of vibration of a piezoelectric crystal plate under specified conditions.

crystal-audio receiver Similar to the crystal-video receiver, except for the path detection bandwidth which is audio rather than video.

crystal blank The result of the final cutting operation on a piezoelectric or semiconductor crystal.

crystal calibrator A crystal-controlled oscillator used as a reference standard to check frequencies.

crystal control Control of the frequency of an oscillator by means of a quartz crystal unit.

crystal-controlled oscillator An oscillator whose frequency of operation is controlled by a crystal unit.

crystal-controlled transmitter A transmitter whose carrier frequency is directly controlled by the electromechanical characteristics of a quartz crystal unit.

crystal current The actual alternating current flowing through a crystal unit.

crystal detector 1. A crystal diode, or an equivalent earlier crystal-catwhisker combination, used to rectify a modulated radio-frequency signal to obtain the audio or video signal directly. 2. A crystal diode used in a microwave receiver to combine an incoming radio-frequency signal with a local oscillator signal to produce an intermediate-frequency signal.

crystal diode *See* semiconductor diode.

crystal filter A highly selective tuned circuit employing one or more quartz crystals; sometimes used in intermediate-frequency amplifiers of communication receivers to improve the selectivity.

crystal harmonic generator A type of crystalcontrolled oscillator which produces an output rich in harmonics (overtones or multiples) of its fundamental frequency.

crystal lattice filter A crystal filter that uses two matched pairs of series crystals and a higher-frequency matched pair of shunt or lattice crystals.

crystalline anisotropy The tendency of crystals to have different properties in different directions; for example, a ferromagnet will spontaneously magnetize along certain crystallographic axes.

crystal mixer A mixer that uses the nonlinear characteristic of a crystal diode to mix two frequencies; widely used in radar receivers to convert the received radar signal to a lower intermediate-frequency value by mixing it with a local oscillator signal.

crystal operation Operation using crystal-controlled oscillators.

crystal oscillator An oscillator in which the frequency of the alternating-current output is determined by the mechanical properties of a piezoelectric crystal. Also known as piezoelectric oscillator.

crystal plate A precisely cut slab of quartz crystal that has been lapped to final dimensions, etched to improve stability and efficiency, and coated with metal on its major surfaces for connecting purposes. Also known as quartz plate.

crystal rectifier *See* semiconductor diode.

crystal resonator A precisely cut piezoelectric crystal whose natural frequency of vibration is used to control or stabilize the frequency of an oscillator. Also known as piezoelectric resonator.

crystal set A radio receiver having a crystal detector stage for demodulation of the received signals, but no amplifier stages.

crystal-stabilized transmitter A transmitter employing automatic frequency control, in which the reference frequency is that of a crystal oscillator.

crystal transducer A transducer in which a piezoelectric crystal serves as the sensing element.

crystal unit A complete assembly of one or more quartz plates in a crystal holder.

crystal video receiver A broad-tuning radar or other microwave receiver consisting only of a crystal detector and a video or audio amplifier.

crystal video rectifier A crystal rectifier transforming a high-frequency signal directly into a video-frequency signal.

C scan *See* C scope.

C scope A cathode-ray scope on which signals appear as spots, with bearing angle as the horizontal coordinate and elevation angle as the vertical coordinate. Also known as C indicator; C scan.

CSW *See* channel status word.

Cuccia coupler *See* electron coupler.

cue circuit A one-way communication circuit used to convey program control information.

cumulative ionization *See* avalanche.

current amplification The ratio of output-signal current to input-signal current for an electron tube, transistor, or magnetic amplifier, the multiplier section of a multiplier phototube, or any other amplifying device; often expressed in decibels by multiplying the common logarithm of the ratio by 20.

current amplifier An amplifier capable of delivering considerably more signal current than is fed in.

current attenuation The ratio of input-signal current for a transducer to the current in a specified load impedance connected to the transducer; often expressed in decibels.

current awareness system A system for notifying users on a periodic basis of the acquisition, by a central file or library, of information (usually literature) which should be of interest to the user.

current-controlled switch A semiconductor device in which the controlling bias sets the resistance at either a very high or very low value, corresponding to the "off" and "on" conditions of a switch.

current feed Feed to a point where current is a maximum, as at the center of a half-wave antenna.

current feedback Feedback introduced in series with the input circuit of an amplifier.

current feedback circuit A circuit used to eliminate effects of amplifier gain instability in an indirect-acting recording instrument, in which the voltage input (error signal) to an amplifier is the difference between the measured quantity and the voltage drop across a resistor.

current gain The fraction of the current flowing into the emitter of a transistor which flows through the base region and out the collector.

current generator A two-terminal circuit element whose terminal current is independent of the voltage between its terminals.

current hogging A condition in which the largest fraction of a current passes through one of several parallel logic circuits because it has a lower resistance than the others.

current-instruction register *See* instruction register.

current limiter A device that restricts the flow of current to a certain amount, regardless of applied voltage. Also known as demand limiter.

current location reference A symbolic expression, such as a star, which indicates the current location reached by the program; a transfer to * + 2 would bring control to the second statement after the current statement.

current-mode logic Integrated-circuit logic in which transistors are paralleled so as to eliminate current hogging.

current noise Electrical noise of uncertain origin which is observed in certain resistances when a direct current is present, and which increases with the square of this current.

current regulator A device that maintains the output current of a voltage source at a predetermined, essentially constant value despite changes in load impedance.

current saturation *See* anode saturation.

cursor A movable spot of light that appears on the screen of a visual display terminal and can be positioned horizontally and vertically through keyboard controls to instruct the computer at what point a change is to be made.

curtate A group of adjacent rows on a punch card.

curvature effect Generally, the condition in which the dielectric strength of a liquid or vacuum separating two electrodes is higher for electrodes of smaller radius of curvature.

curve follower A device in which a photoelectric, capacitive or inductive pick-off guided by a servomechanism reads data in the form of a graph, such as a curve drawn on paper with suitable ink. Also known as graph follower.

custom-designed device An integrated logic circuit element that is generated by a series of steps resembling photographic development from highly complicated artwork patterns.

cut and paste An editing function of a word processing system in which a portion of text is marked with a particular character at the beginning and at the end and is then copied to another location within the text.

cut form In optical character recognition, any document form, receipt, or such, of standard dimensions which must be issued a separate read command in order to be recognized.

cutoff 1. The minimum value of negative grid bias that will prevent the flow of anode current in an electron tube. 2. *See* cutoff frequency.

cutoff bias The direct-current bias voltage that must be applied to the grid of an electron tube to stop the flow of anode current.

cutoff field *See* critical field.

cutoff frequency A frequency at which the attenuation of a device begins to increase sharply, such as the limiting frequency below which a traveling wave in a given mode cannot be maintained in a waveguide, or the frequency above which an electron tube loses efficiency rapidly. Also known as critical frequency; cutoff.

cutoff limiting Limiting the maximum output voltage of a vacuum tube circuit by driving the grid beyond cutoff.

cutoff voltage 1. The electrode voltage value that reduces the dependent variable of an electron-tube characteristic to a specified low value. 2. *See* critical voltage.

cut-signal-branch operation In systems where radio reception continues without cutting off the carrier, the cut-signal-branch operation technique disables a signal branch in one direction when it is enabled in the other to preclude unwanted signal reflections.

cycle count The operation of keeping track of the number of cycles a computer system goes through during processing time.

cycle criterion Total number of times a cycle in a computer program is to be repeated.

cycle delay selector An electromechanical device in a sorter which causes a cycle to be skipped so that the card out of sequence may be directed to a different pocket.

cycle index 1. The number of times a cycle has been carried out by a computer. 2. The difference, or its negative, between the number of executions of a cycle which are desired and the number which have actually been carried out.

cycle index counter A device that counts the number of times a given cycle of instructions in a computer program has been carried out.

cycle reset The resetting of a cycle index to its initial or other specified value.

cycle stealing A technique for memory sharing whereby a memory may serve two autonomous masters, commonly a central processing unit and an input-output channel or device controller, and in effect provide service to each simultaneously.

cycle time The shortest time elapsed between one store (or fetch) and the next store (or fetch) in the same memory unit. Also known as memory cycle.

cycle timer A timer that opens or closes circuits according to a predetermined schedule.

cyclic check One of the two-byte elements replacing the parity bit stripped off each byte transferred from main storage to disk volume (the other element is the bit count appendage); these two elements are appended to the block during the write operation; on a subsequent read operation these elements are calculated and compared to the appended elements for accuracy.

cyclic code A code, such as a binary code, that changes only in one digit when going from one number to the number immediately following, and in that digit by only one unit.

cyclic feeding In character recognition, a system employed by character readers in which each input document is issued to the document transport in a predetermined and constant period of time.

cyclic shift A computer shift in which the digits dropped off at one end of a word are returned at the other end of the word. Also known as circuit shift; circular shift; end-around shift; nonarithmetic shift; ring shift.

cyclic storage A computer storage device, such as a magnetic drum, whose storage medium is arranged in such a way that information can be read into or extracted from individual locations at only certain fixed times in a basic cycle.

cyclic transfer The automatic transfer of data from some medium to memory or from memory to some medium until all the data are read.

cyclophon *See* beam-switching tube.

cyclotron-frequency magnetron A magnetron whose frequency of operation depends on synchronism between the alternating-current electric field and the electrons oscillating in a direction parallel to this field.

cyclotron resonance maser *See* gyrotron.

cylinder 1. The virtual cylinder represented by the tracks of equal radius of a set of disks on a disk drive. 2. *See* seek area.

cylindrical array An electronic scanning antenna that may consist of several hundred columns of vertical dipoles mounted in cylindrical radomes arranged in a circle.

cylindrical-film storage A computer storage in which each storage element consists of a short length of glass tubing having a thin film of nickel-iron alloy on its outer surface.

D

dac *See* digital-to-analog converter.

daisy chain A means of connecting devices (readers, printers, and so on) to a central processor by party-line input/output buses which join these devices by male and female connectors, the last female connector being shorted by a suitable line termination.

daisy wheel printer A serial printer in which the printing element is a plastic hub that has a large number of flexible radial spokes, each spoke having one or more different raised printing characters; the wheel is rotated as it is moved horizontally step by step under computer control, and stops when a desired character is in a desired print position so a hammer can drive that character against an inked ribbon.

damper A diode used in the horizontal deflection circuit of a television receiver to make the sawtooth deflection current decrease smoothly to zero instead of oscillating at zero; the diode conducts each time the polarity is reversed by a current swing below zero.

dangling ELSE A situation in which it is not clear to which part of a compound conditional statement an ELSE instruction belongs.

dark conduction Residual conduction in a photosensitive substance that is not illuminated.

dark current *See* electrode dark current.

dark-current pulse A phototube dark-current excursion that can be resolved by the system employing the phototube.

dark discharge An invisible electrical discharge in a gas.

dark resistance The resistance of a selenium cell or other photoelectric device in total darkness.

dark space A region in a glow discharge that produces little or no light.

dark spot A spot on a television receiver tube that results from a spurious signal generated in the television camera tube during rescan, generally from the redistribution of secondary electrons over the mosaic in the tube.

dark-trace tube A cathode-ray tube with a bright face that does not necessarily luminesce, on which signals are displayed as dark traces or dark blips where the potassium chloride screen is hit by the electron beam. Also known as skiatron.

Darlington amplifier A current amplifier consisting essentially of two separate transistors and often mounted in a single transistor housing.

data 1. General term for numbers, letters, symbols, and analog quantities that serve as input for computer processing. 2. Any representations of characters or analog quantities to which meaning, if not information, may be assigned.

data acquisition computer A computer used to acquire and analyze data generated by instruments.

data aggregate The set of data items within a record.

data analysis The evaluation of digital data.

data automation The use of electronic, electromechanical, or mechanical equipment and associated techniques to automatically record, communicate, and process data and to present the resultant information.

data bank A complete collection of information such as contained in automated files, a library, or a set of computer disks. Also known as data base.

data base See data bank.

data-base machine A computer that handles the storage and retrieval of data into and out of a data base.

data-base management system A special data-processing system, or part of a data-processing system, which aids in the storage, manipulation, reporting, management, and control of data.

data break A facility which permits input/output transfers to occur without disturbing program execution in a computer.

data carrier A medium on which data can be recorded, and which is usually easily transportable, such as cards, tape, paper, or disks.

data carrier storage Any type of storage in which the storage medium is outside the computer, such as tape, cards, or disks, in contrast to inherent storage.

data cartridge A tape cartridge used for nonvolatile and removable data storage in small digital systems.

data cell drive A large-capacity storage device consisting of strips of magnetic tape which can be individually transferred to the read-write head.

data center An organization established primarily to acquire, analyze, process, store, retrieve, and disseminate one or more types of data.

data chain Any combination of two or more data elements, data items, data codes, and data abbreviations in a prescribed sequence to yield meaningful information; for example, "date" consists of data elements year, month, and day.

data chaining A technique used in scatter reading or scatter writing in which new storage areas are defined for use as soon as the current data transfer is completed.

data channel A bidirectional data path between input/output devices and the main memory of a digital computer permitting one or more input/output operations to proceed concurrently with computation.

data circuit A telephone facility allowing transmission of digital data pulses with minimum distortion.

data code A number, letter, character, symbol, or any combination thereof, used to represent a data item.

data collection The process of sending data to a central point from one or more locations.

data communication network A set of nodes, consisting of computers, terminals, or some type of communication control units in various locations, connected by links consisting of communication channels providing a data path between the nodes.

data communications processor A small computer used to control the flow of data between machines and terminals over communications channels.

data compression Any means of increasing the quantity of data that can be stored in a given space, or decreasing the space needed to store a given quantity of data. Also known as compression.

data concentrator A device, such as a microprocessor, that takes data from several different teletypewriter or other slow-speed lines and feeds them to a single higher-speed line.

data conversion The changing of the representation of data from one form to another, as from binary to decimal, or from one physical recording medium to another, as from card to disk. Also known as conversion.

data conversion line The channel, electronic or manual, through which data elements are transferred between data banks.

data converter *See* converter.

data dependence graph A chart that represents a program in a data flow language, in which each node is a function and each arc carries a value.

data descriptor A pointer indicating the memory location of a data item.

data dictionary A catalog containing the names and structures of all data types.

data display Visual presentation of processed data by specially designed electronic or electromechanical devices through interconnection (either on- or off-line) with digital computers or component equipments; although line printers and punch cards may display data, they are not usually categorized as displays but as output equipments.

data distribution Data transmission to one or more locations from a central point.

data division The section of a program (written in the COBOL language) which describes each data item used for input, output, and storage.

data-driven execution A mode of carrying out a program in a data flow system, in which an instruction is carried out whenever all its input values are present.

data element A set of data items pertaining to information of one kind, such as months of a year.

data entry terminal A portable keyboard and small numeric display designed for interactive communication with a computer.

data error A deviation from correctness in data, usually an error, which occurred prior to processing the data.

data field An area in the main memory of the computer in which a data record is contained.

data flow The transfer of data from an external storage device, through the processing unit and memory, and out to an external storage device.

data flow language A programming language used in a data flow system.

data flow system An alternative to conventional programming languages and architectures which is able to achieve a high degree of parallel computation, in which values rather than value containers are dealt with, and in which all processing is achieved by applying functions to values to produce new values.

data formatting Structuring the presentation of data as numerical or alphabetic and specifying the size and type of each datum.

data generator A specialized word generator in which the programming is designed to test a particular class of device, the pulse parameters and timing are adjustable, and selected words may be repeated, reinserted later in the sequence, omitted, and so forth.

data-handling system Automatically operated equipment used to interpret data gathered by instrument installations. Also known as data-reduction system.

data independence Separation of data from processing, either so that changes in the size or format of the data elements require no change in the computer programs processing them or so that these changes can be made automatically by the database management system.

data-initiated control The automatic handling of a program dependent only upon the value of input data fed into the computer.

data interchange Switching of data in and out of storage units.

data item A single member of a data element. Also known as datum.

data level The rank of a data element in a source language with respect to other elements in the same record.

data library A center for the storage of data not in current use by the computer.

data logging Conversion of electrical impulses from process instruments into digital data to be recorded, stored, and periodically tabulated.

data management The collection of functions of a control program that provide access to data sets, enforce data storage conventions, and regulate the use of input/output devices.

data management program A computer program that keeps track of what is in a computer system and where it is located, and of the various means to store and access the data efficiently.

data manipulation The standard operations of sorting, merging, input/output, and report generation.

datamation A shortened term for automatic data processing; taken from data and automation.

data move instruction An instruction in a computer program to transfer data between memory locations and registers or between the central processor and peripheral devices.

data name A symbolic name used to represent an item of data in a source program, in place of the address of the data item.

data organization Any one of the data-management conventions for physical and spatial arrangement of the physical records of a data set. Also known as data set organization.

data origination The process of putting data in a form that can be read by a machine.

data plotter A device which plots digital information in a continuous fashion.

data processing Any operation or combination of operations on data, including everything that happens to data from the time they are observed or collected to the time they are destroyed. Also known as information processing.

data-processing center A computer installation providing data-processing service for others, sometimes called customers, on a reimbursable or nonreimbursable basis.

data-processing inventory An identification of all major data-processing areas in an agency for the purpose of selecting and focusing upon those in which the use of automatic data-processing (ADP) techniques appears to be potentially advantageous, establishing relative priorities and schedules for embarking on ADP studies, and identifying significant relationships among areas to pinpoint possibilities for the integration of systems.

data-processing machine A computer or a component of a data-processing system, such as a card reader or tape unit.

data processor **1.** Any device capable of performing operations on data, for instance, a desk calculator, an analog computer, or a digital computer. **2.** Person engaged in processing data.

data purification The process of removing as many inaccurate or incorrect items as possible from a mass of data before automatic data processing is begun.

data record A collection of data items related in some fashion and usually contiguous in location.

data reduction The transformation of raw data into a more useful form.

data-reduction system *See* data-handling system.

data retrieval The searching, selecting, and retrieving of actual data from a personnel file, data bank, or other file.

data rules Conditions which must be met by data to be processed by a computer program.

data security The protection of data against the deliberate or accidental access of unauthorized persons. Also known as file security.

data set 1. A named collection of similar and related data records recorded upon some computer-readable medium. 2. A data file in IBM 360 terminology. 3. (Also, as one word) *See* modem.

dataset coupler The interface between a parallel computer input-output bus and the serial input-output of a modem.

data set label A data element that describes a data set, and usually includes the name of the data set, its boundaries in physical storage, and certain characteristics of data items within the set.

data set migration The process of moving inactive data sets from on-line storage to back up storage in a time-sharing environment.

data set organization. *See* data organization.

data sink A memory or recording device capable of accepting data signals from a data transmission device and storing data for future use.

data source A device capable of originating data signals for a data transmission device.

data stabilization Stabilization of the display of radar signals with respect to a selected reference, regardless of changes in radar-carrying vehicle attitude, as in azimuth-stabilized plan-position indicator.

data statement An instruction in a source program that identifies an item of data in the program and specifies its format.

data station A remote input/output device which handles a variety of transmissions to and from certain centralized computers.

data station control The supervision of a data station by means of a program resident in the central computer.

data structure A collection of data components that are constructed in a regular and characteristic way.

data system The means, either manual or automatic, of converting data into action or decision information, including the forms, procedures, and processes which together provide an organized and interrelated means of recording, communicating, processing, and presenting information relative to a definable function or activity.

data system interface 1. A common aspect of two or more data systems involving the capability of intersystem communications. 2. A common boundary between automatic data-processing systems or parts of a single system.

data systems integration Achievement through systems design of an improved or broader capability by functionally or technically relating two or more data systems, or by incorporating a portion of the functional or technical elements of one data system into another.

data system specifications 1. The delineation of the objectives which a data system is intended to accomplish. **2.** The data-processing requirements underlying that accomplishment; includes a description of the data output, the data files and record content, the volume of data, the processing frequencies, training, and such other facts as may be necessary to provide a full description of the system.

data tablet *See* electronic tablet.

data tracks Information storage positions on drum storage devices; information is stored on the drum surface in the form of magnetized or nonmagnetized areas.

data transcription equipment Those devices or equipment designed to convey data from its original state to a data-processing media.

data transfer The technique used by the hardware manufacturer to transmit data from computer to storage device or from storage device to computer; usually under specialized program control.

data transmission equipment The communications equipment used in direct support of data-processing equipment.

data type The manner in which a sequence of bits represents data in a computer program.

data unit A set of digits or characters treated as a whole.

data validation The checking of data for correctness, or the determination of compliance with applicable standards, rules, and conventions.

data word A computer word that is part of the data which the computer is manipulating, in contrast with an instruction word. Also known as information word.

datum *See* data item.

day clock An internal binary counter, with a resolution usually of a microsecond and a cycle measured in years, providing an accurate measure of elapsed time independent of system activity.

DCTL *See* direct-coupled transistor logic.

D display In radar, a C display in which the blips extend vertically to give a rough estimate of distance.

deaccentuator A circuit used in a frequency-modulation receiver to offset the preemphasis of higher audio frequencies introduced at the transmitter.

dead halt *See* drop-dead halt.

deadlock A situation in which a task in a multiprogramming system cannot proceed because it is waiting for an event that will never occur. Also known as deadly embrace; interlock; knot.

deadly embrace *See* deadlock.

dead spot A portion of the tuning range of a receiver in which stations are heard poorly or not at all, due to improper design of tuning circuits.

dead zone unit An analog computer device that maintains an output signal at a constant value over a certain range of values of the input signal.

debatable time In the keeping of computer usage statistics, time that cannot be attributed with certainty to any one of various categories of computer use.

deblocking Breaking up a block of records into individual records.

debug 1. To test for, locate, and remove mistakes from a program or malfunctions from a computer. **2.** To detect and remove secretly installed listening devices popularly known as bugs.

debugging routine A routine to aid programmers in the debugging of their routines; some typical routines are storage printout, tape printout, and drum printout routines.

debugging statement Temporary instructions inserted into a program being tested so as to pinpoint problem areas.

debug on-line **1.** To detect and correct errors in a computer program by using only certain parts of the hardware of a computer, while other routines are being processed simultaneously. **2.** To detect and correct errors in a program from a console distant from a computer in a multiaccess system.

debunching A tendency for electrons in a beam to spread out both longitudinally and transversely due to mutual repulsion; the effect is a drawback in velocity modulation tubes.

decade bridge Electronic apparatus for measurement of unknown values of resistances or capacitances by comparison with known values (bridge); one secondary section of the oscillator-driven transformer is tapped in decade steps, the other in 10 uniform steps.

decade counter *See* decade scaler.

decade scaler A scaler that produces one output pulse for every 10 input pulses. Also known as counter decade; decade counter; scale-of-ten circuit.

decelerating electrode Of an electron-beam tube, an electrode to which a potential is applied to decrease the velocity of the electrons in the beam.

deceleration time For a storage medium, such as magnetic tape that must be physically moved in order for reading or writing to take place, the minimum time that must elapse between the completion of a reading or writing operation and the moment that motion ceases. Also known as stop time.

decentralized data processing An arrangement comprising a data-processing center for each division or location of a single organization.

deception The deliberate radiation, reradiation, alteration, absorption, or reflection of electromagnetic energy in a manner intended to mislead an enemy in the interpretation of information received by his electronic systems.

decibel adjusted *See* adjusted decibel.

decimal attenuator System of attenuators arranged so that a voltage or current can be reduced decimally.

decimal code A code in which each allowable position has one of 10 possible states; the conventional decimal number system is a decimal code.

decimal-coded digit One of 10 arbitrarily selected patterns of 1 and 0 used to represent the decimal digits. Also known as coded decimal.

decimal processor A digital computer organized to calculate by decimal arithmetic.

decimal-to-binary conversion The mathematical process of converting a number written in the scale of 10 into the same number written in the scale of 2.

decision The computer operation of determining if a certain relationship exists between words in storage or registers, and taking alternative courses of action; this is effected by conditional jumps or equivalent techniques.

decision box A flow-chart symbol indicating a decision instruction; usually diamond-shaped.

decision element A circuit that performs a logical operation such as "and," "or," "not," or "except" on one or more binary digits of input information representing "yes" or "no" and that expresses the result in its output. Also known as decision gate.

decision gate *See* decision element.

decision instruction *See* conditional jump.

decision mechanism In character recognition, that component part of a character reader which accepts the finalized version of the input character and makes an assessment as to its most probable identity.

decision support system A computer-based system that enables management to interrogate the computer system on an ad hoc basis for various kinds of information on the organization and to predict the effect of potential decisions beforehand. Abbreviated DSS.

decision table **1.** A table of contingencies to be considered in the definition of a problem, together with the actions to be taken; sometimes used in place of a flow chart for program documentation. **2.** *See* DETAB.

deck A set of punched cards.

declarative macroinstruction An instruction in an assembly language which directs the compiler to take some action or take note of some condition and which does not generate any instruction in the object program.

declarative statement Any program statement describing the data which will be used or identifying the memory locations which will be required.

decoder **1.** A matrix of logic elements that selects one or more output channels, depending on the combination of input signals present. **2.** *See* decoder circuit; matrix; tree.

decoder circuit A circuit that responds to a particular coded signal while rejecting others. Also known as decoder.

decoding gate The use of combinatorial logic in circuitry to select a device identified by a binary address code. Also known as recognition gate.

decollator A device which separates the sheets of continuous stationery that form the output of a computer printer into separate stacks.

decometer An adding-type phasemeter which rotates continuously and adds up the total number of degrees of phase shift between two signals, such as those received from two transmitters in the Decca navigation system.

decommutation The process of recovering a signal from the composite signal previously created by a commutation process.

decommutator The section of a telemetering system that extracts analog data from a time-serial train of samples representing a multiplicity of data sources transmitted over a single radio-frequency link.

decoupling filter One of a number of low-pass filters placed between each of several amplifier stages and a common power supply.

decoy transponder A transponder that returns a strong signal when triggered directly by a radar pulse, to produce large and misleading target signals on enemy radar screens.

decrement A specific part of an instruction word in some binary computers, thus a set of digits.

decrement field That part of an instruction word which is used to modify the contents of a storage location or register.

decrypt To convert a crypotogram or series of electronic pulses into plain text by electronic means.

dedicated line A permanent communications link that is used solely to transmit information between a computer and a data-processing system.

dedicated terminal A computer terminal that is permanently connected to a data-processing system by a communications link that is used only to transmit information between the two.

defect chemistry The study of the dynamic properties of crystal defects under particular conditions, such as raising of the temperature or exposure to electromagnetic particle radiation.

defect conduction Electric conduction in a semiconductor by holes in the valence band.

defective track Any circular path on the surface of a magnetic disk which is detected by the system as unable to accept one or more bits of data.

deferred addressing A type of indirect addressing in which the address part of an instruction specifies a location containing an address, the latter in turn specifies another location containing an address, and so forth, the number of iterations being controlled by a preset counter.

deferred entry The passing of control of the central processing unit to a subroutine or to an entry point as the result of an asynchronous event.

deferred processing The making of computer runs which are postponed until nonpeak periods.

definite network A sequential network in which no feedback loops exist.

definition The extent to which the fine-line details of a printed circuit correspond to the master drawing.

deflection The displacement of an electron beam from its straight-line path by an electrostatic or electromagnetic field.

deflection circuit A circuit which controls the deflection of an electron beam in a cathode-ray tube.

deflection coil One of the coils in a deflection yoke.

deflection defocusing Defocusing that becomes greater as deflection is increased in a cathode-ray tube, because the beam hits the screen at a greater slant and the beam spot becomes more elliptical as it approaches the edges of the screen.

deflection electrode An electrode whose potential provides an electric field that deflects an electron beam. Also known as deflection plate.

deflection factor The reciprocal of the deflection sensitivity in a cathode-ray tube.

deflection plate *See* deflection electrode.

deflection polarity Relationship between the direction of a displacement of the cathode beam and the polarity of the applied signal wave.

deflection sensitivity The displacement of the electron beam at the target or screen of a cathode-ray tube per unit of change in the deflection field; usually expressed in inches per volt applied between deflection electrodes or inches per ampere in a deflection coil.

deflection voltage The voltage applied between a pair of deflection electrodes to produce an electric field.

deflection yoke An assembly of one or more electromagnets that is placed around the neck of an electron-beam tube to produce a magnetic field for deflection of one or more electron beams. Also known as scanning yoke; yoke.

defocus-dash mode A mode of cathode-ray tube storage of binary digits in which the writing beam is initially defocused so as to excite a small circular area on the screen; for one kind of binary digit it remains defocused, and for the other kind it is suddenly focused to a concentric dot and drawn out into a dash.

defocus-focus mode A variation of the defocus-dash mode in which the focused dot is drawn out into a dash.

defruit To remove random asynchronous replies from the video input of a display unit in a radar beacon system by comparing the video signals on successive sweeps.

degas To drive out and exhaust the gases occluded in the internal parts of an electron tube or other gastight apparatus, generally by heating during evacuation.

degauss To remove, erase, or clear information from a magnetic tape, disk, drum, or core.

degenerate amplifier Parametric amplifier with a pump frequency exactly twice the signal frequency, producing an idler frequency equal to that of the signal input; it is considered as a single-frequency device.

degenerate semiconductor A semiconductor in which the number of electrons in the conduction band approaches that of a metal.

degeneration The loss or gain in an amplifier through unintentional negative feedback.

deglitcher A nonlinear filter or other special circuit used to limit the duration of switching transients in digital converters.

degradation Condition under which a computer operates when some area of memory or some units of peripheral equipment are not available to the user.

degree of current rectification Ratio between the average unidirectional current output and the root mean square value of the alternating current input from which it was derived.

degree of voltage rectification Ratio between the average unidirectional voltage and the root mean square value of the alternating voltage from which it was derived.

deionization The return of an ionized gas to its neutral state after all sources of ionization have been removed, involving diffusion of ions to the container walls and volume recombination of negative and positive ions.

deionization potential The potential at which ionization of the gas in a gas-filled tube ceases and conduction stops.

deionization time The time required for a gas tube to regain its preconduction characteristics after interruption of anode current, so that the grid regains control. Also called recontrol time.

de la Rue and Miller's law The law that in a field between two parallel plates, the sparking potential of a gas is a function of the product of gas pressure and sparking distance only.

delay circuit *See* time-delay circuit.

delay counter A counter which inserts a time delay in a sequence of events.

delay distortion Phase distortion in which the rate of change of phase shift with frequency of a circuit or system is not constant over the frequency range required for transmission. Also called envelope delay distortion.

delayed automatic gain control An automatic gain control system that does not operate until the signal exceeds a predetermined magnitude; weaker signals thus receive maximum amplification. Also known as biased automatic gain control; delayed automatic volume control; quiet automatic volume control.

delayed automatic volume control *See* delayed automatic gain control.

delayed PPI A plan position indicator in which initiation of the time base is delayed a fixed time after each transmitted pulse, to give expansion of the range scale for distant targets so that they show more clearly on the screen.

delayed sweep A sweep whose beginning is delayed for a definite time after the pulse that initiates the sweep.

delay equalizer A corrective network used to make the phase delay or envelope delay of a circuit or system substantially constant over a desired frequency range.

delay flip-flop *See* D flip-flop.

delay line A transmission line (as dissipationless as possible), or an electric network approximation of it, which, if terminated in its characteristic impedance, will reproduce at its output a waveform applied to its input terminals with little distortion, but at a time delayed by an amount dependent upon the electrical length of the line. Also known as artificial delay line.

delay-line memory *See* circulating memory.

delay-line storage *See* circulating memory.

delay multivibrator A monostable multivibrator that generates an output pulse a predetermined time after it is triggered by an input pulse.

delay time The time taken for collector current to start flowing in a transistor that is being turned on from the cutoff condition.

delay unit 1. Unit of a radar system in which pulses may be delayed a controllable amount. 2. *See* transport delay unit.

deleted representation In paper tape codes, the superposition of a pattern of holes upon another pattern of holes representing a character, to effectively remove or obliterate the latter.

deletion operator The part of a data structure which allows components to be deleted.

deletion record A record which removes and replaces an existing record when it is added to a file.

delimiter A character that separates items of data.

delta The difference between a partial-select output of a magnetic cell in a one state and a partial-select output of the same cell in a zero state.

delta-gun tube A color television picture tube in which three electron guns, arranged in a triangle, provide electron beams that fall on phosphor dots on the screen, causing them to emit light in three primary colors; a shadow mask located just behind the screen ensures that each beam excites only dots of one color.

delta modulation A pulse-modulation technique in which a continuous signal is converted into a binary pulse pattern, for transmission through low-quality channels.

delta pulse code modulation A modulation system that converts audio signals into corresponding trains of digital pulses to give greater freedom from interference during transmission over wire or radio channels.

deltic method A method of sampling incoming radar, sonar, seismic, speech, or other waveforms along with reference signals, compressing the samples in time, and comparing them by autocorrelation.

demagnetizer A device for removing undesired magnetism, as from the playback head of a tape recorder or from a recorded reel of magnetic tape that is to be erased.

demand-driven execution A mode of carrying out a program in a data flow system in which no calculation is carried out until its results are demanded as input to another calculation. Also known as lazy evaluation.

demand limiter *See* current limiter.

demand paging The characteristic of a virtual memory system which retrieves only that part of a user's program which is required during execution.

demand processing The processing of data by a computer system as soon as it is received, so that it is not necessary to store large amounts of raw data. Also known as immediate processing.

demand reading A method of carrying out input operations in which blocks of data are transmitted to the central processing unit as needed for processing.

demand staging Moving blocks of data from one storage device to another when programs request them.

demand writing A method of carrying out output operations in which blocks of data are transmitted from the central processing unit as they are needed by the user.

Dember effect Creation of a voltage in a conductor or semiconductor by illumination of one surface. Also known as photodiffusion effect.

demodifier A data element used to restore part of an instruction which has been modified to its original value.

demodulator See detector.

demountable tube High-power radio tube having a metal envelope with porcelain insulation; can be taken apart for inspection and for renewal of electrodes.

demultiplexer A device used to separate two or more signals that were previously combined by a compatible multiplexer and transmitted over a single channel.

demultiplexing circuit A circuit used to separate the signals that were combined for transmission by multiplex.

dense binary code A code in which all possible states of the binary pattern are used.

dense list A list in which all the cells contain records of the file.

density modulation Modulation of an electron beam by making the density of the electrons in the beam vary with time.

density of states A function of energy E equal to the number of quantum states in the energy range between E and $E + dE$ divided by the product of dE and the volume of the substance.

density packing In computers, the number of binary digit magnetic pulses stored on tape or drum per linear inch on a single track by a single head.

depletion Reduction of the charge-carrier density in a semiconductor below the normal value for a given temperature and doping level.

depletion layer An electric double layer formed at the surface of contact between a metal and a semiconductor having different work functions, because the mobile carrier charge density is insufficient to neutralize the fixed charge density of donors and acceptors. Also known as barrier layer (deprecated); blocking layer (deprecated); space-charge layer.

depletion-layer rectification Rectification at the junction between dissimilar materials, such as a *pn* junction or a junction between a metal and a semiconductor. Also known as barrier-layer rectification.

depletion-layer transistor A transistor that relies directly on motion of carriers through depletion layers, such as spacistor.

depletion-mode field-effect transistor See junction field-effect transistor.

depletion region The portion of the channel in a metal oxide field-effect transistor in which there are no charge carriers.

deposit To preserve the contents of a portion of a computer memory by copying it in a backing storage.

deposited carbon resistor A resistor in which the resistive element is a carbon film pyrolytically deposited on a ceramic substrate.

derating The reduction of the rating of a device to improve reliability or to permit operation at high ambient temperatures.

descriptor A word or phrase used to identify a document in a computer-based information storage and retrieval system.

designation An item of data forming part of a computer record that indicates the type of record and thus determines how it is to be processed.

designation hole *See* designation punch.

designation punch A hole in a punched card indicating what is the nature of the data on the card or which functions are to be performed by the computer. Also known as control hole; control punch; designation hole; function hole.

desk calculator A device that is used to perform arithmetic operations and is small enough to be conveniently placed on a desk.

desk check *See* dry run.

destination address The location to which a jump instruction passes control in a program.

destination time The time involved in a memory access plus the time required for indirect addressing.

destination warning mark *See* tape mark.

Destriau effect Sustained emission of light by suitable phosphor powders that are embedded in an insulator and subjected only to the action of an alternating electric field.

destructive breakdown Breakdown of the barrier between the gate and channel of a field-effect transistor, causing failure of the transistor.

destructive read Reading that partially or completely erases the stored information as it is being read.

destructive readout memory A memory type in which reading the contents of a storage location destroys the contents of that location.

DETAB A programming language based on COBOL in which problems can be specified in the form of decision tables. Acronym for decision table.

detachable plugboard A control panel that can be removed from the computer or other system and exchanged for another without altering the positions of the plugs and cords. Also known as removable plugboard.

detail chart A flow chart representing every single step of a program.

detail file A file containing current or transient data used to update a master file or processed with the master file to obtain a specific result. Also known as transaction file.

detail printing The printing of information for each card as the card passes through the machine; the function is used to prepare reports that show complete detail about each card; during this listing operation, the machine adds, subtracts, cross-adds, or cross-subtracts, and prints many combinations of totals.

detectivity The normalized radiation power required to give a signal from a photoconductor that is equal to the noise.

detector The stage in a receiver at which demodulation takes place; in a superheterodyne receiver this is called the second detector. Also known as demodulator; envelope detector.

detector balanced bias Controlling circuit used in radar systems for anticlutter purposes.

deterministic algorithm *See* static algorithm.

detune To change the inductance or capacitance of a tuned circuit so its resonant frequency is different from the incoming signal frequency.

deuterium discharge tube A tube similar to a hydrogen discharge lamp, but with deuterium replacing the hydrogen; source of high-intensity ultraviolet radiation for spectroscopic microanalysis.

device 1. A general-purpose term used, often indiscriminately, to refer to a computer component or the computer itself. 2. An electronic element that cannot be divided without destroying its stated function; commonly applied to active elements such as transistors and transducers.

device address The binary code which corresponds to a unique device, referred to when selecting this specific device.

device assignment The use of a logical device number used in conjunction with an input/output instruction, and made to refer to a specific device.

device driver A subroutine which handles a complete input/output operation.

device-end condition The completion of an input/output operation, such as the transfer of a complete data block, recognized by the hardware in the absence of a byte count.

device flag A flip-flop output which indicates the ready status of an input/output device.

device independence Property of a computer program whose successful execution (without recompilation) does not depend on the type of physical unit associated with a given logical unit employed by the program.

device number The physical or logical number which refers to a specific input/output device.

device selector A circuit which gates data-transfer or command pulses to a specific input/output device.

D flip-flop A flip-flop whose output is a function of the input which appeared one pulse earlier. Also known as delay flip-flop.

DG synchro amplifier Synchro differential generator driven by servosystem.

diac *See* trigger diode.

diagnosis The process of locating and explaining detectable errors in a computer routine or hardware component.

diagnostic check *See* diagnostic routine.

diagnostic routine A routine designed to locate a computer malfunction or a mistake in coding. Also known as diagnostic check; diagnostic subroutine; diagnostic test; error detection routine.

diagnostic subroutine *See* diagnostic routine.

diagnostic test *See* diagnostic routine.

diagnotor A combination diagnostic and edit routine which questions unusual situations and notes the implied results.

diagram A schematic representation of a sequence of subroutines designed to solve a problem; it is a coarser and less symbolic representation than a flow chart, frequently including descriptions in English words.

dial pulse interpreter A device that converts the signaling pulses of a dial telephone to a form suitable for data entry to a computer.

diamond circuit A gate circuit that provides isolation between input and output terminals in its off state, by operating transistors in their cutoff region; in the on state the output voltage follows the input voltage as required for gating both analog and digital signals, while the transistors provide current gain to supply output current on demand.

diathermy machine A radio-frequency oscillator, sometimes followed by rf amplifier stages, used to generate high-frequency currents that produce heat within some part of the body for therapeutic purposes.

dibit A pair of binary digits, used to specify one of four values.

di-cap storage Device capable of holding data in the form of an array of charged capacitors and using diodes for controlling information flow.

DICE *See* digital intercontinental conversion equipment.

dichotomizing search A procedure for searching an item in a set, in which, at each step, the set is divided into two parts, one part being then discarded if it can be logically shown that the item could not be in that part.

dichotomy A division into two subordinate classes; for example, all white and all nonwhite, or all zero and all nonzero.

dicing Sawing or otherwise machining a semiconductor wafer into small squares, or dice, from which transistors and diodes can be fabricated.

Dicke fix Technique designed to protect a receiver from fast sweep jamming.

Dicke radiometer A radiometer-type receiver that detects weak signals in noise by modulating or switching the incoming signal before it is processed by conventional receiver circuits.

dictionary A table establishing the correspondence between specific words and their code representations.

dictionary code An alphabetical arrangement of English words and terms, associated with their code representations.

die The tiny, sawed or otherwise machined piece of semiconductor material used in the construction of a transistor, diode, or other semiconductor device; plural is dice.

dielectric amplifier An amplifier using a ferroelectric capacitor whose capacitance varies with applied voltage so as to give signal amplification.

dielectric breakdown Breakdown which occurs in an alkali halide crystal at field strengths on the order of 10^6 volts per centimeter.

dielectric fatigue The property of some dielectrics in which resistance to breakdown decreases after a voltage has been applied for a considerable time.

difference amplifier *See* differential amplifier.

difference detector A detector circuit in which the output is a function of the difference between the amplitudes of the two input waveforms.

differential amplifier An amplifier whose output is proportional to the difference between the voltages applied to its two inputs. Also called difference amplifier.

differential analyzer A mechanical or electromechanical device designed primarily to solve differential equations.

differential capacitance The derivative with respect to voltage of a charge characteristic, such as an alternating charge characteristic or a mean charge characteristic, at a given point on the characteristic.

differential comparator A comparator having at least two high-gain differential-amplifier stages, followed by level-shifting and buffering stages, as required for converting a differential input to single-ended output for digital logic applications.

differential discriminator A discriminator that passes only pulses whose amplitudes are between two predetermined values, neither of which is zero.

differential duplex system System in which the sent currents divide through two mutually inductive sections of a receiving apparatus, connected respectively to the line and to a balancing artificial line in opposite directions, so that there is substantially no net effect on the receiving apparatus; the received currents pass mainly through one section, or through the two sections in the same direction, and operate the apparatus.

differential gain control Device for altering the gain of a radio receiver according to expected change of signal level, to reduce the amplitude differential between the signals at the output of the receiver. Also known as gain sensitivity control.

differential input Amplifier input circuit that rejects voltages that are the same at both input terminals and amplifies the voltage difference between the two input terminals.

differential-input capacitance The capacitance between the inverting and noninverting input terminals of a differential amplifier.

differential-input impedance The impedance between the inverting and noninverting input terminals of a differential amplifier.

differential-input measurement A measurement in which the two inputs to a differential amplifier are connected to two points in a circuit under test and the amplifier displays the difference voltage between the points.

differential-input resistance The resistance between the inverting and noninverting input terminals of a differential amplifier.

differential-input voltage The maximum voltage that can be applied across the input terminals of a differential amplifier without causing damage to the amplifier.

differential keying Method for obtaining chirp-free break-in keying of continuous wave transmitters by using circuitry that arranges to have the oscillator turn on fast before the keyed amplifier stage can pass any signal, and turn off fast after the keyed amplifier stage has cut off.

differential-mode gain The ratio of the output voltage of a differential amplifier to the differential-mode input voltage.

differential-mode input The voltage difference between the two inputs of a differential amplifier.

differential-mode signal A signal that is applied between the two ungrounded terminals of a balanced three-terminal system.

differential operational amplifier An amplifier that has two input terminals, used with additional circuit elements to perform mathematical functions on the difference in voltage between the two input signals.

differential output voltage The difference between the values of two ac voltages, 180° out of phase, present at the output terminals of an amplifier when a differential input voltage is applied to the input terminals of the amplifier.

differential phase Difference in output phase of a small high-frequency sine-wave signal at two stated levels of a low-frequency signal on which it is superimposed in a video transmission system.

differential stage A symmetrical amplifier stage with two inputs balanced against each other so that with no input signal or equal input signals, no output signal exists, while a signal to either input, or an input signal unbalance, produces an output signal proportional to the difference.

differential voltage gain Ratio of the change in output signal voltage at either terminal, or in a differential device, to the change in signal voltage applied to either input terminal, all voltages being measured to common reference.

differentiator A device whose output function is proportional to the derivative, or rate of change, of the input function with respect to one or more variables.

diffractional pulse-height discriminator *See* pulse-height selector.

diffused-alloy transistor A transistor in which the semiconductor wafer is subjected to gaseous diffusion to produce a nonuniform base region, after which alloy junctions are formed in the same manner as for an alloy-junction transistor; it may also have an intrinsic region, to give a *pnip* unit. Also known as drift transistor.

diffused-base transistor A transistor in which a nonuniform base region is produced by gaseous diffusion; the collector-base junction is also formed by gaseous diffusion, while the emitter-base junction is a conventional alloy junction.

diffused emitter-collector transistor A transistor in which both the emitter and collector are produced by diffusion.

diffused junction A semiconductor junction that has been formed by the diffusion of an impurity within a semiconductor crystal.

diffused-junction rectifier A semiconductor diode in which the *pn* junction is produced by diffusion.

diffused-junction transistor A transistor in which the emitter and collector electrodes have been formed by diffusion by an impurity metal into the semiconductor wafer without heating.

diffused-mesa transistor A diffused-junction transistor in which an *n*-type impurity is diffused into one side of a *p*-type wafer; a second *pn* junction, required for the emitter, is produced by alloying or diffusing a *p*-type impurity into the newly formed *n*-type surface; after contacts have been applied, undesired diffused areas are etched away to create a flat-topped peak called a mesa.

diffused resistor An integrated-circuit resistor produced by a diffusion process in a semiconductor substrate.

diffusion 1. A method of producing a junction by diffusing an impurity metal into a semiconductor at a high temperature. **2.** The actual transport of mass, in the form of discrete atoms, through the lattice of a crystalline solid. **3.** The movement of carriers in a semiconductor.

diffusion capacitance The rate of change of stored minority-carrier charge with the voltage across a semiconductor junction.

diffusion constant The diffusion current density in a homogeneous semiconductor divided by the charge carrier concentration gradient.

diffusion transistor A transistor in which current flow is a result of diffusion of carriers, donors, or acceptors, as in a junction transistor.

digit In a decimal digital computer, the space reserved for storage of one digit of information.

digit absorbing selector Dial switch arranged to set up and then fall back on the first one of two digits dialed; it then operates on the next digit dialed.

digital Pertaining to data in the form of digits.

digital circuit A circuit designed to respond at input voltages at one of a finite number of levels and, similarly, to produce output voltages at one of a finite number of levels.

digital comparator A comparator circuit operating on input signals at discrete levels. Also known as discrete comparator.

digital computer A computer operating on discrete data by performing arithmetic and logic processes on these data.

digital converter A device that converts voltages to digital form; examples include analog-to-digital converters, pulse-code modulators, encoders, and quantizing encoders.

digital counter A discrete-state device (one with only a finite number of output conditions) that responds by advancing to its next output condition.

digital data Data that are electromagnetically stored in the form of discrete digits.

digital data recorder Electronic device that converts continuous electrical analog signals into number (digital) values and records these values onto a data log via a high-speed typewriter.

digital delay generator A high-precision adjustable time-delay generator in which delays may be selected in increments such as 1, 10, or 100 nanoseconds by means of panel switches and sometimes by remote programming.

digital differential analyzer A differential analyzer which uses numbers to represent analog quantities. Abbreviated DDA.

digital display A display in which the result is indicated in directly readable numerals.

digital filter An electrical filter that responds to an input which has been quantified, usually as pulses.

digital format Use of discrete integral numbers in a given base to represent all the quantities that occur in a problem or calculation.

digital frequency meter A frequency meter in which the value of the frequency being measured is indicated on a digital display.

digital incremental plotter A device for converting digital signals in the output of a computer into graphical form, in which the digital signals control the motion of a plotting pen and of a drum that carries the paper on which the graph is drawn.

digital integrator A device for computing definite integrals in which increments in the input variables and output variable are represented by digital signals.

digital intercontinental conversion equipment Equipment which uses pulse-code modulation to convert a 525-line, 60-frame-per-second television signal used in the United States into a 625-line, 50-frame-per-second phase-alternation line signal used in Europe; the 525-line signal is sampled and quantized into a pulse-code modulation signal which is stored in shift registers from which the phase-alternation line signal is read out. Abbreviated DICE.

digital message entry system A system that encodes formatted messages in digital form; it enters the encoded digital information into a voice communications transceiver by frequency shift techniques.

digital multiplier A multiplier that accepts two numbers in digital form and gives their product in the same digital form, usually by making repeated additions; the multiplying process is simpler if the numbers are in binary form wherein digits are represented by a 0 or 1.

digital output An output signal consisting of a sequence of discrete quantities coded in an appropriate manner for driving a printer or digital display.

digital phase shifter Device which provides a signal phase shift by the application of a control pulse; a reversal or phase shift requires a control pulse of opposite polarity.

digital plotter A recorder that produces permanent hard copy in the form of a graph from digital input data.

digital printer A printer that provides a permanent readable record of binary-coded decimal or other coded data in a digital form that may include some or all alphanumeric characters and special symbols along with numerals. Also known as digital recorder.

digital recorder *See* digital printer.

digital recording Magnetic recording in which the information is first coded in a digital form, generally with a binary code that uses two discrete values of residual flux.

digital representation The use of discrete impulses or quantities arranged in coded patterns to represent variables or other data in the form of numbers or characters.

digital resolution The ability of a digital computer to approach a truly correct answer, generally established by the number of places expressed, and the value of the least significant digit in a digitally coded representation.

digital signal analyzer A signal analyzer in which one or more analog inputs are sampled at regular intervals, converted to digital form, and fed to a memory.

digital simulation The representation of a system in a form acceptable to a digital computer as opposed to an analog computer.

digital synchronometer A time comparator that provides a direct-reading digital display of time with high precision by making accurate comparisons between its own digital clock and high-accuracy time transmissions from radio station WWV or a loran C station.

digital system Any of the levels of operation for a digital computer, including the wires and mechanical parts, the logical elements, and the functional units for reading, writing, storing, and manipulating information.

digital telemetering Conversion of a continuous electrical analog signal into a digital (number system) code prior to transmitting the signal to a receiver (such as digital readout, card punch, or tape).

digital television converter A converter used to convert television programs from one system to another, such as for converting 525-line 60-field United States broadcasts to 625-line 50-field European PAL (phase-alternation line) or SECAM (sequential couleur à memoire) standards; the video signal is digitized before conversion.

digital-to-analog converter A converter in which digital input signals are changed to essentially proportional analog signals. Abbreviated dac.

digital-to-synchro converter A converter that changes BCD or other digital input data to a three-wire synchro output signal representing corresponding angular data.

digital transducer A transducer that measures physical quantities and transmits the information as coded digital signals rather than as continuously varying currents or voltages.

digital voltmeter A voltmeter in which the unknown voltage is compared with an internally generated analog voltage, the result being indicated in digital form rather than by a pointer moving over a meter scale.

digit-coded voice A limited, spoken vocabulary, each word of which corresponds to a code and which, upon keyed inquiry, can be strung in meaningful sequence and can be outputted as audio response to the inquiry.

digit compression Any process which increases the number of digits stored at a given location.

digit delay element A logic element that introduces a delay of one digit period in a series of signals or pulses.

digit emitter A character emitter limited to the twelfth-row pulses in a punched card.

digit filter A device used with punched-card equipment that detects the presence of a designation punch in a specified card column.

112   digitize

digitize To convert an analog measurement of a quantity into a numerical value.

digit period The time interval between successive pulses, usually representing binary digits, in a computer or in pulse modulation, determined by the pulse-repetition frequency. Also known as digit time.

digit plane In a computer memory consisting of magnetic cores arranged in a three-dimensional array, a plane containing elements for a particular digit position in various words.

digit pulse An electrical pulse which induces a magnetizing force in a number of magnetic cores in a computer storage, all corresponding to a particular digit position in a number of different words.

digit rearrangement A method of hashing which consists of selecting and shifting digits of the original key.

digit selector A device which separates a card column into individual pulses corresponding to punched row positions.

digit time *See* digit period.

diheptal base A tube base having 14 pins or 14 possible pin positions; used chiefly on television cathode-ray tubes.

dimension declaration statement A FORTRAN statement identifying arrays and specifying the number and bounds of the subscripts.

dina An airborne radar-jamming transmitter operating in the band from 92 to 210 megahertz with an output of 30 watts, radiating noise in one side band for spot or barrage jamming; the carrier and the other side band are suppressed.

D indicator *See* D scope.

diode 1. A two-electrode electron tube containing an anode and a cathode. 2. *See* semiconductor diode.

diode alternating-current switch *See* trigger diode.

diode amplifier A microwave amplifier using an IMPATT, TRAPATT, or transferred-electron diode in a cavity, with a microwave circulator providing the input/output isolation required for amplification; center frequencies are in the gigahertz range, from about 1 to 100 gigahertz, and power outputs are up to 20 watts continuous-wave or more than 200 watts pulsed, depending on the diode used.

diode bridge A series-parallel configuration of four diodes, whose output polarity remains unchanged whatever the input polarity.

diode-capacitor transistor logic A circuit that uses diodes, capacitors, and transistors to provide logic functions.

diode characteristic The composite electrode characteristic of an electron tube when all electrodes except the cathode are connected together.

diode clamp *See* diode clamping circuit.

diode clamping circuit A clamping circuit in which a diode provides a very low resistance whenever the potential at a certain point rises above a certain value in some circuits or falls below a certain value in others. Also known as diode clamp.

diode clipping circuit A clipping circuit in which a diode is used as a switch to perform the clipping action.

diode-connected transistor A bipolar transistor in which two terminals are shorted to give diode action.

diode demodulator A demodulator using one or more crystal or electron tube diodes to provide a rectified output whose average value is proportional to the original modulation. Also known as diode detector.

diode detector *See* diode demodulator.

diode drop *See* diode forward voltage.

diode forward voltage The voltage across a semiconductor diode that is carrying current in the forward direction; it is usually approximately constant over the range of currents commonly used. Also known as diode drop; diode voltage; forward voltage drop.

diode function generator A function generator that uses the transfer characteristics of resistive networks containing biased diodes; the desired function is approximated by linear segments.

diode gate An AND gate that uses diodes as switching elements.

diode limiter A peak-limiting circuit employing a diode that becomes conductive when signal peaks exceed a predetermined value.

diode logic An electronic circuit using current-steering diodes, such that the relations between input and output voltages correspond to AND or OR logic functions.

diode matrix A two-dimensional array of diodes used for a variety of purposes such as decoding and read-only memory.

diode mixer A mixer that uses a crystal or electron tube diode; it is generally small enough to fit directly into a radio-frequency transmission line.

diode modulator A modulator using one or more diodes to combine a modulating signal with a carrier signal; used chiefly for low-level signaling because of inherently poor efficiency.

diode pack Combination of two or more diodes integrated into one solid block.

diode peak detector Diode used in a circuit to indicate when peaks exceed a predetermined value.

diode-pentode Vacuum tube having a diode and a pentode in the same envelope.

diode rectifier A half-wave rectifier of two elements between which current flows in only one direction.

diode rectifier-amplifier meter The most widely used vacuum tube voltmeter for measurement of alternating-current voltage; has separate tubes for rectification and direct-current amplification, permitting an optimum design for each.

diode-switch Diode which is made to act as a switch by the successive application of positive and negative biasing voltages to the anode (relative to the cathode), thereby allowing or preventing, respectively, the passage of other applied waveforms within certain limits of voltage.

diode transistor logic A circuit that uses diodes, transistors, and resistors to provide logic functions. Abbreviated DTL.

diode-triode Vacuum tube having a diode and a triode in the same envelope.

diode voltage *See* diode forward voltage.

diode voltage regulator A voltage regulator with a Zener diode, making use of its almost constant voltage over a range of currents. Also known as Zener diode voltage regulator.

DIP *See* dual in-line package.

diplexer A coupling system that allows two different transmitters to operate simultaneously or separately from the same antenna.

direct access *See* random access.

direct-access library A disk-stored set of programs, each of which is directly accessible without sequential search.

direct-access memory *See* random-access memory.

direct-access storage *See* random-access memory.

direct address Any address specifying the location of an operand.

direct-address processing Any computer operation during which data are accessed by means of addresses rather than contents.

direct allocation A system in which the storage locations and peripheral units to be assigned to use by a computer program are specified when the program is written, in contrast to dynamic allocation.

direct code A code in which instructions are written in the basic machine language.

direct control The control of one machine in a data-processing system by another, without human intervention.

direct-coupled amplifier A direct-current amplifier in which a resistor or a direct connection provides the coupling between stages, so small changes in direct currents can be amplified.

direct-coupled transistor logic Integrated-circuit logic using only resistors and transistors, with direct conductive coupling between the transistors; speed can be up to 1 megahertz. Abbreviated DCTL.

direct-current amplifier An amplifier that is capable of amplifying dc voltages and slowly varying voltages.

direct-current coupling That type of coupling in which the zero-frequency term of the Fourier series representing the input signal is transmitted.

direct-current discharge The passage of a direct current through a gas.

direct-current dump Removal of all direct-current power from a computer system or component intentionally, accidentally, or conditionally; in some types of storage, this results in loss of stored information.

direct-current erase Use of direct current to energize an erasing head of a tape recorder.

direct-current inserter A television transmitter stage that adds to the video signal a dc component known as the pedestal level.

direct-current motor control *See* electronic motor control.

direct-current offset A direct-current level that may be added to the input signal of an amplifier or other circuit.

direct-current plate resistance Value or characteristic used in vacuum-tube computations; it is equal to the direct-current plate voltage divided by the direct-current plate current.

direct-current receiver A radio receiver designed to operate directly from a 115-volt dc power line.

direct-current reinsertion *See* clamping.

direct-current restoration *See* clamping.

direct-current restorer A clamp circuit used to establish a dc reference level in a signal without modifying to any important degree the waveform of the signal itself. Also known as clamper; reinserter.

direct-current SQUID A type of superconducting quantum interference device (SQUID) which contains two Josephson junctions in a superconducting loop; its state is determined from direct-current measurements.

direct-current transducer A transducer that requires dc excitation and provides a dc output that varies with the parameter being sensed.

direct-current vacuum-tube voltmeter The amplifying and indicating portions of the diode rectifier-amplifier meter, which are usually designed so that the diode rectifier can be disconnected for dc measurements.

direct-entry terminal A device from which data are received into a computer immediately, and which edits data at the time of receipt, allowing computer files to be accessed to validate the information entered, and allowing the terminal operator to be notified immediately of any errors.

direct-gap semiconductor A semiconductor in which the minimum of the conduction band occurs at the same wave vector as the maximum of the valence band, and recombination radiation consequently occurs with relatively large intensity.

direct grid bias *See* grid bias.

direct hierarchy control A method of manipulating data in a computer storage hierarchy in which data transfer is completely under the control of built-in algorithms and the user or programmer is not concerned with the various storage subsystems.

direct-insert subroutine A body of coding or a group of instructions inserted directly into the logic of a program, often in multiple copies, whenever required.

direct instruction An instruction containing the address of the operand on which the operation specified in the instruction is to be performed.

direct interelectrode capacitance *See* interelectrode capacitance.

directional coupler A device that couples a secondary system only to a wave traveling in a particular direction in a primary transmission system, while completely ignoring a wave traveling in the opposite direction. Also known as directive feed.

directional filter A low-pass, band-pass, or high-pass filter that separates the bands of frequencies used for transmission in opposite directions in a carrier system. Also known as directional separation filter.

directional separation filter *See* directional filter.

direct ionization *See* extrinsic photoemission.

direction rectifier A rectifier that supplies a direct-current voltage whose magnitude and polarity vary with the magnitude and relative polarity of an alternating-current synchro error voltage.

directive An instruction in a source program that guides the compiler in making the translation to machine language, and is usually not translated into instructions in the object program.

directive feed *See* directional coupler.

directivity The ability of a logic circuit to ensure that the input signal is not affected by the output signal.

direct keying device A computer input device which enables direct entry of information by means of a keyboard.

directly heated cathode *See* filament.

direct memory access The use of special hardware for direct transfer of data to or from memory to minimize the interruptions caused by program-controlled data transfers. Abbreviated dma.

direct numerical control The use of a computer to program, service, and log a process such as a machine-tool cutting operation.

director Telephone switch which translates the digits dialed into the directing digits actually used to switch the call.

direct organization A type of processing in which records within data sets stored on direct-access devices may be fetched directly if their physical locations are known.

director-type computer A gunsight computer used in the director-sight system which, in response to the gunner's action of tracking, computes the angle at which a gun must be fired in order to hit a target.

directory The listing and description of all the fields of the records making up a file.

direct piezoelectricity Name sometimes given to the piezoelectric effect in which an electric charge is developed on a crystal by the application of mechanical stress.

direct point repeater Telegraph repeater in which the receiving relay controlled by the signals received over a line repeats corresponding signals directly into another line or lines without the interposition of any other repeating or transmitting apparatus.

direct resistance-coupled amplifier Amplifier in which the plate of one stage is connected either directly or through a resistor to the control grid of the next stage, with the plate-load resistor being common to both stages; used to amplify small changes in direct current.

direct symbol recognition Recognition by sensing the unique geometrical properties of symbols.

direct-view storage tube A cathode-ray tube in which secondary emission of electrons from a storage grid is used to provide an intensely bright display for long and controllable periods of time. Also known as display storage tube; viewing storage tube.

disc *See* disk.

discharge The passage of electricity through a gas, usually accompanied by a glow, arc, spark, or corona. Also known as electric discharge.

discharge lamp A lamp in which light is produced by an electric discharge between electrodes in a gas (or vapor) at low or high pressure. Also known as electric-discharge lamp; gas-discharge lamp; vapor lamp.

discharge tube An evacuated enclosure containing a gas at low pressure, through which current can flow when sufficient voltage is applied between metal electrodes in the tube. Also known as electric-discharge tube.

discontinuous amplifier Amplifier in which the input waveform is reproduced on some type of averaging basis.

discrete comparator *See* digital comparator.

discrete sampling Sampling in which the individual samples are of such long duration that the frequency response of the channel is not deteriorated by the sampling process.

discrimination *See* conditional jump.

discriminator A circuit in which magnitude and polarity of the output voltage depend on how an input signal differs from a standard or from another signal.

discriminator transformer A transformer designed to be used in a stage where frequency-modulated signals are converted directly to audio-frequency signals or in a stage where frequency changes are converted to corresponding voltage changes.

disintegration voltage The lowest anode voltage at which destructive positive-ion bombardment of the cathode occurs in a hot-cathode gas tube.

disjunctive search A search to find items that have at least one of a given set of characteristics.

disk Also spelled disc. A rotating circular plate having a magnetizable surface on which information may be stored as a pattern of polarized spots on concentric recording tracks.

disk cartridge A removable module that contains a single magnetic disk platter which remains attached to the housing when placed into the disk drive.

disk drive The physical unit that holds, spins, reads, and writes the magnetic disks. Also known as disk unit.

diskette *See* floppy disk.

disk file An organized collection of records held on a magnetic disk.

disk memory *See* disk storage.

disk operating system An operating system which uses magnetic disks as its primary on-line storage.

disk pack A set of magnetic disks that can be removed from a disk drive as a unit.

disk-seal tube An electron tube having disk-shaped electrodes arranged in closely spaced parallel layers, to give low interelectrode capacitance along with high power output, up to 2500 megahertz. Also known as lighthouse tube; megatron.

disk storage An external computer storage device consisting of one or more disks spaced on a common shaft, and magnetic heads mounted on arms that reach between the disks to read and record information on them. Also known as disk memory; magnetic disk storage.

disk thermistor A thermistor which is produced by pressing and sintering an oxide binder mixture into a disk, 0.2–0.6 inch (5–15 millimeters) in diameter and 0.04–0.5 inch (1.0–13 millimeters) thick, coating the major surfaces with conducting material, and attaching leads.

disk unit *See* disk drive.

dispatching The control of priorities in a queue of requests in a multiprogramming or multitasking environment.

dispatching priority In a multiprogramming or multitasking environment, the priority assigned to an active (non–real time, nonforeground) task.

dispenser cathode An electron tube cathode having provisions for continuously replacing evaporated electron-emitting material.

disperse A data-processing operation in which grouped input items are distributed among a larger number of groups in the output.

display **1.** A visible representation of information, in words, numbers, or drawings, as on the cathode-ray tube screen of a radar set, navigation system, or computer console. **2.** The device on which the information is projected. Also known as display device. **3.** The image of the information.

display console A cathode-ray tube or other display unit on which data being processed or stored in a computer can be presented in graphical or character form; sometimes equipped with a light pen with which the user can alter the information displayed.

display control A unit in a computer system consisting of channels and associated control circuitry that connect a number of visual display units with a central processor.

display device *See* display.

display information processor Computer used to generate situation displays in a combat operations center.

display loss *See* visibility factor.

display packing An efficient means of transmitting the x and y coordinates of a point packed in a single word to halve the time required to freshen the spot on a cathode-ray tube display.

display processor A section of a computer, or a minicomputer which handles the routines required to display an output on a cathode-ray tube.

display storage tube *See* direct-view storage tube.

display system The total system, combining hardware and software, needed to achieve a visible representation of information in a data-processing system.

display terminal A computer output device in which characters, and sometimes graphic information, appear on the screen of a cathode-ray tube. Also known as display unit; video display terminal (VDT).

display tube A cathode-ray tube used to provide a visual display. Also known as visual display unit.

display unit *See* display terminal.

dissector tube Camera tube having a continuous photo cathode on which is formed a photoelectric emission pattern which is scanned by moving its electron-optical image over an aperture.

dissipative tunneling Quantum-mechanical tunneling of individual electrons, rather than pairs, across a thin insulating layer separating two superconducting metals when there is a voltage across this layer, resulting in partial disruption of cooperative motion.

dissymmetrical network *See* dissymmetrical transducer.

dissymmetrical transducer A transducer whose input and output image impedances are not equal. Also known as dissymmetrical network.

distance mark A movable point produced on a radar display by a special signal generator, so that when the mark is moved to a target position on the screen the range to the target can be read on the calibrated dial of the signal generator; usually used for gun laying where highly accurate distance is important.

distortion Any undesired change in the waveform of an electric signal passing through a circuit or other transmission medium.

distributed amplifier A wide-band amplifier in which tubes are distributed along artificial delay lines made up of coils acting with the input and output capacitances of the tubes.

distributed circuit A film circuit whose effective components cannot be easily recognized as discrete.

distributed-emission photodiode A broad-band photodiode proposed for detection of modulated laser beams at millimeter wavelengths; incident light falls on a photocathode strip that generates a traveling wave of photocurrent having the same wave velocity as the transmission line which the photodiode feeds.

distributed free space Empty spaces in a data layout to allow new data to be inserted at a future time.

distributed intelligence The existence of processing capability in terminals and other peripheral devices of a computer system.

distributed paramp Paramagnetic amplifier that consists essentially of a transmission line shunted by uniformly spaced, identical varactors; the applied pumping wave excites the varactors in sequence to give the desired traveling-wave effect.

distributed processing system An information processing system consisting of two or more programmable devices, connected so that information can be exchanged.

distributing frame Structure for terminating permanent wires of a central office, private branch exchange, or private exchange, and for permitting the easy change of connections between them by means of cross-connecting wires.

distributing terminal assembly Frame situated between each pair of selector bays to provide terminal facilities for the selector bank wiring and facilities for cross-connection to trunks running to succeeding switches.

distribution amplifier A radio-frequency power amplifier used to feed television or radio signals to a number of receivers, as in an apartment house or a hotel.

distribution control *See* linearity control.

distribution deck A card file which duplicates all or part of a master card file and used for disseminating or decentralizing.

distributor The electronic circuitry which acts as an intermediate link between the accumulator and drum storage.

disturbed-one output One output of a magnetic cell to which partial-read pulses have been applied since that cell was last selected for writing.

divergence The spreading of a cathode-ray stream due to repulsion of like charges (electrons).

diversity receiver A radio receiver designed for space or frequency diversity reception.

divide check An error signal indicating that an illegal division (such as dividing by zero) was attempted.

divided slit scan In optical character recognition, a device consisting of a narrow column of photoelectric cells which scans an input character at given intervals for the purpose of obtaining its horizontal and vertical components.

division subroutine A built-in program which achieves division by methods such as repetitive subtraction.

dma *See* direct memory access.

document 1. Any record, printed or otherwise, that can be read by a person or machine. 2. To prepare a written text and charts describing the purpose, nature, usage, and operation of a program or a system of programs.

document alignment The phase of the reading process in which a transverse force is applied to a document to line up its reference edge with that of the reading station.

documentation The collection, organized and stored, of records that describe the purpose, use, structure, details, and operational requirements of a program, for the purpose of making this information easily accessible to the user.

document flow The path taken by documents as they are processed through a record handling system.

document handling In character recognition, the process of loading, feeding, transporting, and unloading a cut-form document that has been submitted for character recognition.

document leading edge In character recognition, that edge which is the foremost one encountered during the reading process and whose relative position defines the document's direction of travel.

document misregistration In character recognition, the improper state of appearance of a document, on site in a character reader, with respect to real or imaginary horizontal baselines.

document number The number given to a document by its originators to be used as a means for retrieval; this number will follow any one of various systems, such as chronological, subject area, or accession.

document reader An optical character reader which reads a limited amount of information (one to five lines) and generally operates from a predetermined format.

document reference edge In character recognition, that edge of a source document which provides the basis of all subsequent reading processes, insofar as it indicates the relative position of registration marks, and the impending text.

docuterm A word or phrase descriptive of the subject matter or concept of an item of information and considered important for later retrieval of information.

doghouse Small enclosure placed at the base of a transmitting antenna tower to house antenna tuning equipment.

Doherty amplifier A linear radio-frequency power amplifier that is divided into two sections whose inputs and outputs are connected by quarter-wave networks; for all values of input signal voltage up to one-half maximum amplitude, section no. 1 delivers all the power to the load; above this level, section no. 2 comes into operation.

do loop A FORTRAN iterative technique which enables any number of instructions to be executed repeatedly.

domain A region in a solid within which elementary atomic or molecular magnetic or electric moments are uniformly arrayed.

domain growth A stage in the process of magnetization in which there is a growth of those magnetic domains in a ferromagnet oriented most nearly in the direction of an applied magnetic field.

domain rotation The stage in the magnetization process in which there is rotation of the direction of magnetization of magnetic domains in a ferromagnet toward the direction of a magnetic applied field and against anisotropy forces.

domain theory A theory of the behavior of ferromagnetic and ferroelectric crystals according to which changes in the bulk magnetization and polarization arise from changes in size and orientation of domains that are each polarized to saturation but which point in different directions.

domain-tip memory A computer memory in which the presence or absence of a magnetic domain in a localized region of a thin magnetic film designates a 1 or 0. Abbreviated DOT memory. Also known as magnetic domain memory.

domain wall *See* Bloch wall.

donor An impurity that is added to a pure semiconductor material to increase the number of free electrons. Also known as donor impurity; electron donor.

donor impurity *See* donor.

donor level An intermediate energy level close to the conduction band in the energy diagram of an extrinsic semiconductor.

dopant *See* doping agent.

dope *See* doping agent.

doped junction A junction produced by adding an impurity to the melt during growing of a semiconductor crystal.

doping The addition of impurities to a semiconductor to achieve a desired characteristic, as in producing an n-type or p-type material. Also known as semiconductor doping.

doping agent An impurity element added to semiconductor materials used in crystal diodes and transistors. Also known as dopant; dope.

doping compensation The addition of donor impurities to a p-type semiconductor or of acceptor impurities to an n-type semiconductor.

dot *See* button.

dot character printer A computer printer that uses the dot matrix technique to generate characters.

dot generator A signal generator that produces a dot pattern on the screen of a three-gun color television picture tube, for use in convergence adjustments.

dot matrix A method of generating characters with a matrix of dots.

DOT memory *See* domain-tip memory.

dot-sequential color television A color television system in which the red, blue, and green primary-color dots are formed in rapid succession along each scanning line.

dot system Manufacturing technique for producing microelectronic circuitry.

double-amplitude-modulation multiplier A multiplier in which one variable is amplitude-modulated by a carrier, and the modulated signal is again amplitude-modulated by the other variable; the resulting double-modulated signal is applied to a balanced demodulator to obtain the product of the two variables.

double-base diode *See* unijunction transistor.

double-base junction diode *See* unijunction transistor.

double-base junction transistor A tetrode transistor that is essentially a junction triode transistor having two base connections on opposite sides of the central region of the transistor. Also known as tetrode junction transistor.

double-beam cathode-ray tube A cathode-ray tube having two beams and capable of producing two independent traces that may overlap; the beams may be produced by splitting the beam of one gun or by using two guns.

double-bounce calibration Method of radar calibration which is used to determine the zero set error by using round-trip echoes; the correct range is the difference between the first and second echoes.

double-buffered data transfer The transmission of data into the buffer register and from there into the device register proper.

double-diffused transistor A transistor in which two pn junctions are formed in the semiconductor wafer by gaseous diffusion of both p-type and n-type impurities; an intrinsic region can also be formed.

double diode *See* binode; duodiode.

double-diode limiter Type of limiter which is used to remove all positive signals from a combination of positive and negative pulses, or to remove all the negative signals from such a combination of positive and negative pulses.

double-doped transistor The original grown-junction transistor, formed by successively adding p-type and n-type impurities to the melt during growing of the crystal.

double image A television picture consisting of two overlapping images due to reception of the signal over two paths of different length so that signals arrive at slightly different times.

double-length number A number having twice as many digits as are ordinarily used in a given computer. Also known as double-precision number.

double limiter *See* cascade limiter.

double-list sorting A method of internal sorting in which the entire unsorted list is first placed in one portion of main memory and sorting action then takes place, creating a sorted list, generally in another area of memory.

double moding Undesirable shifting of a magnetron from one frequency to another at irregular intervals.

double precision The use of two computer words to represent a double-length number.

double-precision hardware Special arithmetic units in a computer designed to handle double-length numbers, employed in operations in which greater accuracy than normal is desired.

double-precision number *See* double-length number.

double-pulse recording A technique for recording binary digits in magnetic cells in which each cell consists of two regions that can be magnetized in opposite directions and the value of each bit (0 or 1) is determined by the order in which the regions occur.

doubler *See* frequency doubler; voltage doubler.

double screen Three-layer cathode-ray tube screen consisting of a two-layer screen with the addition of a second long-persistence coating having a different color and different persistence from the first.

double-stream amplifier Microwave traveling-wave amplifier in which amplification occurs through interaction of two electron beams having different average velocities.

double triode An electron tube having two triodes in the same envelope. Also known as duotriode.

doublet trigger A trigger signal consisting of two pulses spaced a predetermined amount for coding purposes.

double-tuned amplifier Amplifier of one or more stages in which each stage uses coupled circuits having two frequencies of resonance, to obtain wider bands than those obtainable with single tuning.

double-tuned circuit A circuit that is resonant to two adjacent frequencies, so that there are two approximately equal values of peak response, with a dip between.

double-tuned detector A type of frequency-modulation discriminator in which the limiter output transformer has two secondaries, one tuned above the resting frequency and the other tuned an equal amount below.

double word A unit containing twice as many bits as a word.

double-word addressing An addressing mode in computers with short words (less than 16 bits) in which the second of two consecutive instruction words contains the address of a location.

doubly linked ring A cycle arrangement of data elements in which searches are possible in both directions.

down-load To transfer a program or data file from a central computer to a remote computer or to the memory of an intelligent terminal.

downward compatibility The ability of an older or smaller computer to accept programs from a newer or larger one.

Dow oscillator *See* electron-coupled oscillator.

drain One of the electrodes in a thin-film transistor.

dress The arrangement of connecting wires in a circuit to prevent undesirable coupling and feedback.

drift The movement of current carriers in a semiconductor under the influence of an applied voltage.

drift-corrected amplifier A type of amplifier that includes circuits designed to reduce gradual changes in output, used in analog computers.

drift error An error arising in the use of an analog computer due to gradual changes in the output of circuits (such as amplifiers) in the computer.

drift mobility The average drift velocity of carriers per unit electric field in a homogeneous semiconductor. Also known as mobility.

drift space A space in an electron tube which is substantially free of externally applied alternating fields and in which repositioning of electrons takes place.

drift transistor 1. A transistor having two plane parallel junctions, with a resistivity gradient in the base region between the junctions to improve the high-frequency response. 2. *See* diffused-alloy transistor.

drift velocity The average velocity of a carrier that is moving under the influence of an electric field in a semiconductor, conductor, or electron tube.

drive *See* excitation.

drive control *See* horizontal drive control.

driven blocking oscillator *See* monostable blocking oscillator.

drive pulse An electrical pulse which induces a magnetizing force in an element of a magnetic core storage, reversing the polarity of the core.

driver The amplifier stage preceding the output stage in a receiver or transmitter.

driver sweep Sweep triggered only by an incoming signal or trigger.

driver transformer A transformer in the input circuit of an amplifier, especially in the transmitter.

drive winding A coil of wire that is inductively coupled to an element of a magnetic memory. Also known as drive wire.

drive wire *See* drive winding.

driving point impedance The complex ratio of applied alternating voltage to the resulting alternating current in an electron tube, network, or other transducer.

driving signal Television signal that times the scanning at the pickup point.

drop-dead halt A machine halt from which there is no recovery; such a halt may occur through a logical error in programming; examples in which a drop-dead halt could occur are division by zero and transfer to a nonexistent instruction word. Also known as dead halt.

drop-in The accidental appearance of an unwanted bit, digit, or character on a magnetic recording surface or during reading from or writing to a magnetic storage device.

dropout A reduction in output signal level during reproduction of recorded data, sufficient to cause a processing error.

dropout error Loss of a recorded bit or any other error occurring in recorded magnetic tape due to foreign particles on or in the magnetic coating or to defects in the backing.

dropping fraction In punched cards, the chance that a given sorting operation will cause a card taken at random to be selected.

drop repeater Microwave repeater that is provided with the necessary equipment for local termination of one or more circuits.

drum A computer storage device consisting of a rapidly rotating cylinder with a magnetizable external surface on which data can be read or written by many read/write heads floating a few millionths of an inch off the surface. Also known as drum memory; drum storage; magnetic drum; magnetic drum storage.

drum mark A character indicating the termination of a record on a magnetic drum.

drum memory *See* drum.

drum parity error Parity error occurring during transfer of information onto or from drums.

drum printer An impact printer in which a complete set of characters for each print position on a line is on a continuously rotating drum behind an inked ribbon, with paper in front of the ribbon; identical characters are printed simultaneously at all required positions on a line, on the fly, by signal-controlled hammers.

drum recorder A facsimile recorder in which the record sheet is mounted on a rotating drum or cylinder.

drum storage *See* drum.

drum transmitter A facsimile transmitter in which the subject copy is mounted on a rotating drum or cylinder.

dry-disk rectifier *See* metallic rectifier.

dry flashover voltage Voltage at which the air surrounding a clean dry insulator or shell completely breaks down between electrodes.

dry-plate rectifier *See* metallic rectifier.

dry run A check of the logic and coding of a computer program in which the program's operations are followed from a flow chart and written instructions, and the results of each step are written down, before the program is run on a computer. Also known as desk check.

D scan *See* D scope.

D scope A cathode-ray scope which combines the features of B and C scopes, the signal appearing as a spot with bearing angle as the horizontal coordinate and elevation angle as the vertical coordinate, but with each spot expanded slightly in a vertical direction to give a rough range indication. Also known as D indicator; D scan.

DSS *See* decision support system.

DTL *See* diode transistor logic.

dual diversity receiver A diversity radio receiver in which the two antennas feed separate radio-frequency systems, with mixing occurring after the converter.

dual-emitter transistor A passivated *pnp* silicon planar epitaxial transistor having two emitters, for use in low-level choppers.

dual-gun cathode-ray tube A dual-trace oscilloscope in which beams from two electron guns are controlled by separate balanced vertical-deflection plates and also have separate brightness and focus controls.

dual in-line package Microcircuit package with two rows of seven vertical leads that are easily inserted into an etched circuit board. Abbreviated DIP.

duality principle Also known as principle of duality. The principle that analogies may be drawn between a transistor circuit and the corresponding vacuum tube circuit.

dual-trace amplifier An oscilloscope amplifier that switches electronically between two signals under observation in the interval between sweeps, so that waveforms of both signals are displayed on the screen.

dual-trace oscilloscope An oscilloscope which can compare two waveforms on the face of a single cathode-ray tube, using any one of several methods.

ducod punched card A punched card that has 12 rows of punching positions in each column, designated 0 through 9 and X and Y, and in which numbers from 0 through 99 are punched as two holes in positions 0 through 9, while digit order or digit duplication is indicated by punching or not punching in positions X and Y.

dull emitter An electron tube whose cathode is a filament that does not glow brightly.

dumb terminal A computer input/output device that lacks the capability to process or formate data, and is thus entirely dependent on the main computer for these activities.

dummy An artificial address, instruction, or other unit of information inserted in a digital computer solely to fulfill prescribed conditions (such as word length or block length) without affecting operations.

dummy antenna A device that has the impedance characteristic and power-handling capacity of an antenna but does not radiate or receive radio waves; used chiefly for testing a transmitter. Also known as artificial antenna.

dummy argument The variable appearing in the definition of a macro or function which will be replaced by an address at call time.

dummy deck Complete set of tabulating cards containing only punched, coded information (nonaperture); used as machine-handling set for sorting, reproducing, and interpreting in conjunction with an aperture card system.

dummy instruction An artificial instruction or address inserted in a list to serve a purpose other than the execution as an instruction.

dummy load A dissipative device used at the end of a transmission line or waveguide to convert transmitted energy into heat, so that essentially no energy is radiated outward or reflected back to its source.

dump 1. To copy the contents of all or part of a storage, usually from an internal storage device into an external storage device. 2. To withdraw all power from a system or component accidentally or intentionally.

dump check A computer check that usually consists of adding all the digits during dumping, and verifying the sum when retransferring.

duodiode An electron tube having two diodes in the same envelope, with either a common cathode or separate cathodes. Also known as double diode.

duodiode-pentode An electron tube having two diodes and a pentode in the same envelope, generally with a common cathode.

duodiode-triode An electron tube having two diodes and a triode in the same envelope, generally with a common cathode.

duoplasmatron An ion-beam source in which electrons from a hot filament are accelerated sufficiently to ionize a gas by impact; the resulting positive ions are drawn out by high-voltage electrons and focused into a beam by electrostatic lens action.

duoprimed word A computer word containing a representation of the sixth, seventh, eighth, and ninth rows of information from an 80-column card.

duotriode See double triode.

duplex computer Two identical computers, either one of which can ensure continuous operation of the system when the other is shut down.

duplexer A switching device used in radar to permit alternate use of the same antenna for both transmitting and receiving; other forms of duplexers serve for two-way radio communication using a single antenna at lower frequencies. Also known as duplexing assembly.

duplexing assembly See duplexer.

duplex tube Combination of two vacuum tubes in one envelope.

duplicate field A series of 12 punches in a program card.

duplicate key A key on the card punch which, when depressed, will copy a card in the reading station onto a card in the write station.

duplicate record An unwanted record that has the same key as another record in the same file.

duplication check A check based on the identity in results of two independent performances of the same task.

duration control Control for adjusting the time duration of reduced gain in a sensitivity-time control circuit.

Dushman equation *See* Richardson-Dushman equation.

dust core *See* ferrite core.

duty cycle *See* duty ratio.

duty ratio In a pulse radar or similar system, the ratio of average to peak pulse power. Also known as duty cycle.

dyadic processor A type of multiprocessor that includes two processors which operate under control of the same copy of the operating system.

dynamic address translator A hardware device used in a virtual memory system to automatically identify a virtual address inquiry in terms of segment number, page number within the segment, and position of the record with reference to the beginning of the page.

dynamic algorithm An algorithm whose operation is, to some extent, unpredictable in advance, generally because it contains logical decisions that are made on the basis of quantities computed during the course of the algorithm. Also known as heuristic algorithm.

dynamic allocation *See* dynamic storage allocation.

dynamic characteristic *See* load characteristic.

dynamic circuit An MOS circuit designed to make use of its high input impedance to store charge temporarily at certain nodes of the circuit and thereby increase the speed of the circuit.

dynamic convergence The process whereby the locus of the point of convergence of electron beams in a color-television or other multibeam cathode-ray tube is made to fall on a specified surface during scanning.

dynamic debugging routine A debugging routine which operates in conjunction with the program being checked and interacts with it while the program is running.

dynamic dump A dump performed during the execution of a program.

dynamic error Error in a time-varying signal resulting from inadequate dynamic response of a transducer.

dynamic focusing The process of varying the focusing electrode voltage for a color picture tube automatically so the electron-beam spots remain in focus as they sweep over the flat surface of the screen.

dynamicizer A device that converts a collection of data represented by a spatial arrangement of bits in a computer storage device into a series of signals occurring in time.

dynamic memory *See* dynamic storage.

dynamic memory allocation *See* dynamic storage allocation.

dynamic pickup A pickup in which the electric output is due to motion of a coil or conductor in a constant magnetic field. Also known as dynamic reproducer; moving-coil pickup.

dynamic plate impedance Internal resistance to the flow of alternating current between the cathode and plate of a tube.

dynamic plate resistance Opposition that the plate circuit of a vacuum tube offers to a small increment of plate voltage; it is the ratio of a small change in plate voltage to the resulting change in the plate current, other tube voltages remaining constant.

dynamic printout A printout of data which occurs during the machine run as one of the sequential operations.

dynamic problem check Any dynamic check used to ascertain that the computer solution satisfies the given system of equations in an analog computer operation.

dynamic program relocation The act of moving a partially executed program to another location in main memory, without hindering its ability to finish processing normally.

dynamic random-access memory A read-write random-access memory whose storage cells are based on transistor-capacitor combinations, in which the digital information is represented by charges that are stored on the capacitors and must be repeatedly replenished in order to retain the information.

dynamic range The ratio of the specified maximum signal level capability of a system or component to its noise level; usually expressed in decibels.

dynamic regulator Transmission regulator in which the adjusting mechanism is in self-equilibrium at only one or a few settings and requires control power to maintain it at any other setting.

dynamic relocation The ability to move computer programs or data from auxiliary memory into main memory at any convenient location.

dynamic reproducer See dynamic pickup.

dynamic sequential control Method of operation of a digital computer through which it can alter instructions as the computation proceeds, or the sequence in which instructions are executed, or both.

dynamic shift register A shift register that stores information by using temporary charge storage techniques.

dynamic stop A loop in a computer program which is created by a branch instruction in the presence of an error condition, and which signifies the existence of this condition.

dynamic storage 1. Computer storage in which information at a certain position is not always available instantly because it is moving, as in an acoustic delay line or magnetic drum. Also known as dynamic memory. 2. Computer storage consisting of capacitively charged circuit elements which must be continually refreshed or recharged at regular intervals.

dynamic storage allocation A computer system in which memory capacity is made available to a program on the basis of actual, momentary need during program execution, and areas of storage may be reassigned at any time. Also known as dynamic allocation; dynamic memory allocation.

dynamic subroutine Subroutine that involves parameters, such as decimal point position or item size, from which a relatively coded subroutine is derived by the computer itself.

dynatron A screen-grid tube in which secondary emission of electrons from the anode causes the anode current to decrease as anode voltage increases, resulting in a negative resistance characteristic. Also known as negatron.

dynatron oscillator An oscillator in which secondary emission of electrons from the anode of a screen-grid tube causes the anode current to decrease as anode voltage is increased, giving the negative resistance characteristic required for oscillation.

dynode An electrode whose primary function is secondary emission of electrons; used in multiplier phototubes and some types of television camera tubes. Also known as electron mirror.

E

EAM *See* electric accounting machine.

EAROM *See* electrically alterable read-only memory.

Easter-egging An undirected procedure for checking electronic equipment, which derives its name from the children's activity of searching for hidden eggs at Eastertime.

EBAM *See* electron-beam memory.

EBCDIC *See* extended binary-coded decimal interchange code.

echo 1. The signal reflected by a radar target, or the trace produced by this signal on the screen of the cathode-ray tube in a radar receiver. Also known as radar echo; return. 2. *See* ghost signal.

echo amplitude In radar, an empirical measure of the strength of a target signal as determined from the appearance of the echo; the amplitude of the echo waveform usually is measured by the deflection of the electron beam from the base line of an amplitude-modulated indicator.

echo attenuation The power transmitted at an output terminal of a transmission line, divided by the power reflected back to the same output terminal.

echo box A calibrated high-Q resonant cavity that stores part of the transmitted radar pulse power and gradually feeds this energy into the receiving system after completion of the pulse transmission; used to provide an artificial target signal for test and tuning purposes. Also known as phantom target.

echo check A method of ascertaining the accuracy of transmission of data in which the transmitted data are returned to the sending end for comparison with original data. Also known as read-back check.

echo contour A trace of equal signal intensity of the radar echo displayed on a range height indicator or plan position indicator scope.

echo frequency The number of fluctuations, per unit time, in the power or amplitude of a radar target signal.

echo intensity The brightness or brilliance of a radar echo as displayed on an intensity-modulated indicator; echo intensity is, within certain limits, proportional to the voltage of the target signal or to the square root of its power.

echoplex technique A technique for detecting errors in a data communication system with full duplex lines, in which the signal generated when a character is typed on a keyboard is transmitted to a receiver and retransmitted to a display terminal, enabling the operator to check if the character displayed is the same as the character typed.

echo power The electrical strength, or power, of a radar target signal, normally measured in watts or dBm (decibels referred to 1 milliwatt).

echo pulse A pulse of radio energy received at the radar after reflection from a target; that is, the target signal of a pulse radar.

echo suppressor 1. A circuit that desensitizes radar navigation equipment for a fixed period after the reception of one pulse, for the purpose of rejecting delayed pulses arriving from longer, indirect reflection paths. 2. A relay or other device used on a transmission line to prevent a reflected wave from returning to the sending end of the line.

echo talker The interference created by the retransmission of a message back to its source while the source is still transmitting.

ECL See emitter-coupled logic.

ECM See electronic countermeasure.

eco See electron-coupled oscillator.

economy The ratio of the number of characters to be coded to the maximum number available with the code; for example, binary-coded decimal using 4 bits provides 16 possible characters but uses only 10 of them.

ECSW See extended channel status word.

edge-notched card A card with a series of holes along one or more edges, and notches which open one or more holes, so that long needles inserted in specific holes in a deck of such cards let fall only cards with a desired type of data.

edge-punched card A card with one or more rows of holes, representing binary data, punched along the edges.

Edison effect See thermionic emission.

E display A rectangular radar display in which targets appear as blips with distance indicated by the horizontal coordinate, and elevation by the vertical coordinate.

edit 1. To modify the form or format of an output or input by inserting or deleting characters such as page numbers or decimal points. 2. A computer instruction directing that this step be performed.

edit capability The degree of sophistication available to the programmer to modify his statements while in the time-sharing mode.

edit mask The receiving word through which a source word is filtered, allowing for the suppression of leading zeroes, the insertion of floating dollar signs and decimal points, and other such formatting.

editor program A special program by means of which a user can easily perform corrections, insertions, modifications, or deletions in an existing program or data file.

EDP See electronic data processing.

EDP center See electronic data-processing center.

edulcorate To eliminate irrelevant data from a data file.

EDVAC The first stored program computer, built in 1952. Derived from electron discrete variable automatic compiler.

effective address The address that is obtained by applying any specified indexing or indirect addressing rules to the specified address; the effective address is then used to identify the current operand.

effective bandwidth The bandwidth of an assumed rectangular band-pass having the same transfer ratio at a reference frequency as a given actual band-pass filter, and passing the same mean-square value of a hypothetical current having even distribution of energy throughout that bandwidth.

effective instruction The computer instruction that results from changing a basic instruction during program modification. Also known as actual instruction.

effective mass A parameter with the dimensions of mass that is assigned to electrons in a solid; in the presence of an external electromagnetic field the electrons behave in many respects as if they were free, but with a mass equal to this parameter rather than the true mass.

effectiveness level A measure of the effectiveness of data-processing equipment, equal to the ratio of the operational use time to the total performace period, expressed as a percentage. Also known as average effectiveness level.

effective thermal resistance Of a semiconductor device, the effective temperature rise per unit power dissipation of a designated junction above the temperature of a stated external reference point under conditions of thermal equilibrium. Also known as thermal resistance.

effective time The time during which computer equipment is in actual use and produces useful results.

EFL *See* error frequency limit.

e format A decimal, normalized form of a floating point number in FORTRAN in which a number such as 18.756 appears as .18756E + 02, which stands for .18756 $\times$ 10^2.

eighty-column card A card with 80 columns of punch positions, and 12 punch positions in each column.

E indicator *See* E scope.

electret transducer An electroacoustic or electromechanical transducer in which a foil electret, stretched out to form a diaphragm, is placed next to a metal or metal-coated plate, and motion of the diaphragm is converted to voltage between diaphragm and plate, or vice versa.

electric accounting machine Data-processing equipment that is predominantly electromechanical in nature, such as sorters, collectors, and tabulators. Abbreviated EAM.

electrically alterable read-only memory A read-only memory that can be reprogrammed electrically in the field a limited number of times, after the entire memory is erased by applying an appropriate electric field. Abbreviated EAROM.

electrical resonator *See* tank circuit.

electric delay line A delay line using properties of lumped or distributed capacitive and inductive elements; can be used for signal storage by recirculating information-carrying wave patterns.

electric discharge *See* discharge.

electric discharge lamp *See* discharge lamp.

electric discharge tube *See* discharge tube.

electric eye *See* cathode-ray tuning indicator; phototube.

electric filter 1. A network that transmits alternating currents of desired frequencies while substantially attenuating all other frequencies. Also known as frequency-selective device. 2. *See* filter.

electric forming The process of applying electric energy to a semiconductor or other device to modify permanently its electrical characteristics.

electric quadrupole lens A device for focusing beams of charged particles which has four electrodes with alternately positive and negative polarity; used in electron microscopes and particle accelerators.

electric scanning Scanning in which the required changes in radar beam direction are produced by variations in phase or amplitude of the currents fed to the various elements of the antenna array.

electric transducer A transducer in which all of the waves are electric.

electric tuning Tuning a receiver to a desired station by switching a set of preadjusted trimmer capacitors or coils into the tuning circuits.

electric-wave filter *See* filter.

electric wind *See* convective discharge.

electroacoustic effect *See* acoustoelectric effect.

electrochemical recording Recording by means of a chemical reaction brought about by the passage of signal-controlled current through the sensitized portion of the record sheet.

electrochromic display A solid-state passive display that uses organic or inorganic insulating solids which change color when injected with positive or negative charges.

electrode admittance Quotient of dividing the alternating component of the electrode current by the alternating component of the electrode voltage, all other electrode voltages being maintained constant.

electrode capacitance Capacitance between one electrode and all the other electrodes connected together.

electrode characteristic Relation between the electrode voltage and the current to an electrode, all other electrode voltages being maintained constant.

electrode conductance Quotient of the in-phase component of the electrode alternating current by the electrode alternating voltage, all other electrode voltage being maintained constant; this is a variational and not a total conductance. Also known as grid conductance.

electrode current Current passing to or from an electrode, through the interelectrode space within a vacuum tube.

electrode dark current The electrode current that flows when there is no radiant flux incident on the photocathode in a phototube or camera tube. Also known as dark current.

electrode dissipation Power dissipated in the form of heat by an electrode as a result of electron or ion bombardment.

electrode drop Voltage drop in the electrode due to its resistance.

electrode impedance Reciprocal of the electrode admittance.

electrode inverse current Current flowing through an electrode in the direction opposite to that for which the tube is designed.

electrode potential The instantaneous voltage of an electrode with respect to the cathode of an electron tube. Also known as electrode voltage.

electrode resistance Reciprocal of the electrode conductance; this is the effective parallel resistance and is not the real component of the electrode impedance.

electrode voltage *See* electrode potential.

electrogram A record of an image of an object made by sparking, usually on paper.

electrographic pencil A pencil used to make a conductive mark on paper, for detection by a conductive-mark sensing device.

electroluminescence The emission of light, not due to heating effects alone, resulting from application of an electric field to a material, usually solid.

electroluminescent cell *See* electroluminescent panel.

electroluminescent display A display in which various combinations of electroluminescent segments may be activated by applying voltages to produce any desired numeral or other character.

electroluminescent lamp *See* electroluminescent panel.

electroluminescent panel A surface-area light source employing the principle of electroluminescence; consists of a suitable phosphor placed between sheet-metal electrodes, one of which is essentially transparent, with an alternating current applied between the electrodes. Also known as electroluminescent cell; electroluminescent lamp; light panel; luminescent cell.

electrolytic recording Electrochemical recording in which the chemical change is made possible by the presence of an electrolyte.

electromagnetic cathode-ray tube A cathode-ray tube in which electromagnetic deflection is used on the electron beam.

electromagnetic compatibility The capability of electronic equipment or systems to be operated in the intended electromagnetic environment at design levels of efficiency.

electromagnetic countermeasure *See* electronic countermeasure.

electromagnetic current Motion of charged particles (for example, in the ionosphere) giving rise to electric and magnetic fields.

electromagnetic deflection Deflection of an electron stream by means of a magnetic field.

electromagnetic focusing Focusing the electron beam in a telelvision picture tube by means of a magnetic field parallel to the beam; the field is produced by sending an adjustable value of direct current through a focusing coil mounted on the neck of the tube.

electromagnetic lens An electron lens in which electron beams are focused by an electromagnetic field.

electromagnetic reconnaissance Reconnaissance for the purpose of locating and identifying potentially hostile transmitters of electromagnetic radiation, including radar, communication, missile-guidance, and navigation-aid equipment.

electromagnetic susceptibility The tolerance of circuits and components to all sources of interfering electromagnetic energy.

electromagnetic transducer *See* electromechanical transducer.

electromechanical dialer Telephone dialer which activates one of a set of desired numbers, precoded into it, when the user selects and presses a start button.

electromechanical plotter An automatic device used in conjunction with a digital computer to produce a graphic or pictorial representation of computer data on hard copy.

electromechanical recording Recording by means of a signal-actuated mechanical device, such as a pen arm or mirror attached to the moving coil of a galvanometer.

electromechanical transducer A transducer for receiving waves from an electric system and delivering waves to a mechanical system, or vice versa. Also known as electromagnetic transducer.

electrometer amplifier A low-noise amplifier having sufficiently low current drift and other characteristics required for measuring currents smaller than 10^{-12} ampere.

electrometer tube A high-vacuum electron tube having a high input impedance (low control-electrode conductance) to facilitate measurement of extremely small direct currents or voltages.

electron acceptor *See* acceptor.

electron beam A narrow stream of electrons moving in the same direction, all having about the same velocity.

electron-beam-accessed memory *See* electron-beam memory.

electron-beam channeling The technique of transporting high-energy, high-current electron beams from an accelerator to a target through a region of high-pressure gas by creating a path through the gas where the gas density may be temporarily reduced; the gas may be ionized; or a current may flow whose magnetic field focuses the electron beam on the target.

electron-beam drilling Drilling of tiny holes in a ferrite, semiconductor, or other material by using a sharply focused electron beam to melt and evaporate or sublimate the material in a vacuum.

electron-beam generator Velocity-modulated generator, such as a klystron tube, used to generate extremely high frequencies.

electron-beam ion source A source of multiply charged heavy ions which uses an intense electron beam with energies of 5 to 10 kiloelectronvolts to successively ionize injected gas. Abbreviated EBIS.

electron-beam memory A memory that uses a high-resolution electron beam to store information on a target in a vacuum tube. Also known as electron-beam-accessed memory (EBAM).

electron-beam parametric amplifier A parametric amplifier in which energy is pumped from an electrostatic field into a beam of electrons traveling down the length of the tube, and electron couplers impress the input signal at one end of the tube and translate spiraling electron motion into electric output at the other.

electron-beam pumping The use of an electron beam to produce excitation for population inversion and lasing action in a semiconductor laser.

electron-beam recorder A recorder in which a moving electron beam is used to record signals or data on photographic or thermoplastic film in a vacuum chamber.

electron-beam tube An electron tube whose performance depends on the formation and control of one or more electron beams.

electron-bombardment-induced conductivity In a multimode display-storage tube, a process using an electron gun to erase the image on the cathode-ray tube interface.

electron collector *See* collector.

electron-coupled oscillator An oscillator employing a multigrid tube in which the cathode and two grids operate as an oscillator; the anode-circuit load is coupled to the oscillator through the electron stream. Abbreviated eco. Also known as Dow oscillator.

electron coupler A microwave amplifier tube in which electron bunching is produced by an electron beam projected parallel to a magnetic field and, at the same time, subjected to a transverse electric field produced by a signal generator. Also known as Cuccia coupler.

electron coupling A method of coupling two circuits inside an electron tube, used principally with multigrid tubes; the electron stream passing between electrodes in one circuit transfers energy to electrodes in the other circuit. Also known as electronic coupling.

electron cyclotron resonance source A source of multiply charged heavy ions that uses microwave power to heat electrons to energies of tens of kilovolts in two magnetic mirror confinement chambers in series; ions formed in the first chamber drift into the second chamber, where they become highly charged. Abbreviated ECR source.

electron device A device in which conduction is principally by electrons moving through a vacuum, gas, or semiconductor, as in a crystal diode, electron tube, transistor, or selenium rectifier.

electron discrete variable automatic compiler *See* EDVAC.

electron donor *See* donor.

electron efficiency The power which an electron stream delivers to the circuit of an oscillator or amplifier at a given frequency, divided by the direct power supplied to the stream. Also known as electronic efficiency.

electron emission The liberation of electrons from an electrode into the surrounding space, usually under the influence of heat, light, or a high electric field.

electron emitter The electrode from which electrons are emitted.

electron gun An electrode structure that produces and may control, focus, deflect, and converge one or more electron beams in an electron tube.

electron-gun density multiplication Ratio of the average current density at any specified aperture through which the electron stream passes to the average current density at the cathode surface.

electron hole *See* hole.

electronic Pertaining to electron devices or to circuits or systems utilizing electron devices, including electron tubes, magnetic amplifiers, transistors, and other devices that do the work of electron tubes.

electronic alternating-current voltmeter A voltmeter consisting of a direct-current milliammeter calibrated in volts and connected to an amplifier-rectifier circuit.

electronic azimuth marker On an airborne radar plan position indicator (PPI) a bright rotatable radial line used for bearing determination. Also known as azimuth marker.

electronic bearing cursor Of a marine radar set, the bright rotatable radial line on the plan position indicator used for bearing determination. Also known as electronic bearing marker.

electronic bearing marker *See* electronic bearing cursor.

electronic calculating punch A card-handling machine that reads a punched card, performs a number of sequential operations, and punches the result on the card.

electronic calculator A calculator in which integrated circuits perform calculations and show results on a digital display; the displays usually use either seven-segment light-emitting diodes or liquid crystals.

electronic camouflage Use of electronic means, or exploitation of electronic characteristics to reduce, submerge, or eliminate the radar echoing properties of a target.

electronic chart reader A device which scans curves by a graphical recorder on a continuous paper form and converts them into digital form.

electronic circuit An electric circuit in which the equilibrium of electrons in some of the components (such as electron tubes, transistors, or magnetic amplifiers) is upset by means other than an applied voltage.

electronic commutator An electron-tube or transistor circuit that switches one circuit connection rapidly and successively to many other circuits, without the wear and noise of mechanical switches.

electronic component A component which is able to amplify or control voltages or currents without mechanical or other nonelectrical command, or to switch currents or voltages without mechanical switches; examples include electron tubes, transistors, and other solid-state devices.

electronic computing units The sensing sections of tabulating equipment which enable the machine to handle the contents of punched cards in a prescribed manner.

electronic control The control of a machine or process by circuits using electron tubes, transistors, magnetic amplifiers, or other devices having comparable functions.

electronic controller Electronic device incorporating vacuum tubes or solid-state devices and used to control the action or position of equipment; for example, a valve operator.

electronic counter A circuit using electron tubes or equivalent devices for counting electric pulses. Also known as electronic tachometer.

electronic countermeasure An offensive or defensive tactic or device using electronic and reflecting apparatus to reduce the military effectiveness of enemy equipment involving electromagnetic radiation, such as radar, communication, guidance, or other radio-wave devices. Abbreviated ECM. Also known as electromagnetic countermeasure.

electronic coupling *See* electron coupling.

electronic data processing Processing data by using equipment that is predominantly electronic in nature, such as an electronic digital computer. Abbreviated EDP.

electronic data-processing center The complex formed by the computer, its peripheral equipment, the personnel related to the operation of the center and control functions, and, usually, the office space housing hardware and personnel. Abbreviated EDP center. Also known as computer center.

electronic data-processing management science The field consisting of a class of management problems capable of being handled by computer programs.

electronic data-processing system A system for data processing by means of machines using electronic circuitry at electronic speed, as opposed to electromechanical equipment.

electronic defense evaluation A mutual evaluation of radar and aircraft, with the aircraft trying to penetrate the radar's area of coverage in an electronic countermeasure environment.

electronic differential analyzer A form of analog computer using interconnected electronic integrators to solve differential equations.

electronic efficiency Ratio of the power at the desired frequency, delivered by the electron stream to the circuit in an oscillator or amplifier, to the average power supplied to the stream.

electronic interference Any electrical or electromagnetic disturbance that causes undesirable response in electronic equipment.

electronic jammer *See* jammer.

electronic jamming *See* jamming.

electronic line scanning Method which provides motion of the scanning spot along the scanning line by electronic means.

electronic listening device A device used to capture the sound waves of conversation originating in an ostensibly private setting in a form, usually as a magnetic tape recording, which can be used against the target by adverse interests.

electronic locator *See* metal detector.

electronic locking A technique for preventing the operation of a switch until a specific electrical signal (the unlocking signal) is introduced into circuitry associated with the switch; usually, but not necessarily, the unlocking signal is a binary sequence.

electronic microradiography Microradiography of very thin specimens in which the emission of electrons from an irradiated object, either the specimen or a lead screen behind it, is used to produce a photographic image of the specimen, which is then enlarged.

electronic motor control A control circuit used to vary the speed of a direct-current motor operated from an alternating-current power line. Also known as direct-current motor control; motor control.

electronic multimeter A multimeter that uses semiconductor or electron-tube circuits to drive a conventional multiscale meter.

electronic noise jammer An electronic jammer which emits a radio-frequency carrier modulated with a white noise signal usually derived from a gas tube; used against enemy radar.

Electronic Numerical Integrator and Calculator *See* ENIAC.

electronic organ A musical instrument which uses electronic circuits to produce music similar to that of a pipe organ.

electronic phase-angle meter A phasemeter that makes use of electronic devices, such as amplifiers and limiters, that convert the alternating-current voltages being measured to square waves whose spacings are proportional to phase.

electronic piano A piano without a sounding board, in which vibrations of each string affect the capacitance of a capacitor microphone and thereby produce audio-frequency signals that are amplified and reproduced by a loudspeaker.

electronic power supply *See* power supply.

electronic radiography Radiography in which the image is detached by direct image converter tubes or by the use of television pickup or electronic scanning, and the resultant signals are amplified and presented for viewing on a kinescope.

electronic-raster scanning *See* electronic scanning.

electronic reconnaissance The detection, identification, evaluation, and location of foreign, electromagnetic radiations emanating from other than nuclear detonations or radioactive sources.

electronic recording The process of making a graphical record of a varying quantity or signal (or the result of such a process) by electronic means, involving control of an electron beam by electric or magnetic fields, as in a cathode-ray oscillograph, in contrast to light-beam recording.

electronic scanning Scanning in which an electron beam, controlled by electric or magnetic fields, is swept over the area under examination, in contrast to mechanical or electromechanical scanning. Also known as electronic-raster scanning.

electronic sculpturing Procedure for constructing a model of a system by using an analog computer, in which the model is devised at the console by interconnecting components on the basis of analogous configuration with real system elements; then, by adjusting circuit gains and reference voltages, dynamic behavior can be generated that corresponds to the desired response, or is recognizable in the real system.

electronic security Protection resulting from all measures designed to deny to unauthorized persons information of value which might be derived from the possession and study of electromagnetic radiations.

electronic sky screen equipment Electronic device that indicates the departure of a missile from a predetermined trajectory.

electronic surge arrester Device used to switch to ground high-energy surges, thereby reducing transient energy to a level safe for secondary protectors, for example, Zener diodes, silicon rectifiers and so on.

electronic switch 1. Vacuum tube, crystal diodes, or transistors used as an on and off switching device. 2. Test instrument used to present two wave shapes on a single gun cathode-ray tube.

electronic switching The use of electronic circuits to perform the functions of a high-speed switch.

electronic tablet A data-entry device consisting of stylus, writing surface, and circuitry that produces a pair of digital coordinate values corresponding continuously to the position of the stylus upon the surface. Also known as data tablet.

electronic tachometer *See* electronic counter.

electronic tuning Tuning of a transmitter, receiver, or other tuned equipment by changing a control voltage rather than by adjusting or switching components by hand.

electronic video recording The recording of black and white or color television visual signals on a reel of photographic film as coded black and white images. Abbreviated EVR.

electronic voltage regulator A device which maintains the direct-current power supply voltage for electronic equipment nearly constant in spite of input alternating-current line voltage variations and output load variations.

electronic warfare Military action involving the use of electromagnetic energy to determine, exploit, reduce, or prevent hostile use of the electromagnetic spectrum, and action which retains friendly use of electromagnetic spectrum.

electronic warfare support measures That division of electronic warfare involving actions taken to search for, intercept, locate, record, and analyze radiated electromagnetic energy for the purpose of exploiting such radiations in support of military operations.

electronic writing The use of electronic circuits and electron devices to reproduce symbols, such as an alphabet, in a prescribed order on an electronic display device for the purpose of transferring information from a source to a viewer of the display device.

electron image tube See image tube.

electron injection 1. The emission of electrons from one solid into another. 2. The process of injecting a beam of electrons with an electron gun into the vacuum chamber of a mass spectrometer, betatron, or other large electron accelerator.

electron lens An electric or magnetic field, or a combination thereof, which acts upon an electron beam in a manner analogous to that in which an optical lens acts upon a light beam. Also known as lens.

electron microscope A device for forming greatly magnified images of objects by means of electrons, usually focused by electron lenses.

electron mirror See dynode.

electron mobility The drift mobility of electrons in a semiconductor, being the electron velocity divided by the applied electric field.

electron multiplier An electron-tube structure which produces current amplification; an electron beam containing the desired signal is reflected in turn from the surfaces of each of a series of dynodes, and at each reflection an impinging electron releases two or more secondary electrons, so that the beam builds up in strength. Also known as multiplier.

electron-multiplier phototube See multiplier phototube.

electronographic tube An image tube used in astronomy in which the electron image formed by the tube is recorded directly upon film or plates.

electronography The use of image tubes to form intensified electron images of astronomical objects and record them directly on film or plates.

electronoluminescence See cathodoluminescence.

electron optics The study of the motion of free electrons under the influence of electric and magnetic fields.

electron-ray indicator See cathode-ray tuning indicator.

electron-ray tube See cathode-ray tube.

electron-stream potential At any point in an electron stream, the time average of the potential difference between that point and the electron-emitting surface.

electron-stream transmission efficiency At an electrode through which the electron stream (beam) passes, the ratio of the average stream current through the electrode to the stream current approaching the electrode.

electron telescope A telescope in which an infrared image of a distant object is focused on the photosensitive cathode of an image converter tube; the resulting electron image is enlarged by electron lenses and made visible by a fluorescent screen.

electron trap A defect or chemical impurity in a semiconductor or insulator which captures mobile electrons in a special way.

electron tube An electron device in which conduction of electricity is provided by electrons moving through a vacuum or gaseous medium within a gastight envelope. Also known as radio tube; tube; valve (British usage).

electron-tube amplifier An amplifier in which electron tubes provide the required increase in signal strength.

electron-tube generator A generator in which direct-current energy is converted to radio-frequency energy by an electron tube in an oscillator circuit.

electron-tube heater *See* heater.

electron tube static characteristic Relation between a pair of variables such as electrode voltage and electrode current with all other voltages maintained constant.

electrooptical character recognition *See* optical character recognition.

electroosmotic driver A type of solion for converting voltage into fluid pressure, which uses depolarizing electrodes sealed in an electrolyte and operates through the streaming potential effect. Also known as micropump.

electrophotoluminescence Emission of light resulting from application of an electric field to a phosphor which is concurrently, or has been previously, excited by other means.

electroresistive effect The change in the resistivity of certain materials with changes in applied voltage.

electrosensitive recording Recording in which the image is produced by passing electric current through the record sheet.

electrostatic accelerator Any instrument which uses an electrostatic field to accelerate charged particles to high velocities in a vacuum.

electrostatic analyzer A device which filters an electron beam, permitting only electrons within a very narrow velocity range to pass through.

electrostatic cathode-ray tube A cathode-ray tube in which electrostatic deflection is used on the electron beam.

electrostatic deflection The deflection of an electron beam by means of an electrostatic field produced by electrodes on opposite sides of the beam; used chiefly in cathode-ray tubes for oscilloscopes.

electrostatic detection The detection and location of any type of solid body, such as a mineral deposit or a mine, by measuring the associated electrostatic field which arises spontaneously or is induced by the detection equipment.

electrostatic focus Production of a focused electron beam in a cathode-ray tube by the application of an electric field.

electrostatic lens An arrangement of electrostatic fields which acts upon beams of charged particles similar to the way a glass lens acts on light beams.

electrostatic memory *See* electrostatic storage.

electrostatic octupole lens A device for controlling beams of electrons or other charged particles, consisting of eight electrodes arranged in a circular pattern with alternating polarities; commonly used to correct aberrations of quadrupole lens systems.

electrostatic quadrupole lens A device for focusing beams of electrons or other charged particles, consisting of four electrodes arranged in a circular pattern with alternating polarities.

electrostatic scanning Scanning that involves electrostatic deflection of an electron beam.

electrostatic storage A storage in which information is retained as the presence or absence of electrostatic charges at specific spot locations, generally on the screen of a special type of cathode-ray tube known as a storage tube. Also known as electrostatic memory.

electrostatic storage tube *See* storage tube.

electrothermal recording Type of electrochemical recording, used in facsimile equipment, wherein the chemical change is produced principally by signal-controlled thermal action.

element A circuit or device performing some specific elementary data-processing function.

elemental area *See* picture element.

elementary item An item considered to have no subordinate item in the COBOL language.

eleven punch *See* X punch.

elimination factor In information retrieval, the ratio obtained in dividing the number of documents that have not been retrieved by the total number of documents in the file.

eliminator Device that takes the place of batteries, generally consisting of a rectifier operating from alternating current.

ellipticity *See* axial ratio.

ELSE instruction An instruction in a programming language which tells a program what actions to take if previously specified conditions are not met.

ELSE rule A convention in decision tables which spells out which action to take in the case specified conditions are not met.

emanation security The protection resulting from all measures designed to deny unauthorized persons information of value which might be derived from unintentional emissions from other than telecommunications systems.

embedded pointer A pointer set in a data record instead of in a directory.

embossed plate printer In character recognition, a data preparation device which accomplishes printing by allowing a raised character behind the paper to push the paper against the printing ribbon in front of the paper.

emission characteristics Relation, usually shown by a graph, between the emission and a factor controlling the emission, such as temperature, voltage, or current of the filament or heater.

emission electron microscope An electron microscope in which thermionic, photo, secondary, or field electrons emitted from a metal surface are projected on a fluorescent screen, with or without focusing.

emission security That component of communications security which results from all measures taken to protect any unintentional emissions of a telecommunications system from any form of exploitation other than cryptanalysis.

emitter 1. A time pulse generator found in some equipment, such as a card punch. 2. A transistor region from which charge carriers that are minority carriers in the base are injected into the base, thus controlling the current flowing through the collector; corresponds to the cathode of an electron tube. Symbolized E. Also known as emitter region.

emitter barrier One of the regions in which rectification takes place in a transistor, lying between the emitter region and the base region.

emitter bias A bias voltage applied to the emitter electrode of a transistor.

emitter-coupled logic A form of current-mode logic in which the emitters of two transistors are connected to a single current-carrying resistor in such a way that only one transistor conducts at a time. Abbreviated ECL.

emitter follower A grounded-collector transistor amplifier which provides less than unity voltage gain but high input resistance and low output resistance, and which is similar to a cathode follower in its operations.

emitter junction A transistor junction normally biased in the low-resistance direction to inject minority carriers into a base.

emitter pulse In a punch-card machine, one of a set of pulses associated with a particular row of punch positions on a punch card.

emitter region *See* emitter.

emitter resistance The resistance in series with the emitter lead in an equivalent circuit representing a transistor.

emphasizer *See* preemphasis network.

empty medium A material which has been prepared to have data recorded on it by the entry of some preliminary data, such as feed holes punched in a paper tape or header labels written on a magnetic tape; in contrast to a virgin medium.

emulation mode A method of operation in which a computer actually executes the instructions of a different (simpler) computer, in contrast to normal mode.

emulator The microprogram-assisted macroprogram which allows a computer to run programs written for another computer.

enable To authorize an activity which would otherwise be suppressed, such as to write on a tape.

enabled instruction An instruction in a program in data flow language, all of whose input values are present, so that the instruction may be carried out.

enabling pulse A pulse that prepares a circuit for some subsequent action.

encode To prepare a routine in machine language for a specific computer.

encoded abstract An abstract prepared to be scanned by automatic electronic machines.

encoded question A question set up and encoded in the form appropriate for operating, programming, or conditioning a searching device.

encoder **1.** In character recognition, that class of printer which is usually designed for the specific purpose of printing a particular type font in predetermined positions on certain size forms. **2.** In an electronic computer: a network or system in which only one input is excited at a time and each input produces a combination of outputs. **3.** *See* matrix.

encoding strip In character recognition, the area reserved for the inscription of magnetic-ink characters, as in bank checks.

encryption The coding of a clear text message by a transmitting unit so as to prevent unauthorized eavesdropping along the transmission line; the receiving unit uses the same algorithm as the transmitting unit to decode the incoming message.

end-around carry A carry from the most significant digit place to the least significant digit place.

end-around shift *See* cyclic shift.

end-cell rectifier Small trickle charge rectifier used to maintain voltage of the storage battery end cells.

end instrument A pickup used in telemetering to convert a physical quantity to an inductance, resistance, voltage, or other electrical quantity that can be transmitted over wires or by radio.

endless loop A sequence of instructions in a computer program that is repeated over and over without end, due to a mistake in the programming.

end mark A mark which signals the end of a unit of information.

end-of-data-mark A character or word signaling the end of all data held in a particular storage unit.

end-of-field-mark A data item signaling the end of a field of data, generally a variable-length field.

end of file 1. Termination or point of completion of a quantity of data; end of file marks are used to indicate this point. 2. Automatic procedures to handle tapes when the end of an input or output tape is reached; a reflective spot, called a record mark, is placed on the physical end of the tape to signal the end.

end-of-file gap A gap of precise dimension to indicate the end of a file on tape. Abbreviated EOF gap.

end-of-file indicator 1. A device that indicates the end of a file on tape. 2. *See* end-of-file mark.

end-of-file mark A control character which signifies that the last record of a file has been read. Also known as end-of-file indicator.

end-of-file routine A program which checks that the contents of a file read into the computer were correctly read; may also start the rewind procedure.

end-of-file spot A reflective piece of tape indicating the end of the tape.

end-of-job control card The last card in a deck, normally punched with a distinctive code indicating that no additional cards are required for the job.

end-of-record gap A gap of precise dimension (shorter than the end-of-file gap) which indicates the physical end of a record on a magnetic tape. Abbreviated EOR gap.

end-of-record word The last word in a record, usually written in a special format that enables identification of the end of the record.

end-of-run routine A routine that carries out various housekeeping operations such as rewinding tapes and printing control totals before a run is completed.

end-of-tape mark *See* tape mark.

end-of-tape routine A program which is brought into play when the end of a tape is reached; may involve a series of validity checks and initiate the tape rewind.

end-of-transmission recognition The capability of a computer to recognize the end of transmission of a data string even if the buffer area is not filled.

endorser A special feature available on most magnetic-ink character-recognition readers that imprints a bank's endorsement on successful document reading.

end printing Printing across one end of a punched card the information punched on the card.

energy gap A range of forbidden energies in the band theory of solids.

engineering time The nonproductive time of a computer, reserved for maintenance and servicing.

enhanceable language A computer language that has a modest degree of semantic extensibility.

enhancement An increase in the density of charged carriers in a particular region of a semiconductor.

enhancement mode Operation of a field-effect transistor in which no current flows when zero gate voltage is applied, and increasing the gate voltage increases the current.

ENIAC The first digital computer in the modern sense of the word, built 1942–1945. Derived from Electronic Numerical Integrator and Calculator.

entrance The location of a program or subroutine at which execution is to start. Also known as entry point.

entry Input data fed during the execution of a program by means of a terminal.

entry block The area of main memory reserved for the data which will be introduced at execution time.

entry condition A requirement that must be met before a program or routine can be entered by a computer program. Also known as initial condition.

entry instruction The first instruction to be executed in a subroutine.

entry point *See* entrance.

entry portion The right-hand portion of a decision table, which comprises the condition entries and action entries, and whose columns are the decision rules.

entry sorting A method of internal sorting in which records or blocks of records are placed, one at a time, in a buffer area and then integrated into the sorted list before the next record is placed in the buffer.

envelope delay distortion *See* delay distortion.

envelope detector *See* detector.

environment division The section of a program written in COBOL which defines the hardware and files to be used by the program.

environment pointer 1. A component of a task descriptor that designates where the instructions and data code for the task are located. 2. A control component element belonging to the stack model of block structure execution that points to the current environment.

EOF gap *See* end-of-file gap.

EOR gap *See* end-of-record gap.

epitaxial diffused-junction transistor A junction transistor produced by growing a thin, high-purity layer of semiconductor material on a heavily doped region of the same type.

epitaxial diffused-mesa transistor A diffused-mesa transistor in which a thin, high-resistivity epitaxial layer is deposited on the substrate to serve as the collector.

epitaxial layer A semiconductor layer having the same crystalline orientation as the substrate on which it is grown.

epitaxial transistor Transistor with one or more epitaxial layers.

EPROM *See* erasable programmable read-only memory.

equality gate *See* equivalence gate.

equalization The effect of all frequency-discriminating means employed in transmitting, recording, amplifying, or other signal-handling systems to obtain a desired overall frequency response. Also known as frequency-response equalization.

equalizer A network designed to compensate for an undesired amplitude-frequency or phase-frequency response of a system or component; usually a combination of coils, capacitors, and resistors. Also known as equalizing circuit.

equalizing circuit *See* equalizer.

equalizing pulses In television, pulses at twice the line frequency, occurring just before and after the vertical synchronizing pulses, which minimize the effect of line frequency pulses on the interlace.

equal-zero indicator A circuit component which is on when the result of an operation is zero.

equation solver A machine, usually analog, for solving systems of simultaneous equations, which may be linear, nonlinear, or differential, and for finding roots of polynomials.

equilibrium brightness Viewing screen brightness occurring when a display storage tube is in a fully written condition.

equipment augmentation 1. Procuring additional automatic data-processing equipment capability to accommodate increased work load within an established data system. 2. Obtaining additional sites or locations.

equipment compatibility The ability of a device to handle data prepared or handled by other equipment, without alteration of the code or of the form of the data.

equipment failure A fault in equipment that results in its improper behavior or prevents the execution of a job as scheduled.

equipment-misuse error An erroneous programming instruction, such as a read command addressed to a card punch.

equipotential cathode *See* indirectly heated cathode.

equivalence element *See* equivalence gate.

equivalence gate A logic circuit that produces a binary output signal of 1 if its two binary input signals are the same, and an output signal of 0 if the input signals differ. Also known as biconditional gate; equality gate; equivalence element; exclusive-NOR gate; match gate.

equivalent binary digits The number of binary positions required to enumerate the elements of a given set.

equivalent noise conductance Spectral density of a noise current generator measured in conductance units at a specified frequency.

equivalent noise resistance Spectral density of a noise voltage generator measured in ohms at a specified frequency.

equivalent noise temperature Absolute temperature at which a perfect resistor, of equal resistance to the component, would generate the same noise as does the component at room temperature.

erasability of storage Ability to erase data that are recorded in a particular location and replace them with new data; storage media are said to be erasable (for example, magnetic tape) or nonerasable (for example, punched cards).

erasable programmable read-only memory A read-only memory in which stored data can be erased by ultraviolet light or other means and reprogrammed bit by bit with appropriate voltage pulses. Abbreviated EPROM.

erasable storage Any storage medium which permits new data to be written in place of the old, such as magnetic disk or tape, but not punched card or punched tape.

erase 1. To change all the binary digits in a digital computer storage device to binary zeros. 2. To remove recorded material from magnetic tape by passing the tape through a strong, constant magnetic field (dc erase) or through a high-frequency alternating magnetic field (ac erase). 3. To eliminate previously stored information in a charge-storage tube by charging or discharging all storage elements.

erase character *See* ignore character.

erase oscillator The oscillator used in a magnetic recorder to provide the high-frequency signal needed to erase a recording on magnetic tape; the bias oscillator usually serves also as the erase oscillator.

erasing head A magnetic head used to obliterate material previously recorded on magnetic tape.

erasing speed In charge-storage tubes, the rate of erasing successive storage elements.

error An incorrect result arising from approximations used in numerical methods, rather than from a human mistake or computer malfunction.

error analysis In the solution of a problem on a digital computer, the estimation of the cumulative effect of rounding or truncation errors associated with basic arithmetic operations.

error burst The condition when more than one bit is in error in a given number of bits.

error character A character that indicates the existence of an error in the data being processed or transmitted, and usually specifies that a certain amount of preceding or following data is to be ignored.

error checking and recovery An automatic procedure which checks for parity and will proceed with the execution after error correction.

error-checking code *See* self-checking code.

error code A specific character punched into a card or tape to indicate that a conscious error was made in the associated block of data; machines reading the error code may be programmed to throw out the entire block automatically.

error-correcting code Data representation that allows for error detection and error correction if the error is of a specific kind.

error correction Computer device for automatically locating and correcting a machine error of dropping a bit or picking up an extraneous bit, without stopping the machine or having it go to a programmed recovery routine.

error correction routine A program which corrects specific error conditions in another program, routine, or subroutine.

error-detecting code *See* self-checking code.

error-detecting system An automatic system which detects an error due to a lack of data, or erroneous data during transmission.

error detection and feedback system An automatic system which retransmits a piece of data detected by the computer as being in error.

error detection routine *See* diagnostic routine.

error diagnostic A computer printout of an instruction or data statement, pinpointing an error in the instruction or statement and spelling out the type of error involved.

error frequency limit The maximum number of single bit errors per unit of time that a computer will accept before a machine check interrupt is initiated. Abbreviated EFL.

error-indicating system Built-in circuits designed to indicate automatically that certain computational errors have occurred.

error interrupt The halt in execution of a program because of errors which the computer is not capable of correcting.

error list A list generated by a compiler showing invalid or erroneous instructions in a source program.

error message A message indicating detection of an error.

error range A range of values such that an error condition will result if a specified data item falls within it.

error report A list produced by a computer showing the error conditions, such as overflows and errors resulting from incorrect or unmatched data, that are generated during program execution.

error routine A routine which takes control of a program and initiates corrective actions when an error is detected.

error signal A voltage that depends on the signal received from the target in a tracking system, having a polarity and magnitude dependent on the angle between the target and the center of the scanning beam.

error tape The magnetic tape on which erroneous records are stored during processing.

Esaki tunnel diode *See* tunnel diode.

E scan *See* E scope.

escape character A character used to indicate that the succeeding character or characters are expressed in a code different from the code currently in use.

E scope A cathode-ray scope on which signals appear as spots, with range as the horizontal coordinate and elevation angle or height as the vertical coordinate. Also known as E indicator; E scan.

ESD *See* external symbol dictionary.

even parity check A parity check in which the number of 0's or 1's in each word is expected to be even.

event The moment of time at which a specified change of state occurs; usually marks the completion of an asynchronous input/output operation.

EVR *See* electronic video recording.

exalted-carrier receiver Receiver that counteracts selective fading by maintaining the carrier at a high level at all times; this minimizes the second harmonic distortion that would otherwise occur when the carrier drops out while leaving most of the sidebands at their normal amplitudes.

except gate A gate that produces an output pulse only for a pulse on one or more input lines and the absence of a pulse on one or more other lines.

exception-item encoding A technique which allows the uninterrupted flow of a process by the automatic shunting of erroneous records to an error tape for later corrections.

exception-principle system A technique which assumes no printouts except when an error is encountered.

exception reporting A form of programming in which only values that are outside predetermined limits, representing significant changes, are selected for printout at the output of a computer.

excess conduction Electrical conduction by excess electrons in a semiconductor.

excess electron Electron introduced into a semiconductor by a donor impurity and available for conduction.

excess-fifty code A number code in which the number n is represented by the binary equivalent of $n + 50$.

excess-three code A number code in which the decimal digit n is represented by the four-bit binary equivalent of $n + 3$.

exchange The interchange of contents between two locations.

exchangeable disk storage A type of disk storage, used as a backing storage, in which the disks come in capsules, each containing several disks; the capsules can be replaced during operation of the computer and can be stored until needed.

exchange buffering An input/output buffering technique that avoids the internal moving of data.

exchange message A device, placed between a communication line and a computer, in order to take care of certain communication functions and thereby free the computer for other work.

excitation 1. The signal voltage that is applied to the control electrode of an electron tube. Also known as drive. 2. Application of signal power to a transmitting antenna.

excitation anode An anode used to maintain a cathode spot on a pool cathode of a gas tube when output current is zero.

exciter A crystal oscillator or self-excited oscillator used to generate the carrier frequency of a transmitter.

exciton An excited state of an insulator or semiconductor which allows energy to be transported without transport of electric charge; may be thought of as an electron and a hole in a bound state.

excitron A single-anode mercury-pool tube provided with means for maintaining a continuous cathode spot.

exclusive-NOR gate *See* equivalence gate.

exclusive or An instruction which performs the "exclusive or" operation on a bit-by-bit basis for its two operand words, usually storing the result in one of the operand locations.

exclusive segments Parts of an overlay program structure that cannot be resident in main memory simultaneously.

execute Usually, to run a compiled or assembled program on the computer; by extension, to compile or assemble and to run a source program.

execution control program The program delivered by the manufacturer which permits the computer to handle the programs fed to it.

execution cycle The time during which an elementary operation takes place.

execution error detection The detection of errors which become apparent only during execution time.

execution time The time during which actual work, such as addition or multiplication, is carried out in the execution of a computer instruction.

executive communications The routine information transmitted to the operator on the status of programs being executed and of the requirements made by these programs of the various components of the system.

executive-control language The generic term for a finite set of instructions which enables the programmer to run a program more efficiently.

executive file-control system The assignment of intermediate storage devices performed by the computer, and over which the programmer has no control.

executive guard mode A protective technique which prevents the programmer from accessing, or using, the executive instructions.

executive instruction Instruction to determine how a specially written computer program is to operate.

executive logging The automatic bookkeeping of time utilization by programs of the various components of a computer system.

executive routine A digital computer routine designed to process and control other routines. Also known as main program; master routine; monitor routine.

executive schedule maintenance The scheduling of jobs to be run according to priorities as established and maintained by the control executive or executive supervisor.

executive supervisor The component of the computer system which controls the sequencing, setup, and execution of the jobs presented to it.

executive system A set of programs and routines which guides a computer in the performance of its tasks, assists the programs (and programmers) with certain supporting functions, and increases the usefulness of the computer's hardware. Also known as monitor system; operating system.

executive-system concurrency The capability of the executive of a computer system to handle more than one job at the same time if these jobs do not require the same components at the same time.

executive-system control The control exerted over the executive system by means of job control cards or commands issued at a terminal.

executive-system utilities The set of programs, such as diagnostic programs or file utility programs, which enables the executive to handle the jobs efficiently and completely.

exhaustion region A layer in a semiconductor, adjacent to its contact with a metal, in which there is almost complete ionization of atoms in the lattice and few charge carriers, resulting in a space-charge density.

exit 1. A way of terminating a repeated cycle of operations in a computer program. **2.** A place at which such a cycle can be stopped.

expanded batch A level of computer processing more complex than basic batch, in which computer programs perform complex computations and produce reports that analyze performance in addition to reporting it.

expanded position indicator display Display of an expanded sector from a plan position indicator presentation.

expanded scope Magnified portion of a given type of cathode-ray tube presentation.

expanded sweep A cathode-ray sweep in which the movement of the electron beam across the screen is speeded up during a selected portion of the sweep time.

expander A transducer that, for a given input amplitude range, produces a larger output range.

expandor The part of a compandor that is used at the receiving end of a circuit to return the compressed signal to its original form; attenuates weak signals and amplifies strong signals.

expansion A process in which the effective gain of an amplifier is varied as a function of signal magnitude, the effective gain being greater for large signals than for small signals; the result is greater volume range in an audio amplifier and greater contrast range in facsimile.

exponential amplifier An amplifier capable of supplying an output signal proportional to the exponential of the input signal.

expression A mathematical or logical statement written in a source language, consisting of a collection of operands connected by operations in a logical manner.

extended binary-coded decimal interchange code A computer code that uses eight binary positions to represent a single character, giving a possible maximum of 256 characters. Abbreviated EBCDIC.

extended channel status word Stored information which follows an input/output interrupt. Abbreviated ECSW.

extended-entry decision table A decision table in which the condition stub cites the identification of the condition but not the particular values, which are entered directly into the condition entries.

extended-interaction tube Microwave tube in which a moving electron stream interacts with a traveling electric field in a long resonator; bandwidth is between that of klystrons and traveling-wave tubes.

extended-precision word A piece of data of 16 bytes in floating-point arithmetic when additional precision is required.

extended time scale *See* slow time scale.

extend flip-flop A special flag set when there is a carry-out of the most significant bit in the register after an addition or a subtraction.

extensible language A programming language which can be modified by adding new features or changing existing ones.

extensible system A computer system in which users may extend the basic system by implementing their own languages and subsystems and making them available for others to use.

extension mechanism One of the components of an extensible language which allows the definition of new language features in terms of the primitive facilities of the base language.

extent The physical locations in a mass-storage device or volume allocated for use by a particular data set.

extern A pseudoinstruction found in several assembly languages which explicitly tells an assembler that a symbol is external, that is, not defined in the program module.

external delay Time during which a computer cannot be operated due to circumstances beyond the reasonable control of the operators and maintenance engineers, such as a failure of the public power supply.

external-device address The address of a component such as a tape drive.

external-device control The capability of an external device to create an interrupt during the execution of a job.

external-device operands The part of an instruction referring to an external device such as a tape drive.

external-device response The signal from an external device, such as a tape drive, that it is not busy.

external error An error sensed by the computer when this error occurs in a device such as a disk drive.

external interrupt Any interrupt caused by the operator or by some external device such as a tape drive.

external-interrupt status word The content of a special register which indicates, among other things, the source of the interrupt.

external label A reference to a variable not defined in a program segment.

externally stored program A program achieved by wiring plugboards, as in some tabulating equipment.

external memory Any storage device not an integral part of a computer system, such as a magnetic tape or a deck of cards.

external photoelectric effect *See* photoemission.

external Q The inverse of the difference between the loaded and unloaded Q values of a microwave tube.

external signal Any message to an operator for which no printout is required but which is self-explanatory, such as a light condition indicating whether the equipment is on or off.

external sorting The sorting of a list of items by a computer, in which the list is too large to be brought into the memory at one time, and instead is brought into the memory a piece at a time so as to produce a collection of ordered sublists which are subsequently reordered by the computer to produce a single list.

external storage Large-capacity, slow-access data storage attached to a digital computer and used to store information that exceeds the capacity of main storage.

external symbol dictionary A list of external symbols and their relocatable addresses which allows the linkage editor to resolve interprogram references. Abbreviated ESD.

extinction voltage The lowest anode voltage at which a discharge is sustained in a gas tube.

extract 1. To form a new computer word by extracting and putting together selected segments of given words. 2. To remove from a computer register or memory all items that meet a specified condition.

extract instruction An instruction that requests the formation of a new expression from selected parts of given expressions.

extractor *See* mask.

extra-high tension British term for the high direct-current voltage applied to the second anode in a cathode-ray tube, ranging from about 4000 to 50,000 volts in various sizes of tubes. Abbreviated eht.

extraneous emission Any emission of a transmitter or transponder, other than the output carrier fundamental, plus only those sidebands intentionally employed for the transmission of intelligence.

extraneous response Any undersired response of a receiver, recorder, or other susceptible device, due to the desired signals, undersired signals, or any combination or interaction among them.

extrinsic photoconductivity Photoconductivity that occurs for photon energies smaller than the band gap and corresponds to optical excitation from an occupied imperfection level to the conduction band, or to an unoccupied imperfection level from the valence band, of a material.

extrinsic photoemission Photoemission by an alkali halide crystal in which electrons are ejected directly from negative ion vacancies, forming color centers. Also known as direct ionization.

extrinsic properties The properties of a semiconductor as modified by impurities or imperfections within the crystal.

extrinsic semiconductor A semiconductor whose electrical properties are dependent on impurities added to the semiconductor crystal, in contrast to an intrinsic semiconductor, whose properties are characteristic of an ideal pure crystal.

Faber flaw A deformation in a superconducting material that acts as a nucleation center for the growth of a superconducting region.

face *See* faceplate.

face-bonding Method of assembling hybrid microcircuits wherein semiconductor chips are provided with small mounting pads, turned facedown, and bonded directly to the ends of the thin-film conductors on the passive substrate.

faceplate The transparent or semitransparent glass front of a cathode-ray tube, through which the image is viewed or projected; the inner surface of the face is coated with fluorescent chemicals that emit light when hit by an electron beam. Also known as face.

facility assignment The allocation of core memory and external devices by the executive as required by the program being executed.

facsimile posting The process of transferring by a duplicating process a printed line of information from a report, such as a listing of transactions prepared on an accounting machine, to a ledger or other recorded sheet.

facsimile receiver The receiver used to translate the facsimile signal from a wire or radio communication channel into a facsimile record of the subject copy.

facsimile recorder The section of a facsimile receiver that performs the final conversion of electric signals to an image of the subject copy on the record medium.

facsimile signal level Maximum facsimile signal power or voltage (root mean square or direct current) measured at any point in a facsimile system.

facsimile synchronizing Maintenance of predetermined speed relations between the scanning spot and the recording spot within each scanning line.

facsimile transmitter The apparatus used to translate the subject copy into facsimile signals suitable for delivery over a communication system.

factory-data collection The continuous input of data achieved in a working area by having the worker insert a precoded card into a device connected to a computer.

fader A multiple-unit level control used for gradual changeover from one microphone, audio channel, or television camera to another.

failsafe tape *See* incremental dump tape.

failure logging The automatic recording of the state of various components of a computer system following detection of a machine fault; used to initiate corrective procedures, such as repeating attempts to read or write a magnetic tape, and to aid customer engineers in diagnosing errors.

fallback The system, electronic or manual, which is substituted for the computer system in case of breakdown.

false alarm In radar, an indication of a detected target even though one does not exist, due to noise or interference levels exceeding the set threshold of detection.

false drop *See* false retrieval.

false retrieval An item retrieved in an automatic library search which is unrelated or vaguely related to the subject of the search. Also known as false drop.

false sorts Entries irrelevant to the subject sought which are retrieved in a search.

false target A nonexistent target which shows up on a radar scope as the result of time delay.

false target generator An electronic countermeasure device that generates a delayed return signal on an enemy radar frequency to give erroneous position information.

fan-in The number of inputs that can be connected to a logic circuit.

fan-out The number of parallel loads that can be driven from one output mode of a logic circuit.

Faraday dark space The relatively nonluminous region that separates the negative glow from the positive column in a cold-cathode glow-discharge tube.

Farnsworth image dissector tube *See* image dissector tube.

fast-access storage The section of a computer storage from which data can be obtained most rapidly.

fast automatic gain control Radar automatic gain control method characterized by a response time that is long with respect to a pulse width, and short with respect to the time on target.

fast time constant Circuit with short time constant used to emphasize signals of short duration to produce discrimination against low-frequency components of clutter in radar.

fast time scale In simulation by an analog computer, a scale in which the time duration of a simulated event is less than the actual time duration of the event in the physical system under study.

fatal error An error in a computer program which causes running of the program to be terminated.

fatigue The decrease of efficiency of a luminescent or light-sensitive material as a result of excitation.

fault Any physical condition that causes a component of a data-processing system to fail in performance.

fault masking Any type of hardware redundancy in which faults are corrected immediately and the operations of fault detection, location, and correction are indistinguishable.

F band The optical absorption band arising from F centers.

FB data set A data set which has F-format logical records and whose physical records are all some multiple of the size of the logical record, except possibly for a few truncated blocks. Also known as blocked F-format data set.

FBM data set An FB data set which has a machine-control (M) character in its first byte of information.

FBSA data set An FBS data set which has an ASCII (American Standard Code for Information Interchange) control (A) character in its first byte of information.

FBS data set An FB data set which has at most one truncated block, which must be the last one in the data set. Also known as standard blocked F-format data set.

F center A color center consisting of an electron trapped by a negative ion vacancy in an ionic crystal, such as an alkali halide or an alkaline-earth fluoride or oxide.

F display A rectangular display in which a target appears as a centralized blip when the radar antenna is aimed at it; horizontal and vertical aiming errors are respectively indicated by the horizontal and vertical displacement of the blip.

feasible solution In linear programming, any set of values for the variables x_j, $j = 1$, $2, \ldots, n$, that (1) satisfy the set of restrictions

$$\sum_{j=1}^{n} a_{ij}x_j \leq b_i, \; i=1, 2, \ldots, m$$

$$\left(\text{alternatively}, \sum_{j=1}^{n} a_{ij}x_j \geq b_i, \text{ or } \sum_{j=1}^{n} a_{ij}x_j = b_i\right)$$

where the b_i are numerical constants known collectively as the right-hand side and the a_{ij} are coefficients of the variables x_j, and (2) satisfy the restrictions $x_j \geq 0$.

feature extraction-classification model A method of automatic pattern recognition in which recognition is achieved by making measurements on the patterns to be recognized, and then deriving features from these measurements.

fedsim star The starlike shape that is characteristic of the Kiviat graph of a well-balanced computer system.

feed 1. To supply the material to be operated upon to a machine. **2.** A device capable of so feeding. **3.** To supply a signal to the input of a circuit, transmission line, or antenna.

feedback The return of a portion of the output of a circuit or device to its input.

feedback admittance Short-circuit transadmittance from the output electrode to the input electrode of an electron tube.

feedback amplifier An amplifier in which a passive network is used to return a portion of the output signal to its input so as to change the performance characteristics of the amplifier.

feedback circuit A circuit that returns a portion of the output signal of an electronic circuit or control system to the input of the circuit or system.

feedback factor The fraction of the output voltage of an oscillator which is applied to the feedback network.

feedback oscillator An oscillating circuit, including an amplifier, in which the output is fed back in phase with the input; oscillation is maintained at a frequency determined by the values of the components in the amplifier and the feedback circuits.

feedback winding A winding to which feedback connections are made in a magnetic amplifier.

feeder reactor A small inductor connected in series with a feeder in order to limit and localize the disturbances due to faults on the feeder.

feed shelf 1. A device for supporting documents for manual sensing. **2.** The first few feet of a tape reel, used to prime the tape drive.

feed-tape A mechanism which will feed tape to be read or sensed.

feed track The longitudinal channel on a paper tape that contains the feed holes.

femitrons Class of field-emission microwave devices.

fence *See* fence cell.

fence cell A criterion for dividing a list into two equal or nearly equal parts in the course of a binary search. Also known as fence.

Fermi distribution Distribution of energies of electrons in a semiconductor or metal as given by the Fermi-Dirac distribution function; nearly all energy levels below the Fermi level are filled, and nearly all above this level are empty.

Fermi hole A region surrounding an electron in a solid in which the energy band theory predicts that the probability of finding other electrons is less than the average over the volume of the solid.

Fermi surface A constant-energy surface in the space containing the wave vectors of states of members of an assembly of independent fermions, such as electrons in a semiconductor or metal, whose energy is that of the Fermi level.

ferrimagnet *See* ferrimagnetic material.

ferrimagnetic amplifier A microwave amplifier using ferrites.

ferrimagnetic material A material displaying ferrimagnetism; the ferrites are the principal example. Also known as ferrimagnet.

ferrimagnetism A type of magnetism in which the magnetic moments of neighboring ions tend to align nonparallel, usually antiparallel, to each other, but the moments are of different magnitudes, so there is an appreciable resultant magnetization.

ferristor A miniature, two-winding, saturable reactor that operates at a high carrier frequency and may be connected as a coincidence gate, current discriminator, free-running multivibrator, oscillator, or ring counter.

ferrite Any ferrimagnetic material having high electrical resistivity which has a spinel crystal structure and the chemical formula XFe_2O_4, where X represents any divalent metal ion whose size is such that it will fit into the crystal structure.

ferrite bead Magnetic information storage device consisting of ferrite powder mixtures in the form of a bead fired on the current-carrying wires of a memory matrix.

ferrite core A magnetic core made of ferrite material. Also known as dust core; powdered-iron core.

ferrite-core memory A magnetic memory consisting of a matrix of tiny toroidal cores molded from a square-loop ferrite, through which are threaded the pulse-carrying wires and the sense wire.

ferrite-tuned oscillator An oscillator in which the resonant characteristic of a ferrite-loaded cavity is changed by varying the ambient magnetic field, to give electronic tuning.

ferroacoustic storage A delay-line type of storage consisting of a thin tube of magnetostrictive material, a central conductor passing through the tube, and an ultrasonic driving transducer at one end of the tube.

ferroelectric A crystalline substance displaying ferroelectricity, such as barium titanate, potassium dihydrogen phosphate, and Rochelle salt; used in ceramic capacitors, acoustic transducers, and dielectric amplifiers. Also known as seignette-electric.

ferroelectric crystal A crystal of a ferroelectric material.

ferroelectric domain A region of a ferroelectric material within which the spontaneous polarization is constant.

ferroelectricity Spontaneous electric polarization in a crystal; analogous to ferromagnetism.

ferromagnetic amplifier A parametric amplifier based on the nonlinear behavior of ferromagnetic resonance at high radio-frequency power levels; incorrectly known as garnet maser.

ferromagnetic crystal A crystal of a ferromagnetic material. Also known as polar crystal.

ferromagnetic domain A region of a ferromagnetic material within which atomic or molecular magnetic moments are aligned parallel. Also known as magnetic domain.

ferromagnetic film *See* magnetic thin film.

ferromagnetic material A material displaying ferromagnetism, such as the various forms of iron, steel, cobalt, nickel, and their alloys.

ferromagnetics The science that deals with the storage of binary information and the logical control of pulse sequences through the utilization of the magnetic polarization properties of materials.

ferromagnetism A property, exhibited by certain metals, alloys, and compounds of the transition (iron group) rare-earth and actinide elements, in which the internal magnetic moments spontaneously organize in a common direction; gives rise to a permeability considerably greater than that of vacuum, and to magnetic hysteresis.

ferroresonant circuit A resonant circuit in which a saturable reactor provides nonlinear characteristics, with tuning being accomplished by varying circuit voltage or current.

FET *See* field-effect transistor.

fetch To locate and load into main memory a requested load module, relocating it as necessary and leaving it in a ready-to-execute condition.

fetch ahead *See* instruction lookahead.

fetch bit The fifth bit in a storage key; the value of the fetch bit can protect a stored block from destruction or from being accessed by unauthorized programs.

F format 1. In data management, a fixed-length logical record format. 2. In FORTRAN, a real variable formatted as $F\mu.d$, where μ is the width of the field and d represents the number of digits to appear after the decimal point.

field 1. A specified area, such as a group of card columns or a set of bit locations in a computer word, used for a particular category of data. 2. One of the equal parts into which a frame is divided in interlaced scanning for television; includes one complete scanning operation from top to bottom of the picture and back again.

field delimiter Any symbol, such as a slash, colon, tab, or space, which enables an assembler to recognize the end of a field.

field-desorption microscope A type of field-ion microscope in which the tip specimen is imaged by ions that are field-desorbed or field-evaporated directly from the surface rather than by ions obtained from an externally supplied gas.

field discharge A spark discharge due to high potential across a gap.

field-effect capacitor A capacitor in which the effective dielectric is a region of semiconductor material that has been depleted or inverted by the field effect.

field-effect device A semiconductor device whose properties are determined largely by the effect of an electric field on a region within the semiconductor.

field-effect diode A semiconductor diode in which the charge carriers are of only one polarity.

field-effect phototransistor A field-effect transistor that responds to modulated light as the input signal.

field-effect tetrode Four-terminal device consisting of two independently terminated semiconducting channels so displaced that the conductance of each is modulated along its length by the voltage conditions in the other.

field-effect transistor A transistor in which the resistance of the current path from source to drain is modulated by applying a transverse electric field between grid or gate electrodes; the electric field varies the thickness of the depletion layer between the gates, thereby reducing the conductance. Abbreviated FET.

field-effect-transistor resistor A field-effect transistor in which the gate is generally tied to the drain; the resultant structure is used as a resistance load for another transistor.

field-effect varistor A passive, two-terminal, nonlinear semiconductor device that maintains constant current over a wide voltage range.

field emission The emission of electrons from the surface of a metallic conductor into a vacuum (or into an insulator) under influence of a strong electric field; electrons penetrate through the surface potential barrier by virtue of the quantum-mechanical tunnel effect. Also known as cold emission.

field-emission microscope A device that uses field emission of electrons or of positive ions (field-ion microscope) to produce a magnified image of the emitter surface on a fluorescent screen.

field-emission tube A vacuum tube within which field emission is obtained from a sharp metal point; must be more highly evacuated than an ordinary vacuum tube to prevent contamination of the point.

field engineer A professional who installs computer hardware on customers' premises, performs routine preventive maintenance, and repairs equipment when it is out of order. Also known as field service representative.

field-enhanced emission An increase in electron emission resulting from an electric field near the surface of the emitter.

field-free emission current Electron current emitted by a cathode when the electric field at the surface of the cathode is zero. Also known as zero-field emission.

field frequency The number of fields transmitted per second in television; equal to the frame frequency multiplied by the number of fields that make up one frame. Also known as field repetition rate.

field ionization The ionization of gaseous atoms and molecules by an intense electric field, often at the surface of a solid.

field-ion microscope A microscope in which atoms are ionized by an electric field near a sharp tip; the field then forces the ions to a fluorescent screen, which shows an enlarged image of the tip, and individual atoms are made visible; this is the most powerful microscope yet produced. Also known as ion microscope.

field length The number of columns, characters, or bits in a specified field.

field of search The space that a radar set or installation can cover effectively.

field-programmable logic array A programmed logic array in which the internal connections of the logic gates can be programmed once in the field by passing high current through fusible links, by using avalanche-induced migration to short base-emitter junctions at desired interconnections, or by other means. Abbreviated FPLA. Also known as programmable logic array.

field quenching Decrease in the emission of light of a phosphor excited by ultraviolet radiation, x-rays, alpha particles, or cathode rays when an electric field is simultaneously applied.

field repetition rate *See* field frequency.

field scan Television term denoting the vertical excursion of an electron beam downward across a cathode-ray tube face, the excursion being made in order to scan alternate lines.

field section A portion of a field, such as the section formed by the second and third character of a 10-character field.

figurative constant A predefined constant in COBOL which does not require a description in data division, such as ZERO which stands for 0.

figure of merit A performance rating that governs the choice of a device for a particular application; for example, the figure of merit of a magnetic amplifier is the ratio of usable power gain to the control time constant.

filament A cathode made of resistance wire or ribbon, through which an electric current is sent to produce the high temperature required for emission of electrons in a thermionic tube. Also known as directly heated cathode; filamentary cathode; filament-type cathode.

filamentary cathode *See* filament.

filament current The current supplied to the filament of an electron tube for heating purposes.

filament emission Liberation of electrons from a heated filament wire in an electron tube.

filament saturation *See* temperature saturation.

filament transformer A small transformer used exclusively to supply filament or heater current for one or more electron tubes.

filament-type cathode *See* filament.

filament winding The secondary winding of a power transformer that furnishes alternating-current heater or filament voltage for one or more electron tubes.

file A collection of related records treated as a unit.

file control system Software package which handles the transfer of data from any device into any device.

file event A single access to any storage device for either input or output.

file gap An area in a data storage medium which is used mainly to indicate the end of a file and sometimes the beginning of another.

file header A set of words comprising the file name and various characteristics of the file, found at the beginning of a file stored on magnetic tape or disk.

file identification A device, such as a label or tag, used to identify, describe, or name a physical medium, such as a reel of digital magnetic tape or a box of punched cards, which contains data.

file layout A description of the arrangement of the data in a file.

file maintenance Data-processing operation in which a master file is updated on the basis of one or more transaction files.

file name The name given by the programmer to a specific set of data.

file opening The process, carried out by computer software, of identifying a file and comparing the file header with specifications in the program being run to ensure that the file corresponds.

file organization The structure of a file meeting two requirements: to minimize the running time of the program, and to simplify the work involved in modifying the contents of the file.

file organization routine A program which allocates data files into random-access storage devices.

file-oriented system A computer configuration which considers a heavy, or exclusive, usage of data files.

file printout Output from a computer printer consisting of a copy of the contents of a file held in some storage device, usually to assist in debugging a program.

file processing The job of updating, sorting, or validating a data file.

file protection A mechanical device or a computer command which prevents erasing of or writing upon a magnetic tape but allows a program to read the data from the tape.

file protection ring A ring that can be attached to, or detached from, the hub of a reel of magnetic tape, used to identify the reel's status and, in some computer systems, to prevent writing upon the tape when the ring is attached or detached.

file reference An operation involving looking up and retrieving the information on file for a specified item or items.

file search An operation involving looking through the file for information on all items falling in a specified category, extracting the information for any item where the information recorded meets certain criteria, and determining whether or not there exists a specified pattern of information anywhere in the file.

file security *See* data security.

file storage unit The component of a computer system that stores information required for reference.

fill characters Nondata characters or bits which are used to fill out a field on the left if data are right-justified or on the right if data are left-justified.

filled band An energy band, each of whose energy levels is occupied by an electron.

film integrated circuit An integrated circuit whose elements are films formed in place on an insulating substrate.

film optical scanning device for input to computers *See* FOSDIC II.

film optical-sensing device A device capable of digitizing the information stored on a film.

film reader A device for converting a pattern of transparent or opaque spots on a photographic film into a series of electric pulses.

film recorder A device which places data, usually in the form of transparent and opaque spots or light and dark spots, on photographic film.

film scanning The process of converting motion picture film into corresponding electric signals that can be transmitted by a television system.

filter 1. A device or program that separates data or signals in accordance with specified criteria. 2. Any transmission network used in electrical systems for the selective enhancement of a given class of input signals. Also known as electric filter; electric-wave filter.

filter crystal Quartz crystal which is used in an electrical circuit designed to pass energy of certain frequencies.

filter design The design of electrical networks in which the principle of electrical resonance is used to make the network accept wanted frequencies while rejecting unwanted ones.

filter discrimination Difference between the minimum insertion loss at any frequency in a filter attenuation band and the maximum insertion loss at any frequency in the operating range of a filter transmission band.

filtered radar data Radar data from which unwanted returns have been removed by mapping.

filter impedance compensator Impedance compensator which is connected across the common terminals of electric wave filters when the latter are used in parallel to compensate for the effects of the filters on each other.

filter pass band *See* filter transmission band.

filter transmission band Frequency band of free transmission; that is, frequency band in which, if dissipation is neglected, the attenuation constant is zero. Also known as filter pass band.

final amplifier The transmitter stage that feeds the antenna.

financial planning system A decision-support system that allows the financial planner or manager to examine and evaluate many alternatives before making final decisions, and which employs the use of a model, usually a matrix of data elements which is constructed as a series of equations.

finder beam A beam of light projected by a light pen on the spot on the display screen where the light pen photodetector is focused, in order to aid the user in positioning the light pen.

F indicator *See* F scope.

finding circuit *See* lockout circuit.

fine index The more specific of two indices consulted to gain access to a record.

finite clipping Clipping in which the threshold level is large but is below the peak input signal amplitude.

finite precision number A number that can be represented by a finite set of symbols in a given numeration system.

finite state machine An automaton that has a finite number of distinguishable internal configurations.

fire-control circuit An electric circuit in a fire-control system.

fired state The "on" state of a silicon controlled rectifier or other semiconductor switching device, occurring when a suitable triggering pulse is applied to the gate.

firing 1. The gas ionization that initiates current flow in a gas-discharge tube. 2. Excitation of a magnetron or transmit-receive tube by a pulse. 3. The transition from the unsaturated to the saturated state of a saturable reactor.

firing circuit 1. Circuit used with an ignitron to deliver a pulse of current of 5–50 amperes in the forward direction, from the igniter to the mercury, to start a cathode spot and to control the time of firing. 2. By analogy, a similar control circuit of silicon-controlled rectifiers and like devices.

firing point *See* critical grid voltage.

firing potential Controlled potential at which conduction through a gas-filled tube begins.

firmware A computer program or instruction, such as a microprogram, used so often that it is stored in a read-only memory instead of being included in software; often used in computers that monitor production processes.

first detector *See* mixer.

first-generation Denoting electronic hardware, logical organization, and software characteristic of a first-generation computer.

first-generation computer A computer from the earliest stage of computer development, ending in the early 1960s, characterized by the use of vacuum tubes, the performance of one operation at a time in strictly sequential fashion, and elementary software, usually including a program loader, simple utility routines, and an assembler to assist in program writing.

first-item list A series of records that is printed with descriptive information from only the first record of each group.

first level address The location of a referenced operand.

first-order subroutine A subroutine which is entered directly from a main routine or program and which leads back to that program. Also known as first-remove subroutine.

first-remove subroutine *See* first-order subroutine.

first selector Selector which immediately follows a line finder in a switch train and which responds to dial pulses of the first digit of the called telephone number.

five-level code A code which uses five bits to specify each character.

fix A piece of coding that is inserted in a computer program to correct an error.

fixed area That portion of the main storage occupied by the resident portion of the control program.

fixed attenuator *See* pad.

fixed bias A constant value of bias voltage, independent of signal strength.

fixed-bias transistor circuit A transistor circuit in which a current flowing through a resistor is independent of the quiescent collector current.

fixed-block Pertaining to an arrangement of data in which all the blocks of data have the same number of words or characters, as determined by either the hardware requirements of the computer or the programmer.

fixed-cycle operation An operation completed in a specified number of regularly timed execution cycles.

fixed disk A disk drive that permanently holds the disk platters.

fixed echo An echo indication that remains stationary on a radar plan-position indicator display, indicating the presence of a fixed target.

fixed field A field in computers, film selection devices, or punched cards, or a given number of holes along the edge of a marginal punched card, set aside, or "fixed," for the recording of a given type of characteristic.

fixed-field method A method of data storage in which the same type of data is always placed in the same relative position.

fixed form coding Any method of coding a source language in which each part of the instruction appears in a fixed field.

fixed-head disk A disk storage device in which the read-write heads are fixed in position, one to a track, and the arms to which they are attached are immovable.

fixed-length field A field that always has the same number of characters, regardless of its content.

fixed-length record One of a file of records, each of which must have the same specified number of data units, such as blocks, words, characters, or digits.

fixed logic Circuit logic of computers or peripheral devices that cannot be changed by external controls; connections must be physically broken to arrange the logic.

fixed memory Of a computer, a nondestructive readout memory that is only mechanically alterable.

fixed-point arithmetic 1. A method of calculation in which the computer does not consider the location of the decimal or radix point because the point is given a fixed position. 2. A type of arithmetic in which the operands and results of all arithmetic operations must be properly scaled so as to have a magnitude between certain fixed values.

fixed-point calculation A calculation made with fixed-point arithmetic.

fixed-point computer A computer in which numbers in all registers and storage locations must have an arithmetic point which remains in the same fixed location.

fixed-point part *See* mantissa.

fixed-point representation Any method of representing a number in which a fixed-point convention is used.

fixed-point system A number system in which the location of the point is fixed with respect to one end of the numerals, according to some convention.

fixed-position addressing Direct access to an item in a data file on disk or drum, as opposed to a sequential search for this item starting with the first item in the file.

fixed-product area The area in core memory where multiplication takes place for certain types of computers.

fixed-program computer A special-purpose computer having a program permanently wired in.

fixed storage A storage for data not alterable by computer instructions, such as magnetic-core storage with a lockout feature.

fixed transmitter Transmitter that is operated in a fixed or permanent location.

fixed word length The length of a computer machine word that always contains the same number of characters or digits.

flag 1. Any of various types of indicators used for identification, such as a work mark, or a character that signals the occurrence of some condition, such as the end of a word. 2. A small metal tab that holds the getter during assembly of an electron tube.

flag flip-flop A one-bit register which indicates overflow, carry, or sign bit from past or current operations.

flag operand A part of the instruction of some assembly languages denoting which elements of the object instruction will be flagged.

flare A radar screen target indication having an enlarged and distorted shape due to excessive brightness.

flash arc A sudden increase in the emission of large thermionic vacuum tubes, probably due to irregularities in the cathode surface.

flashback voltage Inverse peak voltage at which ionization takes place in a gas tube.

flash lamp A gaseous-discharge lamp used in a photoflash unit to produce flashes of light of short duration and high intensity for stroboscopic photography. Also known as stroboscopic lamp.

flashover voltage The voltage at which an electric discharge occurs between two electrodes that are separated by an insulator; the value depends on whether the insulator surface is dry or wet. Also known as sparkover voltage.

flat file A two-dimensional array.

flatpack Semiconductor network encapsulated in a thin, rectangular package, with the necessary connecting leads projecting from the edges of the unit.

flat top response *See* band-pass response.

flat tuning Tuning of a radio receiver in which a change in frequency of the received waves produces only a small change in the current in the tuning apparatus.

Fleming tube The original diode, consisting of a heated filament and a cold metallic electrode in an evacuated glass envelope; negative current flows from the filament to the cold electrode, but not in the reverse direction.

flexible circuit A printed circuit made on a flexible plastic sheet that is usually die-cut to fit between large components.

flexional symbols Symbols in which the meaning of each component digit is dependent on those which precede it.

flexowriter A typewriterlike device to read in manually or to read out information of a computer to which it is connected; it can also be used to punch paper tape.

flicker effect Random variations in the output current of an electron tube having an oxide-coated cathode, due to random changes in cathode emission.

flight-path computer A computer that includes all of the functions of a course-line computer and also provides means for controlling the altitude of an aircraft in accordance with a desired plan of flight.

flip chip A tiny semiconductor die having terminations all on one side in the form of solder pads or bump contacts; after the surface of the chip has been passivated or otherwise treated, it is flipped over for attaching to a matching substrate.

flip-flop circuit *See* bistable multivibrator.

floating The condition wherein a device or circuit is not grounded and not tied to an established voltage supply.

floating address The symbolic address used prior to its conversion to a machine address.

floating dollar sign A dollar sign used with an edit mask, allowing the sign to be inserted before the nonzero leading digit of a dollar amount.

floating grid Vacuum-tube grid that is not connected to any circuit; it assumes a negative potential with respect to the cathode. Also known as free grid.

floating-point calculation A calculation made with floating-point arithmetic.

floating-point coefficient *See* mantissa.

floating-point package A program which enables a computer to perform arithmetic operations when such capabilities are not wired into the computer. Also known as floating-point routine.

floating-point routine *See* floating-point package.

floating-point system A number system in which the location of the point does not remain fixed with respect to one end of the numerals.

flood To direct a large-area flow of electrons toward a storage assembly in a charge storage tube.

flopover A defect in television reception in which a series of frames move vertically up or down the screen, caused by lack of synchronization between the vertical and horizontal sweep frequencies.

floppy disk A flexible plastic disk about 7½ inches (19 centimeters) in diameter, coated with magnetic oxide and used for data entry to a computer; a slot in its protective envelope or housing, which remains stationary while the disk rotates, exposes the track positions for the magnetic read/write head of the drive unit. Also known as diskette.

flow The sequence in which events take place or operations are carried out.

fluid computer A digital computer constructed entirely from air-powered fluid logic elements; it contains no moving parts and no electronic circuits; all logic functions are carried out by interaction between jets of air.

fluorescent lamp A tubular discharge lamp in which ionization of mercury vapor produces radiation that activates the fluorescent coating on the inner surface of the glass.

fluoroscopic image intensifier An electron-beam tube that converts a relatively feeble fluoroscopic image on the fluorescent input phosphor into a much brighter image on the output phosphor.

flute storage Ferrite storage consisting of a number of parallel lengths of fine prism-shaped tubing, each surrounding an insulated axial conductor that acts as a word line; the lengths of tubing are intersected at right angles by parallel sets of insulated wire bit lines that are displaced slightly from the word lines; each intersection stores one bit.

flux jumping *See* Meissner effect.

flyback The time interval in which the electron beam of a cathode-ray tube returns to its starting point after scanning one line or one field of a television picture or after completing one trace in an oscilloscope. Also known as retrace; return trace.

flyback power supply A high-voltage power supply used to produce the direct-current voltage of about 10,000–25,000 volts required for the second anode of a cathode-ray tube in a television receiver or oscilloscope.

flyback transformer *See* horizontal output transformer.

flying-aperture scanner An optical scanner, used in character recognition, in which a document is flooded with light, and light is collected sequentially spot by spot from the illuminated image.

flying head A read/write head used on magnetic disks and drums, so designed that it flies a microscopic distance off the moving magnetic surface and is supported by a film of air.

flying spot A small point of light, controlled mechanically or electrically, which moves rapidly in a rectangular scanning pattern in a flying-spot scanner.

flying-spot scanner A scanner used for television film and slide transmission, electronic writing, and character recognition, in which a moving spot of light, controlled mechanically or electrically, scans the image field, and the light reflected from or transmitted by the image field is picked up by a phototube to generate electric signals. Also known as optical scanner.

flywheel synchronization Automatic frequency control of a scanning system by using the average timing of the incoming sync signals, rather than by making each pulse trigger the scanning circuit; used in high-sensitivity television receivers designed for fringe-area reception, when noise pulses might otherwise trigger the sweep circuit prematurely.

FM/AM multiplier Multiplier in which the frequency deviation from the central frequency of a carrier is proportional to one variable, and its amplitude is proportional to the other variable; the frequency-amplitude-modulated carrier is then consecutively demodulated for frequency modulation (FM) and for amplitude modulation (AM); the final output is proportional to the product of the two variables.

focus To control convergence or divergence of the electron paths within one or more beams, usually by adjusting a voltage or current in a circuit that controls the electric or magnetic fields through which the beams pass, in order to obtain a desired image or a desired current density within the beam.

focus control A control that adjusts spot size at the screen of a cathode-ray tube to give the sharpest possible image; it may vary the current through a focusing coil or change the position of a permanent magnet.

focusing anode An anode used in a cathode-ray tube to change the size of the electron beam at the screen; varying the voltage on this anode alters the paths of electrons in the beam and thus changes the position at which they cross or focus.

focusing coil A coil that produces a magnetic field parallel to an electron beam for the purpose of focusing the beam.

focusing electrode An electrode to which a potential is applied to control the cross-sectional area of the electron beam in a cathode-ray tube.

focusing magnet A permanent magnet used to produce a magnetic field for focusing an electron beam.

focus projection and scanning Method of magnetic focusing and electrostatic deflection of the electron beam of a hybrid vidicon; a transverse electrostatic field is used for beam deflection; this field is immersed with an axial magnetic field that focuses the electron beam.

folded cavity Arrangement used in a klystron repeater to make the incoming wave act on the electron stream from the cathode at several places and produce a cumulative effect.

folding A method of hashing which consists of splitting the original key into two or more parts and then adding the parts together.

foldover Picture distortion seen as a white line on the side, top, or bottom of a television picture; generally caused by nonlinear operation in either the horizontal or vertical deflection circuits of a receiver.

forbidden band A range of unallowed energy levels for an electron in a solid.

forbidden-character code A bit code which exists only when an error occurs in the binary coding of characters.

forbidden-combination check A test for the occurrence of a nonpermissible code expression in a computer; used to detect computer errors.

force To intervene manually in a computer routine and cause the computer to execute a jump instruction.

forced programming *See* minimum-access programming.

foreground A program or process of high priority that utilizes machine facilities as needed, with less critical, background work performed in otherwise unused time.

fork oscillator An oscillator that uses a tuning fork as the frequency-determining element.

formal language An abstract mathematical object used to model the syntax of a programming or natural language.

format The specific arrangement of data on a printed page, punched card, or such to meet established presentation requirements.

format effector *See* layout character.

formatted tape A magnetic tape which employs a prerecorded timing track by means of which blocks of data can be found after reference to a directory table.

form feed character A control character that determines when a printer or display device moves to the next page, form, or equivalent unit of data.

form feeding The positioning of documents in order to move them past printing or sensing devices, either singly or in continuous rolls.

form of the physical store The code store considered as a physical structure, which can exhibit many different forms: discrete (cards), continuous (tapes), linear (tapes), cylindrical (drums), three-dimensional (array of cores), disks, strips, sheets, reels, and so on.

forms control buffer A reserved storage containing coordinates for a page position on the printer; earlier printers utilized a carriage control tape, allowing the page to be set at a specific position.

form stop A device which stops a machine when its supply of paper has run out.

formula transition *See* FORTRAN.

for-next loop In computer programming, a high-level logic statement which defines a part of a computer program that will be repeated a certain number of times.

FORTRAN A family of procedure-oriented languages used mostly for scientific or algebraic applications; derived from formula translation.

forty-four-type repeater Type of telephone repeater employing two amplifiers and no hybrid arrangements; used in a four-wire system.

forward-acting regulator Transmission regulator in which the adjustment made by the regulator does not affect the quantity which caused the adjustment.

forward-backward counter A counter that has both an add and a subtract input so as to count in either an increasing or a decreasing direction. Also known as bidirectional counter.

forward bias A bias voltage that is applied to a *pn* junction in the direction that causes a large current flow; used in some semiconductor diode circuits.

forward coupler Directional coupler used to sample incident power.

forward current Current which flows upon application of forward voltage.

forward direction Of a semiconductor diode, the direction of lower resistance to the flow of steady direct current.

forward drop The voltage drop in the forward direction across a rectifier.

forward error analysis A method of error analysis based on the assumption that small changes in the input data lead to small changes in the results, so that bounds for the errors in the results caused by rounding or truncation errors in the input can be calculated.

forward recovery time Of a semiconductor diode, the time required for the forward current or voltage to reach a specified value after instantaneous application of a forward bias in a given circuit.

forward voltage drop *See* diode forward voltage.

forward wave Wave whose group velocity is the same direction as the electron stream motion.

FOSDIC II An electronic scanner which reads filmed images of punched cards, searches for cards containing specified information, and copies the selected information onto new cards for computer input. Derived from film optical scanning device for input to computers.

Foster-Seely discriminator *See* phase-shift discriminator.

four-address Pertaining to an instruction address which contains four address parts.

four-layer device A *pnpn* semiconductor device, such as a silicon controlled rectifier, that has four layers of alternating *p*- and *n*-type material to give three *pn* junctions.

four-layer diode A semiconductor diode having three junctions, terminal connections being made to the two outer layers that form the junctions; a Shockley diode is an example.

four-layer transistor A junction transistor having four conductivity regions but only three terminals; a thyristor is an example.

four-plus-one address An instruction that contains four operand addresses and a control address.

four-quadrant multiplier A multiplier in an analog computer in which both the reference signal and the number represented by the input may be bipolar, and the multiplication rules for algebraic sign are obeyed. Also known as quarter-square multiplier.

four-tape To sort input data, supplied on two tapes, into incomplete sequences alternately on two output tapes; the output tapes are used for input on the succeeding pass, resulting in longer and longer sequences after each pass, until the data are all in one sequence on one output tape.

four-wire repeater Telephone repeater for use in a four-wire circuit and in which there are two amplifiers, one serving to amplify the telephone currents in one side of the four-wire circuit, and the other serving to amplify the telephone currents in the other side of the four-wire circuit.

four-wire terminating set Hybrid arrangement by which four-wire circuits are terminated on a two-wire basis for interconnection with two-wire circuits.

Fowler function A mathematical function used in the Fowler-DuBridge theory to calculate the photoelectric yield.

FPLA *See* field-programmable logic array.

fragmenting The breaking up of a document into its various components.

frame 1. A row of recording or punch positions extending across a magnetic or paper tape in a direction at right angles to its motion. 2. One complete coverage of a television picture. 3. A rectangular area representing the size of copy handled by a facsimile system. 4. *See* central processing unit.

frame frequency The number of times per second that the frame is completely scanned in television. Also known as picture frequency.

frame period A time interval equal to the reciprocal of the frame frequency.

framer Device for adjusting facsimile equipment so the start and end of a recorded line are the same as on the corresponding line of the subject copy.

framing 1. Adjusting a television picture to a desired position on the screen of the picture tube. 2. Adjusting a facsimile picture to a desired position in the direction of line progression. Also known as phasing.

framing control 1. A control that adjusts the centering, width, or height of the image on a television receiver screen. 2. A control that shifts a received facsimile picture horizontally.

Franck-Hertz experiment Experiment for measuring the kinetic energy lost by electrons in inelastic collisions with atoms; it established the existence of discrete energy levels in atoms, and can be used to determine excitation and ionization potentials.

free field A property of information retrieval devices which permits recording of information in the search medium without regard to preassigned fixed fields.

free-field storage Data storage that allows recording of the data without regard for fixed or preassigned fields.

free grid *See* floating grid.

free hole Any hole which is not bound to an impurity or to an exciton.

free impedance Impedance at the input of the transducer when the impedance of its load is made zero. Also known as normal impedance.

free motional impedance Of a transducer, the complex remainder after the blocked impedance has been subtracted from the free impedance.

free-running frequency Frequency at which a normally driven oscillator operates in the absence of a driving signal.

free-running sweep Sweep triggered continuously by an internal trigger generator.

free symbol A contextual symbol preceded and followed by a space; it is always meaningful and always used to symbolize both grammatical and nongrammatical meaning; an example is the English "I."

free symbol sequence A symbol sequence either not preceded, or not followed, or neither preceded nor followed by space.

Frenkel defect A crystal defect consisting of a vacancy and an interstitial which arise when an atom is plucked out of a normal lattice site and forced into an interstitial position. Also known as Frenkel pair.

Frenkel pair *See* Frenkel defect.

frequency analysis A determination of the number of times certain parts of an algorithm are executed, indicating which parts of the algorithm consume large quantities of time and hence where efforts should be directed toward improving the algorithm.

frequency analyzer A device which measures the intensity of many different frequency components in some oscillation, as in a radio band; used to identify transmitting sources.

frequency-azimuth intensity Type of radar display in which frequency, azimuth, and strobe intensity are correlated.

frequency bridge A bridge in which the balance varies with frequency in a known manner, such as the Wien bridge; used to measure frequency.

frequency compensation *See* compensation.

frequency conversion Converting the carrier frequency of a received signal from its original value to the intermediate frequency value in a superheterodyne receiver.

frequency counter An electronic counter used to measure frequency by counting the number of cycles in an electric signal during a preselected time interval.

frequency cutoff The frequency at which the current gain of a transistor drops 3 decibels below the low-frequency gain value.

frequency discriminator A discriminator circuit that delivers an output voltage which is proportional to the deviations of a signal from a predetermined frequency value.

frequency distortion Distortion in which the relative magnitudes of the different frequency components of a wave are changed during transmission or amplification. Also known as amplitude distortion; amplitude-frequency distortion; waveform-amplitude distortion.

frequency divider A harmonic conversion transducer in which the frequency of the output signal is an integral submultiple of the input frequency. Also known as counting-down circuit.

frequency doubler An amplifier stage whose resonant anode circuit is tuned to the second harmonic of the input frequency; the output frequency is then twice the input frequency. Also known as doubler.

frequency drift A gradual change in the frequency of an oscillator or transmitter due to temperature or other changes in the circuit components that determine frequency.

frequency-modulated jamming Jamming technique consisting of a constant amplitude radio-frequency signal that is varied in frequency about a center frequency to produce a signal over a band of frequencies.

frequency-modulation detector A device, such as a Foster-Seely discriminator, for the detection or demodulation of a frequency-modulated wave.

frequency-modulation receiver A radio receiver that receives frequency-modulated waves and delivers corresponding sound waves.

frequency-modulation receiver deviation sensitivity Least frequency deviation that produces a specified output power.

frequency-modulation transmitter A radio transmitter that transmits a frequency-modulated wave.

frequency-modulation tuner A tuner containing a radio-frequency amplifier, converter, intermediate-frequency amplifier, and demodulator for frequency-modulated signals, used to feed a low-level audio-frequency signal to a separate af amplifier and loudspeaker.

frequency modulator A circuit or device for producing frequency modulation.

frequency monitor An instrument for indicating the amount of deviation of the carrier frequency of a transmitter from its assigned value.

frequency multiplier A harmonic conversion transducer in which the frequency of the output signal is an exact integral multiple of the input frequency. Also known as multiplier.

frequency-offset transponder Transponder that changes the signal frequency by a fixed amount before retransmission.

frequency pulling A change in the frequency of an oscillator due to a change in load impedance.

frequency relay Relay which functions at a predetermined value of frequency; may be an over-frequency relay, an under-frequency relay, or a combination of both.

frequency-response equalization *See* equalization.

frequency run A series of tests made to determine the amplitude-frequency response characteristic of a transmission line, circuit, or device.

frequency scanning Type of system in which output frequency is made to vary at a mechanical rate over a desired frequency band.

frequency-selective device *See* electric filter.

frequency separation multiplier Multiplier in which each of the variables is split into a low-frequency part and a high-frequency part that are multiplied separately, and the results added to give the required product; this system makes it possible to get high accuracy and broad bandwidth.

frequency separator The circuit that separates the horizontal and vertical synchronizing pulses in a monochrome or color television receiver.

frequency shift A change in the frequency of a radio transmitter or oscillator. Also known as radio-frequency shift.

frequency-shift converter A device that converts a received frequency-shift signal to an amplitude-modulated signal or a direct-current signal.

frequency-shift keyer A lever to effect a frequency shift, that is, a change in the frequency of a radio transmitter, oscillator, or receiver.

frequency splitting One condition of operation of a magnetron which causes rapid alternating from one mode of operation to another; this results in a similar rapid change in oscillatory frequency and consequent loss in power at the desired frequency.

frequency stability The ability of an oscillator to maintain a desired frequency; usually expressed as percent deviation from the assigned frequency value.

frequency standard A stable oscillator, usually controlled by a crystal or tuning fork, that is used primarily for frequency calibration.

frequency synthesizer A device that provides a choice of a large number of different frequencies by combining frequencies selected from groups of independent crystals, frequency dividers, and frequency multipliers.

frequency-time-intensity Type of radar display in which the frequency, time, and strobe intensity are correlated.

frequency tolerance Of a radio transmitter, extent to which the carrier frequency of the transmitter may be permitted to depart from the frequency assigned.

frequency-to-voltage converter A converter that provides an analog output voltage which is proportional to the frequency or repetition rate of the input signal derived from a flowmeter, tachometer, or other alternating-current generating device. Abbreviated F/V converter.

frequency-type telemeter Telemeter that employs frequency of an alternating current or voltage as the translating means.

frequency variation The change over time of the deviation from assigned frequency of a radio-frequency carrier (or power supply system); usually tightly controlled because of national or industry standards.

frogging repeater Carrier repeater having provisions for frequency frogging to permit use of a single multipair voice cable without having excessive crosstalk.

front-end Of a minicomputer, under programmed instructions, performing data transfers and control operations to relieve a larger computer of these routines.

front-end processor A computer which connects to the main computer at one end and communications channels at the other, and which directs the transmitting and receiving of messages, detects and corrects transmission errors, assembles and disassembles messages, and performs other processing functions so that the main computer receives pure information.

front-to-back ratio Ratio of resistance of a crystal to current flowing in the normal direction to current flowing in the opposite direction.

F scan *See* F scope.

F scope A cathode-ray scope on which a single signal appears as a spot with bearing error as the horizontal coordinate and elevation angle error as the vertical coordinate, with cross hairs on the scope face to assist in bringing the system to bear on the target. Also known as F indicator; F scan.

full adder A logic element which operates on two binary digits and a carry digit from a preceding stage, producing as output a sum digit and a new carry digit.

full duplex The complete duplication of any data-processing facility.

full section filter A filter network whose graphical representation has the shape of the Greek letter pi, connoting capacitance in the upright legs and inductance or reactance in the horizontal member.

full subtracter A logic element which operates on three binary input signals representing a minuend, subtrahend, and borrow digit, producing as output a difference digit and a new borrow digit. Also known as three-input subtracter.

full-wave amplifier An amplifier without any clipping.

full-wave bridge A circuit having a bridge with four diodes, which provides full-wave rectification and gives twice as much direct-current output voltage for a given alternating-current input voltage as a conventional full-wave rectifier.

full-wave control Phase control that acts on both halves of each alternating-current cycle, for varying load power over the full range from 0 to the full-wave maximum value.

full-wave rectification Rectification in which output current flows in the same direction during both half cycles of the alternating input voltage.

full-wave rectifier A double-element rectifier that provides full-wave rectification; one element functions during positive half cycles and the other during negative half cycles.

full-word boundary In the IBM 360 system, any address which ends in 00, and is therefore a natural boundary for a four-byte machine word.

function In FORTRAN, a subroutine of a particular kind which returns a computational value whenever it is called.

functional In a linear programming problem involving a set of variables x_j, $j = 1, 2, ..., n$, a function of the form $c_1x_1 + c_2x_2 + ... + c_nx_n$ (where the c_j are constants) which one wishes to optimize (maximize or minimize, depending on the problem) subject to a set of restrictions.

functional design A level of the design process in which subtasks are specified and the relationships among them defined, so that the total collection of subsystems performs the entire task of the system.

functional diagram A diagram that indicates the functions of the principal parts of a total system and also shows the important relationships and interactions among these parts.

functional generator *See* function generator.

functional interleaving Alternating the parts of a number of sequences in a cyclic fashion, such as a number of accesses to memory followed by an access to a data channel.

functional multiplier *See* function multiplier.

functional requirement The documentation which accompanies a program and states in detail what is to be performed by the system.

functional specifications The documentation for the design of an information system, including the data base; the human and machine procedures; and the inputs, outputs, and processes for each data entry, query, update, and report program in the system.

functional switching circuit One of a relatively small number of types of circuits which implements a Boolean function and constitutes a basic building block of a switching system; examples are the AND, OR, NOT, NAND, and NOR circuits.

functional unit The part of the computer required to perform an elementary process such as an addition or a pulse generation.

function code Special code which appears on a medium such as a paper tape and which controls machine functions such as a carriage return.

function-evaluation routine A canned routine such as a log function or a sine function.

function generator Also known as functional generator. 1. An analog computer device that indicates the value of a given function as the independent variable is increased. 2. A signal generator that delivers a choice of a number of different waveforms, with provisions for varying the frequency over a wide range.

function hole *See* designation punch.

function key A special key on a keyboard to control a mechanical function, initiate a specific computer operation, or transmit a signal that would otherwise require multiple key strokes.

function multiplier An analog computer device that takes in the changing values of two functions and puts out the changing value of their product as the independent variable is changed. Also known as functional multiplier.

function switch A network having a number of inputs and outputs so connected that input signals expressed in a certain code will produce output signals that are a function of the input information but in a different code.

function table 1. Sets of computer information arranged so an entry in one set selects one or more entries in the other sets. 2. A computer device that converts multiple inputs into a single output or encodes a single input into multiple outputs.

function unit In computer systems, a device which can store a functional relationship and release it continuously or in increments.

functor *See* logic element.

fuse diode A diode that opens under specified current surge conditions.

fused junction *See* alloy junction.

fused-junction diode *See* alloy junction diode.

fused-junction transistor *See* alloy-junction transistor.

fused semiconductor Junction formed by recrystallization on a base crystal from a liquid phase of one or more components and the semiconductor.

future address patch A computer output containing the address of a symbol and the address of the last reference to that symbol.

future label An address referenced in the operand field of an instruction, but which has not been previously defined.

F/V converter *See* frequency-to-voltage converter.

G

g_m *See* transconductance.

G_m *See* transconductance.

gain The increase in signal power that is produced by an amplifier; usually given as the ratio of output to input voltage, current, or power, expressed in decibels. Also known as transmission gain.

gain-bandwidth product The midband gain of an amplifier stage multiplied by the bandwidth in megacycles.

gain control A device for adjusting the gain of a system or component.

gain reduction Diminution of the output of an amplifier, usually achieved by reducing the drive from feed lines by use of equalizer pads or reducing amplification by a volume control.

gain sensitivity control *See* differential gain control.

gallium arsenide semiconductor A semiconductor having a forbidden-band gap of 1.4 electronvolts and a maximum operating temperature of 400°C when used in a transistor.

gallium phosphide semiconductor A semiconductor having a forbidden-band gap of 2.4 electronvolts and a maximum operating temperature of 870°C when used in a transistor.

ganged control Controls of two or more circuits mounted on a common shaft to permit simultaneous control of the circuits by turning a single knob.

gang-punch To punch identical or constant information into all of a group of punched cards.

gap A uniformly magnetized area in a magnetic storage device (tape, disk), used to indicate the end of an area containing information.

gap digit A digit in a machine word that does not represent data or instructions, such as a parity bit or a digit included for engineering purposes.

gap factor Ratio of the maximum energy gained in volts to the maximum gap voltage in a tube employing electron accelerating gaps, that is, a traveling-wave tube.

gapless tape A magnetic tape upon which raw data is recorded in a continuous manner; the data are streamed onto the tape without the word gaps; the data still may contain signs and end-of-record marks in the gapless form.

gapped tape A magnetic tape upon which blocked data has been recorded; it contains all of the flag bits and format to be read directly into a computer for immediate use.

gap scatter The deviation from the exact distance required between read/write heads and the magnetized surface.

garbage *See* hash.

garbage collection In a computer program with dynamic storage allocation, the automatic process of identifying those memory cells whose contents are no longer useful for the computation in progress and then making them available for some other use.

garbage in, garbage out A phrase often stressed during introductory courses in computer utilization as a reminder that, regardless of the correctness of the logic built into the program, no answer can be valid if the input is erroneous. Abbreviated GIGO.

garnet maser A name incorrectly applied to a ferromagnetic amplifier.

gas current A positive-ion current produced by collisions between electrons and residual gas molecules in an electron tube. Also known as ionization current.

gas discharge Conduction of electricity in a gas, due to movements of ions produced by collisions between electrons and gas molecules.

gas-discharge display A display in which seven or more cathode elements form the segments of numerical or alphameric characters when energized by about 160 volts direct current; the segments are vacuum-sealed in a neon-mercury gas mixture.

gas-discharge lamp *See* discharge lamp.

gas doping The introduction of impurity atoms into a semiconductor material by epitaxial growth, by using streams of gas that are mixed before being fed into the reactor vessel.

gas-filled diode A gas tube which is a diode, such as a cold-cathode rectifier or phanotron.

gas-filled rectifier *See* cold-cathode rectifier.

gas-filled triode A gas tube which has a grid or other control element, such as a thyratron or ignitron.

gas focusing A method of concentrating an electron beam by utilizing the residual gas in a tube; beam electrons ionize the gas molecules, forming a core of positive ions along the path of the beam which attracts beam electrons and thereby makes the beam more compact. Also known as ionic focusing.

gas ionization Removal of the planetary electrons from the atoms of gas filling an electron tube, so that the resulting ions participate in current flow through the tube.

gas magnification Increase in current through a phototube due to ionization of the gas in the tube.

gas phototube A phototube into which a quantity of gas has been introduced after evacuation, usually to increase its sensitivity.

gas scattering The scattering of electrons or other particles in a beam by residual gas in the vacuum system.

gassiness Presence of unwanted gas in a vacuum tube, usually in relatively small amounts, caused by the leakage from outside or evolution from the inside walls or elements of the tube.

gassy tube A vacuum tube that has not been fully evacuated or has lost part of its vacuum due to release of gas by the electrode structure during use, so that enough gas is present to impair operating characteristics appreciably. Also known as soft tube.

gas tetrode *See* tetrode thyratron.

gas tube An electron tube into which a small amount of gas or vapor is admitted after the tube has been evacuated; ionization of gas molecules during operation greatly increases current flow.

gas vacuum breakdown Ionization of residual gas in a vacuum, causing reverse conduction in an electron tube.

gate 1. A circuit having an output and a multiplicity of inputs and so designed that the output is energized only when a certain combination of pulses is present at the inputs. **2.** A circuit in which one signal, generally a square wave, serves to switch another signal on and off. **3.** One of the electrodes in a field-effect transistor. **4.** An output element of a cryotron. **5.** To control the passage of a pulse or signal. **6.** In radar, an electric waveform which is applied to the control point of a circuit to alter the mode of operation of the circuit at the time when the waveform is applied. Also known as gating waveform.

gate-array device An integrated logic circuit that is manufactured by first fabricating a two-dimensional array of logic cells, each of which is equivalent to one or a few logic gates, and then adding final layers of metallization that determine the exact function of each cell and interconnect the cells to form a specific network when the customer orders the device.

gate-controlled rectifier A three-terminal semiconductor device, such as a silicon controlled rectifier, in which the unidirectional current flow between the rectifier terminals is controlled by a signal applied to a third terminal called the gate.

gate-controlled switch A semiconductor device that can be switched from its nonconducting or "off" state to its conducting or "on" state by applying a negative pulse to its gate terminal and that can be turned off at any time by applying reverse drive to the gate. Abbreviated GCS.

gated-beam tube A pentode electron tube having special electrodes that form a sheet-shaped beam of electrons; this beam may be deflected away from the anode by a relatively small voltage applied to a control electrode, thus giving extremely sharp cutoff of anode current.

gated sweep Sweep in which the duration as well as the starting time is controlled to exclude undesired echoes from the indicator screen.

gate equivalent circuit A unit of measure for specifying relative complexity of digital circuits, equal to the number of individual logic gates that would have to be interconnected to perform the same function as the digital circuit under evaluation.

gate generator A circuit used to generate gate pulses; in one form it consists of a multivibrator having one stable and one unstable position.

gate multivibrator Rectangular-wave generator designed to produce a single positive or negative gate voltage when triggered and then to become inactive until the next trigger pulse.

gate pulse A pulse that triggers a gate circuit so it will pass a signal.

gate turnoff A *pnpn* switching device comparable to a silicon-controlled rectifier, but having a more complex gate structure that permits easy and fast turnoff as well as turn-on from its gate input terminal, at frequencies up to 100 kilohertz.

gate-turnoff silicon-controlled rectifier A silicon-controlled rectifier that can be turned off by applying a current to its gate; used largely for direct-current switching, because turnoff can be achieved in a fraction of a microsecond.

gate winding A winding used in a magnetic amplifier to produce on-off action of load current.

gather write An operation that creates a single output record from data items gathered from nonconsecutive locations in main memory.

gating The process of selecting those portions of a wave that exist during one or more selected time intervals or that have magnitudes between selected limits.

gating waveform *See* gate.

Gaussian noise generator A signal generator that produces a random noise signal whose frequency components have a Gaussian distribution centered on a predetermined frequency value.

GCS *See* gate-controlled switch.

G display A rectangular radar display in which horizontal and vertical aiming errors are indicated by horizontal and vertical displacement, respectively, and range is indicated by the length of wings appearing on the blip, with length increasing as range decreases.

Geissler tube An experimental discharge tube with two electrodes at opposite ends, used to demonstrate and study the luminous effects of electric discharges through various gases at low pressures.

generalized routine A routine which can process a wide variety of jobs; for example, a generalized sort routine which will sort in ascending or descending order on any number of fields whether alphabetic or numeric, or both, and whether binary coded decimals or pure binaries.

general program A computer program designed to solve a specific type of problem when values of appropriate parameters are supplied.

general-purpose automatic test system Modular, computer-type, automatic electronic checkout system capable of finding faults in electronic equipment at the system, subsystem, line replaceable unit, module, and piece part levels.

general-purpose computer A device that manipulates data without detailed, step-by step control by human hand and is designed to be used for many different types of problems.

general-purpose function generator A function generator which can be adjusted to generate many different functions, rather than being designed for a particular function. Also known as arbitrary function generator.

general routine In computers, a routine, or program, applicable to a class of problems; it provides instructions for solving a specific problem when appropriate parameters are supplied.

generate To create a particular program by selecting parts of a general-program skeleton (or outline) and specializing these parts into a cohesive entity.

generate and test A computer problem-solving method in which a sequence of candidate solutions is generated, and each is tested to determine if it is an appropriate solution.

generated address An address calculated or determined by instructions contained in a computer program for subsequent use by that program. Also known as calculated address; synthetic address.

generating routine *See* generator.

generation 1. Any one of three groups used to historically classify computers according to their electronic hardware components, logical organization and software, or programming techniques; computers are thus known as first-, second-, or third-generation; a particular computer may possess characteristics of all generations simultaneously. **2.** One of a family of data sets, related to one another in that each is a modification of the next most recent data set.

generation number A number contained in the file label of a reel of magnetic tape that indicates the generation of the data set of the tape.

generation rate In a semiconductor, the time rate of creation of electron-hole pairs.

generative grammar A set of rules that describes the valid expressions in a formal language on the basis of a set of the parts of speech (formally called the set of metavariables or phrase names) and the alphabet or character set of the language.

generator 1. A program that produces specific programs as directed by input parameters. Also known as generating routine. **2.** A vacuum-tube oscillator or any other nonrotating device that generates an alternating voltage at a desired frequency when energized with direct-current power or low-frequency alternating-current power. **3.** A circuit that generates a desired repetitive or nonrepetitive waveform, such as a pulse generator.

generator reactor A small inductor connected between power-plant generators and the rest of an electric power system in order to limit and localize the effects of voltage transients.

geophone A transducer, used in seismic work, that responds to motion of the ground at a location on or below the surface of the earth.

germanium diode A semiconductor diode that uses a germanium crystal pellet as the rectifying element. Also known as germanium rectifier.

germanium rectifier *See* germanium diode.

germanium transistor A transistor in which the semiconductor material is germanium, to which electric contacts are made.

getter sputtering The deposition of high-purity thin films at ordinary vacuum levels by using a getter to remove contaminants remaining in the vacuum.

ghost algebraic manipulation language An algebraic manipulation language which externally gives the appearance of manipulating quite general mathematical expressions, although internally it is functioning with canonically represented data, much like the simpler seminumerical languages.

ghost image 1. An undesired duplicate image at the right of the desired image on a television receiver; due to multipath effect, wherein a reflected signal traveling over a longer path arrives slightly later than the desired signal. 2. *See* ghost pulse.

ghost pulse An unwanted signal appearing on the screen of a radar indicator and caused by echoes which have a basic repetition frequency differing from that of the desired signals. Also known as ghost image; ghost signal.

ghost signal 1. The reflection-path signal that produces a ghost image on a television receiver. Also known as echo. 2. *See* ghost pulse.

gibberish *See* hash.

GIGO *See* garbage in, garbage out.

Gilbert circuit A circuit that compensates for nonlinearities and instabilities in a monolithic variable-transconductance circuit by using the logarithmic properties of diodes and transistors.

G indicator *See* G scope.

Ginzburg-London superconductivity theory A modification of the London superconductivity theory to take into account the boundary energy.

glassivation Method of transistor passivation by a pyrolytic glass-deposition technique, whereby silicon semiconductor devices, complete with metal contact systems, are fully encapsulated in glass.

glass switch An amorphous solid-state device used to control the flow of electric current. Also known as ovonic device.

glass-to-metal seal An airtight seal between glass and metal parts of an electron tube, made by fusing together a special glass and special metal alloy having nearly the same temperature coefficients of expansion.

glint 1. Pulse-to-pulse variation in amplitude of a reflected radar signal, owing to the reflection of the radar from a body that is rapidly changing its reflecting surface, for example, a spinning airplane propeller. **2.** The use of this effect to degrade tracking or seeking functions of an enemy weapons system.

glitch 1. An undesired transient voltage spike occurring on a signal being processed. **2.** A minor technical problem arising in electronic equipment.

global search and replace A text-editing function of a word-processing system in which text is scanned for a given combination of characters, and each such combination is replaced by another set of characters.

global variable A variable which can be accessed (used or changed) throughout a computer program and is not confined to a single block.

glow discharge A discharge of electricity through gas at relatively low pressure in an electron tube, characterized by several regions of diffuse, luminous glow and a voltage drop in the vicinity of the cathode that is much higher than the ionization voltage of the gas. Also known as cold-cathode discharge.

glow-discharge cold-cathode tube *See* glow-discharge tube.

glow-discharge tube A gas tube that depends for its operation on the properties of a glow discharge. Also known as glow-discharge cold-cathode tube; glow tube.

glow-discharge voltage regulator Gas tube that varies in resistance, depending on the value of the applied voltage; used for voltage regulation.

glow lamp A two-electrode electron tube containing a small quantity of an inert gas, in which light is produced by a negative glow close to the negative electrode when voltage is applied between the electrodes.

glow potential The potential across a glow discharge, which is greater than the ionization potential and less than the sparking potential, and is relatively constant as the current is varied across an appreciable range.

glow tube *See* glow-discharge tube.

glow-tube oscillator A circuit using a glow-discharge tube which functions as a simple relaxation oscillator, generating a fixed-amplitude periodic sawtooth waveform.

gold doping A technique for controlling the lifetime of minority carriers in a transistor; gold is diffused into the base and collector regions to reduce storage time in transistor circuits.

golden section search A dichotomizing search in which, in each step, the remaining items are divided as closely as possible according to the golden section.

Goto pair Two tunnel diodes connected in series in such a way that when one is in the forward conduction region, the other is in the reverse tunneling region; used in high-speed gate circuits.

g parameter One of a set of four transistor equivalent-circuit parameters; they are the inverse of the h parameters.

graceful degradation A programming technique to prevent catastrophic system failure by allowing the machine to operate, though in a degraded mode, despite failure or malfunction of several integral units or subsystems.

graded-junction transistor *See* rate-grown transistor.

graded periodicity technique A technique for modifying the response of a surface acoustic wave filter by varying the spacing between successive electrodes of the interdigital transducer.

grain direction In character recognition, the arrangement of paper fibers in relation to a document's travel through a character reader.

grandfather A data set that is two generations earlier than the data set under consideration.

grandfather cycle The period during which records are kept but not used except to reconstruct other records which are accidentally lost.

graphechon A storage tube having two electron guns, one for writing and the other for reading and simultaneous erasing, on opposite sides of the storage medium, which consists of an insulator or semiconductor deposited on a thin substratum of metal supported by a fine mesh.

graph follower *See* curve follower.

graphical design Methods of obtaining operating data for an electron tube or semiconductor circuit by using graphs which plot the relationship between two variables, such as plate voltage and grid voltage, while another variable, such as plate current, is held constant.

graphical visual display device A computer input-output device which enables the user to manipulate graphic material in a visible two-way, real-time communication with the computer, and which consists of a light pen, keyboard, or other data entry devices, and a visual display unit monitored by a controller. Also known as graphoscope.

graphic display The display of data in graphical form on the screen of a cathode-ray tube.

graphic terminal A cathode-ray-tube or other type of computer terminal capable of producing some form of line drawing based on data being processed by or stored in a computer.

graphite anode 1. The rod of graphite which is inserted into the mercury-pool cathode of an ignitron to start current flow. 2. The collector of electrons in a beam power tube or other high-current tube.

graphoscope *See* graphical visual display device.

grass Clutter due to circuit noise in a radar receiver, seen on an A scope as a pattern resembling a cross section of turf. Also known as hash.

Gratz rectifier Three-phase, full-wave rectifying circuit using six rectifiers connected in a bridge circuit.

grid In optical character recognition, a system of two groups of parallel lines, perpendicular to each other, used to measure or specify character images.

grid-anode transconductance *See* transconductance.

grid bias The direct-current voltage applied between the control grid and cathode of an electron tube to establish the desired operating point. Also known as bias; C bias; direct grid bias.

grid-bias cell *See* bias cell.

grid blocking 1. Method of keying a circuit by applying negative grid bias several times cutoff value to the grid of a tube during key-up conditions; when the key is down, the blocking bias is removed and normal current flows through the keyed circuit. 2. Blocking of capacitance-coupled stages in an amplifier caused by the accumulation of charge on the coupling capacitors due to grid current passed during the reception of excessive signals.

grid blocking capacitor *See* grid capacitor.

grid cap A top-cap terminal for the control grid of an electron tube.

grid capacitor A small capacitor used in the grid circuit of an electron tube to pass signal current while blocking the direct-current anode voltage of the preceding stage. Also known as grid blocking capacitor; grid condenser.

grid cathode capacitance Capacitance between the grid and the cathode in a vacuum tube.

grid characteristic Relationship of grid current to grid voltage of a vacuum tube.

grid circuit The circuit connected between the grid and cathode of an electron tube.

grid condenser *See* grid capacitor.

grid conductance *See* electrode conductance.

grid control Control of anode current of an electron tube by variation (control) of the control grid potential with respect to the cathode of the tube.

grid-controlled mercury-arc rectifier A mercury-arc rectifier in which one or more electrodes are employed exclusively to control the starting of the discharge. Also known as grid-controlled rectifier.

grid-controlled rectifier *See* grid-controlled mercury-arc rectifier.

grid control tube Mercury-vapor-filled thermionic vacuum tube with an external grid control.

grid current Electron flow to a positive grid in an electron tube.

grid-dip meter A multiple-range electron-tube oscillator incorporating a meter in the grid circuit to indicate grid current; the meter reading dips (reads lower grid current) when an external resonant circuit is tuned to the oscillator frequency. Also known as grid-dip oscillator.

grid-dip oscillator *See* grid-dip meter.

grid drive A signal applied to the grid of a transmitting tube.

grid driving power Average product of the instantaneous value of the grid current and of the alternating component of the grid voltage over a complete cycle; this comprises the power supplied to the biasing device and to the grid.

grid-glow tube A glow-discharge tube in which one or more control electrodes initiate but do not limit the anode current except under certain operating conditions.

gridistor Field-effect transistor which uses the principle of centripetal striction and has a multichannel structure, combining advantages of both field-effect transistors and minority carrier injection transistors.

grid leak A resistor used in the grid circuit of an electron tube to provide a discharge path for the grid capacitor and for charges built up on the control grid.

grid-leak detector A detector in which the desired audio-frequency voltage is developed across a grid leak and grid capacitor by the flow of modulated radio-frequency current; the circuit provides square-law detection on weak signals and linear detection on strong signals, along with amplification of the audio-frequency signal.

grid limiter Limiter circuit which operates by limiting positive grid voltages by means of a large ohmic value resistor; as the exciting signal moves in a positive direction with respect to the cathode, current through the resistor causes an IR drop which holds the grid voltage essentially at cathode potential; during negative excursions no current flows in the grid circuit, so no voltage drop occurs across the resistor.

grid locking Defect of tube operation in which the grid potential becomes continuously positive due to excessive grid emission.

grid modulation Modulation produced by feeding the modulating signal to the control-grid circuit of any electron tube in which the carrier is present.

grid neutralization Method of amplifier neutralization in which a portion of the grid-cathode alternating-current voltage is shifted 180° and applied to the plate-cathode circuit through a neutralizing capacitor.

grid-plate capacitance Direct capacitance between the grid and the plate in a vacuum tube.

grid-plate transconductance *See* transconductance.

grid-pool tube An electron tube having a mercury-pool cathode, one or more anodes, and a control electrode or grid that controls the start of current flow in each cycle; the excitron and ignitron are examples.

grid pulse modulation Modulation produced in an amplifier or oscillator by applying one or more pulses to a grid circuit.

grid pulsing Circuit arrangement of a radio-frequency oscillator in which the grid of the oscillator is biased so negatively that no oscillation takes place even when full plate voltage is applied; pulsing is accomplished by removing this negative bias through the application of a positive pulse on the grid.

grid resistor A general term used to denote any resistor in the grid circuit.

grid return External conducting path for the return grid current to the cathode.

grid suppressor Resistor of low ohmic value inserted in the grid circuit of a radio-frequency amplifier to prevent low-frequency parasitic oscillations.

grid swing Total variation in grid-cathode voltage from the positive peak to the negative peak of the applied signal voltage.

grid transformer Transformer to supply an alternating voltage to a grid circuit or circuits.

grid-type level detector A detector using a vacuum tube with input applied to a grid.

grid voltage The voltage between a grid and the cathode of an electron tube.

grinding 1. A mechanical operation performed on silicon substrates of semiconductors to provide a smooth surface for epitaxial deposition or diffusion of impurities. **2.** A mechanical operation performed on quartz crystals to alter their physical size and hence their resonant frequencies.

Grosh's law The law that the processing power of a computer is proportional to the square of its cost.

gross index The first of two indexes consulted to gain access to a record.

grounded-anode amplifier *See* cathode follower.

grounded-base amplifier An amplifier that uses a transistor in a grounded-base connection.

grounded-base connection A transistor circuit in which the base electrode is common to both the input and output circuits; the base need not be directly connected to circuit ground. Also known as common-base connection.

grounded-cathode amplifier Electron-tube amplifier with a cathode at ground potential at the operating frequency, with input applied between control grid and ground, and with the output load connected between plate and ground.

grounded-collector connection A transistor circuit in which the collector electrode is common to both the input and output circuits; the collector need not be directly connected to circuit ground. Also known as common-collector connection.

grounded-emitter amplifier An amplifier that uses a transistor in a grounded-emitter connection.

grounded-emitter connection A transistor circuit in which the emitter electrode is common to both the input and output circuits; the emitter need not be directly connected to circuit ground. Also known as common-emitter connection.

grounded-gate amplifier Amplifier that uses thin-film transistors in which the gate electrode is connected to ground; the input signal is fed to the source electrode and the output is obtained from the drain electrode.

grounded-grid amplifier An electron-tube amplifier circuit in which the control grid is at ground potential at the operating frequency; the input signal is applied between cathode and ground, and the output load is connected between anode and ground.

grounded-grid-triode circuit Circuit in which the input signal is applied to the cathode and the output is taken from the plate; the grid is at radio-frequency ground and serves as a screen between the input and output circuits.

grounded-grid-triode mixer Triode in which the grid forms part of a grounded electrostatic screen between the anode and cathode, and is used as a mixer for centimeter wavelengths.

grounded-plate amplifier *See* cathode follower.

ground junction *See* grown junction.

ground-up read-only memory A read-only memory which is designed from the bottom up, and for which all fabrication masks used in the multiple mask process are custom-generated.

group A kits Normally those items of electronic equipment which may be permanently or semipermanently installed in an aircraft for supporting, securing, or interconnecting the components and controls of the equipment, and which will not in any manner compromise the security classification of the equipment.

group B kits Normally, the operating or operable component of the electronic equipment in an aircraft which, when installed on or in connection with group A parts, constitute the complete operable equipment.

group code *See* systematic error-checking code.

group-coded record A method of recording data on magnetic tape with eight tracks of data and one parity track, in which every eighth byte in conjunction with the parity track is used for detection and correction of all single-bit errors.

grouped records Two or more records placed together and identified by a single key, to save storage space or reduce access time.

group-indicate To print indicative information from only the first record of a group.

grouping of records Placing records together in a group to either conserve storage space or reduce access time.

group mark A character signaling the beginning or end of a group of data.

group printing The printing of information summarizing the data on a group of cards or other records when a key change occurs.

grown-diffused transistor A junction transistor in which the final junctions are formed by diffusion of impurities near a grown junction.

grown junction A junction produced by changing the types and amounts of donor and acceptor impurities that are added during the growth of a semiconductor crystal from a melt. Also known as ground junction.

grown-junction photocell A photodiode consisting of a bar of semiconductor material having a pn junction at right angles to its length and an ohmic contact at each end of the bar.

grown-junction transistor A junction transistor in which different impurities are placed in the melt in sequence as the silicon or germanium seed crystal is slowly withdrawn, to produce the alternate pn and np junctions.

G scan *See* G scope.

G scope A cathode-ray scope on which a single signal appears as a spot on which wings grow as the distance to the target is decreased, with bearing error as the horizontal coordinate and elevation angle error as the vertical coordinate. Also known as G indicator; G scan.

guard band A narrow frequency band provided between adjacent channels in certain portions of the radio spectrum to prevent interference between stations.

guard ring A ring-shaped auxiliary electrode used in an electron tube or other device to modify the electric field or reduce insulator leakage; in a counter tube or ionization chamber a guard ring may also serve to define the sensitive volume.

guard shield Internal floating shield that surrounds the entire input section of an amplifier; effective shielding is achieved only when the absolute potential of the guard is stabilized with respect to the incoming signal.

guard signal A signal used in digital-to-analog converters, analog-to-digital converters, or other converters which permits values to be read or converted only when the values are not changing, usually to avoid ambiguity error.

Gudden-Pohl effect The momentary illumination produced when an electric field is applied to a phosphor previously excited by ultraviolet radiation.

guidance tape A magnetic tape or punched paper tape that is placed in a missile or its computer to program desired events during flight.

guide edge The edge of a paper or magnetic tape, punch card, printed sheet, or other medium used to properly align its position.

guide holes One or more rows of holes prepunched around the margins of hand-sorted cards.

guide margin The distance between the guide edge of a paper tape and the center line of the track of holes that is closest to this edge.

Guillemin line A network or artificial line used in high-level pulse modulation to generate a nearly square pulse, with steep rise and fall; used in radar sets to control pulse width.

gulp A series of bytes considered as a unit.

Gunn amplifier A microwave amplifier in which a Gunn oscillator functions as a negative-resistance amplifier when placed across the terminals of a microwave source.

Gunn diode *See* Gunn oscillator.

Gunn effect Development of a rapidly fluctuating current in a small block of a semiconductor (perhaps *n*-type gallium arsenide) when a constant voltage above a critical value is applied to contacts on opposite faces.

Gunn oscillator A microwave oscillator utilizing the Gunn effect. Also known as Gunn diode.

gyrator filter A highly selective active filter that uses a gyrator which is terminated in a capacitor so as to have an inductive input impedance.

gyromagnetic coupler A coupler in which a single-crystal yig (yttrium iron garnet) resonator provides coupling at the required low signal levels between two crossed strip-line resonant circuits.

gyrotron 1. A device that detects motion of a system by measuring the phase distortion that occurs when a vibrating tuning fork is moved. 2. A type of microwave tube in which microwave amplification or generation results from cyclotron resonance coupling between microwave fields and an electron beam in vacuum. Also known as cyclotron resonance maser.

H

halation An area of glow surrounding a bright spot on a fluorescent screen, due to scattering by the phosphor or to multiple reflections at front and back surfaces of the glass faceplate.

half-adder A logic element which operates on two binary digits (but no carry digits) from a preceding stage, producing as output a sum digit and a carry digit.

half-adjust A rounding process in which the least significant digit is dropped and, if the least significant digit is one-half or more of the number base, one is added to the next more significant digit and all carries are propagated.

half block The unit of transfer between main storage and the buffer control unit; it consists of a column of 128 elements, each element 16 bytes long.

half-duplex repeater Duplex telegraph repeater provided with interlocking arrangements which restrict the transmission of signals to one direction at a time.

half-power frequency One of the two values of frequency, on the sides of an amplifier response curve, at which the voltage is $1/\sqrt{2}$ (0.707) of a midband or other reference value. Also known as half-power point.

half-power point 1. A point on the graph of some quantity in an antenna, network, or control system, versus frequency, distance, or some other variable at which the power is half that of a nearby point at which power is a maximum. 2. *See* half-power frequency.

half-pulse-repetition-rate delay In the loran navigation system, an interval of time equal to half the pulse repetition rate of a pair of loran transmitting stations, introduced as a delay between transmission of the master and slave signals, to place the slave station signal on the B trace when the master station signal is mounted on the A trace pedestal.

half-shift register Logic circuit consisting of a gated input storage element, with or without an inverter.

half-subtracter A logic element which operates on two digits from a preceding stage, producing as output a difference digit and a borrow digit. Also known as one-digit subtracter; two-input subtracter.

half-wave amplifier A magnetic amplifier whose total induced voltage has a frequency equal to the power supply frequency.

half-wave rectification Rectification in which current flows only during alternate half cycles.

half-wave rectifier A rectifier that provides half-wave rectification.

half-word I/O buffer A buffer, the upper half being used to store the upper half of a word for both input and output characters, the lower half of the buffer being used for purposes such as the storage of constants.

Hall-effect modulator A Hall-effect multiplier used as a modulator to give an output voltage that is proportional to the product of two input voltages or currents.

Hall-effect multiplier A multiplier based on the Hall effect, used in analog computers to solve such problems as finding the square root of the sum of the squares of three independent variables.

Hall-effect switch A magnetically activated switch that uses a Hall generator, trigger circuit, and transistor amplifier on a silicon chip.

Hall mobility The product of conductivity and the Hall constant for a conductor or semiconductor; a measure of the mobility of the electrons or holes in a semiconductor.

Hall voltage The no-load voltage developed across a semiconductor plate due to the Hall effect, when a specified value of control current flows in the presence of a specified magnetic field.

halo An undesirable bright or dark ring surrounding an image on the fluorescent screen of a television cathode-ray tube; generally due to overloading or maladjustment of the camera tube.

halt The cessation of the execution of the sequence of operations in a computer program resulting from a halt instruction, hang-up, or interrupt.

halt instruction *See* program stop.

hamming distance *See* signal distance.

ham radio *See* amateur radio.

hand-feed punch *See* hand punch.

handie-talkie Two-way radio communications unit small enough to be carried in the hand.

hand punch A device which punches holes in punch cards and moves the cards as they are punched as a direct result of pressure on the keys of a keyboard, and which requires feeding and removal of cards by hand, one at a time. Also known as hand-feed punch.

hang-up A nonprogrammed stop in a computer routine caused by a human mistake or a computer malfunction.

hard copy Human-readable typewritten or printed characters produced on paper at the same time that information is being keyboarded in a coded machine language, as when punching cards or paper tape.

hard disk A magnetic disk made of rigid material.

hardened circuit A circuit that uses components whose tolerance to radiation released by a nuclear explosion has been increased by various radiation-hardening procedures.

hard tube *See* high-vacuum tube.

hardware The physical, tangible, and permanent components of a computer or a data-processing system.

hardware compatibility Property of two computers such that the object code from one machine can be loaded and executed on the other to produce exactly the same results.

hardware control The control of, and communications between, the various parts of a computer system.

hardware diagnostic A computer program designed to determine whether the components of a computer are operating properly.

hardware monitor A system used to evaluate the performance of computer hardware; it collects information such as central processing unit usage from voltage level sensors that are attached to the circuitry and measure the length of time or the number of times various signals occur, and displays this information or stores it on a medium that is then fed into a special data-reduction program.

hardware multiplexing A procedure in which a servicing unit interleaves its attention among a family of serviced units in such a way that the serviced units appear to be receiving constant attention.

hard-wired Having a fixed wired program or control system built in by the manufacturer and not subject to change by programming.

hard x-ray An x-ray having high penetrating power.

harmonica bug A surreptitious interception technique applied to telephone lines; the target instrument is modified so that a tuned relay bypasses the switch hook and ringing circuit when a 500-hertz tone is received; this tone was originally generated by use of a harmonica.

harmonic analyzer An instrument that measures the strength of each harmonic in a complex wave. Also known as harmonic wave analyzer.

harmonic attenuation Attenuation of an undesired harmonic component in the output of a transmitter.

harmonic conversion transducer A conversion transducer of which the useful output frequency is a multiple or a submultiple of the input frequency.

harmonic detector Voltmeter circuit so arranged as to measure only a particular harmonic of the fundamental frequency.

harmonic distortion Nonlinear distortion in which undesired harmonics of a sinusoidal input signal are generated because of circuit nonlinearity.

harmonic filter A filter that is tuned to suppress an undesired harmonic in a circuit.

harmonic generator A generator operated under conditions such that it generates strong harmonics along with the fundamental frequency.

harmonic oscillator *See* sinusoidal oscillator.

harmonic producer Tuning-fork controlled oscillator device capable of producing odd and even harmonics of the fundamental tuning-fork frequency; used to provide carrier frequencies for broad-band carrier systems.

harmonic telephone ringer Telephone ringer which responds only to alternating current within a very narrow frequency band.

harmonic wave analyzer *See* harmonic analyzer.

Harris flow Electron flow in a cylindrical beam in which a radial electric field is used to overcome space charge divergence.

Hartley oscillator A vacuum-tube oscillator in which the parallel-tuned tank circuit is connected between grid and anode; the tank coil has an intermediate tap at cathode potential, so the grid-cathode portion of the coil provides the necessary feedback voltage.

Hartree equation An equation which gives the lowest anode voltage at which it is theoretically possible to maintain oscillation in the different modes of a magnetron.

hash 1. Data which are obviously meaningless, caused by human mistakes or computer malfunction. Also known as garbage; gibberish. **2.** *See* grass.

hash coding *See* hashing.

hashing 1. A direct addressing technique which derives the required address from a random number table. **2.** Any computer operation which transforms one or more fields into a different arrangement which is usually more compact and easily manipulated. Also known as hash coding.

hash total A sum obtained by adding together numbers having different meanings; the sole purpose is to ensure that the correct number of data have been read by the computer.

H attenuator *See* H network.

head 1. A device that reads, records, or erases data on a storage medium such as a drum or tape; examples are a small electromagnet or a sensing or punching device. 2. The photoelectric unit that converts the sound track on motion picture film into corresponding audio signals in a motion picture projector.

head crash The collision of the read-write head and the magnetic recording surface of a hard disk.

header card A card that contains supplemental information related to the data on the succeeding cards.

header label A block of data at the beginning of a magnetic tape file containing descriptive information to identify the file.

header record Computer input record containing common, constant, or identifying information for records that follow.

head gap The space between the read/write head and the recording medium, such as a disk in a computer.

heading-upward plan position indicator A plan position indicator in which the heading of the craft appears at the top of the indicator at all times.

head-per-track An arrangement having one read/write head for each magnetized track on a disk or drum to eliminate the need to move a single head from track to track.

heads-up display An electronic display that presents critical aircraft performance, such as speed and altitude, on a combining glass at the wind screen for pilot monitoring, while permitting the pilot to look out the window for other aircraft on the runway.

heater An electric heating element for supplying heat to an indirectly heated cathode in an electron tube. Also known as electron-tube heater.

heater-type cathode *See* indirectly heated cathode.

heat of emission Additional heat energy that must be supplied to an electron-emitting surface to maintain it at a constant temperature.

heavy-ion source Any source of ionized molecules or atoms of elements heavier than helium.

Heidelberg capsule A radio pill for telemetering pH values of gastric acidity.

height control The television receiver control that adjusts picture height.

height gain A radio-wave interference phenomenon which results in a more or less periodic signal strength variation with height; this specifically refers to interference between direct and surface-reflected waves; maxima or minima in these height-gain curves occur at those elevations at which the direct and reflected waves are exactly in phase or out of phase respectively.

height input Radar height information on target received by a computer from height finders and relayed via ground-to-ground data link or telephone.

height overlap coverage Height-finder coverage within which there is an area of overlapping coverage from adjacent height finders or other radar stations.

height-position indicator Radar display which shows simultaneously angular elevation, slant range, and height of objects detected in the vertical sight plane.

height-range indicator 1. Radar display which shows an echo as a bright spot on a rectangular field, slant range being indicated along the X axis, height above the horizontal plane being indicated (on a magnified scale) along the Y axis, and height above the earth being shown by a cursor. 2. Cathode-ray tube from which altitude and range measurements of flightborne objects may be viewed.

Heisenberg exchange coupling The exchange forces between electrons in neighboring atoms which give rise to ferromagnetism in the Heisenberg theory.

Heisenberg theory of ferromagnetism A theory in which exchange forces between electrons in neighboring atoms are shown to depend on relative orientations of electron spins, and ferromagnetism is explained by the assumption that parallel spins are favored so that all the spins in a lattice have a tendency to point in the same direction.

helical traveling-wave tube *See* helix tube.

helitron An electrostatically focused, low-noise backward-wave oscillator; the microwave output signal frequency can be swept rapidly over a wide range by varying the voltage applied between the cathode and the associated radio-frequency circuit.

helix tube A traveling-wave tube in which the electromagnetic wave travels along a wire wound in a spiral about the path of the beam, so that the wave travels along the tube at a velocity approximately equal to the beam velocity. Also known as helical traveling-wave tube.

helmet-mounted display An electronic display that presents, on a combining glass within the visor of the helmet of a helicopter gunner, primary information for directing firepower; the angular direction of the helmet is sensed and used to control weapons to point in the same direction as the gunner is looking. Also known as visually coupled display.

help screen Instructions that explain how to use the software of a computer system and that can be presented on the screen of a video display terminal at any time.

heptode A seven-electrode electron tube containing an anode, a cathode, a control electrode, and four additional electrodes that are ordinarily grids. Also known as pentagrid.

herringbone pattern An interference pattern sometimes seen on television receiver screens, consisting of a horizontal band of closely spaced V- or S-shaped lines.

Hertz effect Increase in the length of a spark induced across a spark gap when the gap is irradiated with ultraviolet light.

hesitation A brief automatic suspension of the operations of a main program in order to perform all or part of another operation, such as rapid transmission of data to or from a peripheral unit.

Hesser's variation A variation of a Kiviat graph in which all variables are arranged so that their plots approach the circumference of the graph as the system being evaluated approaches saturation, and the scales on the various axes may not cover the full 0–100% range, or may be in units other than percent.

heterodyne To mix two alternating-current signals of different frequencies in a nonlinear device for the purpose of producing two new frequencies, the sum of and difference between the two original frequencies.

heterodyne conversion transducer *See* converter.

heterodyne detector A detector in which an unmodulated carrier frequency is combined with the signal of a local oscillator having a slightly different frequency, to provide an audio-frequency beat signal that can be heard with a loudspeaker or headphones; used chiefly for code reception.

heterodyne frequency meter A frequency meter in which a known frequency, which may be adjustable or fixed, is heterodyned with an unknown frequency to produce a zero beat or an audio-frequency signal whose value is measured by other means. Also known as heterodyne wavemeter.

heterodyne measurement A measurement carried out by a type of harmonic analyzer which employs a highly selective filter, at a frequency well above the highest frequency to be measured, and a heterodyning oscillator.

heterodyne modulator *See* mixer.

heterodyne oscillator **1.** A separate variable-frequency oscillator used to produce the second frequency required in a heterodyne detector for code reception. **2.** *See* beat-frequency oscillator.

heterodyne reception Radio reception in which the incoming radio-frequency signal is combined with a locally generated rf signal of different frequency, followed by detection. Also known as beat reception.

heterodyne repeater A radio repeater in which the received radio signals are converted to an intermediate frequency, amplified, and reconverted to a new frequency band for transmission over the next repeater section.

heterodyne wavemeter *See* heterodyne frequency meter.

heterojunction The boundary between two different semiconductor materials, usually with a negligible discontinuity in the crystal structure.

heuristic algorithm *See* dynamic algorithm.

heuristic program A program in which a computer tries each of several methods of solving a problem and judges whether the program is closer to solution after each attempt. Also known as heuristic routine.

heuristic programming *See* conceptual modeling.

heuristic routine *See* heuristic program.

hexadecimal notation A notation in the scale of 16, using decimal digits 0 to 9 and six more digits that are sometimes represented by A, B, C, D, E, and F.

hexode A six-electrode electron tube containing an anode, a cathode, a control electrode, and three additional electrodes that are ordinarily grids.

hierarchical distributed processing system A type of distributed processing system in which processing functions are distributed outward from a central computer to intelligent terminal controllers or satellite information processors. Also known as host-centered system; host/satellite system.

hierarchical file A file with a grandfather-father-son structure.

high boost *See* high-frequency compensation.

high-current rectifier A solid-state device, gas tube, or vacuum tube used to convert alternating to direct current for powering low-impedance loads.

higher-level language *See* high-level language.

higher-order language *See* high-level language.

higher than high-level language A programming language, such as an application development language, report program, or financial planning language, that is oriented toward a particular application and is much easier to use for that application than a conventional programming language.

high-frequency compensation Increasing the amplification at high frequencies with respect to that at low and middle frequencies in a given band, such as in a video band or an audio band. Also known as high boost.

high-frequency transformer A transformer which matches impedances and transmits a frequency band in the carrier (or higher) frequency ranges.

high-frequency triode A triode designed for operation at high frequency, having small spacings between the grid and the cathode and anode, large emission and power densities, and low active and inactive capacitances.

high-frequency voltmeter A voltmeter designed to measure currents alternating at high frequencies.

high level The more positive of the two logic levels or states in a binary digital logic system.

high-level language A computer language whose instructions or statements each correspond to several machine language instructions, designed to make coding easier. Also known as higher-level language; higher-order language.

highlights Bright areas occurring in a television image.

high-low bias test A routine maintenance procedure that tests equipment over and under normal operating conditions in order to detect defective units.

high-mu tube A tube having a very high amplification factor.

high-order Pertaining to a digit location in a numeral, the leftmost digit being the highest-order digit.

high-pass filter A filter that transmits all frequencies above a given cutoff frequency and substantially attenuates all others.

high-positive indicator A component in some computers whose status is "on" if the number tested is positive and nonzero.

high-pressure mercury-vapor lamp A discharge tube containing an inert gas and a small quantity of liquid mercury; the initial glow discharge through the gas heats and vaporizes the mercury, after which the discharge through mercury vapor produces an intensely brilliant light.

high Q A characteristic wherein a component has a high ratio of reactance to effective resistance, so that its Q factor is high.

high-side capacitance coupling Taking the output of an oscillator or amplifier from a point of high potential, using a capacitor to block direct current flow.

high-speed carry A technique in parallel addition to speed up the propagation of carries.

high-speed data acquisition system A system which collects and transmits data rapidly to a monitoring and controlling center.

high-speed oscilloscope An oscilloscope with a very fast sweep, capable of observing signals with rise times or periods on the order of nanoseconds.

high-speed printer A printer which can function at a high rate, relative to the state of the art; 600 lines per minute is considered high speed. Abbreviated HSP.

high-speed reader The fastest input device existing at a particular time in the state of the technology.

high-speed relay A relay specifically designed for short operate time, short release time, or both.

high-speed storage See rapid storage.

high-vacuum rectifier Vacuum-tube rectifier in which conduction is entirely by electrons emitted from the cathode.

high-vacuum switching tube A microwave transmit-receive (TR) tube of the high-vacuum variety, as contrasted with gas-tube or semiconductor devices.

high-vacuum tube Electron tube evacuated to such a degree that its electrical characteristics are essentially unaffected by gaseous ionization. Also known as hard tube.

high-voltage electron microscope An electron microscope whose accelerating voltage is on the order of 10^6 volts, as compared with 40–100 kilovolts for an ordinary electron microscope; it has the advantages of increased specimen penetration, reduced specimen damage, better theoretical resolution, and more efficient dark-field operation.

hill bandwidth The difference between the upper and lower frequencies at which the gain of an amplifier is 3 decibels less than its maximum value.

hit The obtaining of a correct answer in a mechanical information-retrieval system.

hit-on-the-fly system A printer in a computer system where either the print roller or the paper is in continuous motion.

hit rate The ratio of the number of records accessed in a run to the number of records in the file, expressed as a percentage.

Hittorf dark space *See* cathode dark space.

Hittorf principle The principle that a discharge between electrodes in a gas at a given pressure does not necessarily occur between the closest points of the electrodes if the distance between these points lies to the left of the minimum on a graph of spark potential versus distance. Also known as short-path principle.

H network An attenuation network composed of five branches and having the form of the letter H. Also known as H attenuator; H pad.

hold 1. To retain information in a computer storage device for further use after it has been initially utilized. 2. To maintain storage elements at equilibrium voltages in a charge storage tube by electron bombardment.

hold circuit A circuit in a sampled-data control system that converts the series of impulses, generated by the sampler, into a rectangular function, in order to smooth the signal to the motor or plant.

hold control A manual control that changes the frequency of the horizontal or vertical sweep oscillator in a television receiver, so that the frequency more nearly corresponds to that of the incoming synchronizing pulses.

hold facility The ability of a computer to operate in a hold mode.

holding anode A small auxiliary anode used in a mercury-pool rectifier to keep a cathode spot energized during the intervals when the main-anode current is zero.

holding beam A diffused beam of electrons used to regenerate the charges stored on the dielectric surface of a cathode-ray storage tube.

holding coil A separate relay coil that is energized by contacts which close when a relay pulls in, to hold the relay in its energized position after the orginal operating circuit is opened.

holding current The minimum current required to maintain a switching device in a closed or conducting state after it is energized or triggered.

hold mode The state of an analog computer in which its operation is interrupted without altering the values of the variables it is handling, so that computation can continue when the interruption is over. Also known as interrupt mode.

hold-over command A command punched at the end of each card to cause machines to treat the several cards as if they were one continuous record.

hole A vacant electron energy state near the top of an energy band in a solid; behaves as though it were a positively charged particle. Also known as electron hole.

hole conduction Conduction occurring in a semiconductor when electrons move into holes under the influence of an applied voltage and thereby create new holes.

hole injection The production of holes in an n-type semiconductor when voltage is applied to a sharp metal point in contact with the surface of the material.

hole mobility A measure of the ability of a hole to travel readily through a semiconductor, equal to the average drift velocity of holes divided by the electric field.

hole site The area on a punch card where a hole may be punched.

hole trap A semiconductor impurity capable of releasing electrons to the conduction or valence bands, equivalent to trapping a hole.

holistic masks In character recognition, that set of characters which resides within a character reader and theoretically represents the exact replicas of all possible input characters.

Hollerith code A code used to represent letters, numbers, or special symbols to be punched in standard 80-column punch cards.

Hollerith string A sequence of characters preceded by an H and a character count in FORTRAN, as 4HSTOP.

hollow cathode A cathode which is hollow and closed at one end in a discharge tube filled with inert gas, designed so that radiation is emitted from the cathode glow inside the cathode.

holographic memory A memory in which information is stored in the form of holographic images on thermoplastic or other recording films.

home address A technique used to identify each disk track uniquely by means of a 9-byte record immediately following the index marker; the record contains a flag (good or defective track), cylinder number, head number, cyclic check, and bit count appendage.

home-on-jam A feature that permits radar to track a jamming source in angle.

home record The first record in the chaining method of file organization.

hometaxial-base transistor Transistor manufactured by a single-diffusion process to form both emitter and collector junctions in a uniformly doped silicon slice; the resulting homogeneously doped base region is free from accelerating fields in the axial (collector-to-emitter) direction, which could cause undesirable high current flow and destroy the transistor.

homing device A control device that automatically starts in the correct direction of motion or rotation to achieve a desired change, as in a remote-control tuning motor for a television receiver.

homodyne reception A system of radio reception for suppressed-carrier systems of radiotelephony, in which the receiver generates a voltage having the original carrier frequency and combines it with the incoming signal. Also known as zero-beat reception.

homopolar generator A direct-current generator in which the poles presented to the armature are all of the same polarity, so that the voltage generated in active conductors has the same polarity at all times; a pure direct current is thus produced, without commutation. Also known as acyclic machine; homopolar machine; unipolar machine.

homopolar machine *See* homopolar generator.

hook A circuit phenomenon occurring in four-zone transistors, wherein hole or electron conduction can occur in opposite directions to produce voltage drops that encourage other types of conduction.

hook collector transistor A transistor in which there are four layers of alternating n- and p-type semiconductor material and the two interior layers are thin compared to the diffusion length. Also known as hook transistor; pn hook transistor.

hook transistor *See* hook collector transistor.

hoot stop A closed loop that generates an audible signal; usually employed to signal an error or for operating convenience.

hopper *See* card hopper.

horizontal blanking Blanking of a television picture tube during the horizontal retrace.

horizontal blanking pulse The rectangular pulse that forms the pedestal of the composite television signal between active horizontal lines and causes the beam current of the picture tube to be cut off during retrace. Also known as line-frequency blanking pulse.

horizontal centering control The centering control provided in a television receiver or cathode-ray oscilloscope to shift the position of the entire image horizontally in either direction on the screen.

horizontal convergence control The control that adjusts the amplitude of the horizontal dynamic convergence voltage in a color television receiver.

horizontal definition *See* horizontal resolution.

horizontal deflection electrode One of a pair of electrodes that move the electron beam horizontally from side to side on the fluorescent screen of a cathode-ray tube employing electrostatic deflection.

horizontal deflection oscillator The oscillator that produces, under control of the horizontal synchronizing signals, the sawtooth voltage waveform that is amplified to feed the horizontal deflection coils on the picture tube of a television receiver. Also known as horizontal oscillator.

horizontal distributed processing system A type of distributed system in which two or more computers which are logically equivalent are connected together, with no hierarchy or master/slave relationship.

horizontal drive control The control in a television receiver, usually at the rear, that adjusts the output of the horizontal oscillator. Also known as drive control.

horizontal feed A card feed in which punch cards are placed in a hopper and enter and pass through a card track, all in a horizontal position.

horizontal flow chart A graphical representation of the movement of forms, punch cards, and other recording media through an organization, showing the movement of each medium from the time it is first used to the time it is destroyed.

horizontal flyback Flyback in which the electron beam of a television picture tube returns from the end of one scanning line to the beginning of the next line. Also known as horizontal retrace.

horizontal frequency *See* line frequency.

horizontal hold control The hold control that changes the free-running period of the horizontal deflection oscillator in a television receiver, so that the picture remains steady in the horizontal direction.

horizontal instruction An instruction in machine language to carry out independent operations on various operands in parallel or in a well-defined time sequence.

horizontal linearity control A linearity control that permits narrowing or expanding of the width of the left half of a television receiver image, to give linearity in the horizontal direction so that circular objects appear as true circles.

horizontal line frequency *See* line frequency.

horizontal oscillator *See* horizontal deflection oscillator.

horizontal output stage The television receiver stage that feeds the horizontal deflection coils of the picture tube through the horizontal output transformer; may also include a part of the second-anode power supply for the picture tube.

horizontal output transformer A transformer used in a television receiver to provide the horizontal deflection voltage, the high voltage for the second-anode power supply of the picture tube, and the filament voltage for the high-voltage rectifier tube. Also known as flyback transformer; horizontal sweep transformer.

horizontal resolution The number of individual picture elements or dots that can be distinguished in a horizontal scanning line of a television or facsimile image. Also known as horizontal definition.

horizontal retrace *See* horizontal flyback.

horizontal scanning frequency The number of horizontal lines scanned by the electron beam in a television receiver in 1 second.

horizontal sweep The sweep of the electron beam from left to right across the screen of a cathode-ray tube.

horizontal sweep transformer *See* horizontal output transformer.

horizontal synchronizing pulse The rectangular pulse transmitted at the end of each line in a television system, to keep the receiver in line-by-line synchronism with the transmitter. Also known as line synchronizing pulse.

horizontal system A programming system in which instructions are written horizontally, that is, across the page.

hospital information system The collection, evaluation or verification, storage, and retrieval of information about a patient.

host-centered system *See* hierarchical distributed processing system.

host computer The computer upon which depends a specialized computer handling the input/output functions in a real-time system.

host language data-base management system A data-base management system that, from a programmer's point of view, represents an extension of an existing programming language.

host processor The central computer in a hierarchical distributed processing system, which is typically located at some central site where it serves as a focal point for the collection of data, and often for the provision of services which cannot economically be distributed.

host/satellite system *See* hierarchical distributed processing system.

hot carrier A carrier, which may be either an electron or a hole, that has relatively high energy with respect to the carriers normally found in majority-carrier devices such as thin-film transistors.

hot-carrier diode *See* Schottky barrier diode.

hot cathode A cathode in which electron or ion emission is produced by heat. Also known as thermionic cathode.

hot-cathode gas-filled tube *See* thyratron.

hot-cathode tube *See* thermionic tube.

hot electron An electron that is in excess of the thermal equilibrium number and, for metals, has an energy greater than the Fermi level; for semiconductors, the energy must be a definite amount above that of the edge of the conduction band.

hot-electron triode Solid-state, evaporated thin-film structure directly equivalent to a vacuum triode.

hot-filament ionization gage An ionization gage in which electrons emitted by an incandescent filament, and attracted toward a positively charged grid electrode, collide with gas molecules to produce ions which are then attracted to a negatively charged electrode; the ion current is a measure of the number of gas molecules.

hot hole A hole that can move at much greater velocity than normal holes in a semiconductor.

hot junction The heated junction of a thermocouple.

housekeeping Those operations or routines which do not contribute directly to the solution of a computer program, but rather to the organization of the program.

housekeeping run The performance of a program or routine to maintain the structure of files, such as sorting, merging, addition of new records, or deletion or modification of existing records.

howler An audio device used to warn a radar operator that signals are appearing on a radar screen.

H pad *See* H network.

h parameter One of a set of four transistor equivalent-circuit parameters that conveniently specify transistor performance for small voltages and currents in a particular circuit. Also known as hybrid parameter.

HSP *See* high-speed printer.

hub An electric socket in a plugboard into which one may insert or connect leads or may plug wires.

hue control A control that varies the phase of the chrominance signals with respect to that of the burst signal in a color television receiver, in order to change the hues in the image. Also known as phase control.

hum An electrical disturbance occurring at the power supply frequency or its harmonics, usually 60 or 120 hertz in the United States.

hum bar A dark horizontal band extending across a television picture due to excessive hum in the video signal applied to the input of the picture tube.

humidity capacitor A device for measuring ambient relative humidity by sensing a change in capacitance.

hum modulation Modulation of a radio-frequency signal or detected audio-frequency signal by hum; heard in a radio receiver only when a station is tuned in.

hunting Operation of a selector in moving from terminal to terminal until one is found which is idle.

hunting circuit *See* lockout circuit.

hybrid algebraic manipulation language The most ambitious type of algebraic manipulation language, which accepts the broadest spectrum of mathematical expressions but possesses, in addition, special representations and special algorithms for particular special classes of expressions.

hybrid computer A computer designed to handle both analog and digital data. Also known as analog-digital computer.

hybrid distributed processing system A distributed processing system that includes both horizontal and hierarchical distribution.

hybrid hardware control The control of and communication between the various parts of a hybrid computer.

hybrid input/output The routines required to handle inputs to and outputs from a computer system comprising digital and analog computers.

hybrid integrated circuit A circuit in which one or more discrete components are used in combination with integrated-circuit construction.

hybrid interface A device that joins a digital to an analog computer, converting digital signals transmitted serially by the digital computer into analog signals that are transmitted simultaneously to the various units of the analog computer, and vice versa.

hybrid junction A transformer, resistor, or waveguide circuit or device that has four pairs of terminals so arranged that a signal entering at one terminal pair divides and emerges from the two adjacent terminal pairs, but is unable to reach the opposite terminal pair. Also known as bridge hybrid.

hybrid microcircuit Microcircuit in which thin-film, thick-film, or diffusion techniques are combined with separately attached semiconductor chips to form the circuit.

hybrid parameter *See* h parameter.

hybrid problem analysis The determination of the parts of a problem best suited for the digital computer.

hybrid programming Hybrid system routines that handle timing, function generation, and simulation.

hybrid redundancy A synthesis of triple modular redundancy and standby replacement redundancy, consisting of a triple modular redundancy system (or, in general, an N-modular redundancy system) with a bank of spares so that when one of the units in the triple modular redundancy system fails it is replaced by a spare unit.

hybrid simulation The use of a hybrid computer for purposes of simulation.

hybrid system checkout The static check of a hybrid system and of the digital program and analog wiring required to solve a problem.

hybrid thin-film circuit Microcircuit formed by attaching discrete components and semiconductor devices to networks of passive components and conductors that have been vacuum-deposited on glazed ceramic, sapphire, or glass substrates.

hydraulic computer A computer in which electric current and gates are replaced by fluid and valves.

hydrogen-discharge lamp A discharge lamp containing hydrogen and used as a source of ultraviolet radiation.

hydrogen thyratron A thyratron containing hydrogen instead of mercury vapor to give freedom from effects of changes in ambient temperature; used in radar pulse circuits and stroboscopic photography.

hygristor A resistor whose resistance varies with humidity; used in some types of recording hygrometers.

hyperbolic sweep generator A sweep generator that generates a waveform resembling a hyperbola.

hyperbolic waveform A waveform which is an approximate hyperbola.

hyperdisk A mass-storage technique which uses a large-capacity storage and a disk for overflow.

hyperpure germanium detector A variant of the lithium-drifted germanium crystal which uses high-purity germanium, making it possible to store the detector at room temperature rather than liquid nitrogen temperature.

hypersensor Single-component, resettable circuit breaker which operates as a majority-carrier tunneling device, and is used for overcurrent or overvoltage protection of integrated circuits.

hypertape control unit *See* tape control unit.

hypertape drive *See* cartridge tape drive.

hypervisor A control program enabling two operating systems to share a common computing system.

hysteresis An oscillator effect wherein a given value of an operating parameter may result in multiple values of output power or frequency.

I

IC *See* integrated circuit.

iconoscope A television camera tube in which a beam of high-velocity electrons scans a photoemissive mosaic that is capable of storing an electric charge pattern corresponding to an optical image focused on the mosaic. Also known as storage camera; storage-type camera tube.

ICS system *See* intercarrier sound system.

ideal bunching Theoretical condition in which the bunching of electrons in a velocity-modulated tube would give a single infinitely large current peak during each cycle.

ideal network An interconnection of lumped, constant electrical quantities analyzed without consideration of noise and distributed parameters that would exist in actual settings.

I demodulator Stage of a color television receiver which combines the chrominance signal with the color oscillator output to restore the *I* signal.

identification division The section of a program, written in the COBOL language, which contains the name of the program and the name of the programmer.

identifier A symbol whose purpose is to specify a body of data.

identifier word A full-length computer word associated with a search function.

identity gate *See* identity unit.

identity unit A logic element with several binary input signals and a single binary output signal whose value is 1 if all the input signals have the same value and 0 if they do not. Also known as identity gate.

I display A radarscope display in which a target appears as a complete circle when the radar antenna is correctly pointed at it, the radius of the circle being proportional to target distance; when the antenna is not aimed at the target, the circle reduces to a circle segment.

idler frequency Of a parametric device, a sum or difference frequency generated within the parametric device other than the input, output, or pump frequencies which require specific circuit consideration to achieve the desired device performance; it is called an idler frequency since, in conventional parametric amplifiers, it is more or less a useless by-product of the parametric process.

idle time The time during which a piece of hardware in good operating condition is unused.

IDP *See* integrated data processing.

i-f *See* intermediate frequency.

i-f amplifier *See* intermediate-frequency amplifier.

IF canceler In radar, a moving-target indicator canceler that operates at intermediate frequencies.

if then else A logic statement in a high-level programming language that defines the data to be compared and the actions to be taken as the result of a comparison.

i-f transformer *See* intermediate-frequency transformer.

ignitor 1. An electrode used to initiate and sustain the discharge in a switching tube. Also known as keep-alive electrode (deprecated). 2. A pencil-shaped electrode, made of carborundum or some other conducting material that is not wetted by mercury, partly immersed in the mercury-pool cathode of an ignitron and used to initiate conduction at the desired point in each alternating-current cycle.

ignitron A single-anode pool tube in which an ignitor electrode is employed to initiate the cathode spot on the surface of the mercury pool before each conducting period.

ignitron contactor A circuit containing an ignitron and control contacts that serves as a heavy-duty switch in the primary of a resistance-welding transformer.

ignore character Also known as erase character. 1. A character indicating that no action whatever is to be taken, that is, a character to be ignored; often used to obliterate an erroneous character. 2. A character indicating that the preceding or following character is to be ignored, as specified. 3. A character indicating that some specified action is not to be taken.

I indicator *See* I scope.

I²L *See* integrated injection logic.

ill-conditioned problem A problem in which a small error in the data or in subsequent calculation results in much larger errors in the answers.

illegal character A character or combination of bits that is not accepted as a valid representation by a computer or by a specific routine; commonly detected and used as an indication of a machine malfunction.

illumination control A photoelectric control that turns on lights when outdoor illumination decreases below a predetermined level.

image A copy of the information contained in a punched card (or other data record) recorded on a different data medium.

image attenuation constant The real part of the image transfer constant.

image card A representation in storage of the holes punched in a card, in such a manner that the holes are represented by one binary digit, and the unpunched spaces are represented by the other binary digit.

image converter *See* image tube.

image converter camera A camera consisting of an image tube and an optical system which focuses the image produced on the phosphorescent screen of the tube onto photographic film.

image dissection photography A method of high-speed photography in which an image is split in any one of various ways into interlaced space and time elements which can be unscrambled or played back through the system either to be viewed or to give a master negative.

image dissector In optical character recognition, a device that optically examines an input character for the purpose of breaking it down into its prescribed elements.

image dissector tube A television camera tube in which an electron image produced by a photoemitting surface is focused in the plane of the defining aperture and is scanned past that aperture. Also known as Farnsworth image dissector tube.

image enhancement Improvement of the quality of a picture, with the aid of a computer, by giving it higher contrast or making it less blurred or less noisy.

image frequency An undesired carrier frequency that differs from the frequency to which a superheterodyne receiver is tuned by twice the intermediate frequency.

image iconoscope A camera tube in which an optical image is projected on a semitransparent photocathode, and the resulting electron image emitted from the other side of the photocathode is focused on a separate storage target; the target is scanned on the same side by a high-velocity electron beam, neutralizing the elemental charges in sequence to produce the camera output signal at the target. Also known as superemitron camera (British usage).

image impedance One of the impedances that, when connected to the input and output of a transducer, will make the impedances in both directions equal at the input terminals and at the output terminals.

image intensifier *See* light amplifier.

image isocon A television camera tube which is similar to the image orthicon but whose return beam consists of scanning beam electrons that are scattered by positive stored charges on the target.

image load Load parameters reflected back to the source by line discontinuities.

image orthicon A television camera tube in which an electron image is produced by a photoemitting surface and focused on one side of a separate storage tube that is scanned on its opposite side by a beam of low-velocity electrons; electrons that are reflected from the storage tube, after positive stored charges are neutralized by the scanning beam, form a return beam which is amplified by an electron multiplier.

image parameter design A method of filter design using image impedance and image transfer functions as the fundamental network functions.

image parameter filter A filter constructed by image parameter design.

image phase constant The imaginary part of the image transfer constant.

image processing A technique in which the data from an image are digitized and various mathematical operations are applied to the data, generally with a digital computer, in order to create an enhanced image that is more useful or pleasing to a human observer, or to perform some of the interpretation and recognition tasks usually performed by humans. Also known as picture processing.

image ratio In a heterodyne receiver, the ratio of the image frequency signal input at the antenna to the desired signal input for identical outputs.

image reject mixer Combination of two balanced mixers and associated hybrid circuits designed to separate the image channel from the signal channels normally present in a conventional mixer; the arrangement gives image rejection up to 30 decibels without the use of filters.

image response The response of a superheterodyne receiver to an undesired signal at its image frequency.

image restoration Operation on a picture with a digital computer to make it more closely resemble the original object.

image-storage array A solid-state panel or chip in which the image-sensing elements may be a metal oxide semiconductor or a charge-coupled or other light-sensitive device that can be manufactured in a high-density configuration.

image transfer constant One-half the natural logarithm of the complex ratio of the steady-state apparent power entering and leaving a network terminated in its image impedance.

image tube An electron tube that reproduces on its fluorescent screen an image of the optical image or other irradiation pattern incident on its photosensitive surface. Also known as electron image tube; image converter.

imitative deception Introduction of electromagnetic radiations into enemy channels which imitate their own emissions, in order to mislead them.

immediate-access 1. Pertaining to an access time which is relatively brief, or to a relatively fast transfer of information. 2. Pertaining to a device which is directly connected with another device.

immediate address The value of an operand contained in the address part of an instruction and used as data by this instruction.

immediate operand An operand contained in the instruction which specifies the operation.

immediate processing *See* demand processing.

immersion electron microscope An emission electron microscope in which the specimen is a flat conducting surface which may be heated, illuminated, or bombarded by high-velocity electrons or ions so as to emit low-velocity thermionic, photo-, or secondary electrons; these are accelerated to a high velocity in an immersion objective or cathode lens and imaged as in a transmission electron microscope.

immersion electrostatic lens *See* bipotential electrostatic lens.

impact avalanche and transit time diode *See* IMPATT diode.

impact ionization Ionization produced by the impact of a high-energy charge carrier on an atom of semiconductor material; the effect is an increase in the number of charge carriers.

IMPATT amplifier A diode amplifier that uses an IMPATT diode; operating frequency range is from about 5 to 100 gigahertz, primarily in the C and X bands, with power output up to about 20 watts continuous-wave or 100 watts pulsed.

IMPATT diode A *pn* junction diode that has a depletion region adjacent to the junction, through which electrons and holes can drift, and is biased beyond the avalanche breakdown voltage. Derived from impact avalanche and transit time diode.

impedance-admittance matrix A four-element matrix used to describe analytically a transistor in terms of impedances or admittances.

imperative statement A statement in a symbolic program which is translated into actual machine-language instructions by the assembly routine.

implanted atom An atom introduced into semiconductor material by ion implantation.

implanted device A resistor or other device that is fabricated within a silicon or other semiconducting substrate by ion implantation.

implementation The installation of a computer system or an information system.

impulse separator In a television receiver, the circuit that separates the horizontal synchronizing impulses in the received signal from the vertical synchronizing impulses.

impurity A substance that, when diffused into semiconductor metal in small amounts, either provides free electrons to the metal or accepts electrons from it.

impurity semiconductor A semiconductor whose properties are due to impurity levels produced by foreign atoms.

incandescent readout A readout in which each character is formed by energizing an appropriate combination of seven bar-shaped incandescent lamps.

incident wave A current or voltage wave that is traveling through a transmission line in the direction from source to load.

incorporate To place in storage.

incremental compiler A compiler that generates code for a statement, or group of statements, which is independent of the code generated for other statements.

incremental computer A special-purpose computer designed to process changes in variables as well as absolute values; for instance, a digital differential analyzer.

incremental digital recorder Magnetic tape recorder in which the tape advances across the recording head step by step, as in a punched-paper-tape recorder; used for recording an irregular flow of data economically and reliably.

incremental dump tape A safety technique used in time-sharing which consists in copying all files (created or modified by a user during a day) on a magnetic tape; in case of system failure, the file storage can then be reconstructed. Also known as failsafe tape.

incremental mode The plotting of a curve on a cathode-ray tube by illuminating a fixed number of points at a time.

incremental representation A way of representing variables used in incremental computers, in which changes in the variables are represented instead of the values of the variables themselves.

independent sector A device on some punched-card tabulators that allows only the first of a series of similar data items to be printed and prevents printing of the rest.

independent-sideband receiver A radio receiver designed for the reception of independent-sideband modulation, having provisions for restoring the carrier.

independent-sideband transmitter A transmitter which produces independent-sideband modulated signals.

index 1. A list of record surrogates arranged in order of some attribute expressible in machine-orderable form. **2.** To produce a machine-orderable set of record surrogates, as in indexing a book. **3.** To compute a machine location by indirection, as is done by index registers. **4.** The portion of a computer instruction which indicates what index register (if any) is to be used to modify the address of an instruction.

index arithmetic unit A section of some computers that performs addition or subtraction operations on address parts of instructions for the purpose of indexing, boundary tests for memory protection, and so forth.

index array A group of registers corresponding one-for-one with the buffer registers, each register containing the main storage address of the data contained in the corresponding buffer register.

indexed address An address which is modified, generally by means of index registers, before or during execution of a computer instruction.

indexed sequential data set A collection of related data items that are stored sequentially on a key, but are also accessible through index tables maintained by the system.

indexed sequential organization A sequence of records arranged in collating sequence used with direct-access devices.

index marker The beginning (and end) of each track in a disk, which is recognized by a special sensing device within the disk mechanism.

index point A hardware reference mark on a disk or drum for use in timing.

index register A hardware element which holds a number that can be added to (or, in some cases, subtracted from) the address portion of a computer instruction to form an effective address. Also known as base register; B box; B line; B register; B store; modifier register.

index word *See* modifier.

indicative data Data which describe a specific item.

indicator 1. A device announcing an error or failure. 2. A cathode-ray tube or other device that presents information transmitted or relayed from some other source, as from a radar receiver.

indicator element A component whose variability under conditions of manufacture or use is likely to cause the greatest variation in some measurable parameter.

indicator gate Rectangular voltage waveform which is applied to the grid or cathode circuit of an indicator cathode-ray tube to sensitize or desensitize it during a desired portion of the operating cycle.

indicator tube An electron-beam tube in which useful information is conveyed by the variation in cross section of the beam at a luminescent target.

indirect address An address in a computer instruction that indicates a location where the address of the referenced operand is to be found. Also known as multilevel address.

indirect addressing A programming device whereby the address part of an instruction is not the address of the operand but rather the location in storage where the address of the operand may be found.

indirect control The control of one peripheral unit by another through some sequence of events that involves human intervention.

indirectly heated cathode A cathode to which heat is supplied by an independent heater element in a thermionic tube; this cathode has the same potential on its entire surface, whereas the potential along a directly heated filament varies from one end to the other. Also known as equipotential cathode; heater-type cathode; unipotential cathode.

induced anisotropy A type of uniaxial anisotropy in a magnetic material produced by annealing the magnetic material in a magnetic field.

inductive feedback 1. Transfer of energy from the plate circuit to the grid circuit of a vacuum tube by means of induction. 2. Transfer of energy from the output circuit to the input circuit of an amplifying device through an inductor, or by means of inductive coupling.

inductive filter A low-pass filter used for smoothing the direct-current output voltage of a rectifier; consists of one or more sections in series, each section consisting of an inductor on one of the pair of conductors in series with a capacitor between the conductors. Also known as LC filter.

inductive neutralization Neutralizing an amplifier whereby the feedback susceptance due to an interelement capacitance is canceled by the equal and opposite susceptance of an inductor. Also known as coil neutralization; shunt neutralization.

inductive tuning Tuning involving the use of a variable inductance.

ineffective time Time during which a computer can operate normally but which is not used effectively because of mistakes or inefficiency in operating the installation or for other reasons.

infinity Any number larger than the maximum number that a computer is able to store in any register.

infinity transmitter A device used to tap a telephone; the telephone instrument is so modified that an interception device can be actuated from a distant source without the caller's becoming aware.

infix operation An operation carried out within an operation, as the addition of a and b prior to the multiplication by c or division by d in the operation $(a+b)c/d$.

information flow The graphic representation of data collection, data processing, and report distribution throughout an organization.

information precedence relation A statement that some specified piece of data is required for the production of another piece of data.

information processing 1. The manipulation of data so that new data (implicit in the original) appear in a useful form. 2. *See* data processing.

Information Processing Language *See* IPL.

information redundancy The use of more information than is absolutely necessary, such as the application of error-detection and error-correction codes, in order to increase the reliability of a computer system.

information requirements Actual or anticipated questions which may be posed to an information retrieval system.

information retrieval The technique and process of searching, recovering, and interpreting information from large amounts of stored data.

information selection systems A class of information processing systems which carry out a sequence of operations necessary to locate in storage one or more items assumed to have certain specified characteristics and to retrieve such items directly or indirectly, in whole or in part.

information separator A character that separates items or fields of information in a record, especially a variable-length record.

information word *See* data word.

infradyne receiver A superheterodyne receiver in which the intermediate frequency is higher than the signal frequency, so as to obtain high selectivity.

infrared bolometer A bolometer adapted to detecting infrared radiation, as opposed to microwave radiation.

infrared communications set Components required to operate a two-way electronic system using infrared radiation to carry intelligence.

infrared detector A device responding to infrared radiation, used in detecting fires, or overheating in machinery, planes, vehicles, and people, and in controlling temperature-sensitive industrial processes.

infrared-emitting diode A light-emitting diode that has maximum emission in the near-infrared region, typically at 0.9 micrometer for *pn* gallium arsenide.

infrared heterodyne detector A heterodyne detector in which both the incoming signal and the local oscillator signal frequencies are in the infrared range and are combined in a photodetector to give an intermediate frequency in the kilohertz or megahertz range for conventional amplification.

infrared image converter A device for converting an invisible infrared image into a visible image, consisting of an infrared-sensitive, semitransparent photocathode on one end of an evacuated envelope and a phosphor screen on the other, with an electrostatic lens system between the two. Also known as infrared image tube.

infrared image tube *See* infrared image converter.

infrared jamming An attempt to confuse heat-seeking missiles by emissions which overload their inputs or misdirect them.

infrared phosphor A phosphor which, when exposed to infrared radiation during or even after decay of luminescence resulting from its usual or dominant activator, emits light having the same spectrum as that of the dominant activator; sulfide and selenide phosphors are the most important examples.

infrared photoconductor A conductor whose conductivity increases when it is exposed to infrared radiation.

infrared receiver A device that intercepts or demodulates infrared radiation that may carry intelligence. Also known as nancy receiver.

infrared scanner An infrared detector mounted on a motor-driven platform which causes it to scan a field of view line by line, much as in television.

infrared thermistor A thermistor used to measure the power of infrared radiation.

infrared transmitter A transmitter that emits energy in the infrared spectrum; may be modulated with intelligence signals.

infrared vidicon A vidicon whose photoconductor surface is sensitive to infrared radiation.

inherent storage Any type of storage in which the storage medium is part of the hardware of the computer medium.

inherited error The error existing in the data supplied at the beginning of a step in a step-by-step calculation as executed by a program.

inhibit-gate Gate circuit whose output is energized only when certain signals are present and other signals are not present at the inputs.

inhibiting input A gate input which, if in its prescribed state, prevents any output which might otherwise occur.

inhibiting signal A signal, which when entered into a specific circuit will prevent the circuit from exercising its normal function; for example, an inhibit signal fed into an AND gate will prevent the gate from yielding an output when all normal input signals are present.

inhibit pulse A drive pulse that tends to prevent flux reversal of a magnetic cell by certain specified drive pulses.

initial condition *See* entry condition.

initial condition mode *See* reset mode.

initial instructions A routine stored in a computer to aid in placing a program in memory. Also known as initial orders.

initial inverse voltage Of a rectifier tube, the peak inverse anode voltage immediately following the conducting period.

initialize 1. To set counters, switches, and addresses to zero or other starting values at the beginning of, or at prescribed points in, a computer routine. **2.** To begin an operation, and more specifically, to adjust the environment to the required starting configuration.

initial orders *See* initial instructions.

initial program load button *See* bootstrap button.

initiate *See* trigger.

injection 1. The method of applying a signal to an electronic circuit or device. **2.** The process of introducing electrons or holes into a semiconductor so that their total number exceeds the number present at thermal equilibrium.

injection efficiency A measure of the efficiency of a semiconductor junction when a forward bias is applied, equal to the current of injected minority carriers divided by the total current across the junction.

injection electroluminescence Radiation resulting from recombination of minority charge carriers injected in a *pn* or *pin* junction that is biased in the forward direction. Also known as Lossev effect; recombination electroluminescence.

injection grid Grid introduced into a vacuum tube in such a way that it exercises control over the electron stream without causing interaction between the screen grid and control grid.

injection locking The capture or synchronization of a free-running oscillator by a weak injected signal at a frequency close to the natural oscillator frequency or to one of its subharmonics; used for frequency stabilization in IMPATT or magnetron microwave oscillators, gas-laser oscillators, and many other types of oscillators.

injection luminescent diode Gallium arsenide diode, operating in either the laser or the noncoherent mode, that can be used as a visible or near-infrared light source for triggering such devices as light-activated switches.

injector An electrode through which charge carriers (holes or electrons) are forced to enter the high-field region in a spacistor.

ink bleed In character recognition, the capillary extension of ink beyond the original edges of a printed or handwritten character.

ink smudge In character recognition, the overflow of ink beyond the original edges of a printed or handwritten character.

ink squeezeout In character recognition, the overflow of ink from the stroke centerline to the edges of a printed or handwritten character.

in-line coding Any group of instructions within the main body of a program.

in-line guns An arrangement of three electron guns in a horizontal line; used in color picture tubes that have a slot mask in front of vertical color phosphor stripes.

in-line procedure A short body of coding or instruction which accomplishes some purpose.

in-line processing The processing of data in random order, not subject to preliminary editing or sorting.

in-line subroutine A subroutine which is an integral part of a program.

in-line tuning Method of tuning the intermediate-frequency strip of a superheterodyne receiver in which all the intermediate-frequency amplifier stages are made resonant to the same frequency.

in-phase rejection *See* common-mode rejection.

in-phase signal *See* common-mode signal.

input 1. The information that is delivered to a data-processing device from the external world, the process of delivering this data, or the equipment that performs this process. 2. The power or signal fed into an electrical or electronic device. 3. The terminals to which the power or signal is applied.

input area A section of internal storage reserved for storage of data or instructions received from an input unit such as cards or tape. Also known as input block; input section; input storage.

input block 1. A block of data read or transferred into a computer. 2. *See* input area.

input capacitance The short-circuited transfer capacitance that exists between the input terminals and all other terminals of an electron tube (except the output terminal) connected together.

input data Data employed as input.

input equipment 1. The equipment used for transferring data and instructions into an automatic data-processing system. 2. The equipment by which an operator transcribes original data and instructions to a medium that may be used in an automatic data-processing system.

input gap An interaction gap used to initiate a variation in an electron stream; in a velocity-modulated tube it is in the buncher resonator.

input-limited Pertaining to a system or operation whose speed or efficiency depends mainly on the speed of input into the machine rather than the speed of the machine itself.

input magazine A part of a card-handling device which supplies the cards to the processing portion of the machine. Also known as magazine.

input/output Pertaining to all equipment and activity that transfers information into or out of a computer. Abbreviated I/O.

input/output adapter A circuitry which allows input/output devices to be attached directly to the central processing unit.

input/output bound Pertaining to a system or condition in which the time for input and output operation exceeds other operations. Also known as input/output limited.

input/output buffer An area of a computer memory used to temporarily store data and instructions transferred into and out of a computer, permitting several such transfers to take place simultaneously with processing of data.

input/output channel The physical link connecting the computer to an input device or to an output device.

input/output controller An independent processor which provides the data paths between input and output devices and main memory.

input/output control system A set of flexible routines that supervise the input and output operations of a computer at the detailed machine-language level. Abbreviated IOCS.

input/output control unit The piece of hardware which controls the operation of one or more of a type of devices such as tape drives or disk drives; this unit is frequently an integral part of the input/output device itself.

input/output device A unit that accepts new data, sends it into the computer for processing, receives the results, and translates them into a usable medium.

input/output instruction An instruction in a computer program that causes transfer of data between peripheral devices and main memory, and enables the central processing unit to control the peripheral devices connected to it.

input/output interrupt A technique by which the central processor needs only initiate an input/output operation and then handle other matters, while other units within the system carry out the rest of the operation.

input/output interrupt identification The ascertainment of the device and channel taking part in the transfer of information into or out of a computer that causes a particular input/output interrupt, and of the status of the device and channel.

input/output interrupt indicator A device which registers an input/output interrupt associated with a particular input/output channel; it can be used in input/output interrupt identification.

input/output library A set of programs which take over the job from the programmer of creating the required instructions to access the various peripheral devices. Also known as input/output routines.

input/output limited See input/output bound.

input/output order A procedure of transferring data between main memory and peripheral devices which is assigned to and performed by an input/output controller.

input/output referencing The use of symbolic names in a computer program to indicate data on input/output devices, the actual devices allocated to the program being determined when the program is executed.

input/output register Computer register that provides the transfer of information from inputs to the central computer, or from it to output equipment.

input/output routines See input/output library.

input/output switching A technique in which a number of channels can connect input and output devices to a central processing unit; each device may be assigned to any available channel, so that several different channels may service a particular device during the execution of a program.

input/output traffic control The coordination, by both hardware and software facilities, of the actions of a central processing unit and the input, output, and storage devices under its control, in order to permit several input/output devices to operate simultaneously while the central processing unit is processing data.

input/output wedge The characteristic shape of a Kiviat graph of a system which is approaching complete input/output boundedness.

input record 1. A record that is read from an input device into a computer memory during the performance of a program or routine. 2. A record that has been stored in an input area and is ready to be processed.

input register A register that accepts input information from a computer at one speed and supplies the information to the central processing unit at another speed, usually much greater.

input resistance *See* transistor input resistance.

input resonator *See* bunching resonator.

input routine A routine which controls the loading and reading of programs, data, and other routines into a computer for storage or immediate use. Also known as loading routine.

input section 1. The part of a program which controls the reading of data into a computer memory from external devices. 2. *See* input area.

input station A terminal in an in-plant communications system at which data can be entered into the system directly as events take place, enabling files to be immediately updated.

input storage *See* input area.

inquiry A request for the retrieval of a particular item or set of items from storage.

inquiry and communications system A computer system in which centralized records are maintained with data transmitted to and from terminals at remote locations or in an in-plant system, and which immediately responds to inquiries from remote terminals.

inquiry and subscriber display An inquiry display unit that is distant from its computer and communicates with it over wire lines.

inquiry display terminal A cathode-ray-tube terminal which allows the user to query the computer through a keyboard, the answer appearing on the screen.

inquiry station A remote terminal from which an inquiry may be sent to a computer over wire lines.

inquiry unit Any terminal which enables a user to query a computer and get a hard-copy answer.

inscribe To rewrite data on a document in a form which can be read by an optical or magnetic ink character recognition machine.

insertion gain The ratio of the power delivered to a part of the system following insertion of an amplifier, to the power delivered to that same part before insertion of the amplifier; usually expressed in decibels.

insertion loss The loss in load power due to the insertion of a component or device at some point in a transmission system; generally expressed as the ratio in decibels of the power received at the load before insertion of the apparatus, to the power received at the load after insertion.

insertion switch Process by which information is inserted into the computer by an operator who manually operates switches.

installation processing control A system that automatically schedules the processing of jobs by a computer installation, in order to minimize waiting time and time taken to prepare equipment for operation.

installation tape number A number that is permanently assigned to a reel of magnetic tape to identify it.

instantaneous automatic gain control Portion of a radar system that automatically adjusts the gain of an amplifier for each pulse to obtain a substantially constant output-pulse peak amplitude with different input-pulse peak amplitudes; the circuit is fast enough to act during the time a pulse is passing through the amplifier.

instantaneous companding Companding in which the effective gain variations are made in response to instantaneous values of the signal wave.

instantaneous description For a Turing machine, the set of machine conditions at a given point in the computation, including the contents of the tape, the position of the read-write head on the tape, and the internal state of the machine.

instantaneous frequency-indicating receiver A radio receiver with a digital, cathode-ray, or other display that shows the frequency of a signal at the instant it is picked up anywhere in the band covered by the receiver.

instant-on switch A switch that applies a reduced filament voltage to all tubes in a television receiver continuously, so the picture appears almost instantaneously after the set is turned on.

instant replay *See* video replay.

instruction A pattern of digits which signifies to a computer that a particular operation is to be performed and which may also indicate the operands (or the locations of operands) to be operated on.

instruction address The address of the storage location in which a given instruction is stored.

instruction address register A special storage location, forming part of the program controller, in which addresses of instructions are stored in order to control their sequential retrieval from memory during the execution of a program.

instruction area A section of storage used for storing program instructions.

instruction code That part of an instruction which distinguishes it from all other instructions and specifies the action to be performed.

instruction constant A dummy instruction of the type K = 1, where K is irrelevant to the program.

instruction counter A counter that indicates the location of the next computer instruction to be interpreted. Also known as location counter; program counter; sequence counter.

instruction deck Set of cards punched to contain a symbolic coded program to be read into a computer.

instruction format Any rule which assigns various functions to the various digits of an instruction.

instruction length The number of bits or bytes (eight bits per byte) which defines an instruction.

instruction lookahead A technique for speeding up the process of fetching and decoding instructions in a computer program, and of computing addresses of required operands and fetching them, in which the control unit fetches any unexecuted instructions on hand, to the extent this is feasible. Also known as fetch ahead.

instruction modification A change, carried out by the program, in an instruction so that, upon being repeated, this instruction will perform a different operation.

instruction pointer 1. A component of a task descriptor that designates the next instruction to be executed by the task. 2. An element of the control component of the stack model of block structure execution, which points to the current instruction.

instruction register A hardware element that receives and holds an instruction as it is extracted from memory; the register either contains or is connected to circuits that interpret the instruction (or discover its meaning). Also known as current-instruction register.

instruction repertory *See* instruction set.

instruction set Also known as instruction repertory. 1. The set of instructions which a computing or data-processing system is capable of performing. 2. The set of instructions which an automatic coding system assembles.

instruction time The time required to carry out an instruction having a specified number of addresses in a particular computer.

instruction transfer An instruction which transfers control to one or another subprogram, depending upon the value of some operation.

instruction word A computer word containing an instruction rather than data. Also known as coding line.

instrumentation amplifier An amplifier that accepts a voltage signal as an input and produces a linearly scaled version of this signal at the output; it is a closed-loop fixed-gain amplifier, usually differential, and has high input impedance, low drift, and high common-mode rejection over a wide range of frequencies.

insulated-gate field-effect transistor *See* metal oxide semiconductor field-effect transistor.

insulated-substrate monolithic circuit Integrated circuit which may be either an all-diffused device or a compatible structure so constructed that the components within the silicon substrate are insulated from one another by a layer of silicon dioxide, instead of reverse-biased *pn* junctions used for isolation in other techniques.

insulator A substance in which the normal energy band is full and is separated from the first excitation band by a forbidden band that can be penetrated only by an electron having an energy of several electronvolts, sufficient to disrupt the substance.

integer constant A constant that uses the values 0, 1, ..., 9 with no decimal point in FORTRAN.

integer data type A scalar date type which is used to represent whole numbers, that is, values without fractional parts.

integer variable A variable in FORTRAN whose first character is normally I, J, K, L, M, or N.

integral discriminator A circuit which accepts only pulses greater than a certain minimum height.

integrated circuit An interconnected array of active and passive elements integrated with a single semiconductor substrate or deposited on the substrate by a continuous series of compatible processes, and capable of performing at least one complete electronic circuit function. Abbreviated IC. Also known as integrated semiconductor.

integrated-circuit capacitor A capacitor that can be produced in a silicon substrate by conventional semiconductor production processes.

integrated-circuit memory *See* semiconductor memory.

integrated-circuit resistor A resistor that can be produced in or on an integrated-circuit substrate as part of the manufacturing process.

integrated data processing Data processing that has been organized and carried out as a whole, so that intermediate outputs may serve as inputs for subsequent processing with no human copying required. Abbreviated IDP.

integrated data retrieval system A section of a data-processing system that provides facilities for simultaneous operation of several video-data interrogations in a single line and performs required communications with the rest of the system; it provides storage and retrieval of both data subsystems and files and standard formats for data representation.

integrated electronics A generic term for that portion of electronic art and technology in which the interdependence of material, device, circuit, and system-design consideration is especially significant; more specifically, that portion of the art dealing with integrated circuits.

integrated information processing System of computers and peripheral systems arranged and coordinated to work concurrently or independently on different problems at the same time.

integrated injection logic Integrated-circuit logic that uses a simple and compact bipolar transistor gate structure which makes possible large-scale integration on silicon for logic arrays, memories, watch circuits, and various other analog and digital applications. Abbreviated I^2L. Also known as merged-transistor logic.

integrated semiconductor *See* integrated circuit.

integrating amplifier An operational amplifier with a shunt capacitor such that mathematically the waveform at the output is the integral (usually over time) of the input.

integrating detector A frequency-modulation detector in which a frequency-modulated wave is converted to an intermediate-frequency pulse-rate modulated wave, from which the original modulating signal can be recovered by use of an integrator.

integrating filter A filter in which successive pulses of applied voltage cause cumulative buildup of charge and voltage on an output capacitor.

integrating network A circuit or network whose output waveform is the time integral of its input waveform. Also known as integrator.

integrator 1. A computer device that approximates the mathematical process of integration. 2. *See* integrating network.

integrity Property of data which can be recovered in the event of its destruction through failure of the recording medium, user carelessness, program malfunction, or other mishap.

intelligent terminal A computer input/output device with its own memory and logic circuits which can perform certain operations normally carried out by the computer. Also known as smart terminal.

intensifier electrode An electrode used to increase the velocity of electrons in a beam near the end of their trajectory, after deflection of the beam. Also known as postaccelerating electrode; postdeflection accelerating electrode.

intensifier image orthicon An image orthicon combined with an image intensifier that amplifies the electron stream originating at the photocathode before it strikes the target.

intensity control *See* brightness control.

intensity modulation Modulation of electron beam intensity in a cathode-ray tube in accordance with the magnitude of the received signal.

interaction space A region of an electron tube in which electrons interact with an alternating electromagnetic field.

interactive graphical input Information which is delivered to a computer by using hand-held devices, such as writing styli used with electronic tablets and light-pens used with cathode-ray tube displays, to sketch a problem description in an on-line inter-active mode in which the computer acts as a drafting assistant with unusual powers, such as converting rough freehand motions of a pen or stylus to accurate picture elements.

interactive information system An information system in which the user communicates with the computing facility through a terminal and receives rapid responses which can be used to prepare the next input.

interactive processing Computer processing in which the user can modify the operation appropriately while observing results at critical steps.

interactive terminal A computer terminal designed for two-way communication between operator and computer.

interbase current The current that flows from one base connection of a junction tetrode transistor to the other, through the base region.

interblock A device or system that prevents one part of a computing system from interfering with another.

interblock gap A space separating two blocks of data on a magnetic tape.

intercarrier noise suppression Means of suppressing the noise resulting from increased gain when a high-gain receiver with automatic volume control is tuned between stations; the suppression circuit automatically blocks the audio-frequency input of the receiver when no signal exists at the second detector. Also known as interstation noise suppression.

intercarrier sound system A television receiver arrangement in which the television picture carrier and the associated sound carrier are amplified together by the video intermediate-frequency amplifier and passed through the second detector, to give the conventional video signal plus a frequency-modulated sound signal whose center frequency is the 4.5 megahertz difference between the two carrier frequencies. Abbreviated ICS system.

intercycle A cycle of operation of a punched-card tabulator or other punched-card machine during which card feeding is stopped to permit calculation and printing of control totals or to effect a change in control.

interdigital magnetron Magnetron having axial anode segments around the cathode, alternate segments being connected together at one end, remaining segments connected together at the opposite end.

interdigital structure A structure in which the length of the region between two electrodes is increased by an interlocking-finger design for metallization of the electrodes. Also known as interdigitated structure.

interdigital transducer Two interlocking comb-shaped metallic patterns applied to a piezoelectric substrate such as quartz or lithium niobate, used for converting microwave voltages to surface acoustic waves, or vice versa.

interdigitated structure *See* interdigital structure.

interelectrode capacitance The capacitance between one electrode of an electron tube and the next electrode on the anode side. Also known as direct interelectrode capacitance.

interelectrode transit time   Time required for an electron to traverse the distance between the two electrodes.

interface **1.** Some form of electronic device that enables one piece of gear to communicate with or control another. **2.** A device linking two otherwise incompatible devices, such as an editing terminal of one manufacturer to typesetter of another.

interface control module   Relocatable modularized compiler allowing for efficient operation and easy maintenance.

interference analyzer   An instrument that discloses the frequency and amplitude of unwanted input.

interference blanker   Device that permits simultaneous operation of two or more pieces of radio or radar equipment without confusion of intelligence, or that suppresses undesired signals when used with a single receiver.

interference filter **1.** A filter used to attenuate artificial interference signals entering a receiver through its power line. **2.** A filter used to attenuate unwanted carrier-frequency signals in the tuned circuits of a receiver.

interference pattern   Pattern produced on a radarscope by interference signals.

interference prediction   Process of estimating the interference level of a particular equipment as a function of its future electromagnetic environment.

interference reduction   Reduction of interference from such causes as power lines and equipment, radio transmitters, and lightning, usually through the use of electric filters. Also known as interference suppression.

interference rejection   Use of a filter to reject (to bypass to ground) unwanted input.

interference source suppression   Techniques applied at or near the source to reduce its emission of undesired signals.

interference spectrum   Frequency distribution of the jamming interference in the propagation medium external to the receiver.

interference suppression   *See* interference reduction.

interferometer systems   Method of determining the position of a target in azimuth by using an interferometer to compare the phases of signals at the output terminals of a pair of antennas receiving a common signal from a distant source.

interfix   A technique for describing relationships of key words in an item or document in a way which prevents crosstalk from causing false retrievals when very specific entries are made.

interior label   A label attached to the data that it identifies.

interlace   To assign successive memory location numbers to physically separated locations on a storage tape or magnetic drum of a computer, usually to reduce access time.

interlaced scanning   A scanning process in which the distance from center to center of successively scanned lines is two or more times the nominal line width, so that adjacent lines belong to different fields. Also known as line interlace.

interlace operation   System of computer operation where data can be read out or copied into memory without interfering with the other activities of the computer.

interleave **1.** To alternate parts of one sequence with parts of one or more other sequences in a cyclic fashion such that each sequence retains its identity. **2.** To arrange the members of a sequence of memory addresses in different memory modules of a computer system, in order to reduce the time taken to access the sequence.

interlock **1.** A mechanism, implemented in hardware or software, to coordinate the activity of two or more processes within a computing system, and to ensure that one process has reached a suitable state such that the other may proceed. **2.** *See* deadlock.

interlude A small routine or program which is designed to carry out minor preliminary calculations or housekeeping operations before the main routine begins to operate, and which can usually be overwritten after it has performed its function.

intermediate control change A change of function that is of average or relatively moderate magnitude of importance such as the printing of intermediate totals by a punched-card tabulator, resulting from a change in intermediate control data between one card and the next.

intermediate control data Control data at a level which is neither the most nor the least significant, or which is used to sort records into groups that are neither the largest nor the smallest used; for example, if control data are used to specify state, town, and street, then the data specifying town would be intermediate control data.

intermediate frequency The frequency produced by combining the received signal with that of the local oscillator in a superheterodyne receiver. Abbreviated i-f.

intermediate-frequency amplifier The section of a superheterodyne receiver that amplifies signals after they have been converted to the fixed intermediate-frequency value by the frequency converter. Abbreviated i-f amplifier.

intermediate-frequency jamming Form of continuous wave jamming that is accomplished by transmitting two continuous wave signals separated by a frequency equal to the center frequency of the radar receiver intermediate-frequency amplifier.

intermediate-frequency response ratio In a superheterodyne receiver, the ratio of the intermediate-frequency signal input at the antenna to the desired signal input for identical outputs. Also known as intermediate-interference ratio.

intermediate-frequency signal A modulated or continuous wave signal whose frequency is the intermediate-frequency value of a superheterodyne receiver and is produced by frequency conversion before demodulation.

intermediate-frequency stage One of the stages in the intermediate-frequency amplifier of a superheterodyne receiver.

intermediate-frequency strip A receiver subassembly consisting of the intermediate-frequency amplifier stages, installed or replaced as a unit.

intermediate-frequency transformer The transformer used at the input and output of each intermediate-frequency amplifier stage in a superheterodyne receiver for coupling purposes and to provide selectivity. Abbreviated i-f transformer.

intermediate-interference ratio *See* intermediate-frequency response ratio.

intermediate memory storage An electronic device for holding working figures temporarily until needed and for releasing final figures to the output.

intermediate repeater Repeater for use in a trunk or line at a point other than an end.

intermediate result A quantity or value derived from an operation performed in the course of a program or subroutine which is itself used as an operand in further operations.

intermediate storage The portion of the computer storage facilities that usually stores information in the processing stage.

intermediate total A sum that is produced when there is a change in the value of control data at a level that is neither the most nor the least significant.

intermittent scanning Scans of an antenna beam at irregular intervals to increase difficulty of detection by intercept receivers.

intermodulation Modulation of the components of a complex wave by each other, producing new waves whose frequencies are equal to the sums and differences of integral multiples of the component frequencies of the original complex wave.

intermodulation distortion Nonlinear distortion characterized by the appearance of output frequencies equal to the sums and differences of integral multiples of the input frequency components; harmonic components also present in the output are usually not included as part of the intermodulation distortion.

intermodulation interference Interference that occurs when the signals from two undesired stations differ by exactly the intermediate-frequency value of a superheterodyne receiver, and both signals are able to pass through the preselector due to poor selectivity.

internal arithmetic Arithmetic operations carried out in a computer's arithmetic unit within the central processing unit.

internal cycle time The time required to change the information in a single register of a computer, usually a fraction of the cycle time of the main memory. Also known as clock time.

internally stored program A sequence of instructions, stored inside the computer in the same storage facilities as the computer data, as opposed to external storage on tape, disk, drum, or cards.

internal memory *See* internal storage.

internal photoelectric effect A process in which the absorption of a photon in a semiconductor results in the excitation of an electron from the valence band to the conduction band.

internal sorting The sorting of a list of items by a computer in which the entire list can be brought into the main computer memory and sorted in memory.

internal storage The total memory or storage that is accessible automatically to a computer without human intervention. Also known as internal memory.

internal storage capacity The quantity of data that can be retained simultaneously in internal storage.

interphase transformer Autotransformer or a set of mutually coupled reactors used in conjunction with three-phase rectifier transformers to modify current relations in the rectifier system to increase the number of anodes of different phase relations which carry current at any instant.

interpret To print on a punched card the infomation punched in that card.

interpreter 1. A program that translates and executes each source program statement before proceeding to the next one. Also known as interpretive routine. 2. A machine that senses a punched card and prints the punched information on that card. Also known as punched-card interpreter. 3. *See* conversational compiler.

interpretive code *See* interpretive language.

interpretive language A computer programming language in which each instruction is immediately translated and acted upon by the computer, as opposed to a compiler which decodes a whole program before a single instruction can be executed. Also known as interpretive code; pseudocode.

interpretive programming The writing of computer programs in an interpretive language, which generally uses mnemonic symbols to represent operations and operands and must be translated into machine language by the computer at the time the instructions are to be executed.

interpretive routine *See* interpreter.

interpretive trace program An interpretive routine that provides a record of the machine code into which the source program is translated and of the result of each step, or of selected steps, of the program.

interrecord gap *See* record gap.

interrogating typewriter A typewriter designed to insert data into a computer program in main memory or receive output from the program.

interrogator 1. A radar transmitter which sends out a pulse that triggers a transponder; usually combined in a single unit with a responsor, which receives the reply from a transponder and produces an output suitable for actuating a display of some navigational parameter. Also known as challenger; interrogator-transmitter. **2.** *See* interrogator-responsor.

interrogator-responsor A transmitter and receiver combined, used for sending out pulses to interrogate a radar beacon and for receiving and displaying the resulting replies. Also known as interrogator.

interrogator-transmitter *See* interrogator.

interrupt 1. To stop a running program in such a way that it can be resumed at a later time, and in the meanwhile permit some other action to be performed. **2.** The action of such a stoppage.

interrupt-driven system An operating system in which the interrupt system is the mechanism for reporting all changes in the states of hardware and software resources, and such changes are the events that induce new assignments of these resorces to meet work-load demands.

interrupt handling A computer system's accepting and storing interrupt requests and responding to the requests by calling appropriate programs.

interrupt mask A technique of suppressing certain interrupts and allowing the control program to handle these masked interrupts at a later time.

interrupt mode *See* hold mode.

interrupt signal A control signal which requests the immediate attention of the central processing unit.

interrupt system The means of interrupting a program and proceeding with it at a later time; this is accomplished by saving the contents of the program counter and other specific registers, storing them in reserved areas, starting the new instruction sequence, and upon completion, reloading the program counter and registers to return to the original program, and reenabling the interrupt.

interrupt trap A program-controlled technique which either recognizes or ignores an interrupt, depending upon a switch setting.

intersection data Data which are meaningful only when associated with the concatenation of two segments.

interstage punching A system of card punching in which only odd-numbered rows of the cards are used.

interstage transformer A transformer used to provide coupling between two stages.

interstation noise suppression *See* intercarrier noise suppression.

interstitial impurity An atom which is not normally found in a solid, and which is located at a position in the lattice structure where atoms or ions normally do not exist.

intersystem communications The ability of two or more computer systems to share input, output, and storage devices, and to send messages to each other by means of shared input and output channels or by channels that directly connect central processors.

interval arithmetic A method of numeric computation in which each variable is specified as lying within some closed interval, and each arithmetic operation computes an interval containing all values that can result from operating on any numbers selected from the intervals associated with the operands. Also known as range arithmetic.

intrinsic-barrier diode A *pin* diode, in which a thin region of intrinsic material separates the *p*-type region and the *n*-type region.

intrinsic-barrier transistor A *pnip* or *npin* transistor, in which a thin region of intrinsic material separates the base and collector.

intrinsic conductivity The conductivity of a semiconductor or metal in which impurities and structural defects are absent or have a very low concentration.

intrinsic layer A layer of semiconductor material whose properties are essentially those of the pure undoped material.

intrinsic mobility The mobility of the electrons in an intrinsic semiconductor.

intrinsic photoconductivity Photoconductivity associated with excitation of charge carriers across the band gap of a material.

intrinsic procedure *See* built-in function.

intrinsic semiconductor A semiconductor in which the concentration of charge carriers is characteristic of the material itself rather than of the content of impurities and structural defects of the crystal. Also known as *i*-type semiconductor.

intrinsic temperature range In a semiconductor, the temperature range in which its electrical properties are essentially not modified by impurities or imperfections within the crystal.

inverse current The current resulting from an inverse voltage in a contact rectifier.

inverse direction The direction in which the electron flow encounters greater resistance in a rectifier, going from the positive to the negative electrode; the opposite of the conducting direction. Also known as reverse direction.

inverse electrode current Current flowing through an electrode in the direction opposite to that for which the tube is designed.

inverse limiter A transducer, the output of which is constant for input of instantaneous values within a specified range and a linear or other prescribed function of the input for inputs above and below that range.

inverse peak voltage 1. The peak value of the voltage that exists across a rectifier tube or x-ray tube during the half cycle in which current does not flow. 2. The maximum instantaneous voltage value that a rectifier tube or x-ray tube can withstand in the inverse direction (with anode negative) without breaking down and becoming conductive.

inverse piezoelectric effect The contraction or expansion of a piezoelectric crystal under the influence of an electric field, as in crystal headphones; also occurs at *pn* junctions in some semiconductor materials.

inverse voltage The voltage that exists across a rectifier tube or x-ray tube during the half cycle in which the anode is negative and current does not normally flow.

inversion The production of a layer at the surface of a semiconductor which is of opposite type from that of the bulk of the semiconductor, usually as the result of an applied electric field.

inverted amplifier A two-tube amplifier in which the control grids are grounded and the input signal is applied between the cathodes; the grid then serves as a shield between the input and output circuits.

inverted file 1. A file, or method of file organization, in which labels indicating the locations of all documents of a given type are placed in a single record. 2. A file whose usual order has been inverted.

inverter *See* phase inverter.

inverter circuit *See* NOT circuit.

inverting amplifier Amplifier whose output polarity is reversed as compared to its input; such an amplifier obtains its negative feedback by a connection from output to input, and with high gain is widely used as an operational amplifier.

inverting function A logic device that inverts the input signal, so that the output is out of phase with the input.

inverting parametric device Parametric device whose operation depends essentially upon three frequencies, a harmonic of the pump frequency and two signal frequencies, of which the higher signal frequency is the difference between the pump harmonic and the lower signal frequency.

inverting terminal The negative input terminal of an operational amplifier; a positive-going voltage at the inverting terminal gives a negative-going output voltage.

I/O *See* input/output.

I/O-bound *See* peripheral-limited.

IOCS *See* input/output control system.

ion-beam scanning The process of analyzing the mass spectrum of an ion beam in a mass spectrometer either by changing the electric or magnetic fields of the mass spectrometer or by moving a probe.

ion burn *See* ion spot.

ion gage *See* ionization gage.

ion gun *See* ion source.

ionic conduction Electrical conduction of a solid due to the displacement of ions within the crystal lattice.

ionic focusing *See* gas focusing.

ionic-heated cathode Hot cathode heated primarily by ionic bombardment of the emitting surface.

ionic semiconductor A solid whose electrical conductivity is due primarily to the movement of ions rather than that of electrons and holes.

ionization current *See* gas current.

ionization density The density of ions in a gas.

ionization gage An instrument for measuring low gas densities by ionizing the gas and measuring the ion current. Also known as ion gage; ionization vacuum gage.

ionization source *See* ion source.

ionization time Of a gas tube, the time interval between the initiation of conditions for and the establishment of conduction at some stated value of tube voltage drop.

ionization vacuum gage *See* ionization gage.

ion microscope *See* field-ion microscope.

ionospheric recorder A radio device for determining the distribution of virtual height with frequency, and the critical frequencies of the various layers of the ionosphere.

ion pump A vacuum pump in which gas molecules are first ionized by electrons that have been generated by a high voltage and are spiraling in a high-intensity magnetic field, and the molecules are then attracted to a cathode, or propelled by electrodes into an auxiliary pump or an ion trap.

ion source A device in which gas ions are produced, focused, accelerated, and emitted as a narrow beam. Also known as ion gun; ionization source.

ion spot Of a cathode-ray tube screen, an area of localized deterioration of luminescence caused by bombardment with negative ions. Also known as ion burn.

ion trap 1. An arrangement whereby ions in the electron beam of a cathode-ray tube
are prevented from bombarding the screen and producing an ion spot, usually employing a magnet to bend the electron beam so that it passes through the tiny
aperture of the electron gun, while the heavier ions are less affected by the magnetic
field and are trapped inside the gun. 2. A metal electrode, usually of titanium, into
which ions in an ion pump are absorbed.

IPL Collective term for a series of list-processing languages developed principally by
Newell, Simon, and Shaw. Derived from Information Processing Language.

IPL button See bootstrap button.

IRG See record gap.

I scan See I scope.

I scope A cathode-ray scope on which a single signal appears as a circular segment
whose radius is proportional to the range and whose circular length is inversely
proportional to the error of aiming the antenna, true aim resulting in a complete
circle; the position of the arc, relative to the center, indicates the position of the
target relative to the beam axis. Also known as broken circle indicator; I indicator;
I scan.

I signal The in-phase component of the chrominance signal used in color television,
having a bandwidth of 0 to 1.5 megahertz, and consisting of $+0.74(R - Y)$ and
$-0.27(B - Y)$, where Y is the luminance signal, R is the red camera signal, and B
is the blue camera signal.

isobits Binary digits having the same value.

isograph An electronic calculator that ascertains both real and imaginary roots for
algebraic equations.

isolated camera 1. A television camera that views a particular portion of a scene of
action and produces a tape which can then be used either immediately for instant
replay or for video replay at a later time. 2. The technique of video replay involving
such a camera.

isolated location A location in a computer memory which is protected by some hardware device so that it cannot be addressed by a computer program and its contents
cannot be accidentally altered.

isolation The ability of a logic circuit having more than one input to ensure that each
input signal is not affected by any of the others.

isolation amplifier An amplifier used to minimize the effects of a following circuit on
the preceding circuit.

isolation diode A diode used in a circuit to allow signals to pass in only one direction.

isolator A passive attenuator in which the loss in one direction is much greater than
that in the opposite direction; a ferrite isolator for waveguides is an example.

isolith Integrated circuit of components formed on a single silicon slice, but with the
various components interconnected by beam leads and with circuit parts isolated by
removal of the silicon between them.

item A set of adjacent digits, bits, or characters which is treated as a unit and conveys
a single unit of information.

item advance A technique of efficiently grouping records to optimize the overlap of
read, write, and compute times.

item design The specification of what fields make up an item, the order in which the
fields are to be recorded, and the number of characters to be allocated to each field.

item size The length of an item expressed in characters, words, or blocks.

iteration process The process of repeating a sequence of instructions with minor modifications between successive repetitions.

iterations per second In computers, the number of approximations per second in iterative division; the number of times an operational cycle can be repeated in 1 second.

iterative array In a computer, an array of a large number of interconnected identical processing modules, used with appropriate driver and control circuits to permit a large number of simultaneous parallel operations.

iterative division In computers, a method of dividing by use of the operations of addition, subtraction, and multiplication; a quotient of specified precision is obtained by a series of successively better approximations.

iterative filter Four-terminal filter that provides iterative impedance.

iterative impedance Impedance that, when connected to one pair of terminals of a four-terminal transducer, will cause the same impedance to appear between the other two terminals.

iterative routine A computer program that obtains a result by carrying out a series of operations repetitiously until some specified condition is met.

i-type semiconductor *See* intrinsic semiconductor.

J

jam In punched-card equipment, a feed malfunction causing blockage of passages with crumpled cards.

jammer A transmitter used in jamming of radio or radar transmissions. Also known as electronic jammer.

jammer finder Radar which attempts to obtain the range of the target by training a highly directional pencil beam on a jamming source. Also known as burn-through.

jamming Radiation or reradiation of electromagnetic waves so as to impair the usefulness of a specific segment of the radio spectrum that is being used by the enemy for communication or radar. Also known as active jamming; electronic jamming.

J display A modified radarscope A display in which the time base is a circle; the target signal appears as an outward radial deflection from the time base.

JFET *See* junction field-effect transistor.

jitter Small, rapid variations in a waveform due to mechanical vibrations, fluctuations in supply voltages, control-system instability, and other causes.

J-K flip-flop A storage stage consisting only of transistors and resistors connected as flip-flops between input and output gates, and working with charge-storage transistors; gives a definite output even when both inputs are 1.

job A unit of work to be done by the computer; it is a single entity from the standpoint of computer installation management, but may consist of one or more job steps.

job class The set of jobs on a computer system whose resource requirements (for the central processing unit, memory, and peripheral devices) fall within specified ranges.

job control block A group of data containing the execution-control data and the job identification when the job is initiated as a unit of work to the operating system.

job control language *See* command language.

job control statement Any of the statements used to direct an operating system in its functioning, as contrasted to data, programs, or other information needed to process a job but not intended directly for the operating system itself. Also known as control statement.

job flow control Control over the order in which jobs are handled by a computer in order to use the central processing units and the units under the computer's control as efficiently as possible.

job library A partitioned data set, or a concatenation of partitioned data sets, used as the primary source of object programs (load modules) for a particular job, and more generally, as a source of runnable programs from which all or most of the programs for a given job will be selected.

job mix The distribution of the jobs handled by a computer system among the various job classes.

job-oriented terminal A terminal, such as a point-of-sale terminal, at which data taken directly from a source can enter a communication network directly.

job processing control The section of the control program responsible for initiating operations, assigning facilities, and proceeding from one job to the next.

job stacking The presentation of jobs to a computer system, each job followed by another.

job step A unit of work from the viewpoint of the user.

Johnson noise *See* thermal noise.

JOSS A time-sharing language, designed for concurrent use by a number of people, each at his own console typewriter, and for programs of moderate size and running time.

JOVIAL A procedure-oriented language derived from ALGOL, commonly used in programming command and control procedures.

J scan *See* J scope.

J scope A modification of an A scope in which the trace appears as a circular range scale near the circumference of the cathode-ray tube face, the signal appearing as a radial deflection of the range scale; no bearing indication is given. Also known as J indicator; J scan.

jump A transfer of control which terminates one sequence of instructions and begins another sequence at a different location. Also known as branch; change of control; transfer.

jumping trace routine A trace routine which is primarily concerned with providing a record of jump instructions in order to show the sequence of program steps that the computer followed.

junction A region of transition between two different semiconducting regions in a semiconductor device, such as a *pn* junction, or between a metal and a semiconductor.

junction capacitor An integrated-circuit capacitor that uses the capacitance of a reverse-biased *pn* junction.

junction diode A semiconductor diode in which the rectifying characteristics occur at an alloy, diffused, electrochemical, or grown junction between *n*-type and *p*-type semiconductor materials. Also known as junction rectifier.

junction field-effect transistor A field-effect transistor in which there is normally a channel of relatively low-conductivity semiconductor joining the source and drain, and this channel is reduced and eventually cut off by junction depletion regions, reducing the conductivity, when a voltage is applied between the gate electrodes. Abbreviated JFET. Also known as depletion-mode field-effect transistor.

junction isolation Electrical isolation of a component on an integrated circuit by surrounding it with a region of a conductivity type that forms a junction, and reverse-biasing the junction so it has extremely high resistance.

junction phenomena Phenomena which occur at the boundary between two semiconductor materials, or a semiconductor and a metal, such as the existence of an electrostatic potential in the absence of current flow, and large injection currents which may arise when external voltages are applied across the junction in one direction.

junction rectifier *See* junction diode.

junction station Microwave relay station that joins a microwave radio leg or legs to the main or through route.

junction transistor A transistor in which emitter and collector barriers are formed between semiconductor regions of opposite conductivity type.

justify To shift data so that they assume a particular position relative to one or more reference points, lines, or marks in a storage medium.

K

K *See* cathode.

Karnaugh map A truth table that has been rearranged to show a geometrical pattern of functional relationships for gating configurations; with this map, essential gating requirements can be recognized in their simplest form.

Karp circuit A slow-wave circuit used at millimeter wavelengths for backward-wave oscillators.

K band An optical absorption band which appears together with an F-band and has a lower intensity and shorter wavelength than the latter.

K display A modified radarscope A display in which a target appears as a pair of vertical deflections instead of as a single deflection; when the radar antenna is correctly pointed at the target in azimuth, the deflections are of equal height; when the antenna is not correctly pointed, the difference in pulse heights is an indication of direction and magnitude of azimuth pointing error.

keep-alive circuit A circuit used with a transmit-receive (TR) tube or anti-TR tube to produce residual ionization for the purpose of reducing the initiation time of the main discharge.

keep-alive electrode *See* ignitor.

key A data item that serves to uniquely identify a data record.

keyboard entry A piece of information fed manually into a computing system by means of a set of keys, such as a typewriter.

keyboard inquiry A question asked a computer concerning the status of a program being run, or concerning the value achieved by a specific variable, by means of a console typewriter.

keyboardless typesetter An automatic typesetting machine that has no keyboard and is operated by perforated tape at a speed of 12–15 lines per minute; the text is punched on tape at separate keyboard machines.

keyboard lockout An arrangement for preventing transmission from a particular keyboard while other transmissions are taking place on the same circuit.

keyboard printer A computer input device that includes a keyboard and a printer that prints the keyed-in data and often also prints computer output information.

keyboard send/receive A manual teleprinter that can transmit or receive. Abbreviated KSR. Also known as keyboard teleprinter.

keyboard teleprinter *See* keyboard send/receive.

key cabinet A case, installed on a customer's premises, to permit different lines to the control office to be connected to various telephone stations; it has signals to indicate originating calls and busy lines.

key change The occurrence, in a file of records which have been sorted according to their keys and are being read into a computer, of a record whose key differs from that of its immediate predecessor.

key compression A technique used to reduce the number of bits contained in a key.

key-disk machine A keyboard machine used to record data directly on a magnetic disk.

key-driven calculator A mechanical desk calculator in which numeric selection keys, arranged in columns, are coupled directly to accumulator dials on which the results are visible.

keyed clamp Clamping circuit in which the time of clamping is determined by a control signal.

keyed clamp circuit A clamp circuit in which the time of clamping is controlled by separate voltage or current sources, rather than by the signal itself. Also known as synchronous clamp circuit.

keyer Device which changes the output of a transmitter from one condition to another according to the intelligence to be transmitted.

keyer adapter Device which detects a modulated signal and produces the modulating frequency as a direct-current signal of varying amplitude.

key punch A keyboard-actuated device that punches holes in a card; it may be a hand-feed punch or an automatic feed punch.

keystoning Producing a keystone-shaped (wider at the top than at the bottom, or vice versa) scanning pattern because the electron beam in the television camera tube is at an angle with the principal axis of the tube.

keyswitch A switch that is operated by depressing a key on the keyboard of a data entry terminal.

key-to-disk system A data-entry system in which information entered on several keyboards is collected on different sections of a magnetic disk, and the data are extracted from the disk when complete, and are copied onto a magnetic tape or another disk for further processing on the main computer.

key-to-tape system A data-entry system consisting of several keyboards connected to a central controlling unit, typically a minicomputer, which collects information from each keyboard and then directs it to a magnetic tape.

key verify The use of a key punch verifier to ascertain that the data punched on a card corresponds to the data of the original document.

key-word-in-context index A computer-generated listing of titles of documents, produced on a line printer, with the key words lined up vertically in a fixed position within the title and arranged in alphabetical order. Abbreviated KWIC index.

key-word-out-of-context index A computer-generated listing of document titles with their keywords listed separately, arranged in the alphabetical order of the keywords. Abbreviated KWOC index.

killer circuit Vaccum tube or tubes and associated circuits in which are generated the blanking pulses used to temporarily disable a radar set.

killer pulse Blanking pulse generated by a killer circuit.

killer stage *See* color killer circuit.

kilovolts peak The peak voltage applied to an x-ray tube, expressed in kilovolts. Abbreviated kVp.

K indicator *See* K scope.

kinescope *See* picture tube.

Kiviat graph A circular diagram used in computer performance evaluation, in which variables are plotted on axes of the circle with 0% at the center of the circle and 100% at the circumference, and variables which are "good" and "bad" as they approach 100% are plotted on alternate axes.

Kleinschmidt printer A page printer capable of receiving ASCII (American Standard Code for Information Interchange) or Baudot code from transmission circuits exceeding 300 bits per second.

kludge A poorly designed data-processing system composed of ill-fitting mismatched components.

klystron An evacuated electron-beam tube in which an initial velocity modulation imparted to electrons in the beam results subsequently in density modulation of the beam; used as an amplifier in the microwave region or as an oscillator.

klystron generator Klystron tube used as a generator, with its second cavity or catcher directly feeding waves into a waveguide.

klystron oscillator *See* velocity-modulated oscillator.

klystron repeater Klystron tube operated as an amplifier and inserted directly in a waveguide in such a way that incoming waves velocity-modulate the electron stream emitted from a heated cathode; a second cavity converts the energy of the electron clusters into waves of the original type but of greatly increased amplitude and feeds them into the outgoing guide.

knock-on atom An atom which is knocked out of its equilibrium position in a crystal lattice by an energetic bombarding particle, and is displaced many atomic distances away into an interstitial position, leaving behind a vacant lattice site.

knot *See* deadlock.

K scan *See* K scope.

K scope A modified form of A scope on which one signal appears as two pips, the relative amplitudes of which indicate the error of aiming the antenna. Also known as K indicator; K scan.

KSR *See* keyboard send/receive.

kVp *See* kilovolts peak.

KWIC index *See* key-word-in-context index.

KWOC index *See* key-word-out-of-context index.

L

label A data item that serves to identify a data record (much in the same way as a key is used), or a symbolic name used in a program to mark the location of a particular instruction or routine.

label constant *See* location constant.

label data type A scalar data type that refers to locations in the computer program.

label record A tape record containing information concerning the file on that tape, such as format, record length, and block size.

labile oscillator An oscillator whose frequency is controlled from a remote location by wire or radio.

lace To punch all the holes in some area of a punch card, such as a card row or card column.

laced card A punched card in which several holes appear in all or nearly all of the card columns; it usually carries no information but is used for testing purposes or to indicate the end of a file of cards.

lacing Extra multiple punching in a card column to signify the end of a specific card run; the term is derived from the lacework appearance of the card.

ladder attenuator A type of ladder network designed to introduce a desired, adjustable loss when working between two resistive impedances, one of which has a shunt arm that may be connected to any of various switch points along the ladder.

ladder network A network composed of a sequence of H, L, T, or pi networks connected in tandem; chiefly used as an electric filter. Also known as series-shunt network.

laddic Multiaperture magnetic structure resembling a ladder, used to perform logic functions; operation is based on a flux change in the shortest available path when adjacent rungs of the ladder are initially magnetized with opposite polarity.

lag A persistence of the electric charge image in a camera tube for a small number of frames.

laminography *See* sectional radiography.

land *See* terminal area.

Langevin ion-mobility theories Two theories developed to calculate the mobility of ions in gases; the first assumes that atoms and ions interact through a hard-sphere collision and have a constant mean free path, while the second assumes that there is an attraction between atoms and ions arising from the polarization of the atom in the ion's field, in addition to hard-sphere repulsion for close distances of approach.

Langevin ion-recombination theory A theory predicting the rate of recombination of negative with positive ions in an ionized gas on the assumption that ions of opposite sign approach one another under the influence of mutual attraction, and that their relative velocities are determined by ion mobilities; applicable at high pressures, above 1 or 2 atmospheres.

Langmuir-Child equation *See* Child's law.

Langmuir dark space A nonluminous region surrounding a negatively charged probe inserted in the positive column of a glow discharge.

language The set of words and rules used to construct sentences with which to express and process information for handling by computers and associated equipment.

language converter A device which translates a form of data (such as that on microfilm) into another form of data (such as that on magnetic tape).

language translator 1. Any assembler or compiler that accepts human-readable statements and produces equivalent outputs in a form closer to machine language. **2.** A program designed to convert one computer language to equivalent statements in another computer language, perhaps to be executed on a different computer. **3.** A routine that performs or assists in the performance of natural language translations, such as Russian to English, or Chinese to Russian.

lap dissolve Changeover from one television scene to another so that the new picture appears gradually as the previous picture simultaneously disappears.

lapping Moving a quartz, semiconductor, or other crystal slab over a flat plate on which a liquid abrasive has been poured, to obtain a flat polished surface or to reduce the thickness a carefully controlled amount.

large-scale integrated circuit A very complex integrated circuit, which contains well over 100 interconnected individual devices, such as basic logic gates and transistors, placed on a single semiconductor chip. Abbreviated LSI circuit. Also known as chip circuit; multiple-function chip.

large-scale integrated memory *See* semiconductor memory.

LASCR *See* light-activated silicon controlled rectifier.

LASCS *See* light-activated silicon controlled switch.

laser amplifier A laser which is used to increase the output of another laser. Also known as light amplifier.

laser flash tube A high-power, air-cooled or water-cooled xenon flash tube designed to produce high-intensity flashes for pumping applications.

laser-holography storage A computer storage technology in which information is stored in microscopic spots burned in a holographic substrate by a laser beam, and is read by sensing a lower-energy laser beam that is transmitted through these spots.

laser memory A computer memory in which a controlled laser beam acts on individual and extremely small areas of a photosensitive or other type of surface, for storage and subsequent readout of digital data or other types of information.

laser radiation detector A photodetector that responds primarily to the coherent visible, infrared, or ultraviolet light of a laser beam.

laser threshold The minimum pumping energy required to initiate lasing action in a laser.

last-mask read-only memory A read-only memory in which the final mask used in the fabrication process determines the connections to the internal transistors, and these connections in turn determine the data pattern that will be read out when the cell is accessed. Also known as contact-mask read-only memory.

latency The waiting time between the order to read/write some information from/to a specified place and the beginning of the data–read/write operation.

lateral parity check The number f one bits counted across the width of the magnetic tape; this number plus a one or a zero must always be odd (or even), depending upon the manufacturer.

lattice filter An electric filter consisting of a lattice network whose branches have L-C parallel-resonant circuits shunted by quartz crystals.

lattice vibration A periodic oscillation of the atoms in a crystal lattice about their equilibrium positions.

lawnmower Type of radio-frequency preamplifier used with radar receivers.

Lawrence tube *See* chromatron.

layer capacitance *See* cathode interface capacitance.

layer impedance *See* cathode interface impedance.

layout character A control character that determines the form in which the output data generated by a printer or display device are arranged. Also known as format effector.

lazy evaluation *See* demand-driven execution.

LCD *See* liquid crystal display.

LC filter *See* inductive filter.

L display A radarscope display in which the target appears as two horizontal pulses or blips, one extending to the right and one to the left from a central vertical time base; when the radar antenna is correctly aimed in azimuth at the target, both blips are of equal amplitude; when not correctly aimed, the relative blip amplitudes indicate the pointing error; the position of the signal along the baseline indicates target distance; the display may be rotated 90° when used for elevation aiming instead of azimuth aiming.

leader A record which precedes a group of detail records, giving information about the group not present in the detail records; for example, "beginning of batch 17."

leader label A record appearing at the beginning of a magnetic tape to uniquely identify the tape as one required by the system.

lead-I-lead junction A Josephson junction consisting of two pieces of lead separated by a thin insulating barrier of lead oxide. Abbreviated Pb-I-Pb junction.

leading edge The edge of a punched card or document which enters a machine first.

leading end The end of a paper or magnetic tape that is read first, or has data entered on it first.

lead sulfide cell A cell used to detect infrared radiation; either its generated voltage or its change of resistance may be used as a measure of the intensity of the radiation.

leakage current The alternating current that passes through a rectifier without being rectified.

leapfrog test A computer test using a special program that performs a series of arithmetical or logical operations on one group of storage locations, transfers itself to another group, checks the correctness of the transfer, then begins the series of operations again; eventually, all storage positions will have been tested.

learning machine A machine that is capable of improving its future actions as a result of analysis and appraisal of past actions.

least significant bit The bit that carries the lowest value or weight in binary notation for a numeral; for example, when 13 is represented by binary 1101, the 1 at the right is the least significant bit. Abbreviated LSB.

least significant character The character in the rightmost position in a number or word.

LED *See* light-emitting diode.

left-justify To shift the contents of a register so that the left, or most significant, digit is at some specified position.

leg The sequence of instructions that is followed in a computer routine from one branch point to the next.

Lenard rays Cathode rays produced in air by a Lenard tube.

Lenard tube An early experimental electron-beam tube that had a thin glass or metallic foil window at the end opposite the cathode, through which the electron beam could pass into the atmosphere.

length block The total number of records, words, or characters contained in one block.

lens *See* electron lens.

letter code A Baudot code function which cancels errors by causing the receiving terminal to print nothing.

level 1. The status of a data item in COBOL language indicating whether this item includes additional items. 2. The difference between a quantity and an arbitrarily specified reference quantity, usually expressed as the logarithm of the ratio of the quantities. 3. A charge value that can be stored in a given storage element of a charge storage tube and distinguished in the output from other charge values. 4. *See* channel.

level compensator 1. Automatic transmission-regulating feature or device used to minimize the effects of variations in amplitude of the received signal. 2. Automatic gain control device used in the receiving equipment of a telegraph circuit.

level converter An amplifier that converts nonstandard positive or negative logic input voltages to standard DTL or other logic levels.

level shifting Changing the logic level at the interface between two different semiconductor logic systems.

lexicographic order *See* row order.

librarian The program which maintains and makes available all programs and routines composing the operating system.

library 1. A computerized facility containing a collection of organized information used for reference. 2. An organized collection of computer programs together with the associated program listings, documentation, users' directions, decks, and tapes.

library routine A computer program that is part of some program library.

library software The collection of programs and routines in the library of a computer system.

library tape A magnetic tape that is kept in a stored, indexed collection for ready use and is made generally available.

light-activated silicon controlled rectifier A silicon-controlled rectifier having a glass window for incident light that takes the place of, or adds to the action of, an electric gate current in providing switching action. Abbreviated LASCR. Also known as photo-SCR; photothyristor.

light-activated silicon controlled switch A semiconductor device that has four layers of silicon alternately doped with acceptor and donor impurities, but with all four of the p and n layers made accessible by terminals; when a light beam hits the active light-sensitive surface, the photons generate electron-hole pairs that make the device turn on; removal of light does not reverse the phenomenon; the switch can be turned off only by removing or reversing its positive bias. Abbreviated LASCS.

light amplifier 1. Any electronic device which, when actuated by a light image, reproduces a similar image of enhanced brightness, and which is capable of operating at very low light levels without introducing spurious brightness variations (noise) into the reproduced image. Also known as image intensifier. **2.** *See* laser amplifier.

light carrier injection A method of introducing the carrier in a facsimile system by periodic variation of the scanner light beam, the average amplitude of which is varied by the density changes of the subject copy. Also known as light modulation.

light chopper A rotating fan or other mechanical device used to interrupt a light beam that is aimed at a phototube, to permit alternating-current amplification of the phototube output and to make its output independent of strong, steady ambient illumination.

light-emitting diode A semiconductor diode that converts electric energy efficiently into spontaneous and noncoherent electromagnetic radiation at visible and near-infrared wavelengths by electroluminescence at a forward-biased *pn* junction. Abbreviated LED. Also known as solid-state lamp.

light-gating cathode-ray tube A cathode-ray tube in which the electron beam varies the transmission or reflection properties of a screen that is positioned in the beam of an external light source.

light gun A light pen mounted in a gun-type housing.

lighthouse tube *See* disk-seal tube.

light modulation *See* light carrier injection.

light modulator The combination of a source of light, an appropriate optical system, and a means for varying the resulting light beam to produce an optical sound track on motion picture film.

light-negative Having negative photoconductivity, hence decreasing in conductivity (increasing in resistance) under the action of light.

lightning recorder *See* sferics receiver.

light-operated switch A switch that is operated by a beam or pulse of light, such as a light-activated silicon controlled rectifier.

light panel *See* electroluminescent panel.

light pen A tiny photocell or photomultiplier, mounted with or without fiber or plastic light pipe in a pen-shaped housing; it is held against a cathode-ray screen to make measurements from the screen or to change the nature of the display.

light-positive Having positive photoconductivity; selenium ordinarily has this property.

light relay *See* photoelectric relay.

light-sensitive Having photoconductive, photoemissive, or photovoltaic characteristics. Also known as photosensitive.

light-sensitive cell *See* photodetector.

light-sensitive detector *See* photodetector.

light-sensitive tube *See* phototube.

light sensor photodevice *See* photodetector.

light stability In optical character recognition, the ability of an image to retain its spectral appearance when exposed to radiant energy.

light valve 1. A device whose light transmission can be made to vary in accordance with an externally applied electrical quantity, such as voltage, current, electric field, or magnetic field, or an electron beam. **2.** Any direct-view electronic display optimized for reflecting or transmitting an image with an independent collimated light source for projection purposes.

limited-access data Data to which only authorized users have access.

limited-entry decision table A decision table in which the condition stub specifies exactly the condition or the value of the variable.

limited integrator A device used in analog computers that has two input signals and one output signal whose value is proportional to the integral of one of the input signals with respect to the other as long as this output signal does not exceed specified limits.

limited signal Radar signal that is intentionally limited in amplitude by the dynamic range of the radar system.

limited space-charge accumulation diode *See* LSA diode.

limiter An electronic circuit used to prevent the amplitude of an electronic waveform from exceeding a specified level while preserving the shape of the waveform at amplitudes less than the specified level. Also known as amplitude limiter; amplitude-limiting circuit; automatic peak limiter; clipper; clipping circuit; limiter circuit; peak limiter.

limiter circuit *See* limiter.

limiting A desired or undesired amplitude-limiting action performed on a signal by a limiter. Also known as clipping.

limit priority An upper bound to the dispatching priority that a task can assign to itself or any of its subtasks.

limit ratio Ratio of peak value to limited value, or comparison of such ratios.

L indicator *See* L scope.

line 1. The path covered by the electron beam of a television picture tube in one sweep from left to right across the screen. 2. One horizontal scanning element in a facsimile system. 3. *See* trace.

linear amplifier An amplifier in which changes in output current are directly proportional to changes in applied input voltage.

linear bounded automaton A nondeterministic, one-tape Turing machine whose read/write head is confined to move only on a restricted section of tape initially containing the input.

linear collision cascade A sputtering event in which the bombarding projectile collides directly with a small number of target atoms, which collide with others, and the sharing of energy then proceeds through many generations before one or more target atoms are ejected; the density of atoms in motion remains sufficiently small so that collisions between atoms can be ignored.

linear comparator A comparator circuit which operates on continuous, or nondiscrete, waveforms. Also known as continuous comparator.

linear detection Detection in which the output voltage is substantially proportional, over the useful range of the detecting device, to the voltage of the input wave.

linear distortion Amplitude distortion in which the output signal envelope is not proportional to the input signal envelope and no alien frequencies are involved.

linear integrated circuit An integrated circuit that provides linear amplification of signals.

linearity control A cathode-ray-tube control which varies the distribution of scanning speed throughout the trace interval. Also known as distribution control.

linear-logarithmic intermediate-frequency amplifier Amplifier used to avoid overload or saturation as a protection against jamming in a radar receiver.

linearly graded junction A *pn* junction in which the impurity concentration does not change abruptly from donors to acceptors, but varies smoothly across the junction, and is a linear function of position.

linear magnetic amplifier A magnetic amplifier employing negative feedback to make its output load voltage a linear function of signal current.

linear-phase Pertaining to a filter or other network whose image phase constant is a linear function of frequency.

linear power amplifier A power amplifier in which the signal output voltage is directly proportional to the signal input voltage.

linear rectifier A rectifier, the output current of voltage of which contains a wave having a form identical with that of the envelope of an impressed signal wave.

linear repeater A repeater used in communication satellites to amplify input signals a fixed amount, generally with traveling-wave tubes or solid-state devices operating in their linear region.

linear sweep A cathode-ray sweep in which the beam moves at constant velocity from one side of the screen to the other, then suddenly snaps back to the starting side.

linear-sweep delay circuit A widely used form of linear time-delay circuit in which the input signal initiates action by a linear sawtooth generator, such as the bootstrap or Miller integrator, whose output is then compared with a calibrated direct-current reference voltage level.

linear-sweep generator An electronic circuit that provides a voltage or current that is a linear function of time; the waveform is usually recurrent at uniform periods of time.

linear time base A time base that makes the electron beam of a cathode-ray tube move at a constant speed along the horizontal time scale.

linear transducer A transducer for which the pertinent measures of all the waves concerned are linearly related.

linear unit An electronic device used in analog computers in which the change in output, due to any change in one of two or more input signals, is proportional to the change in that input and does not depend upon the values of the other inputs.

linear variable-differential transformer A transformer in which a diaphragm or other transducer sensing element moves an armature linearly inside the coils of a differential transformer, to change the output voltage by changing the inductances of the coils in equal but opposite amounts. Abbreviated LVDT.

line code The single instruction required to solve a specific type of problem on a special-purpose computer.

line-controlled blocking oscillator A circuit formed by combining a monostable blocking oscillator with an open-circuit transmission line in the regenerative circuit; it is capable of generating pulses with large amounts of power.

line dot matrix A line printer that uses the dot matrix printing technique. Also known as parallel dot character printer.

line driver An integrated circuit that acts as the interface between logic circuits and a two-wire transmission line.

line editor A text-editing system that stores a file of discrete lines of text to be printed out on the console (or displayed) and manipulated on a line-by-line basis, so that editing operations are limited and are specified for lines identified by a specific number.

line feed 1. Signal that causes a printer to feed the paper up a discrete number of lines. 2. Rate at which paper is fed through a printer.

line finder A device that automatically advances the platen of a line printer or typewriter.

line frequency The number of times per second that the scanning spot sweeps across the screen in a horizontal direction in a television system. Also known as horizontal frequency; horizontal line frequency.

line-frequency blanking pulse *See* horizontal blanking pulse.

line interlace *See* interlaced scanning.

line misregistration In character recognition, the improper appearance of a line of characters, on site in a character reader, with respect to a real or imaginary horizontal line.

line of code A single statement in a programming language.

line pad Pad inserted between a program amplifier and a transmission line, to isolate the amplifier from impedance variations of the line.

line printer A device that prints an entire line in a single operation, without necessarily printing one character at a time.

line printing The printing of an entire line of characters as a unit.

line pulsing Method of pulsing a transmitter in which an artificial line is charged over a relatively long period of time and then discharged through the transmitter tubes in a short interval determined by the line characteristic.

line skew In character recognition, a form of line misregistration, when the string of characters to be recognized appears in a uniformly slanted condition with respect to a real or imaginary baseline.

lines per minute A measure of the speed of the printer. Abbreviated LPM.

line-stabilized oscillator Oscillator in which a section of line is used as a sharply selective circuit element for the purpose of controlling the frequency.

line switching Connecting or disconnecting the line voltage from a piece of electronic equipment.

line synchronizing pulse *See* horizontal synchronizing pulse.

line transducer A special type of electret transducer consisting essentially of a coaxial cable with polarized dielectric, and with the center conductor and shield serving as electrodes; mechanical excitation resulting in a deformation of the shield at any point along the length of the cable produces an electrical output signal.

line unit Electric control device used to send, receive, and control the impulses of a teletypewriter.

linguistic model A method of automatic pattern recognition in which a class of patterns is defined as those patterns satisfying a certain set of relations among suitably defined primitive elements. Also known as syntactic model.

linkage In programming, coding that connects two separately coded routines.

linkage editor A service routine that converts the output of assemblers and compilers into a form that can be loaded and executed.

link field The first word of a message buffer, used to point to the next buffer on the message queue.

linking loader A loader which combines the functions of a relocating loader with the ability to combine a number of program segments that have been independently compiled into an executable program.

lin-log amplifier Automatic gain control amplifier that operates in a linear manner for low-amplitude input signals, but responds in a logarithmic manner to high-amplitude input signals.

LIOCS Set of routines handling buffering, blocking, label checking, and overlap of input/output with processing. Derived from logical input/output control system.

liquid crystal display A digital display that consists of two sheets of glass separated by a sealed-in, normally transparent, liquid crystal material; the outer surface of each glass sheet has a transparent conductive coating such as tin oxide or indium oxide, with the viewing-side coating etched into character-forming segments that have leads going to the edges of the display; a voltage applied between front and back electrode coatings disrupts the orderly arrangement of the molecules, darkening the liquid enough to form visible characters even though no light is generated. Abbreviated LCD.

liquid rheostat A variable-resistance type of voltage regulator in which the variable-resistance element is liquid, usually water; carbon electrodes are raised or lowered in the liquid to change resistance ratings and control voltage flow.

liquid semiconductor An amorphous material in solid or liquid state that possesses the properties of varying resistance induced by charge carrier injection.

LISP An interpretive language developed for the manipulation of symbolic strings of recursive data; can also be used to manipulate mathematical and arithmetic logic. Derived from list processing language.

list 1. A last-in, first-out storage organization, usually implemented by software, but sometimes implemented by hardware. 2. In FORTRAN, a set of data items to be read or written.

list processing A programming technique in which list structures are used to organize memory.

list processing language See LISP.

list structure A set of data items, connected together because each element contains the address of a successor element (and sometimes of a predecessor element).

literal operand An operand, usually occurring in a source language instruction, whose value is specified by a constant which appears in the instruction rather than by an address where a constant is stored.

lithium-drifted germanium crystal A high-resolution junction detector, used especially for more penetrating gamma-radiation and higher-energy electrons, produced by drifting lithium ions through a germanium crystal to produce an intrinsic region where impurity-based carrier generation centers are deactivated, sandwiched between a p layer and an n layer.

live chassis A radio, television, or other chassis that has a direct chassis connection to one side of the alternating-current line.

LLL circuit See low-level logic circuit.

L network A network composed of two branches in series, with the free ends connected to one pair of terminals; the junction point and one free end are connected to another pair of terminals.

load 1. To place data into an internal register under program control. 2. To place a program from external storage into central memory under operator (or program) control, particularly when loading the first program into an otherwise empty computer. 3. An instruction, or operator control button, which causes the computer to initiate the load action. **4.** The device that receives the useful signal output of an amplifier, oscillator, or other signal source.

load-and-go An operating technique with no stops between the loading and execution phases of a program; may include assembling or compiling.

load characteristic Relation between the instantaneous values of a pair of variables such as an electrode voltage and an electrode current, when all direct electrode supply voltages are maintained constant. Also known as dynamic characteristic.

load circuit Complete circuit required to transform power from a source such as an electron tube to a load.

load circuit efficiency Ratio between useful power delivered by the load circuit to the load and the load circuit power input.

loaded motional impedance *See* motional impedance.

loader A computer program that takes some other program from an input or storage device and places it in memory at some predetermined address.

load impedance The complex impedance presented to a transducer by its load.

loading program Program used to load other programs into computer memory. Also known as bootstrap program.

loading routine *See* input routine.

load line A straight line drawn across a series of tube or transistor characteristic curves to show how output signal current will change with input signal voltage when a specified load resistance is used.

load module A program in a form suitable for loading into memory and executing.

load point Preset point on a magnetic tape from which reading or writing will start.

lobe switching *See* beam switching.

local-area network A communications network connecting various hardware devices together within a building by means of a continuous cable or an in-house voice-data telephone system.

local battery telephone set Telephone set for which the transmitter current is supplied from a battery, or other current supply circuit, individual to the telephone set; the signaling current may be supplied from a local hand generator or from a centralized power source.

localization Imposing some physical order upon a set of objects, so that a given object has a greater probability of being in some particular regions of space than in others.

local oscillator The oscillator in a superheterodyne receiver, whose output is mixed with the incoming modulated radio-frequency carrier signal in the mixer to give the frequency conversions needed to produce the intermediate-frequency signal.

local oscillator injection Adjustment used to vary the magnitude of the local oscillator signal that is coupled into the mixer.

local oscillator radiation Radiation of the fundamental or harmonics of the local oscillator of a superheterodyne receiver.

local register One of a relatively small number (usually less than 32) of high-speed storage elements in a computer system which may be directly referred to by the instructions in the programs. Also known as general register.

local storage The collection of local registers in a computer system.

local variable A variable which can be accessed (used or changed) only in one block of a computer program.

locate mode A method of communicating with an input/output control system (IOCS), in which the address of the data involved, but not the data themselves, is transferred between the IOCS routine and the program.

location Any place in which data may be stored; usually expressed as a number.

location constant A number that identifies an instruction in a computer program, written in a higher-level programming language, and used to refer to this instruction at other points in the program. Also known as label constant.

location counter *See* instruction counter.

lock To fasten onto and automatically follow a target by means of a radar beam.

locked oscillator A sine-wave oscillator whose frequency can be locked by an external signal to the control frequency divided by an integer.

locked-oscillator detector A frequency-modulation detector in which a local oscillator follows, or is locked to, the input frequency; the phase difference between local oscillator and input signal is proportional to the frequency deviation, and an output voltage is generated proportional to the phase difference.

lock-in Shifting and automatic holding of one or both of the frequencies of two oscillating systems which are coupled together, so that the two frequencies have the ratio of two integral numbers.

lock-in amplifier An amplifier that uses some form of automatic synchronization with an external reference signal to detect and measure very weak electromagnetic radiation at radio or optical wavelengths in the presence of very high noise levels.

locking Controlling the frequency of an oscillator by means of an applied signal of constant frequency.

lock-on 1. The procedure wherein a target-seeking system (such as some types of radars) is continuously and automatically following a target in one or more coordinates (for example, range, bearing, elevation). 2. The instant at which radar begins to track a target automatically.

lockout 1. In computer communications, the inability of a remote terminal to achieve entry to a computer system until project programmer number, processing authority code, and password have been validated against computer-stored lists. 2. The precautions taken to ensure that two or more programs executing simultaneously in a computer system do not access the same data at the same time, make unauthorized changes in shared data, or otherwise interfere with each other.

lockout circuit A switching circuit which responds to concurrent inputs from a number of external circuits by responding to one, and only one, of these circuits at any time. Also known as finding circuit; hunting circuit.

log A record of computer operating runs, including tapes used, control settings, halts, and other pertinent data.

logarithmic amplifier An amplifier whose output signal is a logarithmic function of the input signal.

logarithmic diode A diode that has an accurate semilogarithmic relationship between current and voltage over wide and forward dynamic ranges.

logarithmic fast time constant Constant false alarm rate scheme which has a logarithmic intermediate-frequency amplifier followed by a fast time constant circuit.

logarithmic multiplier A multiplier in which each variable is applied to a logarithmic function generator, and the outputs are added together and applied to an exponential function generator, to obtain an output proportional to the product of two inputs.

logbook A bound volume in which operating data of a computer is noted.

logic 1. The basic principles and applications of truth tables, interconnections of on/off circuit elements, and other factors involved in mathematical computation in a computer. 2. General term for the various types of gates, flip-flops, and other on/off circuits used to perform problem-solving functions in a digital computer.

logical comparison The operation of comparing two items in a computer and producing a one output if they are equal or alike, and a zero output if not alike.

logical construction A simple logical property that determines the type of characters which a particular code represents; for example, the first two bits can tell whether a character is numeric or alphabetic.

logical data independence A data base structured so that changing the logical structure will not affect its accessibility by the program reading it.

logical data type A scalar data type in which a data item can have only one of two values: true or false. Also known as Boolean data type.

logical decision The ability to select one of many paths, depending upon intermediate programming data.

logical device table A table that is used to keep track of information pertaining to an input/output operation on a logical unit, and that contains such information as the symbolic name of the logical unit, the logical device type and the name of the file currently attached to it, the logical input/output request currently pending on the device, and a pointer to the buffers currently associated with the device.

logical expression Two arithmetic expressions connected by a relational operator indicating whether an expression is greater than, equal to, or less than the other, or connected by a logical variable, logical constant (true or false), or logical operator.

logical file A file as seen by the program accessing it.

logical flow chart A detailed graphic solution in terms of the logical operations required to solve a problem.

logical gate *See* switching gate.

logical input/output control system *See* LIOCS.

logical instruction A digital computer instruction which forms a logical combination (on a bit-by-bit basis) of its operands nd leaves the result in a known location.

logical record A group of adjacent, logically related data items.

logical shift A shift operation that treats the operand as a set of bits, not as a signed numeric value or character representation.

logical sum A computer addition in which the result is 1 when either one or both input variables is 1, and the result is 0 when the input variables are both 0.

logical symbol A graphical symbol used to represent a logic element.

logical unit An abstraction of an input/output device in the form of an additional name given to the device in a computer program.

logic-arithmetic unit *See* arithmetical unit.

logic card A small fiber chassis on which resistors, capacitors, transistors, magnetic cores, and diodes are mounted and interconnected in such a way as to perform some computer function; computers employing this type of construction may be repaired by removing the faulty card and replacing it with a new card.

logic circuit A computer circuit that provides the action of a logic function or logic operation.

logic design The design of a computer at the level which considers the operation of each functional block and the relationships between the functional blocks.

logic diagram A graphical representation of the logic design or a portion thereof; displays the existence of functional elements and the paths by which they interact with one another.

logic element A hardware circuit that performs a simple, predefined transformation on its input and presents the resulting signal as its output. Occasionally known as functor.

logic level One of the two voltages whose values have been arbitrarily chosen to represent the binary numbers 1 and 0 in a particular data-processing system.

logic operation A nonarithmetical operation in a computer, such as comparing, selecting, making references, matching, sorting, and merging, where logical yes-or-no quantities are involved.

logic operator A rule which assigns, to every combination of the values "true" and "false" among one or more independent variables, the value "true" or "false" to a dependent variable.

logic section *See* arithmetical unit.

logic swing The voltage difference between the logic levels used for 1 and 0; magnitude is chosen arbitrarily for a particular system and is usually well under 10 volts.

logic switch A diode matrix or other switching arrangement that is capable of directing an input signal to one of several outputs.

logic unit A separate unit which exists in some computer systems to carry out logic (as opposed to arithmetic) operations.

logic word A machine word which represents an arbitrary set of digitally encoded symbols.

log-on The procedure for users to identify themselves to a computer system for authorized access to their programs and information.

loktal base A special base for small vacuum tubes, so designed that it locks the tube firmly in a corresponding special eight-pin loktal socket; the tube pins are sealed directly into the glass envelope.

London equations Equations for the time derivative and the curl of the current in a superconductor in terms of the electric and magnetic field vectors respectively, derived in the London superconductivity theory.

London penetration depth A measure of the depth which electric and magnetic fields can penetrate beneath the surface of a superconductor from which they are otherwise excluded, according to the London superconductivity theory.

London superconductivity theory An extension of the two-fluid model of superconductivity, in which it is assumed that superfluid electrons behave as if the only force acting on them arises from applied electric fields, and that the curl of the superfluid current vanishes in the absence of a magnetic field.

longitudinal-made delay line A magnetostrictive delay in which signals are propagated by means of longitudinal vibrations in the magnetostrictive material.

long-line effect An effect occurring when an oscillator is coupled to a transmission line with a bad mismatch; two or more frequencies may then be equally suitable for oscillation, and the oscillator jumps from one of these frequencies to another as its load changes.

long-persistence screen A fluorescent screen containing phosphorescent compounds that increase the decay time, so a pattern may be seen for several seconds after it is produced by the electron beam.

long-tail pair A two-tube or transistor circuit that has a common resistor (tail resistor) which gives strong negative feedback.

lookahead A procedure in which a processor is preparing one instruction in a computer program while executing its predecessor.

look-through 1. When jamming, a technique whereby the jamming emission is interrupted irregularly for extremely short periods to allow monitoring of the victim signal during jamming operations. **2.** When being jammed, the technique of observing or monitoring a desired signal during interruptions in the jamming signal.

look-up An operation or process in which a table of stored values is scanned (or searched) until a value equal to (or sometimes, greater than) a specified value is found.

look-up table A stored matrix of data for reference purpose.

loop A sequence of computer instructions which are executed repeatedly, but usually with address modifications changing the operands of each iteration, until a terminating condition is satisfied.

loop body The set of statements to be performed iteratively with the range of a loop.

loop filter A low-pass filter, which may be a simple *RC* filter or may include an amplifier, and which passes the original modulating frequencies but removes the carrier-frequency components and harmonics from a frequency-modulated signal in a locked-oscillator detector.

loop gain Total usable power gain of a carrier terminal or two-wire repeater; maximum usable gain is determined by, and may not exceed, the losses in the closed path.

loop head The first instruction of a loop, which contains the mode of execution, induction variable, and indexing parameters.

loop stop A small closed loop that is entered to stop the progress of a computer program, usually when some condition occurs that requires intervention by the operator or that should be brought to the operator's attention. Also known as stop loop.

loose list A list, some of whose cells are empty and thus do not contain records of the file. Also known as thin list.

Lorentz gas A model of completely ionized gas in which ions are assumed to be stationary and interactions between electrons are neglected.

Lossev effect *See* injection electroluminescence.

loss modulation *See* absorption modulation.

loss of information *See* walk-down.

loudness analyzer An instrument that produces a cathode-ray display which shows the loudness of airborne sounds at a number of subdivisions of part or all of the audio spectrum.

lower curtate The lower or bottom part of a punch card; on a standard punch card, it contains the punch positions designated 1 through 9.

lower half-power frequency The frequency on an amplifier response curve which is smaller than the frequency for peak response and at which the output voltage is $1/\sqrt{2}$ of its midband or other reference value.

lower-sideband upconverter Parametric amplifier in which the frequency, power, impedance, and gain considerations are the same as for the nondegenerate amplifier; here, however, the output is taken at the difference frequency, or the lower sideband, rather than the signal-input frequency.

low-frequency compensation Compensation that serves to extend the frequency range of a broad-band amplifier to lower frequencies.

low-frequency cutoff A frequency below which the gain of a system or device decreases rapidly.

low-frequency gain The gain of the voltage amplifier at frequencies less than those frequencies at which this gain is close to its maximum value.

low-frequency padder In a superheterodyne receiver, a small adjustable capacitor connected in series with the oscillator tuning coil and adjusted during alignment to obtain correct calibration of the circuit at the low-frequency end of the tuning range.

low-frequency transconductance The change in the plate current of a vacuum tube divided by the change in the control-grid voltage that produces it, at frequencies small enough for these two quantities to be considered in phase.

low-frequency tube An electron tube operated at frequencies small enough so that the transit time of an electron between electrodes is much smaller than the period of oscillation of the voltage.

low-impedance measurement The measurement of an impedance which is small enough to necessitate use of indirect methods.

low-impedance switching tube A gas tube which has a static impedance on the order of 10,000 ohms, but zero or negative dynamic impedance, and therefore can be used as a relay and transmits information with negligible loss as well.

low level The less positive of the two logic levels or states in a digital logic system.

low-level language A computer language consisting of mnemonics that directly correspond to machine language instructions; for example, an assembler that converts the interpreted code of a higher-level language to machine language.

low-level logic circuit A modification of a diode-transistor logic circuit in which a resistor and capacitor in parallel are replaced by a diode, with the result that a relatively small voltage swing is required at the base of the transistor to switch it on or off. Abbreviated LLL circuit.

low-level modulation Modulation produced at a point in a system where the power level is low compared with the power level at the output of the system.

low-noise amplifier An amplifier having very low background noise when the desired signal is weak or absent; field-effect transistors are used in audio preamplifiers for this purpose.

low-noise preamplifier A low-noise amplifier placed in a system prior to the main amplifier, sometimes close to the source; used to establish a satisfactory noise figure at an early point in the system.

low-order Pertaining to the digit which contributes the smallest amount to the value of a numeral, or to its position, or to the rightmost position of a word.

low-Q filter A filter in which the energy dissipated in each cycle is a fairly large fraction of the energy stored in the filter.

LPM *See* lines per minute.

LSA diode A microwave diode in which a space charge is developed in the semiconductor by the applied electric field and is dissipated during each cycle before it builds up appreciably, thereby limiting transit time and increasing the maximum frequency of oscillation. Derived from limited space-charge accumulation diode.

LSB *See* least significant bit.

L scan *See* L scope.

L scope A cathode-ray scope on which a trace appears as a vertical or horizontal range scale, the signals appearing as left and right horizontal (or up and down vertical) deflections as echoes are received by two antennas, the left and right (or up and down) deflections being proportional to the strength of the echoes received by the two antennas. Also known as L indicator; L scan.

LSI circuit *See* large-scale integrated circuit.

Lukasiewicz notation *See* Polish notation.

luminescent cell *See* electroluminescent panel.

luminescent center A point-lattice defect in a transparent crystal that exhibits luminescence.

luminescent screen The screen in a cathode-ray tube, which becomes luminous when bombarded by an electron beam and maintains its luminosity for an appreciable time.

luminous sensitivity of phototube Quotient of the anode current by the incident luminous flux.

LVDT *See* linear variable-differential transformer.

MAC *See* message authentication code.

machinable *See* machine-sensible.

machine 1. A mechanical, electric, or electronic device, such as a computer, tabulator, sorter, or collator. **2.** A simplified, abstract model of an internally programmed computer, such as a Turing machine.

machine address The actual and unique internal designation of the location at which an instruction or datum is to be stored or from which it is to be retrieved.

machine available time The time during which a computer has its power turned on, is not undergoing maintenance, and is thought to be operating properly.

machine check A check that tests whether the parts of equipment are functioning properly. Also known as hardware check.

machine-check indicator A protective device which turns on when certain conditions arise within the computer; the computer can be programmed to stop or to run a separate correction routine or to ignore the condition.

machine code 1. A computer representation of a character, digit, or action command in internal form. **2.** A computer instruction in internal format, or that part of the instruction which identifies the action to be performed. **3.** The set of all instruction types that a particular computer can execute.

machine conditions A component of a task descriptor that specifies the contents of all programmable registers in the processor, such as arithmetic and index registers.

machine cycle 1. The shortest period of time at the end of which a series of events in the operation of a computer is repeated. **2.** The series of events itself.

machine error A deviation from correctness in computer-processed data, caused by equipment failure.

machine-independent Referring to programs and procedures which function in essentially the same manner regardless of the machine on which they are carried out.

machine instruction A set of digits, binary bits, or characters that a computer can recognize and act upon, and that, when interpreted or decoded, indicates the action to be performed and which operand is to be involved in the action.

machine instruction statement A statement consisting usually of a tag, an operating code, and one or more addresses.

machine interruption A halt in computer operations followed by the beginning of a diagnosis procedure, as a result of an error detection.

machine language The set of instructions available to a particular digital computer, and by extension the format of a computer program in its final form, capable of being executed by a computer.

machine language code A set of instructions appearing as combinations of binary digits.

machine learning The process or technique by which a device modifies its own behavior as the result of its past experience and performance.

machine logic The structure of a computer, the operation it performs, and the type and form of data used internally.

machine operator The person who manipulates the computer controls, brings up and closes down the computer, and can override a number of computer decisions.

machine-oriented programming system A system written in assembly language (or macro code) directly oriented toward the computer's internal language.

machine processible form Any input medium such as a punch card, paper tape, or magnetic tape.

machine-readable *See* machine-sensible.

machine-recognizable *See* machine-sensible.

machine run *See* run.

machine script Any data written in a form that can immediately be used by a computer.

machine-sensible Capable of being read or sensed by a device, usually by one designed and built specifically for this task. Also known as machinable; machine-readable; machine-recognizable; mechanized.

machine-sensible information Information in a form which can be read by a specified machine.

machine-spoiled time Computer time wasted on production runs that cannot be completed or whose results are made worthless by a computer malfunction, plus extensions of running time on runs that are hampered by a malfunction.

machine switching system *See* automatic exchange.

machine-tool control The computer control of a machine tool for a specific job by means of a special programming language.

machine translation *See* mechanical translation.

machine word The fundamental unit of information in a word-organized digital computer, consisting of a fixed number of binary bits, decimal digits, characters, or bytes.

macroassembler A program made up of one or more sequences of assembly language statements, each sequence represented by a symbolic name.

macroassembly program A set of assembly languages for the IBM 7090 and 7040 series of computers, and the assemblers for these languages; the assemblers operate under the IBSYS systems and prepare relocatable or absolute binary output in computer language. Abbreviated MAP.

macrocode A coding and programming language that assembles groups of computer instructions into single instructions.

macrodefinition A statement that defines a macroinstruction and the set of ordinary instructions which it replaces.

macro flow chart A graphical representation of the overall logic of a computer program in which entire segments or subroutines of the program are represented by single blocks and no attempt is made to specify the detailed operation of the program.

macrogeneration The creation of many machine instructions from one macroword.

macrogenerator *See* macroprocessor.

macroinstruction An instruction in a higher-level language which is equivalent to a specific set of one or more ordinary instructions in the same language.

macrolanguage A computer language that manipulates stored strings in which particular sites of the string are marked so that other strings can be inserted in these sites when the stored string is brought forth.

macrolibrary A collection of prewritten specialized but unparticularized routines (or sets of statements) which reside in mass storage.

macroparameter The character in a macro operand which will complete an open subroutine created by the macroinstruction.

macroprocessor A piece of software which replaces each macroinstruction in a computer program by the set of ordinary instructions which it stands for. Also known as macrogenerator.

macroprogramming The process of writing machine procedure statements in terms of macroinstructions.

macroskeleton A definition of a macroinstruction in a precise but content-free way, which can be particularized by a processor as directed by macroinstruction parameters. Also known as model.

macrosystem A language in which words represent a number of machine instructions.

madistor A cryogenic semiconductor device in which injection plasma can be steered or controlled by transverse magnetic fields, to give the action of a switch.

MADT *See* microalloy diffused transistor.

MAG *See* maximum available gain.

magamp *See* magnetic amplifier.

magazine 1. A holder of microfilm or magnetic recording media strips. 2. *See* input magazine.

magic eye *See* cathode-ray tuning indicator.

magnesium–copper sulfide rectifier Dry-disk rectifier consisting of magnesium in contact with copper sulfide.

magnetic amplifier A device that employs saturable reactors to modulate the flow of alternating-current electric power to a load in response to a lower-energy-level direct-current input signal. Abbreviated magamp. Also known as transductor.

magnetic bubble A cylindrical stable (nonvolatile) region of magnetization produced in a thin-film magnetic material by an external magnetic field; direction of magnetization is perpendicular to the plane of the material. Also known as bubble.

magnetic card A card with a magnetic surface on which data can be stored by selective magnetization.

magnetic card file A direct-access storage device in which units of data are stored on magnetic cards contained in one or more magazines from which they are withdrawn, when addressed, to be carried at high speed past a read/write head.

magnetic cell One unit of a magnetic memory, capable of storing one bit of information as a zero state or a one state.

magnetic character A character printed with magnetic ink, as on bank checks, for reading by machines as well as by humans.

magnetic character reader A character reader that reads special type fonts printed in magnetic ink, such as those used on bank checks, and feeds the character data directly to a computer for processing.

magnetic character sorter A device that reads documents printed with magnetic ink; all data read are stored, and records are sorted on any required field. Also known as magnetic document sorter-reader.

magnetic core A configuration of magnetic material, usually a mixture of iron oxide or ferrite particles mixed with a binding agent and formed into a tiny doughnutlike shape, that is placed in a spatial relationship to current-carrying conductors, and is used to maintain a magnetic polarization for the purpose of storing data, or for its nonlinear properties as a logic element. Also known as core; memory core.

magnetic core multiplexer A device which channels many bit inputs into a single output.

magnetic core storage A computer storage system in which each of thousands of magnetic cores stores one bit of information; current pulses are sent through wires threading through the cores to record or read out data. Also known as core memory; core storage.

magnetic Curie temperature The temperature below which a magnetic material exhibits ferromagnetism, and above which ferromagnetism is destroyed and the material is paramagnetic.

magnetic deflection Deflection of an electron beam by the action of a magnetic field, as in a television picture tube.

magnetic delay line Delay line, used for the storage of data in a computer, consisting essentially of a metallic medium along which the velocity of the propagation of magnetic energy is small compared to the speed of light; storage is accomplished by the recirculation of wave patterns containing information, usually in binary form.

magnetic disk storage *See* disk storage.

magnetic document sorter-reader *See* magnetic character sorter.

magnetic domain *See* ferromagnetic domain.

magnetic-domain memory *See* domain-tip memory.

magnetic drum *See* drum.

magnetic drum receiving equipment Radar developed for detection of targets beyond line of sight using ionospheric reflection and very low power.

magnetic drum storage *See* drum.

magnetic ferroelectric A substance which possesses both magnetic ordering and spontaneous electric polarization.

magnetic film *See* magnetic thin film.

magnetic firing circuit A type of firing circuit in which the capacitor is discharged through the igniter by saturating a reactor, which is connected in series with the capacitor; often used in ignitron rectifiers to obtain longer life and greater reliability than is possible with thyratron firing tubes.

magnetic head The electromagnet used for reading, recording, or erasing signals on a magnetic disk, drum, or tape. Also known as magnetic read/write head.

magnetic-ink character recognition That branch of character recognition which involves the sensing of magnetic-ink characters for the purpose of determining the character's most probable identity. Abbreviated MICR.

magnetic memory *See* magnetic storage.

magnetic-memory plate Magnetic memory consisting of a ferrite plate having a grid of small holes through which the read-in and read-out wires are threaded; printed wiring may be applied directly to the plate in place of conventionally threaded wires, permitting mass production of plates having a high storage capacity.

magnetic modulator A modulator in which a magnetic amplifier serves as the modulating element for impressing an intelligence signal on a carrier.

magnetic printing The permanent and usually undesired transfer of a recorded signal from one section of a magnetic recording medium to another when these sections are brought together, as on a reel of tape. Also known as crosstalk; magnetic transfer.

magnetic read/write head *See* magnetic head.

magnetic recorder An instrument that records information, generally in the form of audio-frequency or digital signals, on magnetic tape or magnetic wire as magnetic variations in the medium.

magnetic recording Recording by means of a signal-controlled magnetic field.

magnetic reproducer An instrument which moves a magnetic recording medium, such as a tape, wire, or disk, past an electromagnetic transducer that converts magnetic signals on the medium into electric signals.

magnetic reproducing The conversion of information on magnetic tape or magnetic wire, which was originally produced by electric signals, back into electric signals.

magnetic shift register A shift register in which the pattern of settings of a row of magnetic cores is shifted one step along the row by each new input pulse; diodes in the coupling loops between cores prevent backward flow of information.

magnetic storage A device utilizing magnetic properties of materials to store data; may be roughly divided into two categories, moving (drum, disk, tape) and static (core, thin film). Also known as magnetic memory.

magnetic striped ledger A ledger sheet used on a special typing device which stores the coded data on a magnetic strip on the sheet while typing out the data on the sheet; the magnetic strip can be read directly by a special reader linked to a computer.

magnetic tape A plastic, paper, or metal tape that is coated or impregnated with magnetizable iron oxide particles; used in magnetic recording.

magnetic tape core Toroidal core formed by winding a strip of thin magnetic-core material around a form.

magnetic tape file operation All the jobs related to creating, sorting, inputting, and maintenance of magnetic tapes in a magnetic tape environment.

magnetic tape group A cabinet containing two or more magnetic tape units, each of which can operate independently, but which sometimes share one or more channels with which they communicate with a central processor. Also known as tape cluster; tape group.

magnetic tape librarian Routine which provides a computer the means to automatically run a sequence of programs.

magnetic tape master file A magnetic tape consisting of a set of related elements such as is found in a payroll, an inventory, or an accounts receivable; a master file is, as a rule, periodically updated.

magnetic tape parity A check performed on the data bits on a tape; usually an odd (or even) condition is expected and the occurrence of the wrong parity indicates the presence of an error.

magnetic tape reader A computer device that is capable of reading information recorded on magnetic tape by transforming this information into electric pulses.

magnetic tape station On-line device that provides write, read, and erase data on magnetic tape to permit high-speed storage of data.

magnetic tape storage Storage of binary information on magnetic tape, generally on 5 to 10 tracks, with up to several thousand bits per inch (more than a thousand bits per centimeter) on each track.

magnetic tape switching unit A device which permits the computer operator to bring into play any number of tape drives as required by the system.

magnetic tape terminal Device which converts pulses in series to pulses in parallel while checking for bit parity prior to the entry in buffer storage.

magnetic tape unit A computer unit that usually consists of a tape transport, reading and recording heads, and associated electric and electronic equipment.

magnetic thin film A sheet or cylinder of magnetic material less than 5 micrometers thick, usually possessing uniaxial magnetic anisotropy; used mainly in computer storage and logic elements. Also known as ferromagnetic film; magnetic film.

magnetic transfer *See* magnetic printing.

magnetooptical switch A thin-film modulator which acts on a laser beam by polarization, causing the beam to emerge from the output prism at a different angle.

magnetoresistor Magnetic field–controlled variable resistor.

magnetostrictive filter Filter network which uses the magnetostrictive phenomena to form high-pass, low-pass, band-pass, or band-elimination filters; the impedance characteristic is the inverse of that of a crystal.

magnetostrictive oscillator An oscillator whose frequency is controlled by a magnetostrictive element.

magnetron One of a family of crossed-field microwave tubes, wherein electrons, generated from a heated cathode, move under the combined force of a radial electric field and an axial magnetic field in such a way as to produce microwave radiation in the frequency range 1–40 gigahertz; a pulsed microwave radiation source for radar, and continuous source for microwave cooking.

magnetron oscillator Oscillator circuit employing a magnetron tube.

magnetron pulling Frequency shift of a magnetron caused by factors which vary the standing waves or the standing-wave ratio on the radio-frequency lines.

magnetron pushing Frequency shift of a magnetron caused by faulty operation of the modulator.

magnetron vacuum gage A vacuum gage that is essentially a magnetron operated beyond cutoff in the vacuum being measured.

magnistor A device that utilizes the effects of magnetic fields on injection plasmas in semiconductors such as indium antimonide.

main bang Transmitted pulse, within a radar system.

main clock *See* master clock.

main frame *See* central processing unit.

main instruction buffer A section of storage in the instruction unit, 16 bytes in length, used to hold prefetched instructions.

main memory *See* main storage.

main path The principal branch of a routine followed by a computer in the process of carrying out the routine.

main program 1. The central part of a computer program, from which control may be transferred to various subroutines and to which control is eventually returned. Also known as main routine. 2. *See* executive routine.

main storage A digital computer's principal working storage, from which instructions can be executed or operands fetched for data manipulation. Also known as main memory.

main sweep On certain fire-control radar, the longest range scale available.

maintenance routine A computer program designed to detect conditions which may give rise to a computer malfunction in order to assist a service engineer in performing routine preventive maintenance.

major cycle The time interval between successive appearances of a given storage position in a serial-access computer storage.

majority carrier The type of carrier, that is, electron or hole, that constitutes more than half the carriers in a semiconductor.

majority element *See* majority gate.

majority emitter Of a transistor, an electrode from which a flow of minority carriers enters the interelectrode region.

majority gate A logic circuit which has one output and several inputs, and whose output is energized only if a majority of its inputs are energized. Also known as majority element; majority logic.

majority logic *See* majority gate.

major relay station Tape relay station which has two or more trunk circuits connected thereto to provide an alternate route or to meet command requirements.

malfunction routine A program used in troubleshooting.

manipulated variable Variable whose value is being altered to bring a change in some condition.

mantissa A fixed point number composed of the most significant digits of a given floating point number. Also known as fixed-point part; floating-point coefficient.

manual input The entry of data by hand into a device at the time of processing.

manual number generator *See* manual word generator.

manual operation Any processing operation performed by hand.

manual rate-aided tracking Radar circuit which tracks individual targets by computing the velocity from position fixes inserted manually into the circuitry.

manual switching Method by which manual connection is made between two or more teletypewriter circuits.

manual system A system involving data processing which does not make use of stored-program computing equipment; by this somewhat arbitrary definition, systems using other types of tabulating equipment, such as the card-programmed calculator, are considered to be manual.

manual telephone set Telephone set not equipped with a dial.

manual word generator A device into which an operator can enter a computer word by hand, either for direct insertion into memory or to be held until it is read during the execution of a program. Also known as manual number generator.

map 1. An output produced by an assembler, compiler, linkage editor, or relocatable loader which indicates the (absolute or relocatable) locations of such elements as programs, subroutines, variables, or arrays. **2.** By extension, an index of the storage allocation on a magnetic disk or drum.

MAP *See* macroassembly program.

marginal checking A preventive-maintenance procedure in which certain operating conditions, such as supply voltage or frequency, are varied about their normal values in order to detect and locate incipient defective units.

marginal test A test of electronic equipment in which conditions are varied until failures occur or faults can be detected, allowing measurement of permissible operating margins.

margin-punched card A card which is punched only along the edges, the remaining area being used for printed or written data.

mark A distinguishing feature used to signal some particular location or condition.

mark detection That class of character recognition systems which employs coded documents, in the form of boxes or windows, in order to convey intended information by means of pencil or ink marks made in specific boxes.

mark reading In character recognition, that form of mark detection which employs a photoelectric device to locate and convey intended information; the information appears as special marks on sites (windows) within the document coding area.

mark sensing In character recognition, that form of mark detection which depends on the conductivity of graphite pencil marks to locate and convey intended information; the information appears as special marks on sites (windows) within the document coding area.

mark-space multiplier A multiplier used in analog computers in which one input controls the mark-to-space ratio of a square wave while the other input controls the amplitude of the wave, and the output, obtained by a smoothing operation, is proportional to the average value of the signal. Also known as time-division multiplier.

mark-space ratio *See* mark-to-space ratio.

mark-to-space ratio The ratio of the duration of the positive-amplitude part of a square wave to that of the negative-amplitude part. Also known as mark-space ratio.

maser amplifier A maser which is used to increase the power produced by another maser.

mask 1. A pattern of characters used to control the retention or elimination of portions of another pattern of characters. Also known as extractor. 2. A thin sheet of metal or other material containing an open pattern, used to shield selected portions of a semiconductor or other surface during a deposition process.

masking 1. Replacing specific characters in one register by corresponding characters in another register. 2. Extracting certain characters from a string of characters. 3. Using a covering or coating on a semiconductor surface to provide a masked area for selective deposition or etching. 4. A programmed procedure for eliminating radar coverage in areas where such transmissions may be of use to the enemy for navigation purposes, by weakening the beam in appropriate directions or by use of additional transmitters on the same frequency at suitable sites to interfere with homing; also used to suppress the beam in areas where it would interfere with television reception.

mask matching In character recognition, a method employed in character property detection in which a correlation or match is attempted between a specimen character and each of a set of masks representing the characters to be recognized.

mask register Filter which determines the parts of a word which are to be tested.

mask word A word modifier used in a logical AND operation.

mass-data multiprocessing The basic concept of time sharing, with many inquiry stations to a central location capable of on-line data retrieval.

mass-memory unit Drum or disk memory that provides rapid access bulk storage for messages that are awaiting availability of outgoing channels.

mass storage A computer storage with large capacity, especially one whose contents are directly accessible to a computer's central processing unit.

mass-storage executive capability The ability of the executive to relieve operators from handling cards, tapes, and the like and achieve a more efficient operation.

mass-storage system A computer system containing a large number of storage devices, with one of these devices containing the master file of the operating system, routines, and library routines.

master card A computer card that contains information about a group of computer cards, and is usually the first card of this group.

master clock The electronic or electric source of standard timing signals, often called clock pulses, required for sequencing the operation of a computer. Also known as main clock; master synchronizer; master timer.

master control A computer program, oriented toward applications, which carries out the highest level of control in a hierarchy of programs, routines, and subroutines.

master control interrupt A signal which causes the master control program to take over control of a computer system.

master data A set of data which are rarely changed, or changed in a known and constant manner.

master file 1. A computer file containing relatively permanent information, usually updated periodically, such as subscriber records or payroll data other than time worked. 2. A computer file that is used as an authoritative source of data in carrying out a particular job on the computer.

master gain Control of overall gain of an amplifying system as opposed to varying the gain of several individual inputs.

master instruction tape A computer magnetic tape on which all programs for a system of runs are recorded.

master mode The mode of operation of a computer system exercised by the operating system or executive system, in which a privileged class of instructions, which user programs cannot execute, is permitted. Also known as monitor mode; privileged mode.

master multivibrator Master oscillator using a multivibrator unit.

master oscillator An oscillator that establishes the carrier frequency of the output of an amplifier or transmitter.

master-oscillator power amplifier Transmitter using an oscillator followed by one or more stages of radio-frequency amplification.

master plan position indicator In a radar system, a plan position indicator which controls remote indicators or repeaters.

master program file The tape record of all programs for a system of runs.

master record The basic updated record which will be used for the next run.

master routine *See* executive routine.

master/slave mode The feature ensuring the protection of each program when more than one program resides in memory.

master/slave system A system of interlinked computers under the control of one computer (master computer).

master synchronizer *See* master clock.

master system tape A monitor program centralizing the control of program operation by loading and executing any program on a system tape.

master tape A magnetic tape that contains data which must not be overwritten, such as an executive routine or master file; updating a master tape means generating a new master tape onto which supplementary data have been added.

master timer *See* master clock.

match A data-processing operation similar to a merge, except that instead of producing a sequence of items made up from the input sequences, the sequences are matched against each other on the basis of some key.

matched filter 1. In character recognition, a method employed in character property detection in which a vertical projection of the input character produces an analog waveform which is then compared to a set of stored waveforms for the purpose of determining the character's identity. 2. A filter with the property that, when the input consists of noise in addition to a specified desired signal, the signal-to-noise ratio is the maximum which can be obtained in any linear filter.

matched load A load having the impedance value that results in maximum absorption of energy from the signal source.

match gate *See* equivalence gate.

matching A computer problem-solving method in which the current situation is represented as a schema to be mapped into the desired situation by putting the two in correspondence.

mathematical check A programmed computer check of a sequence of operations, using the mathematical properties of that sequence.

mathematical function program A set of routinely used mathematical functions, such as square root, which are efficiently coded and called for by special symbols.

mathematical software The set of algorithms used in a computer system to solve general mathematical problems.

mathematical subroutine A computer subroutine in which a well-defined mathematical function, such as exponential, logarithm, or sine, relates the output to the input.

matrix 1. A latticework of input and output leads with logic elements connected at some of their intersections. 2. The section of a color television transmitter that transforms the red, green, and blue camera signals into color-difference signals and combines them with the chrominance subcarrier. Also known as color coder; color encoder; encoder. 3. The section of a color television receiver that transforms the color-difference signals into the red, green, and blue signals needed to drive the color picture tube. Also known as color decoder; decoder.

matrix algebra tableau The current matrix at the end of an iteration while running a linear program.

matrix printing High-speed printing in which characterlike configurations of dots are printed through the proper selection of wire ends from a matrix of wire ends. Also known as stylus printing; wire printing.

matrix storage A computer storage in which coordinates are used to address the locations or circuit elements. Also known as coordinate storage.

mavar *See* parametric amplifier.

maximum available gain The theoretical maximum power gain available in a transistor stage; it is seldom achieved in practical circuits because it can be approached only when feedback is negligible. Abbreviated MAG.

maximum average power output In television, the maximum of radio-frequency output power that can occur under any combination of signals transmitted, averaged over the longest repetitive modulation cycle.

maximum keying frequency In facsimile, the frequency in hertz that is numerically equal to the spot speed divided by twice the horizontal dimension of the spot.

maximum modulating frequency Highest picture frequency required for a facsimile transmission system; the maximum modulating frequency and the maximum keying frequency are not necessarily equal.

maximum operating frequency The highest rate at which the modules perform iteratively and reliably.

maximum retention time Maximum time between writing into and reading an acceptable output from a storage element of a charge storage tube.

maximum signal level In an amplitude-modulated facsimile system, the level corresponding to copy black or copy white, whichever has the highest amplitude.

maximum undistorted power output Of a transducer, the maximum power delivered under specified conditions with a total harmonic output not exceeding a specified percentage.

MBE *See* molecular beam epitaxy.

M center A color center consisting of an *F* center combined with two ion vacancies.

McNally tube Reflex klystron tube, the frequency of which may be electrically controlled over a wide range; used as a local oscillator.

M-derived filter A filter consisting of a series of T or pi sections whose impedances are matched at all frequencies, even though the sections may have different resonant frequencies.

M display A modified radarscope A display in which target distance is determined by moving an adjustable pedestal signal along the baseline until it coincides with the horizontal position of the target deflection.

Mealy machine A sequential machine in which the output depends on both the current state of the machine and the input.

mean carrier frequency Average carrier frequency of a transmitter corresponding to the resting frequency in a frequency-modulated system.

mean power of a radio transmitter Power supplied to the antenna transmission line by a transmitter during normal operation, averaged over a time sufficiently long compared with the period of the lowest frequency encountered in the modulation; a time of 1/10 second during which the mean power is greatest will be selected normally.

means-ends analysis A method of problem solving in which the difference between the form of the data in the present and desired situations is determined, and an operator is then found to transform from one into the other, or, if this is not possible, objects between the present and desired objects are created, and the same procedure is then repeated on each of the gaps between them.

mean time between failures A measure of the reliability of a computer system, equal to average operating time of equipment between failures, as calculated on a statistical basis from the known failure rates of various components of the system. Abbreviated MTBF.

mechanical analog computer A machine aid to computation in which variables are represented as continuously variable displacements or motions of mechanical elements, such as gears and shafts.

mechanical computer A machine such as Charles Babbage's analytical engine.

mechanical dialer *See* automatic dialer.

mechanical differential analyzer An analog computer using interconnected surfaces to solve differential equations, such as the device developed by Vannevar Bush at Massachusetts Institute of Technology.

mechanical filter Filter, used in intermediate-frequency amplifiers of highly selective superheterodyne receivers, consisting of shaped metal rods that act as coupled mechanical resonators when used with piezoelectric input and output transducers. Also known as mechanical wave filter.

mechanical integrator A mechanical device which draws the graph of the integral of a function when a tracing point is passed over a graph of the function.

mechanical jamming *See* passive jamming.

mechanical replacement The replacement of one piece of hardware by another piece of hardware at the instigation of the manufacturer.

mechanical scanner In optical character recognition, a device that projects an input character into a rotating disk, on the periphery of which is a series of small, uniformly spaced apertures; as the disk rotates, a photocell collects the light passing through the apertures.

mechanical tilt 1. Vertical tilt of the mechanical axis of a radar antenna. 2. The angle indicated by the tilt indicator dial.

mechanical translation Automatic translation of one language into another by means of a computer or other machine that contains a dictionary look-up in its memory, along with the programs needed to make logical choices from synonyms, supply missing words, and rearrange word order as required for the new language. Also known as machine translation.

mechanical wave filter *See* mechanical filter.

mechanized *See* machine-sensible.

media conversion The transfer of data from one storage type (such as punched cards) to another storage type (such as magnetic tape).

media conversion buffer Large storage area, such as a drum, on which data may be stored at low speed during nonexecution time, to be later transferred at high speed into core memory during execution time.

medical electronics A branch of electronics in which electronic instruments and equipment are used for such medical applications as diagnosis, therapy, research, anesthesia control, cardiac control, and surgery.

medium The material, or configuration thereof, on which data are recorded; usually not applied to disk, drum, or core, but to storable, removable media, such as paper tape, cards, and magnetic tape.

medium-frequency tube An electron tube operated at frequencies between 300 and 3000 kilohertz, at which the transit time of an electron between electrodes is much smaller than the period of oscillation of the voltage.

medium-scale integration Solid-state integrated circuits having more than about 12 gate-equivalent circuits. Abbreviated MSI.

megabit One million binary bits.

megatron *See* disk-seal tube.

Meissner effect The expulsion of magnetic flux from the interior of a piece of superconducting material as the material undergoes the transition to the superconducting phase. Also known as flux jumping; Meissner-Ochsenfeld effect.

Meissner-Ochsenfeld effect *See* Meissner effect.

Meissner oscillator Electron-tube oscillator in which the grid and plate circuits are inductively coupled through an independent tank circuit which determines the frequency.

melodeon Broadband panoramic receiver used for countermeasures reception; all types of received electromagnetic radiation are presented as vertical pips on a frequency-calibrated cathode-ray indicator screen.

meltback transistor A junction transistor in which the junction is made by melting a properly doped semiconductor and allowing it to solidify again.

memex A hypothetical machine described by Vannevar Bush, which would store written records so that they would be available almost instantly by merely pushing the right button for the information desired.

memory Any apparatus in which data may be stored and from which the same data may be retrieved; especially, the internal, high-speed, large-capacity working storage of a computer, as opposed to external devices. Also known as computer memory.

memory address register A special register containing the address of a word currently required.

memory bank A physical section of a computer memory, which may be designed to handle information transfers independently of other such transfers in other such sections.

memory buffer register A special register in which a word is stored as it is read from memory or just prior to being written into memory.

memory capacity *See* storage capacity.

memory cell A single storage element of a memory, together with associated circuits for storing and reading out one bit of information.

memory contention A situation in which two different programs, or two parts of a program, try to read items in the same block of memory at the same time.

memory core *See* magnetic core.

memory cycle *See* cycle time.

memory dump *See* storage dump.

memory dump routine A debugging routine which produces a listing of a consecutive section of memory, either numbers or instructions, at selected points in a program.

memory element Any component part of core memory.

memory fill *See* storage fill.

memory gap A gulf in access time, capacity, and cost of computer storage technologies between fast, expensive, main-storage devices and slow, high-capacity, inexpensive secondary-storage devices. Also known as access gap.

memory guard Built-in safety devices which prevent a program or a programmer from accessing certain memory areas reserved for the central processor. Also known as memory protect.

memory hierarchy A ranking of computer memory devices, with devices having the fastest access time at the top of the hierarchy, and devices with slower access times but larger capacity and lower cost at lower levels.

memory lockout register A special register containing the limiting addresses of an area in memory which may not be accessed by the program.

memory management 1. The allocation of computer storage in a multiprogramming system so as to maximize processing efficiency. 2. The collection of routines for placing, fetching, and removing pages or segments into or out of the main memory of a computer system.

memory map The list of variables, constants, identifiers, and their memory locations when a FORTRAN program is being run. Also known as memory map list.

memory map list *See* memory map.

memory overlay The efficient use of memory space by allowing for repeated use of the same areas of internal storage during the different stages of a program; for instance, when a subroutine is no longer required, another routine can replace all or part of it.

memory port A logical connection through which data are transferred in or out of main memory under control of the central processing unit.

memory power A relative characteristic pertaining to differences in access time speeds in different parts of memory; for instance, access time from the buffer may be a tenth of the access time from core.

memory print *See* storage dump.

memory printout A listing of the contents of memory.

memory protect *See* memory guard.

memory protection *See* storage protection.

memory-reference instruction A type of instruction usually requiring two machine cycles, one to fetch the instruction, the other to fetch the data at an address (part of the instruction itself) and to execute the instruction.

memory register *See* storage register.

memory search routine A debugging routine which has as an essential feature the scanning of memory in order to locate specified instructions.

memory-segmentation control Address-computing logic to address words in memory with dynamic allocation and protection of memory segments assigned to different users.

memory storage The sum total of the computer's storage facilities, that is, core, drum, disk, cards, and paper tape.

memory switch *See* ovonic memory switch.

memory tube *See* storage tube.

memotron An electrical-visual storage tube which is capable of bistable visual-signal display, controllable in duration from a few milliseconds to infinity, and which is suited to specialized oscillography.

menu A list of computer functions appearing on a video display terminal which indicates the possible operations that a computer can perform next, only one of which can be selected by the operator.

mercury arc An electric discharge through ionized mercury vapor, giving off a brilliant bluish-green light containing strong ultraviolet radiation.

mercury-arc rectifier A gas-filled rectifier tube in which the gas is mercury vapor; small sizes use a heated cathode, while larger sizes rated up to 8000 kilowatts and higher use a mercury-pool cathode. Also known as mercury rectifier; mercury-vapor rectifier.

mercury delay line An acoustic delay line in which mercury is the medium for sound transmission. Also known as mercury memory; mercury storage.

mercury lamp *See* mercury-vapor lamp.

mercury memory *See* mercury delay line.

mercury-pool cathode A cathode of a gas tube consisting of a pool of mercury; an arc spot on the pool emits electrons.

mercury-pool rectifier *See* pool-cathode mercury arc rectifier.

mercury rectifier *See* mercury-arc rectifier.

mercury storage *See* mercury delay line.

mercury tank A container of mercury, with pairs of transducers at opposite ends, used in a mercury delay line.

mercury tube *See* mercury-vapor tube; pool tube.

mercury-vapor lamp A lamp in which light is produced by an electric arc between two electrodes in an ionized mercury-vapor atmosphere; it gives off a bluish-green light rich in ultraviolet radiation. Also known as mercury lamp.

mercury-vapor rectifier *See* mercury-arc rectifier.

mercury-vapor tube A gas tube in which the active gas is mercury vapor. Also known as mercury tube.

merge To create an ordered set of data by combining properly the contents of two or more sets of data, each originally ordered in the same manner as the output data set. Also known as mesh.

merged-transistor logic *See* integrated injection logic.

merge search A procedure for searching a table in which both the table and file records must first be ordered in the same sequence on the key involved, and the table is searched sequentially until a table-record key equal to or greater than the file-record key is found, upon which the file record is processed if its key is equal, and the process is repeated with the next file record, starting at the table position where the previous search terminated.

merge sort To produce a single sequence of items ordered according to some rule, from two or more previously ordered or unordered sequences, without changing the items in size, structure, or total number; although more than one pass may be required for a complete sort, items are selected during each pass on the basis of the entire key.

merging routine A program that creates a single sequence of items, ordered according to some rule, out of two or more sequences of items, each sequence ordered according to the same rule.

merit A performance rating that governs the choice of a device for a particular application; it must be qualified to indicate type of rating, as in gain-bandwidth merit or signal-to-noise merit.

mesa device Any device produced by diffusing the surface of a germanium or silicon wafer and then etching down all but selected areas, which then appear as physical plateaus or mesas.

mesa diode A diode produced by diffusing the entire surface of a large germanium or silicon wafer and then delineating the individual diode areas by a photoresist-controlled etch that removes the entire diffused area except the island or mesa at each junction site.

mesa transistor A transistor in which a germanium or silicon wafer is etched down in steps so the base and emitter regions appear as physical plateaus above the collector region.

MESFET *See* metal semiconductor field-effect transistor.

mesh *See* merge.

message An arbitrary amount of information with beginning and end defined or implied: usually, it originates in one place and is intended to be transmitted to another place.

message authentication code The encrypted personal identification code appended to the message transmitted to a computer; the message is accepted only if the decrypted code is recognized as valid by the computer. Abbreviated MAC.

message buffer One of a number of sections of computer memory, which contains a message that can be transmitted between tasks in the computer system to request service and receive replies from tasks, and which is stored in a system buffer area, outside the address spaces of tasks.

message display console A cathode-ray tube on which is displayed information requested by the user.

message exchange A device which acts as a buffer between a communication line and a computer and carries out communication functions.

message queuing The stacking of messages according to some priority rule as the messages await processing.

meta character A character in a computer programming language system that has some controlling role with respect to other characters with which it may be associated.

metadyne A type of rotating magnetic amplifier having more than one brush per pole, used for voltage regulation or transformation.

metalanguage A set of symbols and words that syntactically describes another programming language (in which these words and symbols do not appear).

metal detector An electronic device for detecting concealed metal objects, such as guns, knives, or buried pipelines, generally by radiating a high-frequency electromagnetic field and detecting the change produced in that field by the ferrous or nonferrous metal object being sought. Also known as electronic locator; metal locator; radio metal locator.

metal halide lamp A discharge lamp in which metal halide salts are added to the contents of a discharge tube in which there is a high-pressure arc in mercury vapor; the added metals generate different wavelengths, to give substantially white light at an efficiency approximating that of high-pressure sodium lamps.

metal-insulator semiconductor Semiconductor construction in which an insulating layer, generally a fraction of a micrometer thick, is deposited on the semiconducting substrate before the pattern of metal contacts is applied. Abbreviated MIS.

metal-insulator transition The change of certain low-dimensional conductors from metals to insulators as the temperature is lowered through a certain value, due to the lattice distortion and band gap accompanying the onset of a charge-density wave.

metallic-disk rectifier *See* metallic rectifier.

metallic rectifier A rectifier consisting of one or more disks of metal under pressure-contact with semiconductor coatings or layers, such as a copper oxide, selenium, or silicon rectifier. Also known as contact rectifier; dry-disk rectifier; dry-plate rectifier; metallic-disk rectifier; semiconductor rectifier.

metal locator *See* metal detector.

metal-nitride-oxide semiconductor A semiconductor structure that has a double insulating layer; typically, a layer of silicon dioxide (SiO_2) is nearest the silicon substrate, with a layer of silicon nitride (Si_3N_4) over it. Abbreviated MNOS.

metal oxide semiconductor A metal insulator semiconductor structure in which the insulating layer is an oxide of the substrate material; for a silicon substrate, the insulating layer is silicon dioxide (SiO_2). Abbreviated MOS.

metal oxide semiconductor field-effect transistor A field-effect transistor having a gate that is insulated from the semiconductor substrate by a thin layer of silicon dioxide. Abbreviated MOSFET; MOST; MOS transistor. Formerly known as insulated-gate field-effect transistor.

metal oxide semiconductor integrated circuit An integrated circuit using metal oxide semiconductor transistors; it can have a higher density of equivalent parts than a bipolar integrated circuit.

metal semiconductor field-effect transistor A field-effect transistor that uses a thin film of gallium arsenide, with a Schottky barrier gate formed by depositing a layer of metal directly onto the surface of the film. Abbreviated MESFET.

metascope An infrared receiver used for converting pulsed invisible infrared rays into visible signals for communication purposes; also used with an infrared source for reading maps in darkness.

metavariable One of the elements of a formal language, corresponding to the parts of speech of a natural language. Also known as component name; phrase name.

MIC *See* microwave integrated circuit.

mickey-mouse To play with something new, such as hardware, software, or a system, until a feel is gotten for it and the proper operating procedure is discovered, understood, and mastered.

MICR *See* magnetic-ink character recognition.

micro *See* microcomputer.

microalloy diffused transistor A microalloy transistor in which the semiconductor wafer is first subjected to gaseous diffusion to produce a nonuniform base region. Abbreviated MADT.

microalloy transistor A transistor in which the emitter and collector electrodes are formed by etching depressions, then electroplating and alloying a thin film of the impurity metal to the semiconductor wafer, somewhat as in a surface-barrier transistor.

microbit A unit of information equal to one-millionth of a bit.

microcapacitor Any very small capacitor used in microelectronics, usually consisting of a thin film of dielectric material sandwiched between electrodes.

microchannel plate A plate that consists of extremely small cylinder-shaped electron multipliers mounted side by side, to provide image intensification factors as high as 100,000.

microcircuitry Electronic circuit structures that are orders of magnitude smaller and lighter than circuit structures produced by the most compact combinations of discrete components. Also known as microelectronic circuitry; microminiature circuitry.

microcode A code that employs microinstructions; not ordinarily used in programming.

microcomputer A microprocessor combined with input/output interface devices, some type of external memory, and the other elements required to form a working computer system; it is smaller, lower in cost, and usually slower than a minicomputer. Also known as micro.

microcomputer development system A complete microcomputer system that is used to test both the software and hardware of other microcomputer-based systems.

microcontroller A microcomputer, microprocessor, or other equipment used for precise process control in data handling, communication, and manufacturing.

microdiagnostic program A microprogram that tests a specific hardware component, such as a bus or store location, for faults.

microelectronic circuitry *See* microcircuitry.

microelectronics The technology of constructing circuits and devices in extremely small packages by various techniques. Also known as microminiaturization; microsystem electronics.

microelement Resistor, capacitor, transistor, diode, inductor, transformer, or other electronic element or combination of elements mounted on a ceramic wafer 0.025 centimeter thick and about 0.75 centimeter square; individual microelements are stacked, interconnected, and potted to form micromodules.

microinstruction The portion of a microprogram that specifies the operation of individual computing elements and such related subunits as the main memory and the input/output interfaces; usually includes a next-address field that eliminates the need for a program counter.

microlock 1. Satellite telemetry system that uses phase-lock techniques in the ground receiving equipment to achieve extreme sensitivity. **2.** A lock by a tracking station upon a minitrack radio transmitter. **3.** The system by which this lock is effected.

micromainframe A main frame of a computer placed on one or more integrated circuit chips.

micromini The central processing unit of a minicomputer placed on one of more integrated circuit chips.

microminiature circuitry *See* microcircuitry.

microminiaturization *See* microelectronics.

micromodule Cube-shaped, plug-in, miniature circuit composed of potted microelements; each microelement can consist of a resistor, capacitor, transistor, or other element, or a combination of elements.

microoperation Any clock-timed step of an operation.

microphonics Noise caused by mechanical vibration of the elements of an electron tube, component, or system. Also known as microphonism.

microphonism *See* microphonics.

microprocessing unit A microprocessor with its external memory, input/output interface devices, and buffer, clock, and driver circuits. Abbreviated MPU.

microprocessor A single silicon chip on which the arithmetic and logic functions of a computer are placed.

microprogram A computer program that consists only of basic elemental commands which directly control the operation of each functional element in a microprocessor.

microprogrammable instruction An instruction that does not refer to a core memory address and that can be microprogrammed, thus specifying various commands within one instruction.

microprogramming Transformation of a computer instruction into a sequence of elementary steps (microinstructions) by which the computer hardware carries out the instruction.

micropump *See* electroosmotic driver.

microradiometer A radiometer used for measuring weak radiant power, in which a thermopile is supported on and connected directly to the moving coil of a galvanometer. Also known as radiomicrometer.

microspec function The set of microinstructions which performs a specific operation in one or more machine cycles.

microsystem electronics *See* microelectronics.

microvoltmeter A voltmeter whose scale is calibrated to indicate voltage values in microvolts.

microwave amplifier A device which increases the power of microwave radiation.

microwave detector A device that can demonstrate the presence of a microwave by a specific effect that the wave produces, such as a bolometer, or a semiconductor crystal making a pinpoint contact with a tungsten wire.

microwave device Any device capable of generating, amplifying, modifying, detecting, or measuring microwaves, or voltages having microwave frequencies.

microwave generator *See* microwave oscillator.

microwave integrated circuit A microwave circuit that uses integrated-circuit production techniques involving such features as thin or thick films, substrates, dielectrics, conductors, resistors, and microstrip lines, to build passive assemblies on a dielectric. Abbreviated MIC.

microwave oscillator A type of electron tube or semiconductor device used for generating microwave radiation or voltage waveforms with microwave frequencies. Also known as microwave generator.

microwave radiometer *See* radiometer.

microwave receiver Complete equipment that is needed to convert modulated microwaves into useful information.

microwave solid-state device A semiconductor device for the generation or amplification of electromagnetic energy at microwave frequencies.

microwave tube A high-vacuum tube designed for operation in the frequency region from approximately 3000 to 300,000 megahertz.

middle-ultraviolet lamp A mercury-vapor lamp designed to produce radiation in the wavelength band from 2800 to 3200 angstrom units (280 to 320 nanometers) such as sunlamps and photochemical lamps.

mid-frequency gain The maximum gain of an amplifier, when this gain depends on the frequency; for an RC-coupled voltage amplifier the gain is essentially equal to this value over a large range of frequencies.

mid-square generator A procedure for generating a sequence of random numbers, in which a member of a sequence is squared and the middle digits of the resulting number form the next member of the sequence.

migration 1. Movement of frequently used data items to more accessible storage locations, and of infrequently used data items to less accessible locations. **2.** The movement of charges through a semiconductor material by diffusion or drift of charge carriers or ionized atoms. **3.** The movement of crystal defects through a semiconductor crystal under the influence of high temperature, strain, or a continuously applied electric field.

Miller bridge Type of bridge circuit for measuring amplification factors of vacuum tubes.

Miller code A code used internally in some computers, in which a binary 1 is represented by a transition in the middle of a bit (either up or down), and a binary 0 is represented by no transition following a binary 1; a transition between bits represents successive 0's; in this code, the longest period possible without a transition is two bit times.

Miller effect The increase in the effective grid-cathode capacitance of a vacuum tube due to the charge induced electrostatically on the grid by the anode through the grid-anode capacitance.

Miller generator *See* bootstrap integrator.

Miller integrator A resistor-capacitor charging network having a high-gain amplifier paralleling the capacitor; used to produce a linear time-base voltage. Also known as Miller time-base.

Miller time-base *See* Miller integrator.

Millikan meter An integrating ionization chamber in which a gold-leaf electroscope is charged a known amount and ionizing events reduce this charge, so that the resulting angle through which the gold leaf is repelled at any given time indicates the number of ionizing events that have occurred.

M indicator *See* M scope.

miniature electron tube A small electron tube having no base, with tube electrode leads projecting through the glass bottom in positions corresponding to those of pins for either a seven-pin or nine-pin tube base.

miniaturization Reduction in the size and weight of a system, package, or component by using small parts arranged for maximum utilization of space.

minicartridge A self-contained package of reel-to-reel magnetic tape that resembles a cassette or cartridge but is slightly different in design and dimensions.

minicomputer A small computer which in its basic configuration has at least 4096 words of memory, and employs words between 8 and 16 bits in length.

minimal latency coding *See* minimum-access coding.

minimum-access coding Coding in such a way that a minimum time is required to transfer words to and from storage, for a computer in which this time depends on the location in storage. Also known as minimal-latency coding; minimum-delay coding; minimum-latency coding.

minimum-access programming The programming of a digital computer in such a way that minimum waiting time is required to obtain information out of the memory. Also known as forced programming; minimum-latency programming.

minimum-access routine *See* minimum-latency routine.

minimum-delay coding *See* minimum-access coding.

minimum discernible signal Receiver input power level that is just sufficient to produce a discernible signal in the receiver output; a receiver sensitivity test.

minimum-latency coding *See* minimum-access coding.

minimum-latency programming *See* minimum-access programming.

minimum-latency routine A computer routine that is constructed so that the latency in serial-access storage is less than the random latency that would be expected if storage locations were chosen without regard for latency. Also known as minimum-access routine.

minimum-loss attenuator A section linking two unequal resistive impedances which is designed to introduce the smallest attenuation possible. Also known as minimum-loss pad.

minimum-loss matching Design of a network linking two resistive impedances so that it introduces a loss which is as small as possible.

minimum-loss pad *See* minimum-loss attenuator.

minimum signal level In facsimile, level corresponding to the copy white or copy black signal, whichever is the lower.

minitrack A subminiature radio transmitter capable of sending data over 4000 miles (6500 kilometers) on extremely low power.

minor control change A change of function that is of relatively small magnitude or importance, resulting from a difference in minor control data between one card and the next.

minor control data Control data which are at the least significant level used, or which are used to sort records into the smallest groups used; for example, if control data are used to specify state, town, and street, then the data specifying street would be minor control data.

minor cycle The time required for the transmission or transfer of one machine word, including the space between words, in a digital computer using serial transmission. Also known as word time.

minority carrier The type of carrier, electron, or hole that constitutes less than half the total number of carriers in a semiconductor.

minority emitter Of a transistor, an electrode from which a flow of minority carriers enters the interelectrode region.

minor relay station A tape relay station which has tape relay responsibility but does not provide an alternate route.

minus zone The bit positions in a computer code that represent the algebraic minus sign.

MIS *See* metal-insulator semiconductor.

misfire Failure to establish an arc between the main anode and the cathode of an ignitron or other mercury-arc rectifier during a scheduled conducting period.

mismatch loss Loss of power delivered to a load as a result of failure to make an impedance match of a transmission line with its load or with its source.

misregistration In character recognition, the improper state of appearance of a character, line, or document, on site in a character reader, with respect to a real or imaginary horizontal baseline.

missing error The result of calling for a subroutine not available in the library.

mistake A human action producing an unintended result, in contrast to an error in a computer operation.

mixed congruential generator A congruential generator in which the constant *b* in the generating formula is not equal to zero.

mixed-entry decision table A decision table in which the action entries may be either sequenced or unsequenced.

mixed-mode expression An expression involving operands of more than one data type.

mixer 1. A device having two or more inputs, usually adjustable, and a common output; used to combine separate audio or video signals linearly in desired proportions to produce an output signal. **2.** The stage in a superheterodyne receiver in which the incoming modulated radio-frequency signal is combined with the signal of a local r-f oscillator to produce a modulated intermediate-frequency signal. Also known as first detector; heterodyne modulator; mixer-first detector.

mixer-first detector *See* mixer.

mixer tube A multigrid electron tube, used in a superheterodyne receiver, in which control voltages of different frequencies are impressed upon different control grids, and the nonlinear properties of the tube cause the generation of new frequencies equal to the sum and difference of the impressed frequencies.

mixing Combining two or more signals, such as the outputs of several microphones.

mnemonic code A programming code that is easy to remember because the codes resemble the original words, such as MPY for multiply and ACC for accumulator.

MNOS *See* metal-nitride-oxide semiconductor.

mobile digital computer Large, mobile, fixed-point operation, one-address, parallel-mode type digital computer.

mobile systems equipment Computers located on planes, ships, or vans.

mobility *See* drift mobility.

mode One of several alternative conditions or methods of operation of a device.

mode converter *See* mode transducer.

mode jump Change in mode of magnetron operation from one pulse to the next; each mode represents a different frequency and power level.

model *See* macroskeleton.

model symbol The standard usage of geometrical figures, such as squares, circles, or triangles, to help illustrate the various working parts of a model: each symbol must, nevertheless, be footnoted for complete clarification.

modem A combination modulator and demodulator at each end of a telephone line to convert binary digital information to audio tone signals suitable for transmission over the line, and vice versa. Also known as dataset. Derived from modulator-demodulator.

mode number 1. The number of complete cycles during which an electron of average speed is in the drift space of a reflex klystron. 2. The number of radians of phase in the microwave field of a magnetron divided by 2π as one goes once around the anode.

mode shift Change in mode of magnetron operation during a pulse.

mode skip Failure of a magnetron to fire on each successive pulse.

mode switch 1. A preset control which affects the normal response of various components of a mechanical desk calculator. 2. A microwave control device, often consisting of a waveguide section of special cross section, which is used to change the mode of microwave power transmission in the waveguide.

mode transducer Device for transforming an electromagnetic wave from one mode of propagation to another. Also known as mode converter; mode transformer.

mode transformer *See* mode transducer.

modifier A quantity used to alter the address of an operand in a computer, such as the cycle index. Also known as index word.

modifier register *See* index register.

modify 1. To alter a portion of an instruction so its interpretation and execution will be other than normal; the modification may permanently change the instruction or leave it unchanged and affect only the current execution; the most frequent modification is that of the effective address through the use of index registers. 2. To alter a subroutine according to a defined parameter.

moding Defect of magnetron oscillation in which it oscillates in one or more undesired modes.

modular circuit Any type of circuit assembled to form rectangular or cubical blocks that perform one or more complete circuit functions.

modularity The property of functional flexibility built into a computer system by assembling discrete units which can be easily joined to or arranged with other parts or units.

modular programming The construction of a computer program from a collection of modules, each of workable size, whose interactions are rigidly restricted.

modular structure 1. An assembly involving the use of integral multiples of a given length for the dimensions of electronic components and electronic equipment, as well as for spacings of holes in a chassis or printed wiring board. 2. An assembly made from modules.

modulate To vary the amplitude, frequency, or phase of a wave, or vary the velocity of the electrons in an electron beam in some characteristic manner.

modulated amplifier Amplifier stage in a transmitter in which the modulating signal is introduced and modulates the carrier.

modulated stage Radio-frequency stage to which the modulator is coupled and in which the continuous wave (carrier wave) is modulated according to the system of modulation and the characteristics of the modulating wave.

modulating electrode Electrode to which a potential is applied to control the magnitude of the beam current.

modulation capability Of an aural transmitter, the maximum percentage modulation that can be obtained without exceeding a given distortion figure.

modulation-doped structure An epitaxially grown crystal structure in which successive semiconductor layers contain different types of electrical dopants.

modulation rise Increase of the modulation percentage caused by nonlinearity of any tuned amplifier, usually the last intermediate-frequency stage of a receiver.

modulator 1. The transmitter stage that supplies the modulating signal to the modulated amplifier stage or that triggers the modulated amplifier stage to produce pulses at desired instants as in radar. **2.** A device that produces modulation by any means, such as by virtue of a nonlinear characteristic or by controlling some circuit quantity in accordance with the waveform of a modulating signal. **3.** One of the electrodes of a spacistor.

modulator-demodulator *See* modem.

modulator glow tube Cold cathode recorder tube that is used for facsimile and sound-on-film recording; provides a modulated high-intensity point source of light.

module 1. A distinct and identifiable unit of computer program for such purposes as compiling, loading, and linkage editing. **2.** One memory bank and associated electronics in a computer. **3.** A packaged assembly of wired components, built in a standardized size and having standardized plug-in or solderable terminations.

modulo N check A procedure for verification of the accuracy of a computation by repeating the steps in modulo N arithmetic and comparing the result with the original result (modulo N). Also known as residue check.

modulo-two adder A logical circuit for adding one-digit binary numbers.

molectronics *See* molecular electronics.

molecular beam epitaxy A technique of growing single crystals in which beams of atoms or molecules are made to strike a single-crystalline substrate in a vacuum, giving rise to crystals whose crystallographic orientation is related to that of the substrate. Abbreviated MBE.

molecular circuit A circuit in which the individual components are physically indistinguishable from each other.

molecular electronics The branch of electronics that deals with the production of complex electronic circuits in microminiature form by producing semiconductor devices and circuit elements integrally while growing multizoned crystals in a furnace. Also known as molectronics.

molecular engineering The use of solid-state techniques to build, in extremely small volumes, the components necessary to provide the functional requirements of overall equipments, which when handled in more conventional ways are vastly bulkier.

molecular field theory *See* Weiss theory.

monadic operation An operation on one operand, such as a negation.

monitor To supervise a program, and check that it is operating correctly during its execution, usually by means of a diagnostic routine.

monitor control dump A memory dump routinely carried out by the system once a program has been run.

monitor display The facility of stopping the central processing unit and displaying information of main storage and internal registers; after manual intervention, normal instruction execution can be initiated.

monitoring amplifier A power amplifier used primarily for evaluation and supervision of a program.

monitoring key Key which, when operated, makes it possible for an attendant or operator to listen on a telephone circuit without appreciably impairing transmission on the circuit.

monitor mode *See* master mode.

monitor operating system The control of the routines which achieves efficient use of all the hardware components.

monitor printer Input-output device, capable of receiving coded signals from the computer, which automatically operates the keyboard to print a hard copy and, when desired, to punch paper tape.

monitor routine *See* executive routine.

monitor system *See* executive system.

monitor system components The set of programs which form the complete operating system: the control program (task management, job management, and data management routines) and the processing programs.

monobrid circuit Integrated circuit using a combination of monolithic and multichip techniques by means of which a number of monolithic circuits, or a monolithic device in combination with separate diffused or thin-film components, are interconnected in a single package.

monocharge electret A type of foil electret that carries electrical charge of the same sign on both surfaces.

monochrome channel In a color television system, any path which is intended to carry the monochrome signal; the monochrome channel may also carry other signals.

monochrome signal **1.** A signal wave used for controlling luminance values in monochrome television. **2.** The portion of a signal wave that has major control of the luminance values in a color television system, regardless of whether the picture is displayed in color or in monochrome. Also known as M signal.

monofier Complete master oscillator and power amplifier system in a single evacuated tube envelope; electrically, it is equivalent to a stable low-noise oscillator, an isolator, and a two- or three-cavity klystron amplifier.

monolithic ceramic capacitor A capacitor that consists of thin dielectric layers interleaved with staggered metal-film electrodes; after leads are connected to alternate projecting ends of the electrodes, the assembly is compressed and sintered to form a solid monolithic block.

monolithic integrated circuit An integrated circuit having elements formed in place on or within a semiconductor substrate, with at least one element being formed within the substrate.

monopinch Antijam application of the monopulse technique where the error signal is used to provide discrimination against jamming signals.

monoscope A signal-generating electron-beam tube in which a picture signal is produced by scanning an electrode that has a predetermined pattern of secondary-emission response over its surface. Also known as monotron; phasmajector.

monostable Having only one stable state.

monostable blocking oscillator A blocking oscillator in which the electron tube or other active device carries no current unless positive voltage is applied to the grid. Also known as driven blocking oscillator.

monostable circuit A circuit having only one stable condition, to which it returns in a predetermined time interval after being triggered.

monostable multivibrator A multivibrator with one stable state and one unstable state; a trigger signal is required to drive the unit into the unstable state, where it remains for a predetermined time before returning to the stable state. Also known as one-shot multivibrator; single-shot multivibrator; start-stop multivibrator; univibrator.

monotonicity In an analog-to-digital converter, the condition wherein there is an increasing output for every increasing value of input voltage over the full operating range.

monotron *See* monoscope.

Moore machine A sequential machine in which the output depends uniquely on the current state of the machine, and not on the input.

MOS *See* metal oxide semiconductor

mosaic A light-sensitive surface used in television camera tubes, consisting of a thin mica sheet coated on one side with a large number of tiny photosensitive silver-cesium globules, insulated from each other.

MOS transistor *See* metal oxide semiconductor field-effect transistor.

MOSFET *See* metal oxide semiconductor field-effect transistor.

MOST *See* metal oxide semiconductor field-effect transistor.

most significant bit The left-most bit in a word. Abbreviated msb.

most significant character The character in the leftmost position in a number or word.

motherboard A common pathway over which information is transmitted between the hardware devices (the central processing unit, memory, and each of the peripheral control units) in a microcomputer.

motional impedance Of a transducer, the complex remainder after the blocked impedance has been subtracted from the loaded impedance. Also known as loaded motional impedance.

motion picture pickup Use of a television camera to pick up scenes directly from motion picture film.

motion register The register which controls the go/stop, forward/reverse motion of a tape drive.

motorboating Undesired oscillation in an amplifying system or transducer, usually of a pulse type, occurring at a subaudio or low-audio frequency.

motor control *See* electronic motor control.

move mode A method of communicating between an operating program and an input/output control system in which the data records to be read or written are actually moved into and out of program-designated memory areas; in contrast to locate mode.

moving-coil pickup *See* dynamic pickup.

moving-head disk A disk-storage device in which one or more read-write heads are attached to a movable arm which allows each head to cover many tracks of information.

moving-target indicator A device that limits the display of radar information primarily to moving targets; signals due to reflections from stationary objects are canceled by a memory circuit. Abbreviated MTI.

MPU *See* microprocessing unit.

MQ register Temporary-storage register whose contents can be transferred to or from, or swapped with, the accumulator.

msb *See* most significant bit.

M scan *See* M scope.

MSI *See* medium-scale integration.

M scope A modified form of A scope on which part of the time base is slightly displaced in a vertical direction by insertion of an adjustable step which serves as a range marker. Also known as M indicator; M scan.

M signal *See* monochrome signal.

MTBF *See* mean time between failures.

MTI *See* moving-target indicator.

M-type backward-wave oscillator A backward-wave oscillator in which focusing and interaction are through magnetic fields, as in a magnetron. Also known as M-type carcinotron; type-M carcinotron.

M-type carcinotron *See* M-type backward-wave oscillator.

mu factor Ratio of the change in one electrode voltage to the change in another electrode voltage under the conditions that a specified current remains unchanged and that all other electrode voltages are maintained constant; a measure of the relative effect of the voltages on two electrodes upon the current in the circuit of any specified electrode.

multiaccess computer A computer system in which computational and data resources are made available simultaneously to a number of users who access the system through terminal devices, normally on an interactive or conversational basis.

multiaddress Referring to an instruction that has more than one address part.

multianode tube Electron tube having two or more main anodes and a single cathode.

multiaperture reluctance switch Two-aperture ferrite storage core which may be used to provide a nondestructive readout computer memory.

multiaspect Pertaining to searches or systems which permit more than one aspect, or facet, of information to be used in combination, one with the other to effect identifying or selecting operations.

multicavity klystron A klystron in which there is at least one cavity between the input and output cavities, each of which remodulates the beam so that electrons are more closely bunched.

multicavity magnetron A magnetron in which the circuit includes a plurality of cavities, generally cut into the solid cylindrical anode so that the mouths of the cavities face the central cathode.

multichannel field-effect transistor A field-effect transistor in which appropriate voltages are applied to the gate to control the space within the current flow channels.

multichip microcircuit Microcircuit in which discrete, miniature, active electronic elements (transistor or diode chips) and thin-film or diffused passive components or component clusters are interconnected by thermocompression bonds, alloying, soldering, welding, chemical deposition, or metallization.

multicollector electron tube An electron tube in which electrons travel to more than one electrode.

multicomputer system A system consisting of more than one computer, usually under the supervision of a master computer, in which smaller computers handle input/output and routine jobs while the large computer carries out the more complex computations.

multicoupler A device for connecting several receivers to one antenna and properly matching the impedances of the receivers to the antenna.

multicycle feeding *See* multiread feeding.

multidimensional Turing machine A variation of a Turing machine in which tapes are replaced by multidimensional structures.

multielectrode tube Electron tube containing more than three electrodes associated with a single electron stream.

multielement vacuum tube A vacuum tube which has one or more grids in addition to the cathode and plate electrodes.

multigrid tube An electron tube having two or more grids between cathode and anode, as a tetrode or pentode.

multigun tube A cathode-ray tube having more than one electron gun.

multihead Turing machine A variation of a Turing machine in which more than one head is allowed per tape.

multijob operation The concurrent or interleaved execution of job steps from more than one job.

multilevel indirect addressing A programming device whereby the address retrieved in the memory word may itself be an indirect address that points to another memory location, which in turn may be another indirect address, and so forth.

multilist organization A chained file organization in which each segment is indexed.

multipactor A high-power, high-speed microwave switching device in which a thin electron cloud is driven back and forth between two parallel plane surfaces in a vacuum by a radio-frequency electric field.

multipass sort Computer program designed to sort more data than can be contained within the internal storage of a computer; intermediate storage, such as disk, tape, or drum, is required.

multiple-access computer A computer system whose facilities can be made available to a number of users at essentially the same time, normally through terminals, which are often physically far removed from the central computer and which typically communicate with it over telephone lines.

multiple accumulating registers Special registers capable of handling factors larger than one computer word in length.

multiple-address code A computer instruction code in which more than one address or storage location is specified; the instruction may give the locations of the operands, the destination of the result, and the location of the next instruction.

multiple-address computer A computer whose instruction contains more than one address, for example, an operation code and three addresses A, B, C, such that the content of A is multiplied by the content of B and the product stored in location C.

multiple-address instruction An instruction which has more than one address in a computer; the addresses give locations of other instructions, or of data or instructions that are to be operated upon.

multiple computer operation The utilization of any one computer of a group of computers by means of linkages provided by multiplexor channels, all computers being linked through their channels or files.

multiple-function chip *See* large-scale integrated circuit.

multiple-keyboard point-of-sale system A point-of-sale system consisting of a group of electronic machines, without programming capability, placed at all check points and linked either to one central data collector with a magnetic tape or to a minicomputer with disk storage.

multiple-length arithmetic Arithmetic performed by a computer in which two or more machine words are used to represent each number in the calculations, usually to achieve higher precision in the result.

multiple-length number A number having two or more times as many digits as are ordinarily used in a given computer.

multiple-length working Any processing of data by a computer in which two or more machine words are used to represent each data item.

multiple module access Device which establishes priorities in storage access in a multiple computer environment.

multiple precision arithmetic Method of increasing the precision of a result by increasing the length of the number to encompass two or more computer words in length.

multiple programming The execution of two or more operations simultaneously.

multiple punching The punching of two or more holes in a column of a punch card.

multiple target generator An electronic countermeasures device that produces several false responses in a hostile radar set.

multiple-unit semiconductor device Semiconductor device having two or more sets of electrodes associated with independent carrier streams.

multiple-unit tube *See* multiunit tube.

multiplex mode The utilization of differences in operating speeds between a computer and transmission lines; the multiplexor channel scans each line in sequence, and any transmitted pulse on a line is assembled in an area reserved for this line; consequently, a number of users can be handled by the computer simultaneously. Also known as multiplexor channel operation.

multiplexer A device for combining two or more signals, as for multiplex, or for creating the composite color video signal from its components in color television. Also spelled multiplexor.

multiplexor *See* multiplexer.

multiplexor channel operation *See* multiplex mode.

multiplexor terminal unit Device which permits a large number of data transmission lines to access a single computer.

multiplication An increase in current flow through a semiconductor because of increased carrier activity.

multiplication table In certain computers, a part of memory holding a table of numbers in which the computer looks up values in order to perform the multiplication operation.

multiplication time The time required for a computer to perform a multiplication; for a binary number it will be equal to the total of all the addition times and all the shift times involved in the multiplication.

multiplicative congruential generator A congruential generator in which the constant b in the generating formula is equal to zero.

multiplier 1. A device that has two or more inputs and an output that is a representation of the product of the quantities represented by the input signals; voltages are the quantities commonly multiplied. 2. *See* electron multiplier; frequency multiplier.

multiplier field The area reserved for a multiplication, equal to the length of multiplier plus multiplicand plus one character.

multiplier phototube A phototube with one or more dynodes between its photocathode and the output electrode; the electron stream from the photocathode is reflected off each dynode in turn, with secondary emission adding electrons to the stream at each reflection. Also known as electron-multiplier phototube; photoelectric electron-multiplier tube; photomultiplier; photomultiplier tube.

multiplier-quotient register A register equal to two words in length in which the quotient is developed and in which the multiplier is entered for multiplication.

multiplier traveling-wave photodiode Photodiode in which the construction of a traveling-wave tube is combined with that of a multiplier phototube to give increased sensitivity.

multiplier tube Vacuum tube using secondary emission from a number of electrodes in sequence to obtain increased output current; the electron stream is reflected, in turn, from one electrode of the multiplier to the next.

multiply defined symbol Common assembler or compiler error printout indicating that a label has been used more than once.

multiport memory A memory shared by many processors to communicate among themselves.

multiprecision arithmetic A form of arithmetic similar to double precision arithmetic except that two or more words may be used to represent each number.

multiprocessing Carrying out of two or more sequences of instructions at the same time in a computer.

multiprocessing system See multiprocessor.

multiprocessor A data-processing system that can carry out more than one program, or more than one arithmetic operation, at the same time. Also known as multiprocessing system.

multiprocessor interleaving Technique used to speed up processing time; by splitting banks of memory each with x microseconds access time and accessing each one in sequence $1/n$ of a cycle later, a reference to memory can be had every x/n microseconds; this speed is achieved at the cost of hardware complexity.

multiprogramming The interleaved execution of two or more programs by a computer, in which the central processing unit executes a few instructions from each program in succession.

multiprogramming executive control Control program structure required to handle multiprogramming with either a fixed or a variable number of tasks.

multiread feeding A system of reading punched cards in which the card passes a sensing station several times and successive fields of the card are read on consecutive machine cycles, enabling several lines to be printed from a single card. Also known as multicycle feeding.

multisegment magnetron Magnetron with an anode divided into more than two segments, usually by slots parallel to its axis.

multistable circuit A circuit having two or more stable operating conditions.

multistage amplifier See cascade amplifier.

multistrip coupler A series of parallel metallic strips placed on a surface acoustic wave filter between identical apodized interdigital transducers; it converts the spatially nonuniform surface acoustic wave generated by one transducer into a spatially uniform wave received at the other transducer, and helps to reject spurious bulk acoustic modes.

multitape Turing maching A variation of a Turing machine in which more than one tape is permitted, each tape having its own read-write head.

multitask operation A sophisticated form of multijob operation in a computer which allows a single copy of a program module to be used for more than one task.

multitrack operation The selection of the next read/write head in a cylinder, usually indicated by bit zero of the operation code in the channel command word.

multiunit tube Electron tube containing within one glass or metal envelope, two or more groups of electrodes, each associated with separate electron streams. Also known as multiple-unit tube.

multiuser system A computer system with multiple terminals, enabling several users, each at their own terminal, to use the computer.

multivator An automatic device for analyzing a number of dust samples that might be collected by spacecraft on the moon, Mars, and other planets, to detect the presence of microscopic organisms with a multiplier phototube that measures the fluorescence given off.

multivibrator A relaxation oscillator using two tubes, transistors, or other electron devices, with the output of each coupled to the input of the other through resistance-capacitance elements or other elements to obtain in-phase feedback voltage.

multivolume file A file that consists of more than one physical unit of storage medium.

multiway merge A computer operation in which three or more lists are merged into a single list.

muting circuit 1. Circuit which cuts off the output of a receiver when no radio-frequency carrier greater than a predetermined intensity is reaching the first detector. 2. Circuit for making a receiver insensitive during operation of its associated transmitter.

mutual conductance *See* transconductance.

mutual deadlock A condition in which deadlocked tasks are awaiting resource assignments, and each task on a list awaits release of a resource held by the following task, with the last task awaiting release of a resource held by the first task. Also known as circular wait.

N

nancy receiver *See* infrared receiver.

NAND circuit A logic circuit whose output signal is a logical 1 if any of its inputs is a logical 0, and whose output signal is a logical 0 if all of its inputs are logical 1.

narrow-band amplifier An amplifier which increases the magnitude of signals over a band of frequencies whose bandwidth is small compared to the average frequency of the band.

narrow-band-pass filter A band-pass filter in which the band of frequencies transmitted by the filter has a bandwidth which is small compared to the average frequency of the band.

narrow-sector recorder A radio direction finder with which atmospherics are received from a limited sector related to the position of the antenna; this antenna is usually rotated continuously and the bearings of the atmospherics recorded automatically.

native language Machine language that is executed by the computer for which it is specifically designed, in contrast to a computer using an emulator.

natural binary coded decimal system A particular binary coded decimal system that uses the first ten binary numbers in sequence to represent the digits 0 through 9.

natural frequency The lowest resonant frequency of an antenna, circuit, or component.

natural function generator *See* analytical function generator.

natural language A computer language whose rules reflect and describe current rather than prescribed usage; it is often loose and ambiguous in interpretation, meaning different things to different hearers.

natural law function generator *See* analytical function generator.

navigation receiver An electronic device that determines a ship's position by receiving and comparing radio signals from transmitters at known locations.

Navy Electronics Laboratory International Algol Compilers *See* NELIAC.

n-channel A conduction channel formed by electrons in an n-type semiconductor, as in an n-type field-effect transistor.

N curve A plot of voltage against current for a negative-resistance device; its slope is negative for some values of current or voltage.

N display Radar display in which the target appears as a pair of vertical deflections from a horizontal time base; direction is indicated by relative amplitude of the blips; target distance is determined by moving an adjustable pedestal signal along the base line until it coincides with the horizontal position of the blips; the pedestal control is calibrated in distance.

NDRO *See* nondestructive read.

NEA material *See* negative electron affinity material.

needle A slender rod or probe used to sort decks of edge-punched cards by inserting it through holes along the margin of the deck and vibrating the deck so that cards having that particular hole are retained, but those having a notch cut at that hole position drop out.

needle gap Spark gap in which the electrodes are needle points.

needle scratch *See* surface noise.

Néel point *See* Néel temperature.

Néel's theory A theory of the behavior of antiferromagnetic and other ferrimagnetic materials in which the crystal lattice is divided into two or more sublattices; each atom in one sublattice responds to the magnetic field generated by nearest neighbors in other sublattices, with the result that magnetic moments of all the atoms in any sublattice are parallel, but magnetic moments of two different sublattices can be different.

Néel temperature A temperature, characteristic of certain metals, alloys, and salts, below which spontaneous nonparalleled magnetic ordering takes place so that they become antiferromagnetic, and above which they are paramagnetic. Also known as Néel point.

Néel wall The boundary between two magnetic domains in a thin film in which the magnetization vector remains parallel to the faces of the film in passing through the wall.

negative effective mass amplifiers and generators Class of solid-state devices for broad-band amplification and generation of electrical waves in the microwave region; these devices use the property of the effective masses of charge carriers in semiconductors becoming negative with sufficiently high kinetic energies.

negative electrode *See* cathode.

negative electron affinity material A material, such as gallium phosphide, whose surface has been treated with a substance, such as cesium, so that the surface barrier is reduced, band-bending occurs so that the top of the conduction band lies above the vacuum level, and the elctron affinity of the substance in negative. Abbreviated NEA material.

negative glow The luminous flow in a glow-discharge cold-cathode tube occurring between the cathode dark space and the Faraday dark space.

negative-grid generator Conventional oscillator circuit in which oscillation is produced by feedback from the plate circuit to a grid which is normally negative with respect to the cathode, and which is designed to operate without drawing grid current at any time.

negative-grid thyratron A thyratron with only one grid, which serves to prevent the flow of current until its potential relative to the cathode is made less negative than a certain critical value.

negative impedance An impedance such that when the current through it increases, the voltage drop across the impedance decreases.

negative-impedance repeater A telephone repeater that provides an effective gain for voice-frequency signals by insertion into the line of a negative impedance that cancels out line impedances responsible for transmission losses.

negative indication A hole punched in a specified column and specified punch position on a punch card to indicate that a number represented in a particular field of the card has a negative sign.

negative modulation 1. Modulation in which an increase in brightness corresponds to a decrease in amplitude-modulated transmitter power; used in United States television transmitters and in some facsimile systems. **2.** Modulation in which an increase in brightness corresponds to a decrease in the frequency of a frequency-modulated facsimile transmitter. Also known as negative transmission.

negative picture phase The video signal phase in which the signal voltage swings in a negative direction for an increase in brilliance.

negative resistance The resistance of a negative-resistance device.

negative-resistance device A device having a range of applied voltages within which an increase in this voltage produces a decrease in the current.

negative-resistance oscillator An oscillator in which a parallel-tuned resonant circuit is connected to a vacuum tube so that the combination acts as the negative resistance needed for continuous oscillation.

negative-resistance repeater Repeater in which gain is provided by a series negative resistance or a shunt negative resistance, or both.

negative thermion *See* thermoelectron.

negative-transconductance oscillator Electron-tube oscillator in which the output of the tube is coupled back to the input without phase shift, the phase condition for oscillation being satisfied by the negative transconductance of the tube.

negative transmission *See* negative modulation.

negatron *See* dynatron.

NELIAC An early dialect of ALGOL, which was developed for a specific data-processing application but, unlike ALGOL, is not primarily concerned with being used for complex scientific and engineering calculations. Derived from Navy Electronics Laboratory International Algol Compilers.

neon glow lamp A glow lamp containing neon gas, usually rated between 1/25 and 3 watts, and producing a characteristic red glow; used as an indicator light and electronic circuit component.

neon oscillator Relaxation oscillator in which a neon tube or lamp serves as the switching element.

neon tube An electron tube in which neon gas is ionized by the flow of electric current through long lengths of gas tubing, to produce a luminous red glow discharge; used chiefly in outdoor advertising signs.

nesistor A negative-resistance semiconductor device that is basically a bipolar field-effect transistor.

nest To include data or subroutines in other items of a similar nature with a higher hierarchical level so that it is possible to access or execute various levels of data or routines recursively.

nesting 1. Inclusion of a routine wholly within another routine. **2.** Inclusion of a DO statement within a DO statement in FORTRAN.

nesting storage *See* push-down storage.

network analyzer An analog computer in which networks are used to simulate power line systems or physical systems and obtain solutions to various problems before the systems are actually built.

neuristor A device that behaves like a nerve fiber in having attenuationless propagation of signals; one goal of research is development of a complete artificial nerve cell, containing many neuristors, that could duplicate the function of the human eye and brain in recognizing characters and other visual images.

neutralize To nullify oscillation-producing voltage feedback from the output to the input of an amplifier through tube interelectrode capacitances; an external feedback path is used to produce at the input a voltage that is equal in magnitude but opposite in phase to that fed back through the interelectrode capacitance.

neutralized radio-frequency stage Stage having an additional circuit connected to feed back, in the opposite phase, an amount of energy equivalent to what is causing the oscillation, thus neutralizing any tendency to oscillate and making the circuit function strictly as an amplifier.

neutralizing capacitor Capacitor, usually variable, employed in a radio receiving or transmitting circuit to feed a portion of the signal voltage from the plate circuit of a stage back to the grid circuit.

neutralizing circuit Portion of an amplifier circuit which provides an intentional feedback path from plate to grid to prevent regeneration.

neutralizing voltage Voltage developed in the plate circuit (Hazeltine neutralization) or in the grid circuit (Rice neutralization), used to nullify or cancel the feedback through the tube.

neutral temperature The temperature of the hot junction of a thermocouple at which the electromotive force of the thermocouple attains its maximum value, when the cold junction is maintained at a constant temperature of 0°C.

next-event file A portion of a computer simulation program which maintains a list of all events to be processed and updates the simulated time.

nibble A unit of computer storage or information equal to one-half byte.

nickel delay line An acoustic delay line in which nickel is used to transmit sound signals.

N indicator *See* N scope.

nine's complement The radix-minus-1 complement of a numeral whose radix is 10.

ninety-column card A card, punched or to be punched, divided in half horizontally, éach half containing 45 columns, and each column containing six punch positions.

ninety-six-column card A punch card divided into three parts horizontally, each third containing 32 columns, and each column containing six punch positions.

Nipkow disk In optical character recognition, a disk having one or more spirals of holes around the outer edge, with successive openings positioned so that rotation of the disk provides mechanical scanning, as of a document.

NIXIE display indicator *See* NIXIE Tube.

NIXIE Tube Trademark of Burroughs Corporation for a cold-cathode gas readout tube having a common anode and 10 different metallic cathodes, each formed in the shape of a different numeral, alphabetic character, or special symbol; the desired character is surrounded with a brilliant glow when the corresponding cathode is energized. Also known as NIXIE display indicator.

N-level address A multilevel address specifying N levels of addressing.

N-level logic An arrangement of gates in a digital computer in which not more than N gates are connected in series.

N-modular redundancy A generalization of triple modular redundancy in which there are N identical units, where N is any odd number.

NMRR *See* normal-mode rejection ratio.

nn junction In a semiconductor, a region of transition between two regions having different properties in n-type semiconducting material.

no-address instruction An instruction which a computer can carry out without using an operand from storage.

node A junction point within a network.

noise analyzer A device used for noise analysis.

noise digit A digit, usually 0, inserted into the rightmost position of the mantissa of a floating point number during a left-shift operation associated with normalization. Also known as noisy digit.

noise factor The ratio of the total noise power per unit bandwidth at the output of a system to the portion of the noise power that is due to the input termination, at the standard noise temperature of 290 K. Also known as noise figure.

noise figure See noise factor.

noise filter 1. A filter that is inserted in an alternating-current power line to block noise interference that would otherwise travel through the line in either direction and affect the operation of receivers. 2. A filter used in a radio receiver to reduce noise, usually an auxiliary low-pass filter which can be switched in or out of the audio system.

noise generator A device which produces (usually random) electrical noise, for use in tests of the response of electrical systems to noise, and in measurements of noise intensity. Also known as noise source.

noise jammer 1. An electronic jammer that emits a carrier modulated with recordings or synthetic reproductions of natural atmospheric noise; the radio-frequency carrier may be suppressed; used to discourage the enemy by simulating naturally adverse communications conditions. 2. During World War II, a powerful transmitter modulated with white noise tuned to the approximate frequency of an enemy transmitter and used to obscure intelligible output at the receiver.

noise killer 1. Device installed in a circuit to reduce its interference to other circuits. 2. See noise suicide circuit.

noise limiter A limiter circuit that cuts off all noise peaks that are stronger than the highest peak in the desired signal being received, thereby reducing the effects of atmospheric or man-made interference. Also known as noise silencer; noise suppressor.

noise measurement Any of a wide range of measurements of random and nonrandom electrical noise, but usually noise-power measurement.

noise-metallic In telephone communications, weighted noise current in a metallic circuit at a given point when the circuit is terminated at that point in the nominal characteristic impedance of the circuit.

noise-modulated jamming Random electronic noise that appears at the radar receiver as background noise and tends to mask the desired radar echo or radio signal.

noise-power measurement Measurement of the power carried by electrical noise averaged over some brief interval of time, usually by amplifying noise from the source in a linear amplifier and then using a quadratic detector followed by a low-pass filter and an indicating device.

noise silencer See noise limiter.

noise source See noise generator.

noise suicide circuit A circuit which reduces the gain of an amplifier for a short period whenever a sufficiently large noise pulse is received. Also known as noise killer.

noise suppression Any method of reducing or eliminating the effects of undesirable electrical disturbances, as in frequency modulation whenever the signal carrier level is greater than the noise level.

noise suppressor 1. A circuit that blocks the audio-frequency amplifier of a radio receiver automatically when no carrier is being received, to eliminate background noise. Also known as squelch circuit. **2.** A circuit that reduces record surface noise when playing phonograph records, generally by means of a filter that blocks out the higher frequencies where such noise predominates. **3.** *See* noise limiter.

noise testing The measurement of the power dissipated in a resistance termination of given value joined to one end of a telephone or telegraph circuit when no test power is applied to the circuit.

noise tube A gas tube used as a source of white noise.

noise weighting Use of an electrical network to obtain a weighted average over frequency of the noise power, which is representative of the relative disturbing effects of noise in a communications system at various frequencies.

noisy digit *See* noise digit.

noisy mode A floating-point arithmetic procedure associated with normalization in which "1" bits, rather than "0" bits, are introduced in the low-order bit position during the left shift.

nonarithmetic shift *See* cyclic shift.

nondegenerate amplifier Parametric amplifier that is characterized by a pumping frequency considerably higher than twice the signal frequency; the output is taken at the signal input frequency; the amplifier exhibits negative impedance characteristics, indicative of infinite gain, and is therefore capable of oscillation.

nondegenerative basic feasible solution In linear programming, a basic feasible solution with exactly m positive variables x_i, where m is the number of constraint equations.

nondestructive breakdown Breakdown of the barrier between the gate and channel of a field-effect transistor without causing failure of the device; in a junction field-effect transistor, avalanche breakdown occurs at the pn junction.

nondestructive read A reading process that does not erase the data in memory; the term sometimes includes a destructive read immediately followed by a restorative write-back. Also known as nondestructive readout (NDRO).

nondestructive readout *See* nondestructive read.

nondirectional *See* omnidirectional.

nonerasable storage A device that permits a nondestructive read, such as punched cards, electrically conductive sheets, or paper tape.

nonexecutable statement A statement in a higher-level programming language which cannot be related to the instructions in the machine language program ultimately produced, but which provides the compiler with essential information from which it may determine the allocation of storage and other organizational characteristics of the final program.

nonfatal error An error in a computer program which does not result in termination of execution, but which causes the processor to invent an interpretation, issue a warning, and continue processing.

nonfunctional packages software General-purpose software which permits the user to handle the particular applications requirements with little or no additional program or systems design work, or to perform certain specialized computational functions.

nonhoming tuning system Motor-driven automatic tuning system in which the motor starts up in the direction of previous rotation; if this direction is incorrect for the new station, the motor reverses, after turning to the end of the dial, then proceeds to the desired station.

noninverting amplifier An operational amplifier in which the input signal is applied to the ungrounded positive input terminal to give a gain greater than unity and make the output voltage change in phase with the input voltage.

noninverting parametric device Parametric device whose operation depends essentially upon three frequencies, a harmonic of the pump frequency and two signal frequencies, of which one is the sum of the other plus the pump harmonic.

nonlinear amplifier An amplifier in which a change in input does not produce a proportional change in output.

nonlinear circuit component An electrical device for which a change in applied voltage does not produce a proportional charge in current. Also known as nonlinear device; nonlinear element.

nonlinear coupler A type of frequency multiplier which uses the nonlinear capacitance of a junction diode to couple energy from the input circuit, which is tuned to the fundamental, to the output circuit, which is tuned to the desired harmonic.

nonlinear detection Detection based on the curvature of a tube characteristic, such as square-law detection.

nonlinear device *See* nonlinear circuit component.

nonlinear distortion Distortion in which the output of a system or component does not have the desired linear relation to the input.

nonlinear element *See* nonlinear circuit component.

nonlinear oscillator A radio-frequency oscillator that changes frequency in response to an audio signal; it is the basic circuit used in eavesdropping devices.

nonlinear reactance The behavior of a coil or capacitor whose voltage drop is not proportional to the rate of change of current through the coil, or the charge on the capacitor.

nonlinear resistance The behavior of a substance (usually a semiconductor) which does not obey Ohm's law but has a voltage drop across it that is proportional to some power of the current.

nonmaintenance time The elapsed time during scheduled working hours between the determination of a machine failure and placement of the equipment back into operation.

nonnumeric character Any character except a digit.

nonprint code A bit combination which is interpreted as no printing, no spacing.

nonpriority interrupt Any one of a group of interrupts which may be disregarded by the central processing unit.

nonprocedural language A programming language in which the program does not follow the actual steps a computer follows in executing a program.

nonredundant system A computer system designed in such a way that only the absolute minimum amount of hardware is utilized to implement its function.

nonreproducing code A code which normally does not appear as such in a generated output but will result in a function such as paging or spacing.

nonresident routine Any computer routine which is not stored permanently in the memory but must be read into memory from a data carrier or external storage device.

non-return-to-zero A mode of recording and readout in which it is not necessary for the signal to return to zero after each item of recorded data.

nonshared control unit A control unit which controls only one device. Also known as unipath.

nonstorage camera tube Television camera tube in which the picture signal is, at each instant, proportional to the intensity of the illumination on the corresponding area of the scene.

nonsynchronous timer A circuit at the receiving end of a communications link which restores the time relationship between pulses when no timing pulses are transmitted.

nonsynchronous transmission A data transmission process in which a clock is not used to control the unit intervals within a block or a group of data signals.

nonsynchronous vibrator Vibrator that interrupts a direct-current circuit at a frequency unrelated to the other circuit constants and does not rectify the resulting stepped-up alternating voltage.

nonvolatile memory *See* nonvolatile storage.

nonvolatile random-access memory A semiconductor storage device which has two memory cells for each bit, one of which is volatile, as in a static RAM (random-access memory), and provides unlimited read and write operations, while the other is nonvolatile, and provides the ability to retain information when power is removed. Abbreviated NV RAM.

nonvolatile storage A computer storage medium that retains information in the absence of power, such as a magnetic tape, drum, or core. Also known as nonvolatile memory.

NO OP An instruction telling the computer to do nothing, except to proceed to the next instruction in sequence. Also known as no-operation instruction.

no-operation instruction *See* NO OP.

NOR circuit A circuit in which output voltage appears only when signal is absent from all of its input terminals.

normal direction flow The direction from left to right or top to bottom in flow charting.

normal impedance *See* free impedance.

normalization Breaking down of complex data structures into flat files.

normalize 1. To adjust the representation of a quantity so that this representation lies within a prescribed range. **2.** In particular, to adjust the exponent and mantissa of a floating point number so that the mantissa falls within a prescribed range.

normal mode Operation of a computer in which it executes its own instructions rather than those of a different computer.

normal-mode rejection ratio The ability of an amplifier to reject spurious signals at the power-line frequency or at harmonics of the line frequency. Abbreviated NMRR.

normal orientation In optical character recognition, that determinate position which indicates that the line elements of an inputted source document appear parallel with the document's leading edge.

normal range An interval within which results are expected to fall during normal operations.

normal-stage punching A system of card punching in which only even number rows of the card are used.

notch Rectangular depression extending below the sweep line of the radar indicator in some types of equipment.

notch filter A band-rejection filter that produces a sharp notch in the frequency response curve of a system; used in television transmitters to provide attenuation at the low-frequency end of the channel, to prevent possible interference with the sound carrier of the next lower channel.

NOT circuit A logic circuit with one input and one output that inverts the input signal at the output; that is, the output signal is a logical 1 if the input signal is a logical 0, and vice versa. Also known as inverter circuit.

nought state *See* zero condition.

novar Beam-power tube having a nine-pin base.

npin transistor An *npn* transistor which has a layer of high-purity germanium between the base and collector to extend the frequency range.

N-plus-one address instruction An instruction with N + 1 address parts, one of which gives the location of the next instruction to be carried out.

npnp diode *See* pnpn diode.

npnp transistor An *npn*-junction transistor having a transition or floating layer between *p* and *n* regions, to which no ohmic connection is made. Also known as *pnpn* transistor.

npn semiconductor Double junction formed by sandwiching a thin layer of *p*-type material between two layers of *n*-type material of a semiconductor.

npn transistor A junction transistor having a *p*-type base between an *n*-type emitter and an *n*-type collector; the emitter should then be negative with respect to the base, and the collector should be positive with respect to the base.

np semiconductor Region of transition between *n*- and *p*-type material.

N scan *See* N scope.

N scope A cathode-ray scope combining the features of K and M scopes. Also known as N indicator; N scan.

n-type conduction The electrical conduction associated with electrons, as opposed to holes, in a semiconductor.

N-type crystal rectifier Crystal rectifier in which forward current flows when the semiconductor is negative with respect to the metal.

n-type germanium Germanium to which more impurity atoms of donor type (with valence 5, such as antimony) than of acceptor type (with valence 3, such as indium) have been added, with the result that the conduction electron density exceeds the hole density.

n-type semiconductor An extrinsic semiconductor in which the conduction electron density exceeds the hole density.

nuclear triode detector A type of junction detector that has two outputs which together determine the precise location on the detector where the ionizing radiation was incident, as well as the energy of the ionizing particle.

nucleus 1. That portion of the control program that must always be present in main storage. **2.** The main storage area used in the nucleus (first definition) and other transient control program routines.

null character A control character used as a filler in data processing; may be inserted or removed from a sequence of characters without affecting the meaning of the sequence, but may affect format or control equipment.

null-current circuit A circuit used to measure current, in which the unknown current is opposed by a current resulting from applying a voltage controlled by a slide wire across a series resistor, and the slide wire is continuously adjusted so that the resulting current, as measured by a direct-current detector amplifier, is equal to zero.

null-current measurement Measurement of current using a null-current circuit.

number cruncher A computer with great power to carry out computations, designed to maximize this ability rather than to process large amounts of data.

numeric In computers, pertaining to data composed wholly or partly of digits, as distinct from alphabetic.

numerical display device Any device for visually displaying numerical figures, such as a numerical indicator tube, a device utilizing electroluminescence, or a device in which any one of a stack of transparent plastic strips engraved with digits can be illuminated by a small light at the edge of the strip.

numerical indicator tube An electron tube capable of visually displaying numerical figures; some varieties also display alphabetical characters and commonly used symbols.

numerical tape The tape required by a computer operating a machine tool.

numeric coding Code in which only digits are used, usually binary or octal.

numeric control The action of programs written for specialized computers which operate machine tools.

numeric data Data consisting of digits and not letters of the alphabet or special characters.

numeric printer Old type of printer which positioned its keys to print a field in one operation, rather than one digit at a time.

numeric punch Punching of holes in a column of a computer card so that only one hole in rows zero through nine is punched in the column.

nuvistor Electron tube in which all electrodes are cylindrical, placed one inside the other with close spacing, in a ceramic envelope.

NV RAM *See* nonvolatile random-access memory.

nybble A string of bits, smaller than a byte, operated on as a unit.

Nyquist's theorem The mean square noise voltage across a resistance in thermal equilibrium is four times the product of the resistance, Boltzmann's constant, the absolute temperature, and the frequency range within which the voltage is measured.

O

O attenuator A dissipative attenuator in which the circuit has the form of a ladder with two rungs, and the resistances across the rungs are unequal, so that the impedances across the two pairs of terminals are unequal.

object computer The computer processing an object program; the same computer compiling the source program could, therefore, be called the source computer; such terminology is seldom used in practice.

object deck The set of machine-readable computer instructions produced by a compiler, either in absolute format (that is, containing only fixed addresses) or, more frequently, in relocatable format.

object language The intended and desired output language in the translation or conversion of information from one language to another.

object library *See* object program library.

object module The computer language program prepared by an assembler or a compiler after acting on a programmer-written source program.

object program The computer language program prepared by an assembler or a compiler after acting on a programmer-written source program. Also known as object routine; target program; target routine.

object program library A collection of computer programs in the form of relocatable instructions, which reside on, and may be read from, a mass storage device. Also known as object library.

object routine *See* object program.

object tape A tape, paper or magnetic, containing the machine language instructions resulting from a compiler or assembler, often found in minicomputer environments.

object time The time during which execution of an object program is carried out.

OCR *See* optical character recognition.

octal base Tube base having a central aligning key and positioned for eight equally spaced pins.

octal debugger A simple debugging program which permits only octal (instead of symbolic) address references.

octal loading program Computer utility program providing a method for making changes in programs and tables existing in core memory or drum storage, by reading in words coded in octal notation on punched cards or tape.

octave-band oscillator An oscillator that can be tuned over a frequency range of 2 to 1, so that its highest frequency is twice its lowest frequency.

octode An eight-electrode electron tube containing an anode, a cathode, a control electrode, and five additional electrodes that are ordinarily grids.

odd-even check A means of detecting certain kinds of errors in which an extra bit, carried along with each word, is set to zero or one so that the total number of zeros or ones in each word is always made even or always made odd. Also known as parity check.

odd parity Property of an expression in binary code which has an odd number of ones.

odd parity check A parity check in which the number of 0's or 1's in each word is expected to be odd; if the number is even, the check bit is 1, and if the number is odd, the check bit is 0.

odoriferous homing Homing on the ionized air produced by the exhaust gases of a snorkeling submarine.

off-center plan position indicator A plan position indicator in which the center of the display that represents the location of the radar can be moved from the center of the screen to any position on the face of the PPI.

office automation Use of an electronic computer or computing system for routine clerical jobs.

off-line Describing equipment not connected to a computer, or temporarily disconnected from one.

off-line equipment Peripheral equipment or devices not in direct communication with the central processing unit of a computer.

off-line mode Any operation such as printing, punching, converting which does not involve the main computer.

off-line operation Operation of peripheral equipment in conjunction with, but not under the control of, the central processing unit.

off-line processing Any processing which takes place independently of the central processing unit; for instance, card-to-tape conversion using auxiliary equipment.

off-line storage A storage device not under control of the central processing unit.

off-line unit Any operation device which is not attached to the main computer.

off-lining The process of separating card reading and printing from the actual running of jobs, by transcribing data to and from magnetic tape or other high-speed input/output devices.

off-punch A hole which is not punched in precise position on a computer card.

offset stacker A card stacker which is capable, under machine control, of stacking cards so that some of them stick out from the deck, permitting their identification.

ohmic dissipation Loss of electric energy when a current flows through a resistance due to conversion into heat. Also known as ohmic loss.

ohmic loss See ohmic dissipation.

oil circuit breaker A high-voltage circuit breaker in which the arc is drawn in oil to dissipate the heat and extinguish the arc; the intense heat of the arc decomposes the oil, generating a gas whose high pressure produces a flow of fresh fluid through the arc that furnishes the necessary insulation to prevent a restrike of the arc.

O indicator See O scope.

OL See only loadable.

omegatron A miniature mass spectrograph, about the size of a receiving tube, that can be sealed to another tube and used to identify the residual gases left after evacuation.

omission factor In information retrieval, the ratio obtained in dividing the number of nonretrieved relevant documents by the total number of relevant documents in the file.

omnidirectional Radiating or receiving equally well in all directions. Also known as nondirectional.

OMR *See* optical mark reading.

OMS *See* ovonic memory switch.

ondograph An instrument that draws the waveform of an alternating-current voltage step by step; a capacitor is charged momentarily to the amplitude of a point on the voltage wave, then discharged into a recording galvanometer, with the action being repeated a little further along on the waveform at intervals of about 0.01 second.

ondoscope A glow-discharge tube used to detect high-frequency radiation, as in the vicinity of a radar transmitter; the radiation ionizes the gas in the tube and produces a visible glow.

one-address code In computers, a code using one-address instructions.

one-address instruction A digital computer programming instruction that explicitly describes one operation and one storage location. Also known as single-address instruction.

one condition The state of a magnetic core or other computer memory element in which it represents the value 1. Also known as one state.

one-digit subtracter *See* half-subtracter.

one-ended tape Turing machine A variation of a Turing machine in which the tape can be extended to the right, but not to the left.

one-level address In digital computers, an address that directly indicates the location of an instruction or some data.

one-level code Any code using absolute addresses and absolute operation codes.

one-level subroutine A subroutine that does not use other subroutines during its execution.

one-line adapter A unit connecting central processes and permitting high-speed transfer of data under program control.

one-pass operation An operating method, now standard, which produces an object program from a source program in one pass.

one-plus-one address instruction A digital computer instruction whose format contains two address parts; one address designates the operand to be involved in the operation; the other indicates the location of the next instruction to be executed.

one-quadrant multiplier Of an analog computer, a multiplier in which operation is restricted to a single sign of both input variables.

one's complement A numeral in binary notation, derived from another binary number by simply changing the sense of every digit.

ones-complement code A number coding system used in some computers, where, for any number x, $x = (1 - 2^{n-1}) a_0 + 2^{n-2} a_1 + \ldots + a_{n-1}$, where $a_i = 1$ or 0.

one-shot multivibrator *See* monostable multivibrator.

one-shot operation *See* single-step operation.

one-sided abrupt junction An abrupt junction that is realized by giving one side of the junction a high doping level compared with the other; that is, an n^+p or p^+n junction.

one state *See* one condition.

one-step operation *See* single-step operation.

one-to-one assembler An assembly program which produces a single instruction in machine language for each statement in the source language. Also known as one-to-one translator.

one-to-one translater *See* one-to-one assembler.

on-line 1. Pertaining to equipment capable of interacting with a computer. 2. The state in which a piece of equipment or a subsystem is connected and powered to deliver its proper output to the system.

on-line central file An organized collection of data, such as an on-line disk file, in a storage device under direct control of a central processing unit, that serves as a continually available source of data in applications where real-time or direct-access capabilites are required.

on-line computer system A computer system which is adapted to on-line operation.

on-line data reduction The processing of information as rapidly as it is received by the computing system.

on-line disk file A magnetic disk directly connected to the central processing unit, thereby increasing the memory capacity of the computer.

on-line equipment The equipment or devices in a system whose operation is under control of the central processing unit, and in which information reflecting current activity is introduced into the data-processing system as soon as it occurs.

on-line inquiry A level of computer processing that results from adding to an expanded batch system the capability to immediately access, from any terminal, any record that is stored in the disk files attached to the computer.

on-line mode Mode of operation in which all devices are responsive to the central processor.

on-line operation Computer operation in which input data are fed into the computer directly from observing instruments or other input equipment, and computer results are obtained during the progress of the event.

on-line storage Storage controlled by the central processing unit of a computer.

on-line typewriter A typewriter which transmits information into and out of a computer, and which is controlled by the central processing unit and thus by whatever program the computer is carrying out.

only loadable Attribute of a load module which can be brought into main memory only by a LOAD macroinstruction given from another module. Abbreviated OL.

on the beam Centered on a beam of, or on an equisignal zone of, radiant energy, as a radio range.

on-the-fly printer A high-speed line printer using continuously rotating print wheels and fast-acting hammers to print the letters contained on one line of text so rapidly that the characters appear to be printed simultaneously.

open-ended Of techniques, designed to facilitate or permit expansion, extension, or increase in capability; the opposite of closed-in and artificially constrained.

open-ended system In character recognition, a system in which the input data to be read are derived from sources other than the computer with which the character reader is associated.

open file A file that can be accessed for reading, writing, or both.

open routine 1. A routine which can be inserted directly into a larger routine without a linkage or calling sequence. 2. A computer program that changes the state of a file from closed to open.

open shop A data-processing-center organization in which individuals from outside the data-processing community are permitted to implement their own solutions to problems.

open subroutine A set of computer instructions that collectively perform some particular function and are inserted directly into the program each and every time that particular function is required.

operand Any one of the quantities entering into or arising from an operation.

operand-precision register A special register found in some minicomputers which can be programmed from 8- to 32-bit precision.

operate time The phase of computer operation when an instruction is being carried out.

operating angle Electrical angle of the input signal (for example, portion of a cycle) during which plate current flows in a vacuum tube amplifier.

operating delay Computer time lost because of mistakes or inefficiency of operating personnel or users of the system, excluding time lost because of defects in programs or data.

operating instructions A detailed description of the actions that must be carried out by a computer operator in running a program or group of interrelated programs, usually included in the documentation of a program supplied by a programmer or systems analyst, along with the source program and flow charts.

operating point Point on a family of characteristic curves of a vacuum tube or transistor where the coordinates of the point represent the instantaneous values of the electrode voltages and currents for the operating conditions under study or consideration.

operating range The frequency range over which a reversible transducer is operable.

operating ratio The time during which computer hardware operates and gives reliable results divided by the total time scheduled for computer operation.

operating system *See* executive system.

operating system supervisor The control program of a set of programs which guide a computer in the performance of its tasks and which assist the program with certain supporting functions.

operation 1. A process or procedure that obtains a unique result from any permissible combination of operands. 2. The sequence of actions resulting from the execution of one digital computer instruction.

operational amplifier An amplifier having high direct-current stability and high immunity to oscillation, generally achieved by using a large amount of negative feedback; used to perform analog-computer functions such as summing and integrating.

operational label A combination of letters and digits at the beginning of the tape which uniquely identify the tape required by the system.

operational standby program The program operating in the standby computer when in the duplex mode of operation.

operation code A field or portion of a digital computer instruction that indicates which action is to be performed by the computer. Also known as command code.

operation cycle The portion of a memory cycle required to perform an operation; division and multiplication usually require more than one memory cycle to be completed.

operation decoder A device that examines the operation contained in an instruction of a computer program and sends signals to the circuits required to carry out the operation.

operation number 1. Number designating the position of an operation, or its equivalent subroutine, in the sequence of operations composing a routine. 2. Number identifying each step in a program stated in symbolic code.

operation part That portion of a digital computer instruction which is reserved for the operation code.

operation register A register used to store and decode the operation code for the next instruction to be carried out by a computer.

operation time The time elapsed during the interpretation and execution of an arithmetic or logic operation by a computer.

operator Anything that designates an action to be performed, especially the operation code of a computer instruction.

operator hierarchy A sequence of mathematical operators which designates the order in which these operators are to be applied to any mathematical expression in a given programming language.

operator interrupt A step whereby control is passed to the monitor, and a message, usually requiring a typed answer, is printed on the console typewriter.

operator's console Equipment which provides for manual intervention and monitoring computer operation.

operator subgoaling A computer problem-solving method in which the inability of the computer to take the desired next step at any point in the problem-solving process leads to a subgoal of making that step feasible.

optical bar-code reader A device which uses any of various photoelectric methods to read information which has been coded by placing marks in prescribed boxes on documents with ink, pencil, or other means.

optical branch The vibrations of an optical mode plotted on a graph of frequency versus wave number; it is separated from, and has higher frequencies than, the acoustic branch.

optical character recognition That branch of character recognition concerned with the automatic identification of handwritten or printed characters by any of various photoelectric methods. Abbreviated OCR. Also known as electrooptical character recognition.

optical computer A computer that uses various combinations of holography, lasers, and mass-storage memories for such applications as ultra-high-speed signal processing, image deblurring, and character recognition.

optical coupler *See* optoisolator.

optical coupling Coupling between two circuits by means of a light beam or light pipe having transducers at opposite ends, to isolate the circuits electrically.

optical disk A type of video disk storage device consisting of a pressed disk with a spiral groove at the bottom of which are submicrometer-sized depressions that are sensed by a laser beam.

optical disk storage A computer storage technology in which information is stored in submicrometer-sized holes on a rotating disk, and is recorded and read by laser beams focused on the disk. Also known as video disk storage.

optical electronic reproducer *See* optical sound head.

optical encoder An encoder that converts positional information into corresponding digital data by interrupting light beams directed on photoelectric devices.

optical isolator *See* optoisolator.

optically coupled isolator *See* optoisolator.

optical mark reading Optically sensing information encoded as a series of marks, such as lines or filled-in boxes on a test answer sheet, or some special pattern, such as the Universal Product Code. Abbreviated OMR.

optical mask A thin sheet of metal or other substance containing an open pattern, used to suitably expose to light a photoresistive substance overlaid on a semiconductor or other surface to form an integrated circuit.

optical memory A computer memory that uses optical techniques which generally involve an addressable laser beam, a storage medium which responds to the beam for writing and sometimes for erasing, and a detector which reacts to the altered character of the medium when it uses the beam to read out stored data.

optical mode A type of vibration of a crystal lattice whose frequency varies with wave number only over a limited range, and in which neighboring atoms or molecules in different sublattices move in opposition to each other.

optical phonon A quantum of an optical mode of vibration of a crystal lattice.

optical processing The use of light, including visible and infrared, to handle data-processing information.

optical reader A computer data-entry machine that converts printed characters, bar or line codes, and pencil-shaded areas into a computer-input code format.

optical relay An optoisolator in which the output device is a light-sensitive switch that provides the same on and off operations as the contacts of a relay.

optical scanner *See* flying-spot scanner.

optical sound head The assembly in motion picture projection which reproduces photographically recorded sound; light from an incandescent lamp is focused on a slit, light from the slit is in turn focused on the optical sound track of a film, and the light passing through the film is detected by a photoelectric cell. Also known as optical electronic reproducer.

optical sound recorder *See* photographic sound recorder.

optical sound reproducer *See* photographic sound reproducer.

optical storage Storage of large amounts of data in permanent form on photographic film or its equivalent, for nondestructive readout by means of a light source and photodetector.

optical type font A special type font whose characters are designed to be easily read by both people and optical character recognition machines.

optimize To rearrange the instructions or data in storage so that a minimum number of time-consuming jumps or transfers are required in the running of a program.

optimum bunching Bunching condition required for maximum output in a velocity modulation tube.

optimum code A computer code which is particularly efficient with regard to a particular aspect; for example, minimum time of execution, minimum or efficient use of storage space, and minimum coding time.

optimum filter An electric filter in which the mean square value of the error between a desired output and the actual output is at a minimum.

optimum programming Production of computer programs that maximize efficiency with respect to some criteria such as least cost, least use of storage, least time, or least use of time-sharing peripheral equipment.

optional halt instruction A halt instruction that can cause a computer program to stop either before or after the instruction is obeyed if certain criteria are met. Also known as optional stop instruction.

optional stop instruction *See* optional halt instruction.

optocoupler *See* optoisolator.

optoelectronic isolator *See* optoisolator.

optoelectronics The branch of electronics that deals with solid-state and other electronic devices for generating, modulating, transmitting, and sensing electromagnetic radiation in the ultraviolet, visible-light, and infrared portions of the spectrum.

optoelectronic scanner A scanner in which lenses, mirrors, or other optical devices are used between a light source or image and a photodiode or other photoelectric device.

optoisolator A coupling device in which a light-emitting diode, energized by the input signal, is optically coupled to a photodetector such as a light-sensitive output diode, transistor, or silicon controlled rectifier. Also known as optical coupler; optical isolator; optically coupled isolator; optocoupler; optoelectronic isolator; photocoupler; photoisolator.

or An instruction which performs the logical operation "or" on a bit-by-bit basis for its two or more operand words, usually storing the result in one of the operand locations. Also known as OR function.

OR circuit *See* OR gate.

OR function *See* or.

OR gate A multiple-input gate circuit whose output is energized when any one or more of the inputs is in a prescribed state; performs the function of the logical inclusive-or; used in digital computers. Also known as OR circuit.

orient To change relative and symbolic addresses to absolute form.

origin Absolute storage address in relative coding to which addresses in a region are referenced.

original document *See* source document.

orthicon A camera tube in which a beam of low-velocity electrons scans a photoemissive mosaic that is capable of storing a pattern of electric charges; has higher sensitivity than the iconoscope.

orthogonal parity check A parity checking system involving both a lateral and a longitudinal parity check.

orthotronic error control An error check carried out to ensure correct transmission, which uses lateral and longitudinal parity checks.

O scan *See* O scope.

osciducer Transducer in which information pertaining to the stimulus is provided in the form of deviation from the center frequency of an oscillator.

oscillator 1. An electronic circuit that converts energy from a direct-current source to a periodically varying electric output. 2. The stage of a superheterodyne receiver that generates a radio-frequency signal of the correct frequency to mix with the incoming signal and produce the intermediate-frequency value of the receiver. 3. The stage of a transmitter that generates the carrier frequency of the station or some fraction of the carrier frequency.

oscillator harmonic interference Interference occurring in a superheterodyne receiver due to the interaction of incoming signals with harmonics (usually the second harmonic) of the local oscillator.

oscillator-mixer-first detector *See* converter.

oscillistor A bar of semiconductor material, such as germanium, that will oscillate much like a quartz crystal when it is placed in a magnetic field and is carrying direct current that flows parallel to the magnetic field.

oscillograph tube Cathode-ray tube used to produce a visible pattern, which is the graphical representation of electric signals, by variations of the position of the focused spot or spots according to these signals.

oscilloscope *See* cathode-ray oscilloscope.

O scope An A scope modified by the inclusion of an adjustable notch for measuring range. Also known as O indicator; O scan.

OTS *See* ovonic threshold switch.

O-type backward-wave oscillator A backward-wave tube in which an electron gun produces an electron beam focused longitudinally throughout the length of the tube, a slow-wave circuit interacts with the beam, and at the end of the tube a collector terminates the beam. Also known as O-type carcinotron; type-O carcinotron.

O-type carcinotron *See* O-type backward-wave oscillator.

outer-shell electron *See* conduction electron.

out-of-line coding Instructions in a routine that are stored in a different part of computer storage from the rest of the instructions.

out-plant system A data-processing system that has one or more remote terminals from which information is transmitted to a central computer.

output 1. The data produced by a data-processing operation, or the information that is the objective or goal in data processing. 2. The data actively transmitted from within the computer to an external device, or onto a permanent recording medium (paper, microfilm). 3. The activity of transmitting the generated information. 4. The readable storage medium upon which generated data are written, as in hard-copy output. 5. The current, voltage, power, driving force, or information which a circuit or device delivers. 6. Terminals or other places where a circuit or device can deliver current, voltage, power, driving force, or information.

output area A part of storage that has been reserved for output data. Also known as output block.

output block 1. A portion of the internal storage of a computer that is reserved for receiving, processing, and transmitting data to be transferred out. 2. *See* output area.

output bus driver A device that power-amplifies output signals from a computer to allow them to drive heavy circuit loads.

output capacitance Of an *n*-terminal electron tube, the short-circuit transfer capacitance between the output terminal and all other terminals, except the input terminal, connected together.

output equipment Equipment, such as punched cards, printers, and magnetic tape recorders, which transfers data from within a computer to its outside environment.

output gap An interaction gap by means of which usable power can be abstracted from an electron stream in a microwave tube.

output impedance The impedance presented by a source to a load.

output magazine A mechanism that accumulates cards after they have passed through a machine.

output monitor interrupt A data-processing step in which control is passed to the monitor to determine the precedence order for two requests having the same priority level.

output program *See* output routine.

output punch A device that transcribes data generated by a computer onto paper tape or punch cards.

output record 1. A unit of data that has been transcribed from a computer to an external medium or device. **2.** The unit of data that is currently held in the output area of a computer before being transcribed to an external medium or device.

output resistance The resistance across the output terminals of a circuit or device.

output routine A series of computer instructions which organizes and directs all operations associated with the transcription of data from a computer to various media and external devices by various types of output equipment. Also known as output program.

output stage The final stage in any electronic equipment.

output transformer The iron-core audio-frequency transformer used to match the output stage of a radio receiver or an amplifier to its loudspeaker or other load.

output tube Power-amplifier tube designed for use in an output stage.

output unit In computers, a unit which delivers information from the computer to an external device or from internal storage to external storage.

output word Any running word into which an input word is to be translated.

overall response The ratio between system input and output.

overbunching In velocity-modulated streams of electrons, the bunching condition produced by the continuation of the bunching process beyond the optimum condition.

overcoupled circuits Two resonant circuits which are tuned to the same freqency but coupled so closely that two response peaks are obtained; used to attain broad-band response with substantially uniform impedance.

overcurrent An abnormally high current, usually resulting from a short circuit.

overdriven amplifier Amplifier stage which is designed to distort the input-signal waveform by permitting the grid signal to drive the stage beyond cutoff or plate-current saturation.

overflow 1. The condition that arises when the result of an arithmetic operation exeeds the storage capacity of the indicated result-holding storage. **2.** That part of the result which exceeds the storage capacity.

overflow bucket A unit of storage in a direct-access storage device used to hold an overflow record.

overflow check indicator *See* overflow indicator.

overflow error The condition in which the numerical result of an operation exceeds the capacity of the register.

overflow indicator A bistable device which changes state when an overflow occurs in the register associated with it, and which is designed so that its condition can be determined, and its original condition restored. Also known as overflow check indicator.

overflow record A unit of data whose length is too great for it to be stored in an assigned section of a direct-access storage, and which must be stored in another area from which it may be retrieved by means of a reference stored in the original assigned area in place of the record.

overhead The time a computer system spends doing computations that do not contribute directly to the progress of any user tasks in the system, such as allocation of resources, responding to exceptional conditions, providing protection and reliability, and accounting.

overlap To perform some or all of an operation concurrently with one or more other operations.

overlapped memories An arrangement of computer memory banks in which, to cut down access time, successive words are taken from different memory banks, rewriting in one bank being overlapped by logic operations in another bank, with memory access in still another bank.

overlapping An operation whereby, if the processor determines that the current instruction and the next instruction lie in different storage modules, the two words may be retrieved in parallel.

overlay A technique for bringing routines into high-speed storage from some other form of storage during processing, so that several routines will occupy the same storage locations at different times; overlay is used when the total storage requirements for instructions exceed the available main storage.

overlay transistor Transistor containing a large number of emitters connected in parallel to provide maximum power amplification at extremely high frequencies.

overload A load greater than that which a device is designed to handle; may cause overheating of power-handling components and distortion in signal circuits.

overload current A current greater than that which a circuit is designed to carry; may melt wires or damage elements of the circuit.

overpunch A hole punch in any one of the three rows above the zero row in a punch card, usually combined with a second punch on the same column to represent a character.

overtone crystal Quartz crystal cut in such a manner that it will operate at a higher order than its fundamental frequency, or operate at two frequencies simultaneously as in a synthesizer.

overvoltage The amount by which the applied voltage exceeds the Geiger threshold in a radiation counter tube.

overwrite To enter information into a storage location and destroy the information previously held there.

ovonic device *See* glass switch.

ovonic memory switch A glass switch which, after being brought from the highly resistive state to the conducting state, remains in the conducting state until a current pulse returns it to its highly resistive state. Abbreviated OMS. Also known as memory switch.

ovonic threshold switch A glass switch which, after being brought from the highly resistive state to the conducting state, returns to the highly resistive state when the current falls below a holding current value. Abbreviated OTS.

Ovshinsky effect The characteristic of a special thin-film solid-state switch that responds identically to both positive and negative polarities so that current can be made to flow in both directions equally.

Owen bridge A four-arm alternating-current bridge used to measure self-inductance in terms of capacitance and resistance; bridge balance is independent of frequency.

own coding A series of instructions added to a standard software routine to change or extend the routine so that it can carry out special tasks.

owned program *See* proprietary program.

oxide-coated cathode A cathode that has been coated with oxides of alkaline-earth metals to improve electron emission at moderate temperatures. Also known as Wehnelt cathode.

oxide isolation Isolation of the elements of an integrated circuit by forming a layer of silicon oxide around each element.

oxide passivation Passivation of a semiconductor surface by producing a layer of an insulating oxide on the surface.

P

pack To reduce the amount of storage required to hold information by changing the method of encoding the data.

package A program that is written for a general and widely used application in such a way that its usefulness is not impaired by the problems of data or organization of a particular user.

packaged magnetron Integral structure comprising a magnetron, its magnetic circuit, and its output matching device.

packaging density The number of components per unit volume in a working system or subsystem.

packed decimal A means of representing two digits per character, to reduce space and increase transmission speed.

packing density 1. The amount of information per unit of storage medium, as characters per inch on tape, bits per inch or drum, or bits per square inch in photographic storage. 2. The number of devices or gates per unit area of an integrated circuit.

packing routine A subprogram which compresses data so as to eliminate blanks and reduce the storage needed for a file.

pad 1. An arrangement of fixed resistors used to reduce the strength of a radio-frequency or audio-frequency signal by a desired fixed amount without introducing appreciable distortion. Also known as fixed attenuator. 2. *See* terminal area.

padder A trimmer capacitor inserted in series with the oscillator tuning circuit of a superheterodyne receiver to control calibration at the low-frequency end of a tuning range.

padding The adding of meaningless data (usually blanks) to a unit of data to bring it up to some fixed size.

page 1. A standard quantity of main-memory capacity, usually 512 to 4096 bytes or words, used for memory allocation and for partitioning programs into control sections. 2. A standard quantity of source program coding, usually 8 to 64 lines, used for displaying the coding on a cathode-ray tube.

page boundary The address of the first (lowest) word or byte within a page of memory.

page fault An interruption that occurs while a page which is referred to by the program is being read into memory.

page printer A computer output device which composes a full page of characters before printing the page.

page reader In character recognition, a character reader capable of processing cut-form documents of varying sizes; sometimes capable of reading information in reel forms.

page table A key element in the virtual memory technique; a table of addresses where entries are adjusted for easy relocation of pages.

page turning 1. The process of moving entire pages of information between main memory and auxiliary storage, usually to allow several concurrently executing programs to share a main memory of inadequate capacity. **2.** In conversational time-sharing systems, the moving of programs in and out of memory on a round-robin, cyclic schedule so that each program may use its allotted share of computer time.

paging The scheme used to locate pages, to move them between main storage and auxiliary storage, or to exchange them with pages of the same or other computer programs; used in computers with virtual memories.

paint Vernacular for a target image on a radarscope.

pairing In television, imperfect interlace of lines composing the two fields of one frame of the picture; instead of having the proper equal spacing, the lines appear in groups of two.

Palmer scan Combination of circular or raster and conical radar scans; the beam is swung around the horizon, and at the same time a conical scan is performed.

panadapter *See* panoramic adapter.

panel The face of the console, which is normally equipped with lights, switches, and buttons to control the machine, correct errors, determine the status of the various CPU (central processing unit) parts, and determine and revise the contents of various locations. Also known as control panel; patch panel.

panel display An unconventional method of displaying color television pictures in which luminescent conversion devices, such as light-emitting diodes or electroluminescent devices, are arranged in a matrix array, forming a flat-panel screen, and are controlled by signals sent over vertical and horizontal wires connected to both electrodes of the devices.

panoramic adapter A device designed to operate with a search receiver to provide a visual presentation on an oscilloscope screen of a band of frequencies extending above and below the center frequency to which the search receiver is tuned. Also known as panadapter.

panoramic display A display that simultaneously shows the relative amplitudes of all signals received at different frequencies.

panoramic receiver Radio receiver that permits continuous observation on a cathode-ray-tube screen of the presence and relative strength of all signals within a wide frequency range.

pan-range Intensity-modulated, A-type radar indication with a slow vertical sweep applied to video; stationary targets give solid vertical deflection, and moving targets give broken vertical deflection.

paper tape A paper ribbon in which data may be represented by means of partially or completely punched holes.

paper-tape code The system by which data are represented by means of holes punched on a paper tape.

paper-tape punch Device which places binary characters on a paper tape by punching holes in appropriate channels on the tape; a binary one is placed on the tape by punching a hole; a zero is indicated by the absence of a punched hole.

paper-tape reader A reader used to sense information punched in paper tape as a series of holes. Also known as punched-tape reader; tape reader.

paper-tape Turing machine A variation of a Turing machine in which a blank square can have a nonblank symbol written on it, but this symbol cannot be changed thereafter.

paper-tape unit The mechanism which handles punched paper tape and usually consists of a paper-tape transport, sensing and recording or perforating heads, and associated electrical and electronic equipment.

paper throw The movement of paper through a computer printer for a purpose other than printing, in which the distance traveled, and usually the speed, is greater than that of a single line spacing.

parallel Simultaneous transmission of, storage of, or logical operations on the parts of a word, character, or other subdivision of a word in a computer, using separate facilities for the various parts.

parallel access Transferral of information to or from a storage device in which all elements in a unit of information are transferred simultaneously. Also known as simultaneous access.

parallel addition A method of addition by a computer in which all the corresponding pairs of digits of the addends are processed at the same time during one cycle, and one or more subsequent cycles are used for propagation and adjustment of any carries that may have been generated.

parallel algorithm An algorithm in which several computations are carried on simultaneously.

parallel buffer Electronic device (magnetic core or flip-flop) used to temporarily store digital data in parallel, as opposed to series storage.

parallel by character The handling of all the characters of a machine word simultaneously in separate lines, channels, or storage cells.

parallel computation The simultaneous computation of several parts of a problem.

parallel computer A computer that can carry out more than one logic or arithmetic operation at one time.

parallel digital computer Computer in which the digits are handled in parallel; mixed serial and parallel machines are frequently called serial or parallel, according to the way arithmetic processes are performed; an example of a parallel digital computer is one which handles decimal digits in parallel, although it might handle the bits constituting a digit either serially or in parallel.

parallel dot carrier printer *See* line dot matrix.

parallel element-processing ensemble A powerful electronic computer used by the U.S. Army to simulate tracking and discrimination of reentry vehicles as part of the ballistic missile defense research program. Abbreviated PEPE.

parallel feed 1. Application of a direct-current voltage to the plate or grid of a tube in parallel with an alternating-current circuit, so that the direct-current and the alternating-current components flow in separate paths. Also known as shunt feed. 2. *See* sideways feed.

parallel operation 1. Performance of several actions, usually of a similar nature, by a computer system simultaneously through provision of individual similar or identical devices. 2. The connecting together of the outputs of two or more batteries or other power supplies so that the sum of their output currents flows to a common load.

parallel programming 1. A method for performing simultaneously the normally sequential steps of a computer program, using two or more processors. 2. Method of parallel operation for two or more power supplies in which their feedback terminals (voltage control terminals) are also paralleled; these terminals are often connected to a separate programming source.

parallel rectifier One of two or more rectifiers that are connected to the same pair of terminals, generally in series with small resistors or inductors, when greater current is desired than can be obtained with a single rectifier.

parallel representation The simultaneous appearance of the different bits of a digital variable on parallel bus lines.

parallel resonant interstage A coupling between two amplifier stages achieved by means of a parallel-tuned LC circuit.

parallel-rod oscillator Ultra-high-frequency oscillator circuit in which parallel rods or wires of required length and dimensions form the tank circuits.

parallel running 1. The running of a newly developed system in a data-processing area in conjunction with the continued operation of the current system. 2. The final step in the debugging of a system; this step follows a system test.

parallel search storage A device for very rapid search of a volume of stored data to permit finding a specific item.

parallel storage A storage device in which words (or characters or digits) can be read in or out simultaneously.

parallel transfer Simultaneous transfer of all bits in a storage location constituting a character or word.

parallel transmission The transmission of characters of a word over different lines, usually simultaneously; opposed to serial transmission.

parameter card A punched card containing the values of parameters needed for a program.

parameter tags Constants that are used by several computer programs.

parameter word A word in a computer storage containing one or more parameters that specify the action of a routine or subroutine.

parametric amplifier A highly sensitive ultra-high-frequency or microwave amplifier having as its basic element an electron tube or solid-state device whose reactance can be varied periodically by an alternating-current voltage at a pumping frequency. Also known as mavar; paramp; reactance amplifier.

parametric converter Inverting or noninverting parametric device used to convert an input signal at one frequency into an output signal at a different frequency.

parametric device Electronic device whose operation depends essentially upon the time variation of a characteristic parameter usually understood to be a reactance.

parametric down-converter Parametric converter in which the output signal is at a lower frequency than the input signal.

parametric oscillator An oscillator in which the reactance parameter of an energy-storage device is varied to obtain oscillation.

parametric phase-locked oscillator *See* parametron.

parametric up-converter Parametric converter in which the output signal is at a higher frequency than the input signal.

parametron A resonant circuit in which either the inductance or capacitance is made to vary periodically at one-half the driving frequency; used as a digital computer element, in which the oscillation represents a binary digit. Also known as parametric phase-locked oscillator; phase-locked oscillator; phase-locked subharmonic oscillator.

paramp *See* parametric amplifier.

paraphase amplifier An amplifier that provides two equal output signals 180° out of phase.

parasitic An undesired and energy-wasting signal current, capacitance, or other parameter of an electronic circuit.

parasitic oscillation An undesired self-sustaining oscillation or a self-generated transient impulse in an oscillator or amplifier circuit, generally at a frequency above or below the correct operating frequency.

parasitic suppressor A suppressor, usually in the form of a coil and resistor in parallel, inserted in a circuit to suppress parasitic high-frequency oscillations.

parenthesis-free notation *See* Polish notation.

parity The use of a self-checking code in a computer employing binary digits in which the total number of 1's or 0's in each permissible code expression is always even or always odd.

parity check *See* odd-even check.

parity error A machine error in which an odd number of bits are accidentally changed, so that the error can be detected by a parity check.

parsing A process whereby phrases in a string of characters in a computer language are associated with the component names of the grammar that generated the string.

partial carry A word composed of the carries generated at each position when adding many digits in parallel.

partial function A partial function from a set A to a set B is a correspondence between some subset of A and B which associates with each element of the subset of A a unique element of B.

partial-read pulse Current pulse that is applied to a magnetic memory to select a specific magnetic cell for reading.

partial-select output The voltage response produced by applying partial-read or partial-write pulses to an unselected magnetic cell.

partition 1. A reserved portion of a computer memory, sometimes used for the execution of a single computer program. 2. One of a number of fixed portions into which a computer memory is divided in certain multiprogramming systems.

partitioned data set A single data set, divided internally into a directory and one or more sequentially organized subsections called members, residing on a direct access for each device, and commonly used for storage or program libraries.

partition noise Noise that arises in an electron tube when the electron beam is divided between two or more electrodes, as between screen grid and anode in a pentode.

part operation The part in an instruction that specifies the kind of arithmetical or logical operation to be performed, but not the address of the operands.

party-line bus Parallel input/output bus lines to which are wired all external devices, connected to a processor register by suitable logic.

PASCAL A procedure-oriented programming language whose highly structured design facilitates the rapid location and correction of coding errors.

Paschen's law The law that the sparking potential between two parallel plate electrodes in a gas is a function of the product of the gas density and the distance between the electrodes. Also known as Paschen's rule.

Paschen's rule *See* Paschen's law.

pass A complete cycle of reading, processing, and writing in a computer.

passband A frequency band in which the attenuation of a filter is essentially zero.

pass element Controlled variable resistance device, either a vacuum tube or power transistor, in series with the source of direct-current power; the pass element is driven by the amplified error signal to increase its resistance when the output needs to be lowered or to decrease its resistance when the output must be raised.

passivation Growth of an oxide layer on the surface of a semiconductor to provide electrical stability by isolating the transistor surface from electrical and chemical conditions in the environment; this reduces reverse-current leakage, increases breakdown voltage, and raises power dissipation rating.

passive AND gate *See* AND gate.

passive device A unit of a computer which cannot itself initiate a request for communication with another device, but which honors such a request from another device.

passive electronic countermeasures Electronic countermeasures that do not radiate energy, including reconnaissance or surveillance equipment that detects and analyzes electromagnetic radiation from radar and communications transmitters, and devices such as chaff which return spurious echoes to enemy radar.

passive jamming Use of confusion reflectors to return spurious and confusing signals to enemy radars. Also known as mechanical jamming.

passive system Electronic system which emits no energy, and does not give away its position or existence.

passive transducer A transducer containing no internal source of power.

patch 1. To modify a program or routine by inserting a machine language correction in an object deck, or by inserting it directly into the computer through the console. 2. The section of coding inserted in this way.

patch panel *See* panel.

path The logical sequence of instructions followed by a computer in carrying out a routine.

pattern analysis The phase of pattern recognition that consists of using whatever is known about the problem at hand to guide the gathering of data about the patterns and pattern classes, and then applying techniques of data analysis to help uncover the structure present in the data.

pattern generator A signal generator used to generate a test signal that can be fed into a television receiver to produce on the screen a pattern of lines having usefulness for servicing purposes.

pattern recognition The automatic identification of figures, characters, shapes, forms, and patterns without active human participation in the decision process.

pattern-sensitive fault A fault that appears only in response to one pattern or sequence of data, or certain patterns or sequences.

Pb-I-Pb junction *See* lead-I-lead junction.

PCP *See* primary control program.

PDA *See* postacceleration.

P display *See* plan position indicator.

peak cathode current 1. Maximum instantaneous value of a periodically recurring cathode current. 2. Highest instantaneous value of a randomly recurring pulse of cathode current. 3. Highest instantaneous value of a nonrecurrent pulse of cathode current occurring under fault conditions.

peak detector A detector whose output voltage approximates the true peak value of an applied signal; the detector tracks the signal in its sample mode and preserves the highest input signal in its hold mode.

peak envelope power Of a radio transmitter, the average power supplied to the antenna transmission line by a transmitter during one radio-frequency cycle at the highest crest of the modulation envelope, taken under conditions of normal operation.

peaker A small fixed or adjustable inductance used to resonate with stray and distributed capacitances in a broad-band amplifier to increase the gain at the higher frequencies.

peak forward voltage The maximum instantaneous voltage applied to an electronic device in the direction of lesser resistance to current flow.

peaking circuit A circuit used to improve the high-frequency response of a broad-band amplifier; in shunt peaking, a small coil is placed in series with the anode load; in series peaking, the coil is placed in series with the grid of the following stage.

peaking network Type of interstage coupling network in which an inductance is effectively in series (series-peaking network), or in shunt (shunt-peaking network), with the parasitic capacitance to increase the amplification at the upper end of the frequency range.

peak inverse anode voltage Maximum instantaneous anode voltage in the direction opposite to that in which the tube or other device is designed to pass current.

peak inverse voltage Maximum instantaneous anode-to-cathode voltage in the reverse direction which is actually applied to the diode in an operating circuit.

peak limiter *See* limiter.

peak signal level Expression of the maximum instantaneous signal power or voltage as measured at any point in a facsimile transmission system; this includes auxiliary signals.

pecker The part of a paper tape reader that senses holes in the tape.

pedestal *See* blanking level.

pedestal level *See* blanking level.

peephole masks In character recognition, a set of characters (each character residing in the character reader in the form of strategically placed points) which theoretically render all input characters as being unique regardless of their style.

pel *See* pixel.

pencil follower A device for converting graphic images to digital form; the information to be analyzed appears on a reading table where a reading pencil is made to follow the trace, and a mechanism beneath the table surface transmits position signals from the pencil to an electronic console for conversion to digital form.

pencil tube A small tube designed especially for operation in the ultra-high-frequency band; used as an oscillator or radio-frequency amplifier.

penetration phosphors A system for creating color cathode-ray-tube displays, in which phosphors of two different colors are placed on the screen of a cathode-ray tube in separate layers, and a high-energy beam penetrates the first layer and excites the second, while a low-energy beam is stopped by the first layer and excites it.

Penning gage *See* Philips ionization gage.

pentagrid *See* heptode.

pentode A five-electrode electron tube containing an anode, a cathode, a control electrode, and two additional electrodes that are ordinarily grids.

pentode transistor Point-contact transistor with four-point-contact electrodes; the body serves as a base with three emitters and one collector.

PEPE *See* parallel element-processing ensemble.

percentage differential relay Differential relay which functions when the difference between two quantities of the same nature exceeds a fixed percentage of the smaller quantity. Also known as biased relay; ratio-balance relay; ratio-differential relay.

percentage ripple Ratio of the effective value of the ripple voltage to the average value of the total voltage, expressed as a percentage.

percent make 1. In pulse testing, the length of time a circuit stands closed compared to the length of the test signal. 2. Percentage of time during a pulse period that telephone dial pulse springs are making contact.

perceptron A pattern recognition machine, based on an analogy to the human nervous system, capable of learning by means of a feedback system which reinforces correct answers and discourages wrong ones.

percolation The transfer of needed data back from secondary storage devices to main storage.

perforation rate The rate at which characters, rows, or words are punched in a paper tape.

periodic field focusing Focusing of an electron beam where the electrons follow a trochoidal path and the focusing field interacts with them at selected points.

peripheral buffer A device acting as a temporary storage when transmission occurs between two devices operating at different transmission speeds.

peripheral control unit A device which connects a unit of peripheral equipment with the central processing unit of a computer and which interprets and responds to instructions from the central processing unit.

peripheral equipment Equipment that works in conjunction with a computer but is not part of the computer itself, such as a card or paper-tape reader or punch, magnetic-tape handler, or line printer.

peripheral interface channel A path along which information can flow between a unit of peripheral equipment and the central processing unit of a computer.

peripheral-limited Property of a computer system whose processing time is determined by the speed of its peripheral equipment rather than by the speed of its central processing unit. Also known as I/O-bound.

peripheral processor Auxiliary computer performing specific operations under control of the master computer.

peripheral support computer A computer (on-line or off-line) used primarily for card-to-tape, tape-to-card, and tape-to-printer conversions, control of on-line devices, sorting, merging, and other similar auxiliary operations in support of a large automatic data-processing complex, and compatible with the larger computer to the extent that no required data interchange involves any necessity for conversion.

peripheral transfer The transmission of data between two units of peripheral equipment or between a peripheral unit and the central processing unit of a computer.

peristaltic charge-coupled device A high-speed charge-transfer integrated circuit in which the movement of the charges is similar to the peristaltic contractions and dilations of the digestive system.

permanent-magnet focusing Focusing of the electron beam in a television picture tube by means of the magnetic field produced by one or more permanent magnets mounted around the neck of the tube.

permanent storage A means of storing data for rapid retrieval by a computer; does not permit changing the stored data.

permatron Thermionic gas-discharge diode in which the start of conduction is controlled by an external magnetic field.

persistence A measure of the length of time that the screen of a cathode-ray tube remains luminescent after excitation is removed; ranges from 1 for short persistence to 7 for long persistence.

persistent-image device An optoelectronic amplifier capable of retaining an image for a definite length of time.

persistron A device in which electroluminescence and photoconductivity are used in a single panel capable of producing a steady or persistent display with pulsed signal input.

personal computer A computer for home or personal use.

personal identification code A special number up to six characters in length on a strip of magnetic tape embedded in a plastic card which identifies a user accessing a special-purpose computer. Abbreviated PIC.

persuader Element of storage tube which directs secondary emission to electron multiplier dynodes.

pertinency factor In information retrieval, the ratio obtained in dividing the total number of relevant documents retrieved by the total number of documents retrieved.

perveance The space-charge-limited cathode current of a diode divided by the 3/2 power of the anode voltage.

PFE *See* photoferroelectric effect.

phanotron A hot-filament diode rectifier tube utilizing an arc discharge in mercury vapor or an inert gas, usually xenon.

phantastran A solid-state phantastron.

phantastron A monostable pentode circuit used to generate sharp pulses at an adjustable and accurately timed interval after receipt of a triggering signal.

phantom signals Signals appearing on the screen of a cathode-ray-tube indicator, the cause of which cannot readily be determined and which may be caused by circuit fault, interference, propagation anomalies, jamming, and so on.

phantom target *See* echo box.

phase comparator A comparator that accepts two radio-frequency input signals of the same frequency and provides two video outputs which are proportional, respectively, to the sine and cosine of the phase difference between the two inputs.

phase control 1. A control that changes the phase angle at which the alternating-current line voltage fires a thyratron, ignitron, or other controllable gas tube. Also known as phase-shift control. 2. *See* hue control.

phase-correcting network *See* phase equalizer.

phase detector A circuit that provides a direct-current output voltage which is related to the phase difference between an oscillator signal and a reference signal, for use in controlling the oscillator to keep it in synchronism with the reference signal. Also known as phase discriminator.

phase discriminator *See* phase detector.

phase encoding A method of recording data on magnetic tape in which a logical 1 is defined as the transition from one magnetic polarity to another positioned at the center of the bit cell, and 0 is defined as the transition in the opposite direction, also at the center of the cell.

phase equalizer A network designed to compensate for phase-frequency distortion within a specified frequency band. Also known as phase-correcting network.

phase generator An instrument that accepts single-phase input signals over a given frequency range, or generates its own signal, and provides continuous shifting of the phase of this signal by one or more calibrated dials.

phase inversion Production of a phase difference of 180° between two similar wave shapes of the same frequency.

phase inverter A circuit or device that changes the phase of a signal by 180°, as required for feeding a push-pull amplifier stage without using a coupling transformer, or for changing the polarity of a pulse; a triode is commonly used as a phase inverter. Also known as inverter.

phase jitter Jitter that undesirably shortens or lengthens pulses intermittently during data processing or transmission.

phase lock Technique of making the phase of an oscillator signal follow exactly the phase of a reference signal by comparing the phases between the two signals and using the resultant difference signal to adjust the frequency of the reference oscillator.

phase-locked loop A circuit that consists essentially of a phase detector which compares the frequency of a voltage-controlled oscillator with that of an incoming carrier signal or reference-frequency generator; the output of the phase detector, after passing through a loop filter, is fed back to the voltage-controlled oscillator to keep it exactly in phase with the incoming or reference frequency. Abbreviated PLL.

phase-locked oscillator *See* parametron.

phase-locked subharmonic oscillator *See* parametron.

phase-modulation detector A device which recovers or detects the modulating signal from a phase-modulated carrier.

phase-modulation transmitter A radio transmitter used to broadcast a phase-modulated signal.

phase modulator An electronic circuit that causes the phase angle of a modulated wave to vary (with respect to an unmodulated carrier) in accordance with a modulating signal.

phase response A graph of the phase shift of a network as a function of frequency.

phase shift The phase angle between the input and output signals of a network or system.

phase-shift circuit A network that provides a voltage component which is shifted in phase with respect to a reference voltage.

phase-shift control *See* phase control.

phase-shift discriminator A discriminator that uses two similarly connected diodes, fed by a transformer that is tuned to the center frequency; when the frequency-modulated or phase-modulated input signal swings away from this center frequency, one diode receives a stronger signal than the other; the net output of the diodes is then proportional to the frequency displacement. Also known as Foster-Seely discriminator.

phase-shift oscillator An oscillator in which a network having a phase shift of 180° per stage is connected between the output and the input of an amplifier.

phase splitter A circuit that takes a single input signal voltage and produces two output signal voltages 180° apart in phase.

phasing *See* framing.

phasing line That portion of the length of scanning line set aside for the phasing signal in a television or facsimile system.

phasing signal A signal used to adjust the picture position along the scanning line in a facsimile system.

phasitron An electron tube used to frequency-modulate a radio-frequency carrier; internal electrodes are designed to produce a rotating disk-shaped corrugated sheet of electrons; audio input is applied to a coil surrounding the glass envelope of the tube, to produce a varying axial magnetic field that gives the desired phase or frequency modulation of the rf carrier input to the tube.

phasmajector See monoscope.

Philips ionization gage An ionization gage in which a high voltage is applied between two electrodes, and a strong magnetic field deflects the resulting electron stream, increasing the length of the electron path and thus increasing the chance for ionizing collisions of electrons with gas molecules. Abbreviated pig. Also known as coldcathode ionization gage; Penning gage.

phone patch A device connecting an amateur or citizens'-band transceiver temporarily to a telephone system.

phono jack A jack designed to accept a phono plug and provide a ground connection for the shield of the conductor connected to the plug.

phonon A quantum of an acoustic mode of thermal vibration in a crystal lattice.

phonon-electron interaction An interaction between an electron and a vibration of a lattice, resulting in a change in both the momentum of the particle and the wave vector of the vibration.

phono plug A plug designed for attaching to the end of a shielded conductor, for feeding audio-frequency signals from a phonograph or other a-f source to a mating phono jack on a preamplifier or amplifier.

phosphor dot One of the tiny dots of phosphor material that are used in groups of three, one group for each primary color, on the screen of a color television picture tube.

photocathode A photosensitive surface that emits electrons when exposed to light or other suitable radiation; used in phototubes, television camera tubes, and other lightsensitive devices.

photocell A solid-state photosensitive electron device whose current-voltage characteristic is a function of incident radiation. Also known as electric eye; photoelectric cell.

photocell relay A relay actuated by a signal received when light falls on, or is prevented from falling on, a photocell.

photoconduction An increase in conduction of electricity resulting from absorption of electromagnetic radiation.

photoconductive cell A device for detecting or measuring electromagnetic radiation by variation of the conductivity of a substance (called a photoconductor) upon absorption of the radiation by this substance. Also known as photoresistive cell; photoresistor.

photoconductive device A photoelectric device which utilizes the photoinduced change in electrical conductivity to provide an electrical signal.

photoconductive film A film of material whose current-carrying ability is enhanced when illuminated.

photoconductive gain factor The ratio of the number of electrons per second flowing through a circuit containing a cube of semiconducting material, whose sides are of unit length, to the number of photons per second absorbed in this volume.

photoconductive meter An exposure meter in which a battery supplies power through a photoconductive cell to a milliammeter.

photoconductivity The increase in electrical conductivity displayed by many nonmetallic solids when they absorb electromagnetic radiation.

photoconductivity gain The number of charge carriers that circulate through a circuit involving a photoconductor for each charge carrier generated by light.

photoconductor A nonmetallic solid whose conductivity increases when it is exposed to electromagnetic radiation.

photoconductor diode *See* photodiode.

photocoupler *See* optoisolator.

photodarlington A Darlington amplifier in which the input transistor is a phototransistor.

photodetector A detector that responds to radiant energy; examples include photoconductive cells, photodiodes, photoresistors, photoswitches, phototransistors, phototubes, and photovoltaic cells. Also known as light-sensitive cell; light-sensitive detector; light sensor photodevice; photoelectric detector; photosensor.

photodiffusion effect *See* Dember effect.

photodiode A semiconductor diode in which the reverse current varies with illumination; examples include the alloy-junction photocell and the grown-junction photocell. Also known as photoconductor diode.

photoelectret An electret produced by the removal of light from an illuminated photoconductor in an electric field.

photoelectric Pertaining to the electrical effects of light, such as the emission of electrons, generation of voltage, or a change in resistance when exposed to light.

photoelectric absorption Absorption of photons in one of the several photoelectric effects.

photoelectric cell *See* photocell.

photoelectric constant The ratio of the frequency of radiation causing emission of photoelectrons to the voltage corresponding to the energy absorbed by a photoelectron; equal to Planck's constant divided by the electron charge.

photoelectric control Control of a circuit or piece of equipment by changes in incident light.

photoelectric counter A photoelectrically actuated device used to record the number of times a given light path is intercepted by an object.

photoelectric cutoff register control Use of a photoelectric control system as a longitudinal position regulator to maintain the position of the point of cutoff with respect to a repetitive pattern of moving material.

photoelectric detector *See* photodetector.

photoelectric device A device which gives an electrical signal in response to visible, infrared, or ultraviolet radiation.

photoelectric effect *See* photoelectricity.

photoelectric electron-multiplier tube *See* multiplier phototube.

photoelectric intrusion detector A burglar-alarm system in which interruption of a light beam by an intruder reduces the illumination on a phototube and thereby closes an alarm circuit.

photoelectricity The liberation of an electric charge by electromagnetic radiation incident on a substance; includes photoemission, photoionization, photoconduction, the photovoltaic effect, and the Auger effect (an internal photoelectric process). Also known as photoelectric effect; photoelectric process.

photoelectric lighting control Use of a photoelectric relay actuated by a change in illumination in a given area or at a given point.

photoelectric process *See* photoelectricity.

photoelectric reader A device for reading information stored on paper tape or cards; data are read by sensing the presence or absence of holes.

photoelectric relay A relay combined with a phototube and amplifier, arranged so changes in incident light on the phototube make the relay contacts open or close. Also known as light relay.

photoelectric scanner A device that scans punched cards by photoelectric means, as opposed to the standard brushes or "feelers," or mechanical plungers.

photoelectric tube *See* phototube.

photoelectromagnetic effect The effect whereby, when light falls on a flat surface of an intermetallic semiconductor located in a magnetic field that is parallel to the surface, excess hole-electron pairs are created, and these carriers diffuse in the direction of the light but are deflected by the magnetic field to give a current flow through the semiconductor that is at right angles to both the light rays and the magnetic field.

photoelectromotive force Electromotive force caused by photovoltaic action.

photoelectron An electron emitted by the photoelectric effect.

photoemission The ejection of electrons from a solid (or less commonly, a liquid) by incident electromagnetic radiation. Also known as external photoelectric effect.

photoemission threshold The energy of a photon which is just sufficient to eject an electron from a solid or liquid in photoemission.

photoemissive cell A device which detects or measures radiant energy by measurement of the resulting emission of electrons from the surface of a photocathode.

photoemissivity The property of a substance that emits electrons when struck by light.

photoemitter A material that emits electrons when sufficiently illuminated.

photoferroelectric effect An effect observed in ferroelectric ceramics such as PLZT materials, in which light at or near the band-gap energy of the material has an effect on the electric field in the material created by an applied voltage, and, at a certain value of the voltage, also influences the degree of ferroelectric remanent polarization. Abbreviated PFE.

photoflash unit A portable electronic light source for photographic use, consisting of a capacitor-discharge power source, a flash tube, a battery for charging the capacitor, and sometimes also a high-voltage pulse generator to trigger the flash.

photoglow tube Gas-filled phototube used as a relay by making the operating voltage sufficiently high so that ionization and a flow discharge occur, with considerable current flow, when a certain illumination is reached.

photographic sound recorder A sound recorder having means for producing a modulated light beam and means for moving a light-sensitive medium relative to the beam to give a photographic recording of sound signals. Also known as optical sound recorder.

photographic sound reproducer A sound reproducer in which an optical sound record on film is moved through a light beam directed at a light-sensitive device, to convert the recorded optical variations back into audio signals. Also known as optical sound reproducer.

photoisland grid Photosensitive surface in the storage-type, Farnsworth dissector tube for television cameras.

photoisolator *See* optoisolator.

photomask A film or glass negative that has many high-resolution images, used in the production of semiconductor devices and integrated circuits.

photomultiplier *See* multiplier phototube.

photomultiplier cell A transistor whose *pn*-junction is exposed so that it conducts more readily when illuminated.

photomultiplier counter A scintillation counter that has a built-in multiplier phototube.

photomultiplier tube *See* multiplier phototube.

photon coupled isolator Circuit coupling device, consisting of an infrared emitter diode coupled to a photon detector over a short shielded light path, which provides extremely high circuit isolation.

photon coupling Coupling of two circuits by means of photons passing through a light pipe.

photonegative Having negative photoconductivity, hence decreasing in conductivity (increasing in resistance) under the action of light; selenium sometimes exhibits photonegativity.

photopositive Having positive photoconductivity, hence increasing in conductivity (decreasing in resistance) under the action of light; selenium ordinarily has photopositivity.

photoresistive cell *See* photoconductive cell.

photoresistor *See* photoconductive cell.

photo-SCR *See* light-activated silicon controlled rectifier.

photosensitive *See* light-sensitive.

photosensor *See* photodetector.

photothyristor *See* light-activated silicon controlled rectifier.

phototransistor A junction transistor that may have only collector and emitter leads or also a base lead, with the base exposed to light through a tiny lens in the housing; collector current increases with light intensity, as a result of amplification of base current by the transistor structure.

phototronic photocell *See* photovoltaic cell.

phototropism A reversible change in the structure of a solid exposed to light or other radiant energy, accompanied by a change in color. Also known as phototropy.

phototropy *See* phototropism.

phototube An electron tube containing a photocathode from which electrons are emitted when it is exposed to light or other electromagnetic radiation. Also known as electric eye; light-sensitive tube; photoelectric tube.

phototube cathode The photoemissive surface which is the most negative element of a phototube.

phototube relay A photoelectric relay in which a phototube serves as the light-sensitive device.

photovaristor Varistor in which the current-voltage relation may be modified by illumination, for example, one in which the semiconductor is cadmium sulfide or lead telluride.

photovoltaic Capable of generating a voltage as a result of exposure to visible or other radiation.

photovoltaic cell A device that detects or measures electromagnetic radiation by generating a potential at a junction (barrier layer) between two types of material, upon absorption of radiant energy. Also known as barrier-layer cell; barrier-layer photocell; boundary-layer photocell; photronic photocell.

photovoltaic effect The production of a voltage in a nonhomogeneous semiconductor, such as silicon, or at a junction between two types of material, by the absorption of light or other electromagnetic radiation.

photovoltaic meter An exposure cell in which a photovoltaic cell produces a current proportional to the light falling on the cell, and this current is measured by a sensitive microammeter.

photox cell Type of photovoltaic cell in which a voltage is generated between a copper base and a film of cuprous oxide during exposure to visible or other radiation.

photronic cell Type of photovoltaic cell in which a voltage is generated in a layer of selenium during exposure to visible or other radiation.

photronic photocell *See* photovoltaic cell.

phrase name *See* metavariable.

physical data independence A file structure such that the physical structure of the data can be modified without changing the logical structure of the file.

physical device table A table associated with a physical input/output unit containing such information as the device type, an indication of data paths that may be used to transfer information to and from the device, status information on whether the device is busy, the input/output operation currently pending on the device, and the availability of any storage contained in the device.

physical electronics The study of physical phenomena basic to electronics, such as discharges, thermionic and field emission, and conduction in semiconductors and metals.

physical input/output control system *See* PIOCS.

physical record A set of adjacent data characters recorded on some storage medium, physically separated from other physical records that may be on the same medium by means of some indication that can be recognized by a simple hardware test. Also known as record block.

PIC *See* personal identification code.

pick To select the next card from an input stack for feeding into a card machine.

picker knives The narrow edges of a moving slide which will pick the bottom card from a stack and feed it to a card reader.

picking Identification of information displayed on a screen for subsequent computer processing, by pointing to it with a lightpen.

pickoff A device used to convert mechanical motion into a proportional electric signal.

picture In COBOL, a symbolic description of each data element or item according to specified rules concerning numerals, alphanumerics, location of decimal points, and length.

picture compression The elimination of redundant information from a digital picture through the use of efficient encoding techniques in which frequently occurring gray levels or blocks of gray levels are represented by short codes and infrequently occurring ones by longer codes.

picture element 1. That portion, in facsimile, of the subject copy which is seen by the scanner at any instant; it can be considered a square area having dimensions equal to the width of the scanning line. **2.** In television, any segment of a scanning line, the dimension of which along the line is exactly equal to the nominal line width;

the area which is being explored at any instant in the scanning process. Also known as critical area; elemental area; recording spot; scanning spot.

picture frequency *See* frame frequency.

picture grammar A formalism for carrying out computations on pictures and describing picture structure.

picture processing *See* image processing.

picture segmentation The division of a complex picture into parts corresponding to regions or objects, so that the picture can then be described in terms of the parts, their properties, and their spatial relationships. Also known as scene analysis.

picture synchronizing pulse *See* vertical synchronizing pulse.

picture transmitter *See* visual transmitter.

picture tube A cathode-ray tube used in television receivers to produce an image by varying the electron-beam intensity as the beam is deflected from side to side and up and down to scan a raster on the fluorescent screen at the large end of the tube. Also known as kinescope; television picture tube.

picture-tube brightener A small step-up transformer that can be inserted between the socket and base of a picture tube to increase the heater voltage and thereby increase picture brightness to compensate for normal aging of the tubes.

Pierce oscillator Oscillator in which a piezoelectric crystal unit is connected between the grid and the plate of an electron tube, in what is basically a Colpitts oscillator, with voltage division provided by the grid-cathode and plate-cathode capacitances of the circuit.

piezoelectric effect 1. The generation of electric polarization in certain dielectric crystals as a result of the application of mechanical stress. 2. The reverse effect, in which application of a voltage between certain faces of the crystal produces a mechanical distortion of the material.

piezoelectric element A piezoelectric crystal used in an electric circuit, for example, as a transducer to convert mechanical or acoustical signals to electric signals, or to control the frequency of a crystal oscillator.

piezoelectric oscillator *See* crystal oscillator.

piezoelectric resonator *See* crystal resonator.

piezoelectric transducer A piezoelectric crystal used as a transducer, either to convert mechanical or acoustical signals to electric signals, as in a microphone, or vice versa, as in ultrasonic metal inspection.

pi filter A filter that has a series element and two parallel elements connected in the shape of the Greek letter pi (π).

pig 1. An ion source based on the same principle as the Philips ionization gage. 2. *See* Philips ionization gage.

piggyback twistor Electrically alterable nondestructive-readout storage device that uses a thin narrow tape of magnetic material wound spirally around a fine copper conductor to store information; another similar tape is wrapped on top of the first, piggyback fashion, to sense the stored information; a binary digit or bit is stored at the intersection of a copper strap and a pair of these twistor wires.

pileup A set of moving and fixed contacts, insulated from each other, formed as a unit for incorporation in a relay or switch. Also known as stack.

pilot system A system for evaluating new procedures for handling data in which a sample that is representative of the data to be handled is processed.

pi mode Of a magnetron, the mode of operation for which the phases of the fields of successive anode openings facing the interaction space differ by pi radians.

pin A terminal on an electron tube, semiconductor, integrated circuit, plug, or connector. Also known as base pin; prong.

pinboard A board or panel containing an array of uniform holes into which pins may be inserted to control the operation of equipment.

pinch-off voltage Of a field-effect transistor, the voltage at which the current flow between source and drain is blocked because the channel between these electrodes is completely depleted.

pinch resistor A silicon integrated-circuit resistor produced by diffusing an n-type layer over a p-type resistor; this narrows or pinches the resistive channel, thereby increasing the resistance value.

pincushion distortion Distortion in which all four sides of a received television picture are concave (curving inward).

pin diode A diode consisting of a silicon wafer containing nearly equal p-type and n-type impurities, with additional p-type impurities diffused from one side and additional n-type impurities from the other side; this leaves a lightly doped intrinsic layer in the middle, to act as a dielectric barrier between the n-type and p-type regions. Also known as power diode.

ping A sonic or ultrasonic pulse sent out by an echo-ranging sonar.

ping-pong The programming technique of using two magnetic tape units for multiple reel files and switching automatically between the two units until the complete file is processed.

pin junction A semiconductor device having three regions: p-type impurity, intrinsic (electrically pure), and n-type impurity.

pin sensing Device using a punched card, sensing the opening and closing of switches to generate digital data.

PIOCS An extension of the hardware, constituting an interface between programs and data channels; opposed to LIOCS, logical input/output control system. Derived from physical input/output control system.

pip See blip.

pipelining A procedure for processing instructions in a computer program more rapidly, in which each instruction is divided into numerous small stages, and a population of instructions are in various stages at any given time.

pitch The distance between the centerlines of adjacent rows of hole positions in punched paper tape.

pitch-row The distance between two adjacent holes in a paper tape.

pixel 1. The smallest part of an electronically coded picture image. 2. The smallest addressable element in an electronic display; a short form for picture element. Also known as pel.

PL/1 A multipurpose programming language, developed by IBM for the Model 360 systems, which can be used for both commercial and scientific applications.

PLA See programmed logic array.

planar array An array of ultrasonic transducers that can be mounted in a single plane or sheet, to permit closer conformation with the hull design of a sonar-carrying ship.

planar ceramic tube Electron tube having parallel planar electrodes and a ceramic envelope.

planar device A semiconductor device having planar electrodes in parallel planes, made by alternate diffusion of *p*- and *n*-type impurities into a substrate.

planar diode A diode having planar electrodes in parallel planes.

planar photodiode A vacuum photodiode consisting simply of a photocathode and an anode; light enters through a window sealed into the base, behind the photocathode.

planar transistor A transistor constructed by an etching and diffusion technique in which the junction is never exposed during processing, and the junctions reach the surface in one plane; characterized by very low leakage current and relatively high gain.

plane Screen of magnetic cores; planes are combined to form stacks.

planigraphy *See* sectional radiography.

planning by abstraction A computer problem-solving method in which the task to be accomplished is simplified; the simplified task is solved; and the solution is used as a guide.

plan position indicator A radarscope display in which echoes from various targets appear as bright spots at the same locations as they would on a circular map of the area being scanned, the radar antenna being at the center of the map. Abbreviated PPI. Also known as P display.

plan position indicator repeater Unit which repeats a plan position indicator (PPI) at a location remote from the radar console. Also known as remote plan position indicator.

plant To place a number or instruction that has been generated in the course of a computer program in a storage location where it will be used or obeyed at a later stage of the program.

plasma cathode A cathode in which the source of electrons is a gas plasma rather than a solid.

plasma diode A diode used for converting heat directly into electricity; it consists of two closely spaced electrodes serving as cathode and anode, mounted in an envelope in which a low-pressure cesium vapor fills the interelectrode space; heat is applied to the cathode, causing emission of electrons.

plasma display A display in which sets of parallel conductors at right angles to each other are deposited on glass plates, with the very small space between the plates filled with a gas; each intersection of two conductors defines a single cell that can be energized to produce a gas discharge forming one element of a dot-matrix display.

plasma generator Any device that produces a high-velocity plasma jet, such as a plasma accelerator, engine, oscillator, or torch.

plasma gun A machine, such as an electric-arc chamber, that will generate very high heat fluxes to convert neutral gases into plasma.

plasma sheath An envelope of ionized gas that surrounds a spacecraft or other body moving through an atmosphere at hypersonic velocities; affects transmission, reception, and diffraction of radio waves.

plasmatron A gas-discharge tube in which independently generated plasma serves as a conductor between a hot cathode and an anode; the anode current is modulated by varying either the conductivity or the effective cross section of the plasma.

plastic plate A plate of plastic dielectric material used as a base for a semiconductor device.

plate *See* anode.

plateau The portion of the plateau characteristic of a counter tube in which the counting rate is substantially independent of the applied voltage.

plateau characteristic The relation between counting rate and voltage for a counter tube when radiation is constant, showing a plateau after the rise from the starting voltage to the Geiger threshold. Also known as counting rate–voltage characteristic.

plate circuit *See* anode circuit.

plate-circuit detector *See* anode-circuit detector.

plate current *See* anode current.

plated circuit A printed circuit produced by electrodeposition of a conductive pattern on an insulating base. Also known as plated printed circuit.

plate detector *See* anode detector.

plated printed circuit *See* plated circuit.

plated wire memory A nonvolatile magnetic memory utilizing small zones of thin films plated on wires; such memories are characterized by very fast access and nondestructive readout.

plate efficiency *See* anode efficiency.

plate impedance *See* anode impedance.

plate input power *See* anode input power.

plate-load impedance *See* anode impedance.

plate modulation *See* anode modulation.

plate neutralization *See* anode neutralization.

plate pulse modulation *See* anode pulse modulation.

plate resistance *See* anode resistance.

plate saturation *See* anode saturation.

platinotron A microwave tube that may be used as a high-power saturated amplifier or oscillator in pulsed radar applications; requires permanent magnet just as does a magnetron.

playback head A head that converts a changing magnetic field on a moving magnetic tape into corresponding electric signals. Also known as reproduce head.

pliotron General term for any hot-cathode vacuum tube having one or more grids.

PLL *See* phase-locked loop.

plugboard *See* control panel.

plugboard chart *See* plugging chart.

plug-compatible hardware A piece of equipment which can be immediately connected to a computer manufactured by another company.

plugging chart A printed chart of the sockets in a plugboard on which may be shown the jacks or wires connecting these sockets. Also known as plugboard chart.

plug program patching A relatively small auxiliary plugboard patched with a specific variation of a portion of a program and designed to be plugged into a relatively larger plugboard patched with the main program.

plug-to-plug compatibility Property of a peripheral device that can be made to operate with a computer merely by attachment of a plug or a relatively small number of cables.

plus-90 orientation In optical character recognition, that determinate position which indicates that the line elements of an inputted source document appear perpendicular with the leading edge of the optical reader.

plus zone The bit positions in a computer code which represent the algebraic plus sign.

PMS notation A notation that provides a clear, concise description of the physical structure of computer systems, and that contains only a few primitive components, namely symbols for memory, link, switch, data operation, control unit, and transducer. Acronym for processor-memory-switch notation.

pn hook transistor *See* hook collector transistor.

pnip transistor An intrinsic junction transistor in which the intrinsic region is sandwiched between the n-type base and the p-type collector.

pn junction The interface between two regions in a semiconductor crystal which have been treated so that one is a p-type semiconductor and the other is an n-type semiconductor; it contains a permanent dipole charge layer.

pnpn diode A semiconductor device consisting of four alternate layers of p-type and n-type semiconductor material, with terminal connections to the two outer layers. Also known as *npnp* diode.

pnpn transistor *See npnp* transistor.

pnp transistor A junction transistor having an n-type base between a p-type emitter and a p-type collector.

Pockels readout optical modulator A device for storing data in the form of images; it consists of bismuth silicon oxide crystal coated with an insulating layer of parylene and transparent electrodes evaporated on the surfaces; a blue laser is used for writing and a red laser is used for nondestructive readout or processing. Abbreviated PROM.

pocket One of the several receptacles into which punched cards are fed by a card sorter.

point contact A contact between a specially prepared semiconductor surface and a metal point, usually maintained by mechanical pressure but sometimes welded or bonded.

point-contact diode A semiconductor rectifier that uses the barrier formed between a specially prepared semiconductor surface and a metal point to produce the rectifying action.

point-contact transistor A transistor having a base electrode and two or more point contacts located near each other on the surface of an n-type semiconductor.

pointer The part of an instruction which contains the address of the next record to be accessed.

point jammer Any electronic jammer directed against a specific enemy installation operating on a specific frequency.

point-junction transistor Transistor having a base electrode and both point-contact and junction electrodes.

point-mode display A method of representing information in the form of dots on the face of a cathode-ray tube.

point-of-sale terminal A computer-connected terminal used in place of a cash register in a store, for customer checkout and such added functions as recording inventory data, transferring funds from the customer's bank account to the merchant's bank account, and checking credit on charged or charge-card purchases; the terminals can be modified for many nonmerchandising applications, such as checkout of books in libraries. Abbreviated POS terminal.

poison A material which reduces the emission of electrons from the surface of a cathode.

polarity effect An effect for which the breakdown voltage across a vacuum separating two electrodes, one of which is pointed, is much higher when the pointed electrode is the anode.

polarized ion source A device that generates ion beams in such a manner that the spins of the ions are aligned in some direction.

polar resolution Given the x and y components of a vector, the process of finding the magnitude of the vector and the angle it makes with the x axis.

Polish notation 1. A notation system for digital-computer or calculator logic in which there are no parenthetical expressions and each operator is a binary or unary operator in the sense that it operates on not more than two operands. Also known as Lukasiewicz notation; parenthesis-free notation. 2. The version of this notation in which operators precede the operands with which they are associated. Also known as prefix notation.

polyphase rectifier A rectifier which utilizes two or more diodes (usually three), each of which operates during an equal fraction of an alternating-current cycle to achieve an output current which varies less than that in an ordinary half-wave or full-wave rectifier.

polyvalent number A number, consisting of several figures, used for description, wherein each figure represents one of the characteristics being described.

pool cathode A cathode at which the principal source of electron emission is a cathode spot on a liquid-metal electrode, usually mercury.

pool-cathode mercury-arc rectifier A pool tube connected in an electric circuit; its rectifying properties result from the fact that only the mercury-pool cathode, and not the anode, can emit electrons. Also known as mercury-pool rectifier.

pool-cathode tube *See* pool tube.

pool tube A gas-discharge tube having a mercury-pool cathode. Also known as mercury tube; pool-cathode tube.

popcorn noise Noise produced by erratic jumps of bias current between two levels at random intervals in operational amplifiers and other semiconductor devices.

popping The deletion of the top element of a stack.

port An interface between a communications channel and a unit of computer hardware.

portability Property of a computer program that is sufficiently flexible to be easily transferred to run on a computer of a type different from the one for which it was designed.

portable audio terminal A lightweight, self-contained computer terminal with a typewriter keyboard, which can be attached to a telephone line by placing the telephone handset in a receptacle in the terminal.

posistor A thermistor having a large positive resistance-temperature characteristic.

positional punch The row position of a punched hole in a specific column of a punch card; in an 80-column punch card the rows are designated 0 to 9, or x and y; in a 90-column card the rows are designated 0, 1, 3, 5, 7, and 9.

position pulse *See* commutator pulse.

positive bias A bias such that the control grid of an electron tube is positive with respect to the cathode.

positive column The luminous glow, often striated, that occurs between the Faraday dark space and the anode in a glow-discharge tube. Also known as positive glow.

positive electrode *See* anode.

positive glow *See* positive column.

positive-grid oscillator *See* Barkhausen-Kurz oscillator; retarding-field oscillator.

320   positive-ion sheath

positive-ion sheath Collection of positive ions on the control grid of a gas-filled triode tube.

positive logic Pertaining to a logic circuit in which the more positive voltage (or current level) represents the 1 state; the less positive level represents the 0 state.

positive modulation In an amplitude-modulated television system, that form of television modulation in which an increase in brightness corresponds to an increase in transmitted power.

positive ray A stream of positively charged atoms or molecules, produced by a suitable combination of ionizing agents, accelerating fields, and limiting apertures.

positive zero The zero value reached by counting down from a positive number in the binary system.

postaccelerating electrode *See* intensifier electrode.

postacceleration Acceleration of beam electrons after deflection in an electron-beam tube. Also known as postdeflection acceleration (PDA).

postdeflection accelerating electrode *See* intensifier electrode.

postdeflection acceleration *See* postacceleration.

postedit To edit the output data of a computer.

POS terminal *See* point-of-sale terminal.

postfix notation *See* reverse Polish notation.

postindexing Operation in which the contents of a register indicated by the index bits of an indirect address are added to the indirect address to form the effective address.

posting *See* update.

posting interpreter *See* transfer interpreter.

postmortem Any action taken after an operation is completed to help analyze that operation.

postmortem dump 1. The printout showing the state of all registers and the contents of main memory, taken after a computer run terminates normally or terminates owing to fault. 2. The program which generates this printout.

postmortem program *See* postmortem routine.

postmortem routine A computer routine designed to provide information about the operation of a program after the program is completed. Also known as postmortem program.

posttuning drift In a frequency-agile source such as the fast-tuning oscillators used in set-on jammers for electronic warfare equipment, the increase in frequency brought about by the drop in temperature of the varactor after warm-up time, settling time, and the time when the oscillator has reached a new frequency. Abbreviated PTD.

potting Process of filling a complete electronic assembly with a thermosetting compound for resistance to shock and vibration, and for exclusion of moisture and corrosive agents.

powdered-iron core *See* ferrite core.

power amplification *See* power gain.

power amplifier The final stage in multistage amplifiers, such as audio amplifiers and radio transmitters, designed to deliver maximum power to the load, rather than maximum voltage gain, for a given percent of distortion.

power amplifier tube *See* power tube.

power attenuation *See* power loss.

power detection Form of detection in which the power output of the detecting device is used to supply a substantial amount of power directly to a device such as a loudspeaker or recorder.

power detector Detector capable of handling strong input signals without appreciable distortion.

power diode *See* pin diode.

power factor controller A solid-state electronic device that reduces excessive energy waste in alternating-current induction motors by holding constant the phase angle between current and voltage.

power gain The ratio of the power delivered by a transducer to the power absorbed by the input circuit of the transducer. Also known as power amplification.

power loss The ratio of the power absorbed by the input circuit of a transducer to the power delivered to a specified load; usually expressed in decibels. Also known as power attenuation.

power output The alternating-current power in watts delivered by an amplifier to a load.

power output tube *See* power tube.

power pack Unit for converting power from an alternating- or direct-current supply into an alternating- or direct-current power at voltages suitable for supplying an electronic device.

power semiconductor A semiconductor device capable of dissipating appreciable power (generally over 1 watt) in normal operation; may handle currents of thousands of amperes or voltages up into thousands of volts, at frequencies up to 10 kilohertz.

power supply A source of electrical energy, such as a battery or power line, employed to furnish the tubes and semiconductor devices of an electronic circuit with the proper electric voltages and currents for their operation. Also known as electronic power supply.

power transistor A junction transistor designed to handle high current and power; used chiefly in audio and switching circuits.

power tube An electron tube capable of handling more current and power than an ordinary voltage-amplifier tube; used in the last stage of an audio-frequency amplifier or in high-power stages of a radio-frequency amplifier. Also known as power amplifier tube; power output tube.

PPI *See* plan position indicator.

pp junction A region of transition between two regions having different properties in *p*-type semiconducting material.

P pulse *See* commutator pulse.

preamplifier An amplifier whose primary function is boosting the output of a low-level audio-frequency, radio-frequency, or microwave source to an intermediate level so that the signal may be further processed without appreciable degradation of the signal-to-noise ratio of the system. Also known as preliminary amplifier.

precedence relation A rule stating that, in a given programming language, one of two operators is to be applied before the other in any mathematical expression.

precipitation clutter suppression Technique of reducing, by one of the various devices integral to the radar system, clutter caused by rain in the radar range.

precipitation noise Noise generated in an antenna circuit, generally in the form of a relaxation oscillation, caused by the periodic discharge of the antenna or conductors in the vicinity of the antenna into the atmosphere.

precision attribute A set of one or more integers that denotes the number of symbols used to represent a given number and positional information for determining the base point of the number.

precision sweep Delayed expanded radar sweep for high resolution and range accuracy.

preconduction current Low value of plate current flowing in a thyratron or other grid-controlled gas tube prior to the start of conduction.

predetection combining Method used to produce an optimum signal from multiple receivers involved in diversity reception of signals.

preedit To edit data before feeding it to a computer.

preemphasis A process which increases the magnitude of some frequency components with respect to the magnitude of others to reduce the effects of noise introduced in subsequent parts of the system.

preemphasis network An RC (resistance-capacitance) filter inserted in a system to emphasize one range of frequencies with respect to another. Also known as emphasizer.

preferred numbers A series of numbers adopted by the Electronic Industries Association and the military services for use as nominal values of resistors and capacitors, to reduce the number of different sizes that must be kept in stock for replacements. Also known as preferred values.

preferred values *See* preferred numbers.

prefix notation *See* Polish notation.

preheat fluorescent lamp A fluorescent lamp in which a manual switch or thermal starter is used to preheat the cathode for a few seconds before high voltage is applied to strike the mercury arc.

preindexing Operation in which the address bits of a word are added to the contents of a specified register to determine the pointer address.

preliminary amplifier *See* preamplifier.

preprogramming The prerecording of instructions or commands for a machine, such as an automated tool in a factory.

preread head A read head that is placed near another read head in such a way that it can read data stored on a moving medium such as a tape or disk before these data reach the second head.

prescaler A scaler that extends the upper frequency limit of a counter by dividing the input frequency by a precise amount, generally 10 or 100.

preselection A technique for saving time available in buffered computers by which a block of data is read into computer storage from the next input tape to be called upon before the data are required in the computer; the selection of the next input tape is determined by instructions to the computer.

preselector A tuned radio-frequency amplifier stage used ahead of the frequency converter in a superheterodyne receiver to increase the selectivity and sensitivity of the receiver.

presentation *See* radar display.

preset 1. Of a variable, having a value established before the first time it is used. **2.** To initialize a value of a variable before the value of the variable is used or tested.

preset parameter In computers, a parameter which is fixed for each problem at a value set by the programmer.

presort 1. The first part of a sort program in which data items are arranged into strings that are equal to or greater than some prescribed length. **2.** The sorting of data on off-line equipment before it is processed by a computer.

press-to-talk switch A switch mounted directly on a microphone to provide a convenient means for switching two-way radiotelephone equipment or electronic dictating equipment to the talk position.

pressure pickup A device that converts changes in the pressure of a gas or liquid into corresponding changes in some more readily measurable quantity such as inductance or resistance.

prestore To store a quantity in an available computer location before it is required in a routine.

presumptive address *See* address constant.

presumptive instruction *See* basic instruction.

pre-transmit-receive tube *See* pre-TR tube.

pretrigger Trigger used to initiate sweep ahead of transmitted pulse.

pre-TR tube Gas-filled radio-frequency switching tube used in some radar systems to protect the TR tube from excessively high power and the receiver from frequencies other than the fundamental. Derived from pre-transmit-receive tube.

previewing In character recognition, a process of attempting to gain prior information about the characters that appear on an incoming source document; this information, which may include the range of ink density, relative positions, and so forth, is used as an aid in the normalization phase of character recognition.

prewhitening filter *See* whitening filter.

PRF *See* pulse repetition rate.

primary control program The program which provides the sequential scheduling of jobs and basic operating systems functions. Abbreviated PCP.

primary electron An electron which bombards a solid surface, causing secondary emission.

primary emission Emission of electrons due to primary causes, such as heating of a cathode, and not to secondary effects, such as electron bombardment.

primary flow The current flow that is responsible for the major properties of a semiconductor device.

primary photocurrent A photocurrent resulting from nonohmic contacts unable to replenish charge carriers which pass out of the opposite contact, and whose maximum gain is unity.

primary storage Main internal storage of a computer.

principle of duality *See* duality principle.

printed circuit A conductive pattern that may or may not include printed components, formed in a predetermined design on the surface of an insulating base in an accurately repeatable manner.

printed circuit board A flat board whose front contains slots for integrated circuit chips and connections for a variety of electronic components, and whose back is printed with electrically conductive pathways between the components.

printer A computer output mechanism that prints characters one at a time or one line at a time.

printing calculator A desk-model electronic calculator that provides a printed record on paper tape with or without a digital display.

print member The part of a computer printer that determines the form of a printed character, such as a print wheel or type bar.

printout A printed output of a data-processing machine or system.

print position One of the positions on a printer at which a character can be printed.

print server A computer controlling a series of printers.

printthrough Transfer of signals from one recorded layer of magnetic tape to the next on a reel.

print wheel A disk which has around its rim the letters, numerals, and other characters that are used in printing in a wheel printer.

priority-arbitration circuit A logic circuit which combines all interrupts but allows only the highest-priority request to enable its active flipflop.

priority indicator Data attached to a computer program or job which are used to determine the order in which it will be processed by the computer.

priority interrupt An interrupt procedure in which control is passed to the monitor, the required operation is initiated, and then control returns to the running program, which never knows that it has been interrupted.

priority phase Phase consisting of execution of operations in response to instruments or process interrupts other than clock interrupts.

priority processing A method of computer time-sharing in which the order in which programs are processed is determined by a system of priorities, involving such factors as the length, nature, and source of the programs.

private data Data that are open to a single user only.

private line arrangement The structure of a computer system in which each input/output device has a set of lines leading to the central processing unit for the device's own private use. Also known as radial selector.

privileged instruction A class of instructions, usually including storage protection setting, interrupt handling, timer control, input/output, and special processor status-setting instructions, that can be executed only when the computer is in a special privileged mode that is generally available to an operating or executive system, but not to user programs.

privileged mode *See* master mode.

probabilistic automaton A device, with a finite number of internal states, which is capable of scanning input words over a finite alphabet and responding by successively changing its internal state in a probabilistic way. Also known as stochastic automaton.

probabilistic sequential machine A probabilistic automaton that has the capability of printing output words probabilistically, over a finite output alphabet. Also known as stochastic sequential machine.

problem check One or more tests used to assist in obtaining the correct machine solution to a problem.

problem-defining language A programming language that literally defines a problem and may specifically define the input and output, but does not define the method of transforming one to the other. Also known as problem specification language.

problem definition The art of compiling logic in the form of general flow charts and logic diagrams which clearly explain and present the problem to the programmer in such a way that all requirements involved in the run are presented.

problem-describing language A programming language that describes, in the most general way, the problem to be solved, but gives no indication of the problem's detailed characteristics or its solution.

problem file *See* run book.

problem folder *See* run book.

problem mode A condition of computer operation in which, in contrast to supervisor mode, the privileged instructions cannot be executed, preventing the program from upsetting the supervisor program or any other program.

problem-oriented language A language designed to facilitate the accurate expression of problems belonging to specific sets of problem types.

problem-solving language A programming language that can be used to specify a complete solution to a problem.

problem specification language *See* problem-defining language.

procedural language A programming language made up of macroinstructions, each macroinstruction usually written in assembly language.

procedural representation The representation of certain concepts in a computer by procedures or programs in some appropriate language, rather than by static data items such as numbers or lists.

procedure A sequence of actions (or computer instructions) which collectively accomplish some desired task.

procedure division The section of a program (written in the COBOL language) in which a programmer specifies the operations to be performed with the data names appearing in the program.

procedure-oriented language A language designed to facilitate the accurate description of procedures, algorithms, or routines belonging to a certain set of procedures.

process To assemble, compile, generate, interpret, compute, and otherwise act on information in a computer.

processing interrupt The interruption of the batch processing mode in a real-time system when live data are entered in the system.

processing section The computer unit that does the actual changing of input into output; includes the arithmetic unit and intermediate storage.

process-limited *See* processor-limited.

processor 1. A device that performs one or many functions, usually a central processing unit. 2. A program that transforms some input into some output, such as an assembler, compiler, or linkage editor.

processor error interrupt The interruption of a computer program because a parity check indicates an error in a word that has been transferred to or within the central processing unit.

processor-limited Property of a computer system whose processing time is determined by the speed of its central processing unit rather than by the speed of its peripheral equipment. Also known as process-limited.

processor-memory-switch notation *See* PMS notation.

processor stack pointer A programmable register used to access all temporary-storage words related to an interrupt-service routine which was halted when a new service routine was called in.

processor status word A word comprising a set of flag bits and the interrupt-mask status.

product demodulator A receiver demodulator whose output is the product of the input signal voltage and a local oscillator signal voltage at the input frequency. Also known as product detector.

product detector *See* product demodulator.

production A rule in a grammar of a formal language that describes how parts of a string (or word, phrase, or construct) can be replaced by other strings. Also known as rule of inference.

production program A proprietary program used primarily for internal processing in a business and not generally made available to third parties for profit.

production time Good computing time, including occasional duplication of one case for a check or rerunning of the test run; also including duplication requested by the sponsor, any reruns caused by misinformation or bad data supplied by sponsor, and error studies using different intervals, covergence criteria, and so on.

product modulator Modulator whose modulated output is substantially equal to the carrier and the modulating wave; the term implies a device in which intermodulation between components of the modulating wave does not occur.

program A detailed and explicit set of directions for accomplishing some purpose, the set being expressed in some language suitable for input to a computer, or in machine language.

program card A punched card containing one or more instructions in a computer program in either source language or machine language, in contrast to a card that contains data to be processed according to the instructions.

program check A built-in check system in a program to determine that the program is running correctly.

program compatibility The type of compatibility shared by two computers that can process the identical program or programs written in the same source language or machine language.

program counter *See* instruction counter.

program development time The total time taken on a computer to produce operating programs, including the time taken to compile, test, and debug programs, plus the time taken to develop and test new procedures and techniques.

program editor A computer routine used in time-sharing systems for on-line modification of computer programs.

program element Part of a central computer system that carries out the instruction sequence scheduled by the programmer.

program generator A program that permits a computer to write other programs automatically.

program library An organized set of computer routines and programs.

program logic A particular sequence of instructions in a computer program.

programmable calculator An electronic calculator that has some provision for changing its internal program, usually by inserting a new magnetic card on which the desired calculating program has been stored.

programmable counter A counter that divides an input frequency by a number which can be programmed into decades of synchronous down counters; these decades, with additional decoding and control logic, give the equivalent of a divide-by-N counter system, where N can be made equal to any number.

programmable decade resistor A decade box designed so that the value of its resistance can be remotely controlled by programming logic as required for the control of load, time constant, gain, and other parameters of circuits used in automatic test equipment and automatic controls.

programmable logic array *See* field-programmable logic array.

programmable read-only memory A large-scale integrated-circuit chip for storing digital data; it can be erased with ultraviolet light and reprogrammed, or it can be programmed only once either at the factory or in the field. Abbreviated PROM.

program maintenance The updating of computer programs both by error correction and by alteration of programs to meet changing needs.

programmed check 1. An error-detecting operation programmed by instructions rather than built into the hardware. 2. A computer check in which a sample problem with known answer, selected for having a program similar to that of the next problem to be run, is put through the computer.

programmed dump A storage dump which results from an instruction in a computer program at a particular point in the program.

programmed halt A halt that occurs deliberately as the result of an instruction in the program. Also known as programmed stop.

programmed logic array An array of AND/OR logic gates that provides logic functions for a given set of inputs programmed during manufacture and serves as a read-only memory. Abbreviated PLA.

programmed marginal check Computer program that varies its own voltage to check some piece of electronic computer equipment during a preventive maintenance check.

programmed operators Computer instructions which enable subroutines to be accessed with a single programmed instruction.

programmed stop *See* programmed halt.

programmer A person who prepares sequences of instructions for a computer, without necessarily converting them into the detailed codes.

programmer analyst A person who both writes computer programs and analyzes and designs information systems.

programmer-defined macroinstruction A macroinstruction which is equivalent to a set of ordinary instructions as specified by the programmer for use in a particular computer program.

programming Preparing a detailed sequence of operating instructions for a particular problem to be run on a digital computer. Also known as computer programming.

programming language The language used by a programmer to write a program for a computer.

program module A logically self-contained and discrete part of a larger computer program, for example, a subroutine or a coroutine.

program parameter In computers, an adjustable parameter in a subroutine which can be given a different value each time the subroutine is used.

program register The register in the control unit of a digital computer that stores the current instruction of the program and controls the operation of the computer during the execution of that instruction. Also known as computer control register.

program-sensitive fault A hardware malfunction that appears only in response to a particular sequence (or kind of sequence) of program instructions.

program specification A statement of the precise functions which are to be carried out by a computer program, including descriptions of the input to be processed by the program, the processing needed, and the output from the program.

program status word An internal register to the central processing unit denoting the state of the computer at a moment in time.

program step In computers, some part of a program, usually one instruction.

program stop An instruction built into a computer program that will automatically stop the machine under certain conditions, or upon reaching the end of processing or completing the solution of a program. Also known as halt instruction; stop instruction.

program storage Portion of the internal storage reserved for the storage of programs, routines, and subroutines; in many systems, protection devices are used to prevent inadvertent alteration of the contents of the program storage; contrasted with temporary storage.

program tape Tape containing the sequence of computer instructions for a given problem.

program test A system of checking before running any problem in which a sample problem of the same type with a known answer is run.

program testing time The machine time expended for program testing, debugging, and volume and compatibility testing.

program time The phase of computer operation when an instruction is being interpreted so that it can be carried out.

progressive overflow Retrieval of a randomly stored overflow record by a forward serial search from the home address.

projection cathode-ray tube A television cathode-ray tube designed to produce an intensely bright but relatively small image that can be projected onto a large viewing screen by an optical system.

projection display An electronic system in which an image is generated on a high-brightness cathode-ray tube or similar electronic image generator and then optically projected onto a larger screen.

projection plan position indicator Unit in which the image of a 4-inch (10-centimeter) dark-trace cathode-ray tube is projected on a 24-inch (61-centimeter) horizontal plotting surface; the echoes appear as magenta-colored arcs on white background.

PROM See Pockels readout optical modulator; programmable read-only memory.

PROM programmer A hardware device that writes programmable read-only memory chips in a permanent form.

prong See pin.

proof total One of a group of totals which are compared with each other to check their consistency.

propagated error An error which takes place in one operation and spreads through succeeding operations.

propagation delay The time required for a signal to pass through a given complete operating circuit; it is generally of the order of nanoseconds, and is of extreme importance in computer circuits.

property detector In character recognition, that electronic component of a character reader which processes the normalized signal for the purpose of extracting from it a set of characteristic properties on the basis of which the character can be subsequently identified.

property list A list for describing some object or concept, in which odd-numbered items name a property or attribute of a relevant class of objects, and the item following the property name is the property's value for the described objects.

proportional ionization chamber An ionization chamber in which the initial ionization current is amplified by electron multiplication in a region of high electric-field strength, as in a proportional counter; used for measuring ionization currents or charges over a period of time, rather than for counting.

proprietary program 1. A computer program that is owned by someone, and whose use may thus be restricted in some manner or entail payment of a fee. Also known as owned program. 2. More narrowly, a program that is exploited commercially as a separate product.

protected location A storage cell arranged so that access to its contents is denied under certain circumstances, in order to prevent programming accidents from destroying essential programs and data.

protection code A component of a task descriptor that specifies the protection domain of the task, that is, the authorizations it has to perform certain actions.

protection key An indicator, usually 1 to 6 bits in length, associated with a program and intended to grant the program access to those sections of memory which the program can use but to deny the program access to all other parts of memory.

protective resistance Resistance used in series with a gas tube or other device to limit current flow to a safe value.

protector tube A glow-discharge cold-cathode tube that becomes conductive at a predetermined voltage, to protect a circuit against overvoltage.

Proteus *See* advanced signal-processing system.

protocol 1. A set of hardware and software interfaces in a terminal or computer which allows it to transmit over a communications network, and which collectively forms a communications language. 2. *See* communication protocol.

proton microscope A microscope that is similar to the electron microscope but uses protons instead of electrons as the charged particles.

proving Testing whether a computer is free of faults and capable of functioning normally, usually by having it carry out a check routine or diagnostic routine.

PRR *See* pulse repetition rate.

pseudocode *See* interpretive language.

pseudoinstruction 1. A symbolic representation in a compiler or interpreter. 2. *See* quasi-instruction.

pseudo-operation An operation which is not part of the computer's operation repertoire as realized by hardware; hence, an entension of the set of machine operations.

pseudorandom numbers Numbers produced by a definite arithmetic process, but satisfying one or more of the standard tests for randomness.

psophometric electromotive force The true noise voltage that exists in a circuit.

psophometric voltage The noise voltage as actually measured in a circuit under specified conditions.

PTD *See* posttuning drift.

p-type conductivity The conductivity associated with holes in a semiconductor, which are equivalent to positive charges.

p-type crystal rectifier Crystal rectifier in which forward current flows when the semiconductor is positive with respect to the metal.

p-type semiconductor An extrinsic semiconductor in which the hole density exeeds the conduction electron density.

p$^+$-type semiconductor A p-type semiconductor in which the excess mobile hole concentration is very large.

p-type silicon Silicon to which more impurity atoms of acceptor type (with valence of 3, such as boron) than of donor type (with valence of 5, such as phosphorus) have been added, with the result that the hole density exceeds the conduction electron density.

public data Data that are open to all users, with no security measures necessary as far as reading is concerned.

pulling An effect that forces the frequency of an oscillator to change from a desired value; causes include undesired coupling to another frequency source or the influence of changes in the oscillator load impedance.

pulling figure The total frequency change of an oscillator when the phase angle of the reflection coefficient of the load impedance varies through 360°, the absolute value of this reflection coefficient being constant at 0.20.

pulse analyzer An instrument used to measure pulse widths and repetition rates, and to display on a cathode-ray screen the waveform of a pulse.

pulse circuit An active electrical network designed to respond to discrete pulses of current or voltage.

pulse compression A matched filter technique used to discriminate against signals which do not correspond to the transmitted signal.

pulse counter A device that indicates or records the total number of pulses received during a time interval.

pulse-delay network A network consisting of two or more components such as resistors, coils, and capacitors, used to delay the passage of a pulse.

pulse discriminator A discriminator circuit that responds only to a pulse having a particular duration or amplitude.

pulsed oscillator An oscillator that generates a carrier-frequency pulse or a train of carrier-frequency pulses as the result of self-generated or externally applied pulses.

pulse droop A distortion of an otherwise essentially flat-topped rectangular pulse, characterized by a decline of the pulse top.

pulse-duration discriminator A circuit in which the sense and magnitude of the output are a function of the deviation of the pulse duration from a reference.

pulse-forming network A network used to shape the leading or trailing edge of a pulse.

pulse generator A generator that produces repetitive pulses or signal-initiated pulses.

pulse height The strength or amplitude of a pulse, measured in volts.

pulse-height discriminator A circuit that produces a specified output pulse when and only when it receives an input pulse whose amplitude exceeds an assigned value. Also known as amplitude discriminator.

pulse-height selector A circuit that produces a specified output pulse only when it receives an input pulse whose amplitude lies between two assigned values. Also known as amplitude selector; diffractional pulse-height discriminator.

pulse integrator An RC (resistance-capacitance) circuit which stretches in time duration a pulse applied to it.

pulse interference eliminator Device which removes pulsed signals which are not precisely on the radar operating frequency.

pulse interference separator and blanker Automatic interference blanker that will blank all video signals not synchronous with the radar pulse-repetition frequency.

pulse-link repeater Arrangement of apparatus used in telephone signaling systems for receiving pulses from one E and M signaling circuit, and retransmitting corresponding pulses into another E and M signaling circuit.

pulse operation For microwave tubes, a method of operation in which the energy is delivered in pulses.

pulser A generator used to produce high-voltage, short-duration pulses, as required by a pulsed microwave oscillator or a radar transmitter.

pulse-rate telemetering Telemetering in which the number of pulses per unit time is proportional to the magnitude of the measured quantity.

pulse recurrence rate *See* pulse repetition rate.

pulse regeneration The process of restoring pulses to their original relative timings, forms, and magnitudes.

pulse repeater Device used for receiving pulses from one circuit and transmitting corresponding pulses into another circuit; it may also change the frequencies and waveforms of the pulses and perform other functions.

pulse repetition frequency *See* pulse repetition rate.

pulse repetition rate The number of times per second that a pulse is transmitted. Abbreviated PRR. Also known as pulse recurrence rate; pulse repetition frequency (PRF).

pulse scaler A scaler that produces an output signal when a prescribed number of input pulses has been received.

pulse selector A circuit or device for selecting the proper pulse from a sequence of telemetering pulses.

pulse shaper A transducer used for changing one or more characteristics of a pulse, such as a pulse regenerator or pulse stretcher.

pulse stretcher A pulse shaper that produces an output pulse whose duration is greater than that of the input pulse and whose amplitude is proportional to the peak amplitude of the input pulse.

pulse synthesizer A circuit used to supply pulses that are missing from a sequence due to interference or other causes.

pulse transformer A transformer capable of operating over a wide range of frequencies, used to transfer nonsinusoidal pulses without materially changing their waveforms.

pulse transmitter A pulse-modulated transmitter whose peak-power-output capabilities are usually large with respect to the average-power-output rating.

pulse-width discriminator Device that measures the pulse length of video signals and passes only those whose time duration falls into some predetermined design tolerance.

pump Of a parametric device, the source of alternating-current power which causes the nonlinear reactor to behave as a time-varying reactance.

pumped tube An electron tube that is continuously connected to evacuating equipment during operation; large pool-cathode tubes are often operated in this manner.

pumping frequency Frequency at which pumping is provided in a maser, quadrupole amplifier, or other amplifier requiring high-frequency excitation.

pump oscillator Alternating-current generator that supplies pumping energy for maser and parametric amplifiers; operates at twice or some higher multiple of the signal frequency.

punch 1. A device for making holes representing information in a medium such as cards or paper tape, in response to signals sent to it. 2. A hole in a medium such as a card or paper tape, generally made in an array with other holes (or lack of holes) to represent information.

punch card A medium by means of which data are fed into a computer in the form of rectangular holes punched in the card. Also known as punched card.

punched card *See* punch card.

punched-card accounting machines Machines and equipment, primarily electromechanical in operation, using punched cards as input/output media to record, sort, list, tabulate, select, merge, interpret, or total data.

punched-card equipment Data-processing equipment which is essentially card-oriented and is predominately electromechanical, such as encoders, key punchers, key tapes, mechanical sorters, collators, and tabulators.

punched-card field A set of columns fixed as to number and position into which the same item or items of data are regularly entered.

punched-card interpreter *See* interpreter.

punched-card reader *See* card reader.

punched-card reproducer *See* reproducer.

punched-card sorter *See* card sorter.

punched tape *See* punch tape.

punched-tape reader *See* paper-tape reader.

punching rate The number of cards, characters, blocks, fields, or words of information placed in the form of holes distributed on cards, or paper tape per unit of time.

punching station The position within a punched-card machine at which punching of the cards takes place.

punching track The metal plate along which a punch card moves through a card punch.

punch knife The part of the machinery of a card punch which cuts out a hole in a punch card.

punch position The location of the row in a columnated card; for example, in an 80-column card the rows or punch position may be 0 to 9 or X and Y corresponding to positions 11 and 12.

punch tape A paper or plastic ribbon in which data may be represented by means of partially or completely punched holes; it generally has one row of small sprocket-feed holes and five, seven, or eight rows of larger data-representing holes. Also known as punched tape.

punch-tape code A code used to represent data on punch tape.

punch-through An emitter-to-collector breakdown which can occur in a junction transistor with very narrow base region at sufficiently high collector voltage when the space-charge layer extends completely across the base region.

punctuation bit A binary digit used to indicate the beginning or end of a variable-length record.

pure procedure A procedure that never modifies any part of itself during execution.

purge date The date after which data are released and the storage area can be used for storing other data.

purity coil A coil mounted on the neck of a color picture tube, used to produce the magnetic field needed for adjusting color purity; the direct current through the coil is adjusted to a value that makes the magnetic field orient the three individual electron beams so each strikes only its assigned color of phosphor dots.

purity control A potentiometer or rheostat used to adjust the direct current through the purity coil.

purity magnet An adjustable arrangement of one or more permanent magnets used in place of a purity coil in a color television receiver.

purple plague A compound formed by intimate contact of gold and aluminum, which appears on silicon planar devices and integrated circuits using gold leads bonded to aluminum thin-film contacts and interconnections, and which seriously degrades the reliability of semiconductor devices.

push-button dialing Dialing a number by pushing buttons on the telephone rather than turning a circular wheel; each depressed button causes a transistor oscillator to oscillate simultaneously at two different frequencies, generating a pair of audio tones which are recognized by central-office (or PBX) switching equipment as digits of a telephone number. Also known as tone dialing; touch call.

push-button tuner A device that automatically tunes a radio receiver or other piece of equipment to a desired frequency when the button assigned to that frequency is pressed.

push-down automaton A nondeterministic, finite automaton with an auxiliary tape having the form of a push-down storage.

push-down list An ordered set of data items so constructed that the next item to be retrieved is the item most recently stored; in other words, last-in, first-out (LIFO).

push-down storage A computer storage in which each new item is placed in the first location in the storage and all the other items are moved back one location; it thus follows the principle of a push-down list. Also known as cellar; nesting storage; running accumulator.

pushing The placing of a data element at the top of a stack.

push-pull amplifier A balanced amplifier employing two similar electron tubes or equivalent amplifying devices working in phase opposition.

push-pull electret transducer A type of transducer in which a foil electret is sandwiched between two electrodes and is specially treated or arranged so that the electrodes exert forces in opposite directions on the diaphragm, and the net force is a linear function of the applied voltage.

push-pull magnetic amplifier A realization of a push-pull amplifier using magnetic amplifiers.

push-pull oscillator A balanced oscillator employing two similar electron tubes or equivalent amplifying devices in phase opposition.

push-pull transformer An audio-frequency transformer having a center-tapped winding and designed for use in a push-pull amplifier.

push-pull transistor 1. A realization of a push-pull amplifier using transistors. 2. A Darlington circuit in which the two transistors required for a push-pull amplifier exist in a single substrate.

push-push amplifier An amplifier employing two similar electron tubes with grids connected in phase opposition and with anodes connected in parallel to a common load; usually used as a frequency multiplier to emphasize even-order harmonics; transistors may be used in place of tubes.

push-up list An ordered set of data items so constructed that the next item to be retrieved will be the item that was inserted earliest in the list, resulting in a first-in, first-out (FIFO) structure.

pyroelectricity The property of certain crystals to produce a state of electrical polarity by a change of temperature.

pyrone detector Crystal detector in which rectification occurs between iron pyrites and copper or other metallic points.

Q

Q multiplier A filter that gives a sharp response peak or a deep rejection notch at a particular frequency, equivalent to boosting the Q of a tuned circuit at that frequency.

QPSK *See* quarternary phase-shift keying.

Q signal The quadrature component of the chrominance signal in color television, having a bandwidth of 0 to 0.5 megahertz; it consists of $+0.48(R-Y)$ and $+0.41(B-Y)$, where Y is the luminance signal, R is the red camera signal, and B is the blue camera signal.

quad A series-parallel combination of transistors; used to obtain increased reliability through double redundancy, because the failure of one transistor will not disable the entire circuit.

quadded redundancy A form of redundancy in which each logic gate is quadruplicated, and the outputs of one stage are interconnected to the inputs of the succeeding stage by a connection pattern so that errors made in earlier stages are overridden in later stages, where the original correct signals are restored.

quad in-line An integrated-circuit package that has two rows of staggered pins on each side, spaced closely enough together to permit 48 or more pins per package. Abbreviated QUIL.

quadrature amplifier An amplifier that shifts the phase of a signal 90°; used in a color television receiver to amplify the 3.58-megahertz chrominance subcarrier and shift its phase 90° for use in the Q demodulator.

quadripuntal Having four punches; specifically, having four random punches on an IBM or Hollerith-type punched card.

quadrupole amplifier A low-noise parametric amplifier consisting of an electron-beam tube in which quadrupole fields act on the fast cyclotron wave of the electron beam to produce high amplification at frequencies in the range of 400–800 megahertz.

quad word A word 16 bytes long.

qualified name A name that is further identified by associating it with additional names, usually the names of things that contain the thing being named.

qualifier A name that is associated with another name to give additional information about the latter and distinguish it from other things having the same name.

quantity In computers, a positive or negative real number in the mathematical sense; the term quantity is preferred to the term number in referring to numerical data; the term number is used in the sense of natural number and reserved for "the number of digits," the "number of operations," and so forth.

quantized spin wave *See* magnon.

quantizer A device that measures the magnitude of a time-varying quantity in multiples of some fixed unit, at a specified instant or specified repetition rate, and delivers a proportional response that is usually in pulse code or digital form.

quantum efficiency The average number of electrons photoelectrically emitted from a photocathode per incident photon of a given wavelength in a phototube.

quantum electronics The branch of electronics associated with the various energy states of matter, motions within atoms or groups of atoms, and various phenomena in crystals; examples of practical applications include the atomic hydrogen maser and the cesium atomic-beam resonator.

quarternary phase-shift keying Modulation of a microwave carrier with two parallel streams of nonreturn-to-zero data in such a way that the data is transmitted as 90° phase shifts of the carrier; this gives twice the message channel capacity of binary phase-shift keying in the same bandwidth. Abbreviated QPSK.

quarter-square multiplier A device used to carry out function multiplication in an analog computer by implementing the algebraic identity $xy = \frac{1}{4}[(x+y)^2 - (x-y)^2]$.

quartz crystal A natural or artificially grown piezoelectric crystal composed of silicon dioxide, from which thin slabs or plates are carefully cut and ground to serve as a crystal plate.

quartz-crystal filter A filter which utilizes a quartz crystal; it has a small bandwidth, a high rate of cutoff, and a higher unloaded Q than can be obtained in an ordinary resonator.

quartz-crystal resonator A quartz plate whose natural frequency of vibration is used to control the frequency of an oscillator. Also known as quartz resonator.

quartz delay line An acoustic delay line in which quartz is used as the medium of sound transmission.

quartz-fiber electroscope Electroscope in which a gold-plated quartz fiber serves the same function as the gold leaf of a conventional electroscope.

quartz-iodine lamp An electric lamp having a tungsten filament and a quartz envelope filled with iodine vapor.

quartz lamp A mercury-vapor lamp having a transparent envelope made from quartz instead of glass; quartz resists heat, permitting higher currents, and passes ultraviolet rays that are absorbed by ordinary glass.

quartz oscillator An oscillator in which the frequency of the output is determined by the natural frequency of vibration of a quartz crystal.

quartz plate *See* crystal plate.

quartz resonator *See* quartz-crystal resonator.

quartz strain gage A device used to measure small deformations of a substance by determining the resulting voltage that develops in a quartz attached to it.

quasi-instruction An expression in a source program which resembles an instruction in form, but which does not have a corresponding machine instruction in the object program, and is directed to the assembler or compiler. Also known as pseudoinstruction.

quasi-parallel execution The execution of a collection of coroutines by a single processor that can work on only one coroutine at a time; the order of execution is arbitrary and each coroutine is executed independently of the rest.

quench frequency Number of times per second that a circuit is caused to go in and out of oscillation.

quenching 1. The process of terminating a discharge in a gas-filled radiation-counter tube by inhibiting reignition. 2. Reduction of the intensity of resonance radiation resulting from deexcitation of atoms, which would otherwise have emitted this radiation, in collisions with electrons or other atoms in a gas.

quench oscillator Circuit in a superregenerative receiver which produces the frequency signal.

query A computer instruction to interrogate a data base.

query language A generalized computer language that is used to interrogate a data base.

query program A computer program that allows a user to retrieve information from a data base and have it displayed on a terminal or printed out.

question-answering system An information retrieval system in which a direct answer is expected in response to a submitted query, rather than a set of references that may contain the answers.

queue Any space in main storage or secondry storage reserved to temporarily hold information.

quibinary A numeration system, used in data processing, in which each decimal digit is represented by seven binary digits, a group of five which are coefficients of 8, 6, 4, 2, and 0, and a group of two which are coefficients of 1 and 0.

QUICKTRAN A time-sharing language developed by IBM for use on an IBM 1050 terminal connected to an IBM 7044 computer; as a programming system, it provides concurrent computer access to a maximum of 50 remotely located terminals from a centralized data-processing system having tape, drum, and disk storage.

quiescent Condition of a circuit element which has no input signal, so that it does not perform its active function.

quiescent point The point on the characteristic curve of an amplifier representing the conditions that exist when the input signal equals zero.

quiescent push-pull Push-pull output stage so arranged in a radio receiver that practically no current flows when no signal is being received.

quiescent value The voltage or current value for an electron-tube electrode when no signals are present.

quiet automatic volume control *See* delayed automatic gain control.

quiet battery Source of energy of special design or with added filters which is sufficiently quiet and free from interference that it may be used for speech transmission. Also known as talking battery.

quieting sensitivity Minimum signal input to a frequency-modulated receiver which is required to give a specified output signal-to-noise ratio under specified conditions.

quiet tuning Circuit arrangement for silencing the output of a radio receiver, except when it is accurately tuned to an incoming carrier wave.

QUIL *See* quad in-line.

quinary code A code based on five possible combinations for representing digits.

R

rack panel A panel designed for mounting on a relay rack; its width is 19 inches (48.26 centimeters), height is a multiple of 1¾ inches (4.445 centimeters), and the mounting notches are standardized as to size and position.

radar antijamming Measures taken to counteract radar jamming.

radar constant One of those terms of the radar equation or radar storm-detection equation which are functions of the particular radar to which the equations are applied; these include peak power, antenna gain or aperture, beam width, pulse length, pulse repetition frequency, wavelength, polarization, and noise level of the receiver.

radar control Guidance, direction, or employment exercised over an aircraft, guided missile, gun battery, or the like, by means of, or with the aid of, radar.

radar countermeasure An electronic countermeasure used against enemy radar, such as jamming and confusion reflectors. Abbreviated RCM.

radar data filtering Quality analysis process that causes the computer to reject certain radar data and to alert personnel of mapping and surveillance consoles to the rejection.

radar display The pattern representing the output data of a radar set, generally produced on the screen of a cathode-ray tube. Also known as presentation; radar presentation.

radar distribution switchboard Switching panel for connecting video, trigger, and bearing from any one of five systems, to any or all of 20 repeaters; also contains order lights, bearing cutouts, alarms, test equipment, and so forth.

radar echo *See* echo.

radar image The image of an object which is produced on a radar screen.

radar indicator A cathode-ray tube and associated equipment used to provide a visual indication of the echo signals picked up by a radar set.

radar intelligence item A feature which is radar significant but which cannot be identified exactly at the moment of its appearance as homogeneous.

radar jamming Radiation, reradiation, or reflection of electromagnetic waves so as to impair the usefulness of radar used by the enemy.

radar netting unit Optional electronic equipment that converts the operations central of certain air defense fire distribution systems to a radar netting station.

radar presentation *See* radar display.

radar receiver A high-sensitivity radio receiver that is designed to amplify and demodulate radar echo signals and feed them to a radarscope or other indicator.

radar receiver-transmitter A single component having the dual functions of generating electromagnetic energy for transmission, and of receiving, demodulating, and sometimes presenting intelligence from the reflected electromagnetic energy.

radar repeater A cathode-ray indicator used to reproduce the visible intelligence of a radar display at a remote position; when used with a selector switch, the visible intelligence of any one of several radar systems can be reproduced.

radarscope Cathode-ray tube, serving as an oscilloscope, the face of which is the radar viewing screen. Also known as scope.

radar selector switch Manual or motor-driven switch which transfers a plan-position indicator repeater from one system to another, switching video, trigger, and bearing data.

radar signal spectrograph An electronic device in the form of a scanning filter which provides a frequency analysis of the amplitude-modulated back-scattered signal.

radar transmitter The transmitter portion of a radar set.

radechon A storage tube having a single electron gun and a dielectric storage medium consisting of a sheet of mica sandwiched between a continuous metal backing plate and a fine-mesh screen; used in simple delay schemes, signal-to-noise improvement, signal comparison, and conversion of signal-time bases. Also known as barrier-grid storage tube.

radial-beam tube A vacuum tube in which a radial beam of electrons is rotated past circumferentially arranged anodes by an external rotating magnetic field; used chiefly as a high-speed switching tube or commutator.

radial selector *See* private line arrangement.

radiation cooling Cooling of an electrode resulting from its emission of heat radiation.

radio *See* radio receiver.

radio aid to navigation An aid to navigation which utilizes the propagation characteristics of radio waves to furnish navigation information.

radio command A radio control signal to which a guided missile or other remote-controlled vehicle or device responds.

radio compass *See* automatic direction finder.

radio control The control of stationary or moving objects by means of signals transmitted through space by radio.

radio countermeasures Electrical or other techniques depriving the enemy of the benefits which would ordinarily accrue to him through the use of any technique employing the radiation of radio waves; it includes benefits derived from radar and intercept services.

radio-frequency amplifier An amplifier that amplifies the high-frequency signals commonly used in radio communications.

radio-frequency filter An electric filter which enhances signals at certain radio frequencies or attenuates signals at undesired radio frequencies.

radio-frequency generator A generator capable of supplying sufficient radio-frequency energy at the required frequency for induction or dielectric heating.

radio-frequency measurement The precise measurement of frequencies above the audible range by any of various techniques, such as a calibrated oscillator with some means of comparison with the unknown frequency, a digital counting or scaling device which measures the total number of events occurring during a given time interval, or an electronic circuit for producing a direct current proportional to the frequency of its input signal.

radio-frequency oscillator An oscillator that generates alternating current at radio frequencies.

radio-frequency power supply A high-voltage power supply in which the output of a radio-frequency oscillator is stepped up by an air-core transformer to the high voltage required for the second anode of a cathode-ray tube, then rectified to provide the required high direct-current voltage; used in some television receivers.

radio-frequency reactor A reactor used in electronic circuits to pass direct current and offer high impedance at high frequencies.

radio-frequency shift *See* frequency shift.

radio-frequency signal generator A test instrument that generates the various radio frequencies required for alignment and servicing of radio, television, and electronic equipment. Also known as service oscillator.

radio-frequency SQUID A type of SQUID which has only one Josephson junction in a superconducting loop; its state is determined from radio-frequency measurements of the impedance of the ring.

radiogoniometer A goniometer used as part of a radio direction finder.

radio guidance Guidance of a flight-borne missile or other vehicle from a ground station by means of radio signals.

radio metal locator *See* metal detector.

radiometer A receiver for detecting microwave thermal radiation and similar weak wide-band signals that resemble noise and are obscured by receiver noise; examples include the Dicke radiometer, subtraction-type radiometer, and two-receiver radiometer. Also known as microwave radiometer; radiometer-type receiver.

radiometer-type receiver *See* radiometer.

radiomicrometer *See* microradiometer.

radio pill A device used in biotelemetry for monitoring the physiologic activity of an animal, such as pH values of stomach acid; an example is the Heidelberg capsule.

radio receiver A device that converts radio waves into intelligible sounds or other perceptible signals. Also known as radio; radio set; receiving set.

radio scanner *See* scanning radio.

radio set *See* radio receiver; radio transmitter.

radiosonde commutator A component of a radiosonde consisting of a series of alternate electrically conducting and insulating strips; as these are scanned by a contact, the radiosonde transmits temperature and humidity signals alternately.

radio transmitter The equipment used for generating and amplifying a radio-frequency carrier signal, modulating the carrier signal with intelligence, and feeding the modulated carrier to an antenna for radiation into space as electromagnetic waves. Also known as radio set; transmitter.

radio transponder A transponder which receives and transmits radio waves, in contrast to a sonar transponder, which receives and transmits acoustic waves.

radio tube *See* electron tube.

radix transformation A method of transformation that involves changing the radix or base of the original key and either discarding excess high-order digits (that is, digits in excess of the number desired in the key) or extracting some part of the transformed number.

rail-fence jammer *See* continuous-wave jammer.

railing Radar pulse jamming at high recurrence rates (50 to 150 kilohertz); it results in an image on a radar indicator resembling fence railing.

rainbow Technique which applies pulse-to-pulse frequency changing to identifying and discriminating against decoys and chaff.

RAM *See* random-access memory.

ramp generator A circuit that generates a sweep voltage which increases linearly in value during one cycle of sweep, then returns to zero suddenly to start the next cycle.

random access 1. The ability to read or write information anywhere within a storage device in an amount of time that is constant regardless of the location of the information accessed and of the location of the information previously accessed. Also known as direct access. 2. A process in which data are accessed in nonsequential order and possibly at irregular intervals of time. Also known as single reference.

random-access disk file A file which is contained on a disk having one head per track and in which consecutive records are not necessarily in consecutive locations.

random-access input/output A technique which minimizes seek time and overlaps with processing.

random-access memory A data storage device having the property that the time required to access a randomly selected datum does not depend on the time of the last access or the location of the most recently accessed datum. Abbreviated RAM. Also known as direct-access memory; direct-access storage; random-access storage; random storage; uniformly accessible storage.

random-access programming Programming without regard for the time required for access to the storage positions called for in the program, in contrast to minimum-access programming.

random-access storage *See* random-access memory.

randomized jitter Jitter by means of noise modulation.

randomizing scheme A technique of distributing records among storage modules to ensure even distribution and seek time.

random number generator 1. A mathematical program which generates a set of numbers which pass a randomness test. 2. An analog device that generates a randomly fluctuating variable, and usually operates from an electrical noise source.

random storage *See* random-access memory.

random superimposed coding A system of coding in which a set of random numbers is assigned to each concept to be encoded; with punched cards, each number corresponds to some one hole to be punched in a given field.

range-amplitude display Radar display in which a time base provides the range scale from which echoes appear as deflections normal to the base.

range arithmetic *See* interval arithmetic.

range-bearing display *See* B display.

range calibrator 1. A device with which the operator of a transmitter calculates the distance over which the signal will extend intelligibly. 2. A device for adjusting radar range indications by use of known range targets or delayed signals, so when on target the set will indicate the correct range.

range comprehension In an FM sonar system, valves between the maximum and the minimum ranges.

rangefinder A device which determines the distance to an object by measuring the time it takes for a radio wave to travel to the object and return.

range gate capture Electronic countermeasure technique using a spoofer radar transmitter to produce a false target echo that can make a fire-control tracking radar move off the real target and follow the false one.

range gating The process of selecting those radar echoes that lie within a small range interval.

range-height indicator display A radar display that presents visually the scalar distance between a reference point and a target, along with the vertical distance between a reference plane and the target. Abbreviated RHI display.

range mark offset Displacement of range mark on a type B indicator.

range of a loop The set of instructions contained between the opening and closing statements of a do loop.

range rate The rate at which the distance from the measuring equipment to the target or signal source that is being tracked is changing with respect to time.

range ring Accurate, adjustable, ranging mark on a plan position indicator corresponding to a range step on a type M indicator.

range selection Control on a radar indicator for selection of range scale.

range step Vertical displacement on M-indicator sweep to measure range.

range sweep A sweep intended primarily for measurement of range.

range-tracking element An element in a radar set which measures range and its time derivative; by means of the latter, a range gate is actuated slightly before the predicted instant of signal reception.

range unit Radar system component used for control and indication (usually counters) of range measurements.

range zero Alignment of start sweep trace with zero range.

ranging oscillator Oscillator circuit containing an LC (inductor-capacitor) resonant combination in the cathode circuit, usually used in radar equipment to provide range marks.

rapid access loop A small section of storage, particularly in drum, tape, or disk storage units, which has much faster access than the remainder of the storage.

rapid memory *See* rapid storage.

rapid selector A device which scans codes recorded on microfilm; microimages of the documents associated with the codes may also be recorded on the film.

rapid storage In computers, storage with a very short access time; rapid access is generally gained by limiting storage capacity. Also known as high-speed storage; rapid memory.

raster A predetermined pattern of scanning lines that provides substantially uniform coverage of an area; in television the raster is seen as closely spaced parallel lines, most evident when there is no picture.

raster graphics A computer graphics coding technique which codes each picture element of the picture area in digital form.

raster scanning Radar scan very similar to electron-beam scanning in an ordinary television set; horizontal sector scan that changes in elevation.

rate effect The phenomenon of a *pnpn* device switching to a high-conduction mode when anode voltage is applied suddenly or when high-frequency transients exist.

rate feedback The return of a signal, proportional to the rate of change of the output of a device, from the output to the input.

rate-grown transistor A junction transistor in which both impurities (such as gallium and antimony) are placed in the melt at the same time and the temperature is suddenly raised and lowered to produce the alternate *p*-type and *n*-type layers of rate-grown junctions. Also known as graded-junction transistor.

rate multiplier An integrator in which the quantity to be integrated is held in a register and is added to the number standing in an accumulator in response to pulses which arrive at a constant rate.

rate test A test that verifies that the time constants of the integrators are correct; used in analog computers.

rate transmitter A transmitter in a missile being launched, used with a ground receiver to indicate the rate of speed increase.

ratio-balance relay *See* percentage differential relay.

ratio detector A frequency-modulation detector circuit that uses two diodes and requires no limiter at its input; the audio output is determined by the ratio of two developed intermediate-frequency voltages whose relative amplitudes are a function of frequency.

ratio-differential relay *See* percentage differential relay.

rat race A particular type of radar waveguide configuration which allows the handling of greater power.

Raysistor A device which contains a photosensitive semiconductor and a light source; light source can be used to control the conductivity of the semiconductor.

R-C amplifier *See* resistance-capacitance coupled amplifer.

R-C coupled amplifier *See* resistance-capacitance coupled amplifier.

R-C coupling *See* resistance coupling.

RCM *See* radar countermeasure.

R-C oscillator *See* resistance-capacitance oscillator.

R display Radar display, essentially an expanded A display, in which an echo can be expanded for more detailed examination.

reactance amplifier *See* parametric amplifier.

reactance frequency multiplier Frequency multiplier whose essential element is a nonlinear reactor.

reactance tube Vacuum tube operated in a way that it presents almost a pure reactance to the circuit.

reactance-tube modulator An electron-tube circuit, used to produce phase or frequency modulation, in which the reactance is varied in accordance with the instantaneous amplitude of the modulating voltage.

reactive ion etching A directed chemical etching process used in integrated circuit fabrication in which chemically active ions are accelerated along electric field lines to meet a substrate perpendicular to its surface.

read 1. To acquire information, usually from some form of storage in a computer. 2. To convert magnetic spots, characters, or punched holes into electrical impulses. 3. To generate an output corresponding to the pattern stored in a charge storage tube.

read-around number *See* read-around ratio.

read-around ratio The number of times that a particular bit in electrostatic storage may be read without seriously affecting nearby bits. Also known as read-around number.

read-back check *See* echo check.

Read diode A high-frequency semiconductor diode consisting of an avalanching *pn*-junction, biased to fields of several hundred thousand volts per centimeter, at one end of a high-resistance carrier serving as a drift space for the charge carriers.

reader A device that converts information from one form to another, as from punched paper tape to magnetic tape.

reader-interpreter A service routine that reads an input string, stores programs and data on random-access storage for later processing, identifies the control information contained in the input string, and stores this control information separately in the appropriate control lists.

reader-punch equipment An input/output unit which can punch computer results on cards and read card data into the computer.

read error A condition in which the content of a storage device cannot be electronically identified.

read head A device that converts digital information stored on a magnetic tape, drum, or disk into electrical signals usable by the computer arithmetic unit.

read-in To sense information contained in some source and transmit this information to an internal storage.

readiness review An on-site examination of the adequacy of preparations for effective utilization upon installation of a computer, and to identify any necessary corrective actions.

reading rate Number of characters, words, fields, blocks, or cards sensed by an input sensing device per unit of time.

reading station The position in a punched-card machine at which the data on the card are read, by sensing the positions of the holes, and converted into electrical impulses. Also known as sensing station.

read-in program Computer program that can be put into a computer in a simple binary form and allows other programs to be read into the computer in more complex forms.

read-only memory A device for storing data in permanent, or nonerasable, form; usually a static electronic or magnetic device allowing extremely rapid access to data. Abbreviated ROM. Also known as read-only storage.

read-only storage *See* read-only memory.

readout 1. The presentation of output information by means of lights, printed or punched tape or cards, or other methods. 2. To sense information contained in some computer internal storage and transmit this information to a storage external to the computer.

read-punch unit An input-output unit of a computing system which punches computed results into cards, reads input information into the system, and segregates output cards; the read-punch unit generally consists of a card feed, a read station, a punch station, another read station, and two output card stackers.

read screen In optical character recognition (OCR), the transparent component part of most character readers through which appears the input document to be recognized.

read time The time interval between the instant at which information is called for from storage and the instant at which delivery is completed in a computer.

read-while-writing The reading of a record or group of records into storage from tape at the same time another record or group of records is written from storage to tape.

read/write channel A path along which information is transmitted between the central processing unit of a computer and an input, output, or storage unit under the control of the computer.

read/write check indicator A device incorporated in certain computers to indicate upon interrogation whether or not an error was made in reading or writing; the machine can be made to stop, retry the operation, or follow a special subroutine, depending upon the result of the interrogation.

read/write comb The set of arms mounted with magnetic heads that reach between the disks of a disk storage device to read and record information.

read/write head A magnetic head that both senses and records data. Also known as combined head.

read/write memory A computer storage in which data may be stored or retrieved at comparable intervals.

read/write random-access memory A random access memory in which data can be written into memory as well as read out of memory.

real data type A scalar data type which contains a normalized fraction (mantissa) and an exponent (characteristic) and is used to represent floating-point data, usually decimal.

real-time Pertaining to a data-processing system that controls an ongoing process and delivers its outputs (or controls its inputs) not later than the time when these are needed for effective control; for instance, airline reservations booking and chemical processes control.

real-time clock A pulse generator which operates at precise time intervals to determine time intervals between events and initiate specific elements of processing.

real-time control system A computer system which controls an operation in real time, such as a rocket flight.

real-time operation **1.** Of a computer or system, an operation or other response in which programmed responses to an event are essentially simultaneous with the event itself. **2.** An operation in which information obtained from a physical process is processed to influence or control the physical process.

real-time processing The handling of input data at a rate sufficient to ensure that the instructions generated by the computer will influence the operation under control at the required time.

real-time programming Programming for a situation in which results of computations will be used immediately to influence the course of ongoing physical events.

rear-projection Pertaining to television system in which the picture is projected on a ground-glass screen for viewing from the opposite side of the screen.

recall factor A measure of the efficiency of an information retrieval system, equal to the number of retrieved relevant documents divided by the total number of relevant documents in the file.

receiver The complete equipment required for receiving modulated radio waves and converting them into the original intelligence, such as into sounds or pictures, or converting to desired useful information as in a radar receiver.

receiver bandwidth Spread, in frequency, between the halfpower points on the receiver response curve.

receiver gating Application of operating voltages to one or more stages of a receiver only during that part of a cycle of operation when reception is desired.

receiver incremental tuning Control feature to permit receiver tuning (of a transceiver) up to 3 kilohertz to either side of the transmitter frequency.

receiver noise threshold External noise appearing at the front end of a receiver, plus the noise added by the receiver itself, determines a noise threshold that has to be exceeded by the minimum discernible signal.

receiving set *See* radio receiver.

receiving tube A low-voltage and low-power vacuum tube used in radio receivers, computers, and sensitive control and measuring equipment.

reciprocal transducer Transducer which satisfies the principle of reciprocity.

reciprocation In electronics, a process of deriving a reciprocal impedance from a given impedance, or finding a reciprocal network for a given network.

reclaimer A device that performs dynamic storage allocation, periodically searching memory to locate cells whose contents are no longer useful for computation, and making them available for other uses.

recognition The act or process of identifying (or associating) an input with one of a set of possible known alternatives, as in character recognition and pattern recognition.

recognition gate A logic circuit used to select devices identified by a binary address code. Also known as decoding gate.

recombination coefficient The rate of recombination of positive ions with electrons or negative ions in a gas, per unit volume, divided by the product of the number of positive ions per unit volume and the number of electrons or negative ions per unit volume.

recombination electroluminescence *See* injection electroluminescence.

recombination radiation The radiation emitted in semiconductors when electrons in the conduction band recombine with holes in the valence band.

recombination velocity On a semiconductor surface, the ratio of the normal component of the electron (or hole) current density at the surface to the excess electron (or hole) charge density at the surface.

reconditioned carrier reception Method of reception in which the carrier is separated from the sidebands to eliminate amplitude variations and noise, and is then added at an increased level to the sideband, to obtain a relatively undistorted output.

reconstruction A process in which atoms at the surface of a solid displace and form bands different from those existing in the bulk solid.

recontrol time *See* deionization time.

record A group of adjacent data items in a computer system, manipulated as a unit.

record block *See* physical record.

record density *See* bit density; character density.

record gap An area in a storage medium, such as magnetic tape or disk, which is devoid of information; it delimits records, and, on tape, allows the tape to stop and start between records without loss of data. Also known as interrecord gap (IRG).

record head *See* recording head.

recording head A magnetic head used only for recording. Also known as record head.

recording lamp A lamp whose intensity can be varied at an audio-frequency rate, for exposing variable-density sound tracks on motion picture film and for exposing paper or film in photographic facsimile recording.

recording level Amplifier output level required to secure a satisfactory recording.

recording noise Noise that is introduced during a recording process.

recording spot *See* picture element.

recording storage tube Type of cathode-ray tube in which the electric equivalent of an image can be stored as an electrostatic charge pattern on a storage surface; there is no visual display, but the stored information can be read out at any later time as an electric output signal.

record length The number of characters required for all the information in a record.

record mark A symbol that signals a record's beginning or end.

record storage mark A special character which appears only in the record storage unit of the card reader to limit the length of the record read into storage.

recovery interrupt A type of interruption of program execution which provides the computer with access to subroutines to handle an error and, if successful, to continue with the program execution.

recovery system A system for recognizing a malfunction in a data-base management system, reporting it, reconstructing the damaged part of the data base, and resuming processing.

recovery time 1. The time required for the control electrode of a gas tube to regain control after anode-current interruption. 2. The time required for a fired TR (transmit-receive) or pre-TR tube to deionize to such a level that the attenuation of a low-level radio-frequency signal transmitted through the tube is decreased to a specified value. 3. The time required for a fired ATR (anti-transmit-receive) tube to deionize to such a level that the normalized conductance and susceptance of the tube in its mount are within specified ranges. 4. The interval required, after a sudden decrease in input signal amplitude to a system or component, to attain a specified percentage (usually 63%) of the ultimate change in amplification or attenuation due to this decrease. 5. The time required for a radar receiver to recover to half sensitivity after the end of the transmitted pulse, so it can receive a return echo.

rectangular pulse A pulse in which the wave amplitude suddenly changes from zero to another value at which it remains constant for a short period of time, and then suddenly changes back to zero.

rectangular scanning Two-dimensional sector scanning in which a slow sector scanning in one direction is superimposed on a rapid sector scanning in a perpendicular direction.

rectangular wave A periodic wave that alternately and suddenly changes from one to the other of two fixed values. Also known as rectangular wave train.

rectangular wave train *See* rectangular wave.

Rectenna A device that converts microwave energy in direct-current power; consists of a number of small dipoles, each having its own diode rectifier network, which are connected to direct-current buses.

rectification factor Quotient of the change in average current of an electrode by the change in amplitude of the alternating sinusoidal voltage applied to the same electrode, the direct voltages of this and other electrodes being maintained constant.

rectifier filter An electric filter used in smoothing out the voltage fluctuation of an electron tube rectifier, and generally placed between the rectifier's output and the load resistance.

rectifier rating A performance rating for a semiconductor rectifier, usually on the basis of the root-mean-square value of sinusoidal voltage that it can withstand in the reverse direction and the average current density that it will pass in the forward direction.

rectifier stack A dry-disk rectifier made up of layers or stacks of disks of individual rectifiers, as in a selenium rectifier or copper-oxide rectifier.

rectifier transformer Transformer whose secondary supplies energy to the main anodes of a rectifier.

rectilinear scanning Process of scanning an area in a predetermined sequence of narrow parallel strips.

recursion A technique in which an apparently circular process is used to perform an iterative process.

recursive macro call A call to a macroinstruction already called when used in conjunction with conditional assembly.

recursive procedure A method of calculating a function by deriving values of it which become more elementary at each step; recursive procedures are explicitly outlawed in most systems with the exception of a few which use languages such as ALGOL and LISP.

recursive subroutine A reentrant subroutine whose partial results are stacked, with a processor stack pointer advancing and retracting as the subroutine is called and completed.

recycling Returning to an original condition, as to 0 or 1 in a counting circuit.

redistribution The alteration of charges on an area of a storage surface by secondary electrons from any other area of the surface in a charge storage tube or television camera tube.

red-tape operation *See* bookkeeping operation.

reduction Any process by which data are condensed, such as changing the encoding to eliminate redundancy, extracting significant details from the data and eliminating the rest, or choosing every second or third out of the totality of available points.

reduction rule The principal computation rule in the lambda calculus; it states that an operator-operand combination of the form $(\lambda x M A)$ may be transformed into the expression $S^x_A M$, obtained by substituting the lambda expression A for all instances of x in M, provided there are no conflicts of variable names. Also known as beta rule.

reductive grammar A set of syntactic rules for the analysis of strings to determine whether the strings exist in a language.

redundancy Any deliberate duplication or partial duplication of circuitry or information to decrease the probability of a system or communication failure.

redundancy bit A bit which carries no information but which is added to the information-carrying bits of a character or stream of characters to determine their accuracy.

redundancy check A forbidden-combination check that uses redundant digits called check digits to detect errors made by a computer.

redundant character A character specifically added to a group of characters to ensure conformity with certain rules which can be used to detect computer malfunction.

redundant digit Digit that is not necessary for an actual computation but serves to reveal a malfunction in a digital computer.

reel number A number identifying a reel of magnetic tape in a file containing more than one reel and indicating the order in which the reel is to be used. Also known as reel sequence number.

reel sequence number *See* reel number.

reenterable The attribute that describes a program or routine which can be shared by several tasks concurrently.

reentrant program A subprogram in a time-sharing or multiprogramming system that can be shared by a number of users, and can therefore be applied to a given user program, interrupted and applied to some other user program, and then reentered at the point of interruption of the original user program.

reentry system In character recognition, a system in which the input data to be read are printed by the computer with which the reader is associated.

reference address *See* address constant.

reference block A block within a computer program governing a numerically controlled machine which has enough data to allow resumption of the program following an interruption.

reference burst *See* color burst.

reference listing A list printed by a compiler showing the instructions in the machine language program which it generates.

reference mark One of the marks used in a design of a printed circuit, giving scale dimensions and indicating the edges of the circuit board.

reference noise The power level used as a basis of comparison when designating noise power expressed in decibels above reference noise (dBrn); the reference usually used is 10^{-12} watt (-90 decibels above 1 milliwatt; dBm) at 1000 hertz.

reference record Output of a compiler that lists the operations and their positions in the final specific routine and contains information describing the segmentation and storage allocation of the routine.

reference supply A source of stable and constant voltage, such as a Zener diode, used in analog computers, regulated power supplies, and a variety of other circuits for comparison with a varying voltage.

reference time The instant near the beginning of switching that is chosen as a reference for time measurements in a digital computer.

reference white level In television, the level at the point of observation corresponding to the specified maximum excursion of the picture signal in the white direction.

reflectance In optical character recognition, the relative brightness of the inked area that forms the printed or handwritten character; distinguished from background reflectance and brightness.

reflected binary A particular form of gray code which is constructed according to the following rule: Let the first 2^N code patterns be given, for any N greater than 1; the next 2^N code patterns are derived by changing the $(N+1)$-th bit from the right from 0 to 1 and repeating the original 2^N patterns in reverse order in the N rightmost positions. Also known as reflected code.

reflected code *See* reflected binary.

reflecting electrode Tabular outer electrode or the repeller plate in a microwave oscillator tube, corresponding in construction but not in function to the plate of an ordinary triode; used for generating extremely high frequencies.

reflector *See* repeller.

reflector characteristic A chart of power output and frequency deviation of a reflex klystron as a function of reflector voltage.

reflector voltage Voltage between the reflector electrode and the cathode in a reflex klystron.

reflex bunching The bunching that occurs in an electron stream which has been made to reverse its direction in the drift space.

reflex circuit A circuit in which the signal is amplified twice by the same amplifier tube or tubes, once as an intermediate-frequency signal before detection and once as an audio-frequency signal after detection.

reflex klystron A single-cavity klystron in which the electron beam is reflected back through the cavity resonator by a repelling electrode having a negative voltage; used as a microwave oscillator. Also known as reflex oscillator.

reflex oscillator *See* reflex klystron.

regenerate 1. To restore pulses to their original shape. 2. To restore stored information to its original form in a storage tube in order to counteract fading and disturbances.

regeneration Replacement or restoration of charges in a charge storage tube to overcome decay effects, including loss of charge by reading.

regenerative amplifier An amplifier that uses positive feedback to give increased gain and selectivity.

regenerative clipper A type of monostable multivibrator which is a modification of a Schmitt trigger; used for pulse generation.

regenerative detector A vacuum-tube detector circuit in which radio-frequency energy is fed back from the anode circuit to the grid circuit to give positive feedback at the carrier frequency, thereby increasing the amplification and sensitivity of the circuit.

regenerative divider Frequency divider which employs modulation, amplification, and selective feedback to produce the output wave.

regenerative read A read operation in which the data are automatically written back into the locations from which they are taken.

regenerative receiver A radio receiver that uses a regenerative detector.

regenerative storage A storage unit, such as a delay line or storage tube, in which the stored data must be constantly read and restored to prevent decay or loss.

regenerative track Track on a magnetic drum with interconnected reading and writing heads; information stored on these tracks is continuously read from the drum, transmitted round a closed circuit, and recorded back on the drum; consequently, access times to these data are short; operation is analogous to that of the acoustic delay line.

region A group of machine addresses which refer to a base address.

regional address An address of a machine instruction within a series of consecutive addresses; for example, R18 and R19 are specific addresses in an R region of N consecutive addresses, where all addresses must be named.

register The computer hardware for storing one machine word.

register capacity The upper and lower limits of the numbers which may be processed in a register.

register circuit A switching circuit with memory elements that can store from a few to millions of bits of coded information; when needed, the information can be taken from the circuit in the same code as the input, or in a different code.

register length The number of digits, characters, or bits, which a register can store.

registration mark In character recognition, a preprinted indication of the relative position and direction of various elements of the source document to be recognized.

regular expression A formal description of a language acceptable by a finite automaton or for the behavior of a sequential switching circuit.

regulation The difference between the maximum and minimum tube voltage drops within a specified range of anode current in a gas tube.

reimbursed time The machine time which is loaned or rented to another office, agency, or organization, either on a reimbursable or reciprocal basis.

Reinartz crystal oscillator Crystal-controlled vacuum-tube oscillator in which the crystal current is kept low by placing a resonant circuit in the cathode lead tuned to half the crystal frequency; the resulting regeneration at the crystal frequency improves efficiency without the danger of uncontrollable oscillation at other frequencies.

reinserter *See* direct-current restorer.

reinsertion of carrier Combining a locally generated carrier signal in a receiver with an incoming signal of the suppressed carrier type.

rejector *See* trap.

relational operator An operator that indicates whether one quantity is equal to, greater than, or less than another.

relational system A type of data-base management system in which data are represented as tables in which no entry contains more that one value.

relative address The numerical difference between a desired address and a known reference address.

relative attenuation The ratio of the peak output voltage of an electric filter to the voltage at the frequency being considered.

relative bandwidth For an electric filter, the ratio of the bandwidth being considered to a specified reference bandwidth, such as the bandwidth between frequencies at which there is an attenuation of 3 decibels.

relative coding A form of computer programming in which the address part of an instruction indicates not the desired address but the difference between the location of the instruction and the desired address.

relative response In a transducer, the amount (in decibels) by which the response under some particular condition exceeds the response under a reference condition.

relative triple precision The retention of three times as many digits of a quantity as the computer normally handles; for example, a computer whose basic word consists of 10 decimal digits is called upon to handle 30 decimal digit quantities.

relaxation circuit Circuit arrangement, usually of vacuum tubes, reactances, and resistances, which has two states or conditions, one, both, or neither of which may be stable; the transient voltage produced by passing from one to the other, or the voltage in a state of rest, can be used in other circuits.

relaxation inverter An inverter that uses a relaxation oscillator circuit to convert direct-current power to alternating-current.

relaxation oscillator An oscillator whose fundamental frequency is determined by the time of charging or discharging a capacitor or coil through a resistor, producing waveforms that may be rectangular or sawtooth.

relaxation time The travel time of an electron in a metal before it is scattered and loses its momentum.

relieving anode Of a pool-cathode tube, an auxiliary anode which provides an alternative conducting path for reducing the current to another electrode.

reloadable control storage The control storage made up of unit control words necessary for channel multiplexing.

relocatable code A code generated by an assembler or compiler, and in which all memory references needing relocation are either specially marked or relative to the current program-counter reading.

relocatable emulator An emulator which does not require a stand-alone machine but executes in a multiprogramming environment.

relocatable program A program coded in such a way that it may be located and executed in any part of memory.

relocate To establish or change the location of a program routine while adjusting or modifying the address references within the instructions to correctly indicate the new locations.

relocating loader A loader in which some of the addresses in the program to be loaded are expressed relative to the start of the program rather than in absolute form.

relocation hardware Equipment in a multiprogramming system which allows a computer program to be run in any available space in memory.

relocation register A hardware element that holds a constant to be added to the address of each memory location in a computer program running in a multiprogramming system, as determined by the location of the area in memory assigned to the program.

remedial maintenance *See* corrective maintenance.

remember condition Condition of a flip-flop circuit in which no change takes place between a given internal state and the next state.

remodulator A circuit that converts amplitude modulation to audio frequency-shift modulation for transmission of facsimile signals over a voice-frequency radio channel. Also known as converter.

remote batch computing The running of programs, usually during nonprime hours, or whenever the demands of real-time or time-sharing computing slacken sufficiently to allow less pressing programs to be run.

remote batch processing Batch processing in which an input device is located at a distance from the main installation and has access to a computer through a communication link.

remote calculator A keyboard device that can be connected to the central processing unit of a distant computer over an ordinary telephone channel, enabling the user to present programs to the computer.

remote computing system A data-processing system that has terminals distant from the central processing unit, from which users can communicate with the central processing unit and compile, debug, test, and execute programs.

remote computing system exchange A device that handles communications between the central processing unit and remote consoles of a remote computing system, and enables several remote consoles to operate at the same time without interfering with each other.

remote computing system language A computer language used for communications between the central processing unit and remote consoles of a remote computer system, generally incorporating a procedure-oriented language such as FORTRAN, but also containing operating statements, such as instructions to debug or execute programs.

remote computing system log A record of the volumes of data transmitted and of the frequency of various types of events during the operation of remote consoles in a remote computing system.

remote console A terminal in a remote computing system that has facilities for communicating with, and exerting control over, the central processing unit, and which may have devices for reading and punching cards or paper tape, any of various types of display units, printers, and a keyboard device for direct communication with the central processing unit.

remote-cutoff tube *See* variable-mu tube.

remote data station A terminal in a data-processing system at which data can be sent to or received from a central computer over telephone or telegraph circuits, but which exerts no direct operating control over the central computer. Also known as remote data terminal.

remote data terminal *See* remote data station.

remote debugging 1. The testing and correction of computer programs at a remote console of a remote computing system. **2.** *See* remote testing.

remote indicator 1. An indicator located at a distance from the data-gathering sensing element, with data being transmitted to the indicator mechanically, electrically over wires, or by means of light, radio, or sound waves. **2.** *See* repeater.

remote inquiry Interrogation of the content of an automatic data-processing equipment storage unit from a device remotely displaced from the storage unit site.

remote job entry The submission of jobs to a central computer from a location at least a few hundred meters and sometimes many kilometers distant from the computer, requiring the use of a telephone or other common-carrier communications link. Abbreviated RJE.

remote plan position indicator *See* plan position indicator repeater.

remote terminal A computer terminal which is located away from the central processing unit of a data-processing system, at a location convenient to a user of the system.

remote testing A method of testing and correcting computer programs; programmers do not go to the computer center but provide detailed instructions to be carried out by computer operators along with the programs and associated test data. Also known as remote debugging.

repeater 1. An amplifier or other device that receives weak signals and delivers corresponding stronger signals with or without reshaping of waveforms; may be either a one-way or two-way repeater. 2. An indicator that shows the same information as is shown on a master indicator. Also known as remote indicator.

repeater jammer A jammer that intercepts an enemy radar signal and reradiates the signal after modifying it to incorporate erroneous data on azimuth, range, or number of targets.

repeat operator A pseudo instruction using two arguments, a count p and an increment n: the word immediately following the instruction is repeated p times, with the values $0, n, 2n, \ldots, (p-1)n$ added to the successive words.

repeller An electrode whose primary function is to reverse the direction of an electron stream in an electron tube. Also known as reflector.

repetition instruction An instruction that causes one or more other instructions to be repeated a specified number of times, usually with systematic address modification occurring between repetitions.

repetitive addressing A system used on some computers in which, under certain conditions, an instruction is written without giving the address of the operand, and the operand address is automatically that of the location addressed by the last previous instruction.

repetitive analog computer An analog computer which repeatedly carries out the solution of a problem at a rapid rate (10 to 60 times a second) while an operator may vary parameters in the problem.

repetitive unit A type of circuit which appears more than once in a computer.

report An output document prepared by a data-processing system.

report generator A routine which produces a complete data-processing report, given only a description of the desired content and format, plus certain information concerning the input file.

report program A program that prints out an analysis of a file of records, usually arranged by keys, each analysis or total being produced when a key change takes place.

report program generator A nonprocedural programming language that provides a convenient method of producing a wide variety of reports. Abbreviated RPG.

representative calculating time The time required to perform a specified operation or series of operations.

reproduce head *See* playback head.

reproducer A punched-card machine that reads a punched card and duplicates part or all of its contents by punching another card. Also known as punched-card reproducer.

reproducing unit An electromechanical device which will duplicate a deck of cards.

request/grant logic Logic circuitry which, in effect, selects the interrupt line with highest priority.

rerun To run a program or a portion of it again on a computer. Also known as rollback.

rerun point A location in a program from which the program may be started anew after an interruption of the computer run.

rerun routine A routine designed to be used in the wake of a computer malfunction or a coding or operating mistake to reconstitute a routine from the last previous rerun point.

rescue dump The copying of the entire contents of a computer memory into auxiliary storage devices, carried out periodically during the course of a computer program so that in case of a machine failure the program can be reconstituted at the last point at which this operation was executed.

reserve To assign portions of a computer memory and of input/output and storage devices to a specific computer program in a multiprogramming system.

reserved word A word which cannot be used in a programming language to represent an item of data because it has some particular significance to the compiler, or which can be used only in a particular context.

reset *See* clear.

reset condition Condition of a flip-flop circuit in which the internal state of the flip-flop is reset to zero.

reset cycle To restore a cycle index counter to its initial value.

reset input The act of resetting the original conditions of a problem when running on an analog computer.

reset mode The phase of operation of an analog computer during which the required initial conditions are entered into the system and the computing units are inoperative. Also known as initial condition mode.

reset pulse 1. A drive pulse that tends to reset a magnetic cell in the storage section of a digital computer. 2. A pulse used to reset an electronic counter to zero or to some predetermined position.

resettability The ability of the tuning element of an oscillator to retune the oscillator to the same operating frequency for the same set of input conditions.

resident executive The portion of the executive program (sometimes called monitor system) which is permanently stored in core. Also known as resident monitor.

resident monitor *See* resident executive.

resident routine Any computer routine which is stored permanently in the memory, such as the resident executive.

residual current Current flowing through a thermionic diode when there is no anode voltage, due to the velocity of the electrons emitted by the heated cathode.

residue check *See* modulo N check.

residue system A number system in which each digit position corresponds to a different radix, all pairs of radices are relatively prime, and the value of a digit with radix r for an integer A is equal to the remainder when A is divided by r.

resistance-capacitance coupled amplifier An amplifier in which a capacitor provides a path for signal currents from one stage to the next, with resistors connected from each side of the capacitor to the power supply or to ground; it can amplify alternating-current signals but cannot handle small changes in direct currents. Also known as R-C amplifier; R-C coupled amplifier; resistance-coupled amplifier.

resistance-capacitance coupling *See* resistance coupling.

resistance-capacitance oscillator Oscillator in which the frequency is determined by resistance and capacitance elements. Abbreviated R-C oscillator.

resistance-coupled amplifier *See* resistance-capacitance coupled amplifier.

resistance coupling Coupling in which resistors are used as the input and output impedances of the circuits being coupled; a coupling capacitor is generally used between the resistors to transfer the signal from one stage to the next. Also known as R-C coupling; resistance-capacitance coupling; resistive coupling.

resistance noise *See* thermal noise.

resistance strain gage A strain gage consisting of a strip of material that is cemented to the part under test and that changes in resistance with elongation or compression.

resistive coupling *See* resistance coupling.

resistor-capacitor-transistor logic A resistor-transistor logic with the addition of capacitors that are used to enhance switching speed.

resistor termination A thick-film conductor pad overlapping and contacting a thick-film resistor area.

resistor-transistor logic One of the simplest logic circuits, having several resistors, a transistor, and a diode. Abbreviated RTL.

resnatron A microwave-beam tetrode containing cavity resonators, used chiefly for generating large amounts of continuous power at high frequencies.

resolution In television, the maximum number of lines that can be discerned on the screen at a distance equal to tube height; this ranges from 350 to 400 for most receivers.

resolution error An error of an analog computing unit that results from its inability to respond to changes of less than a given magnitude.

resolution factor In information retrieval, the ratio obtained in dividing the total number of documents retrieved (whether relevant or not to the user's needs) by the total number of documents available in the file.

resolver 1. A synchro or other device whose input is the angular position of an object, such as the rotor of an electric machine, and whose output is electric signals, usually proportional to the sine and cosine of an angle, and often in digital form; used to interchange rectangular and polar coordinates, and in servomechanisms to report the orientation of controlled objects. Also known as angular resolver. **2.** A device that accepts a single vector-valued analog input and produces for output either analog or digital signals proportional to two or three orthogonal components of the vector. Also known as vector resolver.

resolving time In computers, the shortest permissible period between trigger pulses for reliable operation of a binary cell.

resonance transformer An electrostatic particle accelerator, used principally for acceleration of electrons, in which the high-voltage terminal oscillates between voltages which are equal in magnitude and opposite in sign.

resonant gate transistor Surface field-effect transistor incorporating a cantilevered beam which resonates at a specific frequency to provide high-Q-frequency discrimination.

resonant-line oscillator Oscillator in which one or more sections of transmission lines are employed as resonant elements.

resonant-line tuner A television tuner in which resonant lines are used to tune the antenna, radio-frequency amplifier, and radio-frequency oscillator circuits; tuning is achieved by moving shorting contacts that change the electrical lengths of the lines.

resonator grid Grid that is attached to a cavity resonator in velocity-modulated tubes to provide coupling between the resonator and the electron beam.

responder The transmitter section of a radar beacon.

responder beacon The radar beacon that serves to emit the signals of the responder in a transponder.

response time The delay experienced in time sharing between request and answer, a delay which increases when the number of users on the system increases.

responsor The receiving section of an interrogator-responsor.

restart To go back to a specific planned point in a routine, usually in the case of machine malfunction, for the purpose of rerunning the portion of the routine in which the error occurred; the length of time between restart points in a given routine should be a function of the mean free error time of the machine itself.

restore 1. In computers, to regenerate, to return a cycle index or variable address to its initial value, or to store again. **2.** Periodic charge regeneration of volatile computer storage systems.

restorer pulses In computers, pairs of complement pulses, applied to restore the coupling-capacitor charge in an alternating-current flip-flop.

retarding-field oscillator An oscillator employing an electron tube in which the electrons oscillate back and forth through a grid that is maintained positive with respect to both the cathode and anode; the field in the region of the grid exerts a retarding effect through the grid in either direction. Also known as positive-grid oscillator.

retard transmitter Transmitter in which a delay period is introduced between the time of actuation and the time of transmission.

retention period The length of time that data must be kept on a reel of magnetic tape before it can be destroyed.

retention time The maximum time between writing into a storage tube and obtaining an acceptable output by reading. Also known as storage time.

retina In optical character recognition, a scanning device.

retina character reader A character reader that operates in the manner of the human retina in recognizing identical letters in different type fonts.

retrace See flyback.

retrace blanking Blanking a television picture tube during vertical retrace intervals to prevent retrace lines from showing on the screen.

retrace line The line traced by the electron beam in a cathode-ray tube in going from the end of one line or field to the start of the next line or field. Also known as return line.

retransmission unit Control unit used at an intermediate station for feeding one radio receiver-transmitter unit for two-way communication.

retrieve To find and select specific information.

retry When a central processing unit error is detected during execution of an instruction, the computer will execute this instruction unless a register was altered by the operation.

return 1. To return control from a subroutine to the calling program. **2.** To go back to a planned point in a computer program and rerun a portion of the program, usually when an error is detected; rerun points are usually not more than 5 minutes apart. **3.** *See* echo.

return interval Interval corresponding to the direction of sweep not used for delineation.

return jump A jump instruction in a subroutine which passes control to the first statement in the program which follows the instruction called the subroutine.

return line *See* retrace line.

return to zero mode Computer readout mode in which the signal returns to zero between each bit indication.

return trace *See* flyback.

reusable Of a program, capable of being used by several tasks without having to be reloaded; it is a generic term, including reenterable and serially reusable.

reverse bias A bias voltage applied to a diode or a semiconductor junction with polarity such that little or no current flows; the opposite of forward bias.

reverse-blocking tetrode thyristor *See* silicon controlled switch.

reverse-blocking triode thyristor *See* silicon controlled rectifier.

reverse code dictionary Alphabetic or alphanumeric arrangement of codes associated with their corresponding English words or terms.

reverse current Small value of direct current that flows when a semiconductor diode has reverse bias.

reverse direction *See* inverse direction.

reverse-direction flow A logical path that runs upward or to the left on a flowchart.

reverse Polish notation The version of Polish notation, used in some calculators, in which operands follow the operators with which they are associated. Abbreviated RPN. Also known as postfix notation; suffix notation.

reversible capacitance Limit, as the amplitude of an applied sinusoidal capacitor voltage approaches zero, of the ratio of the amplitude of the resulting in-phase fundamental-frequency component of transferred charge to the amplitude of the applied voltage, for a given constant bias voltage superimposed on the sinusoidal voltage.

reversible counter A counter which stores a number whose value can be decreased or increased in response to the appropriate control signal.

reversible transducer Transducer whose loss is independent of transmission direction.

rewind 1. The components on a magnetic tape recorder that serve to return the tape to the supply reel at high speed. **2.** To return a magnetic tape to its starting position.

rewrite The process of restoring a storage device to its state prior to reading; used when the information-storing state may be destroyed by reading.

RHI display *See* range-height indicator display.

rice neutralization Development of voltage in the grid circuit of a vacuum tube in order to nullify or cancel feedback through the tube.

rice neutralizing circuit Radio-frequency amplifier circuit that neutralizes the grid-to-plate capacitance of an amplifier tube.

Richardson-Dushman equation An equation for the current density of electrons that leave a heated conductor in thermionic emission. Also known as Dushman equation.

Richardson effect *See* thermionic emission.

Richardson plot A graph of log (J/T^2) against $1/T$, where J is the current density of electrons leaving a heated conductor in thermionic emission, and T is the temperature of the conductor; according to the Richardson-Dushman equation, this is a straight line.

Rieke diagram A chart showing contours of constant power output and constant frequency for a microwave oscillator, drawn on a Smith chart or other polar diagram whose coordinates represent the components of the complex reflection coefficient at the oscillator load.

right-justify To shift the contents of a register so that the right or least significant digit is at some specified position.

R indicator *See* R scope.

ring A cyclic arrangement of data elements, usually including a specified entry pointer.

ring counter A loop of binary scalers or other bistable units so connected that only one scaler is in a specified state at any given time; as input signals are counted, the position of the one specified state moves in an ordered sequence around the loop.

ringing circuit A circuit which has a capacitance in parallel with a resistance and inductance, with the whole in parallel with a second resistance; it is highly underdamped and is supplied with a step or pulse input.

ring modulator A modulator in which four diode elements are connected in series to form a ring around which current flows readily in one direction; input and output connections are made to the four nodal points of the ring; used as a balanced modulator, demodulator, or phase detector.

ring shift *See* cyclic shift.

ring structure A chained file organization such that the end of the chain points to its beginning.

ring time The length of time in microseconds required for a pulse of energy transmitted into an echo box to die out; a measurement of the performance of the radar.

ripple-carry adder A device for addition of two n-bit binary numbers, formed by connecting n full adders in cascade, with the carry output of each full adder feeding the carry input of the following full adder.

ripple filter A low-pass filter designed to reduce ripple while freely passing the direct current obtained from a rectifier or direct-current generator. Also known as smoothing circuit; smoothing filter.

rising-sun magnetron A multicavity magnetron in which resonators having two different resonant frequencies are arranged alternately for the purpose of mode separation; the cavities appear as alternating long and short radial slots around the perimeter of the anode structure, resembling the rays of the sun.

RJE *See* remote job entry.

rocky point effect Transient but violent discharges between electrodes in high-voltage transmitting tubes.

rod thermistor A type of thermistor that has high resistance, long time constant, and moderate power dissipation; it is extruded as a long vertical rod 0.250–2.0 inches (0.63–5.1 centimeters) long and 0.050–0.110 inch (0.13–0.28 centimeter) in diameter, of oxide-binder mix and sintered; ends are coated with conducting paste and leads are wrapped on the coated area.

role indicator In information retrieval, a code assigned to a key word to indicate its part of speech, nature, or function.

rollback *See* rerun.

roll in To restore to main memory a section of program or data that had previously been rolled out.

roll-off Gradually increasing loss or attenuation with increase or decrease of frequency beyond the substantially flat portion of the amplitude-frequency response characteristic of a system or transducer.

roll-out 1. To make available additional main memory for one task by copying another task onto auxiliary storage. 2. To read a computer register or counter by adding a one to each digit column simultaneously until all have returned to zero, with a signal being generated at the instant a column returns to zero.

ROM *See* read-only memory.

roof filter Low-pass filter used in carrier telephone systems to limit the frequency response of the equipment to frequencies needed for normal transmission, thereby blocking unwanted higher frequencies induced in the circuit by external sources; improves runaround cross-talk suppression and minimizes high-frequency singing.

root The origin or most fundamental point of a tree diagram. Also known as base.

root component *See* root symbol.

root segment The master or controlling segment of an overlay structure which always resides in the main memory of a computer.

root symbol An element of a formal language, generally unique, that is not derivable from other language elements. Also known as root component.

rotary calculator A type of mechanical desk calculator that is distinguished from key-driven calculators by virtue of a latching selection keyboard in which the multiplicand or divisor could be indexed and then repeatedly transferred to the accumulator, positively or negatively by turning a crank; the accumulator and a cycle-counting register were mounted in a carriage that could be shifted right or left, relative to the selection keyboard, to accommodate the successive digits of the multiplier or quotient.

rotating-anode tube An x-ray tube in which the anode rotates continuously to bring a fresh area of its surface into the beam of electrons, allowing greater output without melting the target.

rotational latency The time required, following an order to read or write information in disk storage, for the location of the information to revolve beneath the appropriate read/write head.

rotational position sensing A fast disk search method whereby the control unit looks for a specified sector, and then receives the sector number required to access the record.

round-robin scheduling A scheduling algorithm which repeatedly runs through a list of users, giving each user the opportunity to use the central processing unit in succession.

routine A set of digital computer instructions designed and constructed so as to accomplish a specified function.

routine library Ordered set of standard and proven computer routines by which problems or parts of problems may be solved.

row 1. The characters, or corresponding bits of binary-coded characters, in a computer word. 2. Equipment which simultaneously processes the bits of a character, the characters of a word, or corresponding bits of binary-coded characters in a word. 3. Corresponding positions in a group of columns.

row address An index array entry field which contains the main storage address of a data block.

row binary A method of encoding binary information onto punched cards in which successive bits are punched row-wise onto the card.

row binary card A card in which the binary data are punched along the rows.

row order The storage of a matrix $a(m,n)$ as $a(1,1), a(1,2), \ldots, a(1,n), a(2,1), a(2,2), \ldots$ Also known as lexicographic order.

row pitch The distance between the centerlines of adjacent rows of holes in punched cards and paper tapes.

RPG *See* report program generator.

RPN *See* reverse Polish notation.

R scan *See* R scope.

R scope An A scope presentation with a segment of the horizontal trace expanded near the target spot (pip) for greater accuracy in range measurement. Also known as R indicator; R scan.

RTL *See* resistor-transistor logic.

ruggedization Making electronic equipment and components resistant to severe shock, temperature changes, high humidity, or other detrimental environmental influences.

ruggedized computer A computer, especially a minicomputer, built so as to reduce vibrations, resist moisture, and remain unaffected by electromagnetic interferences such as are found in factory, military, or mobile environments.

rule of inference *See* production.

run A single, complete execution of a computer program, or one continuous segment of computer processing, used to complete one or more tasks for a single customer or application. Also known as machine run.

runaway effect The phenomenon whereby an increase in temperature causes an increase in a collector-terminal current in a transistor, which in turn results in a higher temperature and, ultimately, failure of the transistor; the effect limits the power output of the transistor.

runaway electron An electron, in an ionized gas to which an electric field is applied, that gains energy from the field faster than it loses energy by colliding with other particles in the gas.

run book The collection of materials necessary to document a program run on a computer. Also known as problem file; problem folder.

run chart A flow chart for one or more computer runs which shows input, output, and the use of peripheral units, but no details of the execution of the run. Also known as run diagram.

run diagram *See* run chart.

running accumulator *See* push-down storage.

S

Salisbury dark box Isolating chamber used for test work in connection with radar equipment; the walls of the chamber are specially constructed to absorb all impinging microwave energy at a certain frequency.

sample-and-hold circuit A circuit that measures an input signal at a series of definite points in time, and whose output remains constant at a value corresponding to the most recent measurement until the next measurement is made.

sampling gate A gate circuit that extracts information from the input waveform only when activated by a selector pulse.

sanatron circuit A variable time-delay circuit having two pentodes and two diodes, used to produce very short gate waveforms having time durations that vary linearly with a reference voltage.

SANTA *See* systematic analog network testing approach.

satellite computer A computer which, under control of the main computer, handles the input and output routines, thereby allowing the main computer to be fully dedicated to computations.

satellite processor One of the outlying processors in a hierarchical distributed processing system, typically placed at or near point-of-transaction locations, and designed to serve the users at those locations.

saturated diode A diode that is passing the maximum possible current, so further increases in applied voltage have no effect on current.

saturating signal In radar, a signal of an amplitude greater than the dynamic range of the receiving system.

saturation 1. The condition that occurs when a transistor is driven so that it becomes biased in the forward direction (the collector becomes positive with respect to the base, for example, in a *pnp* type of transistor). 2. *See* anode saturation; temperature saturation.

saturation current 1. In general, the maximum current which can be obtained under certain conditions. 2. In a vacuum tube, the space-charge-limited current, such that further increase in filament temperature produces no specific increase in anode current. 3. In a vacuum tube, the temperature-limited current, such that a further increase in anode-cathode potential difference produces only a relatively small increase in current. 4. In a gaseous-discharge device, the maximum current which can be obtained for a given mode of discharge. 5. In a semiconductor, the maximum current which just precedes a change in conduction mode.

saturation limiting Limiting the minimum output voltage of a vacuum-tube circuit by operating the tube in the region of plate current saturation (not to be confused with emission saturation).

sawtooth generator A generator whose output voltage has a sawtooth waveform; used to produce sweep voltages for cathode-ray tubes.

sawtooth modulated jamming Electronic countermeasure technique when a high level jamming signal is transmitted, thus causing large automatic gain control voltages to be developed at the radar receiver that, in turn, cause target pip and receiver noise to completely disappear.

sawtooth pulse An electric pulse having a linear rise and a virtually instantaneous fall, or conversely, a virtually instantaneous rise and a linear fall.

sawtooth waveform A waveform characterized by a slow rise time and a sharp fall, resembling a tooth of a saw.

S-band hiran See shiran.

scalar data type The manner in which a sequence of bits represents a single data item in a computer program.

scale-of-ten circuit See decade scaler.

scale-of-two circuit See binary scaler.

scaler A circuit that produces an output pulse when a prescribed number of input pulses is received. Also known as counter; scaling circuit.

scaling Counting pulses with a scaler when the pulses occur too fast for direct counting by conventional means.

scaling circuit See scaler.

scaling factor The number of input pulses per output pulse of a scaling circuit. Also known as scaling ratio.

scaling ratio See scaling factor.

scan The motion, usually periodic, given to the major lobe of an antenna; the process of directing the radio-frequency beam successively over all points in a given region of space.

scan converter 1. Equipment that converts radar data images at a 3 kilohertz to 10 kilohertz sampling rate that can be sent over telephone line or narrow bandwidth radio circuits and converted into a slow-scan image, through a similar converter, at the receiving end. 2. A cathode-ray tube that is capable of storing radar, television, and data displays for nondestructive readout over prolonged periods of time.

scanistor Integrated semiconductor optical-scanning device that converts images into electrical signals; the output analog signal represents both amount and position of light shining on its surface.

scanner In character recognition, a magnetic or photoelectric device which converts the input character into corresponding electric signals for processing by electronic apparatus.

scanner selector An electronic device interfacing computer and multiplexers when more than one multiplexer is used.

scanning circuit See sweep circuit.

scanning electron microscope A type of electron microscope in which a beam of electrons, a few hundred angstroms in diameter, systematically sweeps over the specimen; the intensity of secondary electrons generated at the point of impact of the beam on the specimen is measured, and the resulting signal is fed into a cathode-ray-tube display which is scanned in synchronism with the scanning of the specimen.

scanning head Light source and phototube combined as a single unit for scanning a moving strip of paper, cloth, or metal in photoelectric side-register control systems.

scanning linearity In television, the uniformity of scanning speed during the trace interval.

scanning radio A radio receiver that automatically scans across public service, emergency service, or other radio bands and stops at the first preselected station which is on the air. Also known as radio scanner.

scanning spot *See* picture element.

scanning transmission electron microscope A type of electron microscope which scans with an extremely narrow beam that is transmitted through the sample; the detection apparatus produces an image whose brightness depends on atomic number of the sample. Abbreviated STEM.

scanning yoke *See* deflection yoke.

scatter loading The process of loading a program into main memory such that each section or segment of the program occupies a single, connected memory area but the several sections of the program need not be adjacent to each other.

scatter read An input operation that places various segments of an input record into noncontiguous areas in central memory.

scene analysis *See* picture segmentation.

scheduling algorithm A systematic method of determining the order in which tasks will be performed by a computer system, generally incorporated into the operating system.

schema A model of the data in a data base.

Schmitt circuit A bistable pulse generator in which an output pulse of constant amplitude exists only as long as the input voltage exceeds a certain value. Also known as Schmitt limiter; Schmitt trigger.

Schmitt limiter *See* Schmitt circuit.

Schmitt trigger *See* Schmitt circuit.

Schottky barrier A transition region formed within a semiconductor surface to serve as a rectifying barrier at a junction with a layer of metal.

Schottky barrier diode A semiconductor diode formed by contact between a semiconductor layer and a metal coating; it has a nonlinear rectifying characteristic; hot carriers (electrons for n-type material or holes for p-type material) are emitted from the Schottky barrier of the semiconductor and move to the metal coating that is the diode base; since majority carriers predominate, there is essentially no injection or storage of minority carriers to limit switching speeds. Also known as hot-carrier diode; Schottky diode.

Schottky defect 1. A defect in an ionic crystal in which a single ion is removed from its interior lattice site and relocated in a lattice site at the surface of the crystal. 2. A defect in an ionic crystal consisting of the smallest number of positive-ion vacancies and negative-ion vacancies which leave the crystal electrically neutral.

Schottky diode *See* Schottky barrier diode.

Schottky noise *See* shot noise.

Schottky theory A theory describing the rectification properties of the junction between a semiconductor and a metal that result from formation of a depletion layer at the surface of contact.

Schottky transistor-transistor logic A transistor-transistor logic circuit in which a Schottky diode with forward diode voltage is placed across the base-collector junction of the output transistor in order to improve the speed of the circuit.

scientific calculator An electronic calculator that has provisions for handling exponential, trigonometric, and sometimes other special functions in addition to performing arithmetic operations.

scientific computer A computer which has a very large memory and is capable of handling extremely high-speed arithmetic and a very large variety of floating-point arithmetic commands.

scientific system A system devoted principally to computations as opposed to business and data-processing systems, the main emphasis of which is on the updating of data records and files rather than the performance of calculations.

scope *See* cathode-ray oscilloscope; radarscope.

scope of a variable The portion of a computer program within which the variable can be accessed (used or changed).

scotoscope A telescope which employs an image intensifier to see in the dark.

Scott connection A type of transformer which transmits power from two-phase to three-phase systems, or vice versa.

SCR *See* silicon controlled rectifier.

scrambler A circuit that divides speech frequencies into several ranges by means of filters, then inverts and displaces the frequencies in each range so that the resulting reproduced sounds are unintelligible; the process is reversed at the receiving apparatus to restore intelligible speech. Also known as speech inverter; speech scrambler.

scratch file A temporary file for future use, created by copying all or part of a data set to an auxiliary memory device.

scratch-pad memory A very fast intermediate storage (in the form of flip-flop register or semiconductor memory) which often supplements main core memory.

scratch tape A reel of magnetic tape containing data that may now be destroyed.

screen 1. To make a preliminary selection from a set of entities, selection criteria being based on a given set of rules or conditions. **2.** The surface on which a television, radar, x-ray, or cathode-ray oscilloscope image is made visible for viewing; it may be a fluorescent screen with a phosphor layer that converts the energy of an electron beam to visible light, or a translucent or opaque screen on which the optical image is projected. Also known as viewing screen. **3.** *See* screen grid.

screen dissipation Power dissipated in the form of heat on the screen grid as the result of bombardment by the electron stream.

screen grid A grid placed between a control grid and an anode of an electron tube, and usually maintained at a fixed positive potential, to reduce the electrostatic influence of the anode in the space between the screen grid and the cathode. Also known as screen.

scribing Cutting a grid pattern of deep grooves with a diamond-tipped tool in a slice of semiconductor material containing a number of devices, so that the slice can be easily broken into individual chips.

scrolling The continuous movement of information either vertically or horizontally on a video screen.

SCS *See* silicon controlled switch.

sealed tube Electron tube which is hermetically sealed.

search To seek a desired item or condition in a set of related or similar items or conditions, especially a sequentially organized or nonorganized set, rather than a multidimensional set.

search gate A gate pulse used to search back and forth over a certain range.

search time Time required to locate a particular field of data in a computer storage device; requires a comparison of each field with a predetermined standard until an identity is obtained.

seasoning Overcoming a temporary unsteadiness of a component that may appear when it is first installed.

SEC *See* secondary electron conduction.

secondary electron 1. An electron emitted as a result of bombardment of a material by an incident electron. 2. An electron whose motion is due to a transfer of momentum from primary radiation.

secondary electron conduction Transport of charge by secondary electrons moving through the interstices of a porous material under the influence of an externally applied electric field. Abbreviated SEC.

secondary emission The emission of electrons from the surface of a solid or liquid into a vacuum as a result of bombardment by electrons or other charged particles.

secondary grid emission Electron emission from a grid resulting directly from bombardment of its surface by electrons or other charged particles.

secondary photocurrent A photocurrent resulting from ohmic contacts that are able to replenish charge carriers which pass out of the opposite contact in order to maintain charge neutrality, and whose maximum gain is much greater than unity.

secondary radar Radar which receives pulses transmitted by an interrogator and makes a return transmission (usually on a different frequency) by its transponder, as opposed to a primary radar which receives pulses returned from illuminated objects.

secondary storage Any means of storing and retrieving data external to the main computer itself but accessible to the program.

second breakdown Destructive breakdown in a transistor, wherein structural imperfections cause localized current concentrations and uncontrollable generation and multiplication of current carriers; reaction occurs so suddenly that the thermal time constant of the collector regions is exceeded, and the transistor is irreversibly damaged.

second detector The detector that separates the intelligence signal from the intermediate-frequency signal in a superheterodyne receiver.

second-generation computer A computer characterized by the use of transistors rather than vacuum tubes, the execution of input/output operations simultaneously with calculations, and the use of operating systems.

second-order subroutine A subroutine that is entered from another subroutine, in contrast to a first-order subroutine; it constitutes the second level of a two-level or higher-level routine. Also known as second-remove subroutine.

second-remove subroutine *See* second-order subroutine.

second-time-around echo A radar echo received after an interval exceeding the pulse interval. Also known as second-trip echo.

second-trip echo *See* second-time-around echo.

sectional radiography The technique of making radiographs of plane sections of a body or an object; its purpose is to show detail in a predetermined plane of the body, while blurring the images of structures in other planes. Also known as laminography; planigraphy; tomography.

sector 1. A portion of a track on a magnetic disk or a band on a magnetic drum. 2. A unit of data stored in such a portion.

sector display A display in which only a sector of the total service area of a radar system is shown; usually the sector is selectable.

sector scan A radar scan through a limited angle, as distinguished from complete rotation.

security The existence and enforcement of techniques which restrict access to data, and the conditions under which data may be obtained.

Seebeck coefficient The ratio of the open-circuit voltage to the temperature difference between the hot and cold junctions of a circuit exhibiting the Seebeck effect.

Seebeck effect The development of a voltage due to differences in temperature between two junctions of dissimilar metals in the same circuit.

seed A small, single crystal of semiconductor material used to start the growth of a large, single crystal for use in cutting semiconductor wafers.

seeing The introduction of atoms with a low ionization potential into a hot gas to increase electrical conductivity.

seek 1. To position the access mechanism of a random-access storage device at a designated location or position. 2. The command that directs the positioning to take place.

seek area An area of a direct-access storage device, such as a magnetic disk file, assigned to hold records to which rapid access is needed, and located so that the physical characteristics of the device permit such access. Also known as cylinder.

segment 1. A single section of an overlay program structure, which can be loaded into the main memory when and as needed. 2. In some direct-access storage devices, a hardware-defined portion of a track having fixed data capacity.

segmentation The division of virtual storage into identifiable functional regions, each having enough addresses so that programs or data stored in them will not assign the same addresses more than once.

segment mark A special character written on tape to separate one section of a tape file from another.

segregating unit A punched-card machine that selects from a group of punched cards those cards satisfying certain criteria; it has only two output hoppers, one for cards satisfying the criteria and one for those that do not, in contrast with a card sorter which has multiple outputs.

seignette-electric *See* ferroelectric.

select 1. To choose a needed subroutine from a file of subroutines. 2. To take one alternative if the report on a condition is of one state, and another alternative if the report on the condition is of another state. 3. To pull from a mass of data certain items that require special attention; selection of individual cards is accomplished automatically by either the sorter or collator, according to the type of selection.

select bit The bit (or bits) in an input/output instruction word which selects the function of a specified device. Also known as subdevice bit.

selection check Electronic computer check, usually automatic, to verify that the correct register, or other device, is selected in the performance of an instruction.

selective dump An edited or nonedited listing of the contents of selected areas of memory or auxiliary storage.

selective identification feature Airborne pulse-type transponder which provides automatic selective identification of aircraft in which it is installed to ground, shipboard, or airborne identification, friend or foe–selective identification feature recognition installations.

selective jamming Jamming in which only a single radio channel is jammed.

selective trace A tracing routine wherein only instructions satisfying certain specified criteria are subject to tracing.

selectivity The ability of a radio receiver to separate a desired signal frequency from other signal frequencies, some of which may differ only slightly from the desired value.

selector Computer device which interrogates a condition and initiates a particular operation dependent upon the report.

selector channel A unit which connects high-speed input/output devices, such as magnetic tapes, disks, and drums, to a computer memory.

selenium cell A photoconductive cell in which a thin film of selenium is used between suitable electrodes; the resistance of the cell decreases when the illumination is increased.

selenium diode A small area selenium rectifier which has characteristics similar to those of selenium rectifiers used in power systems.

selenium rectifier A metallic rectifier in which a thin layer of selenium is deposited on one side of an aluminum plate and a conductive metal coating is deposited on the selenium.

self-bias A grid bias provided automatically by the resistor in the cathode or grid circuit of an electron tube; the resulting voltage drop across the resistor serves as the grid bias. Also known as automatic C bias; automatic grid bias.

self-bias transistor circuit A transistor with a resistance in the emitter lead that gives rise to a voltage drop which is in the direction to reverse-bias the emitter junction; the circuit can be used even if there is zero direct-current resistance in series with the collector terminal.

self-checking code An encoding of data so designed and constructed that an invalid code can be rapidly detected; this permits the detection, but not the correction, of almost all errors. Also known as error-checking code; error-detecting code.

self-checking number A number with a suffix figure related to the figure of the number, used to check the number after it has been transferred from one medium or device to another.

self-complementing code A binary-coded-decimal code in which the combination for the complement of a digit is the complement of the combination for that digit.

self-contained data-base management system A data-base management system that is in no way an extension of any programming language, and is usually quite independent of any language.

self-excited oscillator An oscillator that depends on its own resonant circuits for initiation of oscillation and frequency determination.

self-pulsing Special type of grid pulsing which automatically stops and starts the oscillations at the pulsing rate by a special circuit.

self-quenched detector Superregenerative detector in which the time constant of the grid leak and grid capacitor is sufficiently large to cause intermittent oscillation above audio frequencies, serving to stop normal regeneration each time just before it spills over into a squealing condition.

self-quenching oscillator Oscillator producing a series of short trains of radio-frequency oscillations separated by intervals of quietness.

self-repair Any type of hardware redundancy in which faults are selectively masked and are detected, located, and subsequently corrected by the replacement of the failed unit by an unfailed replica.

self-resetting loop A loop whose termination causes the numbers stored in all locations affected by the loop to be returned to the original values which they had upon entry into the loop.

self-saturation The connection of half-wave rectifiers in series with the output windings of the saturable reactors of a magnetic amplifier, to give higher gain and faster response.

self-scanned image sensor A solid-state device, still in the early stages of development, which converts an optical image into a television signal without the use of an electron beam; it consists of an array of photoconductor diodes, each located at the intersection of mutually perpendicular address strips respectively connected to horizontal and vertical scan generators and video coupling circuits.

self-triggering program A computer program which automatically commences execution as soon as it is fed into the central processing unit.

semantic extension An extension mechanism which introduces new kinds of objects into an extensible language, such as additional data types or operations.

semaphore A memory cell that is shared by two parallel processes which rely on each other for their continued operation, and that provides an elementary form of communication between them by indicating when significant events have taken place.

semialgorithm A procedure for solving a problem that will continue endlessly if the problem has no solution.

semiconducting compound A compound which is a semiconductor, such as copper oxide, mercury indium telluride, zinc sulfide, cadmium selenide, and magnesium iodide.

semiconducting crystal A crystal of a semiconductor, such as silicon, germanium, or gray tin.

semiconductor A solid crystalline material whose electrical conductivity is intermediate between that of a conductor and an insulator, ranging from about 10^5 mhos to 10^{-7} mho per meter, and is usually strongly temperature-dependent.

semiconductor device Electronic device in which the characteristic distinguishing electronic conduction takes place within a semiconductor.

semiconductor diode Also known as crystal diode; crystal rectifier; diode. 1. A two-electrode semiconductor device that utilizes the rectifying properties of a pn junction or a point contact. 2. More generally, any two-terminal electronic device that utilizes the properties of the semiconductor from which it is constructed.

semiconductor-diode parametric amplifier Parametric amplifier using one or more varactors.

semiconductor doping *See* doping.

semiconductor heterostructure A structure of two different semiconductors in junction contact having useful electrical or electrooptical characteristics not achievable in either conductor separately; used in certain types of lasers and solar cells.

semiconductor intrinsic properties Properties of a semiconductor that are characteristic of the ideal crystal.

semiconductor junction Region of transition between semiconducting regions of different electrical properties, usually between p-type and n-type material.

semiconductor memory A device for storing digital information that is fabricated by using integrated circuit technology. Also known as integrated circuit memory; large-scale integrated memory; transistor memory.

semiconductor rectifier *See* metallic rectifier.

semiconductor thermocouple A thermocouple made of a semiconductor, which offers the prospect of operation with high-temperature gradients, because semiconductors are good electrical conductors but poor heat conductors.

semiconductor trap *See* trap.

semidense list A list that can be divided into two contiguous portions, with all the cells in the larger portion filled and all the other cells empty.

seminumerical algebraic manipulation language The most elementary type of algebraic manipulation language, constructed to manipulate data from rigid classes of mathematical objects possessing strictly canonical forms.

semitransparent photocathode Photocathode in which radiant flux incident on one side produces photoelectric emission from the opposite side.

sense To read punched holes in tape or cards.

sense amplifier Circuit used to determine either a phase or voltage change in communications-electronics equipment and to provide automatic control function.

sense light A light which can be turned on or off, its status being the determinant as to which path a program will select.

sense switch *See* alteration switch.

sensing station *See* reading station.

sensistor Silicon resistor whose resistance varies with temperature, power, and time.

sensitivity 1. The minimum input signal required to produce a specified output signal, for a radio receiver or similar device. **2.** Of a camera tube, the signal current developed per unit incident radiation, that is, per watt per unit area.

sensitivity time control In a radar receiver a circuit which greatly reduces the gain at the time that the transmitter emits a pulse; following the pulse, the circuit increases the sensitivity; thus reflection from distant objects will be received and those from nearby objects will be prevented from saturating the receiver.

sensitization *See* activation.

sentinel Symbol marking the beginning or end of an element of computer information such as an item or a tape.

separation filter Combination of filters used to separate one band of frequencies from another.

separator 1. A datum or character that denotes the beginning or ending of a unit of data. **2.** A circuit that separates one type of signal from another by clipping, differentiating, or integrating action.

sequence To put a set of symbols into an arbitrarily defined order; that is, to select A if A is greater than or equal to B, or to select B if A is less than B.

sequence calling The instructions used for linking a closed subroutine with a main routine; that is, standard linkage and a list of the parameters.

sequence check To verify that correct precedence relationships are obeyed, usually by checking for ascending sequence numbers.

sequence-checking routine In computers, a checking routine which records specified data regarding the operations resulting from each instruction.

sequence counter *See* instruction counter.

sequence error An error that arises when the arrangement of items in a set, for example, a deck of punch cards, does not follow some specified order.

sequence monitor The automatic step-by-step check by a computer of the manual actions required for the starting and shutdown of a computer.

sequence number A number assigned to an item to indicate its relative position in a series of related items.

sequencer A machine which puts items of information into a particular order, for example, it will determine whether A is greater than, equal to, or less than B, and sort or order accordingly. Also known as sorter.

sequence register A counter which contains the address of the next instruction to be carried out.

sequential access A process that involves reading or writing data serially and, by extension, a data-recording medium that must be read serially, as a magnetic tape.

sequential batch operating system Software equipment that automatically begins running a new job on a computer system as soon as the current job is completed.

sequential control Manner of operating a computer by feeding orders into the computer in a given order during the solution of a problem.

sequential logic element A circuit element having at least one input channel, at least one output channel, and at least one internal state variable, so designed and constructed that the output signals depend on the past and present states of the inputs.

sequential machine A mathematical model of a certain type of sequential circuit, which has inputs and outputs that can each take on any value from a finite set and are of interest only at certain instants of time, and in which the output depends on previous inputs as well as the concurrent input.

sequential network An idealized model of a sequential circuit that reflects its logical but not its electronic properties.

sequential operation The consecutive or serial execution of operations, without any simultaneity or overlap.

sequential organization The write and read of records in a physical rather than a logical sequence.

sequential processing Processing items in a collection of data according to some specified sequence of keys, in contrast to serial processing.

sequential scheduling system A first-come, first-served method of selecting jobs to be run.

sequential search A procedure for searching a table that consists of starting at some table position (usually the beginning) and comparing the file-record key in hand with each table-record key, one at a time, until either a match is found or all sequential positions have been searched.

serial Pertaining to the internal handling of data in sequential fashion.

serial-access 1. Pertaining to memory devices having structures such that data storage sites become accessible for read/write in time-sequential order; circulating memories and magnetic tapes are examples of serial-access memories. 2. Pertaining to a particular process or program that accesses data items sequentially, without regard to the capability of the memory hardware. 3. Pertaining to character-by-character transmission from an on-line real-time keyboard.

serial bit Digital computer storage in which the individual bits that make up a computer word appear in time sequence.

serial digital computer A digital computer in which the digits are handled serially, although the bits that make up a digit may be handled either serially or in parallel.

serial dot character printer A computer printer in which the dot matrix technique is used to print characters, one at a time, with a movable print head that is driven back and forth across the page.

serial feed The method of placing cards in the feed hopper of a punched-card machine in which one of the short edges of the card enters the machine first, so that the columns of the card are read sequentially.

serial file The simplest type of file organization, in which no subsets are defined, no directories are provided, no particular file order is specified, and a search is performed by sequential comparison of the query with identifiers of all stored items.

serially reusable An attribute possessed by a program that can be used for several tasks in sequence without having to be reloaded into main memory for each additional use.

serial memory A computer memory in which data are available only in the same sequence as originally stored.

serial operation The flow of information through a computer in time sequence, using only one digit, word, line, or channel at a time.

serial parallel 1. A combination of serial and parallel; for example, serial by character, parallel by bits comprising the character. 2. Descriptive of a device which converts a serial input into a parallel output.

serial-parallel conversion The transformation of a serial data representation as found on a disk or drum into the parallel data representation as exists in core.

serial processing Processing items in a collection of data in the order that they appear in a storage device, in contrast to sequential processing.

serial processor A computer in which data are handled sequentially by separate units of the system.

serial programming In computers, programming in which only one operation is executed at one time.

serial storage Computer storage in which time is one of the coordinates used to locate any given bit, character, or word; access time, therefore, includes a variable waiting time, ranging from zero to many word times.

serial transfer Transfer of the characters of an element of information in sequence over a single path in a digital computer.

series feed Application of the direct-current voltage to the plate or grid of a vacuum tube through the same impedance in which the alternating-current flows.

series loading Loading in which reactances are inserted in series with the conductors of a transmission circuit.

series modulation Modulation in which the plate circuits of a modulating tube and a modulated amplifier tube are in series with the same plate voltage supply.

series peaking Use of a peaking coil and resistor in series as the load for a video amplifier to produce peaking at some desired frequency in the passband, such as to compensate for previous loss of gain at the high-frequency end of the passband.

series-shunt network *See* ladder network.

series transistor regulator A voltage regulator whose circuit has a transistor in series with the output voltage, a Zener diode, and a resistor chosen so that the Zener diode is approximately in the middle of its operating range.

serrated pulse Vertical and horizontal synchronizing pulse divided into a number of small pulses, each of which acts for the duration of half a line in a television system.

serrodyne Phase modulator using transit time modulation of a traveling-wave tube or klystron.

service bureau An organization that offers time sharing and software services to its users who communicate with a computer in the bureau from terminals on their premises.

service oscillator *See* radio-frequency signal generator.

service routine A section of a computer code that is used in so many different jobs that it cannot belong to any one job.

servicing time Machine down-time necessary for routine testing, for machine servicing due to breakdown, or for preventive servicing measures; includes all test time (good or bad) following breakdown and subsequent repair or preventive servicing.

servo amplifier An amplifier used in a servomechanism.

servomultiplier An electromechanical multiplier in which one variable is used to position one or more ganged potentiometers across which the other variable voltages are applied.

set 1. A collection of record types. 2. The placement of a storage device in a prescribed state, for example, a binary storage cell in the high or 1 state.

set class The collection of set occurrences that have been or may be created in accordance with a particular set description.

set condition Condition of a flip-flop circuit in which the internal state of the flip-flop is set to 1.

set description For a specified data set, a definition of the set class name, set-owner selection criteria, set-member eligibility rules, and set-member ordering rules.

set occurrence An instance of a set created in accordance with a set description.

set pulse An electronic pulse designed to place a memory cell in a specified state.

setup The ratio between the reference black level and the reference white level in television, both measured from the blanking level; usually expressed as a percentage.

setup time The time before, after, and between computer machine runs, in which manual tasks are carried out, such as changing tape reels or transporting tapes, cards, or supplies to and from the computer equipment, to prepare for a new run.

sferics receiver An instrument which measures, electronically, the direction of arrival, intensity, and rate of occurrence of atmospherics; in its simplest form, the instrument consists of two orthogonally crossed antennas, whose output signals are connected to an oscillograph so that one loop measures the north-south component while the other measures the east-west component; the signals are combined vertically to give the azimuth. Also known as lightning recorder.

shading Television process of compensating for the spurious signal generated in a camera tube during trace intervals.

shading signal Television camera signal that serves to increase the gain of the amplifier in the camera during those intervals of time when the electron beam is on an area corresponding to a dark portion of the scene being televised.

shadow mask A thin, perforated metal mask mounted just back of the phosphor-dot faceplate in a three-gun color picture tube; the holes in the mask are positioned to ensure that each of the three electron beams strikes only its intended color phosphor dot. Also known as aperture mask.

shaft-position encoder An analog-to-digital converter in which the exact angular position of a shaft is sensed and converted to digital form.

shared control unit A control unit which controls several devices with similar characteristics, such as tape devices.

shared file A direct-access storage device that is used by more than one computer or data-processing system.

shared logic The simultaneous use of a single computer by multiple users.

shared resource Peripheral equipment that is simultaneously shared by several users.

sharp-cutoff tube An electron tube in which the control-grid openings are uniformly spaced; the anode current then decreases linearly as the grid voltage is made more negative, and cuts off sharply at a particular grid voltage.

sheath A space charge formed by ions near an electrode in a gas tube.

shield grid A grid that shields the control grid of a gas tube from electrostatic fields, thermal radiation, and deposition of thermionic emissive material; it may also be used as an additional control electrode.

shield-grid thyratron A thyratron having a shield grid, usually operated at cathode potential.

shift A movement of data to the right or left, in a digital-computer location, usually with the loss of characters shifted beyond a boundary.

shift register A computer hardware element constructed to perform shifting of its contained data.

shift-register generator A random-number generator which consists of a sequence of shift operations and other operations, such as no-carry addition.

shiran Specially designed frequency-modulation continuous-wave distance-measuring equipment used for performing distance measurements of an accuracy comparable to first-order triangulation. Derived from S-band hiran.

Shockley diode A *pnpn* silicon controlled switch having characteristics that permit operation as a unidirectional diode switch.

short-gate gain Video gain on short-range gate.

short-path principle *See* Hittorf principle.

shortwave converter Electronic unit designed to be connected between a receiver and its antenna system to permit reception of frequencies higher than those the receiver ordinarily handles.

short word The fixed word of lesser length in computers capable of handling words of two different lengths; in many computers this is referred to as a half-word because the length is exactly the half-length of the full word.

shot effect *See* shot noise.

shot noise Noise voltage developed in a thermionic tube because of the random variations in the number and the velocity of electrons emitted by the heated cathode; the effect causes sputtering or popping sounds in radio receivers and snow effects in television pictures. Also known as Schottky noise; shot effect.

shunt feed *See* parallel feed.

shunt neutralization *See* inductive neutralization.

shunt peaking The use of a peaking coil in a parallel circuit branch connecting the output load of one stage to the input load of the following stage, to compensate for high-frequency loss due to the distributed capacitances of the two stages.

side effect A consistent result of a procedure that is in addition to or peripheral to the basic result.

side-lobe blanking Radar technique which compares relative signal strengths between an omnidirectional antenna and the radar antenna.

sideways feed The method of placing cards in the feed hopper of a punched-card machine in which one of the long edges of the card enters the machine first, so that the columns of the card are read simultaneously. Also known as parallel feed.

sight check A check that holes are punched in the same positions in two or more punched cards by superimposing the cards and looking through the holes.

signal distance The number of bits that are not the same in two binary words of equal length. Also known as hamming distance.

signal distortion generator Instrument designed to apply known amounts of distortion on a signal for the purpose of testing and adjusting communications equipment such as teletypewriters.

signal-shaping network Network inserted in a telegraph circuit, usually at the receiving end, to improve the waveform of the code signals.

signal-strength meter A meter that is connected to the automatic volume-control circuit of a communication receiver and calibrated in decibels or arbitrary S units to read the strength of a received signal. Also known as S meter; S-unit meter.

signal-to-interference ratio The relative magnitude of signal waves and waves which interfere with signal-wave reception.

signal-to-noise ratio The ratio of the amplitude of a desired signal at any point to the amplitude of noise signals at that same point; often expressed in decibels; the peak value is usually used for pulse noise, while the root-mean-square (rms) value is used for random noise. Abbreviated S/N; SNR.

signal tracer An instrument used for tracing the progress of a signal through a radio receiver or an audio amplifier to locate a faulty stage.

sign-and-magnitude code The representation of an integer X by $(-1)^{a_0} (2^{n-2} a_1 + 2^{n-3} a_2 + \dots + a_{n-1})$, where a_0 is 0 for X positive, and a_0 is 1 for X negative, and any a_j is either 0 or 1.

signature The characteristic pattern of a target as displayed by detection and classification equipment.

sign bit A sign digit consisting of one bit.

sign check indicator An error checking device, indicating no sign or improper signing of a field used for arithmetic processes; the machine can, upon interrogation, be made to stop or enter into a correction routine.

sign-control flip-flop In computers, a flip-flop in the arithmetic unit used for storing the sign of the result of an operation.

sign digit A digit containing one to four binary bits, associated with a data item and used to denote an algebraic sign.

signed field A field of data that contains a number which includes a sign digit indicating the number's sign.

significance arithmetic A rough technique for estimating the numbers and positions of the significant digits of the radix approximation that results when an arithmetic operation is applied to operands in radix approximation form.

sign position That position, always at or near the left or right end of a numeral, in which the algebraic sign of the number is represented.

silicide resistor A thin-film resistor that uses a silicide of molybdenum or chromium, deposited by direct-current sputtering in an integrated circuit when radiation hardness or high resistance values are required.

silicon capacitor A capacitor in which a pure silicon-crystal slab serves as the dielectric; when the crystal is grown to have a p zone, a depletion zone, and an n zone, the capacitance varies with the externally applied bias voltage, as in a varactor.

silicon controlled rectifier A semiconductor rectifier that can be controlled; it is a *pnpn* four-layer semiconductor device that normally acts as an open circuit, but switches rapidly to a conducting state when an appropriate gate signal is applied to the gate terminal. Abbreviated SCR. Also known as reverse-blocking triode thyristor.

silicon controlled switch A four-terminal switching device having four semiconductor layers, all of which are accessible; it can be used as a silicon controlled rectifier, gate-turnoff switch, complementary silicon controlled rectifier, or conventional silicon transistor. Abbreviated SCS. Also known as reverse-blocking tetrode thyristor.

silicon detector *See* silicon diode.

silicon diode A crystal diode that uses silicon as a semiconductor; used as a detector in ultra-high- and super-high-frequency circuits. Also known as silicon detector.

silicon image sensor A solid-state television camera in which the image is focused on an array of individual light-sensitive elements formed from a charged-coupled-device semiconductor chip. Also known as silicon imaging device.

silicon imaging device *See* silicon image sensor.

silicon-on-sapphire A semiconductor manufacturing technology in which metal oxide semiconductor devices are constructed in a thin single-crystal silicon film grown on an electrically insulating synthetic sapphire substrate. Abbreviated SOS.

silicon rectifier A metallic rectifier in which rectifying action is provided by an alloy junction formed in a high-purity silicon slab.

silicon resistor A resistor using silicon semiconductor material as a resistance element, to obtain a positive temperature coefficient of resistance that does not appreciably change with temperature; used as a temperature-sensing element.

silicon solar cell A solar cell consisting of p and n silicon layers placed one above the other to form a pn junction at which radiant energy is converted into electricity.

silicon-symmetrical switch Thyristor modified by adding a semiconductor layer so that the device becomes a bidirectional switch; used as an alternating-current phase control, for synchronous switching and motor speed control.

silicon transistor A transistor in which silicon is used as the semiconducting material.

silvered mica capacitor A mica capacitor in which a coating of silver is deposited directly on the mica sheets to serve in place of conducting metal foil.

simple buffering A technique for obtaining simultaneous performance of input/output operations and computing; it involves associating a buffer with only one input or output file (or data set) for the entire duration of the activity on that file (or data set).

simplex structure The structure of an information processing system designed in such a way that only the minimum amount of hardware is utilized to implement its function.

simulation language A computer language used to write programs for the simulation of the behavior through time of such things as transportation and manufacturing systems; SIMSCRIPT is an example.

simulator A routine which is executed by one computer but which imitates the operations of another computer.

simultaneous access *See* parallel access.

simultaneous color television A color television system in which the phosphors for the three primary colors are excited at the same time, not one after another; the shadow-mask color picture tube gives a simultaneous display.

simultaneous computer A computer, usually of the analog or hybrid type, in which separate units of hardware are used to carry out the various parts of a computation, the execution of different parts usually overlap in time, and the various hardware units are interconnected in a manner determined by the computation.

simultaneous lobing A radar direction-finding technique in which the signals received by two partly overlapping antenna lobes are compared in phase or power to obtain a measure of the angular displacement of a target from the equisignal direction.

simultaneous peripheral operations on line *See* spooling.

sine-cosine encoder A shaft-position encoder having a special type of angle-reading code disk that gives an output which is a binary representation of the sine of the shaft angle.

sine potentiometer A potentiometer whose direct-current output voltage is proportional to the sine of the shaft angle; used as a resolver in computer and radar systems.

sine-wave modulated jamming Jamming signal produced by modulating a continuous wave signal with one or more sine waves.

sine-wave oscillator *See* sinusoidal oscillator.

single-address instruction *See* one-address instruction.

single-board computer A computer consisting of a processor and memory on a single printed circuit board.

single-carrier theory A theory of the behavior of a rectifying barrier which assumes that conduction is due to the motion of carriers of only one type; it can be applied to the contact between a metal and a semiconductor.

single-channel multiplier A type of photomultiplier tube in which electrons travel down a cylindrical channel coated on the inside with a resistive secondary-emitting layer, and gain is achieved by multiple electron impacts on the inner surface as the electrons are directed down the channel by an applied voltage over the length of the channel.

single-column punch A system of coding whereby any one of the numerical values 0 to 11 can be represented by a single punch in a column.

single-edged push-pull amplifier circuit Amplifier circuit having two transmission paths designed to operate in a complementary manner and connected to provide a single unbalanced output without the use of an output transformer.

single-end amplifier Amplifier stage which normally employs only one tube or semiconductor or, if more than one tube or semiconductor is used, they are connected in parallel so that operation is asymmetric with respect to ground. Also known as single-sided amplifier.

single-gun color tube A color television picture tube having only one electron gun and one electron beam; the beam is sequentially deflected across phosphors for the three primary colors to form each color picture element, as in the chromatron.

single in-line package A packaged resistor network or other assembly that has a single row of terminals or lead wires along one edge of the package. Abbreviated SIP.

single-keyboard point-of-sale system A point-of-sale system based upon electronic cash registers as stand-alone units, each equipped with a few internal registers and some programming capability.

single knock-on A sputtering event in which target atoms are ejected either directly by the bombarding projectiles or after a small number of collisions.

single-length Pertaining to the expression of numbers in binary form in such a way that they can be included in a single computer word.

single-phase rectifier A rectifier whose input voltage is a single sinusoidal voltage, in contrast to a polyphase rectifier.

single-precision number A number having as many digits as are ordinarily used in a given computer, in contrast to a double-precision number.

single reference *See* random access.

single-shot blocking oscillator Blocking oscillator modified to operate as a single-shot trigger circuit.

single-shot multivibrator *See* monostable multivibrator.

single-shot operation *See* single-step operation.

single-shot trigger circuit Trigger circuit in which one triggering pulse initiates one complete cycle of conditions ending with a stable condition. Also known as single-trip trigger circuit.

single-sided amplifier *See* single-end amplifier.

single-signal receiver A highly selective superheterodyne receiver for code reception, having a crystal filter in the intermediate-frequency amplifier.

single-step operation A method of computer operation, used in debugging or detecting computer malfunctions, in which a program is carried out one instruction at a time, each instruction being performed in response to a manual control device such as a switch or button. Also known as one-shot operation; one-step operation; single-shot operation; step-by-step operation.

single-trip trigger circuit *See* single-shot trigger circuit.

single-tuned amplifier An amplifier characterized by resonance at a single frequency.

single-tuned interstage An interstage circuit which is resonant at a single frequency.

single-unit semiconductor device Semiconductor device having one set of electrodes associated with a single carrier stream.

singly linked ring A cyclic arrangement of data elements in which searches may be performed in either a clockwise or a counterclockwise direction, but not both.

sinusoidal angular modulation *See* angle modulation.

sinusoidal oscillator An oscillator circuit whose output voltage is a sine-wave function of time. Also known as harmonic oscillator; sine-wave oscillator.

SIP *See* single in-line package.

SIT *See* static induction transistor.

site 1. A position available for the symbols of an inscription, for example, a digital place. 2. A location on a tally that can bear either a mark or a blank; for example, a location that can be punched or left unpunched on a card.

situation-display tube Large cathode-ray tube used to display tabular and vector messages pertinent to the various functions of an air defense mission.

six-phase rectifier A rectifier in which transformers are used to produce six alternating electromotive forces which differ in phase by one-sixth of a cycle, and which feed six diodes.

size control A control provided on a television receiver for changing the size of a picture either horizontally or vertically.

skeletal coding A set of incomplete instructions in symbolic form, intended to be completed and specialized by a processing program written for that purpose.

skew 1. In character recognition, a condition arising at the read station whereby a character or a line of characters appears in a "twisted" manner in relation to a real or imaginary horizontal baseline. 2. The deviation of a received facsimile frame from rectangularity due to lack of synchronism between scanner and recorder; expressed numerically as the tangent of the angle of this deviation. 3. The degree of nonsynchronism of supposedly parallel bits when bit-coded characters are read from magnetic tape.

skew failure In character recognition, the condition that exists during document alignment whereby the document reference edge is not parallel to that of the read station.

skiatron *See* dark-trace tube.

skiograph An instrument used to measure the intensity of x-rays

skip 1. In fixed-instruction-length digital computers, to bypass or ignore one or more instructions in an otherwise sequential process. 2. A device on a card punch that causes columns on a punch in fields where no punching is desired to move rapidly past the punching station.

skip chain A programming technique which matches a word against a set of test words; if there is a match, control is transferred (skipped) to a routine, otherwise the word is matched with the next test word in sequence.

skip flag The thirty-fifth bit of a channel command word which suppresses the transfer of data to main storage.

skip-keying Reduction of radar pulse repetition frequency to submultiple of that normally used, to reduce mutual interference between radar or to increase the length of radar time base.

skip-searched chain A chain which has pointers and can therefore be searched without examining each link.

sky-wave correction The correction to be applied to the time difference readings of received sky waves to convert them to an equivalent ground-wave reading.

slab A relatively thick-cut crystal from which blanks are obtained by subsequent transverse cutting.

Slater's rule The ratio of the cathode radius to the anode radius of a magnetron is approximately equal to $(N - 4)/(N + 4)$, where N is the number of resonators.

slave A terminal or computer that is controlled by another computer.

slave mode *See* user mode.

slew rate The maximum rate at which the output voltage of an operational amplifier changes for a square-wave or step-signal input; usually specified in volts per microsecond.

slicer *See* amplitude gate.

slicer amplifier *See* amplitude gate.

slicing Transmission of only those portions of a waveform lying between two amplitude values.

slide-back voltmeter An electronic voltmeter in which an unknown voltage is measured indirectly by adjusting a calibrated voltage source until its voltage equals the unknown voltage.

slip Distortion produced in the recorded facsimile image which is similar to that produced by skew but is caused by slippage in the mechanical drive system.

slit scan In character recognition, a magnetic or photoelectric device that obtains the horizontal structure of an inputted character by vertically projecting its component elements at given intervals.

slot A punched-out area of a hand-sorted card to connect two or more guide holes; slots can be extended to the outside edge with notches.

slot-mask picture tube An in-line gun-type picture tube in which the shadow mask is perforated by short, vertical slots, and the screen is painted with vertical phosphor stripes.

slow death The gradual change of transistor characteristics with time; this change is attributed to ions which collect on the surface of the transistor.

slowed-down video Technique or method of transmitting radar data over narrow-bandwidth circuits; the procedure involves storing the radar video over the time required for the antenna to move through the beam width, and the subsequent sampling of this stored video at some periodic rate at which all of the range intervals of interest are sampled at least once each beam width or per azimuth quantum; the radar returns are quantized at the gap-filler radar site.

slow memory *See* slow storage.

slow-motion video disk recorder A magnetic disk recorder that stores one field of video information per revolution, for instant replay at normal speed or any degree of slow motion down to complete stopping of action.

slow storage In computers, storage with a relatively long access time. Also known as slow memory.

slow time scale Pertaining to simulation by an analog computer in which the time duration of a simulated event is greater than the actual time duration of the event in the physical system under study. Also known as extended time scale.

small-scale integration Integration in which a complete major subsystem or system is fabricated on a single integrated-circuit chip that contains integrated circuits which have appreciably less complexity than for medium-scale integration. Abbreviated SSI.

small-signal parameter One of the parameters characterizing the behavior of an electronic device at small values of input, for which the device can be represented by an equivalent linear circuit.

smart terminal See intelligent terminal.

smear A television-picture defect in which objects appear to be extended horizontally beyond their normal boundaries in a blurred or smeared manner; one cause is excessive attenuation of high video frequencies in the television receiver.

S meter See signal-strength meter.

smoothing choke Iron-core choke coil employed as a filter to remove fluctuations in the output current of a vacuum-tube rectifier or direct-current generator.

smoothing circuit See ripple filter.

smoothing filter See ripple filter.

S/N See signal-to-noise ratio.

snap-off diode Planar epitaxial passivated silicon diode that is processed so a charge is stored close to the junction when the diode is conducting; when reverse voltage is applied, the stored charge then forces the diode to snap off or switch rapidly to its blocking state.

snapshot dump An edited printout of selected parts of the contents of main memory, performed at one or more times during the execution of a program without materially affecting the operation of the program.

sneak path In computers, an undesired circuit through a series-parallel configuration.

snivet Straight, jagged, or broken vertical black line appearing near the right-hand edge of a television receiver screen.

SNOBOL A computer programming language that has significant applications in program compilation and generation of symbolic equations. Derived from String-Oriented Symbolic Language.

snooperscope An infrared source, an infrared image converter, and a battery-operated high-voltage direct-current source constructed in portable form to permit a foot soldier or other user to see objects in total darkness; infrared radiation sent out by the infrared source is reflected back to the snooperscope and converted into a visible image on the fluorescent screen of the image tube.

snow Small, random, white spots produced on a television or radar screen by inherent noise signals originating in the receiver.

SNR See signal-to-noise ratio.

soft copy Information that is displayed on a screen, given by voice, or stored in a form that cannot be read directly by a person, as on magnetic tape, disk, or microfilm.

soft-copy terminal A computer terminal that presents its output through an electronic display, rather than printing it on paper.

soft limiting Limiting in which there is still an appreciable increase in output for increases in input signal strength up into the range at which limiting action occurs.

soft tube 1. An x-ray tube having a vacuum of about 0.000002 atmosphere (0.202650 newton per square meter), the remaining gas being left in intentionally to give less-penetrating rays than those of a more completely evacuated tube. 2. *See* gassy tube.

software The totality of programs usable on a particular kind of computer, together with the documentation associated with a computer or program, such as manuals, diagrams, and operating instructions.

software compatibility Property of two computers, with respect to a particular programming language, in which a source program from one machine in that language will compile and execute to produce acceptably similar results in the other.

software engineering The systematic application of scientific and technological knowledge, through the medium of sound engineering principles, to the production of computer programs, and to the requirements definition, functional specification, design description, program implementation, and test methods that lead up to this code.

software flexibility The ability of software to change easily in response to different user and system requirements.

software interface A computer language whereby computer programs can communicate with each other, and one language can call upon another for assistance.

software maintenance The correction of errors in software systems and the remedying of inadequacies in running the software.

software monitor A system, used to evaluate the performance of computer software, that is similar to accounting packages, but can collect more data concerning usage of various components of a computer system and is usually part of the control program.

software multiplexing A procedure used in a time-sharing or multiprogrammed system in which the central processing unit, acting under control of a software algorithm, interleaves its attention between a family of programs waiting for service, in such a way that the programs appear to be processed in parallel.

software package A program for performing some specific function or calculation which is useful to more than one computer user and is sufficiently well documented to be used without modification on a defined configuration of some computer system.

software piracy The process of copying commercial software without the permission of the originator.

solar battery An array of solar cells, usually connected in parallel and series.

solar cell A *pn*-junction device which converts the radiant energy of sunlight directly and efficiently into electrical energy.

solar sensor A light-sensitive diode that sends a signal to the attitude-control system of a spacecraft when it senses the sun. Also known as sun sensor.

sole Electrode used in magnetrons and backward-wave oscillators to carry a current that generates a magnetic field in the direction wanted.

solid logic technology A method of computer construction that makes use of miniaturized modules, resulting in faster circuitry because of the reduced distances that current must travel.

solid-state circuit Complete circuit formed from a single block of semiconductor material.

solid-state circuit breaker A circuit breaker in which a Zener diode, silicon controlled rectifier, or solid-state device is connected to sense when load terminal voltage exceeds a safe value.

solid-state component A component whose operation depends on the control of electrical or magnetic phenomena in solids, such as a transistor, crystal diode, or ferrite device.

solid-state computer A digital computer which uses diodes and transistors instead of vacuum tubes.

solid-state device A device, other than a conductor, which uses magnetic, electrical, and other properties of solid materials, as opposed to vacuum or gaseous devices.

solid-state image sensor *See* charge-coupled image sensor.

solid-state lamp *See* light-emitting diode.

solid-state memory A computer memory whose elements consist of integrated-circuit bistable multivibrators in which bits of information are stored as one of two states.

solid-state relay A relay that uses only solid-state components, with no moving parts. Abbreviated SSR.

solid-state switch A microwave switch in which a semiconductor material serves as the switching element; a zero or negative potential applied to the control electrode will reverse-bias the switch and turn it off, and a slight positive voltage will turn it on.

solid-state thyratron A semiconductor device, such as a silicon controlled rectifier, that approximates the extremely fast switching speed and power-handling capability of a gaseous thyratron tube.

sonar array An arrangement of several sonar transducers or sonar projectors, appropriately spaced and energized to give proper directional characteristics.

sonar detector *See* sonar receiver.

sonar receiver A receiver designed to intercept and amplify the sound signals reflected by an underwater target and display the accompanying intelligence in useful form; it may also pick up other underwater sounds. Also known as sonar detector.

sonar resolver A resolver used with echo-ranging and depth-determining sonar to calculate and record the horizontal range of a sonar target, as required for depth-bombing.

sonar self-noise Unwanted sonar signals generated in the sonar equipment itself.

sonar transmitter A transmitter that generates electrical signals of the proper frequency and form for application to a sonar transducer or sonar projector, to produce sound waves of the same frequency in water; the sound waves may carry intelligence.

sonic delay line *See* acoustic delay line.

sophisticated vocabulary An advanced and elaborate set of instructions; a computer with a sophisticated vocabulary can go beyond the more common mathematical calculations such as addition, multiplication, and subtraction, and perform operations such as linearize, extract square root, and select highest number.

sort 1. To rearrange a set of data items into a new sequence, governed by specific rules of precedence. 2. The program designed to perform this activity.

sorter *See* card sorter; sequencer.

sort generator A computer program that produces other programs which arrange collections of items into sequences as specified by parameters in the original program.

sort key A key used as a basis for determining the sequence of items in a set.

sort/merge package A set of programs capable of sorting and merging data files.

SOS *See* silicon-on-sapphire.

sound channel The series of stages that handles only the sound signal in a television receiver.

source The terminal in a field-effect transistor from which majority carriers flow into the conducting channel in the semiconductor material.

source address The first address of a two-address instruction (the second address is known as the destination address).

source data automation *See* automation source data.

source data automation equipment Equipment (except paper tape and magnetic tape cartridge typewriters acquired separately and not operated in support of a computer) which, as a by-product of its operation, produces a record in a medium which is acceptable by automatic data-processing equipment.

source data capture Electronic recording of data at its time and place of origination.

source data entry Entry of data into a computer system directly from its source, without transcription.

source document The original medium containing the basic data to be used by a data-processing system, from which the data are converted into a form which can be read into a computer. Also known as original document.

source-follower amplifier *See* common-drain amplifier.

source language The language in which a program (or other text) is originally expressed.

source library A collection of computer programs in compiler language or assembler language.

source module An organized set of statements in any source language recorded in machine-readable form and suitable for input to an assembler or compiler.

source program The form of a program just as the programmer has written it, often on coding forms or machine-readable media; a program expressed in a source-language form.

source program optimizer A routine for examining the source code of a program under development and providing information about use of the various portions of the code, enabling the programmer to modify those sections of the target program that are most heavily used in order to improve performance of the final, operational program.

source time The time involved in fetching the contents of the register specified by the first address of a two-address instruction.

source transition loss The transmission loss at the junction between an energy source and a transducer connecting that source to an energy load; measured by the ratio of the source power to the input power.

sourcing Redesign or the modification of existing equipment to eliminate a source of radio-frequency interference.

space character *See* blank character.

space-charge balanced flow A method of focusing an electron beam in the interaction region of a traveling-wave tube; there is an axial magnetic field in the interaction region which is stronger than that in the gun region; at the transition between the two values of magnetic field strength, the beam is given a rotation in such a direction as to produce an inward force that counterbalances the outward forces from space charge and from the centrifugal forces set up by rotation.

space-charge debunching A process in which the mutual interactions between electrons in a stream spread out the electrons of a bunch.

space-charge effect Repulsion of electrons emitted from the cathode of a thermionic vacuum tube by electrons accumulated in the space charge near the cathode.

space-charge grid Grid operated at a low positive potential and placed between the cathode and control grid of a vacuum tube to reduce the limiting effect of space charge on the current through the tube.

space-charge layer *See* depletion layer.

space-charge limitation The current flowing through a vacuum between a cathode and an anode cannot exceed a certain maximum value, as a result of modification of the electric field near the cathode due to space charge in this region.

space-charge region Of a semiconductor device, a region in which the net charge density is significantly different from zero.

space current Total current flowing between the cathode and all other electrodes in a tube; this includes the plate current, grid current, screen grid current, and any other electrode current which may be present.

space suppression Prevention of the normal movement of paper in a computer printer after the printing of a line of characters.

spacistor A multiple-terminal solid-state device, similar to a transistor, that generates frequencies up to about 10,000 megahertz by injecting electrons or holes into a space-charge layer which rapidly forces these carriers to a collecting electrode.

spanned record A logical record which covers more than one block, used when the size of a data buffer is fixed or limited.

sparkover voltage *See* flashover voltage.

spark transmitter A radio transmitter that utilizes the oscillatory discharge of a capacitor through an inductor and a spark gap as the source of radio-frequency power.

spatial data management A technique whereby users retrieve information in data bases, document files, or other sources by making contact with picture symbols displayed on the screen of a video terminal through the use of such devices as light pens, joy sticks, and heat-sensitive screens for finger-touch activation.

special character A computer-representable character that is not alphabetic, numeric, or blank.

special-purpose computer A digital or analog computer designed to be especially efficient in a certain class of applications.

special-purpose language A programming language designed to solve a particular type of problem.

specific repetition rate The pulse repetition rate of a pair of transmitting stations of an electronic navigation system using various rates differing slightly from each other, as in loran.

specific routine Computer routine to solve a particular data-handling problem in which each address refers to explicitly stated registers and locations.

spectral sensitivity Radiant sensitivity, considered as a function of wavelength.

spectrum-selectivity characteristic Measure of the increase in the minimum input signal power over the minimum detectable signal required to produce an indication on a radar indicator, if the received signal has a spectrum different from that of the normally received signal.

spectrum signature The spectral characteristics of the transmitter, receiver, and antenna of an electronic system, including emission spectra, antenna patterns, and other characteristics.

spectrum signature analysis The evaluation of electromagnetic interference from transmitting and receiving equipment to determine operational and environment compatibility.

speech inverter *See* scrambler.

speech scrambler *See* scrambler.

speed-power product The product of the gate speed or propagation delay of an electronic circuit and its power dissipation.

speromagnetic state The condition of a rare-earth glass in which the spins are oriented in fixed directions which are more or less random because of electric fields which exist in the glass.

spike A sputtering event in which the process from impact of a bombarding projectile to the ejection of target atoms involves motion of a large number of particles in the target, so that collisions between particles become significant.

spin filter A device used in a Lamb-shift polarized ion source to cause those atoms having an undesired nuclear spin orientation to decay from their metastable state to the ground state, while those with the desired spin orientation are allowed to pass through without decay.

spinthariscope An instrument for viewing the scintillations of alpha particles on a luminescent screen, usually with the aid of a microscope.

split-anode magnetron A magnetron in which the cylindrical anode is divided longitudinally into halves, between which extremely high-frequency oscillations are produced.

split-stator variable capacitor Variable capacitor having a rotor section that is common to two separate stator sections; used in grid and plate tank circuits of transmitters for balancing purposes.

splitting In the scope presentation of the standard loran (2000 kilohertz), signals the slow diminution of the leading or lagging edge of the pulse so that it resembles two pulses and eventually a single pulse, which appears to be normal but which may be displaced in time by as much as 10,000 microseconds; this phenomenon is caused by shifting of the E_1 reflections from the ionosphere, and if the deformation is that of the leading edge and is not detected, it will cause serious errors in the reading of the navigational parameter.

split-word operation A computer operation performed with portions of computer words rather than whole words as is normally done.

spoofing Deceiving or misleading the enemy in electronic operations, as by continuing transmission on a frequency after it has been effectively jammed by the enemy, using decoy radar transmitters to lead the enemy into a useless jamming effort, or transmitting radio messages containing false information for intentional interception by the enemy.

spooling The temporary storage of input and output on high-speed input-output devices, typically magnetic disks and drums, in order to increase throughput. Acronym for simultaneous peripheral operations on line.

spot In a cathode-ray tube, the area instantaneously affected by the impact of an electron beam.

spot jammer A jammer that interferes with reception of a specific channel or frequency.

spot noise figure Of a transducer at a selected frequency, the ratio of the output noise power per unit bandwidth to a portion thereof attributable to the thermal noise in the input termination per unit bandwidth, the noise temperature of the input termination being standard (290 K).

spot punch A hand-operated device resembling a pair of pliers, for selectively punching holes in punch cards.

spot-size error The distortion of the radar returns on the radarscope presentation caused by the diameter of the electron beam which displays the returns of the scope and the lateral radiation across the scope of part of the glow produced when the electron beam strikes the phosphorescent coating of the cathode-ray tube.

spottiness Bright spots scattered irregularly over the reproduced image in a television receiver, due to man-made or static interference entering the television system at some point.

spread spectrum transmission Communications technique in which many different signal waveforms are transmitted in a wide band; power is spread thinly over the band so narrow-band radios can operate within the wide-band without interference; used to achieve security and privacy, prevent jamming, and utilize signals buried in noise.

sprocket pulse 1. A pulse generated by a magnetized spot which accompanies every character recorded on magnetic tape; this pulse is used during read operations to regulate the timing of the read circuits, and also to provide a count on the number of characters read from the tape. 2. A pulse generated by the sprocket or driving hole in paper tape which serves as the timing pulse for reading or punching the paper tape.

spurious modulation Undesired modulation occurring in an oscillator, such as frequency modulation caused by mechanical vibration.

spurious response 1. Response of a radio receiver to a frequency different from that to which the receiver is tuned. 2. In electronic warfare, the undesirable signal images in the intercept receiver resulting from the mixing of the intercepted signal with harmonics of the local oscillators in the receiver.

sputtering Also known as cathode sputtering. 1. The ejection of atoms or groups of atoms from the surface of the cathode of a vacuum tube as the result of heavy-ion impact. 2. The use of this process to deposit a thin layer of metal on a glass, plastic, metal, or other surface in vacuum.

square-law demodulator *See* square-law detector.

square-law detector A demodulator whose output voltage is proportional to the square of the amplitude-modulated input voltage. Also known as square-law demodulator.

square-wave amplifier Resistance-coupled amplifier, the circuit constants of which are to amplify a square wave with the minimum amount of distortion.

square-wave generator A signal generator that generates a square-wave output voltage.

square-wave response The response of a circuit or device when a square wave is applied to the input.

squaring circuit 1. A circuit that reshapes a sine or other wave into a square wave. 2. A circuit that contains nonlinear elements proportional to the square of the input voltage.

squealing A condition in which a radio receiver produces a high-pitched note or squeal along with the desired radio program, due to interference between stations or to oscillation in some receiver circuit.

squegger *See* blocking oscillator.

squegging Condition of self-blocking in an electron-tube-oscillator circuit.

squegging oscillator *See* blocking oscillator.

squelch To automatically quiet a receiver by reducing its gain in response to a specified characteristic of the input.

squelch circuit *See* noise suppressor.

SQUID *See* superconducting quantum interference device.

squitter Random firing, intentional or otherwise, of the transponder transmitter in the absence of interrogation.

SSI *See* small-scale integration.

SSR *See* solid-state relay.

stability factor A measure of a transistor amplifier's bias stability, equal to the rate of change of collector current with respect to reverse saturation current.

stabilivolt Gas tube that maintains a constant voltage drop across its terminals, essentially independent of current, over a relatively wide range.

stabilization Feedback introduced into vacuum tube or transistor amplifier stages to reduce distortion by making the amplification substantially independent of electrode voltages and tube constants.

stabistor A diode component having closely controlled conductance, controlled storage charge, and low leakage, as required for clippers, clamping circuits, bias regulators, and other logic circuits that require tight voltage-level tolerances.

stable local oscillator *See* stalo.

stable strobe Series of strobes which behaves as if caused by a single jammer.

stack 1. A portion of a computer memory used to temporarily hold information, organized as a linear list for which all insertions and deletions, and usually all accesses, are made at one end of the list. **2.** *See* pileup.

stack automaton A variation of a pushdown automaton in which the read-only head of the input tape is allowed to move both ways, and the read-write head on the pushdown storage is allowed to scan the entire pushdown list in a read-only mode.

stacked-job processing A technique of automatic job-to-job transition, with little or no operator intervention.

stacker That part (or parts) of a punched-card handling device which arranges the processed cards into an orderly stack and holds them until they are removed by the operator.

stack model A model for describing the run-time execution of programs written in block-structured languages, consisting of a program component, which remains unchanged throughout the execution of the program; a control component, consisting of an instruction pointer and an environment pointer; and a stack of records containing all the data the program operates on.

stack operation A computer system in which flags, return address, and all temporary addresses are saved in the core in sequential order for any interrupted routine so that a new routine (including the interrupted routine) may be called in.

stack pointer A register which contains the last address of a stack of addresses.

stage A circuit containing a single section of an electron tube or equivalent device or two or more similar sections connected in parallel, push-pull, or push-push; it includes all parts connected between the control-grid input terminal of the device and the input terminal of the next adjacent stage.

stage gain The ratio of the output power of an amplifier stage to the input power, usually expressed in decibels.

staggered tuning Alignment of successive tuned circuits to slightly different frequencies in order to widen the overall amplitude-frequency response curve.

stagger-tuned amplifier An amplifier that uses staggered tuning to give a wide bandwidth.

stagger-tuned filter A filter consisting of a cascade of amplifier stages with tuned coupling networks whose resonant frequencies and bandwidths may be easily adjusted to achieve an overall transmission function of desired shape (maximally flat or equal ripple).

staging Moving blocks of data from one storage device to another.

stalo A highly stable local radio-frequency oscillator used for heterodyning signals to produce an intermediate frequency in radar moving-target indicators; only echoes that have changed slightly in frequency due to reflection from a moving target produce an output signal. Derived from stable local oscillator.

stamping A transformer lamination that has been cut out of a strip or sheet of metal by a punch press.

stand-alone machine A machine capable of functioning independently of a master computer, either part of the time or all of the time.

standard form The form of a floating point number whose mantissa lies within a standard specified range of values.

standard interface 1. A joining place of two systems or subsystems that has a previously agreed-upon form, so that two systems may be readily connected together. 2. In particular, a system of uniform circuits and input/output channels connecting the central processing unit of a computer with various units of peripheral equipment.

standardize To replace any given floating point representation of a number with its representation in standard form; that is, to adjust the exponent and fixed-point part so that the new fixed-point part lies within a prescribed standard range.

standard noise temperature The standard reference temperature for noise measurements, equal to 290 K.

standard subroutine In computers, a subroutine which is applicable to a class of problems.

standard test-tone power One milliwatt (0 decibels above one milliwatt) at 1000 hertz.

standby computer A computer in a duplex system that takes over when the need arises.

standby register In computers, a register into which information can be copied to be available in case the original information is lost or mutilated in processing.

standby replacement redundancy A form of redundancy in which there is a single active unit and a reserve of spare units, one of which replaces the active unit if it fails.

standby time 1. The time during which two or more computers are tied together and available to answer inquiries or process intermittent actions on stored data. 2. The elapsed time between inquiries when the equipment is operating on an inquiry application.

standing-on-nines carry In high-speed parallel addition of decimal numbers, an arrangement that causes carry digits to pass through one or more nine digits, while signaling that the skipped nines are to be reset to zero.

star-free expression An expression containing only Boolean operations and concatenation, used to define the language corresponding to a counter-free machine.

start bit The first bit transmitted in asynchronous data transmission to unequivocally indicate the start of the word.

starter An auxiliary control electrode used in a gas tube to establish sufficient ionization to reduce the anode breakdown voltage. Also known as trigger electrode.

startover Program function that causes a computer that is not active to become active.

startover data transfer and processing program Program which controls the transfer of startover data from the active to the standby machine and their subsequent processing by the standby machine.

start-stop multivibrator *See* monostable multivibrator.

star wheel The sensing device of a card punch, which is held in contact with the card under spring tension and which, detecting a hole, closes a contact point.

state graph A directed graph whose nodes correspond to internal states of a sequential machine and whose edges correspond to transitions among these states.

statement An elementary specification of a computer action or process, complete and not divisible into smaller meaningful units; it is analogous to the simple sentence of a natural language.

statement editor A text editor in which the text is divided into superlines, that is, units greater than ordinary lines, resulting in easier editing and freedom from truncation problems.

state table A table that represents a sequential machine, in which the rows correspond to the internal states, the columns to the input combinations, and the entries to the next state.

state vector *See* task descriptor.

static algorithm An algorithm whose operation is known in advance. Also known as deterministic algorithm.

static breeze *See* convective discharge.

static characteristic A relation between a pair of variables, such as electrode voltage and electrode current, with all other operating voltages for an electron tube, transistor, or other amplifying device maintained constant.

static check Of a computer, one or more tests of computing elements, their interconnections, or both, performed under static conditions.

static debugging routin A debugging routine which is used after the program being checked has been run and has stopped.

static dump An edited printout of the contents of main memory or of the auxiliary storage, performed in a fixed way; it is usually taken at the end of a program run either automatically or by operator intervention.

static eliminator Device intended to reduce the effect of atmospheric static interference in a radio receiver.

static induction transistor A type of transistor capable of operating at high current and voltage, whose current-voltage characteristics do not saturate, and are similar in form to those of a vacuum triode. Abbreviated SIT.

staticize 1. To capture transient data in stable form, thus converting fleeting events into examinable information. 2. To extract an instruction from the main computer memory and store the various component parts of it in the appropriate registers, preparatory to interpreting and executing it.

static random-access memory A read-write random-access memory whose storage cells are made up of four or six transistors forming flip-flop elements that indefinitely remain in a given state until the information is intentionally changed, or the power to the memory circuit is shut off.

static regulator Transmission regulator in which the adjusting mechanism is in self-equilibrium at any setting and requires control power to change the setting.

static sensitivity In phototubes, quotient of the direct anode current divided by the incident radiant flux of constant value.

static storage Computer storage such that information is fixed in space and available at any time, as in flip-flop circuits, electrostatic memories, and coincident-current magnetic-core storage.

static subroutine In computers, a subroutine which involves no parameters other than the addresses of the operands.

station 1. One of a series of essentially similar positions or facilities occurring in a data-processing system. 2. A location at which radio, television, radar, or other electric equipment is installed.

stationary ergodic noise A stationary noise for which the probability that the noise voltage lies within any given interval at any time is nearly equal to the fraction of time that the noise voltage lies within this interval if a sufficiently long observation interval is recorded.

stationary noise A random noise for which the probability that the noise voltage lies within any given interval does not change with time.

statistical multiplexer A device which combines several low-speed communications channels into a single high-speed channel, and which can manage more communications traffic than a standard multiplexer by analyzing traffic and choosing different transmission patterns.

status word A word indicating the state of the system or the diagnosis of a state into which the system has entered.

STEM *See* scanning transmission electron microscope.

stenode circuit Superheterodyne receiving circuit in which a piezoelectric unit is used in the intermediate-frequency amplifier to balance out all frequencies except signals at the crystal frequency, thereby giving very high selectivity.

step A single computer instruction or operation.

step attenuator An attenuator in which the attenuation can be varied in precisely known steps by means of switches.

step-by-step operation *See* single-step operation.

step change The change of a variable from one value to another in a single process, taking a negligible amount of time.

step counter In computers, a counter in the arithmetic unit used to count the steps in multiplication, division, and shift operations.

step-function generator A function generator whose output waveform increases and decreases suddenly in steps that may or may not be equal in amplitude.

step-recovery diode A varactor in which forward voltage injects carriers across the junction, but before the carriers can combine, voltage reverses and carriers return to their origin in a group; the result is abrupt cessation of reverse current and a harmonic-rich waveform.

step strobe marker Form of strobe marker in which the discontinuity is in the form of a step in the time base.

stereofluoroscopy A fluoroscopic technique that gives three-dimensional images.

sticking In computers, the tendency of a flip-flop to remain in, or to spontaneously switch to, one of its two stable states.

stiletto An advanced electronic subsystem contained in United States strike aircraft type F-4D for detection, identification, and location of ground-based radars; the location of radar targets is determined by direction finding and passive ranging techniques; it is used for the delivery of guided and unguided weapons against the target radars under all weather conditions.

stimulated emission device A device that uses the principle of amplification of electromagnetic waves by stimulated emission, namely, a maser or a laser.

stochastic automaton *See* probabilistic automaton.

stochastic sequential machine *See* probabilistic sequential machine.

stop bits The last two bits transmitted in asynchronous data transmission to unequivocally indicate the end of a word.

stop instruction *See* program stop.

stop loop *See* loop stop.

stopping capacitor *See* coupling capacitor.

stopping potential Voltage required to stop the outward movement of electrons emitted by photoelectric or thermionic action.

stop time *See* deceleration time.

storage Any device that can accept, retain, and read back one or more times; the means of storing data may be chemical, electrical, magnetic, mechanical, or sonic.

storage allocation The process of assigning storage locations to data or instructions in a digital computer.

storage and retrieval system An organized method of putting items away in a manner which permits their recall or retrieval from storage. Also known as storetrieval system.

storage area A specified set of locations in a storage unit. Also known as zone.

storage block *See* block.

storage camera *See* iconoscope.

storage capacity The quantity of data that can be retained simultaneously in a storage device; usually measured in bits, digits, characters, bytes, or words. Also known as capacity; memory capacity.

storage cell An elementary (logically indivisible) unit of storage; the storage cell can contain one bit, character, byte, digit (or sometimes word) of data.

storage compacting The practice, followed on multiprogramming computers which use dynamic allocation, of assigning and reassigning programs so that the largest possible area of adjacent locations remains available for new programs.

storage cycle 1. Periodic sequence of events occurring when information is transferred to or from the storage device of a computer. 2. Storing, sensing, and regeneration from parts of the storage sequence.

storage cycle time The time required to read and restore one word from a computer storage, or to write one word in computer storage.

storage density The number of characters stored per unit-length of area of storage medium (for example, number of characters per inch of magnetic tape).

storage device A mechanism for performing the function of data storage: accepting, retaining, and emitting (unchanged) data items. Also known as computer storage device.

storage dump A printout of the contents of all or part of a computer storage. Also known as memory dump; memory print.

storage element Smallest part of a digital computer storage used for storing a single bit.

storage fill Storing a pattern of characters in areas of a computer storage that are not intended for use in a particular machine run; these characters cause the machine to stop if one of these areas is erroneously referred to. Also known as memory fill.

storage hierarchy The sequence of storage devices, characterized by speed, type of access, and size for the various functions of a computer; for example, core storage from programs and data, disks or drums for temporary storage of massive amounts of data, tapes and cards for back up storage.

storage integrator In an analog computer, an integrator used to store a voltage in the hold condition for future use while the rest of the computer assumes another computer control state.

storage key A special set of bits associated with every word or character in some block of storage, which allows tasks having a matching set of protection key bits to use that block of storage.

storage location A digital-computer storage position holding one machine word and usually having a specific address.

storage mark The name given to a point location which defines the character space immediately to the left of the most significant character in accumulator storage.

storage medium Any device or recording medium into which data can be copied and held until some later time, and from which the entire original data can be obtained.

storage oscilloscope An oscilloscope that can retain an image for a period of time ranging from minutes to days, or until deliberately erased to make room for a new image.

storage print In computers, a utility program that records the requested core image, core memory, or drum locations in absolute or symbolic form either on the line-printer or on the delayed-printer tape.

storage protection Any restriction on access to storage blocks, with respect to reading, writing, or both. Also known as memory protection.

storage register A register in the main internal memory of a digital computer storing one computer word. Also known as memory register.

storage ripple A hardware function, used during maintenance periods, which reads or writes zeros or ones through available storage locations to detect a malfunctioning storage unit.

storage surface In computers, the surface (screen), in an electrostatic storage tube, on which information is stored.

storage time 1. The time required for excess minority carriers stored in a forward-biased pn junction to be removed after the junction is switched to reverse bias, and hence the time interval between the application of reverse bias and the cessation of forward current. 2. The time required for excess charge carriers in the collector region of a saturated transistor to be removed when the base signal is changed to cut-off level, and hence for the collector current to cease. 3. See retention time.

storage tube An electron tube employing cathode-ray beam scanning and charge storage for the introduction, storage, and removal of information. Also known as electrostatic storage tube; memory tube (deprecated usage).

storage-type camera tube See iconoscope.

store 1. To record data into a (static) data storage device. 2. To preserve data in a storage device.

stored-program computer A digital computer which executes instructions that are stored in main memory as patterns of data.

stored program logic Program that is stored in a memory unit containing logical commands in order to perform the same processes on all problems.

stored routine In computers, a series of instructions in storage to direct the step-by-step operation of the machine.

stored word The actual linear combination of letters (or their machine equivalents) to be placed in the machine memory; this may be physically quite different from a dictionary word.

storethrough The process of updating data in main memory each time the central processing unit writes into a cache.

storetrieval system *See* storage and retrieval system.

straight-line coding A digital computer program or routine (section of program) in which instructions are executed sequentially, without branching, looping, or testing.

strapped magnetron A multicavity magnetron in which resonator segments having the same polarity are connected together by small conducting strips to suppress undesired modes of oscillation.

strapping Connecting together resonator segments having the same polarity in a multicavity magnetron to suppress undesired modes of oscillation.

stray capacitance Undesirable capacitance between circuit wires, between wires and the chassis, or between components and the chassis of electronic equipment.

stream editor A modification of a statement editor to allow superlines that expand and contract as necessary; the most powerful type of text editor. Also known as string editor.

STRESS A problem-oriented programming language used to solve structural engineering problems. Derived from structural engineering system solver.

striation A succession of alternately luminous and dark regions sometimes observed in the positive column of a glow-discharge tube near the anode.

striking potential 1. Voltage required to start an electric arc. 2. Smallest grid-cathode potential value at which plate current begins flowing in a gas-filled triode.

string A set of consecutive, adjacent items of similar type; normally a bit string or a character string.

string break In the sorting of records, the situation that arises when there are no records having keys with values greater than the highest key already written in the sequence of records currently being processed.

string constant An arbitrary combination of letters, digits, and other symbols that is treated in a manner completely analogous to numeric constants.

string editor *See* stream editor.

string manipulation The handling of strings of characters in a computer storage as though they were single units of data.

string manipulation language *See* string processing language.

String-Oriented Symbolic Language *See* SNOBOL.

string processing language A higher-level programming language equipped with facilities to synthesize and decompose character strings, search them in response to arbitrarily complex criteria, and perform a variety of other manipulations. Also known as string manipulation language.

stringy floppy A peripheral storage device for microcomputers that uses a removable magnetic tape cartridge with a $\frac{1}{16}$-inch wide (1.5875-millimeter) loop of magnetic tape.

strobe 1. Intensified spot in the sweep of a deflection-type indicator, used as a reference mark for ranging or expanding the presentation. 2. Intensified sweep on a plan-position indicator or B-scope; such a strobe may result from certain types of interference, or it may be purposely applied as a bearing or heading marker. 3. Line on a console oscilloscope representing the azimuth data generated by a jammed radar site.

strobe circuit A circuit that produces an output pulse only at certain times or under certain conditions, such as a gating circuit or a coincidence circuit.

strobe marker A small bright spot, or a short gap, or other discontinuity produced on the trace of a radar display to indicate that part of the time base which is receiving attention.

strobe pulse Pulse of duration less than the time period of a recurrent phenomenon used for making a close investigation of that phenomenon; the frequency of the strobe pulse bears a simple relation to that of the phenomenon, and the relative timing is usually adjustable.

strobing The technique required to time-synchronize data appearing as pulses at the output of a computer memory.

stroboscopic lamp *See* flash lamp.

stroboscopic tube *See* strobotron.

strobotron A cold-cathode gas-filled arc-discharge tube having one or more internal or external grids to initiate current flow and produce intensely bright flashes of light for a stroboscope. Also known as stroboscopic tube.

stroke 1. A key-depressing operation in keypunching. 2. In optical character recognition, straight or curved portion of a letter, such as is commonly made with one smooth motion of a pen. Also known as character stroke. 3. That segment of a printed or handwritten character which has been temporarily isolated from other segments for the purpose of analyzing it, particularly with regard to its dimensions and relative reflectance. Also known as character stroke. 4. The penlike motion of a focused electron beam in cathode-ray-tube displays.

stroke analysis In character recognition, a method employed in character property detection in which an input specimen is dissected into certain prescribed elements; the sequence, relative positions, and number of detected elements are then used to identify the characters.

stroke center line In character recognition, a line midway between the two average-edge lines; the center line describes the stroke's direction of travel. Also known as center line.

stroke edge In character recognition, a continuous line, straight or otherwise, which traces the outermost part of intersection of the stroke along the two sides of its greatest dimension.

stroke width In character recognition, the distance that obtains, at a given location, between the points of intersection of the stroke edges and a line drawn perpendicular to the stroke center line.

structural engineering system solver *See* STRESS.

structural information Information specifying the number of independently variable features or degrees of freedom of a pattern.

structured data type The manner in which a collection of data items, which may have the same or different scalar data types, is represented in a computer program.

structured programming The use of program design and documentation techniques that impose a uniform structure on all computer programs.

structure of a system Refers to the nature of the chain of command, the origin and type of data collected, the form and destination of results, and the procedures used to control operations.

stub The left-hand portion of a decision table, consisting of a single column, and comprising the condition stub and the action stub.

stylus printing *See* matrix printing.

subalphabet A subset of an alphabet.

subassembly Two or more components combined into a unit for convenience in assembling or servicing equipment; an intermediate-frequency strip for a receiver is an example.

subcarrier oscillator 1. The crystal oscillator that operates at the chrominance subcarrier or burst frequency of 3.579545 megahertz in a color television receiver; this oscillator, synchronized in frequency and phase with the transmitter master oscillator, furnishes the continuous subcarrier frequency required for demodulators in the receiver. 2. An oscillator used in a telemetering system to translate variations in an electrical quantity into variations of a frequency-modulated signal at a subcarrier frequency.

subchannel The portion of an input/output channel associated with a specific input/output operation.

subclutter visibility A measure of the effectiveness of moving-target indicator radar, equal to the ratio of the signal from a fixed target that can be canceled to the signal from a just visible moving target.

subcycle generator Frequency-reducing device used in telephone equipment which furnishes ringing power at a submultiple of the power supply frequency.

subdevice bit *See* select bit.

subharmonic triggering A method of frequency division which makes use of a triggered multivibrator having a period of one cycle which allows triggering only by a pulse that is an exact integral number of input pulses from the last effective trigger.

subminiature tube An extremely small electron tube designed for use in hearing aids and other miniaturized equipment; a typical subminiature tube is about 1½ inches (4 centimeters) long and 0.4 inch (1 centimeter) in diameter, with the pins emerging through the glass base.

subprogram A part of a larger program which can be converted independently into machine language.

subroutine 1. A body of computer instruction (and the associated constants and working-storage areas, if any) designed to be used by other routines to accomplish some particular purpose. 2. A statement in FORTRAN used to define the beginning of a closed subroutine (first definition).

subschema An individual user's partial view of a data base.

substitute mode One method of exchange buffering, in which segments of storage function alternately as buffer and as program work area.

substitutional impurity An atom or ion which is not normally found in a solid, but which resides at the position where an atom or ion would ordinarily be located in the lattice structure, and replaces it.

substrate The physical material on which a microcircuit is fabricated; used primarily for mechanical support and insulating purposes, as with ceramic, plastic, and glass substrates; however, semiconductor and ferrite substrates may also provide useful electrical functions.

substring A sequence of successive characters within a string.

subtracter A computer device that can form the difference of two numbers or quantities.

successive-approximation converter An analog-to-digital converter which operates by successively considering each bit position in the digital output and setting that bit equal to 0 or 1 on the basis of the output of a comparator.

suffix notation *See* reverse Polish notation.

Suhl effect When a strong transverse magnetic field is applied to an n-type semiconducting filament, holes injected into the filament are deflected to the surface, where they may recombine rapidly with electrons or be withdrawn by a probe.

suite A collection of related computer programs run one after another.

summary punching The conversion of information developed by accounting machines into holes in a punch card.

summary recorder In computers, output equipment which records a summary of the information handled.

summation check An error-detecting procedure involving adding together all the digits of some number and comparing this sum to a previously computed value of the same sum.

summing amplifier An amplifier that delivers an output voltage which is proportional to the sum of two or more input voltages or currents.

sun follower A photoelectric pickup and an associated servomechanism used to maintain a sun-facing orientation, as for a space vehicle. Also known as sun seeker.

S-unit meter *See* signal-strength meter.

sun seeker *See* sun follower.

sun sensor *See* solar sensor.

sun strobe The signal display seen on a radar plan-position-indicator screen when the radar antenna is aimed at the sun; the pattern resembles that produced by continuous-wave interference, and is due to radio-frequency energy radiated by the sun.

supercomputer A computer which is among those with the highest speed, largest functional size, biggest physical dimensions, or greatest monetary cost in any given period of time.

superconducting computer A high-performance computer whose circuits employ superconductivity and the Josephson effect to reduce computer cycle time.

superconducting material *See* superconductor.

superconducting quantum interference device A superconducting ring that couples with one or two Josephson junctions; applications include high-sensitivity magnetometers, near-magnetic-field antennas, and measurement of very small currents or voltages. Abbreviated SQUID.

superconductivity A property of many metals, alloys, and chemical compounds at temperatures near absolute zero by virtue of which their electrical resistivity vanishes and they become strongly diamagnetic.

superconductor Any material capable of exhibiting superconductivity; examples include iridium, lead, mercury, niobium, tin, tantalum, vanadium, and many alloys. Also known as cryogenic conductor; superconducting material.

supercurrent In the two-fluid model of superconductivity, the current arising from motion of superconducting electrons, in contrast to the normal current.

superemitron camera *See* image iconoscope.

superhet *See* superheterodyne receiver.

superheterodyne receiver A receiver in which all incoming modulated radio-frequency carrier signals are converted to a common intermediate-frequency carrier value for additional amplification and selectivity prior to demodulation, using heterodyne action; the output of the intermediate-frequency amplifier is then demodulated in the second detector to give the desired audio-frequency signal. Also known as superhet.

superimposed coding A means of placing many keywords in a single card area, where they can be scanned simultaneously.

superlattice 1. A structure consisting of alternating layers of two different semiconductor materials, each several nanometers thick. 2. An ordered arrangement of atoms in a solid solution which forms a lattice superimposed on the normal solid solution lattice. Also known as superstructure.

superline A unit of text longer than an ordinary line, used in some of the more powerful text editors.

supermini A large minicomputer.

superregeneration Regeneration in which the oscillation is broken up or quenched at a frequency slightly above the upper audibility limit of the human ear by a separate oscillator circuit connected between the grid and anode of the amplifier tube, to prevent regeneration from exceeding the maximum useful amount.

superstructure *See* superlattice.

supervisor call A mechanism whereby a computer program can interrupt the normal flow of processing and ask the supervisor to perform a function for the program that the program cannot or is not permitted to perform for itself.

supervisor interrupt An interruption caused by the program being executed which issues an instruction to the master control program.

supervisor mode A method of computer operation in which the computer can execute all its own instructions, including the privileged instruction not normally allowed to the programmer, in contrast to problem mode.

supervisory computer A minicomputer which accepts test results from satellite minicomputers, transmits new programs to the satellite minicomputers, and may further communicate with a larger computer.

supervisory program A program that organizes and regulates the flow of work in a computer system, for example, it may automatically change over from one run to another and record the time of the run.

supervisory routine A program or routine that initiates and guides the execution of several (or all) other routines and programs; it usually forms part of (or is) the operating system.

suppression 1. Removal or deletion usually of insignificant digits in a number, especially zero suppression. 2. Optional function in either on-line or off-line printing devices that permits them to ignore certain characters or groups of characters which may be transmitted through them. 3. Elimination of any component of an emission, as a particular frequency or group of frequencies in an audio-frequency of a radio-frequency signal.

suppressor *See* suppressor grid.

suppressor grid A grid placed between two positive electrodes in an electron tube primarily to reduce the flow of secondary electrons from one electrode to the other; it is usually used between the screen grid and the anode. Also known as suppressor.

suppressor pulse Pulse used to disable an ionized flow field or beacon transponder during intervals when interference would be encountered.

surface acoustic wave device Any device, such as a filter, resonator, or oscillator, which employs surface acoustic waves with frequencies in the range 10^7–10^9 hertz, traveling on the optically polished surface of a piezoelectric substrate, to process electronic signals.

surface acoustic wave filter An electric filter consisting of a piezoelectric bar with a polished surface along which surface acoustic waves can propagate, and on which are deposited metallic transducers, one of which is connected, via thermocompression-bonded leads, to the electric source, while the other drives the load.

surface barrier A potential barrier formed at a surface of a semiconductor by the trapping of carriers at the surface.

surface-barrier diode A diode utilizing thin-surface layers, formed either by deposition of metal films or by surface diffusion, to serve as a rectifying junction.

surface-barrier transistor A transistor in which the emitter and collector are formed on opposite sides of a semiconductor wafer, usually made of n-type germanium, by training two jets of electrolyte against its opposite surfaces to etch and then electroplate the surfaces.

surface-charge transistor An integrated-circuit transistor element based on controlling the transfer of stored electric charges along the surface of a semiconductor.

surface-controlled avalanche transistor Transistor in which avalanche breakdown voltage is controlled by an external field applied through surface-insulating layers, and which permits operation at frequencies up to the 10-gigahertz range.

surface noise The noise component in the electric output of a phonograph pickup due to irregularities in the contact surface of the groove. Also known as needle scratch.

surface passivation A method of coating the surface of a p-type wafer for a diffused junction transistor with an oxide compound, such as silicon oxide, to prevent penetration of the impurity in undesired regions.

surface recombination velocity A measure of the rate of recombination between electrons and holes at the surface of a semiconductor, equal to the component of the electron or hole current density normal to the surface divided by the excess electron or hole volume charge density close to the surface.

surface state An electron state in a semiconductor whose wave function is restricted to a layer near the surface.

surge suppressor A circuit that responds to the rate of change of a current or voltage to prevent a rise above a predetermined value; it may include resistors, capacitors, coils, gas tubes, and semiconducting disks. Also known as transient suppressor.

swamping resistor Resistor placed in the emitter lead of a transistor circuit to minimize the effects of temperature on the emitter-base junction resistance.

swapping A procedure in which a running program is temporarily suspended and moved onto secondary storage, and primary storage is reassigned to a more pressing job, in order to maximize the efficient use of primary storage.

sweep 1. The steady movement of the electron beam across the screen of a cathode-ray tube, producing a steady bright line when no signal is present; the line is straight for a linear sweep and circular for a circular sweep. 2. The steady change in the output frequency of a signal generator from one limit of its range to the other.

sweep amplifier An amplifier used with a cathode-ray tube, such as in a television receiver or cathode-ray oscilloscope, to amplify the sawtooth output voltage of the sweep oscillator, to shape the waveform for the deflection circuits of a television picture tube, or to provide balanced signals to the deflection plates.

sweep circuit The sweep oscillator, sweep amplifier, and any other stage used to produce the deflection voltage or current for a cathode-ray tube. Also known as scanning circuit.

sweep generator Also known as sweep oscillator. 1. An electronic circuit that generates a voltage or current, usually recurrent, as a prescribed function of time; the resulting waveform is used as a time base to be applied to the deflection system of an electron-beam device, such as a cathode-ray tube. Also known as time-base generator; timing-axis oscillator. **2.** A test instrument that generates a radio-frequency voltage whose frequency varies back and forth through a given frequency range at a rapid constant rate; used to produce an input signal for circuits or devices whose frequency response is to be observed on an oscilloscope.

sweeping receivers Automatically and continuously tuned receivers designed to stop and lock on when a signal is found, or to continually plot band occupancy.

sweep jamming Jamming an enemy radarscope by sweeping the region of radar-beam coverage with electromagnetic waves having the same frequency as those received by the radarscope.

sweep oscillator *See* sweep generator.

sweep rate The number of times a radar radiation pattern rotates during 1 minute; sometimes expressed as the duration of one complete rotation in seconds.

sweep test Test given coaxial cable with an oscilloscope to check attenuation.

sweep-through jammer A jamming transmitter which is swept through a radio-frequency band in short steps to jam each frequency briefly, producing a sound like that of an aircraft engine.

sweep voltage Periodically varying voltage applied to the deflection plates of a cathode-ray tube to give a beam displacement that is a function of time, frequency, or other data base.

switch 1. A hardware or programmed device for indicating that one of several alternative states or conditions have been chosen, or to interchange or exchange two data items. **2.** A symbol used to indicate a branch point, or a set of instructions to condition a branch.

switched capacitor An integrated circuit element, consisting of a capacitor with two metal oxide semiconductor (MOS) switches, whose function is approximately equivalent to that of a resistor.

switched-message network A data transmission system in which a user can communicate with any other user of the network.

switch function A circuit having a fixed number of inputs and outputs designed such that the output information is a function of the input information, each expressed in a certain code or signal configuration or pattern.

switching diode A crystal diode that provides essentially the same function as a switch; below a specified applied voltage it has high resistance corresponding to an open switch, while above that voltage it suddenly changes to the low resistance of a closed switch.

switching gate An electronic circuit in which an output having constant amplitude is registered if a particular combination of input signals exists; examples are the OR, AND, NOT, and INHIBIT circuits. Also known as logical gate.

switching pad Transmission-loss pad automatically cut in and out of a toll circuit for different desired operating conditions.

switching theory The theory of circuits made up of ideal digital devices; included are the theory of circuits and networks for telephone switching, digital computing, digital control, and data processing.

switching time 1. The time interval between the reference time and the last instant at which the instantaneous voltage response of a magnetic cell reaches a stated fraction of its peak value. **2.** The time interval between the reference time and the first instant at which the instantaneous integrated voltage response of a magnetic cell reaches a stated fraction of its peak value.

switching transistor A transistor designed for on/off switching operation.

switching tube A gas tube used for switching high-power radio-frequency energy in the antenna circuits of radar and other pulsed radio-frequency systems; examples are ATR tube; pre-TR tube; TR tube.

switch register A manual switch on the control panel by means of which a bit may be entered in a processor register.

syllabic compandor A compandor in which the effective gain variations are made at speeds allowing response to the syllables of speech but not to individual cycles of the signal wave.

symbolic address In coding, a programmer-defined symbol that represents the location of a particular datum item, instruction, or routine. Also known as symbolic number.

symbolic algebraic manipulation language An algebraic manipulation language which admits the most general species of mathematical expressions, usually representing them as general tree structures, but which lacks certain special algorithms found in seminumerical and ghost languages.

symbolic assembly language listing A list that may be produced by a computer during the compilation of a program showing the source language statements together with the corresponding machine language instructions generated by them.

symbolic assembly system A system for forming programs that can be run on a computer, consisting of an assembly language and an assembler.

symbolic coding Instruction written in an assembly language, using symbols for operations and addresses. Also known as symbolic programming.

symbolic debugging A method of correcting known errors in a computer program written in a source language, in which certain statements are compiled together with the program.

symbolic deck Deck of cards punched out in programmer coding language as opposed to binary language.

symbolic language A language which expresses addresses and operation codes of instructions in symbols convenient to humans rather than in machine language.

symbolic number *See* symbolic address.

symbolic programming *See* symbolic coding.

symbol input Includes all contextual symbols that may appear in a source text.

symbol sequence A sequence of contextual symbols not interrupted by space.

symbol table A mapping for a set of symbols to another set of symbols or numbers.

symmetrical avalanche rectifier Avalanche rectifier that can be triggered in either direction, after which it has a low impedance in the triggered direction.

symmetrical band-pass filter A band-pass filter whose attenuation as a function of frequency is symmetrical about a frequency at the center of the pass band.

symmetrical band-reject filter A band-rejection filter whose attenuation as a function of frequency is symmetrical about a frequency at the center of the rejection band.

symmetrical clipper A clipper in which the upper and lower limits on the amplitude of the output signal are positive and negative values of equal magnitude.

symmetrical deflection A type of electrostatic deflection in which voltages that are equal in magnitude and opposite in sign are applied to the two deflector plates.

symmetrical H attenuator An H attenuator in which the impedance near the input terminals equals the corresponding impedance near the output terminals.

symmetrical O attenuator An O attenuator in which the impedance near the input terminals equals the corresponding impedance near the output terminals.

symmetrical pi attenuator A pi attenuator in which the impedance near the input terminals equals the corresponding impedance near the output terminals.

symmetrical T attenuator A T attenuator in which the impedance near the input terminals equals the corresponding impedance near the output terminals.

symmetrical transducer A transducer is symmetrical with respect to a specified pair of terminations when the interchange of that pair of terminations will not affect the transmission.

symmetric list A list with sequencing pointers to previous as well as subsequent items.

sync generator *See* synchronizing generator.

synchronized blocking oscillator A blocking oscillator which is synchronized with pulses occurring at a rate slightly faster than its own natural frequency.

synchronizer 1. A computer storage device used to compensate for a difference in rate of flow of information or time of occurrence of events when transmitting information from one device to another. **2.** The component of a radar set which generates the timing voltage for the complete set.

synchronizing generator An electronic generator that supplies synchronizing pulses to television studio and transmitter equipment. Also known as sync generator; sync-signal generator.

synchronous clamp circuit *See* keyed clamp circuit.

synchronous communications The high-speed transmission and reception of long groups of characters at a time, requiring synchronization of the sending and receiving devices.

synchronous computer A digital computer designed to operate in sequential elementary steps, each step requiring a constant amount of time to complete, and being initiated by a timing pulse from a uniformly running clock.

synchronous demodulator *See* synchronous detector.

synchronous detector 1. A detector that inserts a missing carrier signal in exact synchronism with the original carrier at the transmitter; when the input to the detector consists of two suppressed-carrier signals in phase quadrature, as in the chrominance signal of a color television receiver, the phase of the reinserted carrier can be adjusted to recover either one of the signals. Also known as synchronous demodulator. **2.** *See* cross-correlator.

synchronous gate A time gate in which the output intervals are synchronized with an incoming signal.

synchronous rectifier A rectifier in which contacts are opened and closed at correct instants of time for rectification by a synchronous vibrator or by a commutator driven by a synchronous motor.

synchronous switch A thyratron circuit used to control the operation of ignitrons in such applications as resistance welding.

synchronous working The mode of operation of a synchronous computer, in which the starting of each operation is clock-controlled.

synchroscope A cathode-ray oscilloscope designed to show a short-duration pulse by using a fast sweep that is synchronized with the pulse signal to be observed.

sync separator A circuit that separates synchronizing pulses from the video signal in a television receiver.

sync-signal generator *See* synchronizing generator.

syntactic analysis The problem of associating a given string of symbols through a grammar to a programming language, so that the question of whether the string belongs to the language may be answered.

syntactic extension An extension mechanism which creates new notations for existing or user-defined mechanisms in an extensible language.

syntactic model *See* linguistic model.

syntax The set of rules needed to construct valid expressions or sentences in a language.

syntax-directed compiler A general-purpose compiler that can service a family of languages by providing the syntactic rules for language analysis in the form of data, typically in tabular form, rather than using a specific parsing algorithm for a particular language. Also known as syntax-oriented compiler.

syntax-oriented compiler *See* syntax-directed compiler.

synthesizer An electronic instrument which combines simple elements to generate more complex entities; examples are frequency synthesizer and sound synthesizer.

synthetic address *See* generated address.

synthetic language A pseudocode or symbolic language; fabricated language.

SYSIN The principal input stream of an operating system. Derived from system input.

system A combination of two or more sets generally physically separated when in operation, and such other assemblies, subassemblies, and parts necessary to perform an operational function or functions.

systematic analog network testing approach An on-line minicomputer-based system with an integrated data-based and optimal human intervention, which provides computer printouts used in automatic testing of electronic systems; aimed at maximizing cost effectivity. Abbreviated SANTA.

systematic error checking code A type of self-checking code in which a valid character consists of the minimum number of digits needed to identify the character and distinguish it from any other valid character, and a set of check digits which maintain a minimum specified signal distance between any two valid characters. Also known as group code.

system chart A flowchart that emphasizes the component operations which make up a system.

system check A check on the overall performance of the system, usually not made by built-in computer check circuits; for example, control total, hash totals, and record counts.

system design Determination in detail of the exact operational requirements of a system, resolution of these into file structures and input/output formats, and relation of each to management tasks and information requirements.

system designer A person who prepares final system documentation, analyzes findings, and synthesizes new system design.

system evaluation A periodic evaluation of the system to assess its status in terms of original or current expectations and to chart its future direction.

system generation A process that creates a particular and uniquely specified operating system; it combines user-specified options and parameters with manufacturer-supplied general-purpose or nonspecialized program subsections to produce an operating system (or other complex software) of the desired form and capacity.

system improvement time The machine downtime needed for the installation and testing of new components, large or small, and machine downtime necessary for modification of existing components; this includes all programming tests following the above actions to prove the machine is operating properly.

system input *See* SYSIN.

system master tapes Magnetic tapes containing programmed instructions necessary for preparing a computer prior to running programs.

system operation The administration and operation of an automatic data-processing equipment-oriented system, including staffing, scheduling, equipment and service contract administration, equipment utilization practices, and time-sharing.

cyotomo dofinition A document doscribing a computer bacod cyctem for prooeɛɛing data or solving a problem, including a general description of the aims and benefits of the system and clerical procedures employed, and detailed program specification. Also known as systems specification.

system software Computer software involved with data and program management, including operating systems, control programs, and data-base management systems.

systems programming The development and production of programs that have to do with translation, loading, supervision, maintenance, control, and running of computers and computer programs.

systems specification *See* systems definition.

systems test The running of the whole system against test data, a complete simulation of the actual running system for purposes of testing out the adequacy of the system.

system study A detailed study to determine whether, to what extent, and how automatic data-processing equipment should be used; it usually includes an analysis of the existing system and the design of the new system, including the development of system specifications which provide a basis for the selection of equipment.

system supervisor A control program which ensures an efficient transition in running program after program and accomplishing setups and control functions.

system unit An individual card, section of tape, or the like, which is manipulated during operation of the system; class 1 systems have one unit per document; class 2 systems have one unit per vocabulary term or concept.

table A set of contiguous, related items, each uniquely identified either by its relative position in the set or by some label.

table-driven compiler A compiler in which the source language is described by a set of syntax rules.

table look-up A procedure for calculating the location of an item in a table by means of an algorithm, rather than by conducting a search for the item.

table look-up device A logic circuit in which the input signals are grouped as address digits to a memory device, and, in response to any particular combination of inputs, the memory device location that is addressed becomes the output.

tabular language A part of a program which represents the composition of a decision table required by the problem considered.

tabulate To order a set of data into a table form, or to print a set of data as a table, usually indicating differences and totals, or just totals.

tabulating card Card into which coded holes are punched.

tabulating equipment Machinery to punch, sense, sort, or check coded holes in tabulating cards.

tabulating system Any group of machines which is capable of entering, converting, receiving, classifying, computing, and recording data by means of tabulating cards, and in which tabulating cards are used for storing data and for communicating with the system.

tabulation character A character that controls the action of a computer printer and is not itself printed, although it forms part of the data to be printed.

tabulator A machine that reads information from punched cards and produces lists, tables, and totals on separate forms or continuous paper.

tactical electronic warfare The application of electronic warfare to tactical air operations; tactical electronic warfare encompasses the three major subdivisions of electronic warfare: electronic warfare support measures, electronic countermeasures, and electronic counter-countermeasures.

tag 1. A unit of information used as a label or marker. **2.** The symbol written in the location field of an assembly-language coding form, and used to define the symbolic address of the data or instruction written on that line.

tag converting unit A device capable of reading the perforations of a price tag as input data.

tag format The arrangement of data in a short record inserted in a direct-access storage to indicate the location of an overflow record.

tail 1. A small pulse that follows the main pulse of a radar set and rises in the same direction. **2.** The trailing edge of a pulse.

tail clipping Method of sharpening the trailing edge of a pulse.

takedown The actions performed at the end of an equipment operating cycle to prepare the equipment for the next setup; for example, to remove the tapes from the tape handlers at the end of a computer run is a takedown operation.

takedown time The time required to take down a piece of equipment.

talking battery *See* quiet battery.

tandem connection *See* cascade connection.

tandem system A computing system in which there are two central processing units, usually with one controlling the other, and with data proceeding from one processing unit into the other.

tank 1. A unit of acoustic delay-line storage containing a set of channels, each forming a separate recirculation path. **2.** The heavy metal envelope of a large mercury-arc rectifier or other gas tube having a mercury-pool cathode. **3.** *See* tank circuit.

tank circuit A circuit which exhibits resonance at one or more frequencies, and which is capable of storing electric energy over a band of frequencies continuously distributed about the resonant frequency, such as a coil and capacitor in parallel. Also known as electrical resonator; tank.

tantalum nitride resistor A thin-film resistor consisting of tantalum nitride deposited on a substrate, such as industrial sapphire.

tap crystal Compound semiconductor that stores current when stimulated by light and then gives up energy as flashes of light when it is physically tapped.

tape A ribbonlike material used to store data in lengthwise sequential position.

tape alternation The switching of a computer program back and forth between two tape units in order to avoid interruption of the program during mounting and removal of tape reels.

tape bootstrap routine A computer routine stored in the first block of a magnetic tape that instructs the computer to read certain programs from the tape.

tape cluster *See* magnetic tape group.

tape-controlled carriage A device which uses a loop of punched-paper or plastic mylar tape to control the motion of paper through a computer printer or typewriter.

tape control unit A device which senses which tape unit is to be accessed for read or write purpose and opens up the necessary electronic paths. Formerly known as hypertape control unit.

tape drive A tape reading or writing device consisting of a tape transport, electronics, and controls; it usually refers to magnetic tape exclusively.

tape editor A routine designed to help edit, revise, and correct a routine contained on a tape.

tape group *See* magnetic tape group.

tape label A record appearing at the beginning or at the end of a magnetic tape to uniquely identify the tape as the one required by the system.

tape-limited Pertaining to a computer operation in which the time required to read and write tapes exceeds the time required for computation.

tape mark 1. A special character or coding, an attached piece of reflective material, or other device that indicates the physical end of recording on a magnetic tape. Also known as destination warning mark; end-of-tape mark. **2.** A special character that divides a file of magnetic tape into sections, usually followed by a record with data describing the particular section of the file. Also known as control mark.

tape operating system A computer operating system in which source programs and sometimes incoming data are stored on magnetic tape, rather than in the computer memory. Abbreviated TOS.

tape plotting system A digital incremental plotter in which the digital data are supplied from a magnetic or paper tape.

tape-processing simultaneity A feature of some computer systems whereby reading or writing of data can be carried out on all the tape units at the same time, while the central processing unit continues to process data.

tape punch A machine that punches code holes and feed holes in paper tape.

tape reader *See* paper-tape reader.

tape reading A process of feeding coded tapes through a tape-to-card punch to convert the coded information into punched cards; tapes can be prepared on the typewriter tape punch or on the card-controlled tape punch; the latter is capable of punching tape that can be transmitted by telegraph.

tape search unit Small, fully transistorized, special-purpose, digital data-processing system using a stored program to perform logical functions necessary to search a magnetic tape in off-line mode, in response to a specific request.

tape serial number A number identifying a magnetic tape which remains unchanged throughout the time the tape is used, even though all other information about the tape may change.

tape skip A machine instruction to space forward and erase a portion of tape when a defect on the tape surface causes a write error to persist.

tape station A tape reading or writing device consisting of a tape transport, electronics, and controls; it may use either magnetic tape or paper tape.

tape-to-card The operation, or job step, required to transfer data from magnetic or paper tape to punched card.

tape-to-card converter A machine that converts information directly from punched or magnetic tape to cards.

tape-to-tape conversion A routine which directs a computer to copy information from one tape to another tape of a different kind; for example, from a seven-track onto a nine-track tape.

tape transport The mechanism that physically moves a tape past a stationary head. Also known as transport.

tape unit A tape reading or writing device consisting of a tape transport, electronics, controls, and possibly a cabinet; the cabinet may contain one or more magnetic tape stations.

tape verifier A verifier for checking the accuracy of a punched paper tape by comparing it with a second manual punch of the same data; the machine stops whenever a character being punched the second time differs from that on the first tape.

tapped control A rheostat or potentiometer having one or more fixed taps along the resistance element, usually to provide a fixed grid bias or for automatic bass compensation.

tapped-potentiometer function generator A device used in analog computers for representing a function of one variable, consisting of a potentiometer with a number of taps held at voltages determined by a table of values of the variable; the input variable sets the angular position of a shaft that moves a slide contact, and the output voltage is taken from the slide contact.

target 1. An index card or test document used to assist, reference, or calibrate equipment. 2. In an x-ray tube, the anode or anticathode which emits x-rays when bombarded with electrons. 3. In a television camera tube, the storage surface that is scanned by an electron beam to generate an output signal current corresponding to the charge-density pattern stored there. 4. In cathode-ray tuning indicator tube, one of the electrodes that is coated with a material that fluoresces under electron bombardment.

408 target acquisition

target acquisition 1. The first appearance of a recognizable and useful echo signal from a new target in radar and sonar. **2.** *See* acquire.

target configuration The combination of input, output, and storage units and the amount of computer memory required to carry out an object program.

target-designating system A system for designating to one instrument a target which has already been located by a second instrument; it employs electrical data transmitters and receivers which indicate on one instrument the pointing of another.

target discrimination The ability of a detection or guidance system to distinguish a target from its background or to discriminate between two or more targets that are close together.

target language The language into which a program (or text) is to be converted.

target phase The stage of handling a computer program at which the object program is first carried out after it has been compiled.

target program *See* object program.

target routine *See* object program.

target signature Characteristic pattern of the target displayed by detection and classification equipment.

task A set of instructions, data, and control information capable of being executed by the central processing unit of a digital computer in order to accomplish some purpose; in a multiprogramming environment, tasks compete with one another for control of the central processing unit, but in a nonmultiprogramming environment a task is simply the current work to be done.

task descriptor The vital information about a task in a multitask system which must be saved when the task is interrupted. Also known as state vector.

task management The functions, assumed by the operating system, of switching the processor among tasks, scheduling, sending messages or timing signals between tasks, and creating or removing tasks.

TDR *See* time-domain reflectometer.

TEA *See* transferred-electron amplifier.

technetron High-power multichannel field-effect transistor.

TELCOMP A computer language developed by Bolt, Beranek, and Newman, Inc., expressly as a time-sharing language; the user of the language is connected to a computer by a teletype terminal attached to a telephone line.

telecine camera A television camera used in conjunction with film or slide projectors to televise motion pictures and still images.

telemetering receiver A device in a telemetering system which converts electrical signals into an indication or recording of the value of the quantity being measured at a distance.

telemetering transmitter A device which converts the readings of instruments into electrical signals for transmission to a remote location by means of wires, radio waves, or other means.

telephone data set Equipment interfacing a data terminal with a telephone circuit.

telephone modem A piece of equipment that modulates and demodulates one or more separate telephone circuits, each containing one or more telephone channels; it may include multiplexing and demultiplexing circuits, individual amplifiers, and carrier-frequency sources.

telephone repeater A repeater inserted at one or more intermediate points in a long telephone line to amplify telephone signals so as to maintain the required current strength.

teleprinter Any typewriter-type device capable of being connected to a computer and of printing out a set of messages under computer control.

teleprocessing 1. The use of telecommunications equipment and systems by a computer. **2.** A computer service involving input/output at locations remote from the computer itself.

teleprocessing monitor A computer program that manages the transfer of information between local and remote terminals. Abbreviated TP monitor.

telering In telephony, a frequency-selector device for the production of ringing power.

telesynd Telemeter or remote-control equipment which is synchronous in both speed and position.

television camera The pickup unit used to convert a scene into corresponding electric signals; optical lenses focus the scene to be televised on the photosensitive surface of a camera tube, and the tube breaks down the visual image into small picture elements and converts the light intensity of each element in turn into a corresponding electric signal. Also known as camera.

television monitor 1. A television set connected to the transmitter at a television station, used to continuously check the image picked up by a television camera and the sound picked up by the microphones. **2.** A closed-circuit television system used to provide continuous observation of such things as hazardous or remote locations, the readings of gages for process control, or microscopic or telescopic images, for greater convenience of viewing.

television picture tube See picture tube.

television receiver A receiver that converts incoming television signals into the original scenes along with the associated sounds. Also known as television set.

television relay system See television repeater.

television repeater A repeater that transmits television signals from point to point by using radio waves in free space as a medium, such transmission not being intended for direct reception by the public. Also known as television relay system.

television screen The fluorescent screen of the picture tube in a television receiver.

television set See television receiver.

television transmitter An electronic device that converts the audio and video signals of a television program into modulated radio-frequency energy that can be radiated from an antenna and received on a television receiver.

television tuner A component in a television receiver that selects the desired channel and converts the frequencies received to lower frequencies within the passband of the intermediate-frequency amplifier; for very-high-frequency reception there are 12 discrete positions (channels 2–13); for ultra-high-frequency reception continuous tuning is usually employed.

temperature-compensated Zener diode Positive-temperature-coefficient reversed-bias Zener diode (pn junction) connected in series with one or more negative-temperature forward-biased diodes within a single package.

temperature compensation The process of making some characteristic of a circuit or device independent of changes in ambient temperature.

temperature saturation The condition in which the anode current of a thermionic vacuum tube cannot be further increased by increasing the cathode temperature at a given value of anode voltage; the effect is due to the space charge formed near the cathode. Also known as filament saturation; saturation.

template A prototype pattern against which observed patterns are matched in a pattern recognition system.

temporary storage The storage capacity reserved or used for retention of temporary or transient data.

terminal A site or location at which data can leave or enter a system.

terminal area The enlarged portion of conductor material surrounding a hole for a lead on a printed circuit. Also known as land; pad.

ternary incremental representation A type of incremental representation in which the value of the change in a variable is defined as $+1$, -1, or 0.

tertiary storage Any of several types of computer storage devices, usually consisting of magnetic tape transports and mass storage tape systems, which have slower access times, larger capacity, and lower cost than main storage or secondary storage.

test data A set of data developed specifically to test the adequacy of a computer run or system; the data may be actual data that has been taken from previous operations, or artificial data created for this purpose.

test pack A deck of punch cards that contains both a computer program and test data for carrying out a test run of the program.

test program See check routine.

test routine See check routine.

test run The performance of a computer program to check that it is operating correctly, by using test data to generate results that can be compared with expected answers.

test set A combination of instruments needed for servicing a particular type of electronic equipment.

tetrode A four-electrode electron tube containing an anode, a cathode, a control electrode, and one additional electrode that is ordinarily a grid.

tetrode junction transistor See double-base junction transistor.

tetrode thyratron A thyratron with two control electrodes. Also known as gas tetrode.

tetrode transistor A four-electrode transistor, such as a tetrode point-contact transistor or double-base junction transistor.

text-editing system A computer program, together with associated hardware, for the on-line creation and modification of computer programs and ordinary text.

thallofide cell A photoconductive cell in which the active light-sensitive material is thallium oxysulfide in a vacuum; it has maximum response at the red end of the visible spectrum and in the near infrared.

theater television A large projection-type television receiver used in theaters, generally for closed-circuit showing of important sport events.

thermal converter A device that converts heat energy directly into electric energy by using the Seebeck effect; it is composed of at least two dissimilar materials, one junction of which is in contact with a heat source and the other junction of which is in contact with a heat sink. Also known as thermocouple converter; thermoelectric generator; thermoelectric power generator; thermoelement.

thermal drift Drift caused by internal heating of equipment during normal operation or by changes in external ambient temperature.

thermal imagery Imagery produced by measuring and recording electronically the thermal radiation of objects.

thermal noise Electric noise produced by thermal agitation of electrons in conductors and semiconductors. Also known as Johnson noise; resistance noise.

thermal noise generator A generator that uses the inherent thermal agitation of an electron tube to provide a calibrated noise source.

thermal resistance *See* effective thermal resistance.

thermal resistor *See* thermistor.

thermal runaway A condition that may occur in a power transistor when collector current increases collector junction temperature, reducing collector resistance and allowing a greater current to flow, which, in turn, increases the heating effect.

thermion A charged particle, either negative or positive, emitted by a heated body, as by the hot cathode of a thermionic tube.

thermionic Pertaining to the emission of electrons as a result of heat.

thermionic cathode *See* hot cathode.

thermionic converter A device in which heat energy is directly converted to electric energy; it has two electrodes, one of which is raised to a sufficiently high temperature to become a thermionic electron emitter, while the other, serving as an electron collector, is operated at a significantly lower temperature. Also known as thermionic generator; thermionic power generator; thermoelectric engine.

thermionic current Current due to directed movements of thermions, such as the flow of emitted electrons from the cathode to the plate in a thermionic vacuum tube.

thermionic detector A detector using a hot-cathode tube.

thermionic diode A diode electron tube having a heated cathode.

thermionic emission 1. The outflow of electrons into vacuum from a heated electric conductor. Also known as Edison effect; Richardson effect. 2. More broadly, the liberation of electrons or ions from a substance as a result of heat.

thermionic fuel cell A thermionic converter in which the space between the electrodes is filled with cesium or other gas, which lowers the work functions of the electrodes, and creates an ionized atmosphere, controlling the electron space charge.

thermionic generator *See* thermionic converter.

thermionic power generator *See* thermionic converter.

thermionics The study and applications of thermionic emission.

thermionic triode A three-electrode thermionic tube, containing an anode, a cathode, and a control electrode.

thermionic tube An electron tube that relies upon thermally emitted electrons from a heated cathode for tube current. Also known as hot-cathode tube.

thermionic work function Energy required to transfer an electron from the fermi energy in a given metal through the surface to the vacuum just outside the metal.

thermistor A resistive circuit component, having a high negative temperature coefficient of resistance, so that its resistance decreases as the temperature increases; it is a stable, compact, and rugged two-terminal ceramiclike semiconductor bead, rod, or disk. Derived from thermal resistor.

thermocouple converter *See* thermal converter.

thermoelectric converter A converter that changes solar or other heat energy to electric energy; used as a power source on spacecraft.

thermoelectric engine *See* thermionic converter.

thermoelectric generator *See* thermal converter.

thermoelectric junction *See* thermojunction.

thermoelectric material A material that can be used to convert thermal energy into electric energy or provide refrigeration directly from electric energy; good thermoelectric materials include lead telluride, germanium telluride, bismuth telluride, and cesium sulfide.

thermoelectric power generator See thermal converter.

thermoelectric solar cell A solar cell in which the sun's energy is first converted into heat by a sheet of metal, and the heat is converted into electricity by a semiconductor material sandwiched between the first metal sheet and a metal collector sheet.

thermoelectron An electron liberated by heat, as from a heated filament. Also known as negative thermion.

thermoelement See thermal converter.

thermojunction One of the surfaces of contact between the two conductors of a thermocouple. Also known as thermoelectric junction.

thermomigration A technique for doping semiconductors in which exact amounts of known impurities are made to migrate from the cool side of a wafer of pure semiconductor material to the hotter side when the wafer is heated in an oven.

thermoplastic recording A recording process in which a modulated electron beam deposits charges on a thermoplastic film, and application of heat by radio-frequency heating electrodes softens the film enough to produce deformation that is proportional to the density of the stored electrostatic charges; an optical system is used for playback.

thick-film circuit A microcircuit in which passive components, of a ceramic-metal composition, are formed on a ceramic substrate by successive screen-printing and firing processes, and discrete active elements are attached separately.

thin film A film a few molecules thick deposited on a glass, ceramic, or semiconductor substrate to form a capacitor, resistor, coil, cryotron, or other circuit component.

thin-film circuit A circuit in which the passive components and conductors are produced as films on a substrate by evaporation or sputtering; active components may be similarly produced or mounted separately.

thin-film cryotron A cryotron in which the transition from superconducting to normal resistivity of a thin film of tin or indium, serving as a gate, is controlled by current in a film of lead that crosses and is insulated from the gate.

thin-film integrated circuit An integrated circuit consisting entirely of thin films deposited in a patterned relationship on a substrate.

thin-film material A material that can be deposited as a thin film in a desired pattern by a variety of chemical, mechanical, or high-vacuum evaporation techniques.

thin-film memory See thin-film storage.

thin-film semiconductor Semiconductor produced by the deposition of an appropriate single-crystal layer on a suitable insulator.

thin-film solar cell A solar cell in which a thin film of gallium arsenide, cadmium sulfide, or other semiconductor material is evaporated on a thin, flexible metal or plastic substrate; the rather low efficiency (about 2%) is compensated by the flexibility and light weight, making these cells attractive as power sources for spacecraft.

thin-film storage A high-speed storage device that is fabricated by depositing layers, one molecule thick, of various materials which, after etching, provide microscopic circuits which can move and store data in small amounts of time. Also known as thin-film memory.

thin-film transistor A field-effect transistor constructed entirely by thin-film techniques, for use in thin-film circuits.

thin list See loose list.

thin magnetic film A data storage device consisting of a thin magnetic film of Permalloy deposited by vacuum evaporation or electrochemical deposition.

third-generation computer One of the general purpose digital computers introduced in the late 1960s; it is characterized by integrated circuits and has logical organization and software which permit the computer to handle many programs at the same time, allow one to add or remove units from the computer, permit some or all input/output operations to occur at sites remote from the main processor, and allow conversational programming techniques.

thoriated emitter *See* thoriated tungsten filament.

thoriated tungsten filament A vacuum-tube filament consisting of tungsten mixed with a small quantity of thorium oxide to give improved electron emission. Also known as thoriated emitter.

thrashing An undesirable condition in a multiprogramming system, due to overcommitment of main memory, in which the various tasks compete for pages and none can operate efficiently.

three-address code In computers, a multiple-address code which includes three addresses, usually two addresses from which data are taken and one address where the result is entered; location of the next instruction is not specified, and instructions are taken from storage in preassigned order.

three-address instruction In computers, an instruction which includes an operation and specifies the location of three registers.

three-dimensional display system A radar display which shows range, azimuth, and elevation; for instance, a G display.

three-input subtracter *See* full subtracter.

three-junction transistor A *pnpn* transistor having three junctions and four regions of alternating conductivity; the emitter connection may be made to the *p* region at the left, the base connection to the adjacent *n* region, and the collector connection to the *n* region at the right, while the remaining *p* region is allowed to float.

three-layer diode A junction diode with three conductivity regions.

three-level subroutine A subroutine in which a second subroutine is called, and a third subroutine is called by the second subroutine.

three-phase magnetic amplifier A magnetic amplifier whose input is the sum of three alternating-current voltages that differ in phase by 120°.

three-plus-one address An instruction format containing an operation code, three operand address parts, and a control address.

three-pulse cascaded canceler A moving-target indicator technique in which two "two-pulse cancelers" are cascaded together; this improves the velocity response.

threshold In a modulation system, the smallest value of carrier-to-noise ratio at the input to the demodulator for all values above which a small percentage change in the input carrier-to-noise ratio produces a substantially equal or smaller percentage change in the output signal-to-noise ratio.

threshold element A logic circuit which has one output and several weighted inputs, and whose output is energized if and only if the sum of the weights of the energized inputs exceeds a prescribed threshold value.

threshold frequency The frequency of incident radiant energy below which there is no photoemissive effect.

threshold switch A voltage-sensitive alternating-current switch made from a semiconductor material deposited on a metal substrate; when the alternating-current voltage acting on the switch is increased above the threshold value, the number of free carriers present in the semiconductor material increases suddenly, and the switch changes from a high resistance of about 10 megohms to a low resistance of less than 1 ohm; in other versions of this switch, the threshold voltage is controlled by heat, pressure, light, or moisture.

threshold voltage 1. In general, the voltage at which a particular characteristic of an electronic device first appears. 2. The voltage at which conduction of current begins in a *pn* junction. **3.** The voltage at which channel formation occurs in a metal oxide semiconductor field-effect transistor. **4.** The voltage at which a solid-state lamp begins to emit light.

throughput The productivity of a data-processing system, as expressed in computing work per minute or hour.

through repeater Microwave repeater that is not equipped to provide for connections to any local facilities other than the service channel.

thunk An additional subprogram created by the compiler to represent the evaluation of the argument of an expression in the call-by-name procedure.

thyratron A hot-cathode gas tube in which one or more control electrodes initiate but do not limit the anode current except under certain operating conditions. Also known as hot-cathode gas-filled tube.

thyratron gate In computers, an AND gate consisting of a multielement gas-filled tube in which conduction is initiated by the coincident application of two or more signals; conduction may continue after one or more of the initiating signals are removed.

thyratron inverter An inverter circuit that uses thyratrons to convert direct-current power to alternating-current power.

thyrector Silicon diode that acts as an insulator up to its rated voltage, and as a conductor above rated voltage; used for alternating-current surge voltage protection.

thyristor A transistor having a thyratronlike characteristic; as collector current is increased to a critical value, the alpha of the unit rises above unity to give high-speed triggering action.

tick A time interval equal to 1/60 second, used primarily in discussing computer operations.

ticket converting The process of changing prepunched ticket stubs, 2.7 inches (6.9 centimeters) wide by 1 inch (2.5 centimeters) deep, into punched cards; the ticket is made up of a basic section and one or more stubs that are numerically prepunched and printed with identical information.

tickler coil Small coil connected in series with the plate circuit of an electron tube and inductively coupled to a grid-circuit coil to establish feedback or regeneration in a radio circuit; used chiefly in regenerative detector circuits.

time base A device which moves the fluorescent spot rhythmically across the screen of the cathode-ray tube.

time-base generator *See* sweep generator.

time-code generator A crystal-controlled pulse generator that produces a train of pulses with various predetermined widths and spacings, from which the time of day and sometimes also day of year can be determined; used in telemetry and other data-acquisition systems to provide the precise time of each event.

time-delay circuit A circuit in which the output signal is delayed by a specified time interval with respect to the input signal. Also known as delay circuit.

time-division multiplexing The interleaving of bits or characters in time to compensate for the slowness of input devices as compared to data transmission lines.

time-division multiplier *See* mark-space multiplier.

time-division switching system A type of electronic switching system in which input signals on lines and trunks are sampled periodically, and each active input is associated with the desired output for a specific phase of the period.

time-domain reflectometer An instrument that measures the electrical characteristics of wideband transmission systems, subassemblies, components, and lines by feeding in a voltage step and displaying the superimposed reflected signals on an oscilloscope equipped with a suitable time-base sweep. Abbreviated TDR.

time factor *See* time scale.

time gate A circuit that gives an output only during chosen time intervals.

time-height section A facsimile trace of a vertically directed radar; specifically, a cloud-detection radar.

time-mark generator A signal generator that produces highly accurate clock pulses which can be superimposed as pips on a cathode-ray screen for timing the events shown on the display.

time-of-day clock An electronic device that registers the actual time, generally accurate to 0.1 second, through a 24-hour cycle, and transmits its reading to the central processing unit of a computer upon demand.

time-pulse distributor A device or circuit for allocating timing pulses or clock pulses to one or more conducting paths or control lines in specified sequence.

time quantum *See* time slice.

timer A circuit used in radar and in electronic navigation systems to start pulse transmission and synchronize it with other actions, such as the start of a cathode-ray sweep.

timer clock An electronic device in the central processing unit of a computer which times events that occur during the operation of the system in order to carry out such functions as changing computer time, detecting looping and similar error conditions, and keeping a log of operations.

time redundancy Performing a computation more than once and checking the results in order to increase reliability.

time scale The ratio of the time duration of an event as simulated by an analog computer to the actual time duration of the event in the physical system under study. Also known as time factor.

time-share To perform several independent processes almost simultaneously by interleaving the operations of the processes on a single high-speed processor.

time-shared amplifier An amplifier used with a synchronous switch to amplify signals from different sources one after another.

time-sharing The simultaneous utilization of a computer system from multiple terminals.

time slice A time interval during which a time-sharing system is processing one particular computer program. Also known as time quantum.

timing-axis oscillator *See* sweep generator.

timing error An error made in planning or writing a computer program, usually in underestimating the time that will be taken by input/output or other operations, which causes unnecessary delays in the execution of the program.

timing signal Any signal recorded simultaneously with data on magnetic tape for use in identifying the exact time of each recorded event.

tip A small protuberance on the envelope of an electron tube, resulting from the closing of the envelope after evacuation.

T junction A network of waveguides with three waveguide terminals arranged in the form of a letter T; in a rectangular waveguide a symmetrical T junction is arranged by having either all three broadsides in one plane or two broadsides in one plane and the third in a perpendicular plane.

T²L *See* transistor-transistor logic.

toggle To switch over to an alternate state, as in a flip-flop.

toggle condition Condition of a flip-flop circuit in which the internal state of the flip-flop changes from 0 to 1 or from 1 to 0.

toggle switch 1. An electronically operated circuit that holds either of two states until changed. **2.** Interconnection between stages of an amplifier which employs a transformer for connecting the plate circuit of one stage to the grid circuit of the following stage; a special case of inductive coupling.

token A distinguishable unit in a sequence of characters.

tomography *See* sectional radiography.

tone control A control used in an audio-frequency amplifier to change the frequency response so as to secure the most pleasing proportion of bass to treble; individual bass and treble controls are provided in some amplifiers.

tone dialing *See* push-button dialing.

tone generator A signal generator used to generate an audio-frequency signal suitable for signaling purposes or for testing audio-frequency equipment.

Tonotron Trademark for a type of direct-view storage tube.

top-down analysis A predictive method of syntactic analysis which, starting from the root symbol, attempts to predict the means by which a string was generated.

tornadotron Millimeter-wave device which generates radio-frequency power from an enclosed, orbiting electron cloud, excited by a radio-frequency field, when subjected to a strong, pulsed magnetic field.

torque amplifier An analog computer device having input and output shafts and supplying work to rotate the output shaft in positional correspondence with the input shaft without imposing any significant torque on the input shaft.

torsional mode delay line A device in which torsional vibrations are propagated through a solid material to make use of the propagation time of the vibrations to obtain a time delay for the signals.

TOS *See* tape operating system.

total deadlock A deadlock that involves all the tasks in a multiprogramming system.

total harmonic distortion Ratio of the power at the fundamental frequency, measured at the output of the transmission system considered, to the power of all harmonics observed at the output of the system because of its nonlinearity, when a single frequency signal of specified power is applied to the input of the system; it is expressed in decibels.

total transfer A method of calculating minor, intermediate, and major control totals during preparation of printed results on a punched-card tabulator, in which only minor totals are calculated by adding values in card fields, while intermediate totals are calculated by adding minor totals, and major totals are calculated by adding intermediate totals.

touch call *See* push-button dialing.

Townsend avalanche *See* avalanche.

Townsend characteristic Current-voltage characteristic curve for a phototube at constant illumination and at voltages below that at which a glow discharge occurs.

Townsend coefficient The number of ionizing collisions by an electron per centimeter of path length in the direction of the applied electric field in a radiation counter.

Townsend discharge A discharge which occurs at voltages too low for it to be maintained by the electric field alone, and which must be initiated and sustained by ionization produced by other agents; it occurs at moderate pressures, above about 0.1 torr, and is free of space charges.

Townsend ionization *See* avalanche.

TP monitor *See* teleprocessing monitor.

trace 1. To provide a record of every step, or selected steps, executed by a computer program, and by extension, the record produced by this operation. 2. The visible path of a moving spot on the screen of a cathode-ray tube. Also known as line.

trace interval Interval corresponding to the direction of sweep used for delineation.

trace routine A routine which tracks the execution of a program, step by step, to locate a program malfunction. Also known as tracing routine.

trace sensitivity The ability of an oscilloscope to produce a visible trace on the scope face for a specified input voltage.

trace statement A statement, included in certain programming languages, that causes certain error-checking procedures to be carried out on specified segments of a source program.

tracing routine *See* trace routine.

track 1. The recording path on a rotating surface. 2. A path for recording one channel of information on a magnetic tape, drum, or other magnetic recording medium; the location of the track is determined by the recording equipment rather than by the medium. 3. The trace of a moving target on a plan-position-indicator radar screen or an equivalent plot.

trackball A ball inset in the console of a video display terminal, which can be rotated by the operator, and whose motion is followed by a cursor on the display screen.

tracking The condition in which all tuned circuits in a receiver accurately follow the frequency indicated by the tuning dial over the entire tuning range.

tracking cross A cross displayed on the screen of a video terminal which automatically follows a light pen. Also known as tracking cursor.

tracking cursor *See* tracking cross.

tracking filter Electronic device for attenuating unwanted signals while passing desired signals, by phase-lock techniques that reduce the effective bandwidth of the circuit and eliminate amplitude variations.

track in range To adjust the gate of a radar set so that it opens at the correct instant to accept the signal from a target of changing range from the radar.

track pitch The physical distance between track centers.

track-to-track access time The time required for a read-write head to move between the adjacent cylinders of a disk.

track-while-scan Electronic system used to detect a radar target, compute its velocity, and predict its future position without interfering with continuous radar scanning.

trailer A bright streak at the right of a dark area or dark line in a television picture, or a dark area or streak at the right of a bright part; usually due to insufficient gain at low video frequencies.

trailer card A card that contains supplemental information related to the data on the preceding cards.

trailer label A record appearing at the end of a magnetic tape that uniquely identifies the tape as one required by the system.

trailer record A record which contains data pertaining to an associated group of records immediately preceding it.

trailing edge The major portion of the decay of a pulse.

trainer A piece of equipment used for training operators of radar, sonar, and other electronic equipment by simulating signals received under operating conditions in the field.

training time The machine time expended in training employees in the use of the equipment, including such activities as mounting, console operation, converter operation, and printing operation, and time spent in conducting required demonstrations.

transacter A system in which data from sources in a number of different locations, as in a factory, are transmitted to a data-processing center and immediately processed by a computer.

transaction General description of updating data relevant to any item.

transaction data A set of data in a data-processing area in which the incidence of the data is essentially random and unpredictable; hours worked, quantities shipped, and amounts invoiced are examples from, respectively, the areas of payroll, accounts receivable, and accounts payable.

transaction file *See* detail file.

transaction processing system A system which processes predefined transactions, one at a time, with direct, on-site entry of the transactions into a terminal, and which produces predefined outputs and maintains the necessary data base.

transaction record *See* change record.

transaction tape *See* change tape.

transadmittance A specific measure of transfer admittance under a given set of conditions, as in forward transadmittance, interelectrode transadmittance, short-circuit transadmittance, small-signal forward transadmittance, and transadmittance compression ratio.

transceiver 1. A device which transmits and receives data from punch card to punch card; it is essentially a conversion device which at the sending end reads the card and transmits the data over the wire, and at the receiving end punches the data into a card. 2. A radio transmitter and receiver combined in one unit and having switching arrangements such as to permit use of one or more tubes for both transmitting and receiving. Also known as transmitter-receiver.

transceiver data link Integrated data processing by means of punched cards, using transceivers as terminal equipment; the transmission path can be wire or radio.

transconductance An electron-tube rating, equal to the change in plate current divided by the change in control-grid voltage that causes it, when the plate voltage and all other voltages are maintained constant. Also known as grid-anode transconductance; grid-plate transconductance; mutual conductance. Symbolized G_m; g_m.

transcribe 1. To copy, with or without translating, from one external computer storage medium to another. 2. To record, as to record a radio program by means of electric transcriptions or magnetic tape for future rebroadcasting.

transcriber The equipment used to convert information from one form to another, as for converting computer input data to the medium and language used by the computer.

transducer loss The ratio of the power available to a transducer from a specified source to the power that the transducer delivers to a specified load; usually expressed in decibels.

transductor *See* magnetic amplifier.

transfer *See* jump.

transfer admittance An admittance rating for electron tubes and other transducers or networks; it is equal to the complex alternating component of current flowing to one terminal from its external termination, divided by the complex alternating component of the voltage applied to the adjacent terminal on the cathode or reference side; all other terminals have arbitrary external terminations.

transfer card *See* transition card.

transfer characteristic 1. Relation, usually shown by a graph, between the voltage of one electrode and the current to another electrode, with all other electrode voltages being maintained constant. **2.** Function which, multiplied by an input magnitude, will give a resulting output magnitude. **3.** Relation between the illumination on a camera tube and the corresponding output-signal current, under specified conditions of illumination.

transfer check Check (usually automatic) on the accuracy of the transfer of a word in a computer operation.

transfer conditionally To copy, exchange, read, record, store, transmit, or write data or to change control or jump to another location according to a certain specified rule or in accordance with a certain criterion.

transfer-in-channel command A command used to direct channel control to a specified location in main storage when the next channel command word is not stored in the next location in sequence.

transfer instruction Step in computer operation specifying the next operation to be performed, which is not necessarily the next instruction in sequence.

transfer interpreter A variation of a punched-card interpreter that senses a punched card and prints the punched information on the following card. Also known as posting interpreter.

transfer operation An operation which moves information from one storage location or one storage medium to another (for example, read, record, copy, transmit, exchange).

transfer rate The speed at which data are moved from a direct-access device to a central processing unit.

transferred-electron amplifier A diode amplifier, which generally uses a transferred-electron diode made from doped n-type gallium arsenide, that provides amplification in the gigahertz range to well over 50 gigahertz at power outputs typically below 1 watt continuous-wave. Abbreviated TEA.

transferred-electron device A semiconductor device, usually a diode, that depends on internal negative resistance caused by transferred electrons in gallium arsenide or indium phosphide at high electric fields; transit time is minimized, permitting oscillation at frequencies up to several hundred megahertz.

transferred-electron effect The variation in the effective drift mobility of charge carriers in a semiconductor when significant numbers of electrons are transferred from a low-mobility valley of the conduction band in a zone to a high-mobility valley, or vice versa.

transform To change the form of digital-computer information without significantly altering its meaning.

transformer-coupled amplifier Audio-frequency amplifier that uses untuned iron-core transformers to provide coupling between stages.

transformer coupling Interconnection between stages of an amplifier which employs a transformer for connecting the plate circuit of one stage to the grid circuit of the following stage; a special case of inductive coupling.

transformer read-only store In computers, read-only store in which the presence or absence of mutual inductance between two circuits determines whether a binary 1 or 0 is stored.

transient analyzer An analyzer that generates transients in the form of a succession of equal electric surges of small amplitude and adjustable waveform, applies these transients to a circuit or device under test, and shows the resulting output waveforms on the screen of an oscilloscope.

transient distortion Distortion due to inability to amplify transients linearly.

transient suppressor *See* surge suppressor.

transistance The characteristic that makes possible the control of voltages or currents so as to accomplish gain or switching action in a circuit; examples of transistance occur in transistors, diodes, and saturable reactors.

transistor An active component of an electronic circuit consisting of a small block of semiconducting material to which at least three electrical contacts are made, usually two closely spaced rectifying contacts and one ohmic (nonrectifying) contact; it may be used as an amplifier, detector, or switch.

transistor amplifier An amplifier in which one or more transistors provide amplification comparable to that of electron tubes.

transistor biasing Maintaining a direct-current voltage between the base and some other element of a transistor.

transistor characteristics The values of the impedances and gains of a transistor.

transistor chip An unencapsulated transistor of very small size used in microcircuits.

transistor circuit An electric circuit in which a transistor is connected.

transistor clipping circuit A circuit in which a transistor is used to achieve clipping action; the bias at the input is set at such a level that output current cannot flow during a portion of the amplitude excursion of the input voltage or current waveform.

transistor gain The increase in signal power produced by a transistor.

transistor input resistance The resistance across the input terminals of a transistor stage. Also known as input resistance.

transistor magnetic amplifier A magnetic amplifier together with a transistor preamplifier, the latter used to make the signal strong enough to change the flux in the core of the magnetic amplifier completely during a half-cycle of the power supply voltage.

transistor memory *See* semiconductor memory.

transistor radio A radio receiver in which transistors are used in place of electron tubes.

transistor-transistor logic A logic circuit containing two transistors, for driving large output capacitances at high speed. Abbreviated T^2L; TTL.

transition card In reading a deck of punched cards by a computer, a card that causes the computer to stop reading cards and begin executing a program. Also known as transfer card.

transition function A function which determines the next state of a sequential machine from the present state and the present input.

transition region The region between two homogeneous semiconductors in which the impurity concentration changes.

transitron Thermionic-tube circuit whose action depends on the negative transconductance of the suppressor grid of a pentode with respect to the screen grid.

transitron oscillator A negative-resistance oscillator in which the screen grid is more positive than the anode, and a capacitor is connected between the screen grid and the suppressor grid; the suppressor grid periodically divides the current between the screen grid and the anode, thereby producing oscillation.

transit time The time required for an electron or other charge carrier to travel between two electrodes in an electron tube or transistor.

transit-time microwave diode A solid-state microwave diode in which the transit time of charge carriers is short enough to permit operation in microwave bands.

transit-time mode One of the three operating modes of a transferred-electron diode, in which space-charge domains are formed at the cathode and travel across the drift region to the anode.

translate To convert computer information from one language to another, or to convert characters from one representation set to another, and by extension, the computer instruction which directs the latter conversion to be carried out.

translating circuit *See* translator.

translation algorithm A specific, effective, essentially computational method for obtaining a translation from one language to another.

translator **1.** A computer network or system having a number of inputs and outputs, so connected that when signals representing information expressed in a certain code are applied to the inputs, the output signals will represent the same information in a different code. Also known as translating circuit. **2.** A combination television receiver and low-power television transmitter, used to pick up television signals on one frequency and retransmit them on another frequency to provide reception in areas not served directly by television stations.

translator routine A program which accepts statements in one language and outputs them as statements in another language.

transliterate To represent the characters or words of one language by corresponding characters or words of another language.

transmission **1.** The process of transferring a signal, message, picture, or other form of intelligence from one location to another location by means of wire lines, radio, light beams, infrared beams, or other communication systems. **2.** A message, signal, or other form of intelligence that is being transmitted.

transmission electron microscope A type of electron microscope in which the specimen transmits an electron beam focused on it, image contrasts are formed by the scattering of electrons out of the beam, and various magnetic lenses perform functions analogous to those of ordinary lenses in a light microscope.

transmission electron radiography A technique used in microradiography to obtain radiographic images of very thin specimens; the photographic plate is in close contact with the specimen, over which is placed a lead foil and then a light-tight covering; hardened x-rays shoot through the light-tight covering.

transmission gain *See* gain.

transmission gate A gate circuit that delivers an output waveform that is a replica of a selected input during a specific time interval which is determined by a control signal.

transmission interface converter A device that converts data to or from a form suitable for transfer over a channel connecting two computer systems or connecting a computer with its associated data terminals.

transmission modulation Amplitude modulation of the reading-beam current in a charge storage tube as the beam passes through apertures in the storage surface; the degree of modulation is controlled by the stored charge pattern.

transmission regulator In electrical communications, a device that maintains substantially constant transmission levels over a system.

transmit To move data from one location to another.

transmit-receive tube A gas-filled radio-frequency switching tube used to disconnect a receiver from its antenna during the interval for pulse transmission in radar and other pulsed radio-frequency systems. Also known as TR box; TR cell (British usage); TR switch; TR tube.

transmitter *See* radio transmitter.

transmitter-receiver *See* transceiver.

transmitting mode Condition of an input/output device, such as a magnetic tape when it is actually reading or writing.

transponder dead time Time interval between the start of a pulse and the earliest instant at which a new pulse can be received or produced by a transponder.

transponder set A complete electronic set which is designed to receive an interrogation signal, and which retransmits coded signals that can be interpreted by the interrogating station; it may also utilize the received signal for actuation of additional equipment such as local indicators or servo amplifiers.

transponder suppressed time delay Overall fixed time delay between reception of an interrogation and transmission of a reply to this interrogation.

transport 1. To convey as a whole from one storage device to another in a digital computer. **2.** *See* tape transport.

transport delay unit A device used in analog computers which produces an output signal as a delayed form of an input signal. Also known as delay unit; transport unit.

transport unit *See* transport delay unit.

transrectification characteristic Graph obtained by plotting the direct-voltage values for one electrode of a vacuum tube as abscissas against the average current values in the circuit of that electrode as ordinates, for various values of alternating voltage applied to another electrode as a parameter; the alternating voltage is held constant for each curve, and the voltages on other electrodes are maintained constant.

transrectifier Device, ordinarily a vacuum tube, in which rectification occurs in one electrode circuit when an alternating voltage is applied to another electrode.

transverse recording Technique for recording television signals on magnetic tape using a four-transducer rotating head.

trap 1. An automatic transfer of control of a computer to a known location, this transfer occurring when a specified condition is detected by hardware. **2.** A tuned circuit used in the radio-frequency or intermediate-frequency section of a receiver to reject undesired frequencies; traps in television receiver video circuits keep the sound signal out of the picture channel. Also known as rejector. **3.** Any irregularity, such as a vacancy, in a semiconductor at which an electron or hole in the conduction band can be caught and trapped until released by thermal agitation. Also known as semiconductor trap. **4.** *See* wave trap.

trap address The location at which control is transferred in case of an interrupt as soon as the current instruction is completed.

TRAPATT diode A *pn* junction diode, similar to the IMPATT diode, but characterized by the formation of a trapped space-charge plasma within the junction region; used in the generation and amplification of microwave power. Derived from trapped plasma avalanche transit time diode.

trapezoidal generator Electronic stage designed to produce a trapezoidal voltage wave.

trapezoidal pulse An electrical pulse in which the voltage rises linearly to some value, remains constant at this value for some time, and then drops linearly to the original value.

trapezoidal wave A wave consisting of a series of trapezoidal pulses.

trapped plasma avalanche transit time diode *See* TRAPATT diode.

trapping mode A procedure by means of which the computer, upon encountering a predetermined set of conditions, saves the program in its present status, executes a diagnostic procedure, and then resumes the processing of the program as of the moment of interruption.

traveling-wave amplifier An amplifier that uses one or more traveling-wave tubes to provide useful amplification of signals at frequencies of the order of thousands of megahertz.

traveling-wave magnetron A traveling-wave tube in which the electrons move in crossed static electric and magnetic fields that are substantially normal to the direction of wave propagation, as in practically all modern magnetrons.

traveling-wave magnetron oscillations Oscillations sustained by the interaction between the space-charge cloud of a magnetron and a traveling electromagnetic field whose phase velocity is approximately the same as the mean velocity of the cloud.

traveling-wave parametric amplifier Parametric amplifier which has a continuous or iterated structure incorporating nonlinear reactors and in which the signal, pump, and difference-frequency waves are propagated along the structure.

traveling-wave phototube A traveling-wave tube having a photocathode and an appropriate window to admit a modulated laser beam; the modulated laser beam causes emission of a current-modulated photoelectron beam, which in turn is accelerated by an electron gun and directed into the helical slow-wave structure of the tube.

traveling-wave tube An electron tube in which a stream of electrons interacts continuously or repeatedly with a guided electromagnetic wave moving substantially in synchronism with it, in such a way that there is a net transfer of energy from the stream to the wave; the tube is used as an amplifier or oscillator at frequencies in the microwave region.

TR box *See* transmit-receive tube.

TR cell *See* transmit-receive tube.

tree A set of connected circuit branches that includes no meshes; responds uniquely to each of the possible combinations of a number of simultaneous inputs. Also known as decoder.

tree automaton An automaton that processes inputs in the form of trees, usually trees associated with parsing expressions in context-free languages.

tree diagram A flow diagram which has no closed paths.

tree pruning A strategy for eliminating branches of the complete game tree associated with a given position in a game such as chess or checkers, creating subtrees that explore a limited number of continuations for a limited number of moves.

TRF receiver *See* tuned-radio-frequency receiver.

triad 1. A group of three bits, pulses, or characters forming a unit of data. 2. A triangular group of three small phosphor dots, each emitting one of the three primary colors on the screen of a three-gun color picture tube.

triangular pulse An electrical pulse in which the voltage rises linearly to some value, and immediately falls linearly to the original value.

triangular wave A wave consisting of a series of triangular pulses.

trickling The temporary transfer of momentarily unneeded data from main storage to secondary storage devices.

tricolor picture tube *See* color picture tube.

trigatron Gas-filled, spark-gap switch used in line pulse modulators.

trigger 1. To execute a jump to the first instruction of a program after the program has been loaded into the computer. Also known as initiate. 2. To initiate an action, which then continues for a period of time, as by applying a pulse to a trigger circuit. 3. The pulse used to initiate the action of a trigger circuit. 4. *See* trigger circuit.

trigger action Use of a weak input pulse to initiate main current flow suddenly in a circuit or device.

trigger circuit 1. A circuit or network in which the output changes abruptly with an infinitesimal change in input at a predetermined operating point. Also known as trigger. 2. A circuit in which an action is initiated by an input pulse, as in a radar modulator. 3. *See* bistable multivibrator.

trigger control Control of thyratrons, ignitrons, and other gas tubes in such a way that current flow may be started or stopped, but not regulated as to rate.

trigger diode A symmetrical three-layer avalanche diode used in activating silicon-controlled rectifiers; it has a symmetrical switching mode, and hence fires whenever the breakover voltage is exceeded in either polarity. Also known as diode alternating-current switch (diac).

trigger electrode *See* starter.

triggering Phenomenon observed in some high-performance magnetic amplifiers with very low leakage rectifiers; as the input current is decreased in magnitude, the amplifier remains at cutoff for some time, and the output then suddenly shoots upward.

triggor lovol In a transponder, the minimum input to the receiver which is capable of causing a transmitter to emit a reply.

trigger pulse A pulse that starts a cycle of operation. Also known as tripping pulse.

trigger tube A cold-cathode gas-filled tube in which one or more auxiliary electrodes initiate the anode current but do not control it.

trigistor A *pnpn* device with a gating control acting as a fast-acting switch similar in nature to a thyratron.

trim Fine adjustment of capacitance, inductance, or resistance of a component during manufacture or after installation in a circuit.

triode A three-electrode electron tube containing an anode, a cathode, and a control electrode.

triode clamp A keyed clamp circuit utilizing triodes, such as a circuit which contains a complementary pair of bipolar transistors.

triode clipping circuit A clipping circuit that utilizes a transistor or vacuum triode.

triode laser Gas laser whose light output may be modulated by signal voltages applied to an integral grid.

triode transistor A transistor that has three terminals.

triple-conversion receiver Communications receiver having three different intermediate frequencies to give higher adjacent-channel selectivity and greater image-frequency suppression.

triple-length working Processing of data by a computer in which three machine words are used to represent each data item, in order to achieve the desired precision in the results.

triple modular redundancy A form of redundancy in which the original computer unit is triplicated and each of the three independent units feeds into a majority voter, which outputs the majority signal.

triplexer Dual duplexer that permits the use of two receivers simultaneously and independently in a radar system by disconnecting the receivers during the transmitted pulse.

tripping pulse *See* trigger pulse.

trisistor Fast-switching semiconductor consisting of an alloyed junction *pnp* device in which the collector is capable of electron injection into the base; characteristics resemble those of a thyratron electron tube, and switching time is in the nanosecond range.

tristate logic A form of transistor-transistor logic in which the output stages or input and output stages can assume three states; two are the normal low-impedance 1 and 0 states, and the third is a high-impedance state that allows many tristate devices to time-share bus lines.

tri-tet oscillator Crystal-controlled, electron-coupled, vacuum-tube oscillator circuit which is isolated from the output circuit through use of the screen grid electrode as the oscillator anode; used for multiband operation because it generates strong harmonics of the crystal frequency.

trouble-location problem In computers, a test problem used in a diagnostic routine.

troubleshoot To find and correct errors and faults in a computer, usually in the hardware.

TR switch *See* transmit-receive tube.

TR tube *See* transmit-receive tube.

true-motion radar A radar set which provides a true-motion radar presentation on the plan-position indicator, as opposed to the relative-motion, true-or-relative-bearing, presentation most commonly used.

true-motion radar presentation A radar plan-position indicator presentation in which the center of the scope represents the same geographic position, until reset, with all moving objects, including the user's own craft, moving on the scope.

TTL *See* transistor-transistor logic.

tube *See* electron tube.

tube coefficient Any of the constants that describe the characteristics of a thermionic vacuum tube, such as amplification factor, mutual conductance, or alternating-current plate resistance.

tube heating time Time required for a tube to attain operating temperature.

tube noise Noise originating in a vacuum tube, such as that due to shot effect and thermal agitation.

tube tester A test instrument designed to measure and indicate the condition of electron tubes used in electronic equipment.

tube voltage drop In a gas tube, the anode voltage during the conducting period.

tunable filter An electric filter in which the frequency of the passband or rejection band can be varied by adjusting its components.

tunable magnetron Magnetron which can be tuned mechanically or electronically by varying its capacitance or inductance.

tune To adjust for resonance at a desired frequency.

tuned amplifier An amplifier in which the load is a tuned circuit; load impedance and amplifier gain then vary with frequency.

tuned-anode oscillator A vacuum-tube oscillator whose frequency is determined by a tank circuit in the anode circuit, coupled to the grid to provide the required feedback. Also known as tuned-plate oscillator.

tuned-anode tuned-grid oscillator *See* tuned-grid tuned-anode oscillator.

tuned-base oscillator Transistor oscillator in which the frequency-determining resonant circuit is located in the base circuit; comparable to a tuned-grid oscillator.

tuned circuit A circuit whose components can be adjusted to make the circuit responsive to a particular frequency in a tuning range. Also known as tuning circuit.

tuned-collector oscillator A transistor oscillator in which the frequency-determining resonant circuit is located in the collector circuit; this is comparable to a tuned-anode electron-tube oscillator.

tuned filter Filter that uses one or more tuned circuits to attenuate or pass signals at the resonant frequency.

tuned-grid oscillator Oscillator whose frequency is determined by a parallel-resonant circuit in the grid coupled to the plate to provide the required feedback.

tuned-grid tuned-anode oscillator A vacuum-tube oscillator whose frequency is determined by a tank circuit in the grid circuit, coupled to the anode to provide the required feedback. Also known as tuned-anode tuned-grid oscillator.

tuned-plate oscillator *See* tuned-anode oscillator.

tuned-radio-frequency receiver A radio receiver consisting of a number of amplifier stages that are tuned to resonance at the carrier frequency of the desired signal by a gang capacitor; the amplified signals at the original carrier frequency are fed directly into the detector for demodulation, and the resulting audio-frequency signals are amplified by an a-f amplifier and reproduced by a loudspeaker. Abbreviated TRF receiver.

tuned-radio-frequency transformer Transformer used for selective coupling in radio-frequency stages.

tuner The portion of a receiver that contains circuits which can be tuned to accept the carrier frequency of the alternating current supplied to the primary, thereby causing the secondary voltage to build up to higher values than would otherwise be obtained.

tungar tube A gas tube having a heated thoriated tungsten filament serving as cathode and a graphite disk serving as anode in an argon-filled bulb at a low pressure; used chiefly as a rectifier in battery chargers.

tuning The process of adjusting the inductance or the capacitance or both in a tuned circuit, for example, in a radio, television, or radar receiver or transmitter, so as to obtain optimum performance at a selected frequency.

tuning circuit *See* tuned circuit.

tuning eye *See* cathode-ray tuning indicator.

tuning indicator A device that indicates when a radio receiver is tuned accurately to a radio station, such as a meter or a cathode-ray tuning indicator; it is connected to a circuit having a direct-current voltage that varies with the strength of the incoming carrier signal.

tuning range The frequency range over which a receiver or other piece of equipment can be adjusted by means of a tuning control.

tuning susceptance Normalized susceptance of an anti-transmit-receive tube in its mount due to the deviation of its resonant frequency from the desired resonant frequency.

tunnel diode A heavily doped junction diode that has a negative resistance at very low voltage in the forward bias direction, due to quantum-mechanical tunneling, and a short circuit in the negative bias direction. Also known as Esaki tunnel diode.

tunneling cryotron A low-temperature current-controlled switching device that has two electrodes of superconducting material separated by an insulating film, forming a Josephson junction, and a control line whose currents generate magnetic fields that switch the device between two states characterized by the presence or absence of electrical resistance.

tunnel rectifier Tunnel diode having a relatively low peak-current rating as compared with other tunnel diodes used in memory-circuit applications.

tunnel resistor Resistor in which a thin layer of metal is plated across a tunneling junction, to give the combined characteristics of a tunnel diode and an ordinary resistor.

tunnel triode Transistorlike device in which the emitter-base junction is a tunnel diode and the collector-base junction is a conventional diode.

Turing machine A mathematical idealization of a computing automation similar in some ways to real computing machines; used by mathematicians to define the concept of computability.

turnaround document A document, such as a punch card, that is produced by a computer, can be read by humans, and can be reread into the machine.

turnaround system In character recognition, a system in which the input data to be read have previously been printed by the computer with which the reader is associated; an application is invoice billing and the subsequent recording of payments.

turnaround time The delay between submission of a job for a data-processing system and its completion.

turnkey A complete computer system delivered to a customer in running condition, with all necessary premises, hardware and software equipment, supplies, and operating personnel.

turn-off time The time that is takes a gate circuit to shut off a current.

turn-on time The time that it takes a gate circuit to allow a current to reach its full value.

turret tuner A television tuner having one set of pretuned circuits for each channel, mounted on a drum that is rotated by the channel selector; rotation of the drum connects each set of tuned circuits in turn to the receiver antenna circuit, radio-frequency amplifier, and r-f oscillator.

TV camera scanner In optical character recognition, a device that images an input character onto a sensitive photoconductive target of a camera tube, thereby developing an electric charge pattern on the inner surface of the target; this pattern is then explored by a scanning beam which traces out a rectangular pattern with the result that a waveform is produced which represents the character's most probable identity.

twenty-nine feature A device used on some punched-card machines to represent values from 0 through 29 by a maximum of two punches on a single column; x and y punches represent 10 and 20, and these are added to punches in positions 0 through 9.

twin arithmetic units A feature of some computers where the essential portions of the arithmetic section are virtually duplicated.

twin check Continuous check of computer operation, achieved by the duplication of equipment and automatic comparison of results.

twistor Computer memory element consisting of a helix of a magnetic wire wound under tension at a 45° angle on a short piece of nonmagnetic wire, with a fine-wire solenoid wound over the helix.

two-address code In computers, a code using two-address instructions.

two-address instruction In computers, an instruction which includes an operation and specifies the location of two registers.

two-carrier theory A theory of the conduction properties of a material in bulk or in a rectifying barrier which takes into account the motion of both electrons and holes.

two-dimensional storage A direct-access storage device in which the storage locations assigned to a particular file do not have to be physically adjacent, but instead may be taken from one or more seek areas.

two-gap head One of two separate magnetic tape heads, one for reading and the other for recording data.

two-input subtracter *See* half-subtracter.

two-level subroutine A subroutine in which entry is made to a second, lower-level subroutine.

two-out-of-five code An encoding of the decimal digits using five binary bits and having the property that every code element contains two 1s and three 0s.

two-plus-one address instruction An instruction in a computer program which has two addresses specifying the locations of operands and one address specifying the location in which the result is to be entered.

two-pulse canceler A moving-target indicator canceler which compares the phase variation of two successive pulses received from a target; discriminates against signals with radial velocities which produce a Doppler frequency equal to a multiple of the pulse repetition frequency.

two-quadrant multiplier Of an analog computer, a multiplier in which operation is restricted to a single sign of one input variable only.

two-state Turing machine A variation of a Turing machine in which only two states are allowed, although the number of symbols may be large.

two-symbol Turing machine A variation of a Turing machine in which only two symbols are permitted, although the number of states may be large.

two-wire repeater Repeater that provides for transmission in both directions over a two-wire circuit; in carrier transmission, it usually operates on the principle of frequency separation for the two directions of transmission.

Twystron Very-high-power, hybrid microwave tube, combining the input section of a high-power klystron with the output section of a traveling wave tube, characterized by high operating efficiency and wide bandwidths.

type drum A steel cylinder containing 128 to 144 lateral bands, each band containing the alphabet, the digits 0–9, and the standard set of punctuation marks such as commas and periods, and revolving at high speed; printing is achieved by a hammer facing each band and activated at the right time to cause a character to be printed on the paper flowing between hammers and drum.

type-M carcinotron *See* M-type backward-wave oscillator.

type-O carcinotron *See* O-type backward wave oscillator.

typewriter terminal An electric typewriter combined with an ASCII or other code generator that provides code output for feeding a computer, calculator, or other digital equipment; the terminal also produces hard copy when driven by incoming code signals.

U

U format A record format which the input/output control system treats as completely unknown and unpredictable.

UJT *See* unijunction transistor.

ultra-audion circuit Regenerative detector circuit in which a parallel resonant circuit is connected between the grid and the plate of a vacuum tube, and a variable capacitor is connected between the plate and cathode to control the amount of regeneration.

ultra-audion oscillator Variation of the Colpitts oscillator circuit; the resonant circuit employs a section of transmission line.

ultra-high-frequency tuner A tuner in a television receiver for reception of stations transmitting in the ultra-high-frequency band (channels 14–83); it usually employs continuous tuning.

ultrasonic camera A device which produces a picture display of ultrasonic waves sent through a sample to be inspected or through live tissue; a piezoelectric crystal is used to convert the ultrasonic waves to voltage differences, and the voltage pattern on the crystal modulates the intensity of an electronic beam scanning the crystal; this beam in turn controls the intensity of a beam in a television tube.

ultraviolet lamp A lamp providing a high proportion of ultraviolet radiation, such as various forms of mercury-vapor lamps.

unamplified back bias Degenerative voltage developed across a fast time constant circuit within an amplifier stage itself.

unattended operation An operation in which components in the hardware of a communications terminal or data-processing system operate automatically, allowing handling of signals or data without human intervention.

unattended time Time during which a computer is turned off but is not undergoing maintenance. Also known as unused time.

unblanking pulse Voltage applied to a cathode-ray tube to overcome bias and cause trace to be visible.

unbundling The separate pricing of software products and services from equipment charges.

unconditional Not subject to conditions external to the specific instruction.

unconditional jump A digital-computer instruction that interrupts the normal process of obtaining instructions in an ordered sequence, and specifies the address from which the next instruction must be taken. Also known as unconditional transfer.

unconditional transfer *See* unconditional jump.

underbunching In velocity-modulated electron streams, a condition representing less than the optimum bunching.

underflow The generation of a result whose value is smaller than the smallest quantity that can be represented or stored by a computer.

underpunch A second hole in a card column which is below the original hole in IBM card code.

undisturbed-one output "One" output of a magnetic cell to which no partial-read pulses have been applied since that cell was last selected for writing.

undisturbed-zero output "Zero" output of a magnetic cell to which no partial-write pulses have been applied since that cell was last selected for reading.

unfired tube Condition of a TR, ATR, or pre-TR tube in which there is no radio-frequency glow discharge at either the resonant gap or resonant window.

unidirectional coupler Directional coupler that samples only one direction of transmission.

unidirectional pulses Single polarity pulses which all rise in the same direction.

unidirectional transducer Transducer that measures stimuli in only one direction from a reference zero or rest position. Also known as unilateral transducer.

uniformly accessible storage *See* random-access memory.

unijunction transistor An *n*-type bar of semiconductor with a *p*-type alloy region on one side; connections are made to base contacts at either end of the bar and to the *p*-region. Abbreviated UJT. Formely known as double-base diode; double-base junction diode.

unilateral conductivity Conductivity in only one direction, as in a perfect rectifier.

unilateralization Use of an external feedback circuit in a high-frequency transistor amplifier to prevent undesired oscillation by canceling both the resistive and reactive changes produced in the input circuit by internal voltage feedback; with neutralization, only the reactive changes are canceled.

unilateral transducer *See* unidirectional transducer.

union catalog A merged listing of the contents of two or more catalogs (of libraries, for example).

unipath *See* nonshared control unit.

unipolar machine *See* homopolar generator.

unipolar transistor A transistor that utilizes charge carriers of only one polarity, such as a field-effect transistor.

unipotential cathode *See* indirectly heated cathode.

unipotential electrostatic lens An electrostatic lens in which the focusing is produced by application of a single potential difference; in its simplest form it consists of three apertures of which the outer two are at a common potential, and the central aperture is at a different, generally lower, potential.

unit delay A network whose output is equal to the input delayed by one unit of time.

uniterm A word, symbol, or number used as a description for retrieval of information from a collection; especially, such a description used in a coordinate indexing system.

uniterm system An information retrieval system which uses uniterm cards; cards representing words of interest in a search are selected and compared visually; if identical members are found to appear on the uniterm card undergoing comparison, those numbers represent documents to be examined in connection with the search.

unitor In computers, a device or circuit which performs a function corresponding to the Boolean operation of union.

unit record Any of a collection of records, all of which have the same form and the same data elements.

unit record device Any piece of equipment such as punch card readers, card punch, and line printers.

unit string A string that has only one element.

unity gain bandwidth Measure of the gain-frequency product of an amplifier; unity gain bandwidth is the frequency at which the open-loop gain becomes unity, based on 6 decibels per octave crossing.

universal product code 1. A 10-digit bar code on the outside of a package for electronic scanning at supermarket checkout counters; each digit is represented by the ratio of the widths of adjacent stripes and white areas. 2. The corresponding combinations of binary digits into which the scanned bars are converted for computer processing that provides continuously updated inventory data and printout of the register tape at the checkout counter.

universal receiver *See* ac/dc receiver.

universal Turing machine A Turing machine that can simulate any Turing machine.

univibrator *See* monostable multivibrator.

unloaded Q The Q of a system when there is no external coupling to it.

unloading amplifer Amplifier that is capable of reproducing or amplifying a given voltage signal while drawing negligible current from the voltage source.

unloading circuit In an analog computer, a computing element or combination of computing elements capable of reproducing or amplifying a given voltage signal while drawing negligible current from the voltage source.

unmodified instruction *See* basic instruction.

unpack 1. To recover the individual data items contained in packed data. 2. More specifically, to convert a packed decimal number into individual digits (and sometimes a sign).

unused time *See* unattended time.

unwind In computers, to rearrange and code a sequence of instructions to eliminate red-tape operations.

up-converter Type of parametric amplifier which is characterized by the frequency of the output signal being greater than the frequency of the input signal.

update 1. In computers, to modify an instruction so that the address numbers it contains are increased by a stated amount each time the instruction is performed. 2. To change a record by entering current information; for example, to enter a new address or account number in the record pertaining to an employee or customer. Also known as posting.

upper curtate The upper or top part of a punch card; on a standard card it contains the 11 (or X), 12 (or Y), and 0 punch positions, that is, the zone punch positions.

upper half-power frequency The frequency on an amplifier response curve which is greater than the frequency for peak response and at which the output voltage is $1/\sqrt{2}$ (that is, 0.707) of its midband or other reference value.

up time The time during which equipment is either producing work or is available for productive work.

upward compatibility The ability of a newer or larger computer to accept programs from an older or smaller one.

user Anyone who requires the use of services of a computing system or its products.

user friendly Property of a computer system that is easy to use and sets up an easily understood dialog between the user and the computer.

user group An organization of users of the computers of a particular vendor, which shares information and ideas, and may develop system software and influence vendors to change their products.

user mode The mode of operation exercised by the user programs of a computer system in which there is a class of privileged instructions that is not permitted, since these can be executed only by the operating system or executive system. Also known as slave mode.

utility routine A program or routine of general usefulness, usually not very complicated, and applicable to many jobs or purposes.

utilization ratio The ratio of the effective time on a computer to the total up time.

V

vacancy A defect in the form of an unoccupied lattice position in a crystal.

vacuum diffusion Diffusion of impurities into a semiconductor material in a continuously pumped hard vacuum.

vacuum fluorescent lamp An evacuated display tube in which the anodes are coated with a phosphor that glows when electrons from the cathode strike it, to create a display.

vacuum phototube A phototube that is evacuated to such a degree that its electrical characteristics are essentially unaffected by gaseous ionization; in a gas phototube, some gas is intentionally introduced.

vacuum tube An electron tube evacuated to such a degree that its electrical characteristics are essentially unaffected by the presence of residual gas or vapor.

vacuum-tube amplifier An amplifier employing one or more vacuum tubes to control the power obtained from a local source.

vacuum-tube circuit An electric circuit in which a vacuum tube is connected.

vacuum-tube clipping circuit A circuit in which a vacuum tube is used to achieve clipping action; the bias at the input is set at such a level that output current cannot flow during a portion of the amplitude excursion of the input voltage or current waveform.

vacuum-tube electrometer An electrometer in which the ionization current in an ionization chamber is amplified by a special vacuum triode having an input resistance above 10,000 megohms.

vacuum-tube keying Code-transmitter keying system in which a vacuum tube is connected in series with the plate supply lead of a frequency-controlling stage of the transmitter; when the key is open, the tube blocks, interrupting the plate supply to the output stage; closing the key allows the plate current to flow through the keying tube and the output tubes.

vacuum-tube modulator A modulator employing a vacuum tube as a modulating element for impressing an intelligence signal on a carrier.

vacuum-tube oscillator A circuit utilizing a vacuum tube to convert direct-current power into alternating-current power at a desired frequency.

vacuum-tube rectifier A rectifier in which rectification is accomplished by the unidirectional passage of electrons from a heated electrode to one or more other electrodes within an evacuated space.

valence band The highest electronic energy band in a semiconductor or insulator which can be filled with electrons.

valence electron *See* conduction electron.

validation   The act of testing for compliance with a standard.

validity check   Computer check of input data, based on known limits for variables in given fields.

valid program   A computer program whose statements, individually and together, follow the syntactical rules of the programming language in which it is written, so that they are capable of being translated into a machine language program.

valley attenuation   For an electric filter with an equal ripple characteristic, the maximum attenuation occurring at a frequency between two frequencies where the attenuation reaches a minimum value.

valve   *See* electron tube.

Van de Graaff accelerator   A Van de Graaff generator equipped with an evacuated tube through which charged particles may be accelerated.

Van de Graaff generator   A high-voltage electrostatic generator in which electrical charge is carried from ground to a high-voltage terminal by means of an insulating belt and is discharged onto a large, hollow metal electrode.

Van der Pol oscillator   A type of relaxation oscillator which has a single pentode tube and an external circuit with a capacitance that causes the device to switch between two values of the screen voltage.

vane-anode magnetron   Cavity magnetron in which the walls between adjacent cavities have parallel plane surfaces.

vapor lamp   *See* discharge lamp.

varactor   A semiconductor device characterized by a voltage-sensitive capacitance that resides in the space-charge region at the surface of a semiconductor bounded by an insulating layer. Also known as varactor diode; variable-capacitance diode; varicap; voltage-variable capacitor.

varactor diode   *See* varactor.

varactor tuning   A method of tuning in which varactor diodes are used to vary the capacitance of a tuned circuit.

variable   A data item, or specific area in main memory, that can assume any of a set of values.

variable attenuator   An attenuator for reducing the strength of an alternating-current signal either continuously or in steps, without causing appreciable signal distortion, by maintaining a substantially constant impedance match.

variable-bandwidth filter   An electric filter whose upper and lower cutoff frequencies may be independently selected, so that almost any bandwidth may be obtained; it usually consists of several stages of *RC* filters, each separated by buffer amplifiers; tuning is accomplished by varying the resistance and capacitance values.

variable-block   Pertaining to an arrangement of data in which the number of words or characters in a block can vary, as determined by the programmer.

variable-capacitance diode   *See* varactor.

variable connector   A flow chart symbol representing a sequence connection which is not fixed, but which can be varied by the flow-charted procedure itself; it corresponds to an assigned GO TO in a programming language such as FORTRAN.

variable-cycle operation   An operation that requires a variable number of regularly timed execution cycles for its completion.

variable diode function generator   An improvement of a diode function generator in which fully adjustable potentiometers are used for breakpoint and slope resistances, permitting the programming of analytic, arbitrary, and empirical functions, including inflections. Abbreviated VDFG.

variable field A field of data whose length is allowed to vary within certain specified limits.

variable-length field A data field in which the number of characters varies, the length of the field being stored within the field itself.

variable-length record A data or file format that allows each record to be exactly as long as needed.

variable-mu tube An electron tube in which the amplification factor varies in a predetermined manner with control-grid voltage; this characteristic is achieved by making the spacing of the grid wires vary regularly along the length of the grid, so that a very large negative grid bias is required to block anode current completely. Also known as remote-cutoff tube.

variable point A system of numeration in which the location of the decimal point is indicated by a special character at that position.

variable speech control A method of removing small portions of speech from a tape recording at regular intervals and stretching the remaining sounds to fill the gaps, so that recorded speech can be played back at twice or even 2½ times the original speed without changing pitch and without significant loss of intelligibility. Abbreviated VSC.

variable-speed scanning Scanning method whereby the speed of deflection of the scanning beam in the cathode-ray tube of a television camera is governed by the optical density of the film being scanned.

variable-transconductance circuit A circuit used in four-quadrant multipliers that employs a simple differential transistor pair in which one variable input to the base of one transistor controls the device's gain or transconductance, and one transistor amplifies the other's variable input, applied to the common emitter point, in proportion to the control input.

variable word length A phrase referring to a computer in which the number of characters addressed is not a fixed number but is varied by the data or instruction.

varicap See varactor.

varistor A two-electrode semiconductor device having a voltage-dependent nonlinear resistance; its resistance drops as the applied voltage is increased. Also known as voltage-dependent resistor.

VCO See voltage-controlled oscillator.

VDFG See variable diode function generator.

VDT See display terminal.

vector graphics A computer graphics image-coding technique which codes only the image itself as a series of lines, according to the cartesian coordinates of the lines' origins and terminations.

vector resolver See resolver.

velocity filter Storage tube device which blanks all targets that do not move more than one resolution cell in less than a predetermined number of antenna scans.

velocity-modulated oscillator Oscillator which employs velocity modulation to produce radio-frequency power. Also known as klystron oscillator.

velocity modulation 1. Modulation in which a time variation in velocity is impressed on the electrons of a stream. 2. A television system in which the intensity of the electron beam remains constant throughout a scan, and the velocity of the spot at the screen is varied to produce changes in picture brightness (not in general use).

velocity shaped canceler *See* cascaded feedback canceler.

verb In COBOL, the action indicating part of an unconditional statement.

verification The process of checking the results of one data transcription against the results of another data transcription; both transcriptions usually involve manual operations.

verifier A device for checking card punching semimechanically; it mimics keypunch machine operation, but reads prepunched cards without punching any new holes, and signals if the card does not agree with data entered through the verifier keyboard in some column.

verify To determine whether an operation has been completed correctly, and in particular, to check the accuracy of keypunching by using a verifier.

vernitel Precision device which makes possible the transmission of data with high accuracy over standard frequency modulated-frequency modulated telemetering systems.

versatile automatic test equipment Computer-controlled tester, for missile electronic systems, that troubleshoots faults by deductive logic and isolates them to the plug-in module or component level.

vertical blanking Blanking of a television picture tube during the vertical retrace.

vertical centering control The centering control provided in a television receiver or cathode-ray oscilloscope to shift the position of the entire image vertically in either direction on the screen.

vertical definition *See* vertical resolution.

vertical deflection oscillator The oscillator that produces, under control of the vertical synchronizing signals, the sawtooth voltage waveform that is amplified to feed the vertical deflection coils on the picture tube of a television receiver. Also known as vertical oscillator.

vertical feed A card feed in which punch cards are placed in a hopper and enter and traverse a card track, all in a vertical position.

vertical hold control The hold control that changes the free-running period of the vertical deflection oscillator in a television receiver, so the picture remains steady in the vertical direction.

vertical instruction An instruction in machine language to carry out a single operation or a time-ordered series of a fixed number and type of operation on a single set of operands.

vertical interval reference A reference signal inserted into a television program signal every $1/60$ second, in line 19 of the vertical blanking period between television frames, to provide references for luminance amplitude, black-level amplitude, sync amplitude, chrominance amplitude, and color-burst amplitude and phase. Abbreviated VIR.

vertical linearity control A linearity control that permits narrowing or expanding the height of the image on the upper half of the screen of a television picture tube, to give linearity in the vertical direction so circular objects appear as true circles; usually mounted at the rear of the receiver.

vertical metal oxide semiconductor technology For semiconductor devices, a technology that involves essentially the formation of four diffused layers in silicon and etching of a V-shaped groove to a precisely controlled depth in the layers, followed by deposition of metal over silicon dioxide in the groove to form the gate electrode. Abbreviated VMOS technology.

vertical oscillator *See* vertical deflection oscillator.

vertical resolution The number of distinct horizontal lines, alternately black and white, that can be seen in the reproduced image of a television or facsimile test pattern; it is primarily fixed by the number of horizontal lines used in scanning. Also known as vertical definition.

vertical retrace The return of the electron beam to the top of the screen at the end of each field in television.

vertical sweep The downward movement of the scanning beam from top to bottom of the picture being televised.

vertical synchronizing pulse One of the six pulses that are transmitted at the end of each field in a television system to keep the receiver in field-by-field synchronism with the transmitter. Also known as picture synchronizing pulse.

very-high-frequency oscillator An oscillator whose frequency lies in the range from a few to several hundred megahertz; it uses distributed, rather than lumped, impedances, such as parallel wire transmission lines or coaxial cables.

very-high-frequency tuner A tuner in a television receiver for reception of stations transmitting in the very-high-frequency band; it generally has 12 discrete positions corresponding to channels 2–13.

very-long-baseline interferometry A method of improving angular resolution in the observation of radio sources; these are simultaneously observed by two radio telescopes which are very far apart, and the signals are recorded on magnetic tapes which are combined electronically or on a computer. Abbreviated VLBI.

very-long-range radar Equipment whose maximum range on a reflecting target of 1 square meter normal to the signal path exceeds 800 miles (1300 kilometers), provided line-of-sight exists between the target and the radar.

very-short-range radar Equipment whose range on a reflecting target of 1 square meter normal to the signal path is less than 50 miles (80 kilometers), provided line-of-sight exists between the target and the radar.

vestigial-sideband filter A filter that is inserted between a transmitter and its antenna to suppress part of one of the sidebands.

V format A data record format in which the logical records are of variable length and each record begins with a record length indication.

vibrotron A triode electron tube having an anode that can be moved or vibrated by an externally applied force.

video 1. Pertaining to picture signals or to the sections of a television system that carry these signals in either unmodulated or modulated form. **2.** Pertaining to the demodulated radar receiver output that is applied to a radar indicator.

video amplifier A low-pass amplifier having a bandwidth on the order of 2–10 megahertz, used in television and radar transmission and reception; it is a modification of an RC-coupled amplifier, such that the high-frequency half-power limit is determined essentially by the load resistance, the internal transistor capacitances, and the shunt capacitance in the circuit.

video correlator Radar circuit that enhances automatic target detection capability, provides data for digital target plotting, and gives improved immunity to noise, interference, and jamming.

video discrimination Radar circuit used to reduce the frequency band of the video amplifier stage in which it is used.

video disk recorder A video recorder that records television visual signals and sometimes aural signals on a magnetic, optical, or other type of disk which is usually about the size of a long-playing phonograph record.

video disk storage *See* optical disk storage.

video display terminal *See* display terminal.

Videograph Trademark of A. B. Dick Company for a high-speed cathode-ray character generator and electrostatic printer, used for printing magazine address labels under control of magnetic tape files of computer-processed addresses; the moving electron beam applies a charge on a dielectric-coated paper to form electrostatic images of characters; powder is then attracted to the image areas and fused to give readable addresses.

video integrator 1. Electric counter-countermeasures device that is used to reduce the response to nonsynchronous signals such as noise, and is useful against random pulse signals and noise. 2. Device which uses the redundancy of repetitive signals to improve the output signal-to-noise ratio, by summing the successive video signals.

video masking Method of removing chaff echoes and other extended clutter from radar displays.

video player A player that converts a video disk, videotape, or other type of recorded television program into signals suitable for driving a home television receiver.

video recorder A magnetic tape recorder capable of storing the video signals for a television program and feeding them back later to a television transmitter or directly to a receiver.

video replay Also known as video tape replay. 1. A procedure in which the audio and video signals of a television program are recorded on magnetic tape and then the tape is run through equipment later to rebroadcast the live scene. 2. A similar procedure in which the scene is rebroadcast almost immediately after it occurs. Also known as instant replay.

video sensing In optical character recognition, a scanning technique in which the document is flooded with light from an ordinary light source, and the image of the character is reflected onto the face of a cathode-ray tube, where it is scanned by an electron beam.

video tape A heavy-duty magnetic tape designed primarily for recording the video signals of television programs.

video tape recording A method of recording television video signals on magnetic tape for later rebroadcasting of television programs. Abbreviated VTR.

video tape replay *See* video replay.

video transformer A transformer designed to transfer, from one circuit to another, the signals containing picture information in television.

video transmitter *See* visual transmitter.

vidicon A camera tube in which a charge-density pattern is formed by photoconduction and stored on a photoconductor surface that is scanned by an electron beam, usually of low-velocity electrons; used chiefly in industrial television cameras.

Vienna definition language A language for defining the syntax and semantics of programming languages; consists of a syntactic metalanguage for defining the syntax of programming and data structures, and a semantic metalanguage which specifies programming language semantics operationally in terms of the computations to which programs give rise during execution.

viewfinder An auxiliary optical or electronic device attached to a television camera so the operator can see the scene as the camera sees it.

viewing screen *See* screen.

viewing storage tube *See* direct-view storage tube.

viewing time Time during which a storage tube is presenting a visible output corresponding to the stored information.

viologen display An electrochromic display based on an electrolyte consisting of an aqueous solution of a dipositively charged organic salt, containing a colorless cation that undergoes a one-electron reduction process to produce a purple radical cation, upon application of a negative potential to the electrode.

VIR *See* vertical interval reference.

virgin medium A material designed to have data recorded on it which is as yet completely lacking any information, such as a paper tape without any punched holes, not even feed holes; in contrast to an empty medium.

virtual address A symbol that can be used as a valid address part but does not necessarily designate an actual location.

virtual cathode The locus of a space-charge-potential minimum such that only some of the electrons approaching it are transmitted, the remainder being reflected back to the electron-emitting cathode.

virtual direct-access storage A device used with mass-storage systems, whereby data are retrieved prior to usage by a batch-processing program and automatically transcribed onto disk storage.

virtual memory A combination of primary and secondary memories that can be treated as a single memory by programmers because the computer itself translates a program or virtual address to the actual hardware address.

visibility factor The ratio of the minimum signal input detectable by ideal instruments connected to the output of a receiver, to the minimum signal power detectable by a human operator through a display connected to the same receiver. Also known as display loss.

visual display unit *See* display tube.

visually coupled display *See* helmet-mounted display.

visual scanner Device that optically scans printed or written data and generates an analog or digital signal.

visual storage tube Any electrostatic storage tube that also provides a visual readout.

visual transmitter Those parts of a television transmitter that act on picture signals, including parts that act on the audio signals as well. Also known as picture transmitter; video transmitter.

VLBI *See* very-long-baseline interferometry.

VMOS technology *See* vertical metal oxide semiconductor technology.

vocoder A system of electronic apparatus for synthesizing speech according to dynamic specifications derived from an analysis of that speech.

vodas A voice-operated switching device used in transoceanic radiotelephone circuits to suppress echoes and singing sounds automatically; it connects a subscriber's line automatically to the transmitting station as soon as he starts speaking and simultaneously disconnects it from the receiving station, thereby permitting the use of one radio channel for both transmitting and receiving without appreciable switching delay as the parties alternately talk. Derived from voice-operated device anti-singing.

voder An electronic system that uses electron tubes and filters, controlled through a keyboard, to produce voice sounds artificially. Derived from voice operation demonstrator.

vogad An automatic gain control circuit used to maintain a constant speech output level in long-distance radiotelephony. Derived from voice-operated gain-adjusted device.

voice coder Device that converts speech input into digital form prior to encipherment for secure transmission and converts the digital signals back to speech at the receiver.

voice digitization The conversion of analog voice signals to digital signals.

voice-frequency dialing Method of dialing by which the direct-current pulses from the dial are transformed into voice-frequency alternating-current pulses.

voice-operated device Any of several devices in a telephone system which are brought into operation by a sound signal, or some characteristic of such a signal.

voice-operated device anti-singing *See* vodas.

voice-operated gain-adjusted device *See* vogad.

voice-operated loss control and suppressor Voice-operated device which switches loss out of the transmitting branch and inserts loss in the receiving branch under control of the subscriber's speech.

voice operation demonstrator *See* voder.

voice response A computer-controlled recording system in which basic sounds, numerals, words, or phrases are individually stored for playback under computer control as the reply to a keyboarded query.

voice synthesizer A synthesizer that simulates speech in any language by assembling a language's elements or phonemes under digital control, each with the correct inflection, duration, pause, and other speech characteristics.

void In optical character recognition, an island of insufficiently inked paper within the area of the intended character stroke.

volatile file Any file in which data are rapidly added or deleted.

volatile memory *See* volatile storage.

volatile storage A storage device that must be continuously supplied with energy, or it will lose its retained data. Also known as volatile memory.

voltage amplification The ratio of the magnitude of the voltage across a specified load impedance to the magnitude of the input voltage of the amplifier or other transducer feeding that load; often expressed in decibels by multiplying the common logarithm of the ratio by 20.

voltage amplifier An amplifier designed primarily to build up the voltage of a signal, without supplying appreciable power.

voltage-amplitude-controlled clamp A single diode clamp in which the diode functions as a clamp whenever the potential at point A rises above V_R; the diode is then in its forward-biased condition and acts as a very low resistance.

voltage-controlled oscillator An oscillator whose frequency of oscillation can be varied by changing an applied voltage. Abbreviated VCO.

voltage-dependent resistor *See* varistor.

voltage doubler A transformerless rectifier circuit that gives approximately double the output voltage of a conventional half-wave vacuum-tube rectifier by charging a capacitor during the normally wasted half-cycle and discharging it in series with the output voltage during the next half-cycle. Also known as doubler.

voltage gain The difference between the output signal voltage level in decibels and the input signal voltage level in decibels; this value is equal to 20 times the common logarithm of the ratio of the output voltage to the input voltage.

voltage generator A two-terminal circuit element in which the terminal voltage is independent of the current through the element.

voltage multiplier A rectifier circuit capable of supplying a direct-current output voltage that is two or more times the peak value of the alternating-current voltage.

voltage quadrupler A rectifier circuit, containing four diodes, which supplies a direct-current output voltage which is four times the peak value of the alternating-current input voltage.

voltage regulator A device that maintains the terminal voltage of a generator or other voltage source within required limits despite variations in input voltage or load. Also known as automatic voltage regulator; voltage stabilizer.

voltage-regulator diode A diode that maintains an essentially constant direct voltage in a circuit despite changes in line voltage or load.

voltage-regulator tube A glow-discharge tube in which the tube voltage drop is approximately constant over the operating range of current; used to maintain an essentially constant direct voltage in a circuit despite changes in line voltage or load. Also known as VR tube.

voltage saturation *See* anode saturation.

voltage stabilizer *See* voltage regulator.

voltage-tunable tube Oscillator tube whose operating frequency can be varied by changing one or more of the electrode voltages, as in a backward-wave magnetron.

voltage-variable capacitor *See* varactor.

volume A single unit of external storage, all of which can be read or written by a single access mechanism or input/output device.

volume lifetime Average time interval between the generation and recombination of minority carriers in a homogeneous semiconductor.

volume-limiting amplifier Amplifier containing an automatic device that functions only when the input signal exceeds a predetermined level, and then reduces the gain so the output volume stays substantially constant despite further increases in input volume; the normal gain of the amplifier is restored when the input volume returns below the predetermined limiting level.

volume table of contents An index record near the beginning of each volume, which records the name, location, and extent of every file or data set residing on that particular volume; usually not found on magnetic tapes, but often required on all disk packs and drums. Abbreviated VTOC.

volume test The processing of a volume of actual data to check for program malfunction.

von Neumann machine A stored-program computer equipped with a program counter.

VR tube *See* voltage-regulator tube.

VSC *See* variable speech control.

VTOC *See* volume table of contents.

VTR *See* video tape recording.

wafer A thin semiconductor slice on which matrices of microcircuits can be fabricated, or which can be cut into individual dice for fabricating single transistors and diodes.

wafer lever switch A lever switch in which a number of contacts are arranged on one or both sides of one or more wafers, for engaging one or more contacts on a movable wafer segment actuated by the operating lever.

wafer socket An electron-tube socket consisting of one or two wafers of insulating material having holes in which are spring metal clips that grip the terminal pins of a tube.

wait state The state of a computer program in which it cannot use the central processing unit normally because the unit is waiting to complete an input/output operation.

walk-down A malfunction in a magnetic core of a computer storage in which successive drive pulses or digit pulses cause charges in the magnetic flux in the core that persist after the magnetic fields associated with pulses have been removed. Also known as loss of information.

wall effect The contribution to the ionization in an ionization chamber by electrons liberated from the walls.

wall energy The energy per unit area of the boundary between two ferromagnetic domains which are oriented in different directions.

warning device A visible or audible alarm to inform the operator of a machine condition.

warning-receiver system An electronic countermeasure system, carried on a tactical or transport aircraft, which is programmed to alert a pilot when the aircraft is being illuminated by a specific radar signal above predetermined power thresholds.

washer thermistor A thermistor in the shape of a washer, which may be as large as 0.75 inch (1.9 centimeters) in diameter and 0.50 inch (1.3 centimeters) thick; it is formed by pressing and sintering an oxide-binder mixture.

water-cooled tube An electron tube that is cooled by circulating water through or around the anode structure.

water cooling Cooling the electrodes of an electron tube by circulating water through or around them.

waveform-amplitude distortion *See* frequency distortion.

wavelength shifter A photofluorescent compound used with a scintillator material to increase the wavelengths of the optical photons emitted by the scintillator, thereby permitting more efficient use of the photons by the phototube or photocell.

wave-shaping circuit An electronic circuit used to create or modify a specified time-varying electrical quantity, usually voltage or current, using combinations of electronic devices, such as vacuum tubes or transistors, and circuit elements, including resistors, capacitors, and inductors.

wave tail Part of a signal-wave envelope (in time or distance) between the steady-state value (or crest) and the end of the envelope.

wave trap A resonant circuit connected to the antenna system of a receiver to suppress signals at a particular frequency, such as that of a powerful local station that is interfering with reception of other stations. Also known as trap.

Wehnelt cathode *See* oxide-coated cathode.

weighted area masks In character recognition, a set of characters (each character residing in the character reader in the form of weighted points) which theoretically render all input specimens unique, regardless of the size or style.

weighted code A method of representing a decimal digit by a combination of bits, in which each bit is assigned a weight, and the value of the decimal digit is found by multiplying each bit by its weight and then summing the results.

Weiss molecular field The effective magnetic field postulated in the Weiss theory of ferromagnetism, which acts on atomic magnetic moments within a domain, tending to align them, and is in turn generated by these magnetic moments.

Weiss theory A theory of ferromagnetism based on the hypotheses that below the Curie point a ferromagnetic substance is composed of small, spontaneously magnetized regions called domains, and that each domain is spontaneously magnetized because a strong molecular magnetic field tends to align the individual atomic magnetic moments within the domain. Also known as molecular field theory.

wet flashover voltage The voltage at which an electric discharge occurs between two electrodes that are separated by an insulator whose surface has been sprayed with water to simulate rain.

wetting The coating of a contact surface with an adherent film of mercury.

wheel printer A line printer that prints its characters from the rim of a wheel around which is the type for the alphabet, numerals, and other characters.

wheel static Interference encountered in automobile-radio installations due to static electricity developed by friction between the tires and the street.

whiffletree switch In computers, a multiposition electronic switch composed of gate tubes and flip-flops, so named because its circuit diagram resembles a whiffletree.

White Alice *See* Alaska Integrated Communications Exchange.

whitening filter An electrical filter which converts a given signal to white noise. Also known as prewhitening filter.

wide band Property of a tuner, amplifier, or other device that can pass a broad range of frequencies.

wide-band amplifier An amplifier that will pass a wide range of frequencies with substantially uniform amplification.

wide-band repeater Airborne system that receives a radio-frequency signal for transmission; used in reconnaissance missions when low-altitude reconnaissance aircraft require an airborne relay platform for beyond line-of-sight data transmission to a readout station.

wide-band switching Basically, four-wire circuits using correed matrices with electronic controls capable of switching wide-band facilities up to 50 kilohertz in bandwidth.

wide-open Refers to the untuned characteristic or lack of frequency selectivity.

width control Control that adjusts the width of the pattern on the screen of a cathode-ray tube in a television receiver or oscilloscope.

Wien bridge oscillator A phase-shift feedback oscillator that uses a Wien bridge as the frequency-determining element.

Wierl equation A formula for the intensity of an electron beam scattered through a specified angle by diffraction from the molecules in a gas.

Williams tube A cathode-ray storage tube in which information is stored as a pattern of electric charges produced, maintained, read, and erased by suitably controlled scanning of the screen by the electron beam.

Winchester disk A type of disk storage device characterized by nonremovable or sealed disk packs; extremely narrow tracks; a lubricated surface that allows the head to rest on the surface during start and stop operations; and servomechanisms which utilize a magnetic pattern, recorded on the medium itself, to position the head.

Winchester technology Innovations designed to achieve disks with up to 6×10^8 bytes per disk drive; the technology includes nonremovable or sealed disk packs, a read/write head that weighs only 0.25 gram and floats above the surface, magnetic orientation of iron oxide particles on the disk surface, and lubrication of the disk surface.

wind The manner in which magnetic tape is wound onto a reel; in an A wind, the coated surface faces the hub; in a B wind, the coated surface faces away from the hub.

window A material having minimum absorption and minimum reflection of radiant energy, sealed into the vacuum envelope of a microwave or other electron tube to permit passage of the desired radiation through the envelope to the output device.

windowing The procedure of selecting a portion of a large drawing to be displayed on the screen of a computer graphics system, usually by placing a rectangular window over a compressed version of the entire drawing displayed on the screen.

wing spot generator Electronic circuit that grows wings on the video target signal of a type G indicator; these wings are inversely proportional in size to the range.

wired-program computer A computer in which the sequence of instructions that form the operating program is created by interconnection of wires on a removable control panel.

wire printing *See* matrix printing.

wiring board *See* control panel.

wobbulator A signal generator in which a motor-driven variable capacitor is used to vary the output frequency periodically between two known limits, as required for displaying a frequency-response curve on the screen of a cathode-ray oscilloscope.

word The fundamental unit of storage capacity for a digital computer, almost always considered to be more than eight bits in length. Also known as computer word.

word format Arrangement of characters in a word, with each position or group of positions in the word containing certain specified data.

word length The number of bits, digits, characters, or bytes in one word.

word mark A nondata punctuation bit used to delimit a word in a variable-word-length computer.

word-oriented computer A computer in which the locations of words are addressed, and the bits and characters within the words can be addressed only through use of special instructions.

word processing The creation, dissemination, storage, and retrieval of the written word by typewriter terminals that use magnetic tape for storage, automatic control, editing, and retyping.

word rate In computer operations, the frequency derived from the elapsed period between the beginning of the transmission of one word and the beginning of the transmission of the next word.

word time *See* minor cycle.

work assembly The clerical activities related to organizing collections of data records and computer programs or series of related programs.

working program A valid program which, when translated into machine language, can be executed on a computer.

working set The smallest collection of instruction and data words of a given computer program which should be loaded into the main storage of a computer system so that efficient processing is possible.

working-set window A fixed time interval during which the working set is referenced.

working space *See* working storage.

working storage 1. An area of main memory that is reserved by the programmer for storing temporary or intermediate values. Also known as working space. 2. In COBOL (computer language), a section in the data division used for describing the name, structure, usage, and initial value of program variables that are neither constants nor records of input/output files.

workspace In a string processing language, the portion of computer memory that contains the string currently being processed.

work tape A magnetic tape that is available for general use during data processing.

woven-screen storage Digital storage plane made by weaving wires coated with thin magnetic films; when currents are sent through a selected pair of wires that are at right angles in the screen, storage and readout occur at the intersection of the two wires.

writable control storage A section of the control storage holding microprograms which can be loaded from a console file or under microprogramming control.

write 1. To transmit data from any source onto an internal storage medium. 2. A command directing that an output operation be performed.

write enable ring A file protection ring that must be attached to the hub of a reel of magnetic tape in order to physically allow data to be transcribed onto the reel. Also known as write ring.

write error 1. A condition in which information cannot be written onto or into a storage device, due to dust, dirt, damage to the recording surface, or damaged electronic components. 2. A condition in which there is an inconsistency between the pattern of bits transmitted to the write head of a magnetic tape drive and the pattern sensed immediately afterward by the read head.

write head Device that stores digital information as coded electrical pulses on a magnetic drum, disk, or tape.

write inhibit ring A file protection ring that physically prevents data from being written on a reel of magnetic tape when it is attached to the hub of the reel.

write protection A form of memory protection in which a computer program can read from any area in memory but cannot write outside its own area.

write ring *See* write enable ring.

write time The time required to transcribe a data item into a computer storage device.

writing speed Lineal scanning rate of the electron beam across the storage surface in writing information on a cathode-ray storage tube.

X punch In an 80-column punched card, any hole in the second row from the top. Also known as eleven punch.

x-ray generator A metal from whose surface large amounts of x-rays are emitted when it is bombarded with high-velocity electrons; metals with high atomic weight are the most efficient generators.

x-ray target The metal body with which high-velocity electrons collide, in a vacuum tube designed to produce x-rays.

x-ray tube A vacuum tube designed to produce x-rays by accelerating electrons to a high velocity by means of an electrostatic field, then suddenly stopping them by collision with a target.

XY switching system A telephone switching system consisting of a series of flat bank and wiper switches in which the wipers move in a horizontal plane, first in one direction and then in another under the control of pulses from a subscriber's dial; the switches are stacked on frames, and are operated one after another.

Y

yig device A filter, oscillator, parametric amplifier, or other device that uses an yttrium-iron-garnet crystal in combination with a variable magnetic field to achieve wide-band tuning in microwave circuits. Derived from yttrium-iron-garnet device.

yig filter A filter consisting of an yttrium-iron-garnet crystal positioned in a magnetic field provided by a permanent magnet and a solenoid; tuning is achieved by varying the amount of direct current through the solenoid; the bias magnet serves to tune the filter to the center of the band, thus minimizing the solenoid power required to tune over wide bandwidths.

yig-tuned parametric amplifier A parametric amplifier in which tuning is achieved by varying the amount of direct current flowing through the solenoid of a yig filter.

yig-tuned tunnel-diode oscillator Microwave oscillator in which precisely controlled wide-band tuning is achieved by varying the current through a tuning solenoid that acts on a yig filter in the tunnel-diode oscillator circuit.

yoke *See* deflection yoke.

y parameter One of a set of four transistor equivalent-circuit parameters, used especially with field-effect transistors, that conveniently specify performance for small voltage and current in an equivalent circuit; the equivalent circuit is a current source with shunt impedance at both input and output.

Y punch In a standard punched card, hole in the topmost row.

yttrium-iron-garnet device *See* yig device.

449

Z

Zener breakdown Nondestructive breakdown in a semiconductor, occurring when the electric field across the barrier region becomes high enough to produce a form of field emission that suddenly increases the number of carriers in this region. Also known as Zener effect.

Zener diode A semiconductor breakdown diode, usually constructed of silicon, in which reverse-voltage breakdown is based on the Zener effect.

Zener diode voltage regulator *See* diode voltage regulator.

Zener effect *See* Zener breakdown.

zero-access instruction An instruction consisting of an operation which does not require the designation of an address in the usual sense; for example, the instruction, "shift left 0003," has in its normal address position the amount of the shift desired.

zero-access storage Computer storage for which waiting time is negligible.

zero-address instruction format An instruction format in which the instruction contains no address, used when an address is not needed to specify the location of the operand, as in repetitive addressing. Also known as addressless instruction format.

zero-beat reception *See* homodyne reception.

zero bias The condition in which the control grid and cathode of an electron tube are at the same direct-current voltage.

zero-bias tube Vacuum tube which is designed so that it may be operated as a class B amplifier without applying a negative bias to its control grid.

zero compression Any of a number of techniques used to eliminate the storage of nonsignificant leading zeros during data processing in a computer.

zero condition The state of a magnetic core or other computer memory element in which it represents the value 0. Also known as nought state; zero state.

zero error Delay time occurring within the transmitter and receiver circuits of a radar system; for accurate range data, this delay time must be compensated for in the calibration of the range unit.

zero-field emission *See* field-free emission current.

zero-level address The operand contained in an instruction so structured as to make immediate use of the operand.

zero output 1. Voltage response obtained from a magnetic cell in a zero state by a reading or resetting process. 2. Integrated voltage response obtained from a magnetic cell in a zero state by a reading or resetting process; a ratio of a one output to a zero output is a one-to-zero ratio.

zero state *See* zero condition.

zero suppression A process of replacing leading (nonsignificant) zeros in a numeral by blanks; it is an editing operation designed to make computable numerals easily readable to the human eye.

zero time reference Reference point in time from which the operations of various radar circuits are measured.

zip mode Mode of operation of a plotter in which each input plot command represents a velocity increment and causes an increase or decrease in speed relative to either axis or both axes.

zirconium lamp A high-intensity point-source lamp having a zirconium oxide cathode in an argon-filled bulb, used because of its low emanation of long-wavelength light and its concentrated source.

zone 1. One of the top three rows of a punched card, namely, the 11, 12, and zero rows. 2. *See* storage area.

zone bit A set of bits; for example, it may indicate whether the set of bits represents a numeric or alphabetic character.

zone blanking Method of turning off the cathode-ray tube during part of the sweep of an antenna.

zoned decimal A format for use with EBCDIC input and output permitting a sign overpunch in the low order position of the field; thus, + 1234 would be represented as: 1111/0001/1111/0010/1111/0011/1100/0100.

zone punch In a punched card, the 11 or 12 punch according to any code, the zero punch if another numeric punch is present in the same column, and sometimes the 8 and 9 punches in EBCDIC-coded cards.

Z parameter One of a set of four transistor equivalent-circuit parameters; they are the inverse of the Y parameters.